Critical Acclaim for

MALCOLM

Perry deserves accolades for completing the first major biography of Malcolm X. . . . Perry's biography helps to explain why this "shining black Prince" has continued to be more popular than Dr. Martin Luther King in the streets of black America in the 1990's.

Choice

A lively, critical biography. . . . A complex portrait that successfully illuminates the inner conflicts that drove Malcolm to greatness and destruction.

Kirkus Reviews

Historian Bruce Perry's *Malcolm* is the product of painstaking research. The book is extremely impressive. . . and highly readable.

Philadelphia Inquirer

The Malcolm who emerges from Perry's pages is more complex, more fully human than the man portrayed in previous accounts of his life. . . . Perry's book in no way diminishes Malcolm's achievements; rather, it deepens our understanding of an extraordinary man and his times.

Dow Jones

Exhaustively researched, this compelling biography corrects Malcolm's autobiography at innumerable points as it peels away the black revolutionary's tough-as-steel persona to reveal the hurt, vulnerable man underneath. . . . This portrait of Malcolm X is the most intimate to date.

Publishers Weekly

Malcolm affords an opportunity to re-examine a figure who, in death, exerts more influence on young blacks than anyone living. . . . Mr. Perry provides much new biographical information.

The New York Times Book Review

Perry has done a creditable and believable job. He succeeds not only at chronicling Malcolm's public persona, but at reporting his private experiences and explaining the links between the two. Well-organized, fluidly written and filled with significant details, *Malcolm* also brings vibrantly alive Malcolm's visionary spirit.

Press-Enterprise

Never have I read a biography with so much documented detail about a subject's childhood. . . .

The Kansas City Star

Once again, it's time to reexamine Malcolm X, and this well-written book does a fine job.

The West Coast Review of Books

Perry's work shares with the reader, for the first time, the growth of one of the greatest leaders who ever lived.

Philadelphia Tribune

What is made clear in Perry's book is that Malcolm's eloquent outrage exposed the flaws in a system of democracy that for generations spoke of freedom but imprisoned the aspirations and opportunities of millions of blacks. . . . Perry's book is highly readable.

The Macon Telegraph

By delineating for the first time the actual distance Malcolm had to travel simply to survive, and by exploring the roots of the blind rancor he had just begun to overcome when he was struck down, Perry has provided heroism enough for any fair-minded reader.

American Heritage

Unquestionably, he has produced an important book. . . . It is extraordinarily detailed in its tracing of Malcolm's childhood and youth.

Hudson Valley Literary Supplement

MALCOLM

The Life of a Man Who Changed Black America

BRUCE PERRY

Station Hill

First paperback edition 1992.

Published by Station Hill Press, Inc., Barrytown, New York 12507.

Text and cover design by Susan Quasha.

Photographic acknowledgements appear on page 543.

Distributed by The Talman Company, 131 Spring Street, Suite 20 E-N, New York, New York 10012.

Library of Congress Cataloging-in-Publication Data

Perry, Bruce.
    Malcolm : The life of a man who changed Black America / Bruce Perry.
        p.   cm.
    Includes bibliographical references and index.
    ISBN 0-88268-103-6 (cloth)
    ISBN 0-88268-121-4 (paper)
    1. X, Malcolm, 1925-1965.   2. Black Muslims — Biography.   3. Afro- Americans — Biography.   I. Title.
BP223.Z8L5766   1991
297'.87'092--dc20
[B]
                                                                                      91-
23350
                                                                                      CIP

Manufactured in the United States of America.

AUTHOR'S NOTE

At their request, I have changed the names of several of the people portrayed in this book.

The thoughts and feelings of those described in the narrative will be included only where they have been confirmed by sufficient evidence. Wherever appropriate, the sources for that evidence will be cited in the Notes.

Many people contributed substantially to this book. But neither my editor, my publisher, nor my sources are responsible for its contents.

CONTENTS

*To my parents,
Harry and Alice Perry,
with gratitude*

INTRODUCTION

A quarter of a century has elapsed since Malcolm X's assassination, and his stature has grown, not diminished. Published writings furnish an exciting, though incomplete and inaccurate account of his life and exploits. But they fail to probe beneath the surface of the young firebrand who raised the banner of resistance while millions of other African-Americans—many of whom encountered far more racial persecution than he did—quietly submitted. What, then, inspired Malcolm to become the standard-bearer for an entire generation of militant blacks?

In part, Malcolm's war against the white power structure evolved from the same inner needs that had spawned earlier rebellions against his teachers, the law, established religion, and other symbols of authority. He gravitated from one variety of rebellion to another. Each "phase of rebellion," as he called it, enabled him to adapt, as successfully as he knew how, to the demands of his internal, psychic environment as well as to those of his external environment.

During the 1950s, as white and black Americans began to take notice of Malcolm X, they generally did so through biased spectacles and condemned or esteemed him accordingly. Few explored further. Malcolm probably would not have wanted them to. He had been hurt too often and too deeply to want to reveal himself. For personal and political reasons, his public image was carefully contrived.

His splendidly written autobiography is a case in point. Its exaggerated portrayal of his youthful criminality enhanced his tough image and dramatized the transformation of the pseudo-masculine, criminal Malcolm into the manly, political Malcolm. It inspired his followers to feel that, no matter how far they had fallen, they could still raise themselves up and surmount their handicaps.

Like others who have been deprived of nurture and acceptance, as well as food and clothing, Malcolm coped with painful, youthful memories by forgetting or altering them, or by asserting that his boyhood had been rosier than it actually had been. An instructive example was his autobiographical portrait of his father. So was his selective account of the events that had precipitated his mother's emotional collapse, which was apparently so painful for him that he later felt compelled to retell it differently. The difficulty he had coping with his father's death apparently prompted him to rewrite it too.

The reader will encounter, in this biography, far more about the subject's childhood than one does in most biographies. But that is precisely the point. One cannot adequately understand the adult, political Malcolm without thoroughly understanding the youthful Malcolm and the legacy that was bequeathed him by the people who raised him. Most of the people who decisively shaped his outlook are still alive. Thus, far more information is available about his early, formative years than about those of most political figures. Much of that information has been gleaned from interviews with members of Malcolm's family, including his mother and four of his five brothers. Moreover, since 1970, I have been interviewing and reinterviewing hundreds of other people who knew Malcolm, including most of his childhood neighbors and playmates, the majority of his teachers, and dozens of former classmates. I have also spoken at length with his former partners-in-crime, prison-mates, "Black Muslim" colleagues, and political associates. The resultant testimony, together with material from his letters and countless documents, reveals the real Malcolm—the one nobody knew, perhaps not even Malcolm himself.

Malcolm was a man in conflict—a living microcosm of the racial discord that corrodes American life. The story of his inner struggle to decide what color he wanted to "be" enables us to see beyond fashionable shibboleths about racism to bigotry's hidden roots.

Malcolm was plagued by other, equally trying inner conflicts. He yearned for happiness and love, yet deprived himself of both. He craved success but courted failure. He longed for freedom but shunned it until it was too late. Deep down, he hungered for the approval of the very authority figures he defied.

He tried to be tough and insensitive but really wasn't, and was eventually murdered by enemies who lacked his underlying humanity. His self-destructiveness contributed to his premature death.

Despite his efforts to attribute his unhappiness and his youthful delinquency solely to white "society," they originated largely in his loveless, conflict-ridden home. His subsequent moral, intellectual, and emotional growth was a triumphant victory over the ravages of a childhood that, until now, has been enshrouded in fiction and myth.

This biography is a narrative about one man's struggle to liberate himself inwardly by liberating his people politically. It is a book about his evolution from youthful waywardness to greatness. But it is also a book about young drug addicts and what breeds them. And about what really spawns criminality, notwithstanding the accepted wisdom that pervades our criminological journals. It is a book about anti-Semites and similar religious and racial fanatics, whatever their color. And rebels, good and bad. It is a book about men who tyrannize women and who hate their fellow men.

The story of Malcolm's life is a biographical testament to both the worst and best in human nature and will comfort neither his detractors nor his idolaters. Nor will it please those who allow heroic myths about him to obscure his real heroism or his knack for transforming youthful weakness into political strength.

Malcolm, who liked to say that "crime is prevented in the high chair, not in the electric chair,"* began his life without the material and educational advantages that young Martin Luther King, Jr. had enjoyed. But he raised himself up and overcame most of his youthful handicaps. Had he lived longer, there is abundant reason to believe he would have accomplished even more than he did before he was killed at the age of thirty-nine. He transformed blackness from what had commonly been regarded as a badge of shame into a symbol of pride. He made Islam a force to be reckoned with in black America. And he articulated its bitterness and anger as no one else did, before or after him. He defended his beleaguered people far better than he defended himself. And by transforming his youthful fear into political fearlessness, he helped transform America.

---

* The statement has been attributed to J. Edgar Hoover.

A NOTE ABOUT THE SOURCES

Initially, I did not intend to write a biography of Malcolm X. I assumed that the article I planned to write would take me about a year. But in 1971, with the help of John Fitzpatrick, the Massachusetts Commissioner of Correction, I obtained access to Malcolm's voluminous prison record, which led me to Malcolm Jarvis, one of the two or three men Malcolm's autobiography had transformed into the fictional character "Shorty." Jarvis, in turn, led me to dozens of people who had known Malcolm when he was a teen-age hustler. One of them was Gloria Strother, whom he had wanted to marry.

Aided by court records, I located the younger sister of the white woman who had been Malcolm's girlfriend during the 1940s. When I telephoned and requested an interview, she was receptive, but she said she'd have to ask her sister, Bea. She did, but Bea (the woman Malcolm's autobiography calls "Sophia") vetoed the idea. So I called Bea myself. Her response was hostile. Her friend Kora, who had also accompanied Malcolm on some of his youthful burglary ventures, later wrote me and said, "The . . . '40s have been a closed chapter of my life. They will remain so."

I flew to Michigan, where Malcolm grew up, expecting to stay for six weeks. But, counting return trips, I spent more than six months there. Ken Mead, who was in charge of student records for the Lansing School District, granted me access to Malcolm's school record. Armed with a list of classmates, I combed Mason, Michigan and its environs for Malcolm's junior high school classmates and teachers. In Lansing and its suburbs, I conducted a similar search for his elementary school classmates and teachers. The Malcolm that some of them described to me was the antithesis of the one whom others described. Which version was real? Eventually, I realized that most of the inconsistencies were attributable to the fact that there were many Malcolms. Around some people he behaved one way; around others, he behaved quite differently.

One relative who had had an enormous impact on Malcolm was his half-sister Ella Collins, the third member of his family I interviewed. The meeting began with her larger-than-life, heroic description of Earl Little, the father she and Malcolm had shared. Then she asked me why so many whites hate blacks. "Because they hate themselves," I answered. I added that people who feel inferior overcompensate by pretending they are superior.

"I can talk to you," Ella replied. She talked for an entire day. During it, not one of the husky young men who accompanied her uttered a single word. I couldn't understand why they just sat there. But today I do.

Later, in Lansing, I began hearing things about Mr. Little that were impossible to reconcile with Ella's glowing portrait of him. At first, I discounted the reports. But they were seconded by so many African-Americans who had known Malcolm's father that I had to investigate further. One interviewee suggested that I examine the records of the 1929 fire that had destroyed Malcolm's Lansing home. What I found prompted me to check the records of the fire that had ravaged his New York City home in 1965, a week before his assassination. The parallels were striking.

But I was still unprepared for the police and court records indicating that Earl Little's family was riddled with criminality. One courthouse contained records describing Malcolm's mother's mental breakdown and her commitment to Kalamazoo State Hospital. But I ran into a brick wall when I tried to obtain access to the hospital records themselves. My frustration was somewhat allayed when I located the nursing home Mrs. Little was in and interviewed her. She seemed so happy to have a visitor. She told me she had always felt alone. But she said she liked being alone and that when Malcolm was a boy, he, too, had kept to himself pretty much. And he didn't like people asking how he was feeling. "I don't blame him," she said.

I had considerable difficulty locating Malcolm's brother Reginald, who spends much of his time living on the street. Finally, someone told me he was temporarily staying with his sister Yvonne. I wrote and requested an interview. Yvonne accompanied him to our initial meeting, but he came alone the second time. As soon as he stepped into my car, he began pouring his heart out; I was so busy trying to take notes that quite some time elapsed before I could even turn on my tape recorder.

By this time, I had gathered so much new information that I realized I had the makings of a full-scale biography. So I began poring through newspapers, such as *Muhammad Speaks*, the New York *Amsterdam News*, the Chicago *Defender*, the Los Angeles *Herald-Dispatch*, the *Herald-Tribune*, the Chicago *Sun-Times*, the *Chicago Tribune*, and the *New York Times*. Scores of newsreels also had to be viewed. And I had to scrutinize more than two thousand pages of FBI reports, as well as documents from the New York City Police Department, the U.S. State Department, the Secret Service, and the CIA.

In 1975, I finally succeeded in locating and interviewing Malcolm's eldest brother Wilfred, whose responses to most of my questions were extremely guarded. But Philbert, Malcolm's next oldest brother, told me so much about his early, formative years that I had to scrap my manuscript and begin anew. By then, it had become clear that I could not adequately understand the adult, political Malcolm unless I thoroughly understood the youthful one.

Though my list of interviewees grew, I couldn't locate James 67X, who had been one of Malcolm's chief aides. None of his former Black Muslim associates seemed to know where he was. His name was not listed in any New York City phone book. James—now Abdullah Abdur-Razzaq—had dropped out of sight.

Eventually, someone told me I might be able to find him through the St. John's Recreational Center, in Brooklyn. One Sunday, I drove there and asked a friendly supervisor named Al Welch if anyone knew Mr. Abdur-Razzaq. Mr. Welch called over two muslims, Bilal Abdullah and Abdul Malik. One of them said he knew the man I was seeking. I wrote my name, address, and phone number on a scrap of paper and asked him to forward it to Abdur-Razzaq. When I telephoned two or three weeks later, I learned that one of my would-be conduits had been killed in a confrontation with some of Elijah Muhammad's followers. The other declined further involvement.

So I was back to square one. I stayed there for three more years. Then I learned that Abdur-Razzaq's wife was supervising a school for young children. When I located it in mid-1977, I was ecstatic.

My joy became despair when Abdur-Razzaq's wife told me that he had moved to South America, where he had carved a farm out of virgin rain forrest. The despair became depression when I learned that the nearest telephone facilities were several days' journey from the Guyana farm.

So I wrote. Abdur-Razzaq's first letter, dated March 13, 1978, arrived eighteen days later. (Other letters took far longer.) We corresponded for about a year. Finally, he agreed to meet me on the Caribbean island of Grenada, where Malcolm's mother had been raised. We spent six days together. After Abdur-Razzaq flew back to Guyana, I made contact with Malcolm's mother's Grenadian relatives, who told me a great deal about her childhood.

One relative I could not locate was Malcolm's older sister Hilda. The only address I had was a post office box, which I staked out after a fruitless attempt to contact her by mail. Each morning, I went to the post office, carrying my lunch in a paper bag. There was no place to sit except a radiator. People came and went, but no one opened Hilda's mailbox. After five days, I had to abandon the effort because I could no longer afford the out-of-town hotel bills.

But I kept trying to find other people who had known Malcolm. By 1990, I had interviewed more than four hundred and twenty. The information they have furnished has greatly enhanced the ensuing narrative.

"People are always speculating: why am I as I am? To understand . . . any person, his whole life, from birth, must be reviewed. All our experiences fuse into our personalities. Everything that ever happened to us is an ingredient."

"I was born in trouble!"

Malcolm X

I

THE FORMATIVE YEARS

PARENTAL DEMANDS

1

Earl Little had great expectations for his forthcoming seventh child. According to a family tradition that sprang from ancient legends ascribing magic power to the number seven, the child would be blessed with the best attributes of the ancestral bloodline. It was destined for greatness, particularly if it were male. In anticipation of the youngster's future achievements, Earl's father wrote from his Georgia farm and directed that the infant be named John, after himself.

The baby was born on May 19, 1925, in Omaha, Nebraska. "It's a boy," Earl wired his parents. "But he's white, just like mama!" The physical similarity between the newborn child and his paternal grandmother went beyond skin color. His eyes, like hers, were blue-green. His ash-blonde hair was tinged with cinnamon; hers turned reddish in the summer sun. The similarities appalled his grandmother, who despised the white blood in her veins. Her dark-skinned husband wept. No "albino" would be named after him.

The baby was christened Malcolm by his mother Louisa, who had been raised on the Caribbean island of Grenada. She had never seen her Scottish father. When she was very young, her unmarried black mother had died giving birth to the last of her three illegitimate children. Louisa's dictatorial grandmother, Mary Jane Langdon, had assumed responsibility for raising her. But since Mary Jane spent considerable time away from home, her daughter Gertrude, Louisa's aunt, became Louisa's surrogate mother.

Aunt Gertie, who habitually flogged her children with straps and makeshift whips, had learned her autocratic child-rearing methods from her parents. On one occasion, her father, Jupiter, had stripped one of her teen-age sisters naked and made her kneel on the ground outside the house, where everyone could see her. Gertrude enforced her own parental decrees with similar indifference to her children's feelings. When she was away—which was much too often, according to one son—young Louisa was put in charge of the household.

Louisa apparently revenged herself by beating her young charges. Ultimately, she outgrew her usefulness to Mary Jane and Gertrude and became an economic liability. She was told she couldn't stay any longer and was sent elsewhere on the tiny British island—exactly where she cannot recall. Her memories of the ensuing period are of emptiness and loneliness. She felt so unwanted that she eventually emigrated to Montreal, where she met Malcolm's father. Earl Little—his real name was Early—was not the only man who found her exceptionally attractive. Her shiny, braided, raven-black hair hung down to her waist and contrasted vividly with her fair complexion. (She was so light-skinned that she was frequently mistaken for white.) Her figure was slim and tall, her bearing proud and erect. Her eyes, which had been sea-blue when she was younger, had turned brown except for the outer rim of the iris, which remained blue.

Earl didn't tell Louisa he had walked out on his first wife and his first three children. Passing himself off as a widower, he married his West Indian girlfriend shortly after they met. But they did not have much in common. While Louisa had had five years of Anglican schooling, Earl was nearly illiterate. She needled him about his ignorance, which he tried to hide with pretensions of learning. They were constantly at odds.

With his new wife in tow, Earl drifted from job to job and city to city. From Montreal, the Littles went to Philadelphia, where they had their first child, Wilfred. Soon afterward, they moved to Omaha, where Louisa gave birth to Malcolm's older sister Hilda, his brother Philbert, and then Malcolm himself.* Earl was a disciple of Marcus Garvey and was elected president of the Omaha branch of Garvey's Universal Negro Improvement Association. Louisa also joined the UNIA, which emphasized that blacks should be proud of their blackness and their African heritage. It urged them to free themselves from their dependence on whites, economically and otherwise. Garvey taught that instead of integrating with whites, blacks should establish their own sovereign nation. His message was so uplifting that hundreds of thousands of American, Caribbean, and other blacks rallied to his cause. Some of them tried resettling in Africa.

Malcolm's father reportedly decided to leave Omaha after Ku Klux Klan horsemen brandishing firearms and blazing torches besieged the Littles' home, shattering the window panes with their gun butts. But Malcolm's mother—who confronted the klansmen, according to his autobiography—says the incident never occurred. Nor does her sister-

---

* Malcolm was Louisa's fourth child but Earl's seventh.

in-law Rose, who lived in Omaha at the time, believe that it occurred. Rose was told by her husband that Earl had impersonated him, purchased clothing in his name, and left him to foot the bill. She also suspected that Earl had stolen the contents of her steamer trunk. But what prompted his departure from Omaha is unclear.*

In Milwaukee, the next stop on Earl's itinerary, he continued playing a prominent role at UNIA gatherings. He also drove his touring car to distant towns and villages, propagating Garvey's teachings and organizing new UNIA chapters. In Indiana Harbor, Indiana, he was evidently met with such enthusiasm that he briefly served as president of that town's UNIA chapter, even though he apparently never lived there.

After Malcolm's brother Reginald was born in August 1927, the Littles trekked from Milwaukee to Albion, Michigan, where Earl's brother Jim bootlegged moonshine. When revenue agents caught up with Jim, Malcolm's father moved the family to the northwestern outskirts of Lansing, where Malcolm's younger sister Yvonne was born. The Littles purchased an aging two-story farmhouse in a semi-rural, all-white neighborhood.

By this time, Malcolm was nearly four. His reddish-blonde hair was so close-cropped it gave his head a roundish, pumpkin-shaped appearance. Though his skin had grown darker, it was still fair. The other children teased him about his "high yellow" appearance. They called him "Chink" and made fun of his bluish eyes, which seemed to change color like his mother's. "We called him a freak of nature," Yvonne recalled years later.

Malcolm's father was as dark as Malcolm was light. Though blacks who heard his crusading oratory thought he hated whites, his white neighbors had a different impression. He greeted them with smiles and gave them fresh, homegrown produce from his vegetable garden. Black acquaintances recall how he shunned them for white ones whenever he found it expedient to do so. And the son he paraded when the church deacons visited was Malcolm, his fair-skinned pride and joy. To the best of Malcolm's recollection, he was the only son his father ever took with

---

* An Earl Little was convicted of larceny in Butler, Georgia, Malcolm's father's birthplace, shortly before Earl's first wife bore her third child in Talbotton, Georgia, twenty miles away. Whether this Earl Little was Malcolm's father is difficult to determine from surviving records, which indicate that the accomplice of the convicted man was named Wright Little. Earl had a cousin whose name was Wright.

him to the Garveyite gatherings where Earl vigorously championed the theme of black pride.

Malcolm's mother, whose American friends called her Louise, was also in conflict about color. Despite the way she extolled the ideal of black pride, she favored her lighter-skinned relatives and proudly insisted she was West Indian, not African-American. Her father, she said, was a white "prince" and plantation owner. She tried to comb the natural curl from her hair in order to make it resemble the hair of the white friends she boasted. Sometimes she scrubbed Malcolm's face and neck violently. "I can make him look almost white if I bathe him enough," she told her white neighbor Anna Stohrer. Anna felt that Louise considered Malcolm superior to her other children because of his light complexion.

But Malcolm felt otherwise, partly because his mother bent over backward to make sure he would not think his fair skin made him superior. She admonished him to get out of the house so that the sun would tan and darken his skin. He thought she favored the darker children, partly because his light skin, like hers, was a painful reminder of her illegitimacy. He felt he was her least favorite child.

Since Louise was so ambivalent about Malcolm's skin color, he could not please her any more than he could please his conflict-ridden father. He had neither parent's unqualified approval. And there was no way he could satisfy their irreconcilable demands.

HOME LIFE

2

Sometimes, Earl beat Louise. He was also brutal to his children. At the slightest pretext, he beat the older ones almost savagely. If one of them violated one of his rules, he grabbed the nearest child—which one didn't seem to matter—and whaled the daylights out of him. Frequently, he administered his beatings with a sapling or a belt. "You'll kill that child, Early," Louise occasionally protested. But she never intervened. She was as afraid of her husband as her young ones were. Even some of the neighbors' children dreaded Earl Little.

Malcolm was spared the brunt of his father's brutality. Years later, he attributed the favoritism to his light skin color. Most of the beatings he received were administered by his mother, who ruled her children with an iron hand, without visible evidence of affection. Like so many autocrats, she tyrannized them the way she had been tyrannized, not only by her husband, but also by Gertrude, Jupiter, and Mary Jane Langdon. Sometimes she used a strap on Malcolm. And at times she punished him with a switch that she made him choose himself. He would try to find one that would snap, but whenever he succeeded, his mother made him fetch another, stouter one. She could hit a boy so hard with the back of her hand that it made him feel as if his head had been split open.

In a partly successful effort to discourage his mother from whipping him, Malcolm protested her beatings loudly enough for the neighbors to hear. He also rebelled in other ways. He refused to let his mother, who was a fanatic about cleanliness, bathe him. He also resisted her attempts to send him outdoors, so that the sun would darken his skin. Yet indoors, he avoided getting too close to her; whenever possible, he stayed in a different part of the house, playing marbles or poring over picture books. He was habitually surly. At times, he refused to speak to his mother. On one occasion, he reproached her for being "all witchy." Clenching his little fists, he screamed, "I could kill you."

Malcolm was learning that verbal protest could achieve results. His mother began yielding to his persistent clamor for the buttered biscuits she impatiently denied her other, less demanding youngsters. Yet his position in the household remained precarious, not only because of Louise's ambivalence about his skin color, but also because his father's favoritism toward him bred resentment in the other children.

The jealousy worked both ways, for Malcolm seemed to envy the children his mother appeared to favor. It galled him that Wilfred, who was such a responsible child, appeared to be her "angel." Malcolm's chief rival, however, was Philbert, the darkest-skinned boy in the family. Nicknamed "Blackie," Philbert was the chromatic antithesis of Malcolm, who was called "Milky." Philbert regarded himself as his mother's favorite, partly because his middle name was Norton, Louise's maiden name. The rivalry between him and Malcolm was so intense that some of their respective friends became near-enemies. Eventually, Philbert would realize that the feud was chiefly about skin color. But he couldn't bring himself to admit that the issue of color was closely linked with the issue of parental approval.

Malcolm's rivalry with Philbert spilled over into the religious sphere, where Philbert had an advantage because he was unusually devout for a youngster. Nor could Malcolm effectively compete with him physically; Philbert was two years older, sturdily built, and determined to learn how to fight back and repay his father for his brutality. Before long, boys who challenged Philbert did so at their peril. The point was made when Malcolm grabbed a hammer in an effort to defend himself against his brother. In the ensuing struggle, Philbert seized the head of the hammer, which rebounded and knocked out the inside corners of Malcolm's two upper front teeth. The inverted, V-shaped gap marred Malcolm's appearance and earned him the nickname "Toothless Blondie."

Malcolm would later deny that he had harbored negative feelings toward any of his brothers and sisters. He asserted he was "very close" to them. But Reginald, the brother to whom he said he felt closest, did not feel close to him at all; he said they communicated very little and did not share their thoughts or feelings. Yet, Reginald, plagued by an inguinal hernia that distended his scrotum until it became as large as a fist, tagged after Malcolm. Though Malcolm often dismissed him impatiently, he enjoyed teaching him and acted as his protector.

Years later, when Malcolm became a public figure, he lauded his father, a "jackleg" (self-ordained) preacher who subsisted largely on the contributions he received for the "visitin' preachin'" that he did in various black churches. He had so many rules that it was hard for his children to remember them all. But according to people who knew him, he failed to observe them himself. In addition to being brutal to his wife and children, he was notoriously unfaithful to Louise—"a natural-born whoremonger," his friend Chester Jones called him. From childhood onward, Malcolm would have great difficulty trying to decide whether to follow the path of virtue his father preached or the path of vice he often practiced.

When he wasn't propagating religion or Garvey's teachings, Earl labored at construction sites. "He worked hard when he worked," says his former co-worker Ray Riddle. But he did it sporadically and gave little financial or emotional support to his family. He arose late, breakfasted on what little remained in the household larder, and spent his day pontificating and preaching in the homes of his avid listeners, who fed him while his wife and children went hungry. When church dignitaries visited his home, he plied them with freshly killed chicken and made his youngsters vie for the leavings. His inability or unwillingness to provide for his children did not deter him from siring more. His aim, his wife told Anna, was to fill his household with young vassals who would do his work for him while he lounged around with fellow Masons or Knights of Pythias. "I do everything around here," she told Anna. Some of Louise's friends helped out by bringing groceries. When Earl found out, he nearly exploded, insisting that he needed no charity and could care for his own.

Earl, who was constantly telling his children they should make something of themselves, had aspirations. "He wanted to be what he couldn't be," recalls Allie Cooper, who belonged to Lansing's tightly-knit black community. In an attempt to explain away his lack of achievement, he claimed he had owned a dress store that had gone bankrupt because its white customers had boycotted it when they discovered its proprietor was black. He could have been a politician, he asserted, were it not for the fact that religion and politics don't mix. (Malcolm would one day prove him wrong.) Earl's pretensions were as transparent as his excuses. He left home dressed in business garb. In one hand, he carried a briefcase. Rapidly, he strode up and down the streets of Lansing's West Side, where most of the city's blacks lived. He told people he was operating an employment agency for jobless blacks, but a number of clients who availed themselves of his services discovered, to their dismay, that he was as unsuccessful procuring employment for them as he was for himself. He was also unable to secure financing for his scheme. Nevertheless, he behaved as if he knew all there was to know about obtaining money. "Money's no problem," he declared.

In September 1929, three months after the Littles moved into their Lansing farmhouse, they were notified that the deed to the property contained a clause stipulating, "This land shall never be rented, leased, sold to, or occupied by . . . persons other than those of the Caucasian race." The owner of the adjacent lots, a land development company that apparently believed the Littles' presence was damaging its efforts to sell to white customers, persuaded James Nicoll, who had sold the farmhouse to the Littles, to collaborate in an effort to evict them. The ensuing lawsuit was all too successful. Judge Leland Carr didn't even give the Littles time to seek new lodgings. He ordered them to vacate "forthwith" and denied them reimbursement. The judge compounded the injustice by levying all the attorneys' fees and court costs against them, despite the absence of culpability on their part. Malcolm's father shook his fist at an unjust God and refused to relinquish his home. His lawyer bought time by posting an appeal bond and serving notice that he intended to appeal to the Supreme Court of Michigan. There was little chance of success; years would elapse before the United States Supreme Court declared racially restrictive land covenants unconstitutional.

Two weeks later, on November 7, Louise warned her children not to sleep upstairs. At about two-thirty in the morning, they were awakened by Earl's shouts. The house was on fire. The Dennises, who lived to the east, had already been awakened by someone who had pounded on their door. Then came an explosion that roused the whole neighborhood. Ernie Wolf, who lived a few yards south of the Littles, peered outside and saw flames leaping fifteen or twenty feet high from the rear of the Littles' home. He pulled on some clothes and rushed outside to find Malcolm's family shivering but safe. With the help of Burt Atkins, another white neighbor, Wolf tried to rescue some furniture from the front of the blazing house. "Let it burn," barked Earl. He warned the two men to stay out of the kitchen, where, it was later discovered, the fire had begun. Joe Nicholson, who ran a grocery stand down the road, telephoned the Lansing fire department, whose firefighters refused to come because the premises lay outside the city limits. (According to Malcolm's version of what happened, the white firemen "came and stood around watching as the house burned down to the ground.") When the state police arrived, they discovered that during the fire Malcolm's father had handed Nicholson a pistol. Earl, who had no permit for the gun, denied it was the one that he had fired at the white men who, he said, had started the fire. He maintained that he had used his shotgun. But the police were skeptical. They were equally skeptical about his assertion that whites had set the fire. There was no need to burn down the house to get the Littles to leave; it was common knowledge that Judge Carr had already ordered them to vacate.

Partly because of the inconsistencies between Earl's testimony and that of his wife and Wilfred, the police jailed him on suspicion of arson and for illegal possession of a revolver.

Subsequent examination of the charred ruins disclosed the presence of a two-gallon oil can. Hours before the fire, Earl had used it to buy kerosene. Louise later testified that she had poured some of the fuel into the kitchen stove and had placed the partly empty can behind the kitchen door. But the fire marshal found the can in the basement, beneath a set of bedsprings. It could not have fallen there during the fire, for there was no cellar beneath the kitchen, which had been added to the back of the farmhouse after it was built.

Had someone inside the house moved the can to the basement just before the fire and placed it beneath the bedsprings? Had the same person stolen outside, knocked on the Dennises' door to make it sound as if strangers were about, run back, and ignited the fuel? Investigators suspected that the answer was yes and that the person was Earl Little. But they were apparently baffled by the question of motive.*

Earl's interrogation by the police suggested a possible motive. In the midst of his denial that he had slipped Nicholson his revolver the night of the fire, he apparently confused him with Nicoll, the man who had sold him the farmhouse and then double-crossed him. Were the eviction and the fire linked? Betty Walker, whose family sheltered the Littles immediately after the fire, thinks they were; Earl seemed to feel that if he couldn't have the house that was rightfully his, neither could Nicoll and his white cohorts. Perhaps he also felt that people would be more willing to assist him financially if they thought he had been burned out rather than kicked out.

But such motives were hard to prove. After several months, the county prosecutor dismissed the arson charge.

Earl apparently quit the construction job he had held when the court handed down the eviction ruling. If he obtained another steady job, no evidence has been found to confirm it. The havoc wrought by the 1929 stock market crash soon made it nearly impossible for anyone to find employment, particularly unskilled blacks. Nevertheless, Earl managed to survive, largely on contributions from individuals and church groups whom he apparently persuaded to accept his version of the fire. The

---

* It is unclear if Earl's two fire insurance policies were still in force.

donations enabled him to move his family to what is now East Lansing, where the Littles were stoned by white neighbors. They relocated in another all-white neighborhood on Lansing's southern outskirts.

The six-acre plot of farmland they bought enabled them to raise chickens and rabbits and grow most of their own food. There are disputed reports that the Littles also received public assistance during this period. Some Lansing blacks gossiped about rumors that Malcolm's father feigned accidents in order to collect insurance. He did seem accident-prone. He was forever mashing his fingers with a hammer. On one occasion, the hammer sideswiped a nail that flew into his eye, which had to be removed. Another time, his automobile, filled with children, skidded into a ditch and overturned; miraculously, no one was seriously hurt.

Self-destructive violence seemed to abound in Earl's family. His brother Herbert committed suicide. Another brother, Oscar, was shot to death by the Pittsburgh police for wounding a white policeman who had attempted to arrest him for allegedly threatening some people with a pistol. John, the third of Earl's six brothers (two of whom had died when they were very young), was shotgunned to death as a result of a quarrel with another African-American. James, the moonshiner, was shot by a black woman whom he had assaulted. He lived to tell the tale and run afoul of the law another day.

Ill fortune continued to plague Earl and Louise Little. The widow who had sold them the six acres had concealed the fact that the northern three acres were encumbered by a tax lien. Malcolm's family found itself embroiled in litigation again. For the second time in eight months, they had to forfeit land they had purchased in the best of faith.

In 1931, Wesley, Louise's seventh child (Earl's tenth), was born. During the same year, Malcolm began kindergarten at Pleasant Grove Elementary School. His teacher, Olive Hicks, was well liked by the Little family, even though she later acknowledged she was somewhat afraid of blacks.

One day late in September, Malcolm returned home from school to find his parents embroiled in one of their habitual arguments. His father was determined to make a feast of one of the rabbits they raised and sold for cash. But Louise objected, not only because they needed the money, but also because she opposed eating rabbit on religious grounds. Enraged, Earl snatched a rabbit from its pen, tore off its head with his bare hands, threw the bleeding carcass at Louise's feet, and stormed out of the house. Suddenly, Malcolm's mother had a premonition that her husband was going to die. Clutching her apron, she ran after him, pleading almost hysterically for him to return. "Early! Early!" she cried. "If you go, you won't come back!" As the day wore on, Malcolm watched her become increasingly distraught, even though hours before she had confided to Anna Stohrer that she was fed up with Earl and on the verge of leaving him.

Bedtime approached without any sign of Earl. Frantically, Malcolm's mother clutched her children. Several miles away, in the no-man's-land separating Lansing from East Lansing, Malcolm's father boarded an interurban trolley. He reached for his changepurse but couldn't find it. At the next stop, he left the vehicle, perhaps to look for the purse. About twelve minutes later, another streetcar came by. There were no street-lamps and the driver failed to see him in the gloom. Minutes later, Earl was discovered lying beside the tracks. His left arm was crushed and blood gushed from his partly severed left leg, which looked as if it had been hacked open by a meat cleaver. The state police were summoned and found him still conscious. He told Trooper Laurence Baril that he had returned to the car stop just as the trolley was passing by and had tried to board the moving vehicle. But he had missed the step and had fallen under the rear wheels.

Shortly thereafter, six-year-old Malcolm awoke to the sound of his mother's screams. Officer Baril and another patrolman were in the living room, trying to calm her. They took her to the emergency room of Sparrow Hospital, where doctors were unable to save her husband. Malcolm, who knew only what he was later told about his father's death, wasn't sure what to believe about its cause. From what he and other members of the family said, his friends got the feeling that Earl's death had been accidental. But as Malcolm grew older, he began leaning towards his mother's theory that her husband had been done in by whites. Malcolm's autobiography gives the impression that his father was assassinated for political reasons by white assailants who bashed in his skull and laid him across the trolley tracks. But Trooper Baril recalls that Earl's skull was not crushed. "If it had been," he says, "Mr. Little would not have been able to explain how his injury had occurred."

Years after the streetcar ran over Earl, Malcolm would contend that his father had been killed by the hooded, black-robed members of a white hate-group called the Black Legion. But the records of the Lansing police and the Michigan state police, as well as newspaper accounts and the recollections of several of Mr. Little's black contemporaries, leave consid-erable doubt about whether the Legion ever operated in the Lansing area.

Some Lansingites wondered whether Earl had attempted to board the moving streetcar because some irate husband was after him. One insurance company even insisted that his death was a suicide. But the state police report, the coroner's report, and the death certificate indicate that his death was accidental.

What struck Malcolm most about his father's funeral was that it wasn't held in a church. Was this because of his unsavory reputation? Louise did her best to hide the truth from her children. "Don't tell anyone what I said about my husband," she admonished Anna Stohrer. "He was a good man." She minimized his failure to keep their bills and life insurance premiums paid up. (Some of the unpaid bills dated back a year or two, despite his admonitions about buying on credit.) Louise went into mourning and portrayed her husband as gallantly as she did her unknown father. As her children watched, Earl received in death the encomiums he had never earned in life.

The black community, many of whose members did not lament Earl Little's death, nevertheless contributed generously to his widow and orphaned children. So did the school PTA. Anna Stohrer, who had "loaned" money to Louise before, paid the overdue premium for one of Earl's two life insurance policies. It had not been cancelled because the insurance agent had advanced the sum out of his own pocket.

Not long after the funeral, Anna went to her front door and found Louise standing there with a raincoat draped over her arm, her eyes smoldering with rage. At first, Louise declined when Anna offered her a chair. Finally, hesitantly, she accepted it. Then, from beneath the coat, she withdrew a butcher knife. She began toying with it, alternately balancing the point of the blade and the tip of the handle on her knee. Suddenly, she rose and pointed the knife at Anna, who instinctively shielded herself with a chair. Just then, Anna's husband returned home through the back door. Without a word, Louise hid the weapon under the coat and hurried out the front door.

When Louise was questioned about her bizarre conduct, she sought to justify it by alleging that whites had murdered Earl. This, she said, impelled her to take a white life. Her insistence that her husband had been a victim of political assassination provided her children with a father-image of which they could at last be proud. Her eagerness to blame others for Earl's death may also have been due to her premonition that her husband was about to die—a premonition that may have been a disguised wish.

Malcolm's autobiography suggests that he shared his mother's premonition. Perhaps he, too, had a guilty conscience. If so, could he relieve it by projecting his angry feelings onto imaginary assassins? His feeling that Earl had been a political martyr enabled him to portray his father as a good man. Occasionally, he buttressed the myth by asserting that Earl had been a policeman—a man who enforced, rather than broke, the law. Years later, after Malcolm Little became Malcolm X, political considerations would reinforce his tendency to idealize his father and portray him as a hero.

But in 1931, when Malcolm was six, he would not talk about his father's death. Tyrannical as Earl Little had been, his absence, according to Reginald, left the children unprotected and afraid, without a strong, reassuring hand to take command. Malcolm refused to eat. When his mother asked him why, he replied that those who try to eat disappear and never return. He also had difficulty sleeping. "Only dead people stretch out," he declared.

Boyhood Fears

arkness terrified Malcolm; at night, he tried to wiggle beneath the slumbering brothers who shared his bed. Daytime, too, had its perils. There was the constant threat of fistfights, which he usually avoided. Even his mother, whose beatings may have contributed to his fear of physical injury, sensed his fear of combat, which caused other youngsters to claim that he was a coward. They said he was "afraid to bleed."

But fights were sometimes unavoidable. When they occurred, Malcolm defended himself as best as he could. If a stick or bottle happened to be handy, he'd use it. Otherwise, he'd try to scare his adversary with bluster, a technique he perfected as he grew older. Occasionally, he threatened boys he disliked through intermediaries, but the confrontations never materialized unless the recipient of the threat was weaker or smaller, or unless the odds were two-to-one in Malcolm's favor. (Reginald sometimes helped him out.)

Yet even during his boyhood, there was a brave, humane side to Malcolm, who defended underdogs better than he defended himself. When neighborhood bullies forced a partly disabled youngster off his bike and into a ditch, Malcolm sprang to the rescue. And he came more than once to the defense of a pint-sized classmate named John Breathour, who was no match for his larger opponents. Philbert, in turn, defended Malcolm against bigger adversaries, despite his deep-rooted differences with his brother. When Malcolm and Al Hildebridle, a tough kid who towered over the other boys, needled each other, it was Philbert who prevented the confrontations from turning violent.

But Philbert was not invincible. During a ball game, a boy named Tom Simmon took him to task for being too rough with the younger participants. The matter was settled, according to custom, atop a spur of railroad track that lay just north of the school. To everyone's surprise, Tom landed the first blow and sent Philbert tumbling down the far side of the railroad embankment. Struggling to his feet, Philbert crawled hand over hand back up the steep, rocky slope, only to be sent sprawling once more. In a flash, Malcolm was on Tom's back, despite the fact that he was older and heavier.

Some white boys picked on Malcolm for racial reasons. Others, like husky, blue-eyed Ores Whitney, defended him. Ores's family was almost as poor as Malcolm's. Nevertheless, he shared his sandwiches with Malcolm at school. A loner, Ores rarely said much to the other children. He'd stand, smile impishly, and watch them play, but he wouldn't take part. Malcolm and Ores, whose middle name was Malcolm, were considered best friends by virtually everyone who knew them. Yet they constantly bickered. No one could figure out how they could squabble so much and still like each other.

Not all the racial confrontations were initiated by whites. On one occasion, Malcolm and Reginald were threatened by blacks who tried to prevent them from passing through West Side turf in the company of white boys. One of the whites was a short, freckle-faced redhead named Bob Bebee. Malcolm, swallowing his fear, successfully stood up for himself and the others. He did it verbally; not a single blow was exchanged.

Some whites ribbed Malcolm about his skin color, calling him "Chinaman," "Snowflake," or "Eskimo." He didn't seem to mind; he just grinned. At home, however, he lamented, "They don't even know my name at school."A white friend of his named Jean_____ felt that he hated his in-between skin color and wished that he could clearly identify with one race or the other. When blacks visited his home and found him frolicking with Jean, he contemptuously dismissed her as white trash and sent her away. She did not take offense because she knew he was grandstanding for his guests and would be back on good terms with her the following day.

But Malcolm turned on her again. At school one day, he learned that Jackie Alexa, whose family owned the dairy farm just south of the Littles' property, was out to get Jean. He advised Jean to avoid Jackie by using the dirt track he customarily took home from school. Then he told Jackie what he had told Jean. The result was predictable. On another occasion, he chided Jean and Geraldine Grill, another neighbor, for being cowards until they donned boxing gloves and began swinging away at each other. Like a spectator at a boxing match, he seemed to enjoy such brawls. He sided with whoever won them.

Another white girl whom Malcolm spent time with was Betty Jean Thiel. Betty was a tomboy who despised dresses and openly admitted she wanted to be a boy. The ideal present, she felt, would be a pair of blue denims with shoulder straps and copper rivets at the stress points. Like Malcolm, she had a gap between her two upper front teeth. It seemed so wide she feared it never would close.

Betty lived across the road from the Littles, a hundred yards or so to the north. She was considered "rich" because she brought her lunch to school in an empty honey can instead of wrapped in newspaper. She had more than one pair of shoes and wore snow-white stockings. Most of the other white girls wore tan ones. The poorest girls wore black.

Malcolm and Betty roamed the neighborhood together. They climbed the Norway maples that commanded the Eaton Rapids road below. From a tree near the road, they sometimes suspended a tattered purse on a string. A passing motorist would spy it, emerge from his car, and bend down to snatch the prize, only to discover it eluding his grasp, as if it had life of its own. Sometimes, Malcolm and Betty "cooned" watermelon, splitting it open upon a rock and scooping out handfuls of the succulent pulp. But even on these occasions, Betty sensed, as others did, that he was not really happy. He laughed at inappropriate times—when he was taken to a surgeon to have a boil lanced, for instance.

Betty liked Malcolm and didn't hide her fondness for him. She admired his physical prowess. He could run faster than she could. He could throw stones farther and leap across the creek that bisected a corner of his yard. Frequently, he had to "rescue" her from its challenging waters. Though he never openly acknowledged that he reciprocated her affection, Malcolm appeared to like Betty—perhaps because she afforded him the unqualified approval his mother denied him. He seemed to enjoy pretending he was Betty's mate when they "played house" on the sturdy limbs of the tall maples. (There were no prescribed criteria as to who was male and who was female. They swapped roles whenever they chose.)

With Malcolm's tacit permission, Betty followed him around. She walked, not beside him, but behind him. "We didn't talk much," she later recalled. "But we must have communicated in some sort of way." Malcolm strode ahead, as if he had no need for his devoted pursuer. Now and then, he concealed himself in the chest-high brome grass, crouching like a jungle cat stalking unwary prey. As his diminutive victim passed his lair, he'd spring. Then the two would start out again, Betty trailing at a respectful distance. Years later, his political followers accorded him similar respect.

HUNGER

4

Lansing, which had been an alternate way-station on the Underground Railroad, boasted fewer than 17,000 inhabitants at the turn of the century, and not a single paved street. But by the time the Littles moved there in 1929, it had become a thriving automotive manufacturing center. It was the proud home of the Merry Oldsmobile, the first gasoline-powered car produced in quantity in America.

During the Depression, however, automotive production plummeted to less than a quarter of what it had been. As a result, the city's residents suffered acutely. By 1933, the industrial unemployment rate for Michigan as a whole was nearly 50%. In Detroit, where the failure of two enormous banks had precipitated a state bank "holiday" (Franklin Delano Roosevelt would soon introduce a nationwide one), little children vied with each other outside one slaughterhouse to catch the discarded cattle lungs that compassionate meatpackers flung outside. A family of four on relief had to exist on sixty cents a week, plus whatever free food was available at the soup kitchens that were located at the city's fire stations. Near Lansing, in the town of Charlotte, men who were fortunate enough to find factory jobs were paid twenty-five cents per hour. Women got fifteen cents. Blacks, many of whom had migrated to Lansing because of the employment opportunities created by the First World War and its prosperous aftermath, often received only half the wages of their white counterparts. Like everyone else, Malcolm's mother scrambled for whatever employment she could find. Her oldest daughter Hilda looked after the children. Eventually, Louise found part-time work as a seamstress. She also worked as a domestic. But as soon as her employers, who had assumed she was white, discovered she was half-black, they fired her. Malcolm never forgot how she came home crying, trying to hide her tears.

Under such conditions, it was difficult for Louise to adequately clothe her brood. In winter, Malcolm wore nothing more than a loosely knit sweater or an insubstantial jacket. The sweater, like his shirts and trousers, looked like a hand-me-down that he was not quite big enough to wear. He stood around shivering, with his gloveless hands clasped in front of him. Yet when he was offered a scarf by his friend Howard Cramer's mother, he declined it. "I'll be all right," he told her.

In summertime, when school wasn't in session, Malcolm went barefoot, for shoes were scarce. The rest of the year, he wore beat-up sneakers; snowshoes or rubber boots were out of the question, and his feet suffered constantly from the Michigan cold. Although many of the white children were just as hard up, some of them chided him about the patches in his "Raggedy Ann" clothes. Some of the blacks who were better off contemptuously called the Littles "farmers." No one, however, could poke fun at them for having dirty clothes. Louise made sure her children were among the cleanest in the neighborhood.

The house the Littles lived in, a small four-room cottage, was in no better shape than their clothing. There was no running water or indoor toilet. Furniture was sparse and the floors were rugless. A single bare lightbulb hung from the ceiling of each room. The uninsulated tar-paper shingle exterior presented virtually no barrier at all to the cold.

Even more difficult to endure than the cold was the hunger, which intensified as the Depression deepened. Every few days, Malcolm and Reginald walked two miles to the Peter Pan bakery. The stale surplus bread they purchased there kept them alive. Whenever possible, Malcolm's overworked mother made it into breadburgers or bread pudding. But at times, they had no bread at all; Louise and her children had to subsist on dandelion greens.

During lunchtime at school, Malcolm sat by himself in a cafeteria corner, furtively pushing two pieces of sandwich bread into his mouth. Between them lay a grayish ooze resembling cat food. Sometimes, there was nothing between the slices but the wild leeks Malcolm gathered on the way to school. One day, a girl who sat beside him in class burst into tears because of the odor. So instructions were given for leek sandwiches to be confiscated and burned.

Some of Malcolm's schoolmates, all of whom were white, tried their best to help out. One hoodwinked her mother into believing she needed more food and passed the extra along to him. Another girl shared her oranges and apples with him. Malcolm repaid her with nickel candy bars that he bought with money he earned delivering newspapers. Two other girls who lived in the neighborhood invited Malcolm and Philbert into their home to share grapefruit. The boys reluctantly turned the offer down; their mother had given strict orders not to "embarrass" whites by eating at their tables.

It was degrading to have to accept handouts. In the school cafeteria,

Malcolm would let the food offerings sit, as if he didn't want them. But when he did let himself eat, he wolfed the food down with both hands. Being a beggar was particularly humiliating at Christmas time, when each pupil contributed a small gift that was placed in a kitty and distributed by lot. Malcolm was unable to contribute. The other children insisted that he receive a present anyway, but when the gifts were handed out, he had to be urged to accept his. He unwrapped it ever so slowly, looking grateful yet ashamed. His attitude toward Christmas was decidedly negative. Years later, he told a friend that children should not be told Santa Claus exists.

Malcolm's reluctance to accept charity echoed his parents' reluctance. Like many people, his mother was apparently ashamed of her poverty and loath to acknowledge it. When friends or social workers asked if they could get her anything, her response was usually negative. She did, however, accept offers to repair and improve the house. But she insisted on giving what little she could in return—a freshly baked pie, if nothing else. And as badly as she and her children needed other peoples' castoff clothes, she gave them back if they had missing buttons. She proudly maintained that the meager public assistance she received was a loan, not a gift.

The charity issue was further aggravated by provincial relief workers who appeared to resent Louise's precise, impeccable English, which frequently put theirs to shame. One would-be benefactor gave her old, stale fig newtons containing worm holes; Malcolm fed them to the chickens. The county's "poor commissioner" was particularly disrespectful to Malcolm's mother, who was not the only welfare recipient he forced to grovel for assistance. But even the compassionate, well-meaning social workers became exasperated by Louise's insistence that money be spent on her broken-down car instead of on necessities. Her kitchen stove, for example, was in dangerous disrepair. A flat-topped, coal- and wood-burning affair, it had two doors—one for fuel, the other for ash-removal. The latter door was partly unhinged, and live coals could have easily fallen out and caused a fire.

The authorities offered to increase Louise's allotment if she would spend the extra funds to fix the stove. No one, however, could tell Louise Little how to run her home. "As long as my back and arms are strong enough," she replied, "I will drive that automobile." The vehicle—a real status symbol in those days—clearly meant a great deal to her, and Philbert labored valiantly to keep it running. The nearest bus stop was about three quarters of a mile away and the busses ran infrequently.

Louise's children could not understand their mother's reluctance to accept the free food the State of Michigan provided. She even refused a large quantity of pork that her next-door neighbor offered, for the church she had recently joined—an offshoot of the Seventh Day Adventist Church called the Seventh Day Church of God—did not permit its members to eat pork. As the economic crunch grew more severe and it became increasingly difficult to cope, she turned more and more to her Job-like religion of self-denial, which gave dignity and meaning to her privation. It was a religion that stressed fasting and cleanliness of mind and body. It discouraged "worldly" pleasures such as movie-going and dancing. In addition, it demanded total abstinence from tobacco, liquor, narcotic drugs, gambling, and, of course, extra-marital sex.

Outwardly, Malcolm did not blame his mother for being proud at her children's expense. He insisted he loved her. But his growing rebellion against her authority suggested otherwise. He ignored her demands for punctuality and became increasingly reluctant to perform his household chores. The part of the vegetable garden that he had once attended so diligently became weedy and unfit for cultivation. The older children tried in vain to get him to mend his ways. But he was not yet ready to assume the responsibility that had been prematurely forced on him by his father's death.

The economic and emotional pressure upon Louise, who had never fully recovered from her husband's death, kept intensifying. Her magnificent ebony hair began to gray. Her face grew expressionless. Neighbors and callers found her unapproachable. Her interest in her children ebbed. She devoted less and less time to them, and her ability to wield authority diminished. The county welfare authorities partly filled the vacuum; as a result, the children were unsure whom to obey. It was the same disconcerting, rudderless feeling they had experienced when their father had died.

Malcolm reacted to his mother's withdrawal by withdrawing himself. He began to steal, not only from his mother's purse but also from grocery stores. He freely acknowledged the latter offense yet concealed the former one. His stealing elicited maternal punishment. But the punishment failed to deter him, perhaps because the attention his thefts provoked was what he craved. Though he had grown big enough to think about resisting the beatings his mother gave him, he never once raised a hand against her. He was very proud of his self-restraint.

Crime and punishment would have additional implications. Every time Malcolm's mother whipped him, he yelled so loudly that the neighbors heard his cries, which, together with his stealing, provided the authorities with ammunition for their accusations that Louise was unfit to raise her children.

EDUCATIONAL AUTHORITY   5

Burdened by seven children and insufficient education, Malcolm's mother never got the opportunity to use her intellectual capacity. She was determined that her young ones would not suffer the same fate. They would be successful—great lawyers or captains of industry. Her aspirations were apparently fueled by the success imperatives of American culture, as well as by those pervading the West Indian culture in which she had been raised.

Believing that she was acting in her children's best interest, Louise pushed them academically. She pushed them hard. Mistakes were not permitted. The perfection she demanded of her youngsters was similar to the perfection that one of her Grenadian teachers had required of her; when she made mistakes in spelling, he beat her. Sometimes, he lashed her bare legs with a strap.

A number of Malcolm's elementary school teachers were nearly as autocratic. One stern taskmaster habitually enforced classroom discipline with a ruler. One day, she decided to use it on Malcolm and his mischievous friend Ores Whitney, who had been exchanging messages via paper airplane. But when she tried to rap Ores's knuckles with the ruler, he drew back his hands so quickly that it struck her kneecap with a resounding smack. Furious, she stood both boys in separate corners and proceeded to stack books on their outstretched arms. Each time their arms collapsed from the resulting pain, she piled the books back on. The "lesson" lasted for nearly the entire class period.

Malcolm also had several confrontations with the school principal, Arthur Delamarter, who didn't like Catholics, blacks, or anyone else who was "different." Delamarter, whose detachable shirt collars never quite matched the color of his shirts, was so enamored of the prerogatives of his position that teachers who ventured to pass through doorways ahead of him were elbowed unceremoniously aside.

Like Malcolm's father, Delamarter demanded absolute adherence to a puritanical moral code, which he enforced with a stout rubber hose. Most of the pupils were petrified of him. He injured the tendons of one boy's neck and thrashed others for offenses they didn't commit. Malcolm was not the only pupil to emerge from his office fighting back tears. Nor was Louise Little the only mother who vainly remonstrated with the Pleasant Grove School Board about his brutality.

Malcolm's grades suffered. It was not because he lacked intellectual curiosity; on the contrary, he'd go to the rear of the classroom, select a book from the library shelf, and eagerly absorb its contents. But when work was assigned, he'd drag his feet. He'd doodle, daydream, and stare out the window. When teachers called on him, he frequently had no idea what the class was doing. Even when he paid attention, he often had trouble completing his work, for he tended to give up as soon as he encountered difficulty. Slouched in his seat, his long legs protruding from beneath his desk, he acted as if he cared nothing about academic achievement or about what his teachers thought of him. He seemed more interested in securing the attention he was not getting at home. If the teacher called on someone else when he had his hand raised, he'd make a scene. If the pupils formed a line, he'd elbow his way to its head. He was the first child inside the school building in the morning, the first outside at recess time, and the first to leave when school was dismissed in the afternoon. Perhaps his determination to be first at school had something to do with his feeling that he came last at home.

Malcolm's harried teachers, at least one of whom felt that he disliked women, tried dealing with him in various ways. They moved his seat in an attempt to isolate him from other troublemakers. They detained him after school. His fifth grade teacher tried pulling his hair but found it too short to grab. Malcolm revenged himself by pulling the pigtails of smaller, less powerful females. He squirted water into their faces at the drinking fountain, shoved them off swings, pinched them, and kicked their shins. He borrowed their bikes without permission, then pretended he was going to run them down. Inside the school building, he concealed himself in the vestibule of the girls' restroom and vexed the unsuspecting pupils who tried to use it.

These pranks may also have been Malcolm's way of pretending that he wasn't interested in the girls he tormented, for he wasn't hostile toward every female. He was very attentive, for instance, to little Helen Bywater, who had roundly thrashed a huge girl who had called Malcolm's sister Hilda a nigger. If Helen dropped her pencilcase, Malcolm was there to retrieve it. If Helen could not reach the coathook, he hung up her jacket. Like a latter-day Sir Walter Raleigh, he chivalrously piggy-backed certain girls across the enormous rain puddles that flooded the path to school. In warm weather, when the girls removed their shoes and waded across, he carried their footwear. On one occasion, he stooped to wipe mud from one girl's shoes with his handkerchief. The boys who witnessed the event chided him unmercifully; they wouldn't be caught dead doing anything so sissified.

Malcolm's second-semester sixth grade teacher had an exceptionally difficult time with him. According to one former colleague, she was not highly interested in teaching; she was primarily interested in the extra income it brought. Nor did she seem to have much sympathy for her students. She publicly ridiculed the penmanship of a pupil who had broken his writing arm and was experiencing difficulty learning how to write with the other.

Malcolm fought ridicule with ridicule. He played the role of class clown to the hilt, flailing his arms like a monkey and amusing his classmates at the teacher's expense. When the class turned to artwork (for which Malcolm displayed a flair despite low grades), he drew lewd caricatures of her. His classmates could scarcely contain themselves.

Malcolm seemed to enjoy outwitting this particular teacher and getting under her skin. He learned that noncompliance, his favorite tactic at home, worked equally well at school. He refused to complete his written themes. And when his exasperated teacher ordered him out of the classroom, he wouldn't budge. She tried to pull him from his chair, but he braced himself and clung to his desk. She then sought help from the new female principal, who fetched the janitor. The small, elderly, anemic-looking custodian, who was the only adult male in the school, was reluctant to use force. Sensing this, perhaps, Malcolm, who was tall for his age, grabbed a foot-long tin of water colors and declared, "I'll club you with this if you lay a hand on me!" His battle against eviction succeeded, but he failed the semester and had to repeat half the sixth grade.

Malcolm's autobiography is as silent about these facts as it is about another crisis that came to a head during 1938 because his mother had become pregnant. By her church's austere standards, she was a hypocrite, as her husband had been.

Shunned by friends and neighbors, Mrs. Little, who had borne the stigma of illegitimacy so long herself, could not bear the additional scandal. She pulled down the windowshades and practically went into hiding, even from her children, who were apparently embarrassed by her condition. She sat alone in a corner in her rocking chair, talking to herself as if the other family members weren't there, lashing out at whichever youngster carelessly ventured within reach. The young ones, who had to fend for themselves, grew unkempt. The once tidy house became disheveled. Bedbugs invaded. Hilda, Malcolm's older sister, had to prepare most of the food. As his last remaining parental anchor gradually gave way, a sense of dread began to overwhelm him.

Late one night, Malcolm woke Reginald, grabbed his father's hunting rifle, and led his younger brother to Levandowski's grocery, where the Littles bought most of the food they couldn't raise themselves. Sheathing his fist in a tattered burlap sack, Malcolm smashed a window and climbed into the store. The climb proved too much for Reginald, whose hernia caused him considerable pain. Malcolm decided to take him home. He stole nothing, not even an apple. According to Reginald, Malcolm's decision to break into the store was prompted, not by hunger, but by a need to do something—anything—to relieve the helplessness they both felt. It was not the last time he'd commit a desperate act of self-assertion in a desperate situation.

THE LONG, HARD ROAD
TO MANHOOD

6

Some of Malcolm's friends called him "the Mountain" because, by the time he had reached puberty, he stood nearly six feet tall. Except for his light complexion, he resembled his father. He had Earl Little's erect frame. He walked the same way. Too often, he behaved the same way, for there was no other man to guide or advise him, or to teach him how to assert his budding manhood constructively.

Malcolm tried to manage with the best male role models he could find—older boys who lived in the neighborhood or in town. He tagged along after them, just as Reginald tagged after him. But he paid the price; because of his size, many of the older boys had no idea he was so much younger than they were. They expected him to perform as well as they did. The competition was frequently more than he could handle. He tried, for example, to pretend he had no time for basketball. Yet he hung around the basketball court watching other boys play. And from the sidelines of a nearby sandlot baseball diamond, he watched Wilfred and his friends play hardball. Though Malcolm appeared eager to join in, he said he wasn't good enough to play. When he finally did agree to participate, his noncompetitive facade fell away. If his team won, he'd gleefully jump up and down or intimate that the other team should have known better than to challenge his. If his team lost, he'd curse. If it was about to lose, he'd quit or find another way to break up the game.

In the outfield, Malcolm hogged every ball he could. Dick Turbin, the captain of the baseball team, declared in jest that he had no need for left and right fielders when Malcolm roamed center. But he didn't complain, for Malcolm caught almost everything that came his way. During the ninth inning of one game, however, Malcolm muffed an easy fly that cost his team the game. Turbin came unglued and gave him a tongue-lashing that the other team members probably would not have tolerated. But Malcolm did. He didn't seem to resent the authority of this teen-ager who had accepted him as a regular member of his team. He seemed to care for Dick. When Dick was felled at home plate by a carelessly thrown bat, Malcolm sprinted all the way from center field to the plate while the other members of the team remained, apparently unconcerned, at their positions. And when the time came to build a new pitcher's mound, Malcolm, who avoided doing chores at home, volunteered his labor.

Since errors, by maternal edict, were impermissible, Malcolm was extremely critical of those who committed them. He was equally intolerant of his own errors, some of which occurred when he tried his luck at ice hockey, which he and his companions played on frozen, flooded gravel pits and sinkholes. If he missed the puck, he'd slam his hockey stick down on the ice and berate himself. One day, he became so overwrought that he failed to notice the rough spots on the ice and tripped and fell. On another occasion, he skated right into a snowbank. The other players laughed, but Malcolm did not respond. Instead, he berated himself.

At football, Malcolm excelled as a pass receiver because of his speed and his big, grabby hands and long arms. But he wouldn't join Turbin's football team. Most of the players were older and huskier, and Malcolm seemed afraid of being trampled. He preferred soccer, which he played with fierce determination, often aiming his kicks at opposing players rather than at the ball. Yet once, when one of his kicks injured a member of the opposite team, he promptly picked up his victim, carried him to a nearby car, and accompanied him right into the doctor's office.

At times, he was equally compassionate with animals. When other boys bloated live frogs by blowing air through tubes of hollow grass into their cloacal cavities, he refused to participate. He befriended the stray dogs and cats that hung around the schoolyard. He knew what it was to feel hungry and unwanted.

One afternoon, Dick Turbin brought his ninety-pound German shepherd to the baseball field. Fritz, a guard dog, did not ordinarily take to strangers. Turbin ordered the shepherd to stay on the hill that overlooked the diamond, while he went off to organize the day's practice. Malcolm summoned the dog, which came right over to him, and put his arm around the animal. When Dick returned, he angrily rebuked Fritz for leaving the hill. Malcolm, who had never before taken issue with his captain, defended Fritz. He reprimanded Dick for being insensitive and dictatorial. The dog apparently understood, for he obeyed Malcolm's command to sit despite the fact that he had been trained to obey only Dick and certain members of Dick's family. Malcolm then asked if he could take Fritz home to show his mother his newfound expertise. Dick agreed and volunteered to join him. The dog walked beside Malcolm instead of taking his appointed place by Dick's heel. When the trio arrived at Malcolm's home, he summoned his mother outside. "Down," he ordered Fritz, who stood without moving. "Speak forcefully and motion downward with your hand," whispered Dick. Malcolm did; the animal obediently sat. His mother was now on notice that he, too, could rule.

Betty Jean Thiel had moved from the neighborhood. As Malcolm grew older, he seemed to become more and more aloof from most of the other white girls, who may have been uneasy about the fact that he wasn't white. It seemed to make no difference to him if they came or went. Yet when other boys engaged their female neighbors or classmates in conversation, Malcolm looked on from afar and grinned in approval, as if he were vicariously enjoying activity from which he apparently felt barred.

One girl he eyed from afar was pretty, slender Betty Girven, who lived directly behind his schoolmate Bob Bebee. Betty, who had matured earlier than many of her classmates, came from a comparatively well-to-do family, as had Betty Jean Thiel. She was outgoing, friendly, popular, and apparently oblivious to Malcolm's interest in her, which had occasionally betrayed itself as empty boasts that he had taken her "into the woods." He claimed she wasn't the only one. Sometimes his allegations took the form of subtle innuendos that this girl or that was seducable. But according to Bob Bebee, there was one girl with whom Malcolm did have sex, a white neighbor who had an evil-tempered stepfather and a mother who was constantly at her throat. Late one night, she met Malcolm and Bob Bebee outside the local Nazarene church. Bob proceeded to have sex with her on the spot. "Quit!" "Quit!" Malcolm implored, "You'll make her pregnant!" But Bob ignored his plea. Finally, he told Malcolm it was his turn. "I can't do that," the girl protested. "Put this cap over your face and make believe it's me," Bob suggested. The girl relented and Malcolm took Bob's place. But he withdrew before ejaculating. He was not going to be guilty of bringing an unwanted child into the world.

Malcolm and Bob performed another experiment one day in the woods. The third participant was a boy they knew named Robert. Physically, Robert was the very image of the all-American boy. He was tall, broad-shouldered, and muscular. But he was also effeminate and considered a sissy. His parents were puritanical. His brother was the apple of their eye. He did everything right. Robert, the black sheep of the family, did everything wrong. Like Malcolm, he was rebellious and stole.

Earlier, Malcolm had stumbled upon Robert masturbating under a tree. Malcolm ordered him to repeat the performance. "He wanted me to see Robert's huge phallus," Bob recalled years later.

Out of fear, perhaps, Robert obeyed. Then Malcolm instructed him to masturbate him. Again Robert obeyed. Malcolm subsequently told Bob that Robert had performed fellatio on him. Bob had no reason to doubt his friend, for Robert had yielded similarly to him.

To Leave or Not to Leave?

7

Shortly after Malcolm turned thirteen, his half-brother "Butch" was born. The event, coupled with rumors of previous maternal love affairs,* apparently provoked him to question his own parentage. He expressed doubt about whether his dark-skinned father could have sired such a light-skinned son. More than once, he suggested that his mother must have been raped by some white lecher. One friend got the feeling that Malcolm believed he had been conceived in iniquity, his very being tainted with some kind of original sin.

In September 1938, Malcolm belatedly began seventh grade at Pleasant Grove School, which the neighborhood children attended up through eighth grade. Olive Roosenraad, the new principal, became his teacher. She was far better educated than most grade school teachers and was well regarded for her dedication and instructional ability. Yet she was stern and cold and insisted on academic perfection. Malcolm responded with the same passive resistance that had exasperated his mother and his previous teachers. He sat sullenly, as if he wanted to curse her but didn't dare. Each time Mrs. Roosenraad returned one of his incomplete papers with a "D" or "E," he grew more and more despondent. He seemed defeated by his previous semester's failure. He would not ask for assistance. Yet when Barbara Hyde, who sat directly behind him, volunteered her help, his chilly exterior vanished. He responded with warmth to her gentle touch. Barbara consid-

---

* A man named Herb Walker boarded at the Littles' after Earl died. Mr. Walker, whose rental payments helped Louise and her children to survive, slept there four or five nights a week; he said it was too far for him to commute to work in Lansing from his home in the town of St. Johns, which is about twenty miles away. Walker reportedly fell in love with Louise, who liked him but refused to marry him; he already had a wife and children.

ered Malcolm to be one of the kindest people she had ever met. Years later, she concluded that his learning difficulties had stemmed from a tendency to shut himself off from the women who had been trying to educate him.

Mrs. Roosenraad suspended Malcolm several times. Each time, he returned to school, only to be suspended again. But one day, Malcolm refused to leave the school grounds. Perhaps he was fed up with being told to get out of his house, his class, his school. Whatever the reason, he stood his ground against eviction, as his father had done. Finally, Mrs. Roosenraad expelled him for good.

Malcolm's apparent inability to decide whether he wanted to be in school or out mirrored his ambivalent feelings about life at home. He didn't want to leave, he would later assert. But time and again, he threatened to run away to the big city, where money, fine clothes, and fancy cars supposedly awaited. Sometimes he sat daydreaming in the front seat of the now-defunct family car, pretending he was driving to Detroit, Chicago, or New York. Though it was only make-believe, his face looked deadly serious.

Prompted by the situation at home, Malcolm and Philbert tried to provoke the authorities to send them away to reform school. "We viewed reform school as a vacation," Philbert later recalled. "We heard they had good beds there. The inmates played ball." And they did not have to worry about where their next meal was coming from. Envisioning such benefits, Malcolm and Philbert temporarily put aside their rivalry and pasted a passing car with ripe tomatoes. But the enraged driver thrashed them and made them wash his automobile.

Their plans for reform school thwarted, Malcolm and Philbert roamed Lansing (separately), dropping in at friends' homes around dinnertime and staying overnight whenever possible. One haven was the home of Arlington Cooper, one of the relatively few boys who liked both Malcolm and Philbert. Arlington's mother, Allie, mothered the entire neighborhood. Philbert actually called her "Mom." He and Malcolm apparently competed with each other for her affection. Allie, who was also poor, understood that it wasn't poverty that drove the two boys from home, but Louise's inability to provide them with the love they needed.

Yet Malcolm's hackles rose if anyone suggested his mother had let him down. Years later, he claimed he was capable of killing, "without hesitation," anyone who uttered disparaging remarks about her.

Malcolm's ambivalence about leaving home was temporarily resolved by his expulsion from Pleasant Grove, which resulted in his transfer to West Junior High School in late October 1938. The decision to send him there in the middle of the semester was apparently predicated upon the fact that West was the only school in Lansing with a sizable black enrollment. Yet the change had little positive impact on Malcolm, who looked neither black nor white. A loner, he mixed infrequently with pupils of either race.

The move to West Junior High was made possible by Mabel and Thornton Gohanna, who, for a fee, agreed to board Malcolm in their West Side home near the school. Malcolm later charged that the move was the first step in a plot by social workers to separate the Little children from their failing mother and place them in foster homes. Surviving records indicate, however, that the decision to relocate Malcolm was not part of any such scheme. It was a short-term expedient designed primarily to enable him to continue his schooling without interruption. His accusations apparently reflected his own divided state of mind.

In many ways, Malcolm liked living at the Gohannas' better than living at home. Mrs. Gohanna, who had no children of her own, took in, fed, and housed everyone from homeless children to ex-cons. The neighborhood kids liked her; so did the adults. Malcolm seemed grateful to the Gohannas, but he appeared to have doubts about whether they really liked him. He dropped hints that living with them was not what it had been cracked up to be. One court record indicates that he got along with them "fairly well," but his stealing continued. He also experienced recurrent headaches. There were disputed reports of conflict between Malcolm and the Gohannas—conflict that may have stemmed from the fact that the Gohannas were straitlaced and sticklers for cleanliness. Moreover, Mrs. Gohanna snooped in her boarders' rooms—a habit Malcolm, who kept things to himself, probably found hard to tolerate.

But the thing Malcolm evidently found most difficult to endure was the Gohannas' religious fervor. They nearly worked themselves into a frenzy at their "Holy Roller" church, which they required him to attend. He refused to criticize them openly for their religious zeal, asserting how nice they were and how much he liked them. Yet, as a rule, he had very little respect for religious people, perhaps because most of those he knew had not set a good example.

One of the boarders at the Gohannas' was a schoolmate of Malcolm's named Dave Roper, who was called "Big Boy." According to Malcolm, the two hit it off nicely; Dave "just wasn't the same" as Malcolm's brothers. Yet, according to Dave, they weren't close. For Malcolm, getting along well apparently meant the absence of conflict.

On weekends, the Gohannas frequently took Malcolm and Big Boy fishing. What little enthusiasm Malcolm had for the sport was soon dampened by an unexpected squall that nearly overturned Mr. Gohanna's rowboat. Malcolm never again ventured into the middle of the lake; he stayed close to shore in Mrs. Gohanna's skiff. He also disliked fishing because it involved so much waiting. And on hunting trips, he impatiently rushed past more game than he sighted. Yet he eventually devised a way to best his adult hunting companions, who used dogs to flush the rabbits from their burrows. The terrified animals instinctively circled right back to their lairs, where the men lay waiting with their rifles. But Malcolm positioned himself in such a way that the fleeing rabbits would likely pass him first. He delighted in the fact he was able to bag most of them before the more experienced hunters could even get in a shot.

The hunting rifle Malcolm used was his father's .22. (He claimed that his mother, who was petrified of guns, had let him have it.) Carelessly, he shot at trees without ascertaining what or who was behind them. He also trudged through thick underbrush with the safety off.

Malcolm spent a good deal of time at the Lincoln Community Center, which provided the underprivileged youngsters of the West Side with a variety of recreational activities. One of them was group discussion. Eagerly, Malcolm participated. He was rarely at a loss for words on these occasions, in contrast to the sullen silence he exhibited at home and school. In fact, it was nearly impossible to silence him once he got the floor. At times, he spoke so fast that he forgot what he had intended to say. Like his father, he was opinionated. If his authority was questioned, he grew angry.

Malcolm also got attention at Lincoln Center in other ways. He made noise in the library. He stole onto the basketball court while the girls were playing and absconded with the ball. If one of the supervisors told him to leave, he'd come back, as he had done at Pleasant Grove. The supervisors who apparently had the most trouble with him were female. One woman repeatedly refused to let him use the Center's facilities. On one occasion, she reportedly dug her fingernails into his neck. Malcolm threatened to kill her. She ordered him to leave and, when he refused, summoned the police.

On some weekends Malcolm visited home. He was glad when Big Boy or one of the Gohannas accompanied him, as it made the ordeal easier. His mother's ordeal was far greater. Her widow's pension had been terminated by county officials who were reportedly incensed by her refusal to disclose the identity of her new baby's father. Grimly, she stuck to her guns and martyred herself for her tall, dark-skinned lover, who abandoned her.

The pressure on Louise became so unbearable that she sought refuge in a world of fantasy. Just before Christmas of 1938, she was discovered walking barefoot along a snow-encrusted road. Her baby, clutched in her arms, was covered head to toe with sores. Disheveled, unwashed, and nearly hysterical, she was taken to the state mental hospital at Kalamazoo for examination. Malcolm subsequently blamed her collapse on the white social workers. He reportedly criticized unnamed family members for agreeing to her hospitalization. At times, he seemed reluctant to admit that she was mentally ill or that the underlying cause of her illness was ascertainable. But he did acknowledge that his delinquent behavior had contributed to her emotional breakdown.

On January 9, 1939, Louise was adjudged insane and formally committed to the Kalamazoo asylum. Three days later, his old friend and fellow classroom rebel Ores Whitney died of a cerebral hemorrhage. When Malcolm was told, he burst into tears. His whole world was coming apart.

Several months before Malcolm's mother was institutionalized, the African-American boxer Joe Louis had k.o.'d Max Schmelling, Adolf Hitler's vaunted master-race pugilist, in one round. According to Malcolm, nearly every black boy in America dreamed of becoming the next heavyweight champ. Philbert had already made quite a reputation for himself in the ring; one of his opponents ended up in the hospital with a broken jaw. Consequently, Reginald began transferring his admiration from Malcolm to Philbert. In hope of stemming this erosion, Malcolm put aside his fear and decided to compete in the local Golden Gloves tournament. He was still doing abysmally in school; perhaps he felt he could do better in another realm.

Malcolm's first opponent was Bill Peterson, a capable fighter who snorted each time he threw a punch. The afternoon of their fight, nearly everyone Malcolm knew was in Lansing's packed Prudden Auditorium, including his brothers and sisters, who were eager to see how he'd fare in comparison to Philbert. Malcolm later admitted he was scared. When Peterson, who was white, emerged from his corner, Malcolm apparently froze, either because he was afraid of injuring Peterson or of being injured himself. His arms fell defenseless by his sides. Bill swung, but the blow struck air, probably because Malcolm was backpedaling so furiously. To the consternation of his brothers and sisters, he fell to the canvas anyway. He covered his head with his hands and stayed put until Peterson had backed away. According to Malcolm's version of the encounter, Bill knocked him down fifty times if he did once. In reality, the fight ended before the sound of the first bell had faded away.

Malcolm's reputation plummeted. Reginald's reaction was particularly humiliating. It wasn't what he said; it was what he didn't say.

Malcolm withdrew into a shell. "He acted as if the whole world was against him," says Barbara Hyde. Yet, after some time, he started training again. He trained diligently. When his preparations were complete, he summoned up his courage and arranged a rematch.

But though he had conquered his fear, Bill defeated him again. The fight lasted less than one round.

Malcolm—who, according to Reginald, was constantly trying to shore up his self-esteem—tried to restore his sagging reputation. He did it by deliberately flouting a time-honored rule and walking into his social studies class with his hat on. The white teacher, Sewell Henry, tried to beat him at his own game. He instructed Malcolm to keep the hat on and to keep walking around the classroom until he was told to stop. "That way, everyone can see you," he said. But when Henry turned his back to the class to write on the blackboard, Malcolm placed a thumbtack on his chair. Henry returned to his desk, sat down, and howled when the tack pierced his flesh.

Malcolm was not expelled, as his autobiography maintains. He remained at West Junior High and managed to squeak through the seventh grade. Some time after the semester ended, he returned to his parentless home, where nineteen-year-old Wilfred was working himself to exhaustion in an effort to keep the family from starving. There was no time for fathering. The burden of cooking, washing, ironing, mending, house-cleaning, and caring for the younger children fell primarily upon sixteen-year-old Hilda, who had been changing diapers since she was nine. Malcolm's attitude toward his "second mother" was ambivalent. He expressed concern about the pressure she was under and said he loved her. Yet he left all the work to her. Moreover, he frequently disobeyed her, perhaps because she was so much like his mother. She nagged him about cleanliness and the need to excel in school. She was also dictatorial, according to Reginald. Like Louise, she told Malcolm to let the sun darken his skin. Nevertheless, Reginald got the feeling that Hilda secretly favored Malcolm because he was so light.

Malcolm slept at home very little that summer. When he did, he frequently asked Arlington Cooper or someone else to keep him company. It wasn't just the loneliness. No one at home cared about him, he told Maynard Allyn, a social worker who periodically dropped in. By mid-August, Malcolm decided he'd be better off elsewhere and asked Allyn if the Ingham County authorities would allow him to live in the county juvenile home, which was a refuge for neglected children as well as a way station for juvenile offenders who were likely candidates for reform school.

Allyn recommended that fourteen-year-old Malcolm be made a ward of the county court, placed on probation, and housed in the juvenile home. Judge John McClellan followed Allyn's recommendations and granted Malcolm's request. Malcolm shed no tears as he departed for the county seat of Mason, where the juvenile home was located. Despite his later assertion that his departure had been forced on him by white officials, he was only too glad to be leaving a home that was so beleaguered and devoid of love.

CHAMELEON

8

The town of Mason, which lies about ten miles south of Lansing, had been hacked out of a forest of hardwood trees: ash, maple, beech, hickory, elm, black walnut, sycamore, tulip, and oak. Some of the settlers who had transformed the forest into farmland served in the Union Army during the Civil War. After the war ended, a number of newly emancipated slaves accompanied the victorious troops back to the North, hoping it would be a more hospitable environment. But one ex-slave who had accompanied a group of Ingham County veterans back to Michigan was jailed on charges of murdering three women. Shortly thereafter, a mob broke into the Mason jail, overpowered the sheriff, and looped a rope around the neck of the black prisoner, who was still in his teens. They dragged him through the streets half a mile or more before they hanged him from a sturdy sycamore. Afterwards, all three of his alleged victims were found alive and well.

When Malcolm arrived in Mason, he was given his own room—the first he had ever had. But the best thing about the Ingham County juvenile home was the jovial, buxom woman who ran it: Lois Swerlein. "Ma" Swerlein was big—bigger than her husband, and probably stronger. But her ability to control her youthful charges was only incidentally related to her bulk. Children respected her authority because she exercised it with wisdom and compassion. Almost invariably, they liked her.

Malcolm was no exception. The disciplined but undictatorial environment was just what he needed. His appetite improved and he put on weight. Mrs. Swerlein, whose friends affectionately called her "Mrs. Gold Dust" because she used lavish quantities of Gold Dust soap powder, was as fanatic about cleanliness as Malcolm's mother had initially been. Yet Malcolm took all the dusting, sweeping, and mopping in stride. With an eagerness that Louise and Hilda would have found hard to believe, he even volunteered for extra chores.

Malcolm was apparently unsure whether his new housemother liked him or just appreciated the diligence with which he performed his household duties. He was soon boasting about his special privileges, both real and imaginary. He incorrectly maintained that he was the only detention home resident who had ever attended Mason Junior High School. Yet because of school and his part-time job, he was the only youth in Mrs. Swerlein's home who was free to come and go as he pleased. And unlike the other youthful residents, he was not transferred to a foster home or a reform school. He later asserted that he had been told he would be sent to reform school. But surviving records make no mention of reform school. Perhaps some officials threatened to send him there in an effort to deter him from further delinquency. But no threat was needed. The juvenile home was the best home Malcolm had ever had. He didn't want to leave it.

Though Judge McClellan was the official who decided where Malcolm would reside, Malcolm attributed his extended stay in the juvenile home entirely to Mrs. Swerlein. It was apparently important for him to feel there was one "ma" in the world who seemed to care.

Smiled on by those in charge at home, Malcolm lost his need to wage war against authority figures at school. He was respectful to his teachers and attentive in class. In his eighth grade class, he ranked third. (Years later, he told one writer that he had invariably ranked first.) His performance may have been partly due to the fact that Mrs. Swerlein wanted him to do well in school, but it was chiefly due to his ability. When his English teacher called on him to recite a theme he had neglected to prepare at home, he stood, looked down at his notebook, and began reciting. Few, if any, of his classmates realized he was ad-libbing from a perfectly blank page.

Since Malcolm was the only eighth grade student who was black, some of his teachers tried hard to make him feel comfortable. But others created obstacles. His history teacher, Otto Grein, welcomed him to class one day by singing, "Way down yonder in the cotton field, some folks say that a nigger won't steal." African feet were so large, Mr. Grein asserted, that they leave holes in the ground. Malcolm, whose feet were large, got the message. Some of his classmates noticed, however, that Mr. Grein's feet were equally large.

"Little Malcolm"—his classmates teased him about his height—dealt with such people as best as he could. He became so adept at making friends that, with Mrs. Swerlein's backing, he was soon "tight" with many members of Mason's youthful upper crust. One friend was the daughter of one of the owners of the town's Chevrolet agency. Another was the son of a bank president. Malcolm became such a good politician that he was elected class president the second semester. He could hardly believe it. He attributed his election to his good grades and his pinkish, non-African appearance. The grades, however, had nothing to do with it. The reason he was so popular was that most of his classmates liked him. But he didn't seem to realize it, perhaps because he had felt unloved for so long.

Another factor contributing to Malcolm's election was that he was a natural leader. He was a year or so older than most of his classmates and well over six feet tall. His voice had a commanding quality. Thus, a group of boys paid heed one wintry afternoon when he spoke in defense of a country boy who had foolishly ignored the unwritten rule that "farmers" were supposed to get out of town after school. The "townies" wanted to seat the intruder on an outdoor drinking fountain. But Malcolm intervened. "Hey, guys," he said, "this fella has a long walk ahead of him before he gets home. If the seat of his pants gets wet in this sub-freezing weather. . . ." The would-be assailants got the point; the boy was allowed to proceed unscathed.

Malcolm exercised his growing authority in school. Periodically, the student body assembled in the auditorium. A teacher was posted in the balcony, where Malcolm's class sat. Malcolm asserted there was no need to station a teacher there to keep order. He said he'd do it himself—and he did. His authority was respected.

Yet his popularity was of little relevance when it came to dating girls. He was a good-looking youth, invariably gentlemanly in deportment, and—despite his modest assertions to the contrary—a good dancer. Outside Matthew's Eatery, where he earned money scrubbing dirty dishes and greasy pots and pans, he entertained bystanders with high-stepping sidewalk solos. But at school dances, he learned not to ask the white girls to dance. The first time he tried it, irate upperclassmen intervened. Malcolm retorted, "You didn't have a chance to choose your ancestors either."

Gradually, he developed ways to deal with the white girl problem. He'd smile, chat with one girl or another, and move on before any of the white boys got upset. When he was alone with a girl, a wall would arise between them. Some girls, oblivious of the constraints under which he labored, thought him cold. Others understood. One of them was a friendly, outgoing girl named Betty Ann Kennedy, who tried her best to make him feel at home. Like Malcolm, she was fatherless. A mutual friend got the feeling that Malcolm was sweet on Betty, who had a lovely figure. If so, she was unaware of it. Black boys were not supposed to be interested in white girls.

But some of the white girls were interested in him. One, Audrey Slagh, lived near the juvenile home and frequently encountered him on the way home from school. She was even taller for her age than Malcolm was—so tall that most boys shied away from her. But Malcolm was just the right height. Half the town knew Audrey cared for him. But Malcolm acted indifferent toward her, even though, by spending time with him, she risked incurring the displeasure of her parents and peers. "If my father discovers that I'm seeing you," she reportedly told him, "he'll kill me."

Then, suddenly, Audrey lost her father in an auto accident. According to one of her close friends, she felt somewhat responsible for his death because she had asked him to venture out onto the icy highway that had apparently contributed to the fatal crash. But she and Malcolm did not share their feelings about their respective losses.

Malcolm did discuss his father's death with his friend Ralph Taylor, who was also fatherless. When Ralph asked him how his father had died, Malcolm's response was hesitant. "Some call it an accident," he said. "Some say it was suicide." His easy-going veneer suddenly vanished. He slammed a fist into the palm of his hand and exclaimed, "We think it was murder!" But his voice betrayed his uncertainty and Ralph got the impression that he was parroting what he had been told by someone else.

The white girl issue was not the only one that marred Malcolm's stay in Mason. When anything was stolen at school, he was the first to be questioned. To get a haircut, he either had to patronize the local barbershops after hours or take a bus into Lansing. Older boys "accidentally" elbowed him as he passed by. Even the Swerleins called him a "nigger." Malcolm tried to let such things roll off his back. They bothered him, he claimed, "only vaguely."

But he later admitted that they bothered him enough to make him wish he were white. He boasted that he was the lightest child in his family.

When Malcolm visited Lansing on weekends, he transformed himself, like a chameleon, to fit into his non-white surroundings. He tailored his behavior to the demands of each color-conscious environment in other ways. For instance, among serious-minded blacks—the ones he seemed to respect—he talked about things that mattered. Among low-lives, he spoke gutter-talk and acted as if he had seduced every white girl in Mason. On one occasion, he dramatized the point by taking a condom out of his pocket and explaining his preference for the lubricated variety. He also participated peripherally in an incident in which a white woman was molested on the street by a number of older black youths. He seemed easily led by such boys, whom he openly envied and imitated. Conversely, younger boys sought his leadership, as did boys his age.

Malcolm was not as successful a politician in Lansing as he was in Mason. The West Side boys called him "Red." The label apparently infuriated Malcolm, who seemed to prefer the nickname "Harpy," which apparently alluded to the fact that he was constantly harping, or mouthing off, about something. The nickname also alluded to a popular comic-strip version of the harpies of Greek mythology—half-human, vulture-like female creatures who liked to steal. The feminine connotation stuck, due to an unconfirmed report that Malcolm had been seen wearing a dress. Though the garment may have been a Halloween costume, "Harpy" became "Madame Harpy," then plain "Madame."

There were other reasons he failed to win the acceptance of the older boys he emulated. During ball games, he became all fingers and thumbs. The other players erroneously concluded that he was unathletic and uncoordinated. They chided him unmercifully about his fear of physical encounter. "Sissy! Sissy! Sissy!" Malcolm smiled back and apparently fought to control the anger that flashed in his eyes. On those rare occasions that his self-control "weakened" and he lashed back, he was soundly thrashed. Street-corner spectators had to intervene to save him from serious harm.

Malcolm fared no better with the West Side girls than he did with the boys. It was partly his fault, for he exhibited no more interest in black girls than he did in white ones. He didn't give the time of day to those who seemed interested in him. If they made overtures, he'd blush or retreat into the nearest corner. Yet he became angry when girls ignored him or showered attention upon Philbert.

Malcolm later acknowledged that there were girls he wanted. But he had a funny way of telling them. At the Palomar Skating Rink, he roller-skated up to vivacious, one-hundred-and-five-pound Zelma Holman, handed her a love-note scribbled on a Mr. Goodbar candy wrapper, and sped away. Zelma didn't take him seriously. Neither did Jean Seaton, whose family had befriended his mother years before. Jean's parents and sister Bethel knew that Malcolm was fond of her. But when he "dropped in," he was uncharacteristically at a loss for words, particularly if older boys were present. He wouldn't speak unless he was spoken to first. Jean's sister sensed that his reticence was due to his feeling that he was not really wanted.

Indeed, he was unwanted by many of Lansing's blacks, particularly those who aspired to middle-class status and looked down on Malcolm because of his poverty and his West Indian background. They wanted their daughters to go with "respectable" boys. But Malcolm's penchant for stealing, his father's unsavory reputation, and his mother's mental illness excluded him from such ranks. He was no more accepted by Lansing's blacks than he was by Mason's whites. At West Side parties, he stood around, watching others jitterbug, bob for apples, or spin the bottle. He was always on the edge of the crowd, a lonely-looking, uncommunicative, forgotten youngster.

DASHED HOPES　9

Ella Little, Malcolm's oldest half-sister, had been an unwanted child. After her father Earl deserted her mother, Ella was foisted off onto her maternal grandparents, who welcomed her without enthusiasm. No doubt they were relieved when Earl retrieved her and gave her to his unmarried sister Sarah Alice. That done, he washed his hands of his eldest daughter. She saw him only once more.

Sarah, who lived in Georgia with Earl's father John Little, raised Ella for the better part of a decade. She was John's seventh, hence favorite, child. Since Ella was so indebted to her, it ultimately fell to her to make sure her father's seventh child, Malcolm, was groomed for the destiny that had been ordained for him.

Louise Little's hospitalization provided an opportunity for Ella, who had moved to Boston in the interim, to discharge her duty. First, she went to Michigan and visited Malcolm and her other half-brothers and sisters. Philbert, who may have sensed Ella's partiality for his rival, was at loggerheads with her from the moment she arrived in Lansing. His refusal to obey one of her edicts prompted her to threaten to scald him with boiling water. When she reached for the hot water kettle in an apparent effort to demonstrate that she was serious, he sent her to her knees with a quick right.

Malcolm, in contrast, was greatly impressed with the purposeful, commanding young woman from Boston, who behaved as if she were accustomed to getting her way. She hugged him, asked him all sorts of questions, and praised him about his grades.

Ella accompanied the family to Kalamazoo to visit Louise. When the two women embraced, the contrast between Malcolm's thin, ailing mother and the big, strapping visitor from Massachusetts was immediately apparent. Louise seemed defeated, a shell of her former self. Ella exuded vigor and confidence. Even her skin color was the antithesis of Malcolm's mother's. According to Malcolm, it was "jet black," like his father's. But in reality, neither Earl nor Ella was that dark. His insistence that they were was indicative of the way he equated blackness with the strength his light-skinned mother had lacked.

Shortly before Malcolm completed the eighth grade, he found himself alone with his English teacher Richard Kaminska, a burly, bushy-moustached ex-football player who ran his classes like coaches run teams. "Kammy's" former college teammates called him "The Bear." He was tall and reddish-complected, like Malcolm. Originally, he'd had hopes of becoming a psychiatrist, but he had been stymied by his inability to afford medical school. He was constantly exhorting his pupils to achieve the success that had eluded him.

Kaminska asked Malcolm whether he had been giving thought to a career.

Though Malcolm's autobiography insists he hadn't been, he replied, "Well, yes, sir. I've been thinking I'd like to be a lawyer." After all, attorneys could prevent evictions. They could keep mothers out of mental institutions. They relished verbal battle, as Malcolm did. They knew how to win over authority figures. And they didn't have to wash dishes to earn money.

The Bear was taken aback by this black boy who aspired to greater heights than he had achieved. He tried to smile as he counseled Malcolm to relinquish his dreams. "Don't misunderstand me," he said:

> We all here like you, you know that. But you've got to be realistic about being a nigger. A lawyer—that's no realistic goal for a nigger. You need to think about something you *can* be. You're good with your hands. . . . Why don't you plan on carpentry?

Malcolm laughed about the incident when he recounted it years later. But it wasn't funny when it occurred. He kept thinking about Kaminska's suggestion that he consider a career of carpentry. The Bear hadn't discouraged the white students who aspired to professional careers. Apparently, there was no place for success-oriented blacks in the white world, no matter how smart or light-skinned they were.

A classmate named Jim Cotton attempted to reassure Malcolm that he could do anything he wanted to do. But since Jim was not an authority figure, Malcolm apparently accorded his statement little weight.

From class president to class carpenter was a comedown Malcolm understandably took very hard. "I just gave up," he ruefully admitted, years later.

He virtually abandoned his schoolwork and turned his attention to sports. His exceptional height helped him land a spot on the junior varsity basketball team. By all reports, he was a better player than he gave himself credit for. He also joined the football team and saw occasional action as an end. He even sparred with other boys in the boxing ring and talked about the possibility of re-entering the Golden Gloves. ("Do what you fear to do," he later advised one associate.)

But Malcolm shrank from confronting what Kaminska had billed as the insuperable obstacles to a successful career. He began hanging around street corners with his intellectual inferiors, outwardly indifferent about the college education he had previously lamented he couldn't afford. At school, he reverted to the self-defeating, defiant noncompliance that had characterized his years at Pleasant Grove. The school band director, Joseph Wyman, had to tell him repeatedly to stop swinging the curtain that formed the auditorium stage backdrop. "Why do you insist?" he asked. Malcolm replied, "I'm blowing all that hot air back where it came from." Mr. Wyman ousted him on the spot.

It was not Malcolm's last eviction. At a class mixer, he took the bit in his mouth and asked a white girl to dance. She turned him down. He asked another. She, too, refused. All at once, Malcolm plopped himself on top of the piano, reached down, and planted his long, bony fingers on the keyboard. The pianist had to stop playing. The other musicians followed suit and the music ground to a halt. If Malcolm couldn't dance, neither would anyone else.

The school principal, Cliff Walcott, hurried over and asked him to desist. There was a lot of commotion and Malcolm was asked to leave. Once again, he had provoked his own ouster.

Spurned by Mason whites and Lansing blacks alike, Malcolm withdrew even further into his shell. Friends like Jim Cotton found him unreceptive and bitter, as if he had a grudge against the entire world. Another person who sensed the anger was Maynard Allyn. "Someday," he said to himself, "this boy is going to explode!"

Whether Malcolm's courageous defiance of the ban on interracial dancing preceded or followed his first trip to Boston is not entirely clear. Ella had invited him to visit her there. Though the journey took him perhaps a day and a half, it seemed like a month to Malcolm, who acknowledged his impatience.

The Boston Malcolm visited had little resemblance to the nineteenth-century city that had boasted William Lloyd Garrison's crusading news paper campaign against slavery. In fact, during the Civil War, Boston's blacks, who numbered no more than three thousand, were somewhat better off than their counterparts in other U.S. cities. As a group, they apparently fared better economically than the despised Irish. According to the historian Oscar Handlin, blacks seemed as reluctant to allow Irish immigrants into their neighborhoods as Boston's Yankees did.

But as the Irish-American population became assimilated and amassed political and economic power, things changed. They changed even more as waves of uneducated, unskilled, southern blacks poured into the city. These black immigrants, unlike their Irish counterparts, found it virtually impossible to join the American mainstream. For instance, when Malcolm arrived in Boston, only six of the city's 1541 insurance agents were black. By virtue of the size of the city's black population, the number should have been nearly ten times that amount. And more than half the city's black males—that is, those who were employed—were still confined to menial occupations. One black Bostonian wrote, "I always thought Boston was above the Mason Dixon line, but I see it has gradually slipped a long ways back."

Nevertheless, the city, with its neon lights, nightclubs, blaring juke-boxes, and large black population, made a powerful impact upon Malcolm. Black men strolled openly with white women, arm in arm. In letters intended for everyone back home, Malcolm wrote and told Wilfred that he would try to describe his experiences when he returned to Michigan. But when he did, he was no more able to tell his brothers and sisters about those experiences than he was able to share his feelings about anything else.

Back in Mason, Lois Swerlein kept asking Malcolm what was wrong. But he wouldn't tell her, partly because she "niggered" him with the same kindly condescension that Kaminska had exuded, and partly because of his inability to trust women—an inability he would later acknowledge.

Unable to crack Malcolm's wall of silence, Mrs. Swerlein persuaded Judge McClellan to board him in the Mason home of another black couple who, she said, liked him very much. But the arrangement didn't work well; Harold and Ivy Lyons already had five children, whom they supported by denying themselves practically everything. Since Malcolm was not their child, he may have felt once again like the least-favored youth in the household. He apparently attempted to deny his second-class position by laying claim to favored status. For example, each week, he monopolized the Sunday funnies and doled them out to the other, younger children, just as Wilfred had doled them out at home.

Word filtered back to the juvenile home that Malcolm thought the Lyonses were nice people, but that he didn't like living with them. The Lyonses evidently had no idea he was unhappy. He laughed at Mr.

Lyons's jokes, even if they weren't funny. He dutifully attended church. When Christmas rolled around, he used his hard-earned money to buy a present for each member of the Lyons family. Like his mother, he made it a practice to repay those to whom he felt indebted.

Mr. Lyons, who kept fit lifting weights, handed Malcolm his two-hundred-pound barbell one evening and stood there laughing as Malcolm vainly tried to raise it above his waist. Beads of sweat hung from his brow. Finally, Mr. Lyons had to rescue him from his embarrassing predicament.

Mr. Lyons was not unsympathetic to Malcolm's needs. But in order to survive, economically and otherwise, he had to get along with Mason's whites, to whom he deferred despite the autocratic way he treated his children. His wife was equally deferential. When she was invited to local weddings, she arrived at church a half hour early and climbed alone to the balcony, where she sat unnoticed to avoid "embarrassing" her white hosts. She and her husband were told, in no uncertain terms, that they would be held responsible if Malcolm made any advances to any white girls.

The precarious acceptance Harold and Ivy Lyons had labored so assiduously to achieve was severely jeopardized by Malcolm's determination to date whomever he pleased. He ignored the nighttime curfew they tried to impose. And he flouted the unwritten rule against interracial couples by walking hand in hand down Maple Street with an independent-minded, older girl named June Palmer. June, like Audrey, Betty Kennedy, and Ralph Taylor, was fatherless.

The situation became unviable, both at the Lyonses's and at the school, whose exasperated administrators petitioned the Probate Court to return Malcolm to Lansing. It was evidently at this juncture that Malcolm was placed in the home of Sidney Grayson, an elderly black resident of Mason. A week or two later, Malcolm asked to be returned to the county juvenile home. The Graysons, like the Gohannas and the Lyonses, were nice people, he said. But he couldn't stand living with them.

Mrs. Swerlein, who may have felt that such a move wouldn't work, did not take Malcolm back. So Malcolm wrote Ella and told her he wanted to come to Boston to live. He did not tell her why. It was not a happy thing to have to admit that no one in Michigan seemed to want him.

II
CRIMEWARD

A HOME AT LAST   10

Ella, who later claimed that Earl Little had been a prosperous landowner and peanut farmer, welcomed Malcolm into her comfortable Harrishof Street home with open arms when he arrived there in early February 1941. She began working hard to mold him to her image of her father. Daily pep talks were just part of her program of elevating her fifteen-year-old half-brother above the hoi polloi. She wanted him to become a successful lawyer. Years later, she talked about running him for President.

Malcolm didn't want to disappoint Ella, whose ambition had been thwarted because she was uneducated, black, and female. He tried very hard to please her, but it was impossible. Ella was as perfectionistic as his mother had been. Instead of encouraging him, she "ripped him apart" in the belief that he'd emerge stronger from the ordeal. He reacted to her disapproval as if he had been hit on the head with a brick.

Moreover, Ella tried to rule him the way she ruled everyone else. Again and again, she made him tidy up his room. When he went out, she demanded to know where he was going. She refused to let him have parties for his friends at her home. Yet she entertained her own friends lavishly in an apparent effort to win the acceptance of the local black upper crust.

At first, Malcolm yielded to Ella's blandishments. He didn't want to upset the one adult who clearly regarded him with favor. He dutifully maintained that he loved his half-sister, who provided the material support his mother had been unable to provide. Privately, however, he complained about her autocratic behavior, which resembled their father's.

As time passed, Malcolm began to rebel. When Ella went on vacation, he hosted a party every night. She returned to find his scribbled confessions. One said, "I broke three cups." Another said something like, "I know I'm going to get killed, but I didn't damage anything."

Gradually, Malcolm became more assertive. When Ella asked him to lend a hand fixing up her summer home, he refused. (Sometime later, she shot a horse she had been stabling there. She used the skin for a rug for the wooden floor. When Malcolm found out, he sank to his knees and cried.)

Malcolm also defied Ella's attempts to persuade him to restrict his contacts to the "nice young people" who lived on "the Hill," the part of upper Roxbury where she lived. The Hill was a mixed neighborhood; that is, until the postwar exodus of Jews and Irish who fled the advancing urban blight. The black portion of the population was stratified and cliquish. The so-called Four Hundred, the Massachusetts-born, self-appointed black elite, despised the southern newcomers who were allegedly causing the neighborhood to decay. Most of these old-timers had menial jobs. Some of them cleaned toilets. Yet they behaved like Boston Brahmins. Malcolm bitterly resented their Earl-Little-like pretensions.

The Hill boys he associated with were unaware of this. He followed around the older ones but led those who were younger, as he had done in Lansing. If someone tried to give him a hard time, he'd fasten him with a menacing glare, stick his square chin within half an inch of his adversary's nose, and snarl, "What did you say?" Somehow, he had learned how to employ fear to combat his own fear. The other boys, who had no way of knowing that he had been considered a sissy in Lansing, didn't call his bluff because he was so big.

But the girls were not inhibited by his size. They snickered because of the way his arms protruded from the sleeves of his apple-green suit, which clashed with his reddish hair. To the teenage female sophisticates of the Hill, he looked as if he had just come from some farm.

Spurned, Malcolm gravitated towards other social rejects—those who inhabited the lower Roxbury ghetto, where people were not measured according to position or family. He said he felt more relaxed among the ghetto dwellers because they accepted him. Besides, downtown Roxbury, with its noisy, gaudy nightspots, was exciting. During one of his exploratory tours, a busy pool joint caught his eye. But he didn't go in; instead, he gazed through the front window at the poolsharks inside, watching them play. Day after day, he returned and stood outside the poolroom the way he had stood around Lansing ballparks and basketball courts, watching other boys play.

Finally, one day Malcolm ventured inside and started talking to a squat-looking young man who had been racking up balls for the customers. Earlier, the attendant, whom Malcolm's autobiography calls "Shorty," had seen him loitering outside. He had been so friendly that Malcolm figured he'd be a good person to ask about where he could find a poolroom job.

Malcolm didn't get a job, but he did make a friend. When "Shorty"—a fictional composite of a number of real-life people—discovered that Malcolm had recently left Mason, he happily exclaimed, "Man, gimme some skin! I'm from Lansing!"

For several hours, Shorty "schooled" Malcolm. He said a half sister who gave him a place to stay without demanding rent in return couldn't be "all bad." He told Malcolm how much he liked gambling. He also acknowledged his penchant for the white prostitutes who worked for some of the pimps who hung around the poolroom. Sheepishly, Malcolm admitted that he had never gambled or slept with a white whore. "Hell, man, don't be ashamed," Shorty declared. Unlike many of the young men and women who lived on the Hill, he treated Malcolm as an equal.

For the next few months, Shorty, who became one of the most influential teachers Malcolm had ever had, gave him his baptism of fast living. He began smoking marijuana and betting a dollar a day on the numbers. Then he decided to buy a zoot suit. The zoot, which had apparently originated as a joke in a small Georgia town and had somehow leap-frogged across the Black Belt to the growing ghettos of the North, was just then coming into vogue.

Shorty induced a Jewish salesman who worked in a nearby clothing store to extend Malcolm the necessary credit. The sales clerk went to a rack and selected a rakish-looking, sky-blue suit. The jacket had huge, padded shoulders and a narrow, constricted waist that made Malcolm's torso look almost triangular.

Malcolm also allowed the salesman to talk him into buying a blue, derby-like hat with a feather protruding from its enormous, saucer-like brim. A string connected the hat to the suit lapel. It was designed to prevent the hat from being blown off his head by the wind.

Dressed impeccably in his new outfit, which flouted the relatively conservative traditions of the Hill, Malcolm stood "profiling" on street corners, twirling his gold-plated keychain like Symphony Sid, the disc jockey who had helped popularize the zoot suit. From time to time, his hand eased into his pocket and conspicuously jangled some loose change.

In an apparent attempt to project the image of a man transformed, he had several photographs made. The first he gave to Ella, who wisely resigned herself to his new attire. He sent another picture of the "new" Malcolm to his brothers and sisters in Lansing.

By this time, Malcolm's hair had grown long enough to be "conked" like Shorty's, so that it would not look African. Following Shorty's instructions, he purchased some lye, two potatoes, and a couple of eggs. Shorty cut up the potatoes and put them in a jar. Then he added the lye and eggs. Malcolm placed a hand against the jar and quickly drew it away. "Damn right, it's hot," said Shorty. "That's the lye."

Malcolm never forgot how it felt when Shorty combed the yellow, starchy paste into his hair:

> My head caught fire. . . . I gritted my teeth and tried to pull the sides
> of the kitchen table together. The comb felt as if it was raking my
> skin off.

But Malcolm's first look in the mirror quenched the pain, for his hair was as smooth and straight "as any white man's." It was also bright red. Now he could be proud of the nickname "Red."

Back on the Hill, Malcolm's flashy attire evoked an enormous amount of interest and commentary. But in the long run, his attention-getting behavior, born of childhood neglect, ensured his rejection by most of those who counted. The girls, especially, were repelled by his loudmouthed antics. Some snubbed him because he didn't have the "right" family background.

Indiscriminantly, Malcolm fought fire with fire. He looked down his nose, not only at the girls who snubbed him, but also at many who didn't. Privately, he boasted how he intended to date some of the girls in whom he was outwardly disinterested. But he did not ask them out. When one of them later died, Malcolm observed at her funeral how lovely she looked, lying there. He said he had always wanted to kiss her. As he turned away from the open coffin, he admitted that he still wanted to kiss her.

One Hill girl who liked Malcolm was Margaret Richmond, whose sinewy six-foot brother John was his best friend on the Hill. She was tall and slim like a model, with long, lustrous hair. Not only was she attractive; she was also a superb dancer. Though Malcolm spent lots of time with her, he seemed indifferent toward her. But his interest perked up after a boy named Gordon Coleman stole her away. When Malcolm found out, he stomped out of Margaret's house and told John to tell Gordon he was displeased. But he did not tell Gordon himself. A week later, he ran into him and promptly offered his hand, as if absolutely nothing had happened.

Everyone knew the girl Malcolm liked best was Gloria Strother, one of the Hill girls who had made fun of his clothes. Gloria belonged to the social set that ranked just below the Four Hundred.

At first, Gloria tried to avoid Malcolm when he showed up at her school library, selected a book, and seated himself near—but not too near—her. "That dude's following you around," whispered her girl-friend. Gloria ducked behind a schoolbook.

Day after day Malcolm returned. For quite some time, he didn't even try to speak to her. Yet there was something about the way he looked at her. Before she realized what was happening, she was going to the library because she knew she'd find him there.

Though Malcolm pursued Gloria hesitantly, it became understood on the Hill that she was Malcolm's girl. He serenaded her with Louis Jordan's popular song about an amorous lad who tells his sweetheart he will spirit her away from her other suitors. He even invited her to Ella's once or twice. Gloria sensed he was proud of Ella's growing affluence.

Malcolm also introduced Gloria to his younger half-sister Mary and his father's sister Sarah, who had been living in Boston for some time. Aunt Sarah prophesied that he would someday be a great man.

In a cautious, roundabout way, Malcolm eventually broached the subject of marriage to Gloria. He wanted children—seven of them, he told her. Gloria didn't take him seriously; most of the time, he acted as if he didn't give a hoot about her or any other girl. For instance, instead of asking her out, he simply showed up at the parties she attended and courted her there. And rather than walk her home, he'd ask some other boy to do it—usually someone in whom she was completely uninterested. He said he didn't mind if she dated other boys when he was away. And the night of her junior prom, he stood her up. He behaved the same way with other girls; if he was supposed to show up at eight, they'd be lucky to see him by ten. Women didn't spurn him—he spurned them.

But despite Malcolm's indifferent facade, his need for Gloria occasionally showed through. If she spent too much time with another boy, he'd pull her aside and protest. "She's my old lady," he told one would-be rival. As a matter of fact, Gloria bore some resemblance to Malcolm's mother, who was the only person about whom he spoke with feeling in her presence. Her skin, like Mrs. Little's, was nearly white. Like Louise, she was tall and exquisitely proportioned. Even the way she spoke was beautiful.

Malcolm acted differently around Gloria than he did around the women he met in lower Roxbury's barrooms. He never tried to have sex with her, or even tried to touch her. Nor did he ever exhibit any anger toward her. In fact, to all appearances, there was little communication between Malcolm and Gloria. He loved her at a very safe distance.

WHITE WOMAN 11

Malcolm successfully defied Ella's efforts to keep him in school. What use was education if success was precluded, as Mr. Kaminska maintained?

Malcolm's first part-time job in Boston, shining shoes in the Roseland State Ballroom's men's room, was not what Ella had in mind for him either. But Roseland was the place where the big-name bands played when they came to Boston. Malcolm was so excited about the opportunity to rub shoulders with famous musicians such as Count Basie and Glenn Miller that he dashed off to the ballroom without even eating dinner.

Like Shorty, the shoeshine boy who trained Malcolm at Roseland was a good teacher. Before the first lesson ended, Malcolm had refurbished the footwear of several drunks who had strayed into the men's room.

The shoeshine boy kept tutoring him as he drove Malcolm home. "Pick up a couple of dozen packs of rubbers," he advised. He said the men who needed them would ask for them; other patrons might want reefers or liquor. "The main thing you got to remember," he added as he dropped Malcolm in front of Ella's, "is that everything in the world is a hustle."

Malcolm learned fast. Before long, he was making more money putting customers in touch with prostitutes than he was polishing their shoes.

When he ran out of customers, he'd sneak downstairs to the dance floor and watch the dance contests that were held in the ballroom. During them, only the best—Malcolm used the word "greatest"—dancers stayed on the floor. The others retired to the sidelines and formed a circle or a big "U" around the lindying contestants.

Occasionally, well-known jazz musicians such as Lionel Hampton, Sonny Greer, and Cootie Williams came to the rest room and grabbed a shine. Malcolm worshipped the ground they walked on. Years later, he would portray many of them as his friends. Some, he said, were his close friends. But they were not really his friends, according to Greer,

Williams, and Hampton's wife, Gladys. The closeness Malcolm described was as fictitious as the closeness he said he had shared with the members of his own family.

Doing menial chores at Roseland was not all peaches and cream; some boys taunted Malcolm about his shoeshine job, which he finally quit. He said he wanted to dance at Roseland himself when the big bands came there.

Malcolm readied himself for the Roseland dance competitions with the same thoroughness that had characterized his preparations for his boxing rematch with Bill Peterson. First, he learned how to lindy at someone's home. Then he attended every party he could in order to practice his footwork.

Soon Malcolm developed such expertise that girls were asking him to lindy. He bought a new zoot suit for his Roseland debut. It was gray, with cuffs so narrow that he had to take off his knob-toed, sweet-po-tato-colored shoes to pull on the tapered Punjab pants.

Ella was so overjoyed when Malcolm informed her he had quit the shoeshine job that she went out and found him work she approved of. The new job was at the Townsend Drugstore, where teenie-boppers from the Hill hung out after school. Malcolm worked behind the soda fountain. It was his first full-time job.

Malcolm's Jewish employers were highly pleased with him. If one of them started to sweep the floor, he'd grab the broom. When their delivery boy was sick, he'd volunteer to deliver medicine. Outwardly, he was a model employee. But inwardly he seethed. It was difficult enough to endure the snobs who lived on the Hill; it was insufferable to have to cater to them.

Not every teen-age customer was a snob, however. One was a quiet, soft-spoken girl named Laura. She came in every weekday afternoon, opened a schoolbook, and devoured its contents as eagerly as she did the ice cream Malcolm served her. The more he watched her, the more uncomfortable he felt about the way he had turned his back on the books he had once read so avidly.

One day, he began chatting with Laura, whose response was warm and friendly. Her parents, he learned, had separated when she was very young. They had entrusted her to a religious zealot of a grandmother who would not even allow her to date.

Laura encouraged Malcolm to talk about himself. In an unguarded moment, he told her that he had once wanted to become a lawyer. As soon as he said it, he regretted it; Laura kept saying he could be one if he put his mind to it. She encouraged him to continue his schooling, and she sensed that Ella would do everything in her power to help financially.

Malcolm looked forward to Laura's after-school visits. One afternoon, she casually mentioned that she loved to lindy. Malcolm asked her to go with him to the next Roseland dance. Laura said she'd love to, but that her strait-laced grandmother would not let her.

But the day of the dance, Laura came into the drugstore and told Malcolm she had decided to accompany him to Roseland. She said she had told her grandmother she was going to attend a school function that evening.

After work, Malcolm stopped by Ella's to change into a suit. He brought Laura with him. Ella was impressed with her excellent manners. But the thing that struck her the most about Laura was her physical similarity to Malcolm's mother. Laura had the same light skin and long, dark, wavy hair. Like Louise, she parted it in the middle. She even had the same long eyelashes and prominent eyebrows. Whether the resemblance had anything to do with the way Malcolm later treated her is unclear.

Despite his limited means, Malcolm squired Laura to the dance in a taxicab. On the dance floor, he soon discovered how gracefully and effortlessly she danced. Like a ballerina, she responded instantaneously to his slightest touch. She didn't appear, however, to have the strength for the long, grueling dance contest that had been scheduled for later that evening.

But a big, strapping woman Malcolm named Mamie Bevels did. She asked Malcolm to team up with her for the contest. Malcolm hesitated— Laura was standing right there. But then he accepted Mamie's invitation. The two of them put on quite a show.

On the way home, Laura said very little. The next time she came into the drugstore, she was very quiet. Malcolm later claimed he wasn't even thinking about her when she approached him and told him Duke Ellington was coming to Roseland. Malcolm agreed to take her. He later asserted that he had no idea what was about to happen.

This time, Laura told her grandmother the truth about where she was going. When she and Malcolm got to the ballroom, she made clear that she intended to participate in the dance contest. Malcolm later described what happened:

> I turned up the steam. Laura's feet were flying . . . . I caught glimpses of the four or five other couples, the girls jungle-strong, animal-like . . . . But little Laura inspired me to drive to new heights. Her hair was all over her face. It was running sweat, and I couldn't believe her strength.

Suddenly, Laura gasped and weakened, like an injured fighter. Malcolm helped her to the sidelines. Just then, he allegedly caught the gaze of a well-built, expensively dressed, blonde-haired, white woman. She was staring at him hard.

Once again, Malcolm left Laura in the lurch. According to his autobiography, he rushed her home, then rendezvoused with the white woman, whom he accompanied to a deserted hideaway.

Laura stopped patronizing the Townsend Drugstore. She began defying her puritanical grandmother more and more, drinking and using drugs. To finance these activities, she became a prostitute. Her clients repelled her so much that she turned to women for sexual satisfaction. She also landed in jail. Malcolm blamed himself for all of this. Two decades later, he said the guilt still plagued him.

The white woman who allegedly approached Malcolm "so boldly" at Roseland was not a natural blonde. According to his friend Larry Neblett, who was with him when he met her, he picked her up at a Tremont Street drinking establishment called the Tic Toc Club. He, not she, initiated the encounter.*

Nor was Beatrice Caragulian the exquisite-looking specimen that Malcolm later said she was. Her face reflected the unhappiness of the broken home from which she came.

The thing that was attractive about Bea, an aspiring nightclub dancer, was the way she dressed. One look at her elegant clothes would have convinced anyone she had access to money. Frequently, she used it to buy Malcolm clothes.

And as Malcolm later pointed out, a white girlfriend who wasn't a known, common whore was, in those days, "a status symbol of the first order." He paraded his white showpiece around lower Roxbury; he seemed to enjoy the fact that other men envied him. He hinted that Bea was the one who came to him for sex, not vice versa. (She told one associate that a woman who had never slept with a "nigger" had never experienced sexual release.) Malcolm seemed to enjoy the role of a stud—a role that may have compensated for the fact that sex with Bea was neither an act of love nor an act of intimacy. It was largely a payment for a payment.

One day, Malcolm brought Bea to Ella's house. Ella later asserted that she threw her down the stairs. She also began treating Malcolm "like a viper." But she did not abandon her efforts to mold him. She tried, for

---

* Malcolm's prison record confirms Neblett's account.

example, to induce him to wear high-top shoes. And one night, as he slept soundly, she tiptoed into his bedroom and cut a swath down the middle of his conked hair. The next morning, when he realized what had happened, he nearly had a coronary.

Some time later—precisely when is unclear—he awoke to find a milky substance seeping from his breast. Ella, who was as alarmed as Malcolm was, hurried him to the doctor, who explained that lactation sometimes occurs in males. He attributed it to endocrinological factors. It is unclear if he was told that Malcolm had been smoking marijuana, which is thought to affect lactation and breast development.

Ella attended church. But, like her father, she frequently disregarded its teachings. For instance, she sent Malcolm to the grocery store without money, but instructed him to bring home food anyway. She stole food herself; her third husband was afraid to accompany her to the market. It wasn't that Ella was poor. She owned her own home, as well as a growing number of rental properties. The value of much of what she stole was negligible. It wasn't the loot that prompted her thievery; it was the act of stealing itself.

Ella had apparently learned her criminality from members of her own family. Her mother had had a number of run-ins with the police. And lawlessness pervaded her father's family. Ultimately, she accumulated a lengthy criminal record that included eighteen or more arrests and ten convictions for offenses ranging from petty larceny to assault and battery. Good lawyers and good luck kept her out of jail, except for a brief tour that lasted a month.

Ella's brother Earl Junior, the eldest of Earl Little's ten children, also did a lot of stealing. His first conviction for burglary occurred when he was twelve. By fourteen, he was in reform school. Though he was released, he went back when he was sixteen. The following year, the police, acting on a tip, went to his room to interrogate him about the theft of some clothing. Then they decided to question Ella, who slept in the adjoining room. They searched it and found the stolen merchandise beneath her mattress. Earl Junior then confessed, maintaining that Ella knew nothing about the hidden loot. He spent the next decade in and out of jail. When he wasn't in prison, he worked as an entertainer at bars and nightclubs, using the stage name Jimmy Carlton. He favored Malcolm with front row seats at his performances and took him backstage to meet the other performers. Malcolm worshipped his good-looking, six-foot-two half-brother. "Someday," he declared, "I'm going to be like Earl!"

SUCCESS OR FAILURE? 12

When Earl, Jr., died of tuberculosis, Malcolm was so grief-stricken that Ella feared he was going to lose his mind. He adamantly refused to accept the fact that his idol, who was twelve or thirteen years older than he was, had died of natural causes. Instead, he insisted that his half-brother had been a victim of foul play, as he had apparently been told his father had been. He said Earl, Jr. had been poisoned.

Malcolm quit his eighteen-dollar-a-week job at the Townsend Drugstore. Bea provided enough money for him to leave Ella's and move in with Shorty. Ella, who was eager to entice Malcolm away from Bea, found him a better paying job with the New Haven Railroad. He raised no objection because he wanted to travel, particularly to New York. Yet he seemed apprehensive as he described his future duties to friends:

> I just got hired as a fourth cook. The funny thing is that I can't cook that well, but I'll make it. Of course, I don't have to cook the big stuff . . . . I'm just fourth cook.

Malcolm was promised the first available Boston-to-New York run. For a while, he worked in the Dover Street railroad yard, loading food requisitions onto trains. He soon learned that fourth cook was a glorified name for a dishwasher, but he said he didn't mind.

At last, Malcolm was assigned to a train that passed through New York City on the way to Washington, D.C. But two and a half months later, he quit; Earl Little's seventh child had bigger fish to fry. He was going to be a lawyer, or perhaps a dancer or an actor—it didn't really matter which as long as the job enabled him to make a name for himself and enough money to buy a Cadillac. His ambition, which belied his easygoing facade, seemed limitless. He seemed determined to conquer the world.

But despite his cocky exterior, Malcolm was terribly afraid of failure, according to Reginald. For one thing, job discrimination made success highly unlikely. The most a black man—even an educated one—could reasonably aspire to during the 1940s was a job in the Post Office. School guidance counselors were reluctant to encourage black pupils to seek professional careers. Black high school graduates were locked out of the trades. Thus, the only work Malcolm could find when he left the railroad in mid-September 1941 was menial. According to imprecise surviving records, he ran through four boring, unchallenging "slaves" in little more than three months.

The first "slave," which Malcolm later portrayed as a foreman's job, was in a South Boston wallpaper company warehouse. He stayed there a month. The second was another dishwashing job, which he said he lost because he was underage. (He was only sixteen.) The third, a small step upward, was in the Parker House Hotel. There, instead of washing dishes, he worked in the dining room in a starched white jacket and carted dirty plates back to the dishwashers who toiled in the kitchen.

But busing tables had no future either. Malcolm came to work so late one December Sunday that he fully expected to be fired. No one noticed, however; Japanese planes had just sunk the bulk of the U.S. Pacific fleet at Pearl Harbor. The navy had already begun a crash shipbuilding program, so Malcolm accompanied some friends to Casco Bay Shipyard in South Portland, Maine, where minesweepers were being built. The one he was assigned to work on was supported, not by the thick, sturdy looking blocks that were later used, but by tall, wooden poles. Malcolm worked beneath the scaffolding. He expressed concern that it might give way. A few days later, he quit. Portland was too dead, he said.

Back in Boston, he stayed at Ella's new house at 72 Dale Street. He gave her mailman—a kindly, elderly man who liked young people— three pairs of warm, woolen socks for Christmas. He also arranged for a woman to knit the postman a scarf. When relatives asked Malcolm what he wanted for Christmas, he said he didn't need anything. Christmas, he told Gloria, was a hoax. He did not tell her that his mother's emotional collapse had occurred just before Christmas.

Early in January, 1942, Malcolm went back to work for the New Haven Railroad, perhaps because he was offered a chance to fill in for the sandwich vendor on the Yankee Clipper, which ran from Boston to New York. Malcolm outperformed his more experienced predecessor, just as he had outperformed his older, more experienced hunting companions. In fact, "Sandwich Red" sold so much food that the man he had replaced was shunted to another train despite his seniority. It was not the last time Malcolm would supplant a rival.

Malcolm's first mesmerizing tour of Harlem's nighspots included a visit to the Savoy Ballroom, which made Roseland look second-rate. He was equally enthralled by Small's Paradise, whose conservatively attired customers quietly conversed like Wall Street bankers.

On the way back to Boston, he lamented his inability to share with Ella his excitement about Harlem. Though he kept part of his growing expensive wardrobe at her home and frequently slept there when his train stopped for the night in Boston, he seemed to prefer staying elsewhere.

Malcolm learned many things on the railroad. The sandwiches that were sold by the kitchen car crew were accounted for by the number of sandwich bags expended. With the connivance of the dining car stewards, who supervised the food preparation, the sandwich salesmen retrieved as many of the used food bags as possible. The cooks filled them with new sandwiches, which were sold in the old wrappers. The profits went into the pockets of the crew members.

The dining car stewards were all white and most of them expected the black help to jump when they snapped their fingers. They resented the fact that Malcolm had a white girlfriend, nor could they tolerate his flamboyant antics. He strutted through Grand Central Station like a zoot-suited peacock. Startled travelers stopped to stare at his garish attire. One weekend, he made an even bigger splash by jumping into Buzzards Bay fully clothed, while hundreds of tourists looked on. "I just want people to notice," he told Alton Cousins, the blue-eyed Yankee Clipper steward. Mr. Cousins, who was called "Pappy," got a kick out of Malcolm's shenanigans. He was probably the only steward with whom Malcolm got along well. Pappy was the kind of boss who didn't disparage subordinates when they made mistakes. He always treated them with respect. "He liked everybody, even me," Malcolm later declared in a statement fraught with self-contempt.

Pappy did like Malcolm. Sensing that he needed someone older to talk to, he lent him a sympathetic paternal ear. Malcolm showed his gratitude to Pappy in various ways. He volunteered for extra duties, as he had done at the Swerleins' and at the Townsend Drugstore. And when two drunken sailors began threatening Pappy, Malcolm grabbed each of them from behind, by the scruff of the neck, and threw them out of the dining car. He defended his new pappy better than he defended himself.

Sometimes, Malcolm's relationship with the passengers he served was even worse than his relationship had been with the snooty Hill youths who had patronized the Townsend Drugstore. He insulted people right and left as he strode up and down the lurching aisles, lugging a five-gallon coffee pot and a sandwich box that was strapped to his shoulder. He later claimed that Pappy protected his job by ignoring the resultant passenger complaints. But Malcolm was mistaken, says Mr. Cousins. Yet Malcolm remained convinced that Pappy had favored him.

In October 1942, Malcolm again quit the railroad. To what extent his decision was prompted by Pappy's transfer to another train is unclear. Wartime demands for manpower were so great that jobs were a dime a dozen, even for blacks, as long as they didn't get too "uppity." Finding another job would have been relatively simple.

But Malcolm didn't appear to want steady employment. He seemed reluctant to assume responsibility. His father had avoided it. His mother, who had been saddled with more responsibility than she could cope with, had relinquished it after a gallant, lonely struggle. "Before I settle down to work," Malcolm declared, "I want to have a little fun."

THE RETURN   13

For the next three years, Malcolm wandered from job to job and city to city, as his peripatetic father had done. When he returned to Lansing sporting the Boston accent he'd later condemn the Hill blacks for using, the people back home couldn't believe it was he. He played the big city slicker to the hilt, lording it over his small-town companions. Older boys whom he had once envied began looking up to him. The girls extolled his high-style dancing. He sailed across Lincoln's Center's dance floor, twirling bobby soxers as if they were tops. Malcolm left them agog with his fancy footwork. The local musicians, who evidently had never seen the "kangaroo" or the "flapping eagle," nearly forgot to keep their eyes on the music.

In short, Malcolm had become the center of attention. But other aspects of his return to Michigan were not so successful. Mrs. Swerlein was repelled by his hipster talk and attire. She invited him in, but she appeared so uncomfortable that he stayed only briefly.

When Malcolm visited Kalamazoo State Hospital, his mother only "half-sensed" who he was. And when he ran into Irene Cooley, who had shared her oranges and apples with him at Pleasant Grove, she, too, failed to recognize him. "I went to school with you," Malcolm told her. He didn't say what school. Irene got the feeling he was hoping she'd remember. When she didn't, Malcolm just smiled. Later, he encountered another former classmate and asked her point-blank, "Do you remember me?"

Malcolm popped in at the home of Betty Girven, who had not laid eyes on him in years. He gave no indication that he was happy to see her, nor did he attempt to stay or chat. He just asked to borrow her camera.

Betty asked Malcolm what he was doing. "Playing in a band," he told her. She inquired how his hair had gotten so red. "By itself," he replied.

Malcolm bumped into other people he knew. Joyce and Lorraine Tellier, the white girls who had invited him into their home to share grapefruit, swapped hellos with him near Shaw's Jewelry Store, where he did janitorial work and odd jobs for two and a half weeks. Shortly after the Tellier sisters arrived home, Malcolm telephoned to offer his apologies for having "embarrassed" them by speaking to them in public. Yet, around his black companions, he bragged about his real or imaginary white conquests.

His accounts of his adventures in other men's bedrooms taxed his listeners' credulity. According to one Henry Miller-like narrative, he was enjoying the charms of Anne the barmaid when her husband unexpectedly came home and started climbing the stairs. Unable to escape, Malcolm grabbed his clothes and scrambled beneath the bed. Anne greeted her husband as enthusiastically as she could and tried to lure him away from the house. Instead, she ended up again in bed with him.

Later, when things were still, Malcolm began edging out from his place of concealment. Anne slid an arm over the side of the bed and motioned him back. After a while, he tried again. Once more, she waved him back. Finally, after what seemed an interminable wait, she bent her head down and signaled him to leave. Out Malcolm crept, bare bottom upward. He slid down the stairway to the front door, which contained two locks. The first made an awful din when he tried to release it. The second made even more noise. He twisted the doorknob. The door wouldn't budge.

Frantically, he worked both locks. The clicking of the tumblers sounded deafening. The big, ebony-skinned man upstairs was bound to hear.

Anne, who realized that Malcolm was having trouble, slipped out of bed, tiptoed downstairs, and saved the day. Out into the chilly night he ran, sweat pouring from his body. He later repeated the tale to another listener, but omitted the part about running naked outdoors.

One of those who saw through Malcolm's macho facade was his friend Weldon Caldwell, who needled him by asserting that women weren't interested in him. Malcolm told a friend he'd "beat Weldon's ass" if he continued to vex him. But he never made the threat directly to Weldon, who had accumulated an impressive record of Golden Gloves victories despite the fact that he stood only five feet four.

Several times during Malcolm's stay in Lansing, he visited Mrs. Gohanna. Whether the visits were prompted by the meals she cooked for him or by the pretty half-black woman who was rooming in her house is hard to tell. The woman, Geraldine Clark, had reddish-blonde hair that was the envy of white and black women alike. Yet both camps spurned her.

Malcolm teased Geraldine, who was married. Gradually, she began to realize that he was interested in her. Despite her efforts to the contrary, she began flirting back. She couldn't help being attracted to the commanding young redhead whose worldly demeanor set him apart from other Lansing blacks. He seemed like a man who could have any woman he wanted.

Malcolm seemed to want Geraldine—so much so that she sometimes felt afraid. Yet, despite the "yellow lights" she flashed, he made no advances. She got the feeling that he put her on a pedestal.

But that did not stop Geraldine's husband from concluding that Malcolm was trying to cuckold him. Whether this had anything to do with his move to Flint, Michigan is unclear. It occurred around Christmas of 1942. He attributed it to a desire to obtain a high-paying defense job. He didn't explain why he preferred Flint's war plants to Lansing's, which were also clamoring for manpower. At Delia Williams' boarding house, Malcolm shared a room with several of his friends. When he applied for employment at the AC Sparkplug factory, he told the personnel office he was of West Indian, not African, descent. In case of emergency, he said, the plant officials should notify, not his family in Lansing, which was less than two hours away, but the mother of his friend Howard Bannister, who lived in Flint.

It was cold that winter in eastern Michigan. Yet, despite Malcolm's sensitivity to icy weather, he wore either a thin, stylish, velvet-collared topcoat or no coat at all. "He'd walk down the street half frozen to look good," says his cousin J. C. Little. But one of his Michigan friends saw it differently. "[Malcolm] dressed more or less in defiance of the elements," he says. "Sissies pulled their coat collars up around their necks."

During Malcolm's stay in Flint, he mingled with black ghetto dwellers as well as with the black elite, as he had done in Boston and Lansing. One of the prettiest members of the local African-American upper crust was sandy-haired, bluish-eyed Blanche Mitchell, who seemed mainly interested in money, stylish clothes, and cars. Blanche, whose voice one friend likened to music, was tall and very light-skinned. According to mutual friends, Malcolm was not the only young man who was captivated by her. Yet, whenever anyone mentioned Blanche, he just laughed. He never stopped by her house. Instead, he hung around her cousin's home, which she visited almost daily.

Though Malcolm refused to compete for Blanche or for the other women he later acknowledged he had "really wanted," he was super-competitive about women who were claimed by other men. It was no big thing, he said, to cuckold another guy. He seemed to regard "woman-theft" as a personal challenge, especially if he disliked his rival.

Sometimes, Malcolm's penchant for other men's women landed him in trouble. One man whose girlfriend Malcolm said he intended to steal threatened to beat him to a pulp, regardless of how much younger he was. Malcolm placed his hands on his hips, threw back his head, and roared. The move disarmed his infuriated would-be rival, who let the matter drop.

But Malcolm was not so fortunate when he spread the rumor that he was having an affair with Blanche's light-skinned cousin. The cousin's boy-friend, Hank Ross,* located him in a Flint barroom. "Let's talk outside," Hank snapped. Malcolm told him to wait a minute, but Hank was not about to wait. He was so mad that he grabbed Malcolm by the collar, dragged him outside on his knees, and hit him once. That's all there was to the fight. Hank, who was older than Malcolm but not quite as tall, couldn't fathom his refusal to defend himself. Years later, he would have difficulty reconciling it with the way Malcolm defended his followers.

Perhaps because of Malcolm's humiliation at Hank's hands, he remained in Flint for only about two months. By March 1943, he was back at work on the New Haven Railroad. Through the grapevine, he learned that Gloria Strother, with whom he had been keeping in touch by mail, was dating someone else. When he returned to Roxbury, he confronted her and bluntly laid it on the line. He told her that his life style was too fast for her and that it would be better for her to find someone who would make her happy. He said he was leaving her for her own good.

Gloria, who was not interested in anyone else, was devastated. But she was darned if she would fight for a guy who didn't seem to want her. It never occurred to her that his chivalry might have been a facade, his martyr-like self-denial a desperate attempt to avoid anticipated rejection. For him to admit that Gloria, Blanche, Geraldine, or Margaret Richmond were important enough to vie for would have been to admit that he was vulnerable. "Never wear your heart on your sleeve," he counseled one friend.

Outwardly, Malcolm's response to the break with Gloria was cold. He did not even mention her in his autobiography.

---

* Hank Ross is a pseudonym that I have used at his request.

SCHOOLING FOR
THE UNSCHOOLED

14

Malcolm apparently had mixed feelings about rejoining the New Haven; seventeen days after he was rehired, he was fired. "It was inevitable," he proclaimed. But he provoked the inevitable. According to his autobiography, he was discharged because of a complaint from an irate passenger. But his prison record suggests that he was canned for flouting the unwritten rule forbidding the railroad's black male employees from fraternizing with the white waitresses who worked in the grill cars. Whatever the case, his discharge left him unable to support himself again.

It may have been at this juncture that good fortune intervened in Harlem. A bartender at Small's Paradise informed Malcolm that one of the waiters was leaving. Malcolm asked Charlie Small, the owner's brother, if he could have the waiter's job. He was concerned about the possibility that Charlie might ask some of the railroad men who frequented Small's about him. But Charlie apparently made up his mind on the basis of what he had seen himself of Malcolm's behavior during his previous visits to Small's. No loud talk. No wild antics, such as those he had exhibited elsewhere. Just a quiet young man sitting and marveling at what he saw.

Charlie laid down the law against any attempt to hustle off customers—particularly men in uniform, whose morals were carefully supervised by a horde of civilian and military functionaries. The hands-off-servicemen rule was observed, not only by Small's, but also by every drinking establishment that wanted to keep its license.

Malcolm was so excited about the opportunity to mingle with the big-timers who patronized Small's that he came to work early. He made himself so useful that, within a week, the cooks and bartenders considered him virtually indispensable.

Malcolm was equally attentive to his customers. "Another drink? . . . Right away, sir . . . . Would you like dinner? . . . Could I get you a menu, sir?" His ingratiating behavior paid off. Grateful customers and co-workers took him aside, when business was slack, and told him about the exploits of the "wolves" and "vultures" who congregated at Small's. The latter included fearless, almost heroic characters like the cat burglar Jumpsteady, who tiptoed from window ledge to window ledge, risking his neck to rob the occupants of elegant high-rise apartment houses. It was rumored that Jumpsteady was so adept at his vocation that he even burgled when his victims were in the adjoining room.

Equally proficient was West Indian Archie, whose infallible memory made him the perfect numbers runner. When a client placed a bet, Archie did not need to record the number on a betting slip. He just did it in his mind; he never put the number in writing until after he had delivered his client's money to the numbers "banker." That way, if police detectives caught him with the cash, they could not prove he was doing anything illegal.

Among the pimps who frequented Small's was "Cadillac" Drake, who joked (or lamented) that his worn-out "chippies" had to work harder than other prostitutes did. Another, older, hustler was the pickpocket Fewclothes, whose arthritic fingers had become so deformed that people shuddered when they saw them. No one knew if his affliction was merely poetic justice or also the result of a guilty conscience.

Each evening, Fewclothes came to Small's to reminisce about happier days. The regular customers took turns buying him drinks. Yet Malcolm, who served Fewclothes his nightly supper with sufficient flourish to gratify a monarch, emphatically denied that he was "on anybody's welfare." His heart went out to the former master pickpocket whose expertise had paled. He had similar empathy for West Indian Archie, whose mathematical talent should have been put to better use. Malcolm seemed to empathize with all the might-have-beens who congregated in Small's for company and solace. White America didn't appear to want them any more than it seemed to want him.

The majority of the customers in Small's Paradise were on the up and up. But it was the hustlers who fascinated Malcolm. One by one, he learned who the successful ones were. He also learned the identity of the strong-arm men who "persuaded" adversaries with blackjacks, brass knuckles, lead pipes, and wet cement.

Many of the tough black cops who policed these hoods were products of similar environments. Some were plainclothesmen. Eventually, Malcolm learned to sense who they were. According to one friend, his ability to smell them out was uncanny.

One gangland "executive" who took a liking to Malcolm belonged to an organization that could deliver to order, for a fraction of the retail price, nearly any garment. Malcolm learned how the thieves operated. A well-dressed customer would enter a store shortly before closing time, conceal himself, and get locked inside. After dark, he'd stuff expensive coats and jackets into bags, deactivate the burglar alarm, and summon the crew of a waiting getaway truck, which would carefully avoid the scheduled police patrols.

One day, the executive whipped out his tape measure and took Malcolm's measurements. The following day, one of the bartenders handed him a package. Inside was a high-priced, conservatively tailored, dark blue suit. Very likely, it was the most expensive gift he had ever received.

And so, in a manner that Malcolm himself characterized as "paternal," his mentors pointed him toward the path that his father, Ella, and Earl Junior had prepared. They didn't test or grade him. He experienced no learning difficulties; he soaked up each lesson like a sponge.

Small's Paradise was not Malcolm's only schoolroom. He spent considerable time in an after-hours speakeasy named Creole Pete's, which opened for business at three in the morning, just before the last of Harlem's legitimate clubs had to close. Pete Robertson, the owner, had a big gap between his upper front teeth, just as Malcolm did. But what made him notice Malcolm was that he didn't buy any drinks. Nor did he try to pick up women. He just stood around the small, cramped makeshift nightclub, studying those who did. Pete, who was not operating a charity, finally cornered him and said, "This is a drinking establishment, young man." "Yes, sir, Mr. Robertson," Malcolm replied. "May I carry those dishes for you? . . . Allow me to hold that tray." Each time Creole Pete made up his mind to put him out, Malcolm ingratiated himself in some other way.

Malcolm also learned a lot at the Harlem rooming house where he slept. Several of the tenants were prostitutes, some of whom Malcolm befriended. He said he trusted them more than he trusted women who weren't prostitutes. After all, a streetwalker couldn't really disappoint you.

Surprisingly, Malcolm's sex education came primarily from the prostitutes, not from Bea, whom he still saw but who was apparently more a showpiece than anything else. The instruction, Malcolm said, was entirely verbal. (A bout he'd had with "the clap" may have had something to do with it.) But though Malcolm said he preferred to sleep with women who cared for him, the sexual partners he picked were women who apparently felt nothing for him. One of them, Dorothy____, slept with everything that wore pants. She later told one of her other lovers that her tryst with Malcolm had not gone well.

One spring afternoon, a black soldier came into Small's, sat down at one of Malcolm's tables, and had several drinks. He seemed depressed. So, despite Malcolm's growing ability to spot police types, he asked the soldier if he wanted a woman.

Malcolm knew he had violated Charlie Small's orders. Perhaps he was sick of taking orders. Waiting tables at Small's Paradise was essentially no different from serving food on trains or in the Townsend Drugstore.

The soldier said yes and Malcolm gave him the phone number of one of the daughters of joy who lived in his rooming house. But Malcolm began feeling uneasy. After enough time had elapsed for the man to reach the house, Malcolm called it. No soldier had been there. Malcolm's premonition had been quite correct.

Instead of trying to hide what he had done, Malcolm went straight to Charlie's office and confessed. He was actually waiting when the police came. They let him off with a warning.

Nevertheless, Malcolm was bitter. Not only was he jobless, he was also barred from Small's, which had become his chief source of "education." It was like being expelled from school. The fact that both expulsions had been self-induced was beside the point.

ADDICT ======================================= 15

Since "slaving" for Charlie Small was no longer an option, Malcolm turned for advice to his dapper friend Sammy McKnight, who was probably the only person he knew who was more clothes-conscious than he was. Sammy wouldn't step outside the door unless his slacks were pressed and his fingernails were manicured. A costly diamond ring graced one of his fingers. His apartment was palatial. People called him "Sammy the Pimp." Outwardly, he exuded manliness and strength, but in reality he was utterly dependent on his prostitutes for sustenance.

Sammy, who was older than Malcolm, was slick. In the restaurant where he had worked as a waiter, he conned female customers into inviting him home. Once he was there, he would insist upon going out to a nearby eating establishment to buy dinner. If he could induce his hostess to let him use her front door key, he'd have it duplicated while he was gone. Then, when she was away, he'd steal nearly everything she owned. When she returned and found out, he'd lend her money to tide her over. Frequently, the loan grew into a financial and emotional dependence that Sammy exploited until the woman practically became his slave.

Malcolm and Sammy, who had also had experience peddling dope, discussed what sort of career Malcolm should pursue. Selling reefers seemed to make sense. No experience was needed and there would be minimal involvement with people who might be under police surveillance. And since jazz musicians tended to be avid purchasers of marijuana, a reefer peddler could spend time with the big bands. He could also make money immediately. Future prospects seemed even brighter; one could earn a hundred dollars a day selling heroin and cocaine. But since selling heavy drugs was more dangerous, it would be some time before Malcolm could "graduate" to that level.

Sammy knew a number of merchant seamen who supplied marijuana to dope pushers. So did Malcolm; some of his Lansing pals had merchant marine jobs that regularly brought them to New York.

Sammy loaned him enough money to buy the requisite supplies. A few hours later, Malcolm returned to Sammy's apartment and repaid the loan.

Pushing reefers had the additional cardinal advantage of allowing Malcolm to satisfy his own growing drug habit at little cost. Except for cocaine, which he inhaled, he took nearly all his drugs orally, like food. This was partly due to his deathly fear of hypodermic injection, which may have stemmed from a movie he had seen in which scores of Africans died after white doctors vaccinated them against disease.

Malcolm occasionally used stronger drugs, such as nembutal, seconal, benzedrine, and opium. But marijuana, which was far less expensive, became his habitual mode of escape. Cocaine was the only other drug that he took with any frequency. Both drugs, Malcolm said, made him feel less estranged. "The weed," which induced a feeling of contentment, also enabled him to hold imaginary conversations with the musicians he idolized. With drugs, he didn't need people. Gratification could be achieved without dependence on anyone or anything—except, of course, his fix.

Malcolm also became habituated to the gambling he had begun in Boston. He bet at least a dollar a day on the numbers. He also played craps, blackjack, and poker, among other things. At times, he squandered forty dollars a day on games of chance. He fantasized what he'd do if he "hit." He wouldn't have to work for what he wanted. He'd be free to do what he pleased. Maybe he'd even buy a fancy car.

The winnings of the numbers players who hit were calculated at the ratio of six hundred to one. But the odds against hitting the jackpot were a thousand to one. To win, a player had to pick the number that matched the last three digits of the following day's dollar volume of sales on the New York Stock Exchange. Alternatively, he could "combinate," or divide, his bet. For instance, six dollars combinated on the number 375 yielded one dollar bets on the numbers 375, 357, 753, 735, 573, and 537. The odds against winning were still $166\frac{2}{3}$ to one. Nevertheless, Malcolm bucked them, just as he bucked authority.

The competitiveness he displayed in gambling dens afforded a vivid contrast to his refusal to compete for the women he wanted. Occasionally, he did win modest sums, but not enough to offset the thousands of dollars he lost over a period of years.

Malcolm admitted it was foolish to gamble. Yet day after day, week after week, he compulsively re-created situations in which loss was virtually inevitable. Perhaps the economic deprivation was less painful to him than emotional deprivation was. Whenever he gambled, the scope and severity of the losses he incurred were subject to his control. Each roll of the dice, each flip of the cards, helped confirm his negative view of the world.

Whenever Malcolm did have cash to spend, he ran through it as if it were going out of style. He flashed big bills and tipped extravagantly. Friends who asked him for twenty dollars got thirty or forty. He loaned one man his last ten dollars and walked away with his chest outstretched, as if he had a hundred more. Later, he quietly borrowed a "fin" from someone else. But his generosity was not prompted solely by a desire to appear more successful than he was. On one occasion, he pawned his suit for a friend who had pawned a watch for him when he had needed a loan. And everyone knew how much his clothes meant to him.

Periodically, Malcolm also became addicted to the movies. Sometimes he viewed as many as five a day. If the film happened to be a detective story, he'd emerge from the theater a cop. After westerns, he'd swagger out like a bow-legged cowboy. He lived vicariously in a world of filmland fantasy. One of his favorite movies was *Stormy Weather*, in which a talented black dancer works for a while as a waiter but finally succeeds in show business and marries a woman who looks almost white. The protagonist of another film he liked, *Cabin in the Sky*, is a compulsive gambler who signs his name with an X.

Malcolm loved the Hollywood tough guys, such as the cold-blooded anti-hero of the movie *Johnny Eager*, a budding, errant genius who might have turned out differently had he had a better childhood. And he was particularly fond of the tough, woman-rejecting hero that Humphrey Bogart played in *Casablanca*—a man who relinquishes love for a vital political cause.

Malcolm's daily rounds of Manhattan's movie palaces were followed by his nightly ones to his stoned reefer customers. He took great precaution against arrest and outfoxed the police more than once. The law specified that a person could not be convicted of a drug violation unless the incriminating evidence was found in his possession. The trick was to make sure it wasn't.

Inside his coat, Malcolm cradled his reefers in his armpit by pressing his arm tightly against his side. Whenever he suspected that a cop was tailing him, he'd turn a corner and unloosen his arm; the small packet of marijuana would drop unnoticed in the dark.

But the reefers he lost cost him money. One day while he was out, his room was searched, apparently by detectives. Fearing that they had planted incriminating evidence with the intent of returning and "discovering" it, he moved to another lair. He also began carrying a pistol.

The police pressure increased. Plainclothesmen searched him in public. Loudly enough for bystanders to hear, Malcolm declared he had no contraband on him and didn't want any planted. The officers didn't try; they may have feared an incident that could have escalated into a riot. Their fear would have been well founded, for Harlem erupted during the summer of 1943 when a white policeman shot an off-duty black soldier who had intervened when the patrolman tried to arrest a black woman for disorderly conduct. The serviceman, Private Robert J. Bandy, grabbed the officer's billy club and hit him on the head with it. As news of the shooting spread through Harlem by word of mouth, it became exaggerated. Within an hour, angry mobs were rampaging in the mistaken belief that Bandy had been killed right in front of his mother. In reality, he was merely wounded in the shoulder and hospitalized, along with the policeman.

Before the looting and stabbing were over, 125th Street and parts of Fifth, Lenox, Seventh, and Eighth Avenue looked like they had been pillaged by an invading army. The sidewalks were littered with glass from broken store windows. Gutters were strewn with appliances that had been too heavy for people to cart away. Thousands of civilian and military policeman converged on the area. Mayor LaGuardia and NAACP Secretary Walter White rode around in a red fire vehicle, pleading over the loudspeaker for the milling throng to disperse. But neither the "Little Flower" nor the head of the National Association for the Advancement of Colored People could sway a crowd the way Malcolm could in his political prime.

Afraid to carry his illicit merchandise with him, Malcolm hid it in various places. Then, after his clients paid him, he told them where to pick it up. He'd put the reefers in an innocent-looking, empty cigarette pack and drop it behind a trash can. But his regular customers, the jazz musicians, took a dim view of such practices; they couldn't be seen scrounging around rubbish cans. So he hawked his wares on Harlem's streets. This was dangerous because addicts lacking money to buy drugs followed him around and waylaid him from doorways. The prudent thing to do in such cases was to yield the reefers. Malcolm lost so many that he was soon in debt. By August 1943, he was again back at work on the railroad—this time the New York Central.

In October, Malcolm was fired again. That same month, as American and Allied forces inched their way up the Italian boot against dogged Nazi resistance, he received orders to report to an army induction center in Manhattan. He admitted he was scared. He said he preferred to be a live coward than a dead hero. And the prospect of being molded into soldierly submission in a racially segregated army must hardly have been appealing.

Like some of the young men who refused to be conscripted to fight in Vietnam a generation later, Malcolm planned his strategy with military precision. Whenever he sensed the presence of the military intelligence operatives who prowled Harlem, he started acting tipsy. He'd pull out his induction notice and read it aloud so that they'd know who he was and when he was supposed to report. He said he was eager to join the army—the Japanese one. The day he reported to the induction center, he costumed himself in his zoot suit and yellow shoes. The show he put on attested to his acting ability:

> I went in skipping and tipping, and I thrust my tattered 'greetings' at that reception desk's white soldier—"Crazy-o, daddy-o, get me moving. I can't wait . . ."

Malcolm was processed, army style, along with several dozen other prospective inductees. Spewing slang, he proclaimed he was going to fight on all fronts. Someday, he bragged, he'd be a general. A number of the other reluctant candidates for flag-draped coffins were as amused by his entertaining antics as the crowds that flocked, years later, to hear him lampoon his political adversaries.

Finally, Malcolm was closeted with an army psychiatrist. He was careful not to rush his attack. Maintaining his verbal barrage, he feinted and parried, letting the physician think he was drawing out of him the very things he wanted him to hear. F.B.I. summaries of Selective Service documents that have apparently been destroyed suggest that the doctor became convinced that Malcolm had engaged in "sexual perversion."

As Malcolm played with the psychiatrist, he kept looking over his shoulder. Suddenly, he stooped and peered under both doors, as if he feared someone else were listening. Then he told the physician:

> Daddy-o, now you and me, we're from up North here, so don't you tell nobody. . . . I want to get sent down South. Organize them nigger soldiers, you dig? Steal us some guns and kill up crackers!

The doctor's couchside manner fell away before Malcolm's ruse de guerre. Groping for his red pencil, he stared at Malcolm in horror. Malcolm knew, then, that his act had succeeded; he was declared psychologically unfit by the draft board. Without firing a shot, he had beaten the whole U.S. army.

ROMANCE WITH FINANCE 16

U nable to secure a job that suited his aspirations, Malcolm, who had been so reluctant to impose on people, began living off them, as his father had done. When mealtime arrived and he just happened to drop by, friends had little alternative but to feed him or to loan him money for food. In fact, Malcolm's criterion for whether a "broad" cared for a man was whether or not she was willing to give him money. He reiterated this viewpoint on numerous occasions. When his five-foot, eleven-and-one-half inch sidekick Malcolm Jarvis declined, for financial reasons, to accompany him to a pre-dawn breakfast after a night of expensive carousing, Malcolm suggested that Jarvis's girlfriend Sophie pay. Sophie got indignant. "You can't think much of your boyfriend," Malcolm replied, "if you're unwilling to spend a dollar on him." On another occasion, Malcolm induced Jarvis, who was older than he was but who invariably followed his suggestions, to test another girlfriend the same way. "Tell her you're broke and you need five dollars," he said. "See how eager she'll be to give it to you."

Even when he was not in Boston, Bea remained a pillar of financial support for Malcolm, who milked his white showpiece dry. He later tried to justify the exploitation by arguing that, in male-female relationships, one had to exploit in order to avoid being exploited.

In early 1944, apparently without warning, Bea married her former dancing partner Mehran Bazarian. The wedding took place while the groom was home on leave from military service. "It made no difference," Malcolm later declared. Sammy had explained to him that white women were quite practical. Some married for financial security; for their pleasure, they looked elsewhere. They weren't necessarily in love with their black paramours. It was just that sex with blacks was better.

Though Malcolm's liaison with Bea continued intermittently, he sought financial support wherever he could find it. Like the pickup artists at Creole Pete's and Small's, he hung around the Braddock Hotel and other Harlem nightspots looking for women. He seemed to prefer white ones or light-skinned black ones. The women he gravitated to were hardly the caliber of Gloria, Betty Kennedy, or Betty Girven. They were easily deceived when the two Malcolms staged their "business executive" act. The two men would seat themselves near two likely-looking prospects. Then Malcolm would ask loudly enough to be overheard, "Will you be able to meet me in St. Louis next week?" "No, Malcolm," Jarvis would reply. "I'll be in L.A." If one of the women took the bait and pulled out a cigarette, Malcolm would reach over, light it, and buy her a drink. Little did she know it was the last one he'd pay for. "Romance without finance" didn't interest him. One source of funds was reportedly a well-to-do Jewish woman whose father owned a number of factories. Another woman apparently lavished gifts on him. A third, an attractive young woman with long black hair, let him live with her for a while, but Malcolm seemed more interested in her books than he did in her. He read everything from Nick Carter thrillers to the Holy Bible. When he had time to spare, which was apparently often, he'd go down to Union Square to watch the street corner orators whom he would one day excel.

Malcolm treated his female providers (he called them "bitches") like his father had treated his mother. Sometimes, he abused them physically, particularly if they exhibited interest in another man. Women, he later asserted, must be dealt with firmly. He said that this was because they were weak and needed male protection. He did not seem to notice the inconsistency between the assertion and his claim that men had to rule their women in order to avoid being ruled by them.

Malcolm went to great lengths to depict himself as a man who subjugated women. He bragged they'd do "anything" for him. And despite his later acknowledgement that he had no interest in pimping, he pretended that he was a big-time pimp when his Lansing friends visited him in New York. Word filtered back to Michigan that he had a chain of white women hustling for him on Manhattan's streets, a myth he fostered in various ways. For example, when a visiting crony asked him where he could contact a woman who was rumored to be in his employ, Malcolm refused to reveal her whereabouts. He used different tactics on Weldon Caldwell. "I'm going to take you to see someone you know," he said. Malcolm wouldn't say who. When Weldon finally realized that the person was Philbert's wife, Mary Bibbs, he grew hot under the collar. Mary and Philbert had separated. But Malcolm did not let the matter rest there. During one of his trips back to Michigan, he asserted, in Philbert's presence, that Mary had been whoring for him back East. With exemplary self-restraint, Philbert refrained from putting him through the wall. After all, they were brothers.

In reality, Mary, who was highly virtuous, was not prostituting herself for Malcolm or anyone else. In fact, Malcolm assumed a protective air towards her. "Be careful when you go here," he'd say. "And for God's sake, don't get caught there. Someone will snatch you up and you'll never be found." Yet he became angry when she refused to wear the flashy clothes he asked her to wear. He would not even walk her home. The only time he offered to do so was when he spotted her browsing along 125th Street in a chic aqua outfit. She had just dyed her hair blonde.

Mary was intrigued by Malcolm's worldly demeanor. But she could tell he wasn't happy.

Bea was apparently not the only person who expected a payment for a payment. In Flint, at Delia Williams' boarding house, one of Malcolm's roomates had jokingly suggested that he might be able to raise some rent money by striking a deal with a fellow boarder called "Miss Jones." Shortly thereafter, the roomate began noticing that Malcolm wasn't sleeping in the room they had been sharing. Instead, he began stealing down the hallway to Miss Jones's room. But Miss Jones, who sported a bright yellow jumper with matching slacks and umbrella, was not a woman. He was a well-known transvestite named Willie Mae. Malcolm's roomate concluded that Willie Mae was sleeping with him.

Later, in New York, there were other incidents. Two of Malcolm's Michigan friends who had joined the merchant marine visited New York one night and went to a YMCA, where they met Malcolm. They asked him what he was doing there. "Hell with all these little 'girls' here, I'm going to make some money," he replied. And when visiting friends ran out of money, Malcolm told them he knew two homosexuals—he called them "queers"—who lived at the Harlem YMCA. It wasn't difficult, he said, to get them to part with their cash. One man demurred. "It's not that bad," Malcolm asserted. "They suck dick!" He arranged a "party" in the six-by-nine-foot YMCA cubicle of a man who called himself "Reverend Witherspoon." The arrangements were businesslike. Each man closeted himself with Witherspoon and emerged, minutes later, with an embarrassed grin on his face. Witherspoon agreed to pay each man's rent for a week and to treat him to a first-rate chicken dinner. After the week had elapsed, one participant sighed, "Boy, we sure are going to be hungry."

The motive for Malcolm's involvement with the men he characterized as "little girls" was apparently financial. Yet there were other ways he could have earned money. His male-to-male encounters, which rendered it unnecessary for him to compete for women, afforded him an opportunity for sexual release without the attendant risk of dependence on women. His flight from women was largely the result of past female tyranny. Due to the hostile attitude toward homosexuality that prevailed at the time, his rebellion against his biologically appointed role may have been purchased at a considerable cost in self-esteem.

PART-TIME HUSTLER 17

I n mid-February 1944, Malcolm applied for work on the Seaboard Railroad. Two days later, he was on his way to Florida on the Silver Meteor, renting pillows to passengers and keeping the coaches clean. But he didn't like the job. At times, he cursed his customers—particularly the servicemen, whom he couldn't tolerate. Perhaps it was their submissiveness to authority, or maybe it had something to do with the fact that Bea's husband was a soldier. Whatever the reasons, Malcolm did not get along with the doughboys who rode the trains. A case in point was an incident that had occurred when he was working on the Yankee Clipper. An inebriated G.I. rose from his seat, blocking the aisle in which Malcolm was working. The man called him a nigger and dared him to fight.

Malcolm laughed and thought fast. "Sure, I'll fight," he replied, "but you have too many clothes on." The soldier discarded his bulky army overcoat. Malcolm kept laughing and protesting that his adversary was still wearing too much woolen armor. Before long, the soldier was naked above the waist, to the amusement of his fellow passengers. Some other servicemen eased him out of the way so that Malcolm could pass by. Verbally, he had beaten his opponent more decisively than he could have beaten him physically. It was a memorable lesson—one he'd later use to great advantage.

Malcolm's tour of duty with the Seaboard Line lasted less than a month—just long enough for him to obtain a railroad identification card. In early March, he took a job with the Atlantic Coast railroad for the same reason. He still had his New Haven Railroad ID card, and perhaps the one from the New York Central. He had learned that if you showed a train conductor your ID and told him you were headed home to see your family, he'd usually let you ride free of charge.

Armed with proper identification, Malcolm set out from New York and ranged up and down the East Coast, selling marijuana. His favorite customers were the big band musicians, many of whom eagerly sought his wares.

But his career as an itinerant dope salesman didn't last long, so he tried his hand at robbery. The stick-ups were small ones—candy stores and the like. (There was none of the bank robbery or murder that he boasted about years later.) As usual, Malcolm followed Sammy's recommendations about proper criminal procedure, steeling himself for each "job" by sniffing cocaine, whose powdery crystals made him feel exceptionally confident and powerful. The "cocaine courage" came in handy; during one heist, he and Sammy narrowly escaped arrest. They were fleeing the scene of the crime when they heard a police car. They immediately stopped running. When the driver saw them and slammed on the brakes, they casually stepped into the street, flagged the car, and asked the occupants for directions. The reverse psychology worked. The policemen, who had apparently expected them to provide information, swore and sped away, unaware that they had been fooled. Once again, brain power had proven more potent than brawn.

During another holdup, Malcolm and Sammy were not so lucky—especially Sammy. A bullet nicked him. He went back to his apartment to recover.

Later, Malcolm joined him there. Sammy's olive-skinned, Spanish mistress Hortense, whose black hair hung halfway down her back, was also there. Her beauty made men gasp.

When Hortense, who was distraught about Sammy's injury, saw Malcolm, she bared her fingernails and sailed into him. Sammy did nothing to call her off. Apparently, he held Malcolm partly responsible for what had happened. Malcolm's autobiography does not tell us why.*

In an attempt to fend off Hortense, Malcolm struck her. It was apparently all the additional provocation Sammy needed. He drew his gun. Hortense screamed and distracted him long enough to allow Malcolm to make a hasty exit.

Superficially, the two men became reconciled. But Malcolm was never again able to really trust Sammy. He said the only person he could trust was Reginald, who sometimes visited him when the merchant ship he worked on docked nearby. Reginald, who admired Malcolm's ability to live by his wits, followed him around Harlem the way he had followed him around Lansing. Malcolm carefully studied his younger, red-haired brother, whom he said he "liked." He finally convinced Reginald to

---

* Nor can Sammy; he's dead.

forsake the merchant marine and become a hustler. He schooled his brother the way Sammy and others had schooled him. And since Reginald had nowhere to live, Malcolm rented an apartment for his brother and himself. To raise the money, he hustled more than usual.

Reginald found himself a mistress who was nearly twice his age. The woman, a waitress in an expensive restaurant, indulged his every whim and even bought his clothes. Malcolm's respect for his brother increased in direct proportion to Reginald's ability to induce the woman to baby him.

Malcolm later asserted that he "got very close" to Reginald in Harlem, and that he confided to him things he had never revealed to anyone. But Reginald disagrees. He found it difficult to express his feelings around Malcolm. How could one get close to a brother who apparently regarded personal questions as unwelcome, probing intrusions? One never knew what he was thinking or feeling. He could be talking with you, looking at you, yet off in some other world.

The next hustle Malcolm tried was safer than robbery. He got involved in it because of his "reputation," he would later maintain. But he didn't explain what a supposedly well-known criminal was doing riding a bus back and forth across the George Washington Bridge, ferrying betting slips for a numbers banker who had been granted a "franchise" in the Bronx.

Malcolm told one visitor from Michigan that he was a big-time gangleader and that his companion was his "lieutenant." Later, he'd claim that he had four to six felons working for him and that he had bribed the police to protect his illegal operation. Instead of feigning morality as his father had done, he exaggerated his immorality. He seemed proud of the fact he wasn't a bible-toting hypocrite.

When his boss's numbers franchise expired, Malcolm started working for him in a gambling den. But he didn't do it for long. He changed hustles the way he changed jobs. His next illegal endeavor was guiding moneyed white customers to Harlem's bawdyhouses. His employer was a madame who arranged for women to gratify the unnatural appetites of her eccentric customers. Among them were men who were commercial, professional, or political pillars of New York City's white community. Years later, after Malcolm became a religious leader, he would severely condemn the apparently fine, upstanding public figures who privately engaged in illicit sex. But he would remain silent about the extra-marital adventures of his own parents.

Night after night, Malcolm viewed the erotic spectacles the madame's clients sponsored. He said he really enjoyed watching two girls "in action" and seeing a man lick a woman from her toes to her forehead.

A man had to "eat pussy" in order to satisfy his mate, he proclaimed to the astonishment of friends. For a youth who didn't seem to care about pleasing women, it was quite a declaration.

Despite his criminal endeavors, Malcolm never completely relinquished his quest for social acceptance. Like his father and Earl Junior, he vacillated between legitimate pursuits and illicit ones. In July 1944, he got a job at a nightclub called the Lobster Pond, where he worked as a bar entertainer and used his dancing ability to good advantage. Occasionally, he played the drums. The stage name he used, Jack Carlton, was virtually a duplicate of Earl Junior's stage name, Jimmy Carlton. The choice may also have been influenced by Malcolm's admiration for black trombonist Carlton Bell Donaldson, alias "Blondie" Donaldson. Like Malcolm, Donaldson had blue eyes and sandy-blonde hair. His skin color was very fair.

Malcolm was secretive about his desire to be a successful entertainer. But during a trip back to Michigan, he confided his ambition to Allie Cooper. He seemed to want to be out front, on stage, entertaining large audiences—making movies rather than watching them.

Malcolm's employer at the Lobster Pond, Abe Goldstein, later characterized him as a "good boy," but somewhat unstable and neurotic. He was pleased with Malcolm's work, but since his need for bar entertainers was largely seasonal, he had to let him go in September.

Malcolm left New York and returned to Boston. In October, he became a twenty-nine-dollar-a-week packer at the Sears Roebuck warehouse in Brookline. Within three weeks, he had failed to report for work six times. In November, he walked off the job for good. He later described himself as "psychologically unsuited" for work, but subsequent events would prove that he meant work that was incompatible with his aspirations. When properly motivated, his capacity for work was enormous.

He began wangling money from Margaret Richmond. He also sold dope to Margaret, who, like Laura, had become a prostitute and reportedly had sex with women as well as men to support her drug habit and her saxophone-playing husband, Lester Shackelford. Considerable time apparently elapsed before Lester realized that Malcolm was cuckolding him. But he didn't seem to mind; he needed the money his wife earned on the street. Malcolm also worked, ostensibly, as a "butler" for a wealthy Boston Brahmin whose living quarters overlooked the Boston Common. His bachelor employer, William Paul Lennon, was hazy about the exact nature of Malcolm's duties when he was questioned about them. Nor did he say why he hired a male to do what he characterized

as "general housework."* There was good reason for Mr. Lennon's lack
of clarity. According to Jarvis, Lennon paid Malcolm to disrobe him,
place him on his bed, sprinkle him with talcum powder, and massage
him until he reached his climax. Lennon, who was virtually the same
age Earl Little would have been if he had lived, was old enough to be
the gentle, loving father Malcolm had never had.

Malcolm would later assert that someone else, not he, was giving
Lennon his satisfaction. Though another man did take part in some of
the rubdowns, Malcolm himself actively participated. He later described
the proceedings to Jarvis. Like a prostitute, he sold himself, as if the best
he had to offer was his body.

Malcolm's income-producing homosexual activity was sporadic. Nevertheless, it may have been an impediment in his quest for a satisfying
masculine self-image. It constituted a key link in a chain of events that
included the absence of appropriate male role models; tyrannical females
at home and school; the excessive demands that had been made on him;
the fact that there was no one to teach him how to meet those demands;
his fear of combat; his unavenged trouncings at the hands of Bill
Peterson, Hank Ross, and others; the shock he apparently felt when he
discovered a milky substance seeping from his breast; his unsatisfying
sexual experiences; and his inability to support himself or to make his
way in a competitive, bigoted world. Perhaps that is why he asserted,
years later, that a man's "greatest urge" is the need to feel masculine.

---

* At the time, nearly all paid housekeepers were women.

MORE HUMILIATION 18

During Malcolm's stay in Boston, he roomed at Ella's with all the advantages and disadvantages that entailed. He was not the only roomer. His father's sister Sarah, whom he affectionately called "Aunt Sassie," had a separate apartment on the ground floor. With her lived another unmarried sister, Malcolm's Aunt Grace.

Grace did not favor Malcolm the way Sassie did. In late November, 1944, he stole a fur coat that was apparently hers and pawned it for five dollars.

Grace attributed Malcolm's growing criminality to Ella's influence. Yet when Ella found out about the stolen coat, she righteously summoned the police, who carted Malcolm away. Years later, she denied having called the police. Asked if she thought Malcolm had deliberately provoked her into ousting him from her home, she grew belligerent and threatened to have her obedient minions work her questioner over.

Judge Samuel Eisenstadt gave Malcolm a three-month suspended sentence and placed him on probation for a year. When Malcolm returned to New York, Abe Goldstein put him to work at one of his nightclubs. But after Christmas, the job, which was merely seasonal, ended.

Malcolm went back to Lansing, dressed in conservative apparel that proclaimed his newest image. Not a trace of hipster slang marred his speech. He told one ex-classmate he had been dancing in New York "in shows." He told another he had just come from California, where he had been acting bit parts in Hollywood movies. He told a third he was "in business" and a fourth that he was associated with a Madison-Avenue-type modeling agency.

Yet his spirits seemed low. The bounce was gone from his step. In contrast to his usual rapid gait, which resembled his father's, he walked slowly, aimlessly. "A man never rises so high," he later declared, "as when he doesn't know where he's going."

For two weeks, Malcolm waited on tables at an East Lansing nightspot called the Coral Gables. He also worked briefly as a busboy at the Mayfair Ballroom. (He later asserted that he had been employed there as a dancer stage-named Rhythm Red.)

He began stealing again. One prospective victim awoke and discovered that he had pilfered her purse. When she demanded her money, which Malcolm had hidden inside his sock, he played innocent. But since the door of the room was still locked, she knew the culprit was still in the room. Cornered, Malcolm swung. It was then, he ruefully acknowledged later, that he discovered that the woman was a professional wrestler. She heaved him across the room. Malcolm staggered to his feet, only to be thrown again. He landed near the door. Hastily, he unbolted it, fled downstairs, and half-ran, half-limped all the way from Maple Street to the Booker T. Washington Club, a distance of about a mile and a half. The limp was due to the fact that, in his eagerness to hurdle a picket fence that was situated along the way, he had cut his shin to the bone. The scar remained with him the rest of his life.

Malcolm received help from Philbert for his injured leg. Then he moved into the home of a two hundred forty pound man named Jimmy Williams, who supplied him with bed and board. But after a while, Malcolm turned on Jimmy, who was homosexual. He held him at gun point and relieved him of his money. When a mutual friend, who would like to be called Vince, found out, he angrily confronted Malcolm, who pleaded with him not to hit him. Vince—who was much shorter than Malcolm, but who hit like a mule—was astonished.

Jimmy Williams declined to press charges. Malcolm then went to Detroit and robbed the man who had been kind enough to put him up for the night.

He took none of the precautions to avoid arrest that he had taken when he was a Harlem drug vendor. In fact, his victims were all people who knew him. His Detroit host, Douglas Haynes, swore out a complaint. The Motor City police alerted Lansing police officials, who apprehended Malcolm in March 1945, after he returned there.

The authorities retrieved several items Malcolm had stolen from Haynes, including a coat that he had pawned. Confronted with the evidence, he asserted that he was innocent. Wilfred generously provided the money he needed to make bail.

After Malcolm was released on bond, he played up his "bad" reputation for all it was worth. The Boston cops, he said, were still after him. He boasted that he had already "done time." Years later, looking back, he'd characterize his youthful, former self as one without a conscience . . . "the personification of evil . . . a predatory animal . . . a vulture." But around people he respected, his amoral facade gave way to the morality that had been pounded into him by his parents. He went to great lengths, for example, to hide his misdeeds from Allie Cooper. On other occasions, he tried to excuse them. "I've got to eat somehow," he told Jean Seaton, the minister's daughter he had liked so much. "If I don't hustle, someone else will," he added. Though he was no longer subject to his mother's furious scrubbing, he took an inordinate number of daily baths, sometimes three or four. Years later, after his religious conversion, he'd talk about physical and moral cleanliness as if they were synonymous. He'd emphatically deny that he had been trying to exaggerate his "sordid" past. But the villainous image he projected enabled him to transform youthful failure into felonious success. By exaggerating how bad he had been, he was able to portray himself as a living symbol of moral uplift, an inspiring example of how wrongdoers could "clean themselves up" and reform themselves.

Malcolm's trial was postponed. Jimmy Williams, who still hadn't given up on him, got him a job in Lansing making mattresses at the Capitol Bedding Company, whose work force he supervised. Malcolm showed up for work intermittently. Nor did he appear to do much for the salary he received.

In July 1945, he quit. Then he worked for about five days at a boring job sweeping floors at the Reo truck factory. The following month, he returned to Harlem. It may have been at this juncture that he began transporting moonshine for a Jewish bootlegger named Hymie. The supposedly reputable New York City drinking establishments that Hymie supplied saved their empty liquor bottles. Malcolm trucked them to Long Island, where they were filled with homemade hootch and then redelivered to tap rooms and cocktail lounges, many of whose customers could not tell the difference between their favorite brands and week-old rot gut.

Hymie, who seemed sympathetic to the plight of black people, chewed Malcolm's ear about the problems of the black and Jewish minorities. Malcolm said his new boss "really liked" him, but qualified the statement with, "He liked me because of something I had managed to do for him."

As Hymie's errand boy, Malcolm sometimes earned hundreds of dollars a week. He earned additional income by supplying Harlem bars with bootleg himself. He later asserted that this was with Hymie's permission and affirmed his loyalty in unswerving terms.

Eventually, the authorities got wind of the bootlegging. A rumor spread about an informant. One day, Hymie failed to show up where he had told Malcolm to meet him. "I never heard from him again,"

Malcolm later recalled. "But I did hear that he was put in the ocean, and I knew he couldn't swim."

Other disturbing incidents occurred. Two Mafia-like toughs mistook Malcolm for a tall, light-skinned black man who had robbed some Italian gangsters. The thugs cornered Malcolm in a barroom phone booth. He tried to bluff them into thinking he was carrying a gun, but the goons called his bluff. They might have done him in then and there had a policeman not entered the taproom.

Malcolm was still shaking when he reached Sammy's apartment. He took no notice when Sammy told him that West Indian Archie, the numbers runner with the computer-like memory, had been looking for him. Archie had been handling Malcolm's bets for some time. Being his client was a sign of prestige, for he serviced only bettors who had established "sound credit." If a customer told him that a number he had bet had "hit," Archie would pay him himself and get reimbursed later by the numbers banker. On one occasion, when he heard that Malcolm was penniless, he had sought him out, handed him some cash, and said, "Stick this in your pocket."

But it was a pistol Archie stuck at Malcolm when he returned to Sammy's.

Malcolm was dumbfounded. Earlier that afternoon, Archie had paid him three hundred dollars on the basis of Malcolm's assurance that the number he had combinated had won. But when Archie had double-checked the betting slip, he discovered that Malcolm had combinated a different number. It would not have been the first time a young, aspiring hustler had tried to make a name for himself by conning an established hood. Nor would it have been the first time Malcolm had attempted to outsmart an older, more experienced competitor.

Still brandishing the gun, Archie issued his ultimatum to Malcolm: "I'll give you until twelve o'clock tomorrow." Then he stalked out the door.

The issue was not just the money; it was one of saving "face." Archie could not let Malcolm get away with what he perceived to be an attempt to "hype" him. Malcolm, whose repuation was also at stake, could not cave in to Archie's threat.

But those who defied Archie, who was a "graduate" of Sing Sing, did so at their peril. Before he was imprisoned, he had been an enforcer for "Dutch" Schultz, who had ruled the Harlem numbers industry until he was liquidated by rivals.

Resolutely, Malcolm prepared to make the rounds of his usual hangouts. (Any refusal to do so would have been interpreted as cowardice.) He began wondering if he had been mistaken about the number he had combinated. If so, it would not have been the last time he provoked a dangerous confrontation with a former benefactor.

Later on, Malcolm took a cab to a St. Nicholas Avenue bar called La Marr-Cheri, one of his favorite nightspots. He hung around, sitting with his back to the front door. Suddenly, West Indian Archie was standing over him, flourishing his pistol.

Malcolm would later claim that he was waiting for Archie to turn around so that he could draw his gun and shoot him. But Archie said:

> You're thinking you're going to kill me first, Red. But I'm going to give you something to think about. I'm sixty. I'm an old man . . . . My life is over. You're a young man. Kill me, you're lost anyway. All you can do is go to prison.

Just then, some people Archie knew eased up beside him. Quietly, they pleaded, "Archie . . . . Archie." Eventually, they maneuvered him toward the rear of the barroom. Leisurely, Malcolm stood, tipped the bartender, and strolled out the door. For several minutes, he waited outside near the entrance with his hand in his pocket. But Archie stayed inside.

Malcolm's account of the incident suggests that Archie was the one who backed down because he didn't follow Malcolm out of the barroom and shoot it out, like the gun-toting heroes of the cowboy films Malcolm loved. But twentieth-century Harlem was a far cry from nineteenth-century Deadwood Gulch. There was organized law to contend with. Professional gunmen did not ordinarily dispatch their victims publicly, where all could see and bear witness. That Archie refrained from such an attempt did not mean he was backing down. On the contrary, he had publicly humiliated Malcolm, who hadn't retaliated. And he had not withdrawn his ultimatum.

The following day, Malcolm stuffed himself full of different drugs: opium, benzedrine, marijuana, cocaine. Archie's noon deadline came and went. People who knew Malcolm avoided him, as if they anticipated a shootout. Then another barroom clash occurred, this one with a total stranger. When Malcolm retold the incident years later, he was uncustomarily silent about the details, except for an assertion that he had to "bust in" his adversary's mouth. Nor did he indicate who provoked whom. The stranger drew a knife. Malcolm later claimed he would have shot him had bystanders not intervened. Over and over, he emphasized his readiness to kill. Yet he gave away his gun to a bystander, even though the knife-wielding youth had threatened to do him in. It turned out to be a smart move. Policemen came, escorted him outside, and frisked him on the sidewalk. Before releasing him, they advised him to leave town.

Malcolm Jarvis (whom Malcolm's autobiography would later transform into the fictional character Shorty) came to his rescue. By chance, he had placed a long distance phone call to Sammy in an attempt to locate Malcolm. When Sammy told Jarvis that Malcolm was in trouble, Jarvis volunteered to come and save him.

Jarvis brought a car.* Malcolm gathered up the few things he had worth taking besides the loose marijuana he had sewn into the lining of his Chesterfield overcoat. He threw them into the car trunk. During the trip to Boston, he babbled incoherently. It was a long time before he admitted that he had been run out of Harlem.

---

* Jarvis and his friends called a car a "short" because it shortened travel time. Perhaps this is why he was called "Shorty" in Malcolm's autobiography.

TOUGH GUY 19

Malcolm insisted that Ella "still liked" him. But he didn't stay with her. Jarvis put him up in his Hollander Street apartment. He, too, had been starved for motherly affection. His father, a jazz musician, was one of upper Roxbury's Four Hundred. In fact, Jarvis was a talented trumpet player himself.

Malcolm renewed his liaison with Bea. She continued giving him money, even though he beat her, just as his father had beaten his mother. Bea would cry and threaten to leave, but Malcolm knew she wouldn't.

Malcolm would later assert that his relationship with her had "nothing to do" with the troubles she was having with her husband, who had recently been discharged from the army because the war had ended. Apparently, he knew nothing about Malcolm.

With Jarvis supplying Malcolm's lodgings and Bea supplying his cash, Malcolm was free to concentrate on rehabilitating his injured reputation. The first breakthrough occurred at the gambling den of an older, experienced cardshark named George Holt. One evening, Malcolm found himself sitting next to George at a poker game. The cards went around the table twice. Malcolm had an ace showing and another in the hole. George's face card was a queen. Since Malcolm had high card, it was up to him to bet first.

He deliberated for quite some time before he passed. The ruse implied that his down card was worthless.

The next player bet. The following one raised him. George, who was sitting with a pair of queens, upped the ante still more.

Malcolm knew his hand was better than anyone else's. But when his turn to bet came, he did not raise George. Instead, he deliberated once more, feigning uncertainty.

Malcolm's final card was another ace, George's another queen. George bet heavily. The other players dropped out, but Malcolm stayed in the game. When George saw the third ace and realized that Malcolm had been acting, he told an aide, "Any time Red comes in here and wants anything, let him have it." He also offered him a job dealing for the house. Though Malcolm turned it down, George kept his word; on several occasions, he lent Malcolm money to gamble with.

One night, however, he refused, apparently because Malcolm had lost too much money. Malcolm exploded. He leaped up from the card table, placed his hand on the pistol inside his suit pocket, threw the weapon on the table, took a step back, and declared, "If I ain't gonna gamble tonight, nobody's gonna gamble!" Then he withdrew a .32 revolver from his shoulder holster, tossed it on the table, and dared anyone to reach for it. No one knew if he was toting a third gun or not. No one wanted to find out. The players all left in a hurry, to George Holt's dismay.

Malcolm flashed his guns at every opportunity. He'd pull back his suit coat so that his shoulder holster lay exposed. In barrooms, he'd "accidentally" drop a pistol, sending patrons scurrying in all directions. Nonchalantly, he'd reach down, retrieve it, and return to his drink as if nothing had happened. Roxbury thought he was the second George Raft.

Malcolm fostered his tough image in other ways. He swaggered when he walked and told Jarvis the scar on his shin had been caused by a gunshot wound. When Jarvis was waylaid by two white sailors, Malcolm volunteered to help track them down. For three weeks, the two Malcolms trekked in and out of every bar on Massachusetts Avenue, looking for Jarvis's assailants. (The likelihood of finding them was slim.) On one occasion, they beat unconscious a young man who had refused to repay some money he owed them. They left the unfortunate welcher in an ash can behind a restaurant. Malcolm also joined in, occasionally, when packs of blacks roamed Roxbury's streets in search of Irishmen or Jews to pummel. During a trip to Michigan, he asked Vince's cousin if he wanted to help him maul a middle-aged drunk who was zigzagging down the other side of the street. When Vince's cousin said no, Malcolm did not pursue the matter.

But when Malcolm was armed, he was what Reginald would later call "the boldest coward" he had ever seen. During November and December, 1945, Malcolm initiated a series of reckless confrontations that were apparently designed to bolster his self-esteem the way he had tried to bolster it after his humiliating encounters with Bill Peterson. When a seaman he knew tried to sell him a machine gun, Malcolm pointed the loaded weapon at him and threatened to drill him full of holes. "He knew I was crazy enough to kill him." Malcolm later asserted. But in reality, it was a carefully calculated craziness, the same kind he had employed in his encounter with the army psychiatrist. Word spread that he was trigger-happy; people grew reluctant to cross him. Yet when his half-sister Mary warned him that one of his pistols might accidentally discharge, he begged her not to say such things. "If you do," he said, "I'll believe them, even though I don't want to."

Looking back years later, Malcolm denied that he had considered the possibility that the people he provoked might retaliate in kind. Yet in virtually the same breath, he acknowledged that he had "deliberately" risked death more willingly than he had risked failure. A case in point occurred as Malcolm and Jarvis were sitting in a Massachusetts Avenue club called the Savoy. Malcolm, mindful of his encounter with Archie, sat facing the door. He had one eye on the telephone booth. At the bar lounged a black plainclothes policeman who had apparently overheard him tell the bartender he was expecting a call.

The telephone rang. Malcolm rose from his seat, but the detective, who was closer to the phone booth, got there first. He picked up the receiver, fixed his gaze on Malcolm, and said, "Hello."

The caller hung up. "Wasn't that call for me?" Malcolm asked. The police officer said yes. "Why didn't you say so?" Malcolm demanded. By this time his hand was inside his coat pocket.

The detective, who disliked Malcolm, gave an uncivil response and inched his hand toward his gun holster. Malcolm knew that the cop wanted to shoot him and was waiting for him to say something that could be interpreted as a threat. So instead of threatening him, he told him, loudly enough for bystanders to hear, that if he wanted to "make history," he'd have to kill him. His deft response left the next move up to the policeman, who let the matter drop.

The Savoy was also the site of another tense incident. Malcolm, Jarvis, Bea, and her heavy-set Armenian girlfriend Kora Marderosian were sitting and chatting when Harvey Yates, one of the meanest black cops in Boston, walked in the door with his light-brown-skinned sidekick. Yates had a habit of frisking Malcolm. It was rumored that he wore a bulletproof vest. People whispered that he'd just as soon blow out your brains as look at you.

Malcolm slipped the gun he was carrying to Bea, who was sitting next to him. "Don't let them arrest me," he said. Bea slipped the pistol inside her fur muff, which she kept pointed at Yates's belly while he searched Malcolm. His partner unconcernedly looked on. The police officers finally departed. Bea turned to Malcolm and said she loved him so much she would have shot Yates. "Damn good thing you didn't," Jarvis replied.

When there was only one cop to contend with, Malcolm provoked the badged representatives of the law the way he had provoked authority figures at home and at school. He was talking with Jarvis and Margaret Richmond's brother John in a club called the Little Dixie when someone summoned a policeman and asked him to evict an inebriated woman who was creating a disturbance. The woman, who was black, resisted. When the police officer tried yanking her out, she stumbled and fell. The patrolman, who was white, reached down and grabbed her by the hair. He was about to drag her out the door when Malcolm confronted the policeman and said, "Take your hands off that woman!" The officer flipped back his jacket, placed his hand on his gun butt, and ordered Malcolm to move on.

Malcolm slid his hand into his coat pocket and replied, "That's all right, friend. I have one of those too. I said, 'Take your hands off that woman!' If she were your mother or your sister, you wouldn't manhandle her like that." The cop, finding himself surrounded by an angry crowd including Jarvis and John (who were also armed), retreated to a call box for help. Quickly, Malcolm bundled the woman into a cab. He flipped the driver five dollars and made himself scarce. The remarkable thing about the incident, which marked the beginning of the evolution of the pseudo-masculine criminal Malcolm into the manly political Malcolm, was that he defended the woman, a stranger, with a determination that had been completely absent when he had been called upon to defend himself against opponents such as Bill Peterson and Hank Ross. Once again, he had mastered, or at least temporarily dispelled, his fear.

Malcolm's tough veneer shielded him from physical attack. But it also protected him from other kinds of hurt. Tough guys didn't cry over the death of a horse, or concern themselves about homeless animals or injured competitors. They had no compunction about torturing captive frogs. They weren't even hurt when their girlfriends dated other men. Like the anti-heroes of his favorite movies, Malcolm was a tough guy with a tear in his eye.

BURGLAR

20

A bout three weeks before Christmas, 1945, Malcolm embarked on a stealing binge, like a Santa Claus in reverse. The type of larceny he chose was house burglary, which had important advantages over armed robbery. If one planned the job carefully so that one wouldn't encounter any of the victims, there would be no witnesses. And the likelihood that one would have to maim or kill anyone would be minimal.

According to Malcolm, the break-ins were highly professional: Bea and her petite eighteen-year-old sister Joyce Caragulian allegedly scouted Boston's suburbs for appropriate targets; "cased" richly appointed homes by posing as pollsters or traveling vendors; reported which targets seemed most promising; and described the layout to the male burglars, who, being black, would have attracted notice had they attempted to reconnoiter white neighborhoods themselves.

But in fact, the burglaries were amateurish and unplanned. One evening, Malcolm, Bea, Joyce, Kora Marderosian, and a tough, feisty twenty-three-year-old ex-con named "Sonny" Brown were cruising around Arlington, a posh Boston suburb. Malcolm and Sonny decided to break into an expensive-looking home and the deed was done before the women had any idea what the two men were doing. Malcolm later admitted that he had qualms about involving the women. The more people who knew what was going on, the more likelihood there was that someone in the group, which he envisioned as a "family unit," would squeal. But he decided to include them anyway. He knew that Bea, whose fascination with him seemed to increase with each new reckless foray, would do whatever he told her to do. Joyce would follow Bea's example. If he got caught, he hoped the Caragulians, who were well heeled, would supply the lawyers and connections that would enable him to get off easy.

Jarvis was later roped into the act the same way the women were. One night Malcolm and Sonny, whose real name was Francis Brown, began filling Jarvis's car with the loot before he knew what was happening. Jarvis protested to no avail. "If I ever get caught," Malcolm told him, "I'll tell the police you were with me."

Malcolm used fear to enforce his authority. On one occasion, he took out his .32, emptied the bullets, reinserted one cartridge, and rotated the cylinder. Then he pointed the pistol at his head, grinned, and squeezed the trigger. The gun went "click."

Malcolm pulled the trigger a second time. Bea and Joyce frantically implored him to stop, but Malcolm pressed the trigger a third time. "Never cross a man not afraid to die," he told them. His companions, who were unaware that he had palmed the bullet he had pretended to put in the gun, took him at his word. Not even Sonny, who was built like Jersey Joe Walcott, ever questioned his authority.

Malcolm seemed unhappy about Sonny's suggestive remarks about Joyce, whom Jarvis later described as the best-looking woman he had ever met, except for Hortense. Jarvis, too, longed for Joyce; Malcolm taunted him about it and wouldn't let him alone with her. Jarvis got the feeling Malcolm wanted her for himself. It was the way he looked at her and hovered over her, ostensibly to protect her. He did nothing that might have compromised his financial arrangement with Bea. But if he couldn't have Joyce, neither would anyone else.

With one or two possible exceptions, the techniques the burglary "ring" employed were always the same. There was no reconnoitering or advance planning; the leads Bea and Joyce obtained resulted from the fact that they knew some wealthy people who were away on vacation. The young burglars drove around until they spotted an unlighted home. One of them rang the doorbell. If no one answered, one or two of the men would sneak to the back door, smash the lock with a hammer, or jimmy open a window with a screwdriver or crowbar while someone kept watch. Malcolm and his companions-in-crime came armed with none of the specialized burglary tools that he would later assert they possessed. They had no glass cutter or lock pick. In fact, according to Jarvis, Malcolm did not even know how to pick a lock.

Malcolm wore gloves, a precaution that should have foreclosed the possibility of fingerprints. But despite his subsequent assertions about the need to avoid detection, he removed the gloves during one or two burglaries; the police reportedly found his prints on a windowsill. They may also have obtained his fingerprints from the flashlight he left behind in one victim's home, or from the batteries that he had inserted into the flashlight shortly before the break-in.

One of the homes that Malcolm burglarized belonged to the people who manufactured the popular Eberhardt fountain pen. Another was the home of his employer Paul Lennon.

As Malcolm and Jarvis emerged from one victim's residence, they noticed a man across the street. He was watching them from behind a tree; his shadow was silhouetted on the moonlit snowbank behind him. Malcolm pulled off his glove, drew his gun, and lowered his arm to take aim at the man, who was walking his dog and was clearly unarmed. "No, don't!" cried Jarvis, knocking Malcolm's arm upward. Later, he rebuked Malcolm for his lack of self-control. Though Malcolm asserted that the pistol hadn't been loaded, he promptly got plastered on some scotch they had stolen.

During one getaway, a cruising police car spotted Jarvis's automobile and began following it. Malcolm used the same reverse psychology that he would later use against some of his political foes. Alighting from the car, he hailed the pursuing vehicle and engaged its uniformed occupants in conversation before the driver could draw abreast of the getaway car, which was full of stolen merchandise. Pretending he was lost, Malcolm asked for directions. The officers obliged him and drove off.

Years later, Malcolm would claim that he had succeeded in getting his new profession "down to a science." He intimated that he had even outdone Jumpsteady, the cat burglar who looted apartments while his victims were in the next room. "It was almost easy," Malcolm boasted as he described how he had waited until he heard the breathing of his sleeping victims and had tiptoed into their bedrooms and emptied them of cash and jewelry. But it was difficult to reconcile his assertions with his insistence on the importance of minimizing the risk of encountering his victims. Moreover, the burglaries occurred during the early evening, before bedtime.

Malcolm would later acknowledge that his thievery had been compulsive; he deprived his burglary victims the way he had been deprived. It was the same kind of revenge mechanism that had prompted the childhood stealing that had caused his harried mother such anguish. He'd later ascribe his stealing to indigence. But Reginald saw through his excuse. Wartime jobs were plentiful, even for unskilled blacks.

Malcolm later claimed that crime stems from the inability of its perpetrators to "stand on their own feet." But he seemed to prefer being supported by others, as if he were determined to be indemnified for the lack of support he had received when he was young and helpless.

Yet he wasn't helpless any more. The criminal Malcolm wielded power over his luckless victims, just as those who had tyrannized him had wielded power over him. He forced his way into locked homes the way a valiant knight might storm a castle. Perhaps he feared the barriers he breached much less than he feared the barriers to the success and acceptance he longed for.

He rebelled against civil authority with a fervor stemming from earlier, unresolved battles against parental and pedagogical authority. If he could not master the law one way, perhaps he could do it another. He preferred to be "bad" rather than an acknowledged failure, and to be condemned by society at large rather than by taskmasters at home and school. The criminal Malcolm was simultaneously a repudiation of everything his father and Ella wanted him to be and an affirmation of everything they were.

SELF-CAUGHT

21

Malcolm's "gang" drove to New York City to live it up for about a week. As the two automobiles sped south along the Merritt Parkway, he yanked out a pistol, leaned out of the window of Bea's convertible, and fired a couple of shots in the direction of Jarvis's black 1938 Buick, which was in the lead. "I could have hit your tires if I had wanted to," he told Jarvis later.

Two days before Christmas, the vacationers returned to Boston. Not long afterward, Malcolm walked into a barroom and saw Bea and Joyce having a drink with a white man. For all he knew, it was Bea's husband, whom he had never seen. There was no reason to barge up to their table and flaunt his familiarity with her—unless he wanted to provoke a confrontation.

Bea's face went pale when she saw him. The man was her husband's best friend. They had gone through the war together.

Alone, later on, at the Cambridge apartment Bea had rented for Malcolm, he became ill. He was nearly asleep when he heard a noise at the door. He scrambled under the bed before he realized he had forgotten his pistol. It was the third time in four or five months that he had abandoned his only effective means of self-defense.

Mehran Bazarian's friend inserted the key in the lock and opened the door. Silently, he surveyed the room, which contained some of Bea's clothing. Finally, he kneeled down, peered under the bed, and saw Malcolm, who forced a laugh. Then Bazarian's friend left.

The break-ins continued for several weeks. But the fence who disposed of the stolen merchandise for Malcolm paid him only a fraction of what it was worth. Malcolm decided to keep some of it in the apartment. He sold just enough of it to keep Jarvis and Brown from suspecting that he was hiding the rest. He hoped the proceeds would become seed money for a legitimate business.

Despite Malcolm's professed determination to avert capture, he later claimed that it was "inevitable" that he'd be rearrested. It was a self-fulfilling prophecy. On, or within days of, the seventh anniversary of his mother's commitment to the Kalamazoo asylum, he initiated the chain of events that led to his own incarceration. He knew very well that the majority of burglars are apprehended, not at the scene of the crime, but trying to market their ill-gotten gains. He was equally aware of the need to remove all identifying marks from each stolen item. Yet for a single dollar, he pawned a wedding band that was clearly stamped with its owner's initials. Malcolm also gave Al Beeman, the proprietor of the jewelry shop where he had pawned the ring, a stolen watch to repair. He supplied his real name and Ella's address and promised to return for the easily identifiable diamond-studded man's watch. Detective Stephen Slack spotted one or both items on one of the reports that Beeman filed daily, or almost daily, with the Boston Police Department.

Detective Slack served the wealthy suburban community of Milton, Massachusetts, where the wedding band had been stolen. Periodically, he drove into Boston to check the reports each jeweler filed. His cousin, Stanley Slack, was a Boston police officer. It was Stanley who staked out Beeman's shop, which was located on Warren Street near the Dudley "el" station.

Malcolm returned to the jewelry store on January 12, 1946, just five days before he was scheduled to appear in court in Michigan, where his conviction was virtually a foregone conclusion.

Later, Malcolm would make a point of the fact that "the Jew Jeweler" accepted payment for fixing the watch before signaling Stanley Slack, who emerged from the rear of the store. "Step into the back," he told Malcolm, who knew he was a police officer. Just then, another black man walked into the store. Thinking that he was Malcolm's companion, Slack turned and confronted him. His back was to Malcolm, whose fully loaded .32 was in its holster.

But though Malcolm would later portray himself as a man who would kill without compunction, he did not draw his gun and shoot Slack. Instead, he surrendered and told him to take his pistol. It was a wise decision. Had he tried using the gun, he would have been shot down by two other armed detectives, who suddenly appeared from nowhere.

Had he not been arrested, he might have been killed by Bea's husband, who had reportedly been told about Malcolm's affair with her and had been gunning for him.

When Malcolm was interrogated by the police, he admitted his role in the break-ins. He implicated his fellow burglars in return for his jailers' promise to persuade Judge Eisenstadt to give him a suspended sentence for the gun-carrying charge that had been filed against him. Later, he asserted that the women had informed on Sonny Brown, whom the cops never caught.

The Boston police turned Malcolm over to the Milton authorities. By the time Stephen Slack questioned him, his tough facade had disintegrated. He seemed like a friendless, scared kid. Slack bought him candy and cigarettes, which Malcolm smoked without stopping. Bea, Joyce, and Kora were released on bail, which was low. But since bail for Malcolm and Jarvis had been set at ten thousand dollars, the requisite bond was beyond their means.

The trial was held during the last week of February, 1946. The three white women sat at the defense table, while the two black Malcolms were locked in a courtroom cage that was reserved for prisoners who were unable to make bail. Inside the cage was a wooden bench. Spectators stared at the two men with a "those are the bastards" look. Some verbalized their feelings: "Nice white girls . . . , goddam niggers!" One sidled up to the bars and snarled, "If we had you coons down south, you'd have been strung up by now."

The moment Judge Allan Buttrick strode into the courtroom, Jarvis knew that he and Malcolm were done for. The judge's face was a mask of stone.

Since some of the burglary victims were in the courtroom, the prosecution did its duty with vigor. The prosecutor even tried to pin a number of unrelated, unsolved burglaries on the five defendants. But Jarvis's lawyer, John Drew, intervened. Some of the other defense attorneys appeared less committed to a spirited defense. When Malcolm observed that he and Jarvis seemed to be on trial for interracial sex, not burglary, one of them angrily exclaimed, "You had no business with white girls!"

Malcolm had no lawyer. Ella, who had already availed herself of counsel in several criminal proceedings, declined to provide him with legal assistance. Years later, she would acknowledge that she wanted him to go to prison. She hoped that a year or two in the clink would straighten him out.

Bea, dressed demurely in black, turned state's evidence and testified that Malcolm had forced her and Joyce to participate in the burglaries. She said he had threatened to kill them unless they continued to cooperate. "We lived in constant fear," she asserted. Malcolm didn't testify. In fact, he put up no defense at all.

Judge Buttrick called the opposing attorneys to the bar. After considerable discussion, a defense lawyer walked over to Jarvis and advised him to change his plea to guilty. "It'll go easier for you if you do," he said. "The judge wants to avoid the time and expense of jury deliberation. Anyway, they've got you dead to rights."

Jarvis reluctantly pleaded guilty. Malcolm, who had formally pleaded not guilty despite his earlier confession, followed suit. Too late, they discovered that Allan Buttrick's conception of leniency was different from theirs: "Count one, eight to ten years at hard labor . . . . Count two, eight to ten years at hard labor . . . . Count three . . . ." The emphasis fell on the word "hard." The judge decreed that the punishment for each count was to run concurrently. Jarvis, who had no idea what the word "concurrently" meant, thought that he was being sentenced to half a century in jail. For a moment, he lost control. He clutched the cage's steel bars and tried to force them apart.

Malcolm received the same sentence. Judge Buttrick made no bones about his feelings about black men who slept with white women. Malcolm later attributed the stiff sentence entirely to the judge's bigotry. He said nothing about his previous arrests and suspended sentences. Even Ella, who was in the courtroom, was unaware of his Michigan arrest. As the enormity of her miscalculation became apparent, she leaped to her feet and nearly started a riot. But Malcolm didn't. He just sat in the cage and smiled.

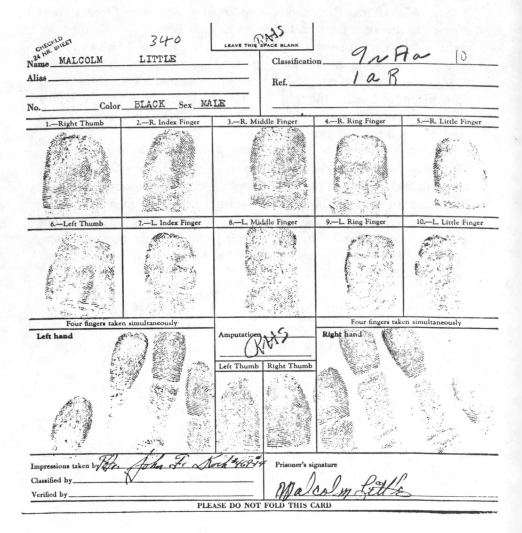

Fingerprints taken from Malcolm's Detroit police record.

III

A NEW HOME

CONVICT

22

Prisoner number 22843 wore the same sardonic smile when he posed for his first Charlestown Prison mug shot that he had worn in the courtroom. Yet within hours of his arrival at the prison, he apparently told the attending physician that his heart was fluttering. The prison doctor, who was not entirely convinced, noted on Malcolm's record the "possibility" of tachycardia, or overly rapid heartbeat. Malcolm was not yet twenty-one years old.

The penitentiary was in the southwestern part of Charlestown, across the Charles River from Boston. Thomas Jefferson had been President when the prison had opened its doors to its first contingent of inmates. Seven years later, during the War of 1812, the warden began making plans to use convict labor to repair the frigate U.S.S. Chesapeake. But before the work could be completed, the British frigate Shannon appeared off Boston harbor with a picked crew and challenged the unready, undermanned American vessel to do battle. The Yankee captain, who was reportedly enraged by the fact that the Union Jack was flying in full view of the bustling city, unwisely accepted the challenge and lost both the battle and his life, but not before uttering the famous rallying cry, "Don't give up the ship!"

In February 1946, when Malcolm entered Charlestown, conditions were not much better than they had been in Jefferson's day. The seven-or-eight-foot-long cells were barely large enough to accommodate a sleeping man. They had no running water or toilets; prisoners had to urinate and defecate in wooden buckets. The excrement was emptied daily, the pails disinfected and scoured. But the stench remained.

Rats were just a minor problem; the white lice were far more troublesome. They bred in the mildew and dampness; sometimes, inmates succeeded in catching the white varmints and squashing them.

In accord with the provisions of Judge Buttrick's sentence, Malcolm spent his first day in Charlestown in solitary confinement. New "fish" customarily spent their first twenty-four hours there, presumably to learn what to expect if they tried to abuse the comparative freedom of ordinary prison life. The day in solitary seemed like ten to Jarvis, who was placed in an adjoining, windowless cubicle. The only time he saw any light was when the guard cracked the solid metal door to deliver some bread and water.

After twenty-four hours, Malcolm was allowed to join the rest of the prison population. His first visitor was Ella. The sight of him in his faded prison uniform shook her. She tried to smile, but neither she nor Malcolm could find much to say.

A representative of the Massachusetts Department of Corrections interviewed Ella, but she refused to answer any questions about the family. When Malcolm was questioned himself, the parents he described were a far cry from the ones who had raised him. He depicted them in heroic, martyr-like terms and said they were "devoted" to each other. The reason they had moved from city to city, he said, was that they had been "missionaries." He characterized his father's financial condition as "good" and asserted that Earl had been studying law at the time of his death. He also declared that Earl's death had been accidental.

Malcolm told the authorities that his mother was white. But he did not tell them that she had borne a child out of wedlock, or that she was in a mental hospital. He said she was living in Lansing at 614 Birch Street. The woman who lived there was her West Indian friend Bea McGuire, who was raising Butch and Yvonne.

Prison psychiatrists tried to question Malcolm about his family on more than one occasion. He told fellow prisoners he resented the probing questions, particularly those about his mother. He called one therapist every foul name he could think of but told another that he feared he was losing his mind. Was he afraid he couldn't cope with a lengthy tour in prison? Or was he merely hoodwinking another psychiatrist?

Asked about his brothers and sisters, Malcolm described his relationship with Philbert as "friendly." When he was questioned about his schooling, he did not mention that he had failed the sixth grade. He characterized his Roseland shoeshine stand as a "business" and asserted he had worked at Small's Paradise as a "bartender and drummer." He also said that he had worked as a master of ceremonies at one of Abe Goldstein's nightclubs.

Malcolm asserted that he had been fully self-supporting since the age of thirteen. He denied that he had ever been dependent on drugs but said that he had left New York a number of times to disassociate himself from companions who had been addicted.

Fellow prisoners enjoyed Malcolm's entertaining exaggerations, just as the crowds who later flocked to hear him speak did. He boasted what a big-time hood he had been and how many women he had conquered.

If someone else began describing his alleged conquests, Malcolm would say, "That's nothing," and let his listener's imagination do the rest. Around weightlifters, whom he seemed to admire, he'd joke that the heaviest thing he had ever lifted was a woman's slip.

Malcolm also tried to impress his fellow convicts with his knowledge. He was so full of instructions about how to do things that Jarvis eventually nicknamed him Mr. Know-How. He also called him the Green-Eyed Monster.

But Malcolm's hostility toward religion prompted most of the men in his cellblock to call him "Satan." He seemed to relish his devilish image, which attracted attention and enhanced his status the way his sinful image had enhanced his status on the streets. Years later, Malcolm would portray himself as a tough, refractory convict who had refused to respond when his prison number was called, dropped his dishes in the dining hall, cursed his guards, and spent considerable time in solitary confinement. But prisoners were addressed by name, not by number. There was no dining hall at Charlestown; each inmate ate locked in his cell. Malcolm's voluminous prison record contains no evidence that he cursed any guards or spent more than his first day in prison in solitary confinement. Nor do any of the officers or guards who were later interviewed recall him doing so. They were well briefed about which inmates caused trouble. They had to be for their own protection.

Most of Malcolm's disciplinary infractions were too minor to warrant disciplinary action. He smoked in prohibited areas and flashed hateful looks at his jailers. He was insolent to certain guards. In the prison workshops, he employed the same passive resistance he had used so effectively against authority figures at home and school. But he was not a real troublemaker. One fellow inmate characterized him as a defiant kid.

For a while, Malcolm seemed curiously optimistic that he'd be "sprung" from jail with the help of Bea's money and her family's supposed influence. He refused to believe that she had testified against him willingly, insisting that the district attorney had forced her to cooperate with him.

But Bea, who had been sentenced to five years in prison, had her hands full getting herself out. Her attorneys, who were well connected, persuaded an appellate court to change her sentence to an indefinite one. This enabled her to win quick parole; she went scot free in seven months. Neither of the other two women spent a single day in jail after the trial; Kora Marderosian's sentence was suspended, and Joyce was placed on probation for two years. A real estate operator who had received some of the stolen goods was also put on probation. Even when Malcolm's past record is taken into consideration, the standard of justice for well-to-do, "respectable" whites was quite different from the one that was applied to poor blacks, especially those who flouted the taboo against interracial sex. The eight to ten year sentence that Judge Buttrick had imposed was far longer than the one that was typically given to burglars who were sent to Charlestown.*

Eventually, Malcolm began to realize that his faith in Bea had been misplaced. His involvement with her had earned him a heavier sentence, not a lighter one. And it was clear that she had no intention of coming to his aid. When the truth hit him with full force, he broke down. The tears streamed down his face. Later, he would blame his imprisonment on Bea, contending that she had turned him in to the police.

Malcolm's last meeting with Bea occurred in April 1946, at his second burglary trial. The first trial, which had taken place in the Middlesex County Courthouse, had involved five burglaries he had committed in the suburbs of Arlington, Belmont, and Newton, which lie west of Boston. The second trial, which was held in Norfolk County Superior Court, dealt with four burglaries he had perpetrated in Milton, Brookline, and Walpole, which lie more or less south of Boston. (The proceedings were held in the same Dedham, Massachusetts courthouse that had housed the famous Sacco-Vanzetti murder trial a quarter of a century earlier.)

By the time the second burglary trial had progressed very far, Bea had mastered the role of the reluctant burglar. With the prosecutor coaxing her along with leading questions, such as, "The real reason you participated was . . . ," she insisted that she had never "loved" Malcolm and that she had taken part in the burglaries only under severe duress. Malcolm exploded. "I might have known you'd brainwash her," he screamed at the D.A. Each time Bea started another lie, Malcolm beat her to the punch with the truth. "If you didn't want to take part, why did you tell us what families were out of town? Why did you rent the apartment? If you didn't love me, why did you come to my place alone? Why did you bring your clothes? I didn't hold a gun on you then." On and on, he raged. "You stole money for me from your own father. You said you knew ways to get more." Malcolm stood up and pointed his finger at Bea's father, who was

---

* In 1945, the only year for which data is presently available, fifty-four men were sentenced to Charlestown Prison for burglary. Just over half received sentences of from two to five years. The average minimum sentence was four years; the average maximum, five and a half. The figures do not indicate which of the fifty-four offenders had been convicted previously.

sitting in the courtroom. "You told me you hated your father and mother and wanted nothing to do with them any more."

The judge sentenced both Malcolms to six to eight years in prison. The sentences proved meaningless, for they ran concurrently with those that had been handed down by Judge Buttrick in Middlesex County.

Initially, in Charlestown, Malcolm sought the company of white convicts. He hardly spoke with Jarvis at all, partly because Jarvis had cold-shouldered him since his arrest. Malcolm laughed aside the rebuff, but Jarvis sensed the hurt in his eyes.

The first prisoner who really impressed Malcolm was a light-reddish-skinned black man named John Elton Bembry. John, who had a superb mind, was the prison guru. He worked in the license plate shop, where Malcolm was on the paint crew. Bembry operated the machine that stamped numbers on the license plates. After work, prisoners and guards would gather around Bembry, listening to him expound on history, theology, and other subjects. He was the first man Malcolm had ever met who commanded attention and respect entirely with words.

One afternoon in the prison courtyard, Malcolm "accidentally" bumped into Bembry, who was seated on a bench playing dominoes. The dominoes fell to the ground. Malcolm didn't say a word; he merely glanced at Bembry and continued walking around "the Circle," the well-worn path around the prison yard.

Minutes later, he came by Bembry's bench and stopped. Bembry put aside the game and stood up, prepared for anything.

But Malcolm just stood there, staring at him. The other domino player finally broke the silence by asking, "Hey, Satan, how you doin', man?" Malcolm grunted affirmatively. "I'm sorry about the dominoes," he said to Bembry. Then he blurted, "Do you believe in God? God the father, God the son, God the Holy Ghost, and all that crap?"

Gradually, the two men became friends. One day, Bembry bluntly told Malcolm that he should start using his brains. Years later, Malcolm acknowledged that it was not the kind of advice he had been looking for. But he began following Bembry around the way Reginald had followed him around. He plied him with questions about everything under the sun. He also began reading books in the prison library. Since his vocabulary was still limited, it was rough going at first. But it wasn't quite as difficult as he later claimed; his assertion that he could hardly read when he entered prison was as unfounded as his autobiographical assertion that he couldn't dance when he first moved to Boston.

The reasons Malcolm later exaggerated his reading difficulties are not altogether clear. Ella told an interviewer that it was due to his lack of confidence. Perhaps it was also due to his desire to inspire his ghetto followers to educate themselves the way he had educated himself.

Malcolm used Bembry's dictionary to improve his reading ability. He borrowed it so often that Bembry finally gave it to him. Later on, Malcolm began studying the dictionary systematically. Using it as an encyclopedia as well as a vocabulary-building device, he scrutinized the definitions and derivations of each word on each page of the book. He also began a correspondence course in English. It took him only two days to finish lessons that took other inmates ten. "When I get out of this place," he told Bembry, "I'm going to be a bad nigger, but I'm going to be . . . a smart bad nigger."

Malcolm began reading everything he could lay his hands on. One of his favorite books was Aesop's Fables, with its didactic parables about wily foxes, hungry wolves, and other creatures who looked like animals but acted like human beings. He was particularly fond of the tale about the old lion who was too weak to hunt for food and pretended to be ill, devouring whoever went into his lair to wish him well. A fox, who saw through the ruse, inquired (from a distance) how he was feeling. "Bad," answered the enfeebled king of the beasts, who asked why the fox didn't visit his cave. "I would have," replied the fox. "But I saw a lot of tracks going in, and none coming out."*

Malcolm did not enjoy everything he read. He would not even finish Romeo and Juliet; it was just a love story, he said. He did read Moby Dick after Bembry told him about Captain Ahab's mad quest for the white whale. "A god damn white whale," he exclaimed after finishing the book. He seemed unable to comprehend how a person could be so self-destructive.

One afternoon, Malcolm saw Bembry reading Macbeth and asked him about it. Bembry described how Macbeth's domineering wife had convinced him to commit criminal acts that he had been reluctant to commit. After some hesitation, Malcolm read the play about the conscience-stricken Scottish nobleman who betrays his leader because of his need to be top dog—a play in which a boy named Malcolm becomes king.

For several days, Malcolm paced around the circle in the penitentiary yard, lost in himself. Then, one afternoon, he walked over to Bembry's metal-stamping machine and shouted above the din, "That bitch was nuts. That's all, just plain nuts."

"Who the heck are you talking about?" asked Bembry.

---

* Recalling Malcolm's fondness for this tale, Jarvis later observed that in order to understand Malcolm, one should visualize him as the fox in each of Aesop's fables.

"That bitch Lady Macbeth," replied Malcolm, who was apparently referring to Lady Macbeth's mental breakdown. Bit by bit, he began telling Bembry about his mother and her emotional breakdown. He asked him whether a mother's insanity affected her children. Bembry could tell that he was deeply distressed by his mother's illness. Tailoring his response accordingly, he assured Malcolm that his mother's collapse had been due to her inability to give her children what they needed.

Bembry's superficial but comforting explanation had a profound effect on Malcolm, who no longer seemed distressed. Years later, he told Bembry that his reassuring explanation was the single most uplifting thing that had happened to him until his religious conversion. He said it had removed a very heavy burden from his mind.

CONVERT

Malcolm became the cellblock's bookie as well as its bookworm. While other prisoners gossiped in the prison yard, he walked around with a pad and pencil, taking bets on ball games, horse races, and boxing matches. Since cash was forbidden as a medium of exchange, his clients used cigarettes or scrip that was later credited or debited against their prison bank accounts.

Malcolm used his profits to purchase nutmeg, which was pilfered from the kitchen by inmates who worked there. Mixed with water, it made one tipsy. Later, he was able to afford the marijuana and benzedrine that were smuggled into the penitentiary by guards who found it difficult to support their families on their low pay. Since the guards accepted only cash, the prisoners devised ingenious methods of sneaking money into the prison. Visitors rolled fifty-dollar bills into tiny wads and wrapped them with tape that was sticky on both sides. At opportune moments, they slipped them to their jailed recipients, who tucked them under their belts as they pretended to hitch up their slacks. Girlfriends passed wadded-up hundred-dollar bills to their boyfriends as they kissed them. Eventually, the authorities discovered what was going on. After each visit, they made each convict open his mouth and stick out his tongue.

In January, 1947, Malcolm was transferred to Concord Reformatory. He complained that the place wasn't tough enough. "They treat you like a baby here," he told Ella. Concord had toilets. It even had a dining hall. Yet in one sense, Concord was tougher than Charlestown; fights broke out there frequently. The perpetrators were usually hot-headed young hoodlums who emulated the older, hardened Charlestown inmates and aspired to "big-house" status. Some of them had been recommitted to Concord four or five times. About forty percent of those who had been released eventually returned to jail.

A month after Malcolm's arrival at the reformatory, which the Massachusetts legislature had condemned as a complete failure, he sought medical assistance for a laceration on his chin, which had to be redressed twice. Later, a rumor began circulating that he was carrying a "shiv" with a six-inch blade. The rumor was never verified, but most of the inmates gave him a wide berth.

For thirteen months, Malcolm worked in Concord's furniture shop. The guard in charge, Arthur Roach, was kinder than most of his colleagues. Good-naturedly, he kidded "Little Malcolm," who retorted, "There's no joking between you and me." He had no use at all for the other officers, many of whom were as calloused as the convicts they were supposedly helping to reform. One device they used to subdue defiant prisoners was the "arm-choker," a collar-shaped instrument that was fashioned from a length of chain. Fastened about a man's arm, it could be twisted so tight that it would break the skin, draw blood, and send him to his knees. No evidence has been found that Malcolm was subjected to such treatment. At Concord, as at Charlestown, he contented himself by committing petty offenses that were reminiscent of his boyhood ones, such as refusing to do his chores. Sometimes, he'd sneak to the front of the line of convicts who were patiently waiting to take their weekly shower. Even in jail, he had to be first.

Malcolm suffered from a variety of illnesses while he was in prison. Stomach distress was one. The headaches that had tormented him when he was younger continued to plague him. He tried to explain them away by comparing the brain to a muscle that aches when you start using it after a long period of inactivity. The prison physician noted that Malcolm's physical symptoms frequently responded to placebo treatment.

The day before the second anniversary of the trial in Middlesex County Court, Malcolm reported something wrong with his penis. Some time later, blood was discovered in his urine. Medical examination failed to disclose any organic cause for the discharge.

Malcolm had recurrent bouts with hemorrhoids, which had to be removed surgically more than once. He also suffered from constipation, for which he took laxatives. Harsh toilet-training may have contributed to these ailments. His mother had responded to her children's lapses of sphincter control with beatings. She was also lax about changing her babies' diapers. Excrement was so repugnant to her that, before sitting down, she reached down with her hand to wipe the chair clean of imaginary filth. Then she smelled her hand. Her aversion was apparently so strong that she is unable to recall potty-training her youngsters. "The clinic fixed them," she told one questioner. "They did not mess."

While Malcolm was languishing at Concord, Philbert, who had

become even more devout than he had been as a child, wrote and told him that he had discovered the "natural religion" for black people. He and Wilfred, Hilda, and Reginald had joined a sect called the Nation of Islam, which envisioned the establishment of a homeland for America's blacks—a place where they would be masters in their own land and would not need to kowtow to whites.

Like Marcus Garvey, the Nation of Islam's leaders taught that the world was headed for a War of Armageddon that would pit the black race against its white oppressors. On the Day of Judgment, Allah would subdue the whites and deliver their black victims from bondage.

He could release Malcolm from bondage too, Philbert said. Malcolm wrote back and told him to keep his religion to himself. The Littles caucused and chose Reginald as their next emissary. Reginald wrote and told Malcolm to stop eating pork and smoking cigarettes. He hinted that if he did, it would help him get out of jail.

The next time pork was served at the dining table, Malcolm refused to eat it. By nightfall, he had become the talk of the cellblock. He felt "very proud." His mother, who had been so opposed to eating pork, would have been proud of him, too.

In the furniture shop, Malcolm befriended a man named Vasquez-telez, who was a member of the Nation of Islam. The two men conversed a lot, but the guards couldn't tell what about.

Periodically, Malcolm requested a transfer to the experimental penal colony at Norfolk, Massachusetts. He wrote, "I only ask that I be given . . . [a] chance . . . until I prove unworthy." In another petition, he pleaded eloquently for a chance to undo his past mistakes. "If I fail," he declared, "I have no one to hate but myself."

Ella lobbied prodigiously in Malcolm's behalf and finally persuaded the authorities to transfer him to Norfolk, which accepted only the best-behaved prisoners, not those who had been in solitary confinement.* Compared to Concord and Charlestown, Norfolk was paradise. There were no cells or iron bars; the prisoners lived in dormitories. Each man had his own room, with a door allowing privacy except for a small window that enabled the guards to peer inside from the corridor. In the

---

* There was one exception to the rule that Norfolk accepted only the best-behaved prisoners. When other penal institutions were overcrowded, Norfolk sometimes received part of the overflow. But Concord was not overcrowded when Malcolm left it in March 1948.

basement of each of the six three-story dormitories, there was a recreation room containing a ping pong table. On the next floor, there was a "common room" containing a radio. (Television was in its infancy.) That luxury of luxuries, a shower room, was located on each of the upper floors; the men could shower as often as they chose. For those who were athletically inclined, there was a ball field. There were garden plots for those who liked to grow their own vegetables. (In warm weather, you could make your own salad and eat lunch outside.) Except for those who were locked up for breaches of prison discipline, the inmates enjoyed considerable freedom of movement within the twenty-foot-high walls—which were manned by guards armed with rifles, shotguns, submachine guns, and grenades.

Though prisoners were not permitted outdoors after dusk, they were free to wander around inside the dorms and engage in a wide variety of activities, including reading. The prison's superb library had been willed to the Commonwealth by State Senator Lewis Parkhurst of Winchester, who had devoted his career to penal reform. There was not enough room on the shelves for all the volumes. Malcolm pored through the books on Buddhism, Hinduism, Islam, and Christianity. He sought out additional information from the Watchtower Bible and Tract Society, which passed his inquiry to J. Prescott Adams, a Jehovah's Witness who lived near Norfolk. Mr. Adams contacted Malcolm, who asked him to teach him about the Bible. For several months, Adams did so. He was struck by Malcolm's interest in Jesus and in the similarities between Christ and the prophet Muhammad. Adams also got the feeling that Malcolm was determined to make a name for himself after he left prison. "He had a great ego that he was feeding," Adams would later recall.

When Ella visited, she admonished Malcolm to settle down and use his time in jail constructively. She hadn't given up hope that he'd go to college and study law. From time to time, Malcolm discussed the possibility. He also expressed interest in teaching political science. He seemed to identify with successful blacks such as Paul Robeson and Marian Anderson. His ear was invariably "glued to the radio" whenever Jackie Robinson came up to bat. He characterized himself as Robinson's "most fanatic fan" and listened to Joe Louis's fights with similar enthusiasm. Although he generally abjured athletics for books, he volunteered to train the boxer whom the black convicts decided to pit against the best fighter the white prisoners could muster. The white contender was a protégé of lightweight champ Willie Pep. Day and night, Malcolm coached the black contender, Boise Philips, and fed him the extra eggs that Jarvis (who had preceded Malcolm to Norfolk) smuggled out of the kitchen. Boise ate them raw, chugged around the makeshift track that encircled the ball field, and beat his opponent almost as badly as Bill Peterson had beaten Malcolm. Earl Little's seventh child was in seventh heaven.

By the time Reginald came to Norfolk to visit, Malcolm was bursting to hear his brother explain why he had instructed him not to eat pork. Gingerly, Reginald broached the subject of Islam, which does not permit its adherents to eat pork. He described the Nation of Islam and some of its teachings, including the doctrine that white people are "devils."

After Reginald left, Malcolm thought long and hard about the whites he had known—Arthur Delamarter; Betty Jean Thiel; the teachers who had stacked books on his outstretched arms and had tried pulling his hair; Bob Bebee; the welfare workers who had badgered his mother; the judge who had incarcerated her; Mrs. Swerlein; Mr. Kaminska; Audrey Slagh; Pappy Cousins; Bea; Hymie; the white policemen who had arrested him; Judge Buttrick.

When Reginald returned to Norfolk, Malcolm was receptive. He listened as his brother described how slavery had deprived America's blacks of their cultural roots and left them "mentally dead." From Michigan, the other Littles who had joined the Nation of Islam bombarded Malcolm with letters urging him to turn to Allah. One relative who wrote was Wilfred's wife, Bertha, who had always welcomed Malcolm when he had needed a meal. But in August 1948, Bertha suddenly died. When Malcolm found out, he burst into tears and refused to eat.

The family scraped together enough cash to send Hilda to visit him. When she arrived at the prison, she ably tilled the soil that Reginald had fertilized. She told him the holy city of Mecca had been founded by blacks. According to the Nation of Islam, the city had fallen on bad times due to the machinations of Yacub, a warped scientist whose name resembled that of the Hebrew patriarch Jacob. Yacub was a genius. Sixty-six hundred years before Gregor Mendel, he had founded the science of genetics.

The authorities finally exiled Yacub and his sixty thousand black followers to a remote island, where he resolved to wreak revenge by breeding a devil-race—a colorless, inferior race of white people.

Yacub never lived to see the final result of his malevolent handiwork, even though he lived to the age of 152. But generations of well-trained, well-disciplined followers executed his decrees to the letter, forbidding pure-blooded blacks from marrying and having children. Only people of mixed blood were allowed to wed. Whenever a dark-skinned infant was born, the midwife plunged a needle into its brain. Light-skinned babies were spared. Gradually, the island's inhabitants grew lighter. Finally, six hundred years after the experiment began, the entire population became devoid of both color and humanity. Some of the resultant white-skinned creatures migrated back to the Arabian Peninsula. Within six months, they had created such dissension that it had become a warring hell.

The Meccans drove out the white devils, who took up residence in Europe, where they lived in caves and walked on all fours. Their naked bodies were hairy, like those of monkeys and gorillas, their nearest relatives.

Eventually, the first wave of European devils—the Jews—ventured out of their caves and became civilized. Others followed suit. Allah agreed to let them rule the world for six thousand years, after which the black "originals" would reassert their innate superiority. White people were unaware of these things because they traced their history only back to Adam and were ignorant of their "pre-Adamite" origins.

Two of Malcolm's fellow prisoners sensed that Hilda's visit had a decisive impact upon him. At her suggestion, he wrote Elijah Muhammad, the Nation of Islam's leader. Before mailing the letter, he redrafted it about two dozen times.

The reply, which was accompanied by a gift of money, was probably similar to the letters that Elijah sent to scores of other convicts—letters that were apparently designed to alleviate their guilt. The real criminal, Elijah told Malcolm, was not the black lawbreaker but the whites who had allegedly made him turn to crime. It was heady medicine. The Nation of Islam and its austere moral code seemed to offer the respect and acceptance the criminal Malcolm had outwardly scorned but secretly coveted.

So Malcolm turned to religion, as his mother had done during a time of troubles. The leap of faith, which he completed before or by early 1949, was not achieved without conflict; the price was complete submission to Allah. The conflict was so intense that it took Malcolm a week to bend his knees and pray for forgiveness. Every time he began to prostrate himself, something drove him back up. But his need for atonement, he later acknowledged, drove him back down.

STUDENT, TEACHER, &
BUDDING ORATOR
24

After his conversion, Malcolm set to work implementing his decision to change his life. He could hardly believe how quickly the criminal Malcolm had become transformed into the religious Malcolm. It was as if the former had been someone else.

He altered his appearance to suit his new Islamic identity. As the spring of 1949 became summer, he began taking the skin-darkening sunbaths his mother had urged upon him. He twitted Jarvis about the fact that he was so dark he didn't need a suntan.

In accord with the custom requiring new male members of Elijah Muhammad's movement to forgo long hair, Malcolm had the prison barber shave his head. Perhaps to compensate for this submissiveness, he grew a beard and a wispy moustache that curved downward at the corners of his mouth. Horace Dow, his house officer, instructed him to shave off the beard, but Malcolm refused on grounds of freedom of religion. To be deprived of one's hair against one's will, he told Jarvis, made a man lose his strength. He cited the example of Samson and Delilah; he did not mention his harrowing encounter with Ella's scissors.

Spurred by religious fervor, Malcolm moved his program of educational self-improvement into high gear. For a while, he attended the prison school, where lectures were given by visiting instructors from nearby universities, including Harvard and M.I.T. But some of the officials who ran the school viewed him as a "disturbing influence." Eventually, Malcolm stopped going to class. While other inmates spent their free time playing ball or attending indifferent movies, he holed up in his room and devoured entire books the way other people devoured food. He subsequently characterized their contents as "intellectual vitamins" for his "hunger-stricken" soul. On weekends, during which most prisoners did no work, he studied twelve or fifteen hours a day. Those who made the mistake of knocking on his door while he was absorbed in a book were greeted stonily or with outright hostility. Years later, he said that he had preferred the hermit-like existence that had allowed him to make constructive use of his penchant for withdrawal.

Each night at ten o'clock, the lights went out in the prisoners' rooms. But that didn't stop Malcolm from studying. He read by the light that filtered from the corridor into his room through the window in the door.

He began a correspondence course in Latin, and, with the help of H.G. Wells and Will Durant, immersed himself in history. Unhindered by the customary emphasis on trivial details, he developed the ability to view political events in historical perspective. Long before ping-pong diplomacy made it fashionable to regard China as something less than a pariah, Malcolm realized that Chinese hostility toward the West was the legacy of more than a century of brazen, successful attempts to impose alien flags and laws on Chinese soil.

But what affected Malcolm the most on his historical tour was the library's extensive collection of books and pamphlets about the captive Africans who had been taken to America in rat-infested ships, sold into slavery, and chained and whipped like miscreant dogs.

In addition to history, Malcolm read philosophy. He waded through Plato, Aristotle, Kant, Spinoza, Nietzsche, and Schopenhauer. Though he had never finished ninth grade, he was already infinitely better read than most American college graduates. With the exception of Bembry and J. Prescott Adams, he had no one to assist him in his lonely struggle to educate himself. All he had was his splendid mind, plus the fact that he didn't have to worry about grades and the possibility of another failure.

As swiftly as Malcolm acquired knowledge, he imparted it to Jarvis and anyone else who would listen. Unlike so many of the men and women who had taught him, he was a patient teacher. At times, he tolerated disagreement, at least in private. In public, he brooked no argument and jealously preserved his new-found pedagogical authority. And though he depicted himself as a man of intellectual humility, other prisoners resented the way he strutted around the prison grounds, pontificating about genius and asserting that "a great man is always willing to be little." He was downright condescending to Jarvis, whose room was across the hall and who was generally considered to be his closest friend. He called him "Jahr-vis," with the emphasis upon the "Jahr." He taunted his friend about his big feet, just as Otto Grein had taunted him.

Malcolm's jibes became even testier when Jarvis, who wrote music, began spending much of his spare time with an Armenian convict who wrote lyrics. But though Malcolm gave Jarvis a hard time, he was fond of him—so fond that, despite his fear of physical encounter, he rose to his defense when a group of white prisoners tried to gang up on him during a lunch hall melee. Malcolm grabbed a knife from the table and shouted, "The first one who tries [anything] gets his throat cut!" No one was interested in finding out if he was bluffing.

One of Malcolm's correspondents, a musician named Bazely Perry, had a friend named Omar Khalil*, who was a member of a Muslim sect called the Amadiya Movement. One Sunday afternoon, Khalil, who also knew Jarvis, accompanied Perry to Norfolk to visit the two Malcolms. At the prison entrance, a guard prohibited Omar from bringing his Qur'an inside, even though a Catholic priest walked right through the entryway with a Bible.

When Malcolm was introduced to Omar Khalil, his mouth fell open. (Jarvis had to tell him to close it.) Speechless, he stared at the bearded Muslim with the moustache and black fez, who cared so little about his clothes that he replaced the buttons that fell off with safety pins. Khalil stared right back with eyes that bored just as deeply as Malcolm's. The two light-skinned, blue-green-eyed six-footers scrutinized each other silently. Even Jarvis could feel the mental heat. At last, he broke the quiet with, "It's a lovely day, isn't it?"

Smiling, Omar Khalil turned toward Jarvis and replied, "Yes, it is." By this time, the entire room was gaping at the strange, magnetic imam, who leaned forward and advised everyone in the group to drop his head and speak softly so that the visiting room guards who were trying to eavesdrop couldn't overhear what they were saying.

Malcolm was visibly impressed and seemed eager to discover the secret of Omar Khalil's charisma. The rest of the afternoon, he listened rather than talked as Khalil schooled both Malcolms in the tenets of orthodox Islam. He did not unfold his hands until he took leave. Subsequently, the good imam had to skip town to avoid paying child support to a woman who had borne his child. It wasn't the last time Malcolm let himself be taken in by a religious charlatan.

When Malcolm wasn't enlightening fellow prisoners, as Bembry had done, he tutored other people by mail. The lectures were carefully prepared; sometimes, he pondered a whole hour before writing a

---

* Omar Khalil is a pseudonym that is being used for legal reasons.

sentence. When the composition was complete, he'd dispatch hand-written facsimiles to nearly everyone he knew—it didn't matter who, as long as they wrote back. "When I write," he said, "I write to all of you . . . for I think of you all as one."

Like chaotic streams of consciousness, the letters tended to ramble, despite the intense preparation. Jarvis felt that Malcolm's letter-writing was his chief emotional outlet, particularly during periods when he lacked visitors. His letters were crammed with biblical and quasi-biblical injunctions. The language was stilted and full of "ah's," "twill's," "unto's," and "wherein's." Instead of "among," he wrote "amongst."

In his correspondence and later in his autobiography, Malcolm described his incarceration, which he characterized as "fortunate," as a liberating experience. "Do not picture us as being in prison," he wrote.

> I was in prison before entering here . . . . The solitude, the long moments of meditative contemplation, have given me the key to my freedom.

He said it was unlikely he could have liberated himself any other way. He also said he felt more contented in jail than people who live outside prison walls do. Perhaps it was the contentment of a man who had been liberated from the nagging tyranny of a guilty conscience. In one letter, he virtually acknowledged he had gotten what he had deserved. Years later, he made the point more bluntly and declared, "When one commits a crime, he should be put in jail." In captivity, there were no sinful "distractions" to tempt him; physical restraint freed him from the necessity of self-restraint. There were no women to tear at his emotions; no irate husbands or vengeful hustlers seeking to do him in. Behind bars, he didn't have to worry about failing or supporting himself—food, clothing, and shelter were automatically provided. Nor did convicts have to grapple with the responsibilities that most adults take for granted. In one letter, Malcolm declared that his imprisonment had enabled him to recapture the contentment he said he had known as a child. It would have been far more accurate to say that his withdrawal into a walled sanctuary afforded him not only the respite that enabled him to educate himself, but also the security that enabled him to muster the strength for battles to come. Prison was the securest home he had ever had, except perhaps for Mrs. Swerlein's.

Malcolm, who later asserted that "cowards don't go to jail," had mixed feelings about life in captivity. He wrote and told Wilfred that he was becoming bitter because of his zoo-like existence. And despite a hint that he thought he might never be ready to forgo the protection of prison walls, his stronger self proclaimed, "I want to get out of here." Reginald, he insisted, knew someone who could spring him for a price. But Malcolm did not ask Wilfred for money directly. He said he felt he had no right to, presumably because his eldest brother had already lost the money he had used to bail Malcolm out of jail after his 1945 Michigan arrest.* Yet the same day, he funneled an ill-disguised plea for funds through Philbert, hinting that Wilfred could buy his way out of jail if he really wanted to. "But I would not let him," he asserted.

Malcolm campaigned for Muslim converts by mail. His letters conveyed the feeling that he had finally found in Allah what he needed to sustain him. Over and over, he depicted his new-found god as "the Father" and himself as "his Son." The Father-Creator was a mighty but merciful ruler who helped and guided those who granted him "divine obedience." He cared for his "children" and protected them so that they were without fear. Those who disobeyed his commandments and incurred his wrath were invariably afflicted, but those who obeyed his divine decrees had nothing to fear. Indeed, Allah had all, or nearly all, the attributes of the good father that Malcolm had never had.

In his letters, Malcolm not only assailed the myth that whites are superior but also claimed that blacks are superior. He said they were god-like.

To buttress his assertions about race, he drew an analogy to the realm of physics, pointing out that black, on the color wheel, is the aggregate of all the colors, while white is the absence of color. White people were therefore inferior. To "prove" the point, Malcolm employed the etymological expertise he had developed studying the dictionary. The word "white," in Spanish, was "blanco," he observed. In French, it was "blanc." The English word "blank" came from the same root. Hence, white meant "blank" or "nothing". But black was the "natural" color of "native" people who were so at one with Mother Nature that they could live either at the Equator or the North Pole. Whites, on the other hand, were "unnatural." Malcolm characterized the white man as a "freak of nature," just as his brothers and sisters had characterized him. "It amuses me to see him look disgustedly at his leprous white skin," he sneered.

He drew a parallel between the pinkish skin of the white man and that of "his nearest relative, the pig." The white "swine," he declared, "love the filth in which they wallow." And since "man is what he eats," pork-eating whites are "walking germs." He explained that this was the

___

* The bail money had been forfeited because Malcolm's imprisonment had precluded his scheduled appearance for trial in Michigan.

reason whites typically found it difficult to tolerate the equatorial climes that black Africans thrived in. Their bodies contained so many dormant germs, he said, that they had to keep themselves "on ice" climatically in order not to spoil; otherwise, hot weather activated the latent microbes, which eventually killed them.

The outlandish character of Malcolm's pronouncements did not appear to disturb him. On the contrary, his correspondence, which was freely peppered with assertions that he spoke the "truth," conveyed the impression of sincere, if credulous, belief. Proof, he maintained, was unnecessary; if you believed deeply enough in something, it substantiated itself. He later told one skeptic:

> I know how you feel . . . . Everything has to be . . . proven to the intellect . . . . You're still in a hole looking for a candle . . . . I'm no longer in that hole. I'm out in the sunshine, finally, bathing in the light of Allah.

Yet there is evidence that Malcolm secretly doubted some of the things he was saying. He characterized the Nation of Islam's teachings as a "blinding light," but verbally equated blindness with ignorance.* Was he unsure if the doctrines he was espousing were illuminating or blinding? Could he dispel his own doubt by spreading the gospel, as true believers characteristically do? Moving swiftly about the prison complex, he buttonholed prospective black converts and told them about his ego-boosting religion. (He avoided the white prisoners to whom he had previously gravitated.) Within a year, he had more than a dozen followers. It was no small achievement; according to one estimate, there were only about eighty blacks in the entire institution.

Another facet of Malcolm's program of self-improvement was his effort to master the difficult art of public speaking. He joined Norfolk's debating club, which had been established in the hope its participants would learn to express their feelings with words, not guns and knives. Standing before his listeners, seeing their upturned, attentive faces, was as exhilarating to Malcolm as the intellectual awakening that had accompanied his reading. He loved matching wits with the teams that came to Norfolk from such schools as Harvard and Yale. Some of the subjects they debated were crucial issues of the day; others were topics such as "Life Is Just a Bowl of Cherries." Before each debate, Malcolm

---

* He also equated blindness with submissiveness.

and Jarvis and a Muslim convert named Osborne Thaxton read everything about the topic they could find. Then they put themselves in their opponents' shoes and tried to anticipate their arguments. Malcolm, who was in charge, did all the talking. Jarvis took notes and shoved them under his nose, like a courtroom aide.

Malcolm became such an accomplished debater that the answers formed on his tongue as fast as his adversaries popped their questions. Though he sometimes lost his temper, he never lost his poise. He informed one friend that he was going to put his growing expertise to work after he left prison. He put it less delicately to Deputy Warden Edward Grennan. "When I leave here," he declared, "I'm going to devote my life to hurting you people."

Prison Philosopher 25

I n the prison yard, Malcolm attempted to outstare the sun's powerful
rays. He tried to persuade Jarvis and others to do the same. The
retina wouldn't burn if you conditioned your eyes gradually, he
said. As authority for that proposition, he cited a book by an Indian guru
entitled *Mind Over Matter*. He claimed that the mind could control the
atmosphere and the weather. He read books on hypnotism and said that
if one could control oneself, one could control others.

Malcolm also declared that the mind could control the body. (One
prison doctor was unable to get a knee jerk out of him.) A person could
train himself, he said, to slow down his heartbeat or his breathing.
Sexuality, too, could be controlled. "One should carry one's brains in
one's head, not between one's legs," he declared.

He talked about temptation and temptresses; Lady Godiva and Eve, he
said, were cases in point. He constantly made unflattering remarks about
women, whom he accused of running the world. His statements evoked
similar comments from Jarvis, who had also been starved for affection when
he was young. When Jarvis asserted that women were bitches, Malcolm
responded by pointing out that Jarvis's mother and sister were women.

Malcolm's views about love reflected his experience. Love, he said, is
painful. One had to suffer before one could obtain it from women, who
made men grovel for affection. The assertion reminded Jarvis of the stories
Malcolm told about the men he had directed to one of Harlem's sex
shops—men who had cringed on their knees while being whipped by a
brawny prostitute. They implored her to stop, yet could hardly wait for their
next rendezvous with her. He later said he couldn't understand why.

He talked a lot about suffering. Since love was impossible without it,
only fools sought love, he told Jarvis. But, on occasion, he passionately
endorsed the pursuit of love and marriage. Love and hate were insepa-
rable, he said. Life was a marriage of opposites. Blackness and whiteness,
morality and criminality, generosity and selfishness, self-deprivation and

greed, loyalty and treachery, submissiveness and tyranny, sensitivity and toughness, homosexuality and heterosexuality, timidity and cour- age—were all part of nature's grand design, Malcolm said. His dualistic philosophy sprang from his painful inner conflicts.

Malcolm also philosophized about happiness. Happy people are too content, he said, to make the sacrifices that inevitably accompany efforts to achieve reform. Yet he insisted that people should be happy. They should live for today and ignore tomorrow. And in an apparent effort to forget the past, he wrote his friend Bazely Perry:

> Ah, how I used to be so happy-go-lucky . . . carefree . . . with no worries . . . fearing nothing. Yes, to romp constantly about the fields from dawn to dusk . . . . T'was then, and only then, I was getting every bit out of life . . . . Oh, how I weep as I think back.

Malcolm had good cause to weep about his boyhood, which he was generally reluctant to discuss. He grew angry when people quizzed him about his mother and made Jarvis swear that he'd never reveal she was in an asylum. "The subject of my mother and father is extremely painful to me," he told him, struggling to hold back tears:

> We love our mother and [the memory of] our father, . . . but life and the hand of fate never permitted us to . . . be cherished by our parents.

Except for a subsequent acknowledgment that his father had never taught him anything worthwhile, Malcolm never spoke disparagingly about his parents, at least in Jarvis's presence. Instead, he quoted didactic poems:

> Three monkeys once dining in a coconut tree,
> Were discussing something they had heard true to be.
> "What do you think? Now listen you two,
> Here, monkeys, is something that cannot be true,
> That humans descended from our pure race
> Why, it's simply shocking—a terrible disgrace
>
> Who ever heard of a monkey deserting his wife?
> Leave a baby to starve and ruin its life?
> And have you ever known of a mother monk
> To leave her darlings with strangers to bunk?
> Their babies are handed from one to another
> And scarce ever know the love of a mother. . . .
>
> And here is another thing a monkey won't do:
> Seek a bootlegger's shanty and get on a stew,
> Carouse and get on a whoopee, disgracing his life,
> Then reel madly home and beat up his wife.

They call this all pleasure and make a big fuss—
They're descended from something, but not from us!"

The following poem by Edgar Guest was another of Malcolm's favorites:

I'd rather see a sermon than hear one any day;
I'd rather one should walk with me than merely show the way.
The eye's a better pupil, and more willing than the ear;
Fine counsel is confusing, but example's always clear.
The best of all the preachers are the men who live their creed.
For to see the good in action is what everybody needs.
I can soon learn how to do it if you'll let me see it done.
I can watch your hands in action, but your tongue too fast may run.
And the lectures you deliver may be very wise and true,
But I'd rather get my lesson by observing what you do,
For I may misunderstand you, and the high advice you give,
But there's no misunderstanding how you act and how you live.

Malcolm wrote poetry himself. But he was reticent about revealing his flair for it. In prison, poets were considered effeminate.

In one letter, he stressed that men are the chief contributors to their own downfall. In another, he wrote:

If one goes against one's conscience, one is only . . . hastening one's own self-destruction.

The subject of death continued to occupy his thoughts. Though he said that man was in "bondage" to it, he told Jarvis he didn't fear it.

He also told Jarvis, "Crime is prevented in the high chair, not in the electric chair." People who become criminals, he declared years later, are usually those who have been "kicked about" as children.

Despite Malcolm's aversion to psychologists, he read psychology books and expressed a desire to change his ways. Ascribing his entertaining, youthful antics to his fear that people considered him a bore, he said he was determined to be himself instead of striving to please others.

Malcolm emphasized that people should strive to turn their faults into assets. Citing a well-known poem, he said that one should not expect to succeed overnight:

When things go wrong, as they sometimes will,
When the road you're trudging seems uphill,
When funds are low and the debts are high,
And you want to smile but you have to sigh,
When care is pressing you down a bit,
Rest if you must, but don't you quit;

Life is queer with its twists and turns,
As every one of us sometimes learns,
And many a failure turns about
When he might have won had he stuck it out,
Don't give up, though the pace seems slow —
You may succeed with another blow.

Often the struggler has given up,
When he might have captured the victor's cup,
And he learned too late, when the night's slipped down,
How close he was to the golden crown.
Success is failure turned inside out —
The silver tint of the clouds of doubt.
And you can never tell how close you are,
It may be near when it seems afar;
So stick to the fight when you're hardest hit —
It's when things seem worst that you mustn't quit.

Malcolm began studying politics. He said he wanted to ascertain what kind of leader would appeal to America's blacks and read biographies of Hannibal, Haile Selassie, Ibn Saud, Karl Marx, Lenin, Stalin, Hitler, Rommel, Gandhi, Patrick Henry, and John Brown. Except for the conquerors, the figures he seemed to admire most were either rebels or tyrants. He ridiculed democracy. Contending that the Greek word "demos," from which the word "democracy" is derived, meant "demon" instead of "people," he argued that democracy meant, not "rule by the people," but rule by white demons. He played similar word games on other occasions. For instance, he equated *Israel*, which is named after the patriarch who allegedly subdued one of God's angels, with *Azrael*, the angel of death. "Both are attributes of the devil," he wrote. He cloaked himself in etymological authority so convincingly that few, if any, questioned him about his linguistic conclusions, which secretly mocked the scholarly authority on which they were supposedly based.

As for the modern-day descendants of the ancient Hebrews, Malcolm claimed that they owned and ran virtually everything. They owned Hollywood, he said. And big business. Harry Truman and Dwight Eisenhower were Jews, he asserted. He told Jarvis that by eliminating the Jews, a German victory in World War II might have benefited blacks.

Malcolm grew distraught when Reginald began intimating that Elijah Muhammad was not everything he was cracked up to be. Mr. Muhammad had suspended Reginald from the Nation of Islam for having extra-marital sex with a Muslim woman. So Malcolm wrote Muhammad on behalf of his younger brother. After mailing the letter, he prayed all night for Allah to relieve his distress.

The following night, as Malcolm lay on his bed, he saw, or thought he saw, a man sitting in his chair. The apparition vanished as swiftly as it had appeared, like the "movies from heaven" Malcolm's hospitalized mother sometimes saw. Malcolm later insisted that he had "no idea whatsoever" who the non-white-skinned man in the chair was. Yet he maintained with equal vigor that "it's impossible" to have a detailed vision of someone you've never seen before.*

Elijah Muhammad's written response to Malcolm's letter arrived, asserting that if Malcolm suddenly doubted "the truth," it was because he was "weak."

So Malcolm put his brother beyond the spiritual pale. But Reginald continued to visit Malcolm, who listened to him with no more empathy than Reginald had exhibited when Malcolm had been humiliated by Bill Peterson. Wilfred, Hilda, and Philbert also cold-shouldered Reginald, for no one in the Nation of Islam was permitted to communicate with suspended members. Reginald apparently tried to revenge himself on Malcolm by drunkenly courting Gloria. Eventually, he suffered the kind of emotional collapse his mother had suffered a decade earlier. Somehow, he found his way back to Michigan, where Philbert quietly defied Elijah Muhammad and took him in. Weeks later, Ella found him standing at her front door. He looked dreadful. "Where did you come from?" she asked. From Detroit, Reginald answered. Ella asked him how he had gotten to Boston. "I walked," Reginald replied.

Reginald began roaming the streets, saying that he, not Elijah Muhammad, was the Messenger of Allah. Then, he began claiming that he was Allah himself. His pitiful attempt to start a rival Islamic movement never got off the ground. Eventually, he was committed to a mental institution. When Jarvis inquired about him, Malcolm snapped, "Reginald's dead!"

Reginald was released and rehospitalized a number of times. He seesawed back and forth between the world of reality and the world of make-believe. At first, Malcolm insisted that his brother's condition was the result of Allah's chastisement. (According to Elijah Muhammad, Allah had burned Reginald's brain.) Eventually, Malcolm realized that Reginald's illness was the result of "the pain he felt when his own family totally rejected him for Elijah Muhammad." Malcolm acknowledged that he felt partly responsible not only for one family member's breakdown, but two.

---

* Later, Malcolm concluded that the apparition had been the "messiah" who had founded the Nation of Islam, Wallace Delaney Fard. But Fard, whose real name was Wallace Dodd Ford, looked white.

SECOND TRY

26

F or a period of several months, Malcolm had no visitors at Norfolk at all. He looked depressed, almost desperate. It was not just the feeling that no one cared. Prisoners without visitors were unlikely to be granted parole, for parole officials were reluctant to release convicts who had no one to turn to for financial or emotional support.

"*You* don't have to worry about convincing the parole board that someone is interested," Malcolm told Jarvis. "You have a mother and a father!" He asked Jarvis if his parents would visit him, too, when they came to the prison.

Clifford and Ethel Jarvis readily assented. Occasionally, they brought along a young woman named Jackie Massie. Jackie, whose real name was Marion, was older than Malcolm. She had a stunning figure, but, according to Jarvis, her oversize nose and boxer-like nostrils severely marred her appearance. Malcolm's opinion of her was not high. However, a visitor was a visitor. He spruced up for each of Jackie's visits. He even wore a tie.

Jackie was the girlfriend of Frank Cooper, who had participated in some of the powdering expeditions at Paul Lennon's home. But that didn't appear to bother Malcolm—nor Jackie, for that matter. She appeared to like Malcolm more than she liked Frank. For a while, she wrote him more than anyone else did. She also gave him money. Nonchalantly, Malcolm nursed the relationship along, perhaps because of the money, perhaps because Jackie belonged to another man. And perhaps because she helped fill the void produced by his lack of contact with the outside world.

The shabby way Malcolm treated Jackie was a far cry from the way he responded to his former girlfriend Gloria Strother, who began corresponding with him after she separated from the man she had married on the rebound following her break with Malcolm. She even wrote him while she was vacationing in New York City. Malcolm wrote back and told her how happy her letter had made him. He said he was deeply gratified to know that, despite New York's allure, she had still remembered him. "That was the test," he declared—the test his luckless mother had apparently failed.

In another letter, Malcolm assured Gloria he was trying to learn all he could. But Gloria did not care how well-read he was. She was mainly concerned about the possibility of a criminal relapse on his part.

Malcolm "discoursed" with her like a prim and proper Victorian suitor. He prefaced each letter with a declaration that he was writing on behalf of Allah and Elijah Muhammad. Yet at times, his real feelings showed through:

> If you wrote every day, I would not be satisfied . . . . I . . . intensely crave your undivided attention."

Instead of playing hard-to-get with her, as he had done in Roxbury, he urged Gloria to visit him every week. When she didn't show up, he needled her with guilt by telling her how much she had made him suffer. "I died inside," he declared in one letter. In another, he responded with sarcasm. When Gloria rebuked him for it, he attributed it to his sense of humor. He said he wouldn't dream of saying anything spiteful to her.

But when Gloria visited Malcolm on February 23, 1950, he had difficulty expressing his feelings. He was cold and distant. He raved about Islam instead of her and lapsed into embarrassed silence. Nor would he look her in the eye when she spoke. She finally became so bored that she left.*

That night, Malcolm wrote Gloria what he had been unable to tell her that day:

> Dearest Glo,
> . . . . My mind was . . . far away [today] when I should have been conversing with you . . . . I was . . . conniving, concocting a plan in which you are the principal character.

He did not elaborate. But he promised that by the time his plan was implemented, Gloria would be ensnared in "its clutches."

Malcolm, who may have anticipated Gloria's unenthusiastic response to this conception of marriage, "hesitatingly" ended his letter, in which he acknowledged that he had been a bore. On February 26, he wrote again and begged her forgiveness for not writing for two—actually

---

* Malcolm was apparently aware of his tendency to clam up around the women he desired. He quoted aphorisms to the effect that people who truly understood one another had no need to communicate verbally.

three—whole days. "You are always on my mind and forever in my heart," he told her. Without asking Gloria what was on her mind, Malcolm gave her the names of two New York City Muslims he wanted her to write. One day, he said, she'd see why he kept urging her to become acquainted with so many of his Islamic friends. He did not broach the subject of marriage directly, and, apparently sensing Gloria's waning interest, stopped signing his letters, "Love." Yet he kept imploring her to visit him. "There is much I have to tell you," he said. "Please don't have me expecting you in vain."

But Malcolm did wait in vain, for Gloria was unable to reconcile the fervor of his letters with his remote, inaccessible behavior, which made it difficult for her to believe the sincerity of his amorous declarations. She never visited him again.

Malcolm wrote once more, noting that Gloria had become "quite a stranger." Mildly rebuking her for her lack of interest in Islam, he renewed his plea for her return. Suddenly, in the midst of the letter, he admitted that he loved her. But he said it so obliquely that Gloria didn't believe it.

J.C.

27

On March 19, 1950, the very day Malcolm made his final, futile plea for Gloria's return, he requested an interview with Assistant Deputy Warden Jeremiah Dacey. He told Dacey he would not agree to take the typhoid inoculation each prisoner was periodically required to have. (Norfolk's well water was chemically untreated and susceptible to contamination by sewage.)

Malcolm told Dacey he was aware of the regulation requiring uninoculated inmates to be transferred to another institution. He said he did not mind being returned to Charlestown Prison. He attributed his readiness to accept transfer—a transfer he'd later blame on the prison administration—to the fact that the Nation of Islam prohibited the ingestion of harmful substances, such as tobacco, alcohol, and street drugs. But inmates subsequently told the prison authorities that Malcolm had run out of potential converts at Norfolk and felt the need to spread the gospel elsewhere.

Were there deeper-seated reasons for his martyr-like eagerness to confront Charlestown's rigors again? Was it a way of reaffirming his manhood? Did the ensuing suffering ease the pain of being rejected by Gloria? Whatever the reasons, Malcolm seemed positively cheerful when he returned to Charlestown Prison on March 23. He played the martyr to the hilt. "They're trying to break me!" he asserted. He claimed that the penal authorities were also trying to starve him to death.

In reality, he ate barely enough to keep healthy.* And he began talking seriously about marrying Jackie Massie "out of obligation," now that

---

* Malcolm skipped many meals altogether, partly because some of the white cooks, knowing that he was forbidden to eat pork, purposely immersed their serving utensils in substances containing pork before dishing out his food. To avoid this problem, he had a friend smuggle bread to him from the kitchen. He ate the bread with cheese purchased from the prison canteen. The resultant diet eventually produced a vitamin deficiency.

Gloria was out of the running. A desire for martyrdom also suggested itself in letters in which Malcolm portrayed himself as a Jesus-like figure who had escaped the "nails of death," and who had been "sent" by God to "lift the crown of thorns" from the heads of his imprisoned black brethren, as well as from his own head. He called himself "J.C." Jarvis assumed that the initials stood for Malcolm's former stage name "Jack Carlton." But another inmate had the feeling that they stood for Jesus Christ—whose name, according to Malcolm, meant "justice crushed."

Malcolm talked about Jesus frequently. He prophesied that Christ would "return again in the flesh." Years later, as he was dictating his autobiography to Alex Haley, he drew a parallel between the way he was being castigated and the way Jesus had been vilified by the majority of his contemporaries. Abruptly, Malcolm rose from his seat, seized Haley's note pad, and ripped out the page on which Haley had written the statement. For the rest of the session, he was unusually guarded.

Occasionally, Malcolm used statements attributed to Jesus to lend authority to his own. He quoted an excerpt from St. Luke that says: "If any man come to me and hate not his father and mother . . . and brethren and sisters . . . he cannot be my disciple." He also cited the passage from St. Matthew that says, "The children shall rise up against their parents." For an Islamic Christ-figure who didn't believe in Christmas, it was revealing language.

Less than a month after his return to Charlestown, Malcolm—along with Jarvis and Osborne Thaxton, both of whom had dutifully followed Malcolm back from Norfolk—demanded cells facing eastward so they could pray toward Mecca. Warden John O'Brien eyed the three Islamic convicts stonily, as if to say, "What the devil do you think this place is? The Waldorf?" He said that he "wasn't sure he could comply immediately" with the request.

Malcolm threatened to appeal to the Egyptian consul. "He'll appreciate our position," he said. "Our religious freedom is being infringed." In Norfolk, he had steeped himself in the relevant constitutional law, using the law books in Parkhurst Library. The books subsequently vanished. Reading material that Ella mailed also disappeared.

The threat of outside intervention worked; the correctional authorities evidently feared a public row. The Muslims were transferred to new cells and the story made the *Boston Post*. Malcolm's autobiography doesn't even mention the episode. Perhaps he felt that he hadn't really succeeded, for he failed to wring any other concessions from the prison administration, which reportedly turned down his requests for a non-pork diet and for time off from work on Islamic holidays. Nor did the warden—whose annual reports to his superiors made no mention of the fact his prison contained Muslims as well as Christians and Jews—accord official recognition to the penitentiary's Islamic minority, so that Muslim convicts could worship communally and receive religious instruction from outside. The authorities feared that the anti-white doctrines of the Nation of Islam would breed dissension and racial violence.

Charlestown's strict regime made it much harder for Malcolm to recruit converts there than it had been for him at Norfolk. He sought them out in the cramped prison yard, where prisoners congregated after work before picking up their supper trays and carrying them to their smelly cells, which were locked until the following morning. After a while, he wangled a transfer from the license plate fabricating shop to the prison laundry, which regularly issued each inmate clean clothes. Malcolm took advantage of the opportunity to court potential converts there. He was so busy trying to interest one black prisoner in Islam that he let the white convict standing next in line wait too long. The latter apparently told a guard, who snarled:

> Any time someone comes here for clothing, black or white, you give
> it to him right away, or you'll end up in seclusion, you black bastard!

Malcolm didn't say a word. But he drilled two holes through the officer with his eyes. Followers of Elijah Muhammad were instructed to behave respectfully toward authority, even white authority. Consequently, Malcolm tailored his Islamic-inspired rebellion to the applicable rules and regulations, which he knew as well as any of the prison officials did. When they tried to make him shorten his six, eight, and ten page letters, which were apparently giving the censor apoplexy, he refused on grounds that they had no authority to do so. The officials retaliated by declining to mail the letters. So Malcolm again threatened to have imaginary allies intercede. The bluff worked.

The authorities also tried to induce Malcolm to stop soliciting converts. He refused. But he did promise that there would be no trouble. He was already exhibiting an uncanny ability to survive in a hostile political environment without losing his grip on his devoted followers.

In mid-1950, Charlestown Prison came alive with the news that war had erupted in a distant place called Korea. For draft-eligible inmates who expected to be released soon, the tidings were ominous; even Charlestown was preferable to a bayonet in the throat.

Two days after President Truman dispatched troops to Pusan, where naval artillery and air power enabled U.S. forces to establish the foothold that prevented the fall of the entire Korean peninsula, Malcolm predicted that Washington would promptly begin conscripting huge numbers of men. But in a letter to a friend, he said he wasn't concerned; even if he enlisted voluntarily, the armed forces wouldn't induct him. "I've always been a communist," he asserted. He said that another reason he was *persona non grata* to the American military was that he had attempted to join the Japanese army during World War II. As he concluded his remarks, which the prison censor dutifully recorded, he admitted he was feigning madness, as he had done during his 1943 encounter with the army psychiatrist. The gambit, which attested to his remarkable ability to argue both sides of an issue simultaneously, may have been designed to discourage possible attempts to consign him to the state "hospital" for the criminally insane at Bridgewater. (Massachusetts law permitted the authorities to commit prisoners there indefinitely.)

Malcolm, who knew his letters were being monitored by the prison authorities, kept up the letter-writing campaign. Alluding to the desperate, death-defying acts he had committed as an aspiring teenage tough, he declared, "I must admit I was crazy." But his ambiguous letters were constructed in such a way that it was impossible for the authorities to tell whether he was really crazy or not. He emphasized that he had no intention of donning a military uniform, except perhaps for a crusade against whites. "If my mother was wearing the devil's uniform," he exclaimed, "she would have to die too."

Malcolm as he probably looked shortly after he joined the Nation of Islam.

IV

POLITICAL SERVITUDE

TO BE OR NOT TO BE FREE?

28

By the autumn of 1950, Malcolm had apparently concluded that he had converted as many Charlestown convicts as he was going to. He wrote Elliott E. McDowell, the Massachusetts Commissioner of Correction, and asked to be retransferred to Norfolk. In tones of pained innocence, he demanded to know why he had been expelled from Norfolk. "Which rule did I break?" he demanded. Emphasizing that he hadn't spent one day in solitary confinement since his first day in Charlestown, Malcolm charged that he had been the victim of "an injustice." Then he abruptly shifted tack and asserted that he couldn't blame the prison officials for doing their duty. Allah would be the final judge, he said. "My heart is without malice," he added. The Commissioner, who denied Malcolm's request for retransfer, was apparently unconvinced, perhaps because of letters Malcolm had written, one of which had warned of the Commissioner's possible "destruction."

So Malcolm started another letter-writing campaign. He sent a letter to Warden O'Brien thanking him and his entire staff for their "kindness" and their readiness to answer the questions of the inmates "with a smile." Each official, Malcolm declared, is "a man with a heart." It was not the last time that he would condemn someone by praising him inordinately.

The warden received the letter exactly one year before Malcolm became eligible for parole. Precisely six months later, he wrote Commissioner McDowell again. He said he was sorry he had pestered him with so many imaginary grievances. "The injustice," Malcolm declared in language that was both highly ironic and highly revealing, "is all within my own mind." He said he was beginning to wonder if he suffered from delusions of persecution:

> I have been too busy thinking everyone is against me to see that I

myself have been against myself.

In another ironic, revealing letter, he wrote:

In my effort to justify my many self-inflicted wrongs, I placed the blame upon everyone except the one who was mainly responsible for all of my troubles . . . myself.

The two Malcolms went before the parole board in mid-1951. The board paroled Jarvis, but not Malcolm. Yet, years later, Malcolm would assert that Jarvis was the one who had experienced difficulty finding someone to sponsor his parole.

Soon after Jarvis was released, he visited Ella, who did not even ask about Malcolm. Jarvis had no way of knowing that she had asked the prison authorities to deny Malcolm's petition for parole. It wasn't just her half-brother's religion that she objected to. She later said she feared that if Malcolm returned to Boston, people would link her with his criminality. Moreover, he was difficult to manage. The best way to help him, she concluded, was to keep him awhile longer behind bars, where she could "do more" with him. She was particularly concerned about the possibility that if Malcolm was released, he might marry Jackie Massie. She preferred him to remain in jail, she candidly admitted years later. "I'd have rather seen him dead than marry Jackie," she bluntly added.

Wilfred, who was always helping people out despite the cost to himself, finally agreed to sponsor Malcolm's parole. He advised his younger brother to tell the parole board what it wanted to hear. It was a lesson, Wilfred says, that Malcolm never forgot.

The board paroled Malcolm. In July 1952, less than three weeks before he was scheduled to be released, one of the guards supervising the prison laundry provoked a laundry strike by ordering a convict to wash a pair of the guard's trousers. "We're not supposed to do guard's clothes," came the defiant reply. Four striking members of the laundry crew were disciplined. The next morning, forty-three convicts seized two guards and held them hostage with improvised weapons. The rebellious prisoners ran amuck until a number of Boston newspapers agreed to publish their demands, which included an end to the practice of keeping inmates in their cells about seventeen hours of every twenty-four. The protesters also demanded a change of clothes at least twice a week and reinstatement of the prison complaint committee. The committee had been discontinued by Warden O'Brien, whom the new Corrections Commissioner stoutly characterized as the "best" in the entire country.

Malcolm did not participate in the riot, which the authorities confined to one portion of the prison. In August 1952, he donned a ten-dollar suit that had been fashioned in the prison tailor shop and walked out the gate a free man. "I never looked back," he later claimed. But his refusal to register for the draft, which could have been construed as a parole violation as well as a violation of the Selective Service laws, nearly resulted, six months after his release, in his reincarceration.

Outwardly, Malcolm's unwillingness to register was the product of his adherence to Elijah Muhammad's teachings, which discouraged participation in the country's armed forces. But Malcolm, who was 27 years old when he left prison, did not have to refuse to register to avoid military service; men who were over twenty-six were legally exempt from military induction unless they were doctors, dentists, or the like. Failure to realize this fact was an uncharacteristic lapse for Malcolm, who had already mastered a considerable amount of law despite his lack of formal legal training.

The oversight provoked the attention of the authorities, who could have sent Malcolm back to jail for five years, not to mention the additional time he would have had to serve had the parole board revoked his parole. But the officials in charge gave him a break and told him they wouldn't prosecute if he agreed to register promptly. Reluctantly, Malcolm consented. His draft board initially classified him 1-A. (In those days, the men who tried to avoid registering were often assigned to active duty, regardless of their age.) A few weeks later, the board agreed to classify Malcolm as a conscientious objector:

> I told them that when the white man asked me to go off somewhere
> and fight and maybe die to preserve the way the white man treated
> the black man in America, then my conscience made me object.

But conscientious objectors were subject to "alternative" service, which meant performing non-military tasks that furthered the nation's welfare. So Malcolm took the armed forces medical examination, which customarily included the kind of psychiatric examination he had received a decade before at the Manhattan induction center. Surviving records indicate that he didn't pass the examination and was consequently reclassified 4-F. According to an FBI summary of Selective Service records that have been destroyed pursuant to legislation permitting the destruction of old records, Malcolm failed to pass because of what the examiner characterized as an "asocial personality with paranoid trends." Perhaps he staged his crazy, trigger-happy act for the examiner. In any event, he was relieved of liability for alternative service, which might have forced him to move someplace that had no Islamic community. Seven years later, he was finally classified, officially, as overage.

From the viewpoint of America's blacks, the year that Malcolm emerged from prison was far from propitious. The national unemployment rate for nonwhites was virtually twice the rate for whites. Median annual income for white families was $5183; for blacks, it was approximately 57% of that, or $2941. Only four-tenths of one percent of the country's black families received more than $15,000 per year.* The infant mortality rate for black babies was 44.8 per thousand live births; for white babies it was 25.5 per thousand. The percentage of nonwhites who had completed four years of college was less than one-fourth the percentage of whites who had done so. The illiteracy rate among whites was 1.8%; among blacks, it was more than 10%. The year before Malcolm left prison, the state of Mississippi spent an average of $122.49 for each white pupil enrolled in its public schools; the figure for black pupils was less than $40. Florida did not permit white and black students to use the same editions of some textbooks. Alabama prohibited white female nurses from ministering to black male hospital patients. Seven states segregated tuberculosis patients by race. Eleven refused to allow blind black people to sit in the same schoolroom with blind white people.

The situation in the Detroit area, where Malcolm was living with Wilfred, was similar to the one that prevailed in other large northern cities. Misleading advertisements drew gullible customers into the "cut-rate" furniture store that Wilfred managed in Inkster, a partly black Detroit suburb. The merchandise in the store, where Malcolm worked as a salesman, was decidedly inferior. Due to the exorbitant interest rates the owners charged the needy blacks who bought on credit, they ended up paying far more for the furniture than it was worth.

Malcolm went to Kalamazoo to visit his mother, who had barely recognized Philbert during Philbert's last visit to the hospital. But Mrs. Little, who hadn't seen Malcolm for about a decade, didn't recognize him at all.

The Detroit temple of the Nation of Islam was called Temple Number One because it was the first one that had been established by Elijah Muhammad's movement, whose members were called "Black Muslims"

---

* The figures cited were calculated on the basis of what the U.S. dollar was worth in 1967.

despite Mr. Muhammad's assertion that they were just ordinary Muslims. The temple was only a storefront in 1952. Yet the meetings that were held there deeply gratified Malcolm, who said he was moved by the respect that the Muslim "brothers" accorded each other. The family-like atmosphere was just one of the distinctive features that drew people to the movement. Another was its stirring vision of an independent black nation that would provide its Muslim inhabitants with food grown on its own farms, clothing made in its own factories, and shelter built on its own land—a nation within a nation that would educate its young in its own schools, keep its people informed with its own publications, and put their money to work in its own banks. The citizens of the nation Muhammad described would not be dependent on whites for any of their needs.

Muhammad's separatism resembled the Garveyism that Malcolm's father had espoused. Even the Messenger's background was somewhat similar to Earl Little's; both men had been raised on a Georgia farm with a minimum of elementary schooling.

The articulate minister of the Detroit temple, Lemuel Hassan, often lectured his flock with the aid of a blackboard. Painted on one side of it was an American flag, beneath which appeared the inscription, "Slavery, Suffering, and Death." On the opposite side was a red flag containing a star, a crescent, and the motto "Islam—Freedom, Justice, Equality." The congregation was told that this was the Islamic flag.

The day before Labor Day, the members of Temple Number One formed a caravan and drove to Chicago to hear Elijah Muhammad speak in Temple Number Two. Reverently, Malcolm gazed for the first time at the man who had given him the hope that his home and schools had failed to furnish. Raptly, he listened as Mr. Muhammad described how his teachings would raise "Original Man" up from the bottom of the white devil's social ladder and place him where his black forefathers had begun—at the pinnacle of civilization.

There was a fatherly quality about the way Mr. Muhammad treated his followers, whom he privately characterized as babies. Even James Baldwin, who described his own stepfather as unloving and "indescribably cruel," was strongly attracted by Muhammad's fatherly demeanor. The Old Man, as he was called behind his back by some of his associates, "was a father to everybody," according to one of his former intimates.

But the kind, fatherly demeanor that constituted a key element of Elijah Muhammad's appeal was a facade. Pursued by real or imaginary assassins, he had drifted, as Earl Little had done, from city to city, fed by his followers. His wife and her eight children, most of whom were Malcolm's contemporaries, had subsisted on handouts, as Louise Little and her eight youngsters had done. For seven years, Mrs. Muhammad and her brood were virtually abandoned by her husband, whose son Wallace later characterized him as dictatorial and cruel. Muhammad, who had been an active member of the Chicago branch of Garvey's UNIA, bluntly told his children that they had to be sacrificed for the good of the movement.

Muhammad's children attended his grade school, which he called the University of Islam. He was eventually arrested for refusing to send them to public school and, eight years later, was imprisoned for refusing to register for the draft. The *Chicago Tribune* reported that the arresting officers found him hiding under his mother's bed, wrapped in a carpet. Publication of the story did not seem to diminish his martyrdom in the eyes of his adoring followers, who were evidently swayed by his stories about how he had suffered "in bondage." He untruthfully claimed that he had not been obliged to register for the draft because he was overage.

Eventually, Elijah Muhammad, whose real name was Robert Poole, accumulated more than a hundred aliases, including Elijah Poole, Elijah Karriem, Mohammed Allah, Elijah Black, Rassoul Mohammed, and Elijah Muck Muck. He also called himself "Black Moses." His mother maintained that, when she was seven, she'd had a vision that she was destined to give birth to a very great man.

Around 1930, Poole met an itinerant door-to-door raincoat and silk peddler named Wallace Dodd Ford, who introduced him to the idea that whites were inherently devils. Ford, who peddled dope as well as fabric, looked white; in fact, he described himself as white to prison officials at San Quentin, where he served time for selling heroin. But he told blacks he was a "light-skinned Negro." At times, he claimed he was an Arab, despite his assertion that his father was British and his mother was Polynesian. On other occasions, he described her as white.

Ford—alias Wallace Delaney Fard, Wali Farrad, Wallie Ford, Ferrad Muhammad, Professor Fard, et cetera—asserted he was from Mecca and that he was a member of the same tribe to which the prophet Muhammad had belonged. Representing himself as Allah's messenger, he established a temple in Detroit and "registered" its members. For a fee, he agreed to replace their slave names—those that had been forced on them by the whites who had enslaved their forebears—with their "original" names. Temporarily, each applicant was given an X that symbolized his or her unknown name. If two or more applicants had the same first name—for instance, James—the first was called James X, the second James 2X, the third James 3X, and so forth. Later, the X was replaced with the appropriate surname. (On one occasion, Ford reportedly bestowed different surnames on three men who happened to be brothers. Confronted with the discrepancy, he said it had been revealed to him that each brother had been sired by a different father.)

In 1933, Ford was arrested in Detroit because one of his followers had killed another during a religious "sacrifice." According to Elijah Muhammad, Ford was later arrested in Chicago, where he had founded another temple. During this period of "persecution," Muhammad traveled around, disseminating Ford's teachings. Eventually, he became Ford's chief minister.

Then in 1934, when Malcolm was nine, Ford vanished. Gentle-looking Elijah Muhammad emerged as his successor after a power struggle with unknown rivals. Attempts to ascertain what happened to Ford, who was called Fard by his followers, have proven unsuccessful. Mr. Muhammad spread word that Fard—believers pronounce the name "Far-*rad*"—had returned to Mecca because his mission had been completed, and that he had appointed Muhammad head of the movement's North American branch. On another occasion, Mr. Muhammad said that Fard had been deported. The conflicting statements, plus Elijah's assertion that Fard had "returned to Allah," lent credence to unconfirmed rumors that Fard had been done in by the very man who had inherited his mantle. Muhammad, who boasted that he knew where Fard was, began to act inordinately afraid of assassination.

Largely because of opposition from Fard's Detroit-based disciples, Elijah Muhammad moved to Chicago, where he assumed the leadership of Temple Number Two. Ultimately, he obtained control of the Detroit temple and founded a few others. He told his followers that by 1936 not a single white would be left alive on the face of the earth. He said that his elderly black believers would then regain their youth and sexual potency.

Eventually, Elijah Muhammad deified his predecessor. He said that Fard had been not only the Islamic messiah, but also an incarnation of Allah. Equating Fard with Allah enabled Muhammad to represent himself, rather than Fard, as Allah's messenger. He claimed he was still in communication with Allah.

Thus, when Elijah Muhammad singled out Malcolm at the Chicago temple and asked him to stand, it was quite an honor. The Messenger explained to the rest of the congregation that Malcolm had recently been released from jail. He described how faithfully Malcolm had corresponded with him from prison. As Malcolm stood there, Elijah recalled the parable of Job, whom God had initially protected from misfortune. But then God removed the protection to see if Job would remain faithful. A similar test faced Malcolm. Now that he was free to do as he pleased, would he revert to his former dissolute ways? "I believe that he is going to remain faithful," Mr. Muhammad declared.

After the meeting, Elijah Muhammad invited the entire Little contingent to dine at his eighteen-room home, which he said his followers had insisted he needed. He prophesied that they would one day live in similar splendor. He promised to lead them to a city where the streets were paved with gold.

At supper, Malcolm sat ruminating about the empty seats he had seen at Temple Number One. He deplored the fact that the movement hadn't been able to fill the tiny place. Its recruitment policy, he felt, seemed based on the assumption that Allah would recruit members.

During a conversation lull, Malcolm asked Mr. Muhammad what was the best way to attract new members. "Go after the young people," the Messenger replied. That was all Malcolm needed. When he returned to Detroit, he broached the idea of a recruitment drive to Wilfred. Then he discussed it with Lemuel Hassan, who responded enthusiastically. That same evening, after work, he began "fishing" for new converts in ghetto poolrooms and bars.

The "fishing" wasn't easy. Most of the people he approached rebuffed him. ("You niggers are crazy!" one asserted.) Less than half of the people who did display interest actually came to the temple. But Malcolm did not quit, as he had done when he was young. His perseverance, plus his knowledge of ghetto psychology, enabled him to attract a slow, steady stream of converts that made it possible for Temple Number One to treble its membership within a few months. The number of vehicles in the auto caravans to Chicago gradually increased.

Like his father, Malcolm did not confine his recruiting forays to one city. On weekends and holidays, he toured Lansing and Flint in an effort to convert former friends and acquaintances into adherents of Islam. Usually, his pitch was low key; if he was rebuffed, he exhibited no resentment. But when his father's friend Ray Riddle, whose skin was so light that he looked virtually white, rejected his overtures, Malcolm exploded. "When we get into power, we're going to kill all you yellow niggers!" he snarled.

As time passed, Malcolm became more proficient at masking his anger. When an irate wife berated him in the erroneous belief that he had called upon her alcoholic husband to go drinking, he politely bowed and promised never to come again.

In January 1953, Malcolm left the Inkster furniture store and took a job on a Lincoln-Mercury assembly line. Despite the high wages, he couldn't stand the monotonous, robot-like work. A week later, he was jobless. Prodded by his parole officer, he accepted another mindless position at a factory where garbage-truck bodies were fabricated. The only place he was enthusiastic about working was at the temple, where

Minister Lemuel, at Elijah Muhammad's behest, encouraged him to address the congregation.

Despite his initial uncertainty, Malcolm did so. The debating expertise he had developed in prison stood him in good stead. "We didn't land on Plymouth Rock," he told his fellow Muslims. "Plymouth Rock landed on *us!*"

Malcolm sang Lemuel Hassan's praises. He told the congregation, "Brother Lemuel is a real good minister. You have a wonderful minister." By June 1953, Malcolm had become one of Mr. Hassan's assistant ministers. He later asserted that it had "never occurred" to him that he might one day become a full-fledged minister. He said he felt unqualified to represent the Messenger and that he was content to serve him "in the lowliest capacity." But he privately told Johnny Davis, Jr., whom he had known for years, "I am going to reach the top. I am going to be Elijah Muhammad's right-hand man."

Malcolm sensed that Mr. Muhammad was interested in his potential. The Messenger began talking about the need to send hard-working young men to other cities to establish new temples. He encouraged Malcolm to come to Chicago as often as he could.

Malcolm did so. For hours at a time, he listened to Elijah, whom he characterized as Allah's "seventh and last prophet," with an attentiveness that would have astounded most of his former teachers. Frequently, Malcolm accompanied Mr. Muhammad as he toured the modest stores that the Nation of Islam owned on Chicago's South Side. Whenever the Messenger tried to sweep a dirty floor in an effort to set a good example, Malcolm tried to grab the broom and sweep the floor himself, as he had done years before at the Townsend Drugstore. He toiled as willingly for Elijah Muhammad as he had once toiled for Ma Swerlein and Pappy Cousins.

Before long, Elijah was treating Malcolm like his seventh son. (Six of the eight children his wife had borne him were male.) The Messenger, who acknowledged that he felt fatherly toward Malcolm, even called him "son." His own children, who were seldom in evidence around his home, had less access to him than Malcolm did. Some of Malcolm's associates observed that Elijah seemed to care more for him than he did for his own children, whom he admitted had not been reared properly. (He attributed it to his wife's "nervous breakdown.")

It became increasingly apparent that, for Malcolm (who seemed to feel adept at penetrating people's facades), Elijah Muhammad was the very image of the loving father he had never had. But as time would tell, he was merely substituting one tyrant for another, and political servitude for penal servitude.

ASCETIC

29

Minister Lemuel, who may have sensed a potential threat to his position from his best recruiter, recommended that Malcolm be sent East to find more converts. By this time, Malcolm had fulfilled his parole obligation and was free to leave his boring factory job. Elijah Muhammad therefore decided to send him to Boston, where the Nation of Islam had been struggling to establish a temple.

In Boston, Malcolm looked up his former cronies. Though he later asserted that he didn't even mention Islam to most of them, he invited nearly everyone he knew to hear him speak at the meetings he held in private homes. He even tried to convert Aunt Sassie and his other relatives. One of them was his cousin Clara, who bluntly told him that she wasn't interested. Malcolm just smiled. He insisted that Ella's refusal to join "didn't bother" him. Yet he later acknowledged that such rebuffs did make him angry—not only at the people who rejected his overtures, but also at himself for his inability to win them over. His tendency to flagellate himself for outcomes beyond his control was a revealing example of the way he turned his anger inward.

Malcolm called on Gloria several times. She sensed that he was still interested in her, but he confined his conversation almost entirely to religion. "I'm going to build a temple," he told one of her friends.

Malcolm kept his word. Within three months, he had attracted enough people to open a makeshift mosque. Among them was Malcolm Jarvis. He and nearly a dozen other aspirants accompanied Malcolm to Chicago to receive the Messenger's personal blessing. But Jarvis, who told Malcolm that he intended to challenge some of Mr. Muhammad's views, did not receive it, nor was he granted the interview his fellow pilgrims were accorded. Jarvis promptly left the Nation. He felt betrayed by Malcolm, who admitted that he had scotched the interview in deference to his chief.

The ascetic life style the Nation of Islam's leaders demanded of their followers was the antithesis of the rebellious licentiousness of Malcolm's youth. Alcohol, drugs—even tobacco—were strictly proscribed, as was gambling and all forms of criminality. Hard work was mandatory. Long vacations were discouraged. Members were encouraged to reduce the amount of time they spent sleeping.

Sporting events, particularly professional ones, were frowned on by Elijah Muhammad, who maintained that his followers should devote themselves to less frivolous pursuits. The proscription was not regarded as a hard and fast rule; Mr. Muhammad's ministers, who were largely responsible for policing the faithful, evidently knew it would be unwise to attempt to enforce an absolute ban on athletics. Watching television was also discouraged by Elijah Muhammad, who taught there was only one source of truth—himself. Later on, when Malcolm became a leading television personality, the members of the Nation of Islam were taught to be discriminating in their choice of television programs. Initially, the attitude toward movies was stricter, perhaps because it was easier to police a ban against unauthorized movies than a ban against TV shows that were viewed in the privacy of members' homes. Malcolm, who had been so addicted to films, avoided movie theaters. But he did attend a few religious movies, one of which dealt with the crucifixion. His cousin "J.C." accompanied him.

Despite Malcolm's love of dancing, he gave it up. But there was sadness in his voice, years later, when he told an interviewer about his former ballroom exploits. Then, abruptly, he arose from his chair, grabbed a tall, vertical pipe with one hand, as if it were his partner, and started jitterbugging. His feet were moving a mile a minute. Suddenly, he stopped short, returned to his seat, and began to sulk.

The use of cosmetics by the Nation of Islam's women was discouraged. Moreover, the sexual mores of the movement were highly circumscribed. At temple meetings, for instance, males and females were required to sit apart "so as not to prohibit concentration." They were forbidden to swim together "to prevent temptation." Dating was regarded as a grave danger. Premarital sex, which was called fornication, was absolutely forbidden. As time passed and the Nation grew, its members began to demolish the myth that the majority of America's blacks were promiscuous, sports-crazy, hard-drinking, indolent lawbreakers.

The movement's dietary code was somewhat similar to that of the fundamentalist religious sect Louise Little had joined after her husband's death. The Nation also insisted upon the same high standards of neatness and cleanliness that Louise had demanded of her children.

Daily baths and purification rituals were mandatory. One had to be clean "internally." The stomach, which the Nation's ideologists likened to a pot-bellied stove, had to be thoroughly cleansed to avoid constipation or "sluggishness," mental or physical. Thus, it was best to eat one meal per day. This would allow the digestive tract to rest, so that it would not "weaken." Malcolm, who faithfully parroted these doctrines, also stressed the dangers of obesity, particularly the strain that excess weight imposes on the heart and circulatory system. He said that excess weight could cause one's heart to flutter.

Malcolm, who had been so accustomed to hunger when he was young, took the fasting the Nation of Islam required in stride. The former fast-living drug addict who had tried to solve the problem of gratification by continual indulgence had become an ascetic who mastered the need for gratification by denying it.

Unlike his father, who had habitually violated the stringent morality he had preached, Malcolm dutifully obeyed Elijah Muhammad's puritanical mandates. He was so unbending in his adherence to the rule restricting believers to one full meal per day that his physician had a hard time persuading him to take vitamin pills more than once a day. (The vitamins were designed to cure the cracked, bleeding gums that resulted from his inadequate diet.) His moral rigidity suggested a need for approval by those who wielded moral authority, as well as a need for external controls to bolster his internal ones, now that there were no prison bars to restrain him. "I only pray," he wrote, "that I do not slip. . .back into the pit."

Malcolm made every effort to guard against backsliding. Though he often exaggerated his criminal past for political reasons, he was some-times reluctant to discuss it.* At times, he ascribed his lengthy prison stay to religious persecution. And when he unexpectedly encountered Betty Walker, whose family had sheltered the Littles after the 1929 fire, he behaved as if he had never been in prison.

Yet, despite its defensive elements, Malcolm's obsessive morality, which barred him from enjoyment as effectively as prison bars, was a striking achievement—one that attested to his ability to transform youthful weakness into adult strength. "We gain strength from the temptations we resist," he said.

Malcolm deprived himself the way others had deprived him. This enabled him to control the severity and the timing of the deprivation. Moreover, there was a certain pride in suffering. While the wayward,

---

* "It sounds as if *I* have done some crime!" he abruptly exclaimed on one occasion.

teen-age Malcolm had "pleasured" himself at the cost of the guilty conscience he had tried so hard to deny, the ascetic Malcolm purchased self-respect at the terrible price of an almost completely joyless existence.

After it became apparent that Gloria was not going to let herself become involved again with Malcolm, he began to exhibit interest in an immaculately dressed Muslim woman who had visited Charlestown Prison with his brother Wesley. Her expressive eyes conveyed intelligence and honesty. She had a warm, winning smile. Her enthusiasm for the Nation of Islam, which she had joined after she realized that the operatic career she had wanted would not materialize, was contagious. Her complexion was as light as Malcolm's, but not as ruddy. "Every time I saw her, she reminded me of my mother," Philbert later recalled. He explained that this was due partly to her skin color and partly to the look that came over her face when she pondered something.

The woman—I'll call her Heather—had been inspired by the way Malcolm had transformed himself in prison. She visited him again and wrote him, not only while he was in prison, but also after he left. When Malcolm moved to Boston, where she lived, their friendship blossomed. They spent hours together at the home of Hilda's friend Dorothy Young, who was Heather's guardian. Like Malcolm, Heather was parentless. Her mother had died shortly after she was born, and her father had remarried and foisted her off on her grandparents. For financial reasons, he eventually moved in with them, but the resultant tensions proved so unbearable that Heather told the attending social worker that she preferred to live elsewhere.

The relationship between Malcolm and Heather deepened as she began to penetrate his tough facade. "He didn't trust anybody," she later recalled. He told her he had been betrayed by women and that a woman had been responsible for his imprisonment. He didn't say who. But on one occasion, he said that the example Ella had set had profoundly influenced his youthful decision to pursue a criminal career. The point was seconded by his Aunt Grace, who bluntly exclaimed, "Ella ruined Malcolm!"

Malcolm, who made no attempt to be physically intimate with Heather, finally began talking about marriage. Quietly, unofficially, they became engaged. Then, in March 1954, he suddenly left Boston without even saying goodbye. Heather wrote and gave him a piece of her mind. When Malcolm returned, he told her that although he loved her, he couldn't marry her. He said he would not be a good husband because he would constantly be away traveling. In short, he was leaving her for her own good, and for the movement's.

Heather felt so shattered that it took years for her to realize that

Malcolm may have felt he was becoming too dependent upon her. (He later characterized a man's need for a woman as "weakness.") She had no way of knowing that Ella had advised him against marrying her. Years later, Ella acknowledged that she felt Heather was too "emotional." She said that Heather's need for love—Ella called it weakness—would have diverted Malcolm from his worldlier objectives.

Malcolm told Heather that Ella was conniving. But, for some reason, he heeded her advice. Heather later realized that Malcolm's decision to forego her love may also have been influenced by his discovery that Wesley loved her. Despite the way he had boasted, years earlier, that he had stolen Philbert's wife, he gallantly relinquished his lovely fiancee to his younger brother.

In Search of a Leader 30

From the moment Malcolm arrived at the Greyhound Bus Terminal, he kept checking his watch. It was his first day as acting minister of Elijah Muhammad's Philadelphia temple, where dissension within the skimpy ranks was making it impossible for the Messenger to establish effective control.

Malcolm rented a room in the North Philadelphia "Jungle," where decomposing debris and refuse had not been swept from the streets in years. He seemed to like the stylish attire of the Messenger's Philadelphia followers. Some believers noticed that his own clothes were too large for him. ("He didn't like anything too close," recalls Wilfred.)

Malcolm took exceptional precautions about his food. He tried not to eat store-bought bread. "If you ever saw how they bake it, you wouldn't eat it," he told an associate. Nor would he eat "tightly-packed" ice cream; he said it contained too many chemicals.

When Malcolm wasn't working—which was rarely—he roamed Philadelphia's Academy of Natural Science and its Parthenon-like art museum. He even read books about opera.

Years later, he said he wouldn't be "one bit ashamed" about returning to school and repeating the ninth grade. He pondered the possibility of combining the study of law with the study of human behavior. He said he'd specialize in international law. Such a venture would have obviously required a commitment of many years and lots of money. His inability to afford the requisite schooling poignantly attested to Eric Hoffer's observation that people who feel thwarted frequently join a mass movement in the hope that its achievements will compensate for their failures.

Yet the Nation of Islam enabled Malcolm to transform youthful failure into success. By the end of May 1954—less than three months after Malcolm's arrival in the racially divided City of Brotherly Love—he had reorganized its Black Muslim temple. During this period, he traveled to other cities on Elijah Muhammad's behalf. In New York, he held discussions with the local minister, Sultan Muhammad. Sultan informed Malcolm that the Messenger was pressing him to discipline or divorce his wife, who had reportedly likened Elijah Muhammad to a dog. "But I love my wife!" Sultan, who was almost in tears, told Malcolm. Shortly thereafter, he was dismissed.

Sultan's dismissal benefited Malcolm, who was made a full minister and placed in charge of Elijah Muhammad's followers in vital New York City, where three quarters of a million black Americans had to coexist with large or larger blocs of Irish-Americans, Italian-Americans, and others. Except for the Puerto Ricans, who constituted the most recent large group of immigrants, most of the African-Americans were near or at the bottom of the social totem pole. In Harlem, the odor of uncollected garbage filled the littered streets. "Downtown," in luxurious midtown and lower Manhattan high-rises, electric garbage disposals obviated such problems. Uptown, the stairwells and hallways of crumbling, overcrowded tenements reeked with the stench of the urine of wandering derelicts. Downtown, air purifiers and air conditioners were the rule of the day. To combat summer heat, Harlemites had to make do with fire escape landings. Hordes of youngsters spent schoolless summers staring out from broken windows, or splashing in water from fire hydrants—in filthy gutters that were so crammed with shattered glass that they glistened in the sunlight. Children who lived downtown frolicked in private swimming pools, or at summer camps, where they used real baseball bats, not broom handles. Their parents browsed at Bloomingdales or Saks, not in pawnshops.

The contrast was equally dismal in the cultural realm: Shakespeare on 47th Street; illiteracy on 147th. The lack of interest in intellectual pursuits that pervaded Harlem and other ghettos was the fault not only of the students but also of the educational establishment, which was so busy trying to preserve existing teaching jobs and to make one subculture conform to another that it virtually ignored the economic and other needs of the pupils. Chemistry and physics continued to be "taught" to students who, at the end of the semester, received high grades although they neither knew nor cared what an atom was. Molecular structure had no discernible relevance to the daily struggle for survival that characterized life in most of Harlem.

Despite the enormous differences between Harlem and the rest of Manhattan, there were hidden similarities. Downtown, workaholic fathers ignored the emotional needs of their youngsters. Uptown, a disproportionate number of children had no father at all. Unwittingly, many of their overworked, unfulfilled mothers took frustration out on them, as Malcolm's mother had apparently done.

Harlem hadn't always been synonymous with privation. The "delightful village" of New Haarlem, as its original, Dutch settlers called it, was situated amidst picturesque farmland. Alexander Hamilton had a country estate there. Though the estate, and others like it, were eventually broken up and replaced by shantytowns of impoverished German, then Irish, immigrants, most of Harlem retained its rural serenity. From the mid-nineteenth century on, affluent New Yorkers went there for Sunday country jaunts. They typically came by horseback through Central Park. Cornelius Vanderbilt exercised his thoroughbred trotters on Harlem Lane, which is now St. Nicholas Avenue.

Then, during the last quarter of the nineteenth century, came the building boom, spurred by Manhattan's industrial, commercial, and demographic growth and the construction of rapid transit facilities from downtown New York City to Harlem. The marshes were filled in. The shanties were replaced by apartment houses and brownstone homes. Electric lights, then telephone lines, were installed. Speculators such as Henry Morgenthau made fortunes buying and reselling Harlem land that, twenty years before, had not been worth paying taxes for. By the last decade of the nineteenth century, Harlem was considered one of the most elegant places in the City of New York, of which it had become an integral part. Many of the elevator-equipped apartment buildings contained servants' quarters. Some of the homes were designed by Stanford White, whose firm had designed the first Madison Square Garden, the central tower of which rose to within nine feet of the dome of what was then the tallest building in New York. The driveways of these distinctive dwellings were ornamented by circular beds of flowers. The rents ranged from eight to fourteen times what working-class families typically paid their landlords.

Consequently, people with means moved to Harlem. They included prominent businessmen, federal judges, Tammany boss Richard Croker, and more than one former mayor. The grammar school their children attended was regarded as New York's "silk stocking" school. Cultural activity flourished. The Harlem Opera House was founded by Oscar Hammerstein I. There was also a Harlem Literary Society, the Harlem Yacht Club, and the Harlem Philharmonic Orchestra, not to mention the Harlem Anti-Litter League. Land values skyrocketed as wealthy speculators competed with each other to buy property along the subway routes that had been, or that were being, constructed. The real estate fever also took firm hold among the Jewish tradesmen and garment workers who left rotting lower East Side tenements in search of better housing in Lower Harlem, part of which became known as "Little Russia." The migration, like the subsequent black one, was adamantly opposed by existing residents, who charged that the neighborhood was growing less "refined." One German-American Harlemite hung out a rental sign reading *"Keine Juden und keine Hunde"* ["No Jews and no dogs"].

The bust came in 1904-05, when it became evident that Harlem had been overbuilt. White landlords frantically competed with one another to reduce rents and attract tenants. As a result, apartment owners began opening their doors to "colored" occupants—not run of the mill tenants, but those who could afford the not-quite-so-high rents: undertakers, realtors, lawyers, entertainers. Some members of New York City's tiny black elite purchased elegant homes, such as those that were situated on 139th Street between Seventh and Eighth Avenues. These immaculate, tree-shaded, Stanford White-designed dwellings, which comprised part of what was known as "Striver's Row," had private garages. A number of nearby apartment houses boasted hall boy service. One wealthy black clergyman was attended and chauffeured about by white servants. Harlem was a place where aspiring blacks dreamed of living, not one from which they longed to escape.

But Harlem's elegance was swiftly undermined by a number of factors, including an influx of nearly indigent southern blacks who had migrated north partly because of disastrous crop failures, partly because of the labor shortage suddenly created by the First World War. Almost overnight, white America had discovered that a favorite target of abuse was a valuable resource. Labor agents were sent South. They brought back huge numbers of blacks from the cotton fields of Mississippi, the coal mines and steel mills of Alabama, and the docks of Norfolk, Savannah, Mobile, and New Orleans. Many of the newcomers settled in the growing, scattered pockets of black poverty that had coexisted with the affluent sections of Harlem since slavery had been abolished. Others found lodgings in the tenements east of Third Avenue, between 110th and 125th Streets. The area was inhabited chiefly by Italians who had come to America during the late nineteenth and early twentieth centuries. Organ grinders walked the neighborhood streets. Sicilian fish peddlers hawked their wares. The district, known as Little Italy, subsequently became a political springboard for Congressman—later Mayor—Fiorello La Guardia.

From Little Italy, the black newcomers spilled over westward into Little Russia and into other parts of Harlem. Whites attempted to stem the invasion by pooling their resources, buying back properties occupied by blacks, and evicting them. Whites put pressure on financial institutions to refuse mortgage money to blacks or to people who rented to them.

The efforts of white property owners to halt the black tide were undermined by "blockbusters"—real estate speculators who purposely placed black families in previously all-white blocks. When the panic-selling began, these speculators bought up nearby properties for a pittance. Then they leased or sold them to blacks for whatever price they could command or sold them to panic-stricken white neighbors who were willing to pay nearly anything to preserve the racial purity of their immediate surroundings. When it became apparent that such techniques would not stem the influx, the panic-selling increased to epidemic proportions. Within a few years, Harlem changed color.

During the 1920s, while much of America prospered, Harlem decayed, to the dismay of its black elite. The causes were multiple. Landlords, among whom were some of Harlem's most prominent black churches, subdivided spacious, multi-story houses into undersized apartments in order to increase the number of rental units.* White property-owners, including Columbia University and some of the largest insurance companies and banks, proceeded similarly in order to maximize their income. One investigator discovered seven children sleeping on pallets on the floor of one tiny, two-room apartment. More typical, perhaps, was the "hot bed" system, which Malcolm and his roomates had used in Delia Williams's Flint, Michigan rooming house during the winter of 1942-43. That is, as soon as one occupant awoke and left a bed, it was taken by another.

Not all the fault lay with the landlords. Some tenants failed to keep the premises in decent, or even sanitary condition. Landlords who made an honest effort to keep their properties in proper repair gave up when it became evident it was largely a losing battle. Hallways, yards, and air shafts were filled with vermin-attracting garbage. Wiring and fixtures were cannibalized from walls and sold for profit. There were more disputes between landlords and tenants in Harlem's Seventh District court than in any municipal court in New York City's five boroughs. Occasionally, conscientious judges inspected the hovels themselves. Nearly always, what they saw horrified them. One civic official found few buildings that were even fit for habitation. Another described the majority of available housing as diseased.

The city, beleaguered by financial burdens caused by the Great Depression, did little to ameliorate the suffering. During the 1930's, for example, Park Commissioner Robert Moses, who was not fond of blacks, authorized the construction of 255 playgrounds in New York City. He had only one built in Harlem, which, at the time, had only two public playgrounds— pathetic little plots containing digging areas so small that the children had to stand in line with their pails and shovels until a spot became available. More often than not, they waited in vain. The one additional facility that was authorized was not enough to make a substantial difference.

---

* One Harlem block contained 3,871 residents.

During the same decade, the city fathers built ten new neighborhood swimming pools. They built one in Harlem. It was located at 146th Street—far away from the sweltering tenements of Lower Harlem. The only other public pool that Harlemites could reach on foot was the one in Thomas Jefferson Park, which was situated in a white neighborhood between First Avenue and East River Drive.

But, as Robert Caro has shown, few of the blacks and Puerto Ricans who lived near Thomas Jefferson Pool ventured there. The attendants and lifeguards, who were all white, scared non-white youngsters half to death with their glowering looks. The pool was purposely kept unheated in the belief that the cold water would deter non-white swimmers. Whether it was the water temperature, the hostility of the pool management, or the fear of being attacked by white swimmers, one could go there on the hottest summer day and not see one non-white face. The blacks and Puerto Ricans of Lower Harlem preferred the 146th Street pool, even though many of them—particularly those who came from large, indigent families—couldn't afford the necessary round-trip bus fare and had to walk two or three miles each way.

Harlem also benefited least from the widely heralded West Side Improvement, which included the completion of the West Side Highway and the transformation of miles of garbage dumps, tar paper shacks, and muddy Hudson riverbank into a majestic park affording New York city residents a respite from the ugliness of the major part of their surroundings. To create the park, which was roughly five miles long, the city removed all the wharves, junk yards, warehouses, and coal bins from the portion of the waterfront that was situated between 72nd Street and 125th Street. By adding landfill, it enlarged this section of the narrow park by 132 acres. But in the section of Riverside Park abutting the part of Harlem that lay north of 125th Street, the authorities let the unsightly industrial facilities remain. They did not add a single acre of landfill. As a result, there was virtually no park at all between 125th Street and 145th Street. Half or more of the Harlem section of the park was a sliver bisected by a sooty railroad track, from which noisy trains emitted smoke and the stench of animals being transported to slaughterhouses.

In contrast, the portion of the park below 110th Street, which was generally regarded as Harlem's southern boundary, was lavishly furnished with trees, shrubs, landscaped terraces, ball fields, marinas, and waterfront promenades. The amount of money per mile allotted to the part of the park bordering most of Harlem was less than a quarter of the sum allotted to the downtown part. There was none of the landscaping or lush foliage that characterized the latter section. Nor were there any of the tennis and horseshoe courts or the biking and roller-skating paths that were located in other parts of the park. In fact, when the West Side Improvement was opened to the public, not a single recreational facility had been built in the Harlem section—not so much as a stanchion with a basketball hoop attached. The inadequate facilities that were later added proved inordinantly difficult to reach from the ghetto they were supposed to serve. The only way to get to them by foot—few Harlemites had cars—was by walking from Riverside Drive down an incredibly long flight of steps, then up another flight to a footbridge that led to two more flights of steps. These led to a highway underpass that provided access to the recreational area. The return trip, which was almost all uphill, was debilitating on hot summer days. Consequently, few Harlemites used the park's facilities. Those who did may have noticed, as Caro later did, that the wrought iron trellises of the comfort station in the Harlem section of Riverside Park were not decorated with the wave-like designs embellishing the comfort stations in other parts of the park. They were adorned with imitation monkeys.

Indicative of Harlem's plight, and that of black America in general, were the armies of African-American women who lined up every morning in the "Slave Market" in the nearby Bronx, where white housewives bid for their services. The going rate for domestics during the Great Depression was between ten and fifteen cents an hour. The cost of lunch was usually deducted from their take-home pay.

The cumulative effect of economic depression, racial oppression, and the neglect engendered by World War II became increasingly evident in Harlem by the late 1940s and early 1950s. The recession of 1953-54 wrought further carnage. So did the Eisenhower Administration's refusal to finance effective remedial programs. Critics joked about the Eisenhower doll, which, after it was wound up, did absolutely nothing for eight years.

The Congress, itself divided innumerable ways, did painfully little to compensate for the lack of executive leadership. In the Senate, the filibuster proved an insuperable obstacle to attempts to establish adequate legislative sanctions against racial discrimination. There were other institutional impediments. A disproportionate number of congressional committee chairmanships were controlled by legislators from Dixie, such as Georgia's Richard B. Russell and Louisiana's Allen J. Ellender. This was due to their congressional seniority, which was the result of the fact that the constituencies they supposedly represented kept returning them to office. One reason for this state of affairs was that, despite the Fourteenth and Fifteenth Amendments, most southern blacks were effectively disenfranchised by gerrymandering, poll taxes, arbitrarily administered voter qualifications tests, and similar devices. Below the Mason-Dixon line, blacks were excluded from white-run hotels, theaters, schools, restaurants, churches, and clubs. Even in the nation's capital, whose black firemen were prohibited from joining white fire companies, many hotels would not admit blacks. The one ray of hope was the U.S. Supreme Court, which in May 1954 declared segregated educational facilities unconstitutional. Whether the high court's decision would be effectively implemented was an open question. Either way, America's blacks were crying for vigorous leadership when Malcolm arrived in Harlem in June 1954 to assume command of Elijah Muhammad's fledgling New York City temple.

BUILDING THE NATION 31

Nearly a decade had elapsed since Malcolm had been run out of New York by West Indian Archie. He combed his old haunts for the numbers runner who had loaned him money when he was penniless. He also scoured Harlem's dingy, crime-ridden streets for the other former benefactor who had nearly killed him—Sammy the Pimp.

The news about Sammy was devastating. He had given up pimping and gone into the numbers racket, where he had done well. But then, not long after he had married, he was discovered dead in his room.

Heartbroken about his former mentor, Malcolm continued inquiring about Archie. No one seemed to know what had happened to him.

Malcolm ran into a number of other hustlers who used to frequent Small's Paradise. Some were working as janitors. Others had been reduced to derelicts or were in jail or dead.

But not everyone Malcolm encountered had gone downhill. Creole Pete had opened a new restaurant and had prospered. When Malcolm saw how successful Pete had become, he became reticent about what he was doing. All he would tell Pete was that he had joined "an organization." He didn't say which one and quickly changed the subject.

Malcolm's inquiries about Archie were relayed about town by the Harlem grapevine. Finally, one day at the temple, an elderly man approached him and told him Archie was ill. He gave Malcolm Archie's Bronx address. Despite the fact that the Bronx was just minutes away by subway, Malcolm took a taxi.

"Red, I'm so glad to see you," Archie exclaimed when he finally realized who the unconked redhead with the brush cut was. Malcolm assisted him back to his bed and proceeded to extol the virtues of the Muslim movement that he had been so reluctant to discuss with Creole Pete.

"I always liked you, Red," Archie said. He told Malcolm that after the confrontation at La Marr-Cheri, he wondered if he had been mistaken about the number Malcolm had combinated. Malcolm explained that he had honestly believed he had combinated the winning number. He said that while he was in jail, he had often thought of Archie and the mathematical contributions he might have made with his computer-like mind.

But it was too late for that; Malcolm sensed that Archie didn't have much time to live. He was so disturbed by the contrast between the Archie he had known and the one who sat beside him that he found it difficult to remain any longer.

New York's Temple Seven—the seventh the Nation of Islam had founded—was just a storefront in 1954. Its membership was minuscule. Very few Harlemites knew that the Nation existed, partly because it had to compete with a bevy of other protest groups, like the "buy black" movement.

Malcolm changed all this. First, he had handbills printed. Then he and his fellow Muslims took to the streets and began fishing on the fringes of the crowds that attended the gatherings of the various black nationalist groups that were scattered throughout Harlem. "Come to hear us too, brother," they cried. The same tactics were employed outside the storefront Christian churches. Each Sunday, as they disgorged their worshippers, Malcolm and his men were waiting. Pointing to the minister, who typically greeted the members of his congregation as they left the church, Malcolm would say, "He represents the white man's god; I represent the black man's god." He'd invite the startled listeners to Temple Seven to hear him. "You don't have to join," he'd assure them. "We may not take you anyway!" The Christian preachers glowered, but there was little they could do.

For nonreligious listeners, Malcolm adjusted his sales pitch accordingly. He advised them to take a long, hard look at their impoverished living conditions:

> When you get through looking at where you live, then . . . take
> a walk across Central Park . . . . Look at the white man's
> apartments. . . . Look at his Wall Street!

In an effort to attract female converts, Malcolm emphasized that black women were beautiful in their own right and shouldn't try to imitate their "dirty," "stinking," "leprous-looking" white counterparts. Black women, he said, should be treated like the "queen-mothers" of civilization they once were. He boasted, as his mother had boasted, that he and his followers were descended from princes and kings. He claimed that Islam, which had originated more than six hundred years after the birth of Christ, was the oldest religion on earth. And that, long before

Columbus had discovered America, a black man named Musa had.* In his effort to demonstrate how history had been "bleached" by historians who had ignored the achievements of the great African empires of the past, such as Ghana and Mali, Malcolm claimed that the ancient Sumerian and Egyptian civilizations had been black. He said the same thing about the Moors and Hannibal's Carthaginians. Malcolm, who privately conceded that he was administering an "overdose" of black culture, even insisted that Beethoven and Haydn had been of African descent. His efforts to unwhiten history included assertions that European cannibals had been "eating up their mothers and fathers" while African culture and science had been flourishing.

Malcolm's "fishing" began to pay off; the Harlem temple grew slowly but surely. In early 1955, he told the Fruit of Islam—the male members of the temple—that Elijah Muhammad wanted a thousand fearless "fruits" by the end of the year.

The Philadelphia mosque, which Malcolm remained in charge of, also grew. He ruled his Islamic dominions the same way he had been ruled. He told his Philadelphia congregation:

> I'd better not hear anyone mentioning my name in criticism or I will give them indefinite time out of the temple . . . . Is there anyone who wants to question me or doesn't think I am being fair? Raise your hand. . . . Good thing you didn't, because you would have gotten [put] out of the temple.

As the membership of the New York, Philadelphia, and Boston temples grew, Malcolm began seeking converts in additional cities. Osborne Thaxton helped him establish Temple Number Thirteen in Springfield, Massachusetts. Temple Number Fourteen was founded in Hartford, Connecticut. Then, in 1955, Malcolm leapfrogged to Atlanta and held the first meeting of Temple Number Fifteen. He was instrumental in organizing the temples that sprang up in Buffalo, Pittsburgh, Atlantic City, Newark, Jersey City, Miami, Cleveland, and Richmond. He had finally learned to put his wanderlust to constructive use.

Yet Malcolm did not neglect his duties in New York. In addition to establishing branches of Temple Seven in Brooklyn and Queens, he launched a building fund for the construction of a new Harlem temple. When a similar effort in Philadelphia foundered, he urged the members

---

* On another occasion, he asserted that Columbus had been half-black.

of the congregation to get extra part-time jobs and to donate the proceeds to the movement. He also called a special meeting and announced that, since the brothers and sisters were not contributing three percent of their earnings as they were supposed to, each Philadelphia Muslim would be required to donate so much per day, regardless of age or employment status. He told the Detroit Fruit of Islam that Elijah Muhammad needed someone who could represent him in distant cities. To finance this person's activities, a fee of fifty cents per week would be levied upon each male member. This sum was to be added to existing assessments, such as the Messenger's "special aid" fund and the requirement that each believer contribute a percentage of his annual income. The new fund, the "laborer's travel expense," was to be called the L.T.E. Every Sunday, "L.T.E." would be written on the blackboard to remind everyone of this new obligation. New, untested members would not be told what "L.T.E." meant.

Shortly after the L.T.E. assessment was levied, Malcolm, whom Elijah Muhammad hailed as his "hardest working minister," toured the country in an effort to promote Elijah's "One Million Dollar" campaign. The slogan he coined for it was, "You can't advance without finance!"

By this time, Malcolm had become not only Muhammad's chief minister and principal trouble shooter—he was officially billed as Elijah's East Coast Representative—but also his chief fund-raiser. Each temple under his control (his jurisdiction extended from Boston to San Diego) had to submit weekly and monthly financial reports to him, as well as to the movement's Chicago headquarters. He exhibited no mercy to subordinates who pleaded indigence. "What kind of a man are you?" he'd ask them. He said that if a man wanted his children to respect him, he should support them.

Within seven years of Malcolm's emergence from prison, the number of black Muslim temples had increased from ten to at least thirty. Before long, the number had grown to about fifty. Membership spiraled from a few hundred to tens of thousands. "Thank Allah for my brother minister Malcolm," a grateful Elijah Muhammad publicly proclaimed.

Even St. Paul, whose religious conversion Malcolm later compared to his own, might have been impressed with his achievements. Some people called him the Islamic St. Paul. But he firmly disclaimed any intention of likening himself to the great Christian evangelist, who had spent time in prison and, by concentrating his efforts in heavily-populated urban centers, had been largely responsible for the rapid growth of his upstart religion.

One of Malcolm's associates likened him to the tall, ascetic Muslim evangelist Omar, who, six centuries after St. Paul popularized Christianity, was chiefly responsible for the rapid spread of Islam: Omar, the protector of the poor; Omar, who had vastly enriched the new nation's treasury; Omar, whose authoritarianism had been countenanced partly because of the respect his integrity had inspired; Omar, who had scoffed at the need for bodyguards and had been killed by an assassin as he was about to address his followers.

In April, 1957, an incident occurred in Harlem that brought the Nation of Islam to the attention of the general public. A drunkard who had been abusing his female companion was stopped by a white policeman. According to the police department, the drunk bit the officer, ran him into a wall, and fastened a bear hug on him. A second policeman intervened and grabbed the drunk, who struck him in the chest. The officer hit him with his nightstick. The blow had no apparent effect on the powerfully built black man, who allegedly kept flailing his arms and legs until the two patrolmen subdued him with their clubs. By the time they had finished pummeling him, his head and clothing were covered with blood.

More than one member of the angry crowd that witnessed the melee protested the behavior of the police. One onlooker shouted, "This isn't Alabama or Georgia; this is New York!"—or words to that effect. Another bystander, a Black Muslim named Johnson Hinton, also remonstrated with the officers. Hinton later testified that as he was leaving the scene, a policeman collared him from the rear, spun him around, and—without saying a word—clobbered him with his billy club. Despite the lack of warning and the impact of the blow, which Hinton later described as "terrific," he said he was able to grab hold of the nightstick as it began to descend upon him again. The officer, who disputed Hinton's testimony, said he had accidentally backed into Hinton after he had finally overpowered the drunk. At first, he claimed that Hinton had seized his nightstick after he had placed him under arrest for refusing to move on. Later, in court, he asserted that Hinton had grabbed his billy club before he had even informed him that he was under arrest. The officer also maintained that Hinton had pushed him. But his description of the confrontation left some doubt whether he or Hinton had initiated the pushing.

The policeman and Hinton struggled for possession of the nightstick. Another patrolman, one of several who had hurried to the scene, tried to help his fellow officer. He later testified that Hinton grabbed him by the throat and started choking him. Other officers joined the fray and clubbed Hinton to the pavement.

Bleeding and handcuffed, Hinton, who had never been arrested before, was taken to the Twenty-eighth Precinct station house, where, he later testified, he was slammed into a chair. (The drunk who had started everything was stretched out on the floor in a pool of blood.) Hinton kept moaning and praying. "Didn't I tell you to shut up with that noise?" one policeman demanded. According to Hinton, the officer struck him in the mouth. When that failed to stop the moaning, another policeman said, "I'll shut you up," and hit him several times in the face with his fist. He stepped back, fetched a nightstick, and began beating Hinton's knees. Then, according to Hinton, whose court testimony was partly contravened by testimony he had given earlier, the officer raised his foot high and kicked him so hard in the chest that he and his chair were propelled back against the wall. His head struck the wall and he blacked out.

Less than half an hour after Temple Seven was notified that Hinton had been beaten and jailed, a contingent of Malcolm's Muslims appeared outside the 123rd Street police station. They stood there in formation.

Malcolm entered the building and asked to see Hinton. At first, he was told Hinton wasn't there. Then he was told Hinton was there, but that he couldn't see him. Malcolm replied that until he was allowed to do so, his men would remain where they were, despite a pointed remark by an official that the police could compel them to move.

By this time, other blacks had gathered behind the Muslims. The crowd swelled to hundreds, then thousands. The police realized they had a potential riot on their hands and quickly summoned a number of influential citizens. One of them was James Hicks, editor of the *Amsterdam News*, the city's most prominent black newspaper. Hicks told the police that only one man could manage the crowd and get it to disperse peacefully: Malcolm X.

The authorities therefore asked Hicks, who was on friendly terms with Malcolm, to arrange a meeting at Hicks's office. When Malcolm arrived there, Deputy Police Commissioner Walter Arm, who was white, told him he wanted the demonstrators removed. He said he was telling him, not begging him. Malcolm rose from his chair, donned his coat, and began walking out. Hicks could hear his heels going "clump," "clump" "clump." He followed Malcolm out and urged him to reconsider. Malcolm returned to his seat, his bargaining position much improved. One official asked him what he wanted in return for removing his men. Malcolm said he wanted access to Johnson Hinton to determine for himself whether he needed medical treatment. He was given assurances that, if Hinton did, he'd be transported to a hospital.

At the police station, Malcolm had to curb himself when he saw Hinton, who was practically unconscious. The police had him taken to Harlem Hospital in an ambulance. The crowd followed on foot. People poured out of bars and eating establishments and enlarged its ranks. An immense throng gathered outside the hospital. Fearing a riot, the hospital authorities released Hinton back to the police, who placed him back in jail. The disciplined Muslims, and the undisciplined spectators accompanying them, resumed their vigil outside the station house. The police, who realized that any attempt to break the cordon by force might precipitate a full-scale riot, then asked Malcolm—who had suddenly become not just a follower of Elijah Muhammad, but also a leader in his own right—if he would use his influence to avert violence. Malcolm agreed on condition that Hinton would continue to receive medical care and that the officers who beat him would be punished. After being told that these things would be done, he strode to the door of the police station, silently stood there, and motioned with his arm. The crowd promptly dispersed. The obedience it accorded him prompted one white official to remark that no man should have that much power. What he meant, Hicks later stressed, was that no black man should have that much power.

In an effort to avert violence, Malcolm reportedly decided that his men would not appear en masse at Hinton's arraignment. He appeared himself, with an attorney and bail money. Hinton was released and staggered out of the courthouse. Malcolm's doctor, Leona Turner, examined him and had him admitted to Sydenham Hospital, where doctors discovered that he had a blood clot on the brain, as well as other injuries.

As Hinton battled for his life, his Muslim colleagues paraded peacefully outside Sydenham Hospital. They were joined by others from Boston, Hartford, Baltimore, and Washington. After a while, uninvited teenagers carrying zip guns began fraternizing with the crowd. When Malcolm found out, he dismissed his followers. He explained that his group had no intention of fomenting violence. Later, he'd admit that many of the rank and file felt differently, and that he'd had a hard time keeping the peace.

Hinton survived with the help of a metal plate that was inserted in his skull. An all-white jury eventually awarded him $75,000. At the time, the award, which was later reduced to $70,000, was the largest made for police brutality in the city's history. Once again, Malcolm had rescued a victim from a dangerous adversary. He had walked into the lion's den and clipped its claws. The achievement made him a hero in Harlem and gained him many non-Muslim followers. Temple Seven's membership soared. Most of this was not lost upon the police, who promptly wired the Massachusetts authorities for information about Malcolm.

The press, too, began to seek information about him. A free lance journalist named Charles Wiley called his home. After several minutes of verbal sparring, Wiley, who had somehow obtained Malcolm's unlisted number, realized it was useless to prolong the conversation. But before he could conclude it, Malcolm's civility dropped away, like a mask. Icily, he said, "Goodbye." He paused a couple of seconds, then hissed, "Mr. Lucifer!" The words sent goose pimples up Wiley's back.

TWO MORE BETTYS

32

E lijah Muhammad made Malcolm his National Representative in 1957 and sent him to Los Angeles, where he supervised the rapid growth of that city's Black Muslim temple. Malcolm also spent a great deal of time at the offices of the *Herald-Dispatch*, a leftist newspaper that had forged an editorial and financial alliance with the Nation of Islam and had begun publishing a weekly column by Malcolm entitled "God's Angry Men." While he was there, he learned as much as he could about the newspaper trade. Eventually, he succeeded in founding the Nation of Islam's own newspaper. He was helped by journalist Louis Lomax, whose assistance he occasionally acknowledged. He prepared himself for his newspaper work as diligently as he had prepared himself for boxing, lindying, and debating. His tutor at the *Herald-Dispatch* was a female taskmaster who bossed him around the way his mother and Ella had. Yet he did not complain, not even once. He accorded his boss the same deference he accorded Elijah Muhammad. When she took him to task for the way he paced about the room—a habit he had developed in cramped prison cells—he obediently desisted.

From Los Angeles, Malcolm shuttled back and forth to his New York temple and the other temples he supervised. Periodically, he passed through Michigan and, during one stopover there, he telephoned a young woman he had known before he had entered prison. She recognized his voice instantly, but he seemed surprised that she had remembered it. Later, he visited her and her husband. After he returned to New York, he mailed her a letter asserting how intelligent and "wonderful" her husband (whose name he couldn't clearly recall) was. But the praise was as sarcastic as the praise he had heaped on the staff of Charlestown State Prison; according to people who knew the husband, he was neither intelligent nor wonderful.

Privately, Malcolm criticized his former mentor Lemuel Hassan, whom he had praised so highly in public. As a result, Elijah Muhammad removed Lemuel as minister of the Detroit temple, which was riddled with dissension. Malcolm was made acting minister. Subsequently, Wilfred was appointed minister. Recalling these events years later, Philbert observed that his younger brother practically praised his rivals to death.

But Malcolm didn't praise women. In sermon after sermon, he reproached the members of the opposite sex, whom he blamed for the ills that befell black males. Women, Malcolm claimed, talk too much. Telling a woman not to talk was like telling a hen not to cackle, he asserted.

Malcolm characterized women as "tricky" and "deceitful." He castigated those who came to the temple "half-naked," using body language to attract members of the opposite sex. He even threatened to expel the bickering female members of the Philadelphia temple and replace them with a bunch of prostitutes. Similar remarks at another temple meeting prompted one outraged woman to stand up and walk out. "Look at the sister," Malcolm taunted. "Hair five different shades!"

It was not easy to reconcile Malcolm's harsh remarks about women with his insistence that black men should respect and protect their women, instead of abusing and exploiting them. Some sisters complained about his negative statements to Elijah Muhammad, who taught that, eons ago, when the moon had separated from the earth, only men had existed. Later on, the genitals of the weaker males had involuted. The result was "wo-men," or weak men—creatures who, Malcolm said, were built, sexually and emotionally, to receive, not to give.

Malcolm, who claimed that women couldn't take criticism, assured the female members of the Philadelphia temple that his purpose was not to criticize them, but to emphasize that they should defer to their men instead of trying to rule them. Women who dominate men, he said, destroy them.

The high regard Malcolm outwardly accorded the institution of motherhood, which he characterized as the key to the future, did not extend to individual mothers. "Your own mother will lie to you," he exclaimed. He reiterated the same theme on another occasion and brusquely added, "No wonder our children do not respect their parents." He stressed that bad mothers produce bad children and denounced women who conceive babies out of wedlock. When a New York reporter attempted to question him about his own mother, he snapped, "As long as you live, don't *ever* mention my mother!"

The women of the Nation of Islam took a back seat to the men in return for the illusory security their protected status afforded them. The majority took Malcolm's anti-feminine diatribes in stride; they attributed them to the leadership's desire to bolster the egos of its male followers by repudiating the matriarchal behavior patterns that are prevalent in America's black community. He took full advantage of the opportunity to disparage females. "The closest thing to a devil is a woman," he asserted. One brother mused, "The woman who marries him will have to be an angel."

But Malcolm insisted he was uninterested in marriage. He said he had no time for it, and that he was already married to his work.

It was not an overstatement; he rarely got more than three or four hours of sleep a night. He telephoned people at one or five in the morning. Sometimes, he went without meals and worked around the clock in an effort to accomplish in twenty-four hours what others couldn't accomplish in seventy-two. He was as addicted to work as he had once been addicted to thievery, gambling, and drugs.

But, despite the self-punishment, the differences between his newest addiction and his earlier ones were profound. His drug and gambling habits had been prompted by the child-like illusion that gratification could be achieved effortlessly. His compulsive work habits reflected a willingness to abandon that wishful illusion. Instead of demanding immediate gratification by chemical means—or by grab-it-fast, get-rich-quick schemes—he had learned to defer gratification. Once again, he had transformed youthful weakness into adult strength.

Malcolm's workaholic habits may also have been prompted by anxiety that, if he stopped working for even a minute, success would elude him; the rewards blacks received were seldom commensurate to the amount of toil they expended.

His preoccupation with work precluded any serious romantic involvement. Yet his apparent disinterest in women, which Philbert later attributed to fear of them, did not fool Jarvis, to whom Malcolm had acknowledged his desire for a wife and children. Jarvis sensed that Malcolm was less interested in marrying, per se, than in fathering sons who could carry on his work after his death. He told Jarvis he would name them after Attillah the Hun and Qubilah Qhan.

Malcolm's indifferent facade was also hard to reconcile with the way he cited St. Paul's assertion that though it is best to remain single, "it is better to marry than to burn" for adultery or fornication. "Malcolm wanted to get married," a Muslim associate later told an interviewer. The man apparently knew what he was talking about, for, some time during the latter part of 1957, Malcolm asked the man's sister, who spelled her named "Bettye," to marry him. Bettye—a worthy successor to Betty Jean Thiel, Betty Girven, and Betty Kennedy—stood straight as an arrow, with the regal bearing befitting an African princess. Her elegant taste in clothes, which enhanced her stunning appearance, prompted more than one of her numerous suitors to observe that it would be less expensive to feed her than to clothe her. The keenness of her mind was apparent from the way she spoke and from the alertness of her lovely, fetching eyes. Lesser men feared her intelligence. But Malcolm didn't.

With a gallantry that may have been prompted by expectation of rejection, Malcolm did not insist on an immediate answer to his proposal; he gave Bettye time to think it over. Then, on October 30, 1957—one of Bettye's brothers thinks it was while Malcolm was awaiting her decision—Malcolm was hospitalized with what he described as a heart attack. He later told Philbert that his heart felt as if it were fluttering. Yet, according to the hospital record, the doctor found nothing wrong with his heart. (The record does mention inflammation in the rib area.)

Days later, Ella, who sometimes complained of heart trouble herself, was hospitalized with what she characterized as a heart attack. (She underwent surgery for something else.) Her illness kept her out of jail, for she had been convicted of assaulting a female friend of her third husband, with whom she was no longer living. The attack followed a similar one against her husband himself, who was hospitalized with eight stitches in his head. She bludgeoned him with a heavy object as he bent to assist a crippled boy who had apparently fallen down when she had given him a prearranged signal. Like young Malcolm, the youth had been entrusted to her care. Ella, who was also convicted for assualting her husband, appealed both convictions. Her husband, Ken Collins, decided not to contest the appeal; later, he explained that he feared that their son Rodnell would have no home if she went to jail. When Collins's friend learned that Ella had been hospitalized, supposedly for a heart ailment, she, too, agreed not to challenge the appeal.

Nevertheless, Ella felt so ill that she did not expect to survive. When Malcolm, who had been discharged from the hospital, found out, he told her it was imperative to find Rodnell another home. He asked if Ella would let Wilfred raise Rodnell if her strength failed. Ella demurred. She said Wilfred would be too "easy" on her son, who cringed when she browbeat him in public. Like Malcolm, he later rebelled against authority and accumulated quite a criminal record.

Despite Malcolm's subsequent insistence that he was the kind of person who would marry only if he wanted to, Ella says he told her, "Well, I guess I'm going to have to get married." He'd marry out of obligation, just as he had threatened to marry Jackie Massie. Ella says he told her, "I can always get a divorce if you get well."

How long Malcolm waited for Bettye to respond to his marriage proposal is unclear. He told Ella about another sister he knew. Her name was Betty Sanders. She was tall. Her skin was dark and she had brown eyes—attributes that were prerequisites for any political leader who wanted to avoid accusations that he had been partial to light-skinned women. She was attractive, though not as slender as Gloria, Heather, Bettye, or the other women he had pursued so ambivalently. Professionally, she outclassed most of the women in the Nation of Islam. She had attended college and was about to embark on a career in nursing, one of the few professions that were then open to blacks. Compared to other black women, nurses earned decent salaries. If anything happened to their husbands, they could always earn enough to support their children. Medically speaking, they made good wives for men who had bad hearts, or who thought they did.

Malcolm made such an impression on Betty Sanders the first time she saw him walk onto the speaker's platform that she sat bolt upright in her chair. She later acknowledged that she wasn't sure if it was his air of authority. (Her reaction, she explained, was "somewhat akin to respect, or maybe even fear.") She was not the only woman who was impressed with the strength Malcolm exuded. To numerous female members of the Nation of Islam—particularly those who were intent on acquiring a hardworking, responsible husband—the tall, lean, muscular celibate whose attractiveness seemed to increase with age was an inviting challenge. He was the movement's most eligible bachelor.

Though Malcolm had known Betty (who had done some typing for him) for some time, he had given no indication that he regarded her as a prospective spouse. Then, out of the blue, he offered to take her to the Museum of Natural History. He said he wanted to show her some exhibits corroborating Elijah Muhammad's teachings on evolution, which included the novel thesis that pigs were giant rodents. Malcolm stressed that the purpose of the visit to the museum was solely to help Betty explain the Messenger's teachings to the students she taught at Temple Seven.

But the day of the trip to the museum, Malcolm called Betty and said he was too busy to go. "Well, you sure waited long enough to tell me," Betty retorted. Her polite but pointed response apparently impressed Malcolm, who suddenly found time to keep the date. At the museum, he plied Betty with various questions. Eventually, he apologetically began venturing personal questions—the kind Reginald had long ago learned not to ask him. Betty, who began to sense that Malcolm was interested in her, repeatedly reassured him that she knew his interest was purely brotherly.

One indication of Malcolm's evolving intent was the way he reacted when Betty told him, in jest, that she had been married before. The look he gave her etched itself in her memory. When she assured him that she had only been spoofing, he brusquely replied, "That is something you never kid about."

She sensed he was afraid of marriage. He described how his parents had constantly been at odds. He said it would be difficult for him to have to account to a woman for his whereabouts.

Malcolm, who had received no response from Bettye, became so alarmed about what he was contemplating that he began avoiding Betty Sanders. When she came into Temple Seven's restaurant, where they had been having dinner together nearly every Sunday, he found ways to occupy himself elsewhere. But he kept weighing the advantages of marrying someone like Betty—"although it could be any sister in any temple," he would later acknowledge. She was the right height. Moreover, she had few relatives—that was "one good thing," Malcolm later asserted. "My feeling about in-laws was that they were outlaws," he added.

Betty also appeared to be the right age, for Elijah Muhammad taught that the ideal age for a bride was half the groom's age plus seven. Malcolm, at the time, was thirty-two. According to Muhammad's formula, Malcolm's bride should have been twenty-three, the age that later appeared on their marriage certificate. But the inconsistent birth dates that subsequently appeared—not only in published interviews and biographical sketches but also in signed documents—made it unclear whether she really was twenty-three when they married.

Betty's list of the things she and Malcolm had in common was not long; the only thing she could later think of was the fact they had both come from Michigan. "That was about it," she said.

Betty, who seemed reluctant to talk about the past, didn't tell Malcolm that her foster parents had threatened to stop financing her education when they learned that she preferred the Nation of Islam's rigorous discipline to theirs. Nor did he reveal himself to her. "I think Malcolm was a very happy child until he was six," she later told the Chicago *Daily News*.

Though Malcolm and Betty talked about marriage, they "never really courted." They were "just friends," she later explained. Malcolm didn't utter a single word of endearment to her. He seemed afraid she would reject him, as he apparently believed Bettye had done:

> I studied about if I just *should* happen to say something to her—what would her position be? Because she wasn't going to get any chance to embarrass me!

He said he'd had "too much experience" with women to risk such humiliation again. He said nothing about his proposal to Bettye. His autobiography is as silent about her as it is about Gloria and Heather.

Malcolm never did get back in touch with Bettye. Instead, shortly after New Year's, he hopped into his car and drove all the way from New York to Michigan, ostensibly to visit Wilfred, the titular head of the family. The date was January 12, 1958—the twelfth anniversary of the self-induced Boston arrest that had resulted in his imprisonment.

The following morning, after Malcolm arrived in Detroit, he called New York City information and asked for the number of the nursing school residence where Betty lived. He had made a point of not memorizing her phone number, even though he had committed "most numbers" to memory.

Malcolm phoned Betty, who said, "Hello, Brother Minister. . . . " Apparently, that was all she had a chance to say. "Look," Malcolm blurted, "Do you want to get married?" He later attributed his long-distance proposal to his aversion to the "romance stuff" that Hollywood incessantly fed its customers. But his former fondness for Hollywood movies and his assertions about love suggested that he secretly craved the romance he outwardly disparaged.

Betty recovered sufficiently to reply affirmatively—"just like I knew she would," Malcolm later boasted, despite his fear of rejection. He instructed her to catch a plane to Michigan because he "didn't have a whole lot time." He asked Wilfred where he could get married "without a whole lot of mess and waiting." Wilfred suggested that he try Indiana.

Betty flew to Detroit and introduced Malcolm to her foster parents. The following morning, he took her to the nearest town in Indiana, which was more than a hundred miles away. But when they got there, they discovered that Indiana's short waiting period had just been lengthened.

Undeterred, Malcolm drove eighty miles or more to Lansing, where he introduced Betty to Philbert's family. He learned that he and Betty could get married that day if they hurried. Within hours, he had obtained the marriage license and had rushed his bride to the office of a justice of the peace. Not one member of his family attended the ceremony, not even a friend.

"Kiss your bride!" the magistrate declared. Malcolm whisked her out. "All of that Hollywood stuff," he later grumbled.

Not long after the wedding, Malcolm unexpectedly encountered one of Bettye's brothers, who told him that his sister, who had been waiting for Malcolm to recontact her, had been looking forward to marrying him. "I didn't know," Malcolm gasped. He broke down and cried. Years later, in his autobiography, he acknowledged that he wasn't in love with his wife when he married her. She did too. "I guess he got lonely," she told a Look reporter.

INTO THE LIMELIGHT   33

B y early 1959, Malcolm was addressing standing-room-only audiences—African-American ones. But an event occurred in July of that year that brought the Black Muslim movement to the attention of white America. It was a television documentary about the movement. The documentary was called *The Hate That Hate Produced*, a title suggesting that black racism is simply a reaction to white racism.

The program, edited for maximum dramatic effect, sent shock waves throughout New York City. One reason was Malcolm's acknowledgment that Elijah Muhammad taught that the serpent in the Garden of Eden was not a snake, but a symbol for the white man. The thing that really frightened white viewers was the footage about the University of Islam—the elementary school the Nation ran in Chicago—where black pupils were taught, from kindergarten on, that whites were devils.

Press reaction was withering. Temple Seven was inundated with angry demands for explanation from news commentators and correspondents from Boston to Tucson. Malcolm lashed back:

> For the white man to ask the black man if he hates him is just like the rapist asking the *raped*—or the wolf asking the *sheep*—"Do you hate me?"

The media spillover caused by the controversial documentary was enormous. Mass circulation weeklies such as *Life*, *Time*, and *Newsweek* began reporting on the Black Muslim movement. A Harlem radio station invited Malcolm to conduct a weekly talk show. Within four years, three books about the Black Muslims were published.

Reporters besieged Malcolm. Their newspapers, which he read assiduously, provided the publicity that quickly propelled him to center stage. Malcolm, who complained that spokesmen for black nationalist groups practically had to "bite their way into print," cultivated the press like an experienced politician. Periodically, he dropped in to see one of the editors at the *Afro-American*, as well as key journalists, whose daily or weekly publication deadlines he had committed to memory. "The reporters . . . were looking for sensationalism—for something that would sell papers. And I gave it to them." On one occasion, he told them, "I rejoice when a white man dies!"

Yet, offstage, Malcolm was courteous to whites. During his first face-to-face meeting with Charles Wiley—the writer he had called "Mr. Lucifer" over the phone—the two got along famously, even though Wiley was a militant, conservative Republican who later directed a movement that put 30,000 white mothers in front of New York City Hall to protest plans to bus black students to white schools. New York *Daily News* reporter Jack Mallon, who was also white, marveled at the cordial way Malcolm greeted white newsmen right after he had delivered a blistering attack upon whites. Malcolm did not tell them he had once toyed with the idea of becoming a Hollywood actor.

Malcolm complained about the "bad" publicity he received; more than once, he accused reporters—"pencil-scratchers," he called them—of misquoting him. Yet he thrived on his fiend-like reputation. He pilloried the press for creating the very image he wanted them to create. His strategy—which Wilfred would later describe as "call me whatever you want, just as long as you keep printing my name"—enabled Malcolm to manipulate his journalistic pursuers so well that they accorded him the political exposure he might otherwise not have received. White America didn't know it yet, but it was dealing with an extraordinarily gifted man.

His oratorical prowess, which surpassed his father's, was partly due to the way he had appropriated and adapted some of the oratorical techniques of Billy Graham, who had been catapulted to national prominence by the mass media. Graham, who was also known for his flawless diction and his pointing, accusatory forefinger, did not read his speeches; except for occasional glances at his notes, his eyes remained fixed on his audience. Likewise, Malcolm, who watched the members of his audiences like a hawk for their reactions, mesmerized his listeners. He knew just how to involve them in his sermons:

> Malcolm: When I say the white man is a devil, I speak with the authority of history.
>
> Audience: That's right!
>
> Malcolm: The record of history shows that the white men, as a people, have never done good.
>
> Audience: Say on, brother, say on.

> Malcolm: He stole our fathers and mothers from their culture of silk and satins and brought them to this land in the belly of a ship—am I right or wrong?
>
> Audience: You are right. God knows you are right.
>
> Malcolm: He brought us here in chains—right?
>
> Audience: Right.
>
> Malcolm: He has kept us in chains ever since we have been here.
>
> Audience: Preach on, Brother Minister, preach on.
>
> Malcolm: Now this blue-eyed devil's time has about run out.

His audience leaped to its feet. There was no longer any reason for him to fear he was a bore.

Malcolm also studied the writings of the Roman orator Cicero, who had emphasized that it is best to sway people by appealing to their emotions, not their intellect. Like Cicero, he used humor to entertain his audiences. Referring to Congolese rebels who had taken white hostages in an effort to deter white pilots from bombing rebel-controlled villages, he quipped:

> [The rebels] weren't keeping [the] . . . hostages because they were cannibals. Or because they thought their flesh was tasty. Some of those [white] missionaries had been over there for forty years and didn't get eaten up. [Audience laughs and applauds.] If they were going to eat them, they would have eaten them when they were young and tender. [Laughter erupts.]

Like Cicero, Malcolm ridiculed his political opponents with his humor, as the proponents of political nonviolence subsequently discovered:

> It's like when you go to the dentist and the man's going to take your tooth. You're going to fight him when he starts pulling. So they squirt some stuff in your jaw called novocaine to make you think they're not doing anything to you. So you sit there. And because you've got all the novocaine in your jaw, you suffer—peacefully. [Audience laughs.] Blood running all down your jaw.

He used Ciceroian irony with equal effectiveness: "I'm not [criticizing the NAACP] . . . . I'm just, uhm, analyzing it." [Audience laughs.] He excelled in the art of political metaphor:

> In the South, they've outright political wolves. In the North, they're political foxes. A fox and a wolf are both canine. Both belong to the dog family. [Audience applauds and cheers.]

Malcolm, who characterized whites as "reptiles" and made fun of their "stringy, dog-like hair," was equally adept at using animal metaphors to counter the charge that he was fomenting hatred. A person who shoots rattlesnakes because a snake bit his daughter shouldn't be accused of hatred, he said. He used another Aesop-like metaphor to mollify a group of Iranian Muslims who had been barred from one of Elijah Muhammad's mosques because of their white skin:

> Let's look at it this way. If a lion is in a cage, his roar will be different from the roar of the lion who is in the forest. That is why you couldn't get in our temple. But both the lion in the forest and the lion in the cage are lions. That is what matters. Lions love lions; they hate leopards.

Now and then, Malcolm would throw back his head and laugh heartily about his entertaining exaggerations, which included the assertion that Khruschev's Russia was merely a satellite of white America. He accused the U.S. of racial "genocide" and said that, racially, there was no difference between New York State and Mississippi. But after he made the assertion over the air, he told his exasperated debating opponent, with a mischievous smile, "Look, you'll never get me to admit there's a difference between New York and Mississippi until we've won our revolution."

Malcolm acknowledged the importance of adapting one's oratory to each set of listeners. Using what he called his "psychic radar," he felt out each audience and fashioned his presentation accordingly. He told prospective converts that Islam was the black man's religion. But he emphatically denied it when he spoke at Michigan State University. He told Elijah Muhammad's followers they were "the descendants of the moon people." The performance of black athletes on U.S. olympic teams demonstrated their superiority, he asserted. He told one group of listeners, "You are better than the white man. . . . Your skin look[s] like gold beside his." He said that blacks were superior in combat: "You just give me ten black ones and we'll eat up fifty of those white ones. Eat them up!"

"The black man will be the dominant man," Malcolm predicted. He intimated that America's whites would one day be the slaves instead of the slavemasters.

Black preachers should be killed and their churches should be burned if they failed to preach black supremacy, Malcolm told the members of Temple Seven. He said that when the showdown between blacks and whites finally came, even the children of the white oppressors would have to be liquidated. Sometimes, he grew so livid that the blackboard, which he used to great advantage when he lectured, went sailing.

Not all of his statements about racial violence, which were prudently couched in terms of the future, countenanced bloodshed. For instance, he told a group of New York Muslims to refrain from violence because the white man would destroy himself. Yet the overall tone of the speeches Malcolm made in Elijah Muhammad's temples was far more belligerent than those he made to educated audiences. At Queens College and Michigan State, he was a model of civility. At Yale, he was sweet reasonability itself. He was equally unpugnacious at Boston University—at least until the end of his prepared remarks. During the ensuing question-and-answer session, his restraint began to fade. At one point, he started pounding the speaker's podium. Afterwards, he begged the audience to forgive him for raising his voice.

A number of B.U. professors were awed by Malcolm's ability to quote lengthy passages of biblical and quranic scripture—a talent he shared with Philbert. Yet, at one point, his supple mind appeared to freeze; he seemed to have difficulty coping with a number of questions from the floor. There were other indications that he felt ill at ease among the educated, whose degrees he alternately praised and ridiculed. At a University of Southern California banquet for Ralph Bunche, for example, he excused himself before dinner and went home. At another, similar function, the woman who had coached him at the *Herald-Dispatch* practically had to hold his hand. He was also visibly nervous the first time he spoke at Harvard Law School. He made derogatory remarks about himself and his lack of formal education, which he later characterized as his greatest shortcoming. His unease, which was unwarranted in view of how he had educated himself, poignantly attested to the way people erroneously equate college degrees with intellectual achievement. When Malcolm was asked what his alma mater was, he replied, "Books!" He always carried reading material in his briefcase. Sometimes he waded through two entire books in a single sleepless night.

With time, Malolm learned to conquer the nervousness he displayed before some of his public appearances. As a teacher, he outperformed most of those who had taught him. He freely acknowledged how much he relished his new professorial role. (He looked like a university professor.) He often lectured his pupils—Malcolm rarely let them forget that's what they were—so hard that he became hoarse. His shirt would become so saturated with perspiration that he'd have to replace it with the spare he carried in his briefcase.

He studied the debating techniques of the lawyers on the Perry Mason-type television shows. Before long, he had become a master of the loaded question and the unresponsive stock answer. He'd parry difficult questions with equally difficult ones of his own. When he was asked whether the Nation of Islam supported the U.S. government, he replied, "Does the government support and protect us?" He became adept at putting his adversaries on the defensive: "We contend that the white man is a devil. If he is not a devil, let him prove it." If someone accused him of inciting blacks to violence, he'd reply that it was a miracle America's blacks hadn't resorted to bloodshed yet.

As he had done in prison, Malcolm prepared for his debates by pretending he was his opponent and by arguing the opposing position as vigorously as possible. In an effort to save time, he sometimes rehearsed his arguments while he was driving his car. At home, he reviewed radio and television playbacks of his speeches. If, despite his preparation, nothing else worked, he'd interrupt his opponent in mid-sentence or simply outtalk him.

Malcolm described debates as battles fought with verbal bullets. His adversaries learned not to debate him.

Malcolm's ability to speak the language of the college campus and the ghetto street corner equally well enabled him to appeal to the educated and the illiterate. His popularity was enhanced by the way he tailored his speeches to each audience, as he had done in Lansing and Mason when he was young. In the Nation of Islam's temples, where Elijah's ministers tape-recorded their sermons and sent them to him, Malcolm spoke in terms of devils and gods. At institutions of higher learning, he talked in terms of the oppressed and their oppressors. Later on, when he began addressing leftist groups, he emphasized the struggle between imperialists and their colonized subjects. Before church groups, he played down Islam; before nonreligious audiences, he played up economic and other secular issues. And on Harlem street corners, he described whites as people who smelled bad.

Like an actor, Malcolm switched roles so skillfully that at least one associate became convinced that he was uninterested in the limelight that was increasingly his. He was impatient with long-winded, flowery introductions. At times, he'd interrupt applauding audiences with a wave of the hand. Or he'd shake his head negatively and exclaim, "Cut that out" or "I don't want to hear that." But others sensed that he enjoyed the adulation and the popping flash bulbs. He collected press clippings about himself. When he passed through Lansing, he'd show them to former cronies and ask, "Did you see this?" The enjoyment he got watching himself perform on television was quite apparent. No longer did he have to lurk on the edges of the crowd, a lonely, forgotten youngster.

Malcolm wasn't exaggerating when he said the Nation of Islam afforded him "every gratification." He was its foremost preacher and teacher, as well as its finest orator. And for the first time in his life, he had a real sense of purpose. He devoted himself to his Black Muslim brothers and sisters with a fervor he had never been able to muster for his biological ones. Malcolm depicted them as members of a big, happy family whose "permanent lodgers" dwelled in harmony in the "House of Allah." The image was a far cry from the divided, unhappy home in which he had been raised.

The Nation enabled Malcolm to achieve the success his parents and Ella had demanded of him. The youth who had dreamed of becoming a great lawyer had become an advocate for an entire people. The youngster who had been unable to protect himself was now the manly protector of an entire flock.

FEAR TRANSFORMED

34

Malcolm's wit—he characterized it as mother-wit—was a potent political weapon. He twitted his black integrationist foes for allegedly endeavoring "to sit down next to white folks on the toilet." He lampooned the Peace Corps as a device for gobbling up pieces of the countries it was supposed to help. His ability to entertain the very whites he pilloried was one of the reasons he eventually became the most sought-after speaker on the college lecture circuit besides Barry Goldwater.

Malcolm poked fun at powerful political figures the same way he had poked fun at authority figures at Pleasant Grove School. Some of his victims were completely unnerved by his scornful grin. His repertory included a host of different smiles: the ingratiating one for reporters, the stiff-lipped one for photographers, the condescending one for debating opponents. There was also the bittersweet smile that concealed the sadness and pain. And the forced television smile which, Jarvis sensed, cloaked seething anger. "Every time I smile," Malcolm told one colleague in a moment of unaccustomed self-revelation, "it doesn't mean I am happy."

The anger showed through in various ways. One could hear it in his voice. His eyes flashed; his face grew taut. The veins bulged on his neck and forehead. His face flushed, making him look even redder than usual. Even the back of his ears turned crimson.

Though he described himself as the angriest Negro in America, he repeatedly denied that he was animated by hatred:

> I don't have hate in me. I have no hate at all. I don't have any hate.

At times, however, he did acknowledge the hate. Some of the admissions were inadvertent; others were quite explicit. He told Associated Press reporter Jules Loh that the hatred had begun before he was born. On occasion, he even acknowledged that hatred was taught at Temple Seven.

He told the members of his congregation they should hate whites. On another occasion, he asserted that Elijah Muhammad's version of Islam was "not all hate."

Malcolm said he made it a cardinal rule never to let his anger get out of hand. People who knew him described him as a man of total control. Yet Malcolm portrayed himself as a man who wanted to break free of control: "You and I don't want anybody to keep us from getting out of control. We want to get out of control."

"Hostility is good!" he exclaimed. "It's been bottled up too long." Outwardly, he was talking about the political tactics African-Americans should employ. But he was also talking about himself.

His ability to identify with his followers and to articulate their anger was central to his charisma. His stature in Harlem was also due to the way he portrayed himself as a child of the ghetto, despite his semi-rural, small-town upbringing and the comfortable lodgings Ella had provided him with in Boston. He incorrectly asserted that the racially mixed neighborhood he lived in was all black. He also claimed that he was living in Harlem, even though he had lived in the section of Queens called East Elmhurst ever since he had come to New York to take command of Temple Seven. A number of his middle-class black neighbors were upset about the fact that he was living near them. Perhaps it was due to the way he made "respectable" blacks uncomfortable by urging them to acknowledge their negative feelings toward whites.

The way he sometimes exaggerated his youthful criminality also contributed to his ghetto following. His appeal was not merely what he had allegedly been, but also what he had become—a man who had risen from the gutter and who wouldn't hold the sins of those who hadn't against them.

Malcolm's virile, fearless demeanor enhanced his stature still further. "I'm the man you think you are!" he boasted to his male followers, for whom he had become a living, breathing symbol of masculinity. For it was Malcolm who stood up to the white establishment and bluntly said what American blacks had been whispering for centuries. It was he who helped them shed their fear and who made their white oppressors fear instead. Outwardly, he seemed unafraid of the death he had apparently dreaded when he was young; his willingness to die for his followers was another part of his charisma. His ability to transform his fear into political fearlessness attested to the skill with which he waged private battles on public battlefields.

Unlike Martin Luther King, Jr., who was determined to "love" the supporters of white supremacy until they yielded, Malcolm harnessed his anger and that of his followers with devastating effectiveness. King was a product of the seminary, not the penitentiary. Even the vocabulary of the two men—one tall and lean, the other short and stocky—reflected their different backgrounds. Malcolm's was earthy and unpretentious; King, by his own admission, was fond of big words. But King's penchant for lofty phrases did not diminish his moving, eloquent appeals for racial brotherhood, which were so unlike Malcolm's machine-gun-like, unbrotherly outbursts. Whereas Malcolm gave his followers leave to express their hatred of their hateful oppressors, King gave his followers the courage to confront them. Eventually, King's "forgive them, they know not what they do" approach would prove more effective politically. But Malcolm's unforgiving, accusatory approach afforded his followers release. It also made King look so "moderate" that many white Americans would eventually embrace him as the lesser of two evils.

The similarities between Malcolm and King were as noteworthy as the differences. Initially, both men followed in the footsteps of their success-oriented, tyrannical fathers, whom they finally eclipsed by rebelling against more powerful tyrants. Both talked incessantly about impending death. (King, whose heroes included Socrates, Jesus, and Gandhi, said he was worried that people would think he was seeking martyrdom.) Both exhibited the drive and keenness of mind that refuted the myth that blacks were lazy and uneducable. Both men exuded moral authority and roused white America's sleeping conscience. Malcolm was apparently so successful at one Ivy League college that one white student cried out and jumped from the balcony during his speech. Malcolm, who omitted the jarring incident from his autobiography, nevertheless kept "telling the truth" about the white man:

> The white man's afraid of truth . . . . Truth takes [away] . . . all his breath. Truth makes him lose all his strength. Just tell him a little truth his face gets all red. Watch him! Yes, yes, yes!

But though he told the truth about white tyranny, he couldn't tell the truth about the tyrants who had raised him. Some things, he told a colleague, are better left unsaid.

Chiefly due to Malcolm, the Nation of Islam, by the late 1950s and early 1960s, had developed many of the attributes of a mass movement—one that enabled its members to lose themselves in the pack and adopt a new, exhilarating corporate sense of identity. No longer were they isolated, helpless human particles, adrift on a lonely sea. The sense of communal strength produced by their union helped to offset whatever feelings of weakness they privately harbored. The security such union afforded apparently outweighed the loss of liberty that individual members sustained when they subjected themselves to Elijah Muhammad's authority. After all, what good was liberty to those who, because of their skin color, had been rendered impotent, politically and otherwise? Elijah's appeal attested to the fact that many victims of oppression outwardly crave freedom but inwardly fear it. The descendants of slaves who flocked to his banner did so partly because the freedom he promised was purely illusory, as events were to demonstrate.

The rallies the Nation periodically held in auditoriums like the Chicago Coliseum were immense, pageant-like affairs. The attendance figures, which sometimes exceeded 10,000, were somewhat misleading, for virtually the entire membership of each temple was obliged, or strongly prodded, to attend. On occasion, Malcolm used similar techniques to pack individual temples. Large turnouts, he explained, were necessary to convince potential members that the movement was dynamic and growing.

The rallies, the inspiration for which had reportedly been Malcolm's, succeeded in creating the desired impression. By automobile and chartered bus, the faithful traveled to the appointed city. Affixed to the busses were colorful banners that advertised the forthcoming proceedings to countless numbers of passing motorists and pedestrians. The lengthy lines that formed outside the meeting hall were kept in order by no-nonsense, grim-faced Muslim ushers, some of whom carried walkie-talkies. Inside, each man, woman, and child who entered was searched by Muslim security officials. (By agreement, the local police kept their uniformed officers outside the auditorium and left the frisking to Mr. Muhammad's followers.) Each person was required to remove everything from his or her pockets. Belts were loosened to determine if they concealed tiny weapons. Ball-point pens were tested to ascertain if they were miniature guns. Nail files were temporarily sequestered on grounds that they could be used as weapons. Women who carried square mirrors in their compacts had to relinquish them. Round mirrors were permitted because they did not have sharp corners. Similar precautions customarily prevailed in each Black Muslim temple.

Those who weathered the search were promptly confronted by believers who were soliciting money: "Help the cause, brother. Contribute at least one dollar. At least!"

During the rally—which was advertised as free—gallon-sized buckets were passed around the hall. As quickly as they were filled with cash, they were emptied and passed up and down the aisles again. Officials such as John 4X, the movement's National Secretary, repeatedly exhorted the faithful to contribute once more: "This is for ourselves. Let's everybody go into our pockets." During one Chicago rally, John pointed to two television cameramen and told the assembled Muslims, "You see, they're using electricity we paid for." Then he addressed the television crew and the other reporters and said:

> You have been exploiting us long enough. If you want to hear, you
> have to give. Otherwise, you'll have to get out of here . . . We'll take
> your equipment out.

Minutes later, two assistants brought a suitcase full of money to the speaker's podium. John dipped a hand into it and exclaimed, "We haven't got enough yet!" He directed his men to pass the buckets again. Malcolm came to his aid and declared, "Dig down into your socks!" The buckets were passed six times that afternoon. According to Malcolm, the sums collected on such occasions "always" equalled or exceeded the rally expenses.

Usually, Malcolm was the one who warmed up the audience for Elijah Muhammad and introduced him. The Messenger was escorted onstage by a phalanx of stiff-legged, marching bodyguards whose military bearing lent credence to the erroneous belief that the Fruit of Islam was a paramilitary force. "*As salaam alaikum* [peace be with you]," Muhammad declared. "*Wa alaikum as salaam* [and unto you peace]," the audience roared back. On occasion, Mr. Muhammad described how he had been "missioned" by Allah to lead America's blacks to a land of deliverance:

> I stand before you as a man who has been chosen for you by God
> himself. I did not choose myself. This must be made clear . . . . I was
> in the presence of God for over three years and I received what I am
> teaching you directly from His mouth.

Having buttressed his position by this appeal to authority, Mr. Muhammad (who told some associates that he had never gone beyond the fifth grade, and others that he had never gone beyond the third or fourth) assured his followers that he would raise them up from the "grave of ignorance" the easy way. They would not have to study or think. Nor would they have to read. (Members were discouraged from reading anything but the Nation's newspaper, *Muhammad Speaks*, and the Messenger's "books," which they had to pay for.) "All you have to do is listen to what I say," Muhammad declared. "I have the ABSOLUTE CURE for all your problems and ailments."

The Messenger, who also claimed that Islam had originated in Africa, made innumerable other pronouncements that might have taxed the credulity of those with less faith:

> According to the word of Allah to me, one of our wise black scientists
> [Yacub] was upset over the dialect the people were speaking, and he

wanted to change the language and make all of the people speak the same dialect . . . . When he saw that he could not accomplish what he wanted, he drilled a huge shaft into this planet for about four or five thousand miles deep, and, filling that hole with high explosives, he set it off with the intention of destroying all civilization . . . . That part of the planet which we call "moon" today was blasted 12,000 miles from its original pocket . . . . [The] part that we call "earth" today dropped 36,000 miles, . . . and found another pocket and started rotating again (it all happened in the twinkling of an eye) . . . . [The] part (moon) that was blasted away dropped all of its water upon this part (earth), and this is why three-fourths of the earth's surface today is covered by water.

Muhammad's followers did not seem perturbed by such assertions, nor did they appear troubled by his grammatical errors. "History don't care anything about your degrees!" he told the college graduates in one audience. His barely literate, often incomprehensible rhetoric contrasted vividly with the eloquence of the youthful orator who had rescued him from historical oblivion. Indeed, Malcolm's oratorical prowess made him virtually indispensable to Elijah Muhammad. At times, he likened himself to the biblical Aaron, who had been Moses's spokesman during his confrontations with the ruling establishment.

Initially, white people were barred from the Nation of Islam's rallies. Later, the policy was changed to allow white reporters, then other whites, entry. They were seated in a separate section of the hall and well guarded by alert marshals, a few of whom looked as if they were hoping one of their light-colored visitors would make a false move. At one rally, the white spectators watched in awe as thousands of Black Muslims stood and cheered as Elijah Muhammad was escorted to the speakers' platform by his forbidding-looking honor guard. Other black members of the audience followed suit. As the applause intensified, more and more people joined in until every black in the huge, jam-packed Philadelphia Arena was standing and clapping. The whites, who suddenly understood what it felt like to be a helpless minority, apparently didn't know what to do. Hesitantly, a number of them rose. Others followed their example. Soon, it was impossible to detect a single white who wasn't standing and applauding the Messenger, who proceeded to flay the "white devils" in the audience for the next three hours.

MARITAL MARTYR   35

The Nation of Islam's Garvey-like call for a separate state—either in Africa or some fenced-off portion of the United States—was unfathomable to most whites. Yet for many American blacks, the separatist argument had the same validity that arguments for independence had had for white Americans back in 1776.

Malcolm's gift for political metaphor reinforced his reputation as the preeminent spokesman for black separatism. Comparing the racial situation in the U.S. to a four hundred [sic] year-old marriage, he said, "We can't get along, so let's be intelligent and get a divorce." Uncle Sam, he declared, had a black lump inside his white body. The cancer-like growth was increasing in size and causing internal pain. If it wasn't removed, it would cause Uncle Sam's death. The surgery would be painful, Malcolm admitted. But failure to excise the racial tumor would prove far worse, he argued.

Again and again, Malcolm compared the independence he was advocating to a grown child's independence from its parents:

> The Negro here in America has been treated like a child. A child stays within the mother until the time of birth. When the time of birth arrives, the child must be separated.

Repeatedly, he warned that if the mother refused to relinquish the child in time, "the doctors" would have to separate it from her forcibly. He paused and added that such measures sometimes precipitated the mother's death.

Malcolm argued so cogently for the separatist position that Martin Luther King, Jr., dean of the integrationist forces, evidently felt constrained to attack his arguments head-on. "We are here in America," he said, " and we are home to stay . . . . We aren't going nowhere."

But Malcolm insisted that blacks were wasting their time trying to integrate. "I know from personal experience," he would subsequently explain in his autobiography, which described his fruitless efforts to achieve acceptance in Mason, Michigan. "I tried hard enough." He told one audience:

> You can't please the white man . . . . You just can't please him. You can't satisfy him. Why, you're out of your mind trying to make love to a white man.

He vigorously disputed the charge that Elijah Muhammad's separatism was a kind of *apartheid*. The latter, he pointed out, was involuntary, compulsory segregation, as opposed to the voluntary separation that the Nation of Islam envisaged.

The inevitable result of racial integration, Malcolm maintained, was intermarriage and interbreeding, which would end up destroying the alleged purity of both races. He expressed pity for the children of interracial unions, whom he characterized as racial freaks.

Malcolm condemned interracial sex and insisted that blacks had no interest in having sex with whites:

> We don't want to be around that old pale thing. We don't want to integrate with that old pale thing. We don't want to sleep next to that old pale thing. No, we can do without him.

He smiled as he said "him," not "her."

Having avoided jail, Ella recovered her health. She even joined the Nation of Islam.

In Boston one day, Malcolm visited his half-sister, who later told an interviewer that, as she and Malcolm were talking, he began laughing. "What are you laughing about?" Ella asked. "It's no joking matter," replied Malcolm. "I'm a married man now."

Yet despite such utterances and despite the fact that Rodnell had a place to live, Malcolm stayed married. He told one associate that Elijah Muhammad had prodded him to get married. But he later acknowledged that Mr. Muhammad had encouraged him to stay single, presumably so that he could devote more time to the movement.

Unlike his father, Malcolm didn't beat his wife. But he was a domineering husband. The strictures he imposed upon Betty, who later characterized their impact as "traumatic," were consistent with those to which she had been conditioned by a lifetime of parental, pedagogical, and "Islamic" discipline. In public, she deferred to him and let him speak for her. Sometimes, she called him "Daddy." (He called her "Girl.")

Malcolm took Betty out to dinner once a week, at least when he was in town. But, perhaps because the Nation of Islam maintained that a woman's place was in the home, he never took her traveling with him. Though they were married for seven years, he took her to only one movie.

Malcolm could have given Betty, who had been raised by a real-estate-owning family that had hired help and two cars, more spending money. He readily acknowledged that he had virtually unlimited access to the ever-expanding Muslim treasury, which paid not only his travel expenses, but also some of his other expenses, including the cost of his home and car. Yet he kept both his expenditures and his salary to a minimum. The $150 he drew each week did not enable him to salt away any nest egg for his rapidly growing family.

He was similarly frugal about his travel expenses. Instead of taking cabs to and from the airport, he called fellow Muslims and asked them for rides. Usually, he avoided expensive restaurants. He made sure that the checks he received for lectures were made out to the Nation rather than to himself. The cash he collected each Sunday at the temple was taken to the post office early each Monday morning, where it was converted into a money order and forwarded to Chicago. He warned about leaders who took advantage of their position, often at the instigation of their wives. Apparently, he tried so hard to convince people that he had relinquished his youthful acquisitive ways that he refused to put his house in his own name, even though Elijah repeatedly urged him to do so. "No, sir, dear Holy Apostle," Malcolm replied. "If anything ever happens to me, I know that the Nation will take care of my family." They were words he would live to regret.

Malcolm seemed to appreciate his home, but he was away from it for days, weeks, sometimes months at a time. He attributed his absences to the demands of the movement.

Before he started out on a trip, he sometimes left Betty extra money in secret hiding places. Afterward, he'd send her a letter saying something like, "Look in the top drawer in the back. There's some money there for you to buy something, and a love letter too." The promised money was always there, but not the love letter.

Whenever Malcolm arrived home from a trip, he hugged his children. But the babysitter never saw him hug or kiss Betty, whom he would later claim was the only woman he had ever thought about loving. He ridiculed women who expected "kissing and hugging," which he characterized as Hollywood-created wants. At times, he slept in his attic studio, into which he retreated nightly, or almost nightly, to work and study. The hideaway was filled with books, which were virtually the only items for which Malcolm expended large sums. He had a desk up there, a tape-recorder, a prayer rug, and a fold-out bed that stayed unfolded more often than not.

On several occasions, he cited a passage from the Qu'ran that says that if a woman is disobedient, her husband should punish her by banishing her from his bed until she submits to his will.

He also asserted that it was better to have a wife who had "been around" than one who had been a virgin at the time of her marriage. An inexperienced woman, he said, would be tempted to sleep with other men. The statement may have been prompted by the fact that his first child was so light-skinned. He was visibly troubled by the fact. His childhood-spawned mistrust manifested itself in other ways. For instance, years later, as he was recalling his Michigan marriage, he exclaimed, "She claims she didn't tell anybody in Temple Seven that we had married." Malcolm, who neglected to tell some of his friends himself, admitted that he only trusted his wife "seventy-five percent." That was far more than he trusted most women; he said Betty was one of the four he had ever trusted at all. Yet his inability to trust apparently made it difficult for him to confide in her.

Malcolm insisted he loved Betty. But a number of his statements were more equivocal. "I guess by now I will say I love Betty," he told one writer. He had to love her, he asserted. Another time, he said he'd love her as long as she raised their children properly.

Malcolm admitted he was not easy to live with and that not many women would have tolerated his behavior, which sometimes reduced Betty to tears. She tried hard to please him. She wore ankle-length dresses, even after the National of Islam decreed that skirt hems could rise to just below the knee. She wore a scarf on her head, even inside the house. She kept her home and her children spotlessly clean. She did her best to preserve the facade of the happy household. But the unhappiness showed through; tacitly, she eventually acknowledged it herself.

Malcolm's marriage was no more unhappy than those of other public figures who shun intimacy for the love of the crowd. Eventually, the marriage nearly broke up, ostensibly over the issue of money. But there were other issues, for Malcolm denied his wife the warmth and emotional support his mother and Ella had unwittingly denied him. He controlled her the way they had controlled him. His male chauvinism was the predictable result of past tyranny.

Despite Elijah Muhammad's anti-white diatribes, he admonished his followers that, until they were liberated from white rule, they should obey existing laws unless those laws violated his teachings. His admonitions discouraged confrontations with the secular authorities and encouraged obedience to his own authority. Nevertheless, confrontations occurred.

During the spring of 1962, about a block away from the Nation of Islam's Los Angeles temple, two police officers stopped and interrogated two Muslims they suspected of peddling stolen suits from a car. The clothing had not been stolen; one suspect was apparently delivering it to the other, who worked for a dry-cleaning establishment. But the suspicions of the policemen, who were under orders to be on the lookout for clothing-store burglars, were not allayed by the fact that it was nearly midnight.

What happened next has been disputed. The policemen, Stanley Kensic and Frank Tomlinson, later maintained that they were merely doing their duty. Malcolm, speaking for the Muslims with characteristic irony, contended that the patrolmen had been angered by the "submissiveness" of the suspects. It was not the last time he cloaked rebellious sentiments in submissive garb.

Officer Kensic, whose testimony was partly contravened by Officer Tomlinson's, later denied that he had provoked the two suspects by calling one a "nigger Muslim." According to the Nation of Islam, Kensic told one of them, "Stop talking with your hands," and twisted his arm. Kensic, who later claimed that he had twisted the man's arm to avoid an anticipated blow, was assaulted by the other suspect, who went for his throat.

As Tomlinson intervened, he heard someone shout, "Get them, brothers!" Other Muslims—at least seventeen—swarmed out of the temple and subdued the patrolmen. Kensic was beaten senseless; his assailants kept kicking him in the head even after he had collapsed in the street. Tomlinson's elbow was shattered by a bullet that was apparently fired from the service revolver that had been taken from Kensic.

An off-duty policeman who passed by grabbed the radio from Tomlinson's squad car and called for help. Reinforcements from three police divisions sped to the scene, among them a young white officer named Donald Weese, who lined up a number of fleeing Muslims against the wall of the temple. "Why? Why?" the Muslims taunted. Several attacked Weese's partner Richard Anderson, who not only lost his pistol but was also bludgeoned in the head with his own nightstick and a five-gallon bottle. According to Weese, he ordered Anderson's assailants to freeze. They apparently didn't, for he and another officer shot about half a dozen of them before the temple secretary, a Korean War veteran named Ronald Stokes, leaped on Weese's back and began choking him. Another policeman pulled Stokes off, then ran off in pursuit of another Muslim, whereupon Weese, who later admitted that he knew Stokes was unarmed, shot him through the heart. He subsequently testified that Stokes had raised his hands menacingly, as if he had intended to try to choke him again. But the Nation of Islam asserted that Stokes had raised his hands in surrender as he begged Weese to stop shooting.

An all-white coroner's jury ruled that Stokes's death was justifiable homicide. Their decision, which took only twenty-three minutes, may have been influenced by the fact that nine of the Black Muslims who had been summoned to testify refused to do so on grounds of possible self-incrimination. Yet when a grand jury convened to consider indictments against the Muslims accused of assaulting Kensic, Tomlinson, Anderson, and a number of other police officers—one of whom testified that a bullet had just missed him and one of whom described how he had nearly been shot with his own gun—the policemen were ordered by their superiors not to talk to reporters or anyone else. Apparently, neither side was confident that it would be completely exonerated if all the relevant facts emerged.

Meanwhile, back at Temple Twenty-Seven, hundreds of blacks gathered, eagerly awaiting word from the Messenger to begin the Battle of Armageddon that Elijah Muhammad promised would end the era of white supremacy. Some were drunks and dope addicts who hadn't been in the mosque for years. At the door, they were not subjected to the customary search for weapons. A number of them were openly sharpening knives. Others had guns in their pockets. Still others were practicing karate chops on imaginary devils' necks.

Brothers from Arizona, New York, and elsewhere phoned and said they were on their way to California to join in the coming battle. Then a message arrived from Elijah Muhammad:

> Hold fast to Islam. Hold fast to Islam. Allah has promised that no devil will ever get away with the death of a Muslim. We are going out into the street now to begin war with the devil. Not the kind of war he expects . . . . No, we are going to let the world know he is the devil. We are going to sell [the movement's] newspapers.

A muffled roar erupted from the disbelieving throng as Edward 2X Sherill, the captain of the Los Angeles temple, continued:

> That's right! We are going to deliver a blow to the devil that he can't get over. We are going to push the Messenger's program like never before. I want all of you brothers to take at least fifty papers. Be sure you pay for them right now at the door.

With obedience that afforded a revealing contrast to their eagerness to defy the city authorities, the Muslims fanned out into the streets to spread the gospel, their arms loaded with copies of *Muhammad Speaks*. Eventually, a number of brothers secretly decided to act on their own. They began hanging out at night on skid row. Vengefully, they fell upon their inebriated, solitary white victims, some of whom did not survive.

News of the mayhem reached Elijah Muhammad, who decided to send Malcolm to Los Angeles. Before Malcolm left New York, he created the impression that he was going to the West Coast to organize the opening skirmish in the promised race war. He told one prominent Harlem black nationalist that the time had come for him to begin practicing what he had been preaching. He said, "I'm going out there to die!"

But according to a Los Angeles Muslim named Hakim Jamal, who was partly responsible for the bloodletting on skid row, Malcolm was under orders to prevent further violence, which might have given the authorities an opportunity to initiate proceedings against the movement. Shortly after he arrived in Los Angeles, he was told about the cowardly killings. The brothers who had perpetrated them expected a pat on the back, or at least an understanding wink. But Malcolm exploded. He was livid. He ordered a stop to the bloodshed despite the fact that he had broken down and cried when he had learned that Ronald Stokes, whom he had known, had died leaving a widow and a fatherless child.

Over and over, Malcolm proclaimed that Stokes's death would be avenged, not by mortals, but by Allah. He told a television interviewer:

> Do you think I'll see violence? . . . . Yes . . . . We, as Muslims, will go to our place of worship . . . and pray to Allah to give us a sign that He can give justice to a people who. . . find it impossible to give . justice to black people. Allah will show us that He can deal with you . . . . sir!

The reporter pressed on: "I mean, Malcolm, will God's justice be enough for you, or will you and your members do more to the white race?"

Icily, Malcolm replied, "We feel that you will begin to see more and more automobile crashes on your freeways, and I also feel that you will see airplane crashes that cannot be explained. This will be the work of God. You will see them, sir!"

The reporter was still unsatisfied. "Are you going to pray that white people die in airplane crashes and things of this sort? Malcolm smiled. "God has power," he said:

> He is enough for us. If I attack you, you'll put me in jail. We'll let God attack you . . . . Let me see you put God in jail.

Partly due to Malcolm's assurance that Allah would exact vengeance, the senseless violence on skid row ended, except for what Jamal subsequently characterized as "little deaths" here and there. Jamal, who left the movement, later described how Malcolm manipulated the emotions of his volatile audiences. The point was illustrated by an incident that had occurred in Harlem. Malcolm had fired up a large outdoor crowd, which began menacing the white policemen who were impassively standing guard on its fringes. Yet when it became apparent that violence might erupt, he shouted, "Wait!" The crowd abruptly turned its attention back to Malcolm, who reminded his black listeners what had happened to Ronald Stokes. "Many of you thought that we should go on out there and make war on the white man," he said. "You wanted to do it yourself, didn't you?" *"Didn't you?"* he pressed when his question failed to elicit much response:

> You wanted some action there, didn't you? 'Cause you don't like the idea of white people shooting black people down, do you? And you're ready to do something about it, aren't you?

Then, with the audience eating out of his hand, Malcolm deftly defused the anger he had skillfully harnessed. "The white man," he said, "should be thankful that God has given the Honorable Elijah Muhammad the control over his followers that he has, so that they can play it cool [he paused for emphasis], calm [he paused again for emphasis and said in a soothing voice], and collected." Malcolm succeeded in quieting the incipient mob. But the achievement, and the similar one he had wrought in Los Angeles, was lost on those who failed to distinguish between what he said and what he actually did.

THE ENEMY
IN THE MIRROR

36

I nspired by the teachings of the Nation of Islam, Malcolm defied established religious and political authority with the same zeal that had characterized his youthful defiance of parental, educational, and civil authority. The black preachers he castigated for failing to practice the Christianity they preached—and for sponging off their gullible followers—bore a striking resemblance to his own father. He accused them of being criminals in disguise and of merely pretending to represent the interests of blacks while they ingratiated themselves with whites. Malcolm declared that the days were gone when the "touring cars" of Christianity could travel the religious roads of black America without impediment. He said the "blind" drivers of such vehicles usually ended up "in the ditch," as his one-eyed father had.

Black Christian women were just as immoral as their male counterparts, Malcolm claimed. For evidence, he cited the superabundance of "bastard babies" in the black community. He said nothing about the child his mother had borne out of wedlock. Instead of expressing his negative feelings about his Christian parents, he vented his wrath upon Christianity itself, which he portrayed as a religion of hypocrisy. He sometimes became so over-wrought during his tirades against Christianity, which he sardonically characterized as his "favorite subject," that he momentarily lost control of his emotions.

At times, Malcolm denounced Freemasonry as well as Christianity. Perhaps the word "Mason" rekindled memories of the Michigan town that had raised his hopes, then dashed them. The intellectual preten-tiousness of Masonry may also have reminded him of his uneducated Masonic father, who had gulled at least one neighbor into believing that he was an educator. Malcolm equated the mentality of thirty-two-degree Masons with the 32-degree-Fahrenheit temperature at which water freezes; their brains were frozen, he said. The Christian churches they attended were "ice-boxes." The ministers who presided over them were "ice-makers" who bred human ice-cubes.

Malcolm's attitude toward Jews was more ambivalent than his attitude toward Christians. Despite his anti-Semitic statements, which were sometimes thinly veiled and sometimes undisguised, he frequently compared the problems of the Jewish minority to those of the black minority. He observed that both peoples had been enslaved and forced to leave their ancestral homeland, and that elements of both groups had sought to return there. (The Garveyism that Earl Little had propagated had been assailed as "Negro Zionism.") Despite Malcolm's empathy for the Palestinian Arabs who had lost their homes, he cited the birth of Israel as an instructive model and legal precedent for the establishment of a separate state for American blacks. He also spoke highly of the achievements of Jewish intellectuals. He seemed particularly impressed with the strong sense of corporate identity that characterized much of the Jewish community. "The biggest difference between the parallel oppression of the Jew and the Negro," he said, "is that the Jew never lost his pride in being a Jew."

Yet Malcolm's public statements were liberally studded with gratuitous gibes about Jews, whom he accused of controlling all of Harlem's liquor stores. He called them "yids" and asserted that they were the worst of the white devils. The Jewish star, he said, was Satan's star.

He was unimpressed by the fact that many Jews were members of the NAACP; he said it was comparable to Jesse James joining the board of trustees of a bank he intended to rob. The main reason Jews were in the forefront of the civil rights movement, he said, was that the more attention they focused upon "the Negro question," the more hostility they could deflect from themselves. He refused to acknowledge the altruistic considerations that prompted most of the Jewish civil rights activists. On the other hand, there was justification for his criticism of Jews who fled to suburbia solely because blacks moved into their neighborhoods.

Malcolm upbraided the Jews for claiming that they were God's chosen people, even though the Nation of Islam taught that, after the promised Day of Judgment, black people would be the only survivors. Despite his empathy for the oppressed, he exhibited no sympathy at all for the downtrodden Jews of the Soviet Union. He characterized their American counterparts as greedy plutocrats who had "bought" Atlantic City and Miami Beach. "When there's something worth owning, the Jew's got it," he asserted. He suggested that Jews were the chief exploiters of America's blacks:

> Goldberg always catches ya'. If Goldberg can't catch ya', Goldstein'll catch ya'. And if Goldstein don't catch ya', Greenberg will catch ya'.

One enterprising reporter took Malcolm to task for blaming all the exploitation on Jews; "What about all the WASPS?" she asked him. Malcolm took her aside and told her that he didn't hate Jews per se but was merely using them as a convenient symbol.

The rich Jew symbolized the avarice that the youthful criminal Malcolm had forsworn when he had become a Muslim ascetic. Jews also symbolized the educational credentials he dreamed of acquiring. He portrayed Jews collectively as brilliant intellectuals. The average Jew, he said, is smarter than the average white.

At times, he was defensive about accusations that he was anti-Jewish. "I know I'll hear 'anti-Semitic' from every direction," he lamented after one anti-Jewish diatribe, "Oh, yes. But truth is truth." He said that condemning someone because he's Jewish is not as bad as condemning him because he's black. The reason, he asserted, is that Jews can hide their beliefs more easily than blacks can hide their skins.

Three decades had elapsed since white lawyers and court officials had evicted the Littles from land they had purchased in the best of faith. Two decades had elapsed since Kaminska had proclaimed that "niggers" couldn't become lawyers. But Malcolm had not forgotten. Nor had he forgotten that Mason's whites hadn't considered him good enough to dance with their daughters.

Prompted by these memories and Elijah Muhammad's teachings, Malcolm bitterly condemned whites en masse, despite the friendship he had shared with Betty Jean Thiel, Bob Bebee, Ores Whitney, Dick Turbin, Audrey Slagh, Pappy Cousins, and other white people. Even white babies were evil, he claimed. At times, he modified this position and argued that even if certain whites were innocent, they were nevertheless guilty collectively. He said that the white population was analogous to a piece of pie, and that if one piece were spoiled, so was the whole pie.

Malcolm denied he was prejudiced, or that he hated white "snakes" or anyone else. "It isn't hate," he asserted. "It is incorrect to clarify that as hate." He did not appear to notice that he had substituted the word "clarify" for the word "classify."

The man who had prided himself on being called Satan insisted that all whites were devils—blonde-haired, pale-skinned, blue- and green-eyed devils whose features bore remarkable similarity to those that had made him *persona non grata* to many Lansing blacks. His catalog of white vices was a mirror image of his own inadequacies, real and imagined. He didn't fear physical combat; the white people were the "cowards." He didn't feel uneducated; the whites were the ignorant ones. He didn't use smiles to mask his anger; the whites were the ones who masked their hatred with friendly grins. Malcolm, who sometimes claimed that black bigotry was solely the result of white bigotry, even accused his white enemies of despising their parents.

He ascribed the sins of his past to whites, whom he depicted as dope-peddling beasts. Again and again, he portrayed them as thieves and criminals. He also characterized them as "vultures," just as the Lansingites who had nicknamed him "Harpy" had characterized him. His hatred of whites eloquently attested to his own self-hatred.

Malcolm acknowledged that racial stereotypes betray the self-image of the racists who employ them. Over and over, he quoted the quasi-biblical injunction, "Judge not, lest ye be judged." Yet he kept condemning "irresponsible" whites for the very things for which he apparently felt partly responsible: his father's death, his mother's breakdown and institutionalization, the moral lapses of his youth, his past failures. He blamed Lansing's white social workers for the dissension in his boyhood home. He attributed his youthful criminality entirely to white oppression. "The white man makes you a drug addict," he told one African-American crowd. He even suggested that his gambling habit had been the fault of the whites who had manufactured the dice. The skill with which he substituted the outer enemy for the inner enemy called conscience gave enormous impetus to the school of thought that claims that whites are responsible for virtually all of the black community's problems. At times, Malcolm propounded that thesis himself. He suggested that whites are responsible for the disproportionate number of illegitimate, unwanted children in our black ghettos. He even asserted that whites are to blame for the fact that many blacks hate their parents.

Just as Malcolm had sought the acceptance of Mason's whites by trying to be "white," he secured the approval of blacks by insisting he was "black," despite his fair complexion. His black self-image enabled him to deny the part of himself that still longed to be part of the dominant white majority. Despite his anti-white rhetoric and his insistence that he had no desire to be anything but black, he made slips of the tongue that indicated he was deeply ambivalent about his skin color. He inadvertently declared—more than once, according to biographer Peter Goldman—that he hated "every drop of black blood" in his body. And when he was asked, during a panel discussion, whether he was in accord with Elijah Muhammad when Elijah said that he hated the white blood that contaminated his light brown body, Malcolm replied, "Yes . . . he hates the few drops of black blood that are in him." Malcolm quickly corrected himself and changed the word "black" to "white."

"That's an interesting slip," interjected the black psychologist Kenneth Clark, whose study of the damaging effects of school segregation had contributed substantially to the Supreme Court's decision to ban it. "Do you say that as a psychologist?" the panel moderator asked. "I say it as a psychologist," replied Dr. Clark.

Malcolm made other slips of the tongue that suggested his inner thoughts were not entirely in concert with his outward ones. On one occasion, his observation that black militancy was not synonymous with black supremacy became a declaration that black militancy was not "white supremacy." His pointed, barbed remarks about blacks who let their neighborhoods decay and who—according to Malcolm—were incapable of dealing with whites "on their intelligence plane" made it difficult to believe he really thought blacks were superior. The black American G.I.s who had fathered mulatto children in England during World War II "messed up the whole country," he asserted.

Malcolm's valiant effort to resolve his ambivalence by cultivating a "black" identity struck a responsive chord among millions of American blacks who, due to slavery's grim legacy, were caught between their desire to be accepted and their desire to be themselves. The niche he ultimately carved for himself in history was largely the result of his unique ability to transform his own personal struggle for identity into a universal one, and to liberate his ardent followers from the kind of conflict about skin color that had afflicted him all his life.

Malcolm X is shown with the dome of the Connecticut Capitol in view as he arrived June 4, 1963 in Hartford for a two day visit.

June 30, 1964. Omaha, Nebraska: Malcolm returned to his native Omaha for the first time on June 30th to say that "in Omaha as in other places the Ku Klux Klan has just changed its bed sheets for policeman's uniform." With Malcolm is the Reverend Rudolph McNair, Omaha leader of the Citizen's Coordinating Commission for Civil Liberties.

V

SUBMISSION OR
REBELLION?

NONE ARE WHITE! 37

Perhaps because his black self-image was so fragile, Malcolm did not disclose that his blue-eyed, blonde-haired paternal grandmother had been part-white. He tried to explain away the white blood on his mother's side of the family by claiming that his maternal grandmother, who had borne three children out of wedlock, had been raped by his mother's Scottish father. No evidence has been found to support this contention, which Louise Little disputes. Nor do any of her Grenadian relatives seem to give the claim credence.

Malcolm asserted that his Scottish grandfather had been a redhead. He also claimed that the man's name was Malcolm, even though no one else in the family (including Malcolm's mother, who never laid eyes on him) seems to know what his first name was.

Malcolm talked about rape quite a bit. He conjured up fearful images of sexual assault:

> *Think* of it—think of that black slave man filled with fear and dread, hearing the screams of his wife, his mother, his daughter being *taken*—in the barn, the kitchen, in the bushes! *Think* of it, my dear brothers and sisters! *Think* of hearing wives mothers, daughters being *raped*!

> A white man don't go nowhere with a black woman in the daytime. But look out here at night and you see him driving through our neighborhood after your mother!

"Yesssssssss," he hissed, "I said he's after your mother!"

In addition to depicting white men as mother-abusers, Malcolm said they had no right to call themselves men. Real men exhibited tenderness toward their wives and children. They provided for their families. White men merely pretended to do these things, Malcolm asserted.

As a rule, Malcolm's white targets were impersonal ones. A white student cornered him one day and asked him, face to face, "Do you really hate me?" Malcolm would not reply. He hated as he loved—at a safe distance.

He also vented his spleen on the acknowledged leaders of the black establishment, whom he characterized as sham leaders. Not even the most venerated dignitaries escaped his scornful tongue. He characterized Booker T. Washington as a "white man's nigger" and lampooned the NAACP as a "black body with a white head." Even Jackie Robinson and Joe Louis, whom he had idolized, were "stooges" for the white establishment, he said. And despite his reluctant admiration for Martin Luther King, Jr., he portrayed him as a "chump, not a champ" and grumbled about the ease with which his gifted rival obtained prime time on television. He also denounced Roy Wilkins, Whitney Young, A. Philip Randolph, and the other prominent black leaders whom President Kennedy invited to the White House.

Malcolm spurned the black bourgeoisie the way the snooty blacks of Lansing and Roxbury had spurned him. He directed many of his bitterest attacks at the blacks whose suspenders, he claimed, dragged the ground with university degrees. "Nincompoops with Ph.D.s," he called them. The word "doctor" was his favorite epithet for his college-educated black rivals, one of whom publicly described him as a racist in reverse. Malcolm got so mad that he nearly forgot his rule about maintaining self-control:

I laid the word down on him, loud: "*Nigger!*"

Malcolm, who later acknowledged how bitter he had been about Kaminska's declaration that "niggers" couldn't become lawyers, also gave black law students and lawyers a hard time. Yet, privately, he urged at least one member of his family to obtain a law degree.

In an effort to purge himself of his ambivalence about skin color, Malcolm projected it onto his black political enemies, whom he characterized as "Quislings" and "Uncle Toms." "They wish they had white skins," he scornfully declared. Portraying them as blacks with white hearts, he reproached them for living in white neighborhoods and for being dependent on white money. He called the civil-rights activists who bravely endured police brutality "masochists" and denounced them for employing the same passive resistance that he had successfully used against authority figures at home, at school, and in prison.

Malcolm's pale complexion did not deter him from describing his integrationist foes as "anemic." Nor did his habit of ingratiating himself with benefactors such as Elijah Muhammad prevent him from characterizing black moderates as obsequious and submissive. He castigated Harry Belafonte and Sammy Davis, Jr. for living with white women. He even criticized one well-known civil rights leader for being a "homo."

He later said similar things about Moise Tshombe, whom he never forgave for the part he played in the murder of Patrice Lumumba:

> Tshombe . . . [is] a bed partner for Lyndon B. Johnson. Yes, a bed partner. They're sleeping together. They're sleeping together.

He said he wasn't speaking literally, but he repeated the accusation again and again.

Privately, Malcolm admitted that he did not believe everything he said publicly. He made clear, for instance, that God didn't work miracles, and that if retribution was to be visited upon the white oppressors, human beings would have to do it. "Look at the Bible," he declared. "Men fought in the Battle of Jericho."

As time passed, it became increasingly evident that he no more believed in the feasibility of racial separation than he believed in the man in the moon. He told Charles 37X, who belonged to Temple Seven, that it was becoming increasingly difficult for him to defend his arguments for a separate black state—arguments that sometimes sounded mechanical and unpersuasive. During one speech, he bluntly questioned whether a nation within another nation could survive. He did not openly admit that it was unlikely to do so, but he hinted as much. He said that Elijah Muhammad "is demanding complete separation where he will . . . ." Malcolm quickly changed the word "he" to "we." When he was asked where the separate state would be, he smiled and replied, "Moses never told the Jews where it was to be!" He responded to one question about the Nation of Islam's separatism by asking the attending newsman not to turn his camera on until after each question was asked—a ploy that made it difficult for those who viewed the resultant newsfilm to discern that some of his answers were evasive. On another occasion, Malcolm characterized separation as a "good talking point." According to Louis Lomax, who frequently interviewed officials of the Nation of Islam, the Messenger privately agreed. It didn't take much political savvy to realize that the U.S. government was not about to permit an independent, potentially hostile black state within its borders.

There were other indications that Malcolm didn't believe everything he was saying. He'd exchange knowing glances with Charles 37X when less sophisticated brothers started rhapsodizing about the "mother plane" that Elijah maintained would lead the final charge during the Battle of Armageddon. Malcolm, who occasionally discussed the mother plane at temple meetings, described it as a wheel-shaped flying saucer that contained hundreds of "baby planes." Each baby plane carried bombs filled with two tons of a powerful explosive. Piloting the planes, he said, were men who had been trained to fly since the age of six—men who had never smiled.

On the Day of Judgment, Malcolm asserted, the mother plane would release its babies, whose lethal cargoes would burrow a mile into the earth and explode with sufficient force to raise mountains a mile high. Each bomb would release poison gas that would destroy every living thing within a radius of fifty miles. The atmosphere would burn for more than three hundred years and would take nearly seven hundred more to cool off. At the end of the thousand-year period, the descendants of the blacks who survived would inherit the earth. At times, Malcolm would smile when he was chided about such statements. The smile, which sometimes assumed an ironic quality that seemed to belie what he was saying, became raucous laughter when one of his less credulous followers privately challenged one of his extravagant utterances. "Malcolm," she exclaimed, "You know you don't believe that!" Except for the laughter, Malcolm did not respond. But at Harvard and Yale, he publicly invited his well-educated audiences to question "the wisdom or folly" of the Messenger's teachings.

Since 1959, orthodox Muslims had been doing just that. Stung by their denunciations, Elijah Muhammad decided to shore up his religious credentials by visiting Mecca. (Only bona fide Muslims are allowed to enter the Holy City.) Malcolm was sent ahead to the Middle East to pave the way. Before he left the United States, he announced his intention to visit Mecca himself. He scheduled his trip to coincide with the annual *hajj*, or sacred pilgrimage, that all devout Muslims endeavor to make at least once.

But Malcolm didn't leave—or wasn't allowed to leave—for the Middle East until July, 1959, after the hajj had ended. While he was there, *The Hate that Hate Produced*, which portrayed Malcolm, not Elijah Muhammad, as the Black Muslim movement's most prominent, dynamic leader, was televised in the United States. A few days later, an official of the Messenger's Buffalo, New York mosque announced that Malcolm "might" go to Mecca, despite pronouncements from New York that he was already there.

Though Malcolm said that the Saudis had authorized him to enter Mecca, he subsequently wrote and admitted that he was leaving Saudi Arabia without visiting the Holy City. He described his disappointment as the kind that "would break the average Muslim's heart."

Malcolm offered several explanations for his failure to visit Mecca. He contended that a severe gastrointestinal ailment had made it impossible to travel the forty-odd miles (he said it was sixty) from Jedda to Mecca in the 110-degree heat. But the claim was reportedly contradicted by a letter that disclosed that he had already recovered from the two-day illness before he had arrived in Jedda. Another letter claimed that he had to cancel his trip to Mecca in order to make a planned tour of Africa. He told a number of people he had to leave the Middle East in order to return home in time for the Harlem rally that Elijah Muhammad had scheduled for July 26. But he returned home at least two days before the rally was held. Later, he would claim that Mecca had never even been on his itinerary.

The reason Malcolm didn't go to Mecca is still unclear. Orthodox Muslim opponents of the Nation of Islam claimed that the city's guardians had refused him entry because the doctrines he was propagating were a perversion of Islam. But Elijah Muhammad's trip to Mecca a few months later suggested that the Saudis were not the ones who had upset Malcolm's plans. So did the rumors that Elijah Muhammad, who was displeased by the fact *The Hate that Hate Produced* had portrayed him far less favorably than it had portrayed Malcolm, had instructed him to bypass Mecca. After Malcolm returned home, he told several people that he had voluntarily elected not to go to Mecca because he didn't want to upstage his teacher-leader, who refused to take him when he went. Malcolm had clearly expressed his desire to accompany Mr. Muhammad. And though he was outwardly left "in charge" while Elijah was away, one of the Messenger's aides obliquely warned the membership to remain on guard during his six-and-a-half week absence.

Malcolm's tour of the Middle East left him with the thorny problem of how to reconcile Elijah Muhammad's insistence that all Muslims are black with the face-to-face contacts he'd had with the fair-skinned inhabitants of the Arab world. He did it with irony:

> The people of Arabia are just like our people in America in facial appearance. They are of many different shades, ranging from regal black to rich brown. But none are white.

He added, "Ninety-nine percent of them would be Jim-Crowed in the United States." He also contended that most of them would be "right at home" in Harlem. His pronouncements, which included the assertion that Gamal Abdel Nasser was "a black man," contrasted sharply with his private acknowledgements to Louis Lomax, to Wilfred, to one of Bettye's brothers, and to others that the Muslim world was not the all-black one Elijah Muhammad depicted. On a couple of occasions, he even said so publicly.

Outwardly, Malcolm continued to maintain that all whites were devils. But he told Philbert that the white-skinned Arabs he had met in the Middle East had not exhibited any animosity toward their darker-skinned Muslim brethren from Africa.

There were other indications that Malcolm had outgrown the white devil theory. He complimented one new Nation of Islam convert for joining it for reasons that apparently had nothing to do with anti-white feeling. He praised another member of the movement for being polite to the whites he encountered, rather than hostile. Moreover, he maintained excellent relations with a number of light-skinned Arab representatives to the United Nations. (Eventually, the guards at the U.N. front gate were instructed to let him enter at will.) At times, his public pronouncements about white devils sounded downright mechanical. He told one television audience, "The Honorable Elijah Muhammad teaches us that God taught him that the white race is a race of devils."

The white devil theory was not the only one of Mr. Muhammad's doctrines that Malcolm frequently prefaced with remarks suggesting that he wasn't entirely in accord with it. An example was the Messenger's claim that Yacub had drilled a shaft into the earth, filled it with explosives, and blasted away the chunk that had produced the moon.

By the early 1960s, there was evidence of political differences, as well as doctrinal ones, between Malcolm and Elijah Muhammad. One bone of contention involved Malcolm's intemperate, attention-getting public utterances, which ran counter to the Messenger's attempts to tone down the pronouncements of his ministers in order to avoid unfavorable publicity and government reprisal. When the nuclear submarine U.S.S. Thresher sank with its crew aboard, Malcolm pictured the incident as an act of divine retribution for the injustices that whites had inflicted upon blacks. (He did not mention that part of the crew was black.) A similar "act of God" occurred in June 1962, when more than 120 Americans from Georgia—Malcolm labeled them "crackers"—were immolated in a jetliner crash near Paris. At the time, it was the worst civil air disaster involving a single plane in aviation history. The only survivors were the two stewardesses who had been sitting in the rear of the plane. Somehow, they were thrown clear of the flaming wreckage.

Malcolm smiled as he stepped to the microphone to report the news to the Los Angeles Muslims who had been waiting for Allah to avenge the killing of Ronald Stokes. "I would like to announce a very beautiful thing," he said. The audience laughed as Malcolm—who still had to contend with believers who wanted to go to war over Stokes' death—described how he had received a telegram directly from God. "We hope that every day another plane falls out of the sky," he declared. The audience applauded and cheered. But Elijah Muhammad didn't.

The Messenger was also upset about Malcolm's efforts to induce the Nation of Islam to abandon its policy of political noninvolvement—a policy that was gradually rendering him politically irrelevant because of the rapid progress the civil rights movement was making. For example, 1962 was the year that James Meredith broke the color bar at the University of

Mississippi. The achievement, which required the help of about 23,000 troops, was another milestone in the protracted struggle that had been buoyed by the Supreme Court's 1954 school desegregation decision and the 1955 bus boycott in Montgomery, Alabama.

The boycott in Montgomery, where the Confederate flag had first been unfurled a century before, was immensely successful. Four days after Rosa Parks was arrested for refusing to relinquish her bus seat to a white man, ninety percent of the city's regular bus riders were "walking with God" to work or using car or taxi pools. One rode a mule to work; another took his horse-drawn buggy. A third, an old woman who hobbled with difficulty, turned down a proferred ride with the explanation, "I'm not walking for myself; I'm walking for my children and grandchildren." Another elderly woman exclaimed, "My feet is tired, but my soul is rested."

The determination of Montgomery's blacks paid off; the bus company's revenues evaporated. The effectiveness of the peaceful boycott, which propelled Martin Luther King, Jr. to national prominence, eventually prompted his Montgomery Improvement Association to combine with similar church-based groups throughout the South to form the Southern Christian Leadership Conference, which provided the civil rights movement with the crusading religious fervor that proved vital to its success.

There were failures as well as successes—the campaign to integrate Little Rock, Arkansas's public schools was a depressing example. But by 1959, the process had been revived. The same year, Bayard Rustin marshalled 25,000 black marchers in his successful effort to integrate Washington, D.C.'s public schools. In Greensboro, North Carolina, the following year, four black college freshmen sat down at a lunch counter that served only white people. They didn't get service. But the next day, they got something even better—the national press coverage that spurred similar sit-ins in fifteen or more Southern cities within two weeks. Within six weeks, black students led by Julian Bond and others had demonstrators sitting in all over downtown Atlanta. The sit-ins gave rise to stand-ins at the entrances of theaters and public parks, read-ins at public libraries, wade-ins at public beaches and pools, and pray-ins at segregated churches. It also inspired the freedom rides, which were designed to integrate transportation facilities that were segregated.

The country first learned about the freedom riders, some of whom were white, when two bus loads of CORE volunteers who were trying to end segregation at Alabama's bus terminals were savagely beaten with lead pipes, baseball bats, and chains. One bus was burned. Subsequently, other freedom riders were greeted with violence in McComb and Jackson, Mississippi, where they attempted to implement new Interstate Commerce

Commission regulations banning segregation in interstate travel.
also lagged in Albany, Georgia, where Martin Luther King re
assumed the titular leadership of a faction-ridden campaign to des
the town's public facilities. The marchers marched, the jails filled
downtown lunch counters remained segregated. Most of the der
tors were relatively well treated by the police, who were under or
to perpetrate the kind of violence that would have produced
martyrs. And since there were no martyrs, it proved impossible to
enough indignation nationally to produce the necessary remedial
tion. One Albany official chuckled, "We killed them with kindnes

The power structure of Birmingham, Alabama, which was
regarded as the most rigidly segregated big city in the United
was not as shrewd; "Bull" Connor's all-white police force was no
for its brutal treatment of the city's blacks. "We're not goin' to have
folks and nigras segregatin' together!" said Commissioner Conno
was also Birmingham's Commissioner of Education. The only
facilities that were not segregated were the city streets, the water s
the sewer system, and some other utilities. "White" radio station:
obliged not to play "Negro" music. A book that depicted black r
commingling with white ones was explicitly banned.

Birmingham wasn't even safe for a universally acclaimed enter
like Nat King Cole, who was slugged onstage by a group of white to
Another black man, who happened to be standing by the wrong wa
at the wrong time, was attacked and castrated; he probably would
died if his assailants had not poured turpentine on his bleeding ger

For such reasons, Birmingham was selected as the site of Martin L
King's next campaign, which began at selected downtown lunch cou
The demonstrators were promptly arrested. Day after day, their places
taken by others. Thousands were eventually jailed. Among them
hundreds of children, including an eight-year-old girl. Malcolm, who
obliged to defend Elijah Muhammad's negative view of racial integra
denounced the campaign leaders for unnecessarily endangering the child

After an initial period of relative restraint, Connor's policemen u
dogs and high-pressure hoses against the marchers. During one me
the Reverend Fred Shuttlesworth, the leader of the local civil rights for
was hurled against the wall of a church by a stream of pressurized w
that was capable of peeling the bark off trees. When Connor was told,
said, "I waited a week to see Shuttlesworths get hit with a hose; I'm sc
I missed it." When someone pointed out that Shuttlesworth had be
carried away in an ambulance, Connor replied, "I wish they'd carried h
away in a hearse."

Five days later, a fragile, tentative desegregation accord was shattered by the bombing of Dr. King's younger brother's home and the motel where King's campaign was headquartered. Using the resultant riot as a pretext, a contingent of shotgun-toting irregulars wearing G.I. helmets descended upon the headquarters. They were joined by Governor George Wallace's Alabama state troopers, who charged into the motel enclosure with carbines, indiscriminantly clubbing its black occupants. The "thonk" of gun butts striking heads could be heard across the street. Dozens of people were injured that day in Birmingham. Glass from broken shop windows littered the streets. So did overturned automobiles and smashed, disabled police cruisers. Helmeted state troopers patrolled the decimated areas in groups of twelve to twenty men. President Kennedy, who had been straddling the political fence in hope of placating the southern Democrats who chaired so many of the congressional committees that were obstructing his New Frontier, dispatched troops to staging areas near Birmingham. Politically, he was torn between his need to retain southern Democratic support for his legislative program (and future reelection), and his need to recement the support of the urban blacks whose votes had enabled him to narrowly defeat Richard Nixon in 1960 in several key states.

Two days after Kennedy threatened to send in the troops, Jeremiah X, who ran Elijah Muhammad's Birmingham temple under Malcolm's supervision, announced that Malcolm (who was unimpressed with Kennedy's belated decision to submit meaningful civil rights legislation to Congress) would soon arrive in Birmingham to hold an unspecified number of public rallies. The next day, in New York, Malcolm disclaimed all knowledge of the announcement, which had been published in the *Herald Tribune.* He said he'd go to Birmingham only if he was directed to do so by Elijah Muhammad or if he was invited there by Jeremiah. But Malcolm, to whom Jeremiah reportedly owed his position, needed no invitation from the officials he supervised to visit their temples or the cities in which they were located. And since Jeremiah's announcement suggested that he favored Malcolm's Birmingham trip, some people began to suspect that Elijah Muhammad had vetoed it.

Mr. Muhammad was reluctant to allow his ministers to engage in political activity for a number of reasons. There was no sense participating, politically or otherwise, in a system that was allegedly doomed to extinction; the Messenger taught that the blacks who refused to separate from white America would be destroyed with it on the Day of Judgment. Moreover, Elijah, who had already spent three and a half years in jail because of his refusal to serve in the U.S. army, was well aware that

political activity on his part could prompt the government to act against him. Whatever tax exemptions his movement claimed could be challenged if such activity enabled the authorities to argue that the Nation of Islam was not really a religious movement. But Malcolm, whose eloquent, militant speeches were attracting so many non-Muslims, chafed at the way the Nation shunned politics.

Yet three months later, when the leading civil rights organizations joined forces to organize the historic March on Washington, Malcolm ridiculed it. The night before the march, he held a press conference outside the hotel where the march organizers were meeting. One of them, Bayard Rustin, emerged from the hotel and good-naturedly cautioned him not to tell the two-hundred-thousand-odd marchers who were scheduled to arrive the next day what he was telling the newsmen. Malcolm looked at Rustin and replied, with a twinkle in his eye, "What I tell them is one thing. What I tell the press is something else."

Malcolm's polemics against what he had dubbed the "Farce on Washington" simultaneously satisfied Elijah Muhammad's demand for political noninvolvement and buttressed Malcolm's position as the chief proponent of greater militancy:

> The whites . . . infiltrated [the March] . . . . They engulfed it. They
> became so much a part of it [that] it lost its original flavor. It ceased
> to be angry. It ceased to be impatient. In fact, it ceased to be a march.
> It became a picnic.

Malcolm characterized it as a circus. He said that most of the marchers looked too happy to be rebels.

Officially, Malcolm continued to support Elijah Muhammad's position on political involvement, which was so rigid that the members of the Nation of Islam—the F.B.I. called it the NOI—were even forbidden to vote. "We're not a political group," he told the NAACP. "We're not politically inclined." Yet Malcolm, who reportedly found it embarrassing to have to sit on the sidelines while others risked their lives, had been trying to nudge the Nation of Islam in the direction of political involvement for some time. There is evidence that suggests he unsuccessfully tried to secure Elijah Muhammad's permission to boycott Harlem stores that refused to hire or promote black employees. The same year, the Messenger made Malcolm apologize publicly for organizing a protest demonstration in nearby Newark. Malcolm kept pressing Mr. Muhammad for permission to engage in demonstrations. The Messenger instructed him not to raise the subject again. Malcolm obeyed. But he publicly endorsed the efforts of the local hospital employees' union to unionize New York City's hospitals, whose black and Puerto Rican janitors, cooks, maids, and laundry-room operators worked six days a week for less than thirty-five dollars—a salary that many of them had to supplement with welfare. He also agreed to participate in a rally that was being organized to protest racial discrimination in the school system of Englewood, New Jersey. Though he insisted that the Black Muslims were "never involved" in boycotts or picketing, he showed up when hundreds of demonstrators picketed a Brooklyn construction site because of the contractor's refusal to hire more minority workers. (He didn't picket himself.) Moreover, Temple Seven's restaurant participated in a "selective buying" campaign to force Sealtest Ice Cream to hire more nonwhites. At the time, the company had about 1,500 employees in New York, but only twelve were black.

In addition, Malcolm attended meetings of certain leftist groups and appeared on speakers' platforms with a number of their members. He donated $100 from Temple Seven's treasury to help offset one group's deficit. According to an F.B.I. informant, he was endeavoring to establish "a working relationship" between his Muslims and the political left. He hinted that he wanted to forge a similar understanding with the leaders of the civil rights movement. The vehicle he employed was a public rally. But when none of the invited dignitaries showed up, the "Unity Rally" degenerated into a poorly disguised attack on the very leaders with whom he had apparently been trying to achieve reconciliation: "Doctor" A. Philip Randolph, "Doctor" Roy Wilkins, "Doctor" Whitney Young, and "the Right Reverend Doctor Martin Luther King."

Both the Unity Rally and Malcolm's appearance at the Brooklyn construction site occurred after Elijah Muhammad forbade him to assist other black organizations in their attempts to secure their constituents their civil rights. Rumors of "minor differences" between Malcolm and Mr. Muhammad began spreading. When they were reported in the *Amsterdam News*, Malcolm told Louis Lomax, "It's a lie!"

> Any article that says there is a "minor" difference between Mr. Muhammad and me is a lie. There is no such thing as a minor difference with the Messenger. Any difference with him is major.

"But I will tell you this," he added:

> The Messenger has seen God. He was with Allah and was given divine patience. . . . He is willing to wait for Allah to deal with this devil. Well, sir, the rest of us Black Muslims have not seen God. We don't have this gift of divine patience with the devil. The younger Black Muslims want to see some action!

UNDER GUISE
OF RELIGION

ad the differences between Malcolm and the Nation of Islam's Chicago-based leadership been merely ideological and political, the rift between them might not have grown as wide as it eventually did. But personal antagonism added fuel to the fire. It was common knowledge, for example, that most of Elijah Muhammad's children deeply resented Malcolm. It wasn't just due to the way Malcolm ordered them around during the movement's 1963 annual convention, which their father was unable to attend because of his bad health. Several members of "the Royal Family," whose visages frequently adorned the pages of *Muhammad Speaks*, reportedly felt that Malcolm was trying to fashion a dynasty of his own that would enable him to take over the movement after his aging superior's death. Wilfred still headed Detroit's Temple Number One, a key mosque. And since Philbert, who was equally capable, had been placed in charge of the temples in Lansing, Grand Rapids, Flint, and Saginaw, the Littles appeared to be in a position to contest Muhammad family control in the State of Michigan, as well as New York, Connecticut, and the City of Boston, where those in charge were regarded as "Malcolm's ministers."

The animosity may also have stemmed partly from the way Mr. Muhammad had taken Malcolm into his home and treated him like a son. According to Wilfred, none of the Messenger's children had the relationship with him that Malcolm had. Instead of flaunting his privileged position, Malcolm donned his noncompetitive facade. He even organized a fund-raising drive that enabled the movement to give jobs to Elijah Muhammad's uneducated children, most of whom had been employed in menial occupations. (One was a cab driver; another, a common laborer.) The ploy, which recalled Malcolm's observation that a wise man will pretend to side with his enemies, backfired. Ultimately, it proved fatal. To the extent that Mr. Muhammad's children owed Malcolm their positions, they may have resented him even more.

In any event, it wasn't difficult for the Messenger's courtiers to poison his mind against Malcolm, whom they accused of taking credit for Elijah Muhammad's achievements. Muhammad appeared envious of the publicity Malcolm had been getting. He took over the weekly column James Hicks had given Malcolm in the *Amsterdam News*. Malcolm's column was transferred to the less prestigious Los Angeles *Herald-Dispatch*. Subsequently, the Messenger appropriated the latter column, too. According to Malcolm, the envy eventually reached such proportions that he was given less and less coverage in *Muhammad Speaks*, which embellished Muhammad's image the way *The Negro World* had embellished Marcus Garvey's. Chicago also tried, unsuccessfully, to discourage Malcolm from holding his own rallies.

Elijah Muhammad also envied Malcolm's popularity on college campuses, where Elijah's intellectual and oratorical inadequacies made him unwelcome. Outside the Nation of Islam, Malcolm overshadowed him in every way. His picture, not Elijah's, appeared on the front cover of Louis Lomax's book *When the Word is Given*, which contained five of Malcolm's speeches but only one by Mr. Muhammad, who was reportedly upset. But the thing that probably galled the Messenger the most was Doubleday's decision to publish Malcolm's autobiography. (Doubleday later sold its publication rights to Grove Press, which actually published the book.) Malcolm's willingness to dedicate the book to his mentor, and to grace his treasury with every cent of his share of the ensuing royalties, made the pill easier to swallow, but not easy.

For some time, neither Lomax nor Alex Haley, the talented black writer to whom Malcolm began dictating his autobiography, was apparently aware that Malcolm was simultaneously working with the other on another book. Lomax secluded himself in a downtown New York hotel to finish his manuscript. He had no idea that, after Malcolm finished meeting with him, he took the hotel elevator to another floor where Haley was temporarily closeted.

For several weeks, Haley vainly tried to get Malcolm to talk about himself instead of Elijah Muhammad and his teachings. As Malcolm mouthed the Messenger's doctrines, he frequently scribbled notes to himself on whatever scrap of paper happened to be available. So Haley began augmenting the paper supply by giving him fresh paper napkins every time he refilled his coffee cup. Some of the pithy statements that Malcolm scrawled on the napkins, which Haley retrieved after each interview, were worthy of Ben Franklin:

Here lies a YM [yellow man], killed by a BM [black man], fighting for the WM [white man], who killed all the RM [red men].

If Christianity had asserted itself in Germany, six million Jews would have lived.

Woman who cries all the time is [doing it] only because she knows she can get away with it.

The latter remark prompted Haley—who was struck by Malcolm's ability to say one thing while he was pondering another—to probe his feelings about women. It soon became apparent, as it had been to Jarvis, that they were mainly negative. Women, Malcolm claimed, were untrustworthy. He wrote on one napkin, "I have a wife who understands, or even if she doesn't, she at least pretends." "You never can fully trust any woman," he exclaimed.

Haley mined the woman theme. One night, Malcolm showed up for an interview so exhausted that his defenses may have been down when Haley interrupted him and said, "I wonder if you'd tell me something about your mother."

Abruptly, Malcolm stopped pacing the floor. The look he gave Haley suggested that Haley had struck a sensitive chord.

Malcolm resumed his pacing. "She was always standing over the stove, he said, "trying to stretch whatever we had to eat. We stayed so hungry we were dizzy." He kept talking about his mother and his boyhood until sunrise. "His talking about his mother triggered something," Haley later recalled.

There was melancholy in Malcolm's voice as he told Haley what he wanted him to know about his youth. He stressed the economic hardship and the racial injustice, but he downplayed the parental neglect. The mother he portrayed in the opening pages of his autobiography, which begins with the spellbinding account of how she fearlessly confronted the torch- and gun-bearing horsemen who are said to have besieged her home, was the strong, protective mother he had never had.

Malcolm's description of his years behind bars was comparatively joyful. "Let me tell you how I'd get those white devil convicts—and the guards, too—to do anything I wanted," he told Haley. "I'd whisper to them, 'If you don't, I'll start a rumor that you're really a light Negro just passing as white.'" He said that, next to college, the best place for a man to be if he had to change himself was prison. Another time, he declared that being imprisoned "was the best thing that could ever have happened" to him.

Malcolm told Haley, "Now, I don't want anything in this book to make it sound that I think I'm somebody important." Apparently referring to his habit of making outrageous statements, he said, "Aristotle shocked people; Charles Darwin outraged people; Aldous Huxley scandalized millions." In the next breath he told Haley, "Don't print that: people would think I'm trying to link myself with them." Yet he told James 67X:

> Brother, I am the seventh son of a seventh son. I spent seventy-seven months in prison—which is seven months less than seven years—and became the minister of Muhammad's Temple Number Seven . . . . There is a sign in all that.*

With regard to his growing prominence, Malcolm told John Bembry, who had left prison and moved to a nearby part of Queens, "They know I'm around!" Bembry asked how Elijah Muhammad was reacting to all the publicity Malcolm was receiving. He asked if the Messenger was envious. Malcolm stood up, straightened his coat, and started toward the door of Bembry's rented room. Bembry could see he was angry. But Malcolm controlled the anger as he explained that the relationship between him and Mr. Muhammad was not subject to such petty considerations. "Black Muslims like myself are all fingers on a giant hand," he declared. "The Honorable Elijah Muhammad is that hand—the right hand of Allah." The hand, Malcolm said, had no need to envy its fingers. Then he stomped out of the room. He didn't even say goodbye.

Malcolm had other enemies in the Nation of Islam besides Elijah Muhammad's children. One of them was John 4X, who was not only an able fundraiser but also a capable administrator. He was regarded as the best administrator in the entire movement.

Malcolm and John, who later changed his name to John Ali, had not always been foes. In fact, he had started out as one of Malcolm's proteges. For a number of years, he was secretary of Temple Seven. (The secretary handled the temple's finances.) He even shared a duplex with Malcolm in Queens. Then he assumed the key post of National Secretary. He said the position, which gave him day-to-day control over a large part of the movement's finances, was unsalaried. "My needs are provided for by Mr. Muhammad," he told the *Chicago Defender*. The Messenger proved generous. Before long, John was sporting well-tailored suits, a new car, a home of his own, and "other things." He characterized the ensuing allegations of corruption as lies and attributed

---

* Malcolm was exaggerating—he was Earl Little's seventh child, not his seventh son. Nor was Earl his father's seventh son; he was just one of seven sons. The exaggerating may have been prompted by the myth that the powers of a seventh son are enhanced if he is directly descended from a seventh son.

his prosperity to his "thrifty nature." He said that he had saved money from his previous "career" in civil service. According to the *Defender*, his government career, which had ended a decade before, had consisted of a stint as a messenger, a job as a budget clerk, and another as "a track man for the Navy Department."

The alliance that John Ali forged with several members of Elijah Muhammad's family contributed to the end of his cordial relationship with Malcolm. So did an incident that occurred when a number of Mr. Muhammad's Jersey City followers visited the Harlem temple. Ulysses X was one of them. As he entered Temple Seven, he noticed a window where money was being collected. John Ali, who was in New York that day, buttonholed him and asked him to make a contribution. Ulysses told him he had already contributed in Jersey City. Ali replied, "Go to the window, brother, and make your donation." Ulysses complied. So did the other Jersey City guests.

But they were upset. "I had to pay to get into your mosque," Ulysses told Malcolm.

"What?" asked Malcolm indignantly. "We were just trying something new," Ali explained. He would not look Ulysses in the eye.

Ulysses demanded his money back. "You want back the money you gave the Messenger?" Ali asked. Malcolm said he didn't think there was anyone in the Nation who had contributed more time and money than Ulysses had. John returned the money.

But he would one day get his revenge. He wasn't the only one of Malcolm's proteges who would turn against him. Another was Temple Seven's chief disciplinarian, Captain Joseph Joseph, who had helped Malcolm build the Boston temple as well as the New York mosque, resented the way Malcolm tyrannized him, according to Ulysses, who worked closely with both men. But what really aroused Joseph's wrath, says Ulysses, was that the woman he wanted to marry—I'll call her Robin—rebuffed him for Malcolm (who was still unmarried at the time). For a long time, Malcolm wielded the upper hand over Joseph. He even removed him as captain, ostensibly for failing to report groundless allegations that Malcolm was having sex with a number of Muslim sisters. But Joseph was reinstated; the Nation issued an edict depriving ministers of authority to dismiss captains, who were made directly responsible to it.

Consequently, a power struggle developed at Temple Seven between Malcolm and Joseph, whom Malcolm tried to remove again. But Joseph stayed. One of the issues reportedly dividing the two men was whether members who committed disciplinary offenses should be routinely subjected to corporal punishment. (Elijah Muhammad's son Wallace characterized his father's followers as children who had to be disciplined physically.) Malcolm was no more able to halt the practice, which was employed throughout the Nation of Islam, than he had been able to put a stop to the beatings his parents had administered in his boyhood home.*

The key issue dividing Joseph and Malcolm was that of authority. Joseph left little doubt that he considered himself in charge. One can imagine how well this sat with Malcolm. As James 67X, who was then one of Joseph's lieutenants, later observed, the two rivals were obliged to work with each other, yet they constantly tread on each other's authoritarian toes. Joseph, who also had a flair for metaphor, told James, "Remember this! . . . . Presidents come, presidents go, but the generals remain."

The struggle between Malcolm and Joseph for control of Temple Seven, which boasted more members than any other temple, was largely a struggle by Joseph's Chicago-based superiors to win control of the money the New York mosque contributed to the movement's national treasury. By comparison, the Chicago mosque, which contributed far less to the Nation's coffers, was in the red. It had been in debt for a number of years and was able to meet its expenses only because other temples—particularly Malcolm's—reportedly kept bailing it out. Malcolm told one gathering of Chicago Muslims about the efforts to "straighten out Number Two." "Everything should be perfect here," he bluntly declared. The thinly veiled criticism was not lost on the F.B.I. informant in the audience, who later told his superiors that although Malcolm praised one of the officials in charge of the mosque, he did not say what the latter had allegedly accomplished.

The fact that money was the prime objective of most of the members of the Muhammad family was no secret to those who knew them. The methods by which they exacted money from the Messenger's compliant followers were subsequently detailed in a *Saturday Evening Post* exposé by a five-and-a-half-foot-tall, former NOI official named Aubrey Barnette. In broad daylight, Barnette had been dragged from his car on a busy thoroughfare by thirteen six-footers, who battered him so severely that he was left with a fractured vertebra, broken ribs, a shattered ankle, and damaged kidneys. His article, which was entitled "The Black Muslims Are a Fraud," described how each Muslim sister had to buy at least three ankle-length Muslim gowns in order to be able to attend social functions that were virtually obligatory. The cost was about two hundred dollars.

---

* Though Malcolm apparently opposed the indiscriminate use of corporal punishment, he approved it in cases where the offender had stolen money from a temple or had publicly defied him or Elijah Muhammad.

The shop that fabricated the gowns was the domain of one of Elijah Muhammad's daughters. She reportedly told a sister-in-law, "We'd better get all we can before these fools who are following my father wake up."

The Muhammads and their associates ran a substantial number of other businesses. They included a clothing store, a combination grocery-restaurant, a barber shop, a laundry-cleaning establishment, an upholstery shop, and a number of bakeries, one of which was one of the largest in Chicago. Other Black Muslims, or the mosques to which they belonged, established business enterprises in other cities. One example was the flourishing restaurant that Temple Seven ran at 116th Street and Lenox Avenue. Temple 7B, which was located in Queens, operated another restaurant. Later on, the New Haven temple opened a Muslim bookstore, a bakery, and an eatery. Other Muslim enterprises appeared in Washington and Cleveland. In Detroit, a furniture and carpet store called Bogans was opened. Gulam Bogans was the alias Elijah Muhammad had used after he was arrested for draft evasion in 1942. On occasion, "Prophet Bogans," who sometimes called himself "Poole the Prophet," substituted "profit" for the word "prophet." The Muslims who patronized the business firms he controlled generally paid higher, not lower, prices for what they bought. The believers these businesses employed received substandard wages and few, if any, fringe benefits.

Despite claims that the Nation's businesses were "not-for-profit," profit considerations apparently prompted Chicago to issue the edict forbidding believers from purchasing Qu'rans from anyone except the captain of the Newark, N.J. mosque, who had obtained a franchise enabling him to import them from Pakistan. The edict superseded one that had prohibited members of the movement from buying Qu'rans at all on the ground that they wouldn't be able to understand them. The Qu'ran contradicted many of Elijah Muhammad's teachings.

In theory, most of the businesses were owned by the Nation itself. But it was no secret that, except for the enterprises under Malcolm's supervision, most of them were run primarily for the benefit of the Muhammads and their business associates. Elijah's son Nathaniel called himself the "proprietor" of the Chicago upholstery shop. Years later, he acknowledged that his father had used his followers' contributions to purchase and operate businesses in his own name and his wife's. The disclosure followed the admission by one of the many law firms the Muhammad family hired that the movement's business ventures and property had become "intertwined" with that of Elijah Muhammad and his children, who claimed that their financial interests were synonymous with those of the Nation at large.

The movement shrouded its financial affairs in secrecy. It kept no books at all, so that it was impossible for the tax authorities or anyone else to ascertain where all the money that was coming into the Nation's coffers was going. Not until the growing rift between Malcolm and the Messenger became irreparable did Malcolm openly complain about the funds Elijah was diverting. The Muhammads maximized their profits but not their taxes. Even the property taxes of many of their Chicago businesses were paid for by the Chicago temple, under whose name the movement was legally incorporated. For federal and other tax purposes, the Nation represented itself as a religious movement. One of its applications for federal income tax exemption contained explicit assurances that none of its income inured to the benefit of Elijah Muhammad, John Ali, or any of the other notables whose names appeared on the application. All but one of them declined to respond to the provision on the exemption application requiring them to disclose the compensation they were receiving. The sole exception—Elijah's son Herbert, the movement's treasurer—said he received no compensation.

The lack of clarity about who owned the business enterprises facilitated the efforts of Elijah and his children to maximize their profits. Yet when the Internal Revenue Service (Malcolm called it the "Eternal Revenue Service") came knocking, the ambiguity about the ownership was used to support the claim that the businesses were owned by a non-profit religious organization and, hence, exempt from income tax. (One year, one of Elijah's wealthiest sons paid no income tax.) The resultant tax benefits would have been jeopardized had the Nation of Islam acceded to Malcolm's attempts to politicize it.

Indicative of the attitude that prevailed in Chicago was an item in *Muhammad Speaks* flaunting the movement's flirtation with wheeler-dealer Billie Sol Estes, who had been indicted for fraud and embezzlement. (He was later convicted for tax evasion and other misdeeds.) With its unpaid newspaper vendors and its captive readership, the newspaper became the most profitable of all the Nation's business ventures. The paper was efficiently run by Herbert Muhammad with the help of John Ali and a number of well-paid professional journalists. Herbert, who shunned the limelight and wielded his financial power behind the scenes, modestly described himself as the "assistant editor."

The pressure to sell the paper was unremitting. Chicago assigned each mosque a sales quota, which had to be met. The New Haven mosque, which had only thirty members, was instructed to sell seven thousand copies of *Muhammad Speaks* every other week. (The paper was published bi-weekly.) The temple assigned mandatory sales quotas to each adult male member. In the Boston mosque, each man was required to take—and pay for—two hundred copies, whether he sold them or not. In Chicago, the quota was three hundred. At eleven cents per copy—a figure that kept rising as the retail price (fifteen cents) was periodically raised to offset inflation—each Chicagoan had to cough up thirty-three dollars every fortnight, or more than sixty-five dollars per month. Since non-Muslim demand for the newspaper was limited, most of the copies ended up in the closets or cellars of the Muslim vendors, some of whom Malcolm helped out by dipping into his own wallet.

Ultimately, the Boston mosque began to have as much trouble collecting from its members as they had getting rid of the papers. The leadership used both carrots and sticks to increase circulation, which was apparently based on the number of copies purchased by the vendors, not the number of copies sold and read. Those who made record sales got their pictures in *Muhammad Speaks*. Brothers who failed to meet their quota were shamed before their Muslim peers. Sometimes, they were invited out for a nighttime ride to Franklin Park, where they were worked over.

With its "circulation" of several hundred thousand—eventually, the figure rose to 900,000—the gross income of *Muhammad Speaks*, which later became a weekly, eventually surpassed $100,000 a week, according to an official of the firm that printed it. The seed money produced by the paper and the other businesses would ultimately enable the movement to build what was reputed to be the largest black-run financial empire in the country—one whose assets would reportedly reach a total of more than forty-five million dollars. (At times, spokesmen would cite larger figures.) The Nation would publish books containing Elijah Muhammad's teachings. It would establish a chain of carry-out restaurants, a meat-packing operation, and a fish-importing business. NOI public relations men would proclaim that a total of twenty-six million pounds of whiting had been imported. The Nation would also purchase control of the Guaranty Bank and Trust, a Chicago bank. Financially, it would begin to resemble a corporate conglomerate. Its elegantly dressed officials had their pictures taken as they sat around board-room tables. They traveled around in a fleet of Cadillacs. "Personally, I would prefer any little old car," Elijah Muhammad told a Nigerian interviewer. He claimed that his near-destitute followers, who proudly waited in line to inspect his twin-engine jet plane at airports throughout the country, didn't want it to appear that their religion had impoverished him.

The Messenger, who frequently invited white "devils" to his dinner table to discuss business matters, used the movement's treasury to buy millions of dollars worth of real estate. But he placed title to much of it in his own name. Many years later, after he died, these "really estate" holdings, as he called them, became part of his estate.

Additional real estate was acquired by two tightly controlled firms that were income-tax-exempt corporate subsidiaries of the Nation. But, according to Nathaniel Muhammad, they were really family-owned corporations. The president of both companies was Elijah Muhammad's son-in-law Raymond Sharrieff, who was also president of the parent corporation. Officially, he was also the movement's Supreme Captain, or Captain Joseph's superior. His wife Ethel, Mr. Muhammad's eldest daughter, wielded similar authority over the female believers. Malcolm claimed that she was the real power behind Sharrieff, who, together with Elijah Muhammad, Herbert Muhammad, and John Ali, supervised the movement's financial affairs.

The real estate holdings were eventually expanded to include farm properties, including a 120-acre farm that had been deeded to "Elijah Muhammad and Sons" instead of the movement. The Nation's spokesmen claimed it was a thousand-acre farm. Then Elijah's press agent announced that the Nation hoped to have 100,000 acres of farmland by the end of the following year. He talked in equally expansive terms of a multi-million-dollar agro-business complex that would furnish food to Muslim food markets and restaurants. The "puffery," as one of Elijah's lawyers called it, echoed the attitude that one had to act rich in order to get rich. It was also designed to impress the ever-credulous believers, many of whom apparently felt that the Black Muslim business empire was really theirs. (One of the supermarkets Elijah Muhammad opened in Chicago was called "Your Supermarket"; the fish restaurant was called "Your Fish House.")

The farms never prospered. Yet some of the officials who managed them somehow amassed enough money to buy prosperous farms nearby. Due to the widespread embezzlement, which was publicly acknowledged by Raymond Sharrieff's son, the Nation had to keep exhorting its members to make up the "deficits" that many of the enterprises incurred despite the fact that their Muslim customers constituted a captive market. The donations were reminiscent of the constant appeals for money Marcus Garvey had made to his followers. They also recalled the statement one defense attorney made when Garvey and several associates were indicted and tried for defrauding the blacks who had invested money in the UNIA's steamship company:

> If every Negro could . . . put every dime, every penny, into the sea, and if he might get in exchange the knowledge that he was somebody

. . . in the world, he would gladly do it. . . . The Black Star Line was
a loss in money, but it was a gain in soul.

The money the believers donated to bail out "their" ailing businesses
was not the only wealth they contributed. In addition to the substantial
sums they forked over bi-weekly to *Muhammad Speaks*, whose financial
health marked the beginning of Herbert Muhammad's prosperity, they
were obliged to give anywhere from eight to fifteen additional dollars
per week, depending on the temple—in other words, four to eight
hundred additional dollars per year. The sum was an enormous one for
most of Elijah Muhammad's followers.

Some of the donated money was used to pay the temple's rent (or
mortgage) and utility bills. It was also used to support the local minister (if
he received pay; part-time ministers often donated their services). But a large
portion of the collected funds went to Chicago, either to the movement's
Central Fund, which was reportedly managed by John Ali, or the "Number
Two Poor Treasury." The latter, which eventually grew to more than three
million dollars, was allegedly used to help the needy. But Ronald Stokes's
widow and child didn't receive a cent from it. Neither did the families of a
number of brothers who died penniless despite the fact that the Messenger
and his courtiers had been living off their contributions for years. "Number
Two Poor is making Number One rich," people quipped. Not until years
later did they learn that Elijah Muhammad called one of the bank accounts
containing the alleged relief funds "my checking account."

The aforementioned levies were not the only ones that were imposed.
Each Sunday at the mosque during services, the members of each temple
were obliged to tithe. They were also saddled with special assessments,
such as the $100 "gift" each Muslim was expected to give to a fund that
was used to finance the Savior's Day Convention that was held each year,
ostensibly to commemorate Wallace D. Fard's birthday. (Elijah's son
Emmanuel would later reveal that the Messenger gave expensive presents
to his children on Savior's Day.) *Muhammad Speaks* repeatedly urged the
faithful to invest their remaining pennies in the Messenger's "Three-Year
Economic Plan." There were also constant appeals for a projected twenty-
million-dollar Islamic Center, which was to house educational facilities as
well as a library, a hospital, and a new mosque. The quality of education
the leadership envisioned was suggested by a description of the monthly
tuition the Nation of Islam charged at one of its schools:

ONE (1) CHILD—$ 55.00	FOUR (4) CHILD—$162.42
TWO (2) CHILD—$ 96.25	FIVE (5)+ CHILD—$176.17
THREE (3) CHILD—$134.92	

Despite an official announcement that construction of the Islamic Center was about to begin in Chicago, the project never moved off the pages of *Muhammad Speaks*. The land on which the Center was allegedly going to be built was appropriated by the Windy City for a park. Evidently, no accounting was given for the three million dollars that had reportedly been collected. To request one was out of the question. People who did such things were labeled "seed planters," a breed that believers were constantly warned about.

Years passed. Periodically, the Nation renewed its appeals for contributions for the Center. It announced other heady projects. There was a benefit drive for a several-hundred-bed hospital that never was built. A spokesman announced that construction was beginning on a nursing home. There was even talk of building facilities to treat the mentally ill. And factories. Yet, despite the fact that none of them materialized, the Nation of Islam somehow found enough money to build a new half million dollar mansion for Elijah Muhammad, who consulted one of his lawyers about the danger of a possible indictment for fraud. The elegant domed structure contained elevators and gold-plated fixtures in the bathrooms. Luxurious homes were also built for several of Elijah's children. After one of them was robbed of $23,000 in cash and costly jewelry, elaborate security measures were taken to protect the new dwellings. They included closed-circuit television scanners and roving patrols of unsmiling Muslim guards in black suits.

In addition to these Chicago dwellings, Elijah purchased a high-priced Phoenix, Arizona home with a swimming pool. He bought at least five other properties in Phoenix, where he spent much of his time trying to recuperate from his chronic asthma. He also purchased a palatial home in Cuernavaca, Mexico. Another $150,000 went for his jewel-studded fez. Eventually, the Messenger, who denounced the "robbers" that exploited America's blacks, amassed more than three and a quarter million dollars in bank deposits.

Chicago's insatiable demands for money prompted the officials in charge of certain mosques to resort to the very criminality they were supposedly combating. Their jobs and privileges depended on their ability to keep money flowing to Chicago. Some ministers and captains virtually bought their positions by funneling large sums to the movement's treasury. For instance, years after the Philadelphia temple was freed from Malcolm's supervision, its officials would forge a marriage of convenience with the local "black Mafia"—a group of alligator-shoed, gun-toting hoods who engaged in bank robbery and other unsavory practices. (Philadelphians who didn't want their automobiles burglarized or stolen would buy copies of *Muhammad Speaks* and leave them on their car seats.) The Federal Bureau of Investigation would estimate that the Muslim mob controlled eighty percent of the heroin sold in the Quaker City. The mob's enforcers would deliver ultimatums to Baptist and Methodist ministers, directing them to pay tribute. Muslim "soldiers" would saunter into black churches and waltz out with the collection plate. They shook down numbers writers, "independent" drug pushers, and neighborhood merchants, many of whom had to raise their prices or go out of business to the detriment of the community. A number of the gunmen who performed these duties joined the Philadelphia temple, which was a fairly safe haven for felons on the lam. It was difficult for the police to obtain warrants to search houses of worship. Experience had demonstrated that such attempts could spark a riot.

The criminality reflected the character of the movement's top leadership. One of Mr. Muhammad's sons broke his lover's jaw in four places when she tried to end their relationship because she had learned he was married. Another son was arrested for armed robbery, reportedly because he was on dope and in need of money due to his differences with his father. According to members of the Chicago temple, he avoided prison only because his underlings threatened the life of his robbery victim, who was "unable" to identify him in court.

Three of Elijah Muhammad's sons did eventually spend time in federal prison—two for draft evasion and one for selling dope, despite the efforts of the rank and file to wean junkies from their needles and pills. Two of the Messenger's grandsons were also arrested on drug charges. The one who was sentenced to prison for transporting 750 pounds of marijuana had extremely wealthy parents.

Malcolm's ascetic life style contrasted vividly with the extravagant one that prevailed in Chicago. According to one insider, many high-ranking movement officials hated him because he turned over all the money he received to the Nation's treasury. He was equally conscientious about making the weekly contributions that were expected of the rank and file. One official later told an interviewer, "I know why John Ali hated Malcolm; he was everything John wasn't!"

And so he was. At one gathering, he reached over and handed a check that he had received to Raymond Sharrieff. He did it right on the speaker's platform, as if to say, "I don't keep anything for myself." Outwardly, he praised Sharrieff and made a point of the fact that Sharrieff took his orders directly from Elijah Muhammad. Malcolm's austere morality, which enhanced his political appeal, was a withering rebuke to the hypocrisy of the Messenger and his entourage. That is, as long as he lived.

Loyalty or Rivalry? 39

J. Edgar Hoover's busy agents eventually compiled more than 2,300 pages of material on Malcolm, who was well aware of the surveillance. Every so often, he'd play with the unknown informer in the audience; he said he wouldn't kill him, but that he'd torture him for a number of days. In the midst of one long, angry tirade against the F.B.I., Malcolm told a Harlem audience:

> One of those old blue-eyed things had the nerve, a couple of years ago, to go to Philadelphia and tell the Muslims, "They say Brother Malcolm is . . . in New York livin' with a white woman." Imagine that! I told the brothers, "Next time the old F.B.I. come and tell you that, you tell him that if I'm in New York livin' with a white woman, it's his mother. [Audience gleefully applauds.] His blue-eyed mother! And since she's livin' with me as he says, I can tell him what his mother is *like*. What she *does*! How *nasty* she is!"

The Federal Bureau of Investigation sensed the friction between Malcolm and Elijah Muhammad long before the rumors about the differences between them reached the press. Some Bureau reports quoted Black Muslim sources to the effect that Malcolm was determined to supplant Mr. Muhammad, just as youthful Sandwich Red had supplanted the older, more experienced sandwich salesman who had preceded him on the Yankee Clipper. After all, the time had long since passed when Malcolm needed to play the obeisant student to Mr. Muhammad's teachings. He had trained long and hard for leadership, just as he had trained long and hard for his youthful boxing, dancing and debating contests. He had already competed successfully against lesser rivals within the Nation of Islam. Was it, perhaps, time for the number two Black Muslim to become Number One? Or had he changed since the days he had endeavored to be first in line at elementary school, first in his junior high school class, and first in line at the entrance to the prison shower room?

Malcolm Jarvis does not believe Malcolm had changed. "He wanted to be top man in anything he did," says Jarvis, emphasizing how Malcolm had insisted on running his burglary team and his prison debating team. Malcolm, who encouraged the NOI rank and file to aspire to the positions of their superiors, told James 67X, "The most difficult position in the orchestra is playing second fiddle." Yet he disclaimed all desire to be Number One, or even Number Two. "All Muslims are number Two after Mr. Muhammad," he declared. At one press conference, he told reporters, "I have seen enough of what happens to people in the number two spot not to have any desire to sit in that hot seat." Perhaps he was referring to Marcus Garvey's chief U.S. organizer James Eason, who had been assassinated by some of Garvey's followers after he had repudiated the UNIA, founded a rival organization, and promised to testify against Garvey in court. Or perhaps Malcolm was thinking of the trouble Elijah Muhammad had been having since the 1930s with some of his top aides. One of them, Hamaas Abdul Khaalis, became openly contemptuous of Mr. Muhammad and his brand of Islam during the 1950s.

In the early 1970s, after he had been expelled from the Nation of Islam and had founded a rival sect, he sent the Messenger's ministers letters denouncing him as a false prophet. The letters reportedly said that Elijah Poole had no more right to change his last name to that of the prophet Muhammad than did Elijah Potts, who had played halfback for the Green Bay Packers. Shortly thereafter, several of the trigger men who had joined the Philadelphia temple drove to Washington, D.C., where Khaalis had his headquarters, and entered his home while he was away. They shot his wife in the head six times. Before they shot his daughter, who miraculously survived, one of them told her that the Khaalises should have expected such retribution for writing such letters. The gunmen drowned Hamaas's nine-day-old granddaughter in a sink. They also drowned three of his children.

Despite the long-running feud between Khaalis and Elijah Muhammad, there was one thing they had always agreed upon; namely, that Malcolm posed the greatest potential threat to Mr. Muhammad's leadership. Elijah, who apparently feared that Malcolm would supplant him the way he had supplanted Wallace Fard, told confidants that though Malcolm was the best minister he had ever had—Malcolm used the word "greatest"—he was "dangerous." Other NOI officials accused him of trying to take over and build an empire within an empire. But the accusations didn't anger him, he said.

It was rumored that Elijah Muhammad tried to get Malcolm out of the country—and away from the spotlight—by offering to send him to Cairo to study orthodox Islam. Mindful that Mr. Muhammad considered him a threat, Malcolm went to great lengths to affirm his loyalty. ("I have always been intensely loyal.") He said he had no political aspirations of his own. To emphasize the point, he began refusing invitations to appear on college campuses. Malcolm also turned down invitations from Life and Newsweek, even though the latter offered to do a cover story on him. And he declined an opportunity to appear on "Meet the Press."

Malcolm's efforts to demonstrate his loyalty had an exaggerated quality about them. When newsmen photographed him, he handed them one of the snapshots of Elijah Muhammad that he carried in his briefcase. Then he'd telephone the newspaper and say, "Please use Mr. Muhammad's picture instead of mine." He said he grew furious whenever he read denunciations of Elijah. "I didn't care what they said about me," he claimed. Over and over, he stressed his willingness to sacrifice himself for Muhammad. "I would have hurled myself between [the Messenger] and an assassin," he asserted. And when a would-be assassin telephoned Temple Seven's restaurant and threatened to kill the Messenger, Malcolm told the Amsterdam News that though he and Elijah's other followers were concerned about such phone calls, "We don't normally let these things excite us":

> It is a known fact that every Muslim will gladly die for Mr. Muhammad, so any fool who wishes to commit suicide is welcome to try to attack him.

On another occasion, he declared that if Elijah Muhammad was not the leader of America's Muslims, "Then who is?" Whether such assertions contributed to the lack of sleep he got trying to merit Elijah Muhammad's confidence is unclear.

Around Mr. Muhammad, Malcolm behaved like a model employee, as he had done at the Townsend Drugstore. He said he had no desire to take credit for any of the Nation of Islam's accomplishments. Claiming that he was "selfless," he asserted that while he had been serving the Messenger, he had never thought "for as much as five minutes" about himself. He stressed his loyalty to Elijah and extolled him. In fact, it was Malcolm who was chiefly responsible for the growing deification of Elijah Muhammad, as opposed to Wallace D. Fard.

Contending that his own oratory was a poor substitute for Elijah Muhammad's and that all his accomplishments were attributable to him, Malcolm (who named his third child Ilyasha after Elijah) seasoned his rhetoric with hosanas about "the Honorable Elijah Muhammad." On one occasion, he used the phrase eleven times in as many sentences. But the word "honorable" sometimes came out "honorbubble." Some of Malcolm's associates began to suspect that the teachings he habitually prefaced with the statement "The Honorable Elijah Muhammad teaches us" were those with which he disagreed. Asked why he used the expression so much, he acidly replied, "Because Mr. Muhammad is everything and I am nothing." He likened his relationship to Elijah to the relationship between television celebrity Edgar Bergen and his puppet Charlie McCarthy:

> When you hear Charlie McCarthy speak, you listen and marvel at what he says. What you forget is that Charlie is nothing but a dummy. He is a hunk of wood sitting on Edgar Bergen's lap. If Bergen quits talking, McCarthy is struck dumb. If Bergen turns [him] loose, McCarthy will fall to the floor, a plank of sawdust fit for nothing but the fire. This is the way it is with the Messenger and me.

The self-denigration, which was so difficult to reconcile with his brother Reginald's observation about Malcolm's constant need to bolster his self-esteem, was reminiscent of a point that Malcolm had emphasized in prison—that one must sometimes stoop to conquer.

Reporters ribbed Malcolm about the exaggerated praise he lavished on Elijah Muhammad. To hear him tell it, Mr. Muhammad was:

> America's wisest black man. America's boldest black man. America's most fearless black man!

Malcolm said Allah had taken the Messenger's heart, cleansed it, and made him sinless. He portrayed Elijah as the last and greatest of the prophets—a "Modern Moses" who would lead the faithful to a land of milk and honey. He characterized Mr. Muhammad as the most important black leader since Marcus Garvey and said he was the foremost living revolutionary figure of the era—greater than Gamal Abdel Nasser or Mao Tse Tung. "No man on earth today is his equal," he proclaimed. The inordinate praise, which appeared to please Elijah Muhammad despite his insistence that he wasn't seeking adulation, was reminiscent of the way Malcolm had extolled Minister Lemuel Hassan and the officials at Charlestown State Prison.

But the adulation was a double-edged sword. While Malcolm subtly undermined Elijah by comparing him to leaders who were truly great, Mr. Muhammad, who was hard to fool, praised Malcolm to his face but condemned him behind his back.

Outwardly, Malcolm continued exalting his mentor. But at Yale, in the midst of a speech praising Elijah Muhammad and his "divine solution" to America's race problem, Malcolm interjected some jarring questions that suggested he was not nearly as enamored of Mr.

Muhammad and his teachings as he asserted:

> If God is going to intervene, will He come Himself, or will He send someone with His solution? . . . How will we know if the Messenger who brings us the solution is really a man from God? . . . Is Mr. Muhammad from God? . . . Does his divine solution fit the events of today?

At Michigan State University, Malcolm said he was "professing to speak for black people by representing the Honorable Elijah Muhammad." On another occasion, he declared:

> Think of this . . . a man born in Georgia, mentally blind, deaf, and dumb, and as ignorant as all the rest of us.

> He tells us constantly that his doctrine . . . is not his own but was authored by . . . God.

He cited the following passage from the Qu'ran:

> Those who follow the Apostle, the unlettered Prophet . . .

But he changed it and said:

> Those who follow the Messenger-Prophet, the ILLITERATE ONE. . . ."

The intellectual differences between him and Elijah Muhammad were as profound as the moral ones.

One thing that underscored the difference in moral standards was the Messenger's attitude toward extra-marital sex. As far back as 1955, Malcolm had heard rumors that Mr. Muhammad was engaging in it. At first, he gave them no credence, for Elijah Muhammad severely disciplined those of his followers who engaged in extra-marital sex. Reginald, for instance, was still forbidden to participate in NOI activities. One day, however, he showed up at Temple Seven's restaurant. Malcolm told Reginald—the brother to whom he said he felt closest—that he was unwelcome. Reginald left. He never saw Malcolm again. Years later, when Reginald was asked about Malcolm, his pent-up resentment toward his older brother, who he said still owed him ten dollars, poured out.

Several of the Messenger's secretaries dined with the Muhammads at their home. Some even lived and slept in the elderly Messenger's spacious mansion. One secretary was Robin, the dark-skinned twenty-six-year-old woman who had spurned Captain Joseph for Malcolm. Robin subsequently told her lawyer that late one night, while she was working in Elijah's private office, he entered the room, locked the door behind him, and pulled her off her seat and down onto the thick-carpeted floor. Afterwards, he asserted that he had not been sexually involved with any woman except his wife since his conversion to Islam.

He said precisely the same thing to Heather, who had moved to Chicago and had begun working for him after it had become clear that Malcolm would not marry her. Muhammad told Heather it had been prophesied that she would become a modern-day variant of Aishah, the favorite wife of the prophet Muhammad. Thus, sex with Elijah wasn't adultery; it was divinely inspired. The Messenger claimed that Allah had told him his wife would produce bad offspring, and that it was his religious duty to lay with virgins who would produce good "seed."

Heather bore Elijah Muhammad several children, the first of whom was born in 1960. Ultimately, the Messenger sired more than a dozen children out of wedlock. The youngsters and their mothers were supported by the tithes of the faithful. When the payments became public knowledge, Mr. Muhammad piously told the Los Angeles *Herald-Dispatch*:

> The Nation of Islam, like the Catholic. . . and the Jewish religious organizations, take[s] care of all of our unwed mothers if they are unable to provide for themselves. Therefore, there is nothing unusual in the fact that both [Heather] and [Robin] were provided for by the Nation of Islam.

He declined to mention that his follower's contributions were used to purchase homes for several of his other mistresses, one of whom apparently spent considerable time with him in his Cuernavaca retreat.

Malcolm later told Alex Haley that he tried hard to push the rumors about Elijah's extra-marital activities out of his mind:

> I totally and absolutely rejected my own intelligence. I simply refused to believe. I didn't want Allah to "burn my brain," as I felt the brain of my brother Reginald had been burned for harboring evil thoughts about Mr. Elijah Muhammad.

But the rumors continued to spread, and people asked Malcolm if he had heard them. He pretended he didn't know what his questioners were talking about.

Malcolm said there was never any specific moment when he acknowledged the truth about Elijah to himself:

> In the way that the human mind can do, somehow I slid over admitting to myself the ugly [truth], even as I began dealing with it.

He later contended that he didn't really admit the truth to himself until late 1962 or 1963. But one of his former Muslim associates later asserted that he had learned about Elijah's philandering in 1957, after two of the Messenger's secretaries became pregnant and gave birth. By 1959 or 1960, four more of Muhammad's secretaries, one of whom was Heather, had borne children out of wedlock. About the same time, Malcolm—who was with Elijah when two of his former secretaries, accompanied by their illegitimate children, paid him a surprise visit— began telling some of his associates why he had been sending Mr. Muhammad additional secretaries (one of whom he had tried to enlist as an informant). He told Charles 37X that he had sent them to Chicago in the hope they would induce "stronger" men to join the Nation of Islam. He told James 67X that he had sent them in the hope of improving the movement's image.

By 1960, even Philbert, who was far less familiar with what was happening in Chicago than Malcolm was, knew about Mr. Muhammad's mistresses, some of whom were reportedly white. Elijah began teaching that it was not the province of ordinary folk to judge him. He told Philbert and some of his other ministers that Allah had ordained that he would follow in the footsteps of certain biblical heroes. He cited the tale of David and Bathsheba as a case in point.

Thus, although Malcolm maintained that he "never" bit his tongue when the truth was at stake, the evidence suggests that he had been holding his tongue about Elijah Muhammad's extra-marital activities for years, just as he had been keeping mum about the improprieties of his skirt-chasing father, his lonely, love-starved mother, and his criminally inclined half-sister. The reasons he apparently feigned ignorance of Elijah's misdeeds were similar to the reasons he had kept silent about the fact that there were whites who were not devils. Once the faithful discovered the truth, the credibility of the Messenger would be gravely impaired. If it became widely known that most of the NOI leadership was morally bankrupt, the discipline that kept many believers from reverting to their former ways might be shattered.

Moreover, if Malcolm revealed the truth about Elijah Muhammad, it would mean the end of his participation in the movement that had become the most important thing in his life. Or, worse still, the end of everything.

SUBMIT OR REBEL?

40

Because of Malcolm's prominence, the press had always assumed that he was Elijah Muhammad's heir-apparent. But Earl Little's seventh child had a rival for that position. He was Mr. Muhammad's boyish-looking seventh child, Wallace Delaney Muhammad. Wallace had been named after Wallace Delaney Fard, the Nation of Islam's founder. Before young Wallace was born, Fard had allegedly chalked "WALLACE" on or near the door of the Muhammad family home. Wallace was reputed to be so special that it was said there had been no afterbirth when he was born. His mother, who said that she had received a telegram from Fard instructing her to name the child after him, constantly reminded him that he was destined to follow in his father's footsteps.

As a child, Wallace didn't take the prophecy very seriously. But his parents groomed him for the future that awaited him as his father's designated successor. At the same time, the Messenger kept Wallace under his thumb by discouraging his efforts to become independent. Though Wallace had his heart set on becoming an electronics technician, Elijah refused to pay his tuition to electronics school. Later, Wallace went to prison because his father wouldn't let him fulfill his military obligation. His brother Emmanuel went to jail for the same reason.

Wallace was considered special not only because he was his father's seventh child, but also because he was one of the few members of Mr. Muhammad's family who even pretended to be religious. "Wallace is not like the rest of my children," the Messenger told one of his ministers. He proudly displayed Wallace as his best son. Even the F.B.I., which tried hard to aggravate the differences between Elijah Muhammad and Malcolm, acknowledged that Wallace was far less interested in money than most of his brothers and sisters were.

Malcolm respected Wallace's sincerity, just as Wallace respected his. Publicly, Malcolm maintained that he shared an "exceptional closeness and trust" with his chief rival for Elijah's favor. Wallace would later dispute the claim, which had no more foundation than Malcolm's contention that he had been "very close" to his brothers. Nor was Wallace taken in by the fact that Malcolm referred to him as Mr. Muhammad's successor. "He wanted to be the boss," Wallace later told one journalist. His father put it less charitably. "He is insane for leadership," he exclaimed.

Yet Malcolm behaved as if he were "desperately" trying to preserve Elijah's reputation, not undermine it. He enlisted Wallace's help in searching the Qu'ran and the Bible for authority for the view that a leader's private failings do not diminish his public achievements. He told Alex Haley how afraid he was that some newspaperman would ask him whether the rumors about his mentor were true. He said he had nightmares in which he could see headlines proclaiming that Elijah Muhammad was a fraud.

Eventually, Malcolm wrote Mr. Muhammad about the fact that his image had become tarnished. Muhammad was too smart to reply in writing. He phoned and told Malcolm he'd discuss the matter with him the next time they met.

In April 1963, they met at Elijah's Phoenix, Arizona home. Bluntly, Malcolm told his mentor the cat was out of the bag. He said that he and Wallace had been scouring the Qu'ran for support for the thesis that the Messenger's· extra-marital activities were the fulfillment of scriptural prophecy. "You always have had such a good understanding of prophecy," Elijah replied:

> . . . . I'm David. When you read about how David took another man's wife, I'm that David. You read about Noah, who got drunk—that's me. You read about Lot, who went and laid up with his own daughters. I have to fulfill all of those things.

The statement placed Malcolm in a position to testify in court that Elijah had acknowledged his illicit affairs.

The Messenger was apparently unmoved by Malcolm's efforts to "help" him. Before the month had ended, Mr. Muhammad had transferred him to Washington, D.C. Malcolm assured his New York followers that he would not forsake Harlem and that he would remain their leader. He said he would serve as interim minister of the Washington temple until Elijah could select a permanent one. Yet he told the Washington press corps that he would eventually leave New York and move to the nation's capital. He said the minister of the Washington temple had been removed. He said he was in danger of removal himself.

The reasons Malcolm advanced for his transfer to Washington were not altogether convincing. He said that he was being transferred there to spread Elijah Muhammad's teachings and to reorganize the Washington mosque, which was reportedly the movement's sixth largest. He claimed that he was sent "to help fight juvenile delinquency." In all likelihood, the motive behind Elijah Muhammad's decision to send Malcolm to Washington—a transfer Chicago depicted as a promotion—was a desire to end Malcolm's control of the activities of the all-important New York City mosques, which provided the movement with so much money and manpower—in other words, an attempt to kick him upstairs and to deprive him of his power base.

But Malcolm apparently maintained control over Temple Seven, whose members continued to regard him as their minister. Day after day, he shuttled back and forth between Washington, New York, and other cities. Then, one day—precisely when is unclear—he called together about half a dozen East Coast Muslim officials and told them about Elijah Muhammad's harem. In his autobiography, he says he did it because he didn't want the Nation to be unprepared if it became necessary for it to teach its members that their leader's love affairs had been divinely ordained. He said he was merely trying to inoculate the Nation against what was likely to occur when the rank and file learned that the Messenger habitually committed the very sins he condemned in others:

> When an epidemic is about to hit somewhere, that community's people are inoculated against exposure with some of the same germs that are anticipated—and this prepares them to resist the oncoming virus.

But Malcolm did not believe in inoculation; his wife had to get their children vaccinated on the sly.

To those who had become accustomed to Malcolm's habit of saying the opposite of what he was really thinking, the "inoculation" meeting looked like the opening gambit of a thinly disguised power play—an effort to outfox Elijah, as young Malcolm had outfoxed older rivals such as Thornton Gohanna and George Holt. The Messenger may also have felt that Malcolm was biting the hand that was feeding him. He reportedly felt as betrayed as Malcolm did.

Before May had ended, Malcolm had written Muhammad a letter of apology. But by June, he had outflanked him politically by authorizing the announcement that Temple Seven would begin a voter registration drive for its members. (Though Malcolm maintained that Mr. Muhammad had given the requisite permission, Muhammad Speaks had merely announced ambiguously that the NOI *might* initiate a nationwide voter registration drive.) By August, Malcolm was publicly advocating a "united black front" with CORE, SCLC, the NAACP, and other black organizations with whom it would have been advantageous for him to work out an accommodation. The crowd cheered when he told them, "You don't need any guns, you just need some unity—and a blade when it gets dark." A few weeks later at a rally at the Philadelphia Arena, Mr. Muhammad embraced Malcolm in front of several thousand attentive Muslims and declared, "This is my most faithful, hardworking minister. He will follow me until he dies."

Less than a month later, Malcolm lost his job as minister of Washington's Temple Number Four. The Nation of Islam, which needed him as much as he needed it, took pains to dispel rumors that he had been demoted because a split had developed between him and Mr. Muhammad. Spokesmen announced that he had relinquished his Washington post because a new resident minister had been found for Temple Four. But Muhammad told *Jet* that the additional responsibilities that Malcolm had assumed in Washington had proven "just too much for him." Yet everyone who was anyone in the movement knew that Malcolm had been supervising the Washington mosque and all the other East Coast mosques for years.

Shortly after Malcolm's Washington assignment ended, he began reappearing on the college lecture circuit. On October 22, he told an audience at Wayne State University that he favored the idea of a black political party. Six days later, he told a New York audience about an incident that had occurred the day before in Flint, Michigan. The Nation had been holding a big rally. Suddenly, police officers attempted to enter the hall. Elijah Muhammad's subordinates apparently asked them to check their weapons at the door. The officers refused. Mr. Muhammad averted potential violence by ending the rally early. Had the Messenger not been divinely guided, Malcolm told his listeners, there would have been war. He said that, had the decision been his, he probably would have handled the situation differently. The thinly veiled criticism helped him portray himself as a more militant leader than his money-minded boss.

Two weeks later in Detroit, Malcolm addressed the Northern Negro Grass Roots Leadership Conference, which had been convened by the recently formed Freedom Now Party, Reverend Albert B. Cleage, Jr., and others in the hope of coordinating anti-Jim Crow efforts outside the South. The conclave opened with an invocation proclaiming "active tolerance and fraternity" between the Christian leadership of the conference and Elijah Muhammad's Nation of Islam. Malcolm told his nearly all-black audience, "If someone puts his hand on you, send him to the cemetery." He said that any white man caught molesting a black woman should be decapitated.

But the part of Malcolm's speech that really electrified the audience was his analysis of the difference between what he disparaged as the Negro revolution and "real" revolution. He cited the Russian revolution as a case in point. "How did they bring it about?" he asked. "Bloodshed!" he thundered:

> . . . . You don't have a peaceful revolution. You don't have a turn-the-other-cheek revolution. There's no such thing as a nonviolent revolution . . . . Revolution is bloody. Revolution is hostile. Revolution knows no compromise. Revolution overturns and destroys everything that gets in its way.

Without explicitly advocating political violence, he convinced most of his listeners that he favored it.

Malcolm also suggested during the speech that the Black Muslims would permit no betrayal of the political candidates the all-black Freedom Now Party and its allies chose to support. The statement implied he was speaking for the Nation of Islam. That impression was reinforced by a Chicago newspaper headline proclaiming, "Black Muslims Join New Militant Negro Organization." It isn't difficult to imagine how Elijah Muhammad reacted to the erroneous report, which appeared in the *Chicago Defender*, the Windy City's leading black newspaper.

Whether these provocations were consciously planned by Malcolm is hard to tell. His behavior was reminiscent of the way he had provoked rivals such as Hank Ross, Philbert, and Bea's husband, as well as former mentors like Bembry and Sammy the Pimp. It also called to mind the ambivalence that had apparently contributed to his ouster from Pleasant Grove Elementary School, Lincoln Community Center, Mason Junior High School, and the experimental penal colony at Norfolk. Similar ambivalence pervaded his feelings about the Nation of Islam, whose refusal to engage in political activity during the zenith of the civil rights struggle was apparently very difficult for him to bear. Moreover, how could he remain in an organization whose financial growth continued to be predicated upon the pauperization of the members it pretended to serve? His dilemma was compounded by the fact that the Nation was encountering increasing difficulty hiding the fact that "the little lamb" who presided over it was a lecherous wolf in disguise. ("Everything is hypocrisy!" Malcolm exclaimed.)

As long as Elijah Muhammad ruled the roost, Malcolm was destined to be his errand boy, despite his ever-growing prominence—a more worldly errand boy than he had been when he had ferried betting slips across the George Washington bridge for his numbers banker—but an errand boy nevertheless. One would think he chafed at the subservience, as he had chafed at the way he had been obliged to cater to the snooty teenagers who had patronized the Townsend Drugstore. In a conversation with Louis Lomax, Malcolm characterized himself as Mr. Muhammad's "slave." He said he could "feel" the might of the man who had subjected him to a servitude that was the very antithesis of the "perfect freedom" he was demanding for his followers.

Difficult as it may have been for Malcolm to stay in the Nation of Islam, it was apparently just as difficult for him to leave the movement, whose by-laws prohibited believers from terminating their membership voluntarily. (Except for dismissal, the by-laws listed death as the only permissible avenue of departure.) How could he repudiate the very man who had raised him up:

> He was the Messenger of Allah. When I was a foul, vicious convict,
> . . . this man had rescued me. He was the man who had trained me,
> who had treated me as if I were his own flesh and blood. He was the
> man who had given me wings."

How could he quit the movement that afforded him "every gratification"?

> I *loved* the Nation and Mr. Muhammad. I *lived* for the Nation, and
> for Mr. Muhammad.

If Malcolm left the Nation, where was he to go? The movement was his sole source of financial and organizational support. According to Lomax, Malcolm was hoping to wait things out until he could take over and "purify" the NOI, which he bitterly declared had been ruined by "niggers." But it was becoming increasingly evident that neither Elijah Muhammad nor anyone else in Chicago would ever allow Malcolm to succeed the Messenger. In short, Malcolm was in conflict. He did not appear able to leave the Nation. Yet, in the long run, he couldn't stay. He couldn't overtly rebel without losing his only secure political base—and perhaps his life. Yet how could he submit much longer? So he did a little of both by continuing to practice the subtle art of political provocation.

SILENCED

41

J ohn Kennedy, the youngest man ever elected President of the United States, was assassinated on November 22, 1963. "The old devil is dead!" exclaimed Malcolm after he was told. It is unclear if he was using the word "old" as an intensive or if he was also talking about one authority figure while he was thinking about another.* At times, he virtually equated one authority-figure with another. The American president, he said, is "almost like a God":

> . . . his powers are so great. Small wonder, then, that every four years the eyes of . . . foreign nations are turned toward America at election time, wondering who is going to be the next "God."

Malcolm also characterized Kennedy (and his predecessor Dwight Eisenhower) as a prison warden. He said Richard Nixon, Eisenhower's vice-president, had been a deputy warden, and that New York City's mayor Robert Wagner was a "screw" (a prison guard).

A few hours after the assassination, Malcolm spoke at Temple Seven. There was standing room only, for many of his expectant listeners knew that he had no sympathy for the fabulously wealthy, Harvard-educated chief executive, who, in addition to being the country's top authority figure, had demonstrated considerable reluctance to implement his campaign promises to press full steam ahead in the area of civil rights. Though the Kennedy Administration had done far more in the racial realm than its predecessors had, the President had waited almost two years before he had signed the executive order that prohibited racial discrimination in housing financed by federal funds. In 1960, he had campaigned in favor of such an executive order. He said it merely

---

* On one occasion, he repeatedly used the word "old" to describe an authority figure who was nearly ten years younger than he was.

required a stroke of the presidential pen. Malcolm took him to task for taking nearly two years to find his pen.

But he went further than that. He characterized Kennedy as "a segregationist" who was more interested in dismantling the Berlin Wall than the "Alabama Wall." He claimed the only difference between Kennedy, whom he depicted as a hypocritical fox, and George Wallace, whom he called a wolf, was that a fox "will eat you with a smile instead of a scowl." Malcolm said that Kennedy's strategy was designed to give blacks a false sense of racial progress. He called the martyred president, whom he accused of trying to act like Jesus, a "crook."

In addition to vilifying John Kennedy, he also criticized Robert and Ted Kennedy. He called the three Kennedys "the K.K.K."

Those who came to Temple Seven that night to hear Malcolm make further disparaging, headline-grabbing statements about the fallen president went away disappointed. He contented himself with an oblique reference to the punishment God had meted out to Pharaoh. He also observed that people reap what they sow. His unwillingness to say more was probably due to two directives he had received from Elijah Muhammad. The directives, which Malcolm relayed to a number of other ministers, were designed to prevent any NOI official from saying anything that might offend the many blacks who had idolized JFK. Elijah's ministers were instructed to refrain from discussing the assassination. He told them that if the press asked them to comment, they should refuse.

Nine days later, on December 1, 1963, Malcolm addressed a throng of about seven hundred at the Manhattan Center. His associate Sharon 10X felt that he was apprehensive about making the speech; he seemed so afraid of what he might say that he had it typed out beforehand. The prepared text was the only one Sharon had ever seen Malcolm use; usually, he spoke extemporaneously from note cards or the yellow note pads that lawyers use. Sometimes, he even spoke from notes he had hurriedly scrawled on paper napkins or scraps of newspaper.

Before Malcolm began speaking, two white reporters entered the Manhattan Center and sat down. James 67X, who was officiating, asked Malcolm what to do, for Elijah Muhammad had recently decided to bar whites from Black Muslim gatherings in an effort to avert the kind of confrontation that had occurred in Flint weeks before. Malcolm hesitated. Then he declared, "Let them stay."

The principal theme of Malcolm's address, which he read word for word, was one he had reiterated countless times: God was wreaking, and would continue to wreak, his vengeance on white America until it let its black population go free. During the latter part of the speech,

Malcolm noted how crucial the black vote had been to President Kennedy. He condemned Kennedy's decision to wait until Birmingham's whites (as opposed to its blacks) had become targets of violence before ordering troops to take up positions near the stricken city. He accused the late president of undermining the original intent of the March on Washington by seeing to it that large sums of money were offered to the civil rights organizations that had staged it:

> When the late President saw that he couldn't stop the March, he joined it; he endorsed it. . . . The government told the marchers what time to arrive in Washington, where to arrive, and how to arrive. The government then channeled them from the arrival point to the feet of a dead president, George Washington, and let them march from there to the feet of another dead president, Abraham Lincoln.

There was no need to add that Abraham Lincoln had also been a victim of assassination.

Having primed his audience, which contained a substantial number of non-Muslim militants who hoped that Malcolm would break free of the political constraints that Elijah Muhammad had imposed on him, Malcolm quickly ended his talk with his customary obeisance to Elijah's teachings and opened the floor to questions. He later asserted it was virtually inevitable that someone in the audience would ask him about Kennedy's assassination.

Someone did. "Without a second thought," Malcolm shed the restraint that had characterized his formal address and described the assassination as case of "chickens coming home to roost." He compared it to the assassinations of Patrice Lumumba, Ngo Dinh Diem, and Ngo Dinh Nhu, all of whom had died in coups the Kennedy Administration had encouraged or condoned. Malcolm said he was "an old farm boy" himself:

> Chickens coming home to roost never did make me sad; they've always made me glad.

A huge grin erupted on his face; one listener later described it as the kind one might expect from a naughty child who knows he's disobeyed. Some members of the audience applauded. Others laughed. They laughed again when Malcolm asserted that the press had been baiting Black Muslim officials with questions about Kennedy's assassination in the hope one of them would exclaim, "Hooray! I'm glad he got it!" But John Ali didn't laugh. Neither did the other NOI officials who were on the stage, for they knew that while Malcolm had been busily denouncing one authority figure, he had simultaneously been defying another.

Malcolm's assault on the dead president afforded Elijah Muhammad a perfect excuse to move against his unproclaimed rival, who flew to Chicago the next day to confer with him. On the plane, Malcolm had another of his premonitions.

As usual, the two men embraced as they greeted each other. But Malcolm could feel the tension.

Elijah took his time getting to the point. Finally, he asked, "Did you see the papers this morning?" Needless to say, Malcolm, who followed the press very closely, had.

Mr. Muhammad told Malcolm his remarks about Kennedy had seriously damaged the Nation of Islam's image. Malcolm was therefore forbidden to make further public statements. This was necessary, Elijah said, to disassociate the movement from his impolitic utterances. (Muzzling Malcolm, who was so popular with the rank and file, was far more politic than sacking him. And it would prevent him from publicizing the details of the Messenger's private life.)

When Malcolm returned to New York, he discovered that Temple Seven had already been told he had been silenced. So had the media. Moreover, when he telephoned Elijah Muhammad on December 4, the Messenger told him that the ban on "public speeching" included the sermons Malcolm customarily gave each week at the temple. When Malcolm tried to mount the speaker's rostrum the following Sunday, Captain Joseph barred the way.

A *New York Times* reporter asked Elijah Muhammad when Malcolm would be ungagged. Somewhat hesitantly, the Messenger replied, "I will decide." He declined to comment further. The F.B.I. agents who tapped his phone learned that he had ordered Malcolm to refrain from making public statements indefinitely. During an interview with the *New York Post*, Malcolm confirmed this. But he told other questioners that he expected to be reinstated "within ninety days." He stressed that he was still in charge of Temple Seven. But "sources close to the Black Muslim movement" told the *Times* that Elijah Muhammad had already chosen a new minister for Temple Seven. They intimated that Malcolm's removal was only a matter of time.

Despite the way Elijah Muhammad had humiliated him, Malcolm concealed his anger as best he could. But the back of his neck was reddish every time he was interviewed by Alex Haley, who could feel Malcolm's hidden rage. Haley was not the only one of Malcolm's associates who sensed it. But others were completely fooled by his contrite facade, which astounded the F.B.I. agents who unsuccessfully tried to offer him money to inform on his NOI foes. "I just should have kept my big mouth shut," he told *Newsweek*'s Peter Goldman. He told CBS that people who disciplined others should learn to discipline themselves. He told *Times* reporter R.W. Apple, who did not appear to sense the political irony, "Anything that Mr. Muhammad does is all right with me. I believe absolutely in his wisdom and his authority."

But each and every one of these submissive-sounding utterances was made in defiance of Mr. Muhammad's directive that Malcolm was forbidden "to speak in public"—a directive that Malcolm interpreted, in fact if not always in theory, as a mere ban on public appearances and public speeches. He canceled all speaking engagements for a number of weeks. Yet, despite the fact that he had also been forbidden to grant interviews, he kept right on making statements to reporters over the telephone. He told one journalist:

> [Elijah Muhammad] suspended me from making public appearances
> for the time being, which I fully understand. I say the same thing to
> you that I have told others—I'm in complete submission.

His talent for clothing rebellion in submissive garb helped him remain in the news despite the fact he had been told to be silent. The press was full of speculation about whether he would stay in the movement or venture out on his own. The *Amsterdam News* even published Harlem businessman Louis Michaux's telegram to Elijah Muhammad, which pointedly described how Pontius Pilate had persecuted Jesus. Michaux died before anyone asked him if Malcolm had inspired him to send the telegram.

Malcolm devised other ways to obtain political exposure. For example, he wrote letters to groups that had invited him to speak, intimating what his future plans were. He leaked a number of newsy items to columnist Jimmy Booker, who published them in the *Amsterdam News*. In addition, he invited Louis Lomax to have coffee with him in Temple Seven's restaurant. As other Muslims looked on, apparently from a discreet distance, Lomax asked him, "How long will the suspension last?"

"It better not last too long," Malcolm replied. "I'm thinking about making a move on my own." He told another questioner, "It's hard to make a rooster stop crowing once the sun has risen." He did not deny that he had a weakness for speaker's platforms—a weakness that was the wellspring of his political strength.

Five weeks after Malcolm made his "chickens roost" speech, Elijah Muhammad reportedly called him on the carpet for his refusal to remain silent and informed him that he was no longer his National Representative or Temple Seven's minister. The press was apparently not told by the Nation of Islam, which was trying to paper over the rift between Malcolm and Chicago. Nor did Malcolm inform the media about his new, diminished status, which was rendered still more precarious by a quietly disseminated decree that he was to be "isolated" from the other believers, as Reginald had been.

Malcolm took the demotion very hard—so hard, in fact, that he broke down and cried. "I was in a state of emotional shock," he later told Alex Haley. "My head felt like it was bleeding inside."

Malcolm consulted his physician, Leona A. Turner, about the splitting headaches he was having. Dr. Turner examined him and told him that the headaches were not due to the brain tumor Malcolm said he thought he had. She explained that the cause of the pain was not physiological. She encouraged Malcolm to forget about Elijah Muhammad. "You don't need him," she said. "You can make it on your own." Malcolm thanked her. A little later, he said his head didn't hurt anymore.

But he said he was still experiencing discomfort in his abdomen, so Dr. Turner referred him to a surgeon, Farrow Allen. Dr. Allen examined him and found nothing wrong with him physically. He concluded that the abdominal cramping was psychosomatic.

Malcolm seemed depressed because of the way Elijah Muhammad had spurned him. Physically, he slumped. His spirit seemed badly broken.

Dr. Turner was not the only woman to whom he turned as everything he had striven for began to crumble. Ella was another. But he told Alex Haley that he relied most heavily on Betty. He said he could feel her comfort envelop him, even though there was no verbal exchange between them:

> Betty said nothing, being the caliber of wife that she is, with the depth of understanding that she has.

Malcolm's wife reportedly continued attending services at Temple Seven, where she had to endure bitter denunciations of her husband. Mrs. Shabazz declined to let me ask whether Malcolm wanted her to attend in order to demonstrate his loyalty to the Nation of Islam. Nor did she grant me an opportunity to ask her anything else.

ANOTHER BOXER

42

Malcolm told one interviewer that he didn't know what he would have done if he had stayed in New York, hounded by reporters. A brief respite was provided by the boxer Cassius Clay, who invited him and his family to visit his Miami fight camp, where he was preparing for a championship bout against heavyweight title-holder Sonny Liston. Clay had come up the hard way. His father, who had been arrested twice for assault and battery, had habitually beaten his wife, who had to ask the police to intervene on three separate occasions. Years later, after Clay had changed his name to Muhammad Ali, he denied one biographer's assertion that his father had beaten him, too; he said, "We were not to be struck by anyone inside the house." But, in other parts of his autobiography, he acknowledged that corporal punishment had been used on him. One maternal "spanking" was apparently so rigorous that he lashed out and struck his mother. He hit her so hard that he loosened two of her front teeth, one or both of which had to be removed.

Cassius said he loved his strict, churchgoing mother, who had complained that, when he was born, he wasn't "nice" like the rest of the babies in her maternity ward. She had a hard time controlling him and "worried about" him and the teenage gang he ran with. On one occasion, he and one of his friends buried iron obstructions in the bed of a railroad track and derailed a diesel engine.

Clay's father, who may have been unaware how sensitive boys are to any suggestion that they are unmasculine, teased him about his "pretty" looks. Occasionally, he used the word "beauty." Yet Mr. Clay, whose aspirations had been thwarted, began telling everyone he knew that Cassius, who had been named after him, was going to be another Joe Louis. Even the boy's mother began noticing a resemblance between him and the Brown Bomber. By the time he was fourteen, he was already dreaming of becoming the heavyweight champion of the world.

The vacation that Clay offered Malcolm and Betty was the only one she had had since she and Malcolm had married. But after three or four days, Malcolm sent her and the children back to New York. The things he said to her and to the people he met in Miami meant "nothing" to him, he later acknowledged. He said he was only mouthing words:

> Whatever I was saying at any time was being handled by a small corner of my mind. The rest of my mind was filled with a parade of a thousand and one different scenes from the past . . . scenes in the Muslim mosques . . . scenes with Mr. Muhammad.

"I walked, I talked, I functioned," he told Alex Haley.

> At the Cassius Clay fight camp, I told the various sportswriters repeatedly what I gradually had come to know within myself was a lie—that I would be reinstated within ninety days.

He said he felt like a man who was married psychologically but divorced physically.

Malcolm also told Haley that he suspected, and that Clay subsequently acknowledged, that Clay's crazy, provocative antics were carefully designed to induce Liston (whom Clay publicly derided as a "big ugly bear") into entering the ring angry, overconfident, and undertrained. The voluble challenger, who also characterized the champ as a "chump," later admitted there were other reasons for his attention-getting pranks, which aroused such indignation that some people were willing to pay top dollar to see Liston put a fist down his hyperactive mouth. The pranks were ingenious. On one occasion, "the Lip" drove his bus, which he called "Big Red," onto the front lawn of Liston's fashionable home at two o'clock in the morning. Blasting the horn, he awakened not only Liston, but also the whole neighborhood. Police officers, accompanied by six dogs, rushed to the scene, along with newsmen. Another time, Big Red, covered with signs containing slogans such as "bear hunting season," invaded Liston's fight camp. The bus was crammed with screaming teenage girls and other Clay supporters. Reporters told Clay, "Stop angering that man; he will literally kill you." "It was music to my ears," Clay acknowledged afterward. He said that as long as Liston stayed angry, he wouldn't be able to concentrate on his boxing. "You got to think to fight," he emphasized. Years before, in Norfolk Prison, Malcolm had given Boise Philips similar advice.

A few weeks before the heavily advertised championship bout, the fight promoter, who reportedly had to shell out half a million dollars or more to stage the fight, started looking for an excuse to cancel it because of sluggish ticket sales. (The day of the bout, the arena in which it was held was only half filled; relatively few people cared to pay up to $250 per ticket for a fight that almost everyone thought Sonny Liston was going to win hands down.) The excuse that the promoter, Bill McDonald, came up with was the presence of Malcolm and the other Black Muslims in Clay's large, expensive retinue. McDonald argued that people might be willing to pay exorbitant prices to see an underdog take on a "killer" like Liston, but they wouldn't spend a dime to see a man who had Black Muslim connections tangle with one who reputedly had Mafia connections. McDonald told Clay that he'd cancel the bout unless Clay publicly renounced his Muslim affiliation, which the press was beginning to play up. But Clay, who nearly sacrificed his boxing career for his convictions more than once, refused to repudiate Islam.

At last, a compromise was hammered out; the fight would take place, but only if Clay promised not to acknowledge his conversion to Islam (which had occurred several years earlier) until after the match. Malcolm, whose presence at Clay's fight camp jeopardized the fragile agreement, helped out by leaving Miami until the bout.

Hours before the fight was scheduled to begin, Clay arrived at the weigh-in ceremony with Sugar Ray Robinson and other members of his retinue. Loudly, he proclaimed that he was ready to rumble there and then. He pounded his cane on the floor of the platform on which the scales were located and nearly went crazy when Liston entered the room. His eyes bulging, his arms wildly jerking, he lunged at the champ, but was restrained by his aides. His body was visibly trembling. When the doctor took his pulse, it was 120—more than twice its normal rate. The doctor attributed Clay's symptoms, which were reminiscent of a heart murmur he had developed before his initial attempt to win the U.S. Golden Gloves championship, to fear. Clay, who later acknowledged that he was "scared to death" before each fight, said his bizarre behavior was another carefully planned provocation.

If his outburst was partly due to fear, it was Malcolm who helped him to overcome it. "This fight," he told Clay, ". . . [is] a modern Crusades—a Christian and a Muslim facing each other, with television to beam it off Telstar for the whole world to see." Malcolm asked if Allah would have allowed the fight in the first place if he didn't intend Islam's champion to win. (Clay proclaimed, at the weigh-in, that he could not be beaten because victory had been prophesied.)

The night of the fight, Malcolm took seat number seven in Miami's spacious Convention Hall and watched as Sonny Liston emerged from his corner almost at a run. The "Dark Destroyer's" face reflected the emotional toll Clay's incessant needling had taken. He lashed out with a couple of lefts. Clay (who was probably the fastest heavyweight titleholder of all time) easily eluded his ominous-looking pursuer by back-pedaling, bobbing, weaving, ducking. He kept watching Liston's eyes, which tipped whenever he was about to throw a haymaker. During round two, the "meanest man in boxing" tried to corner Clay near the ropes, where his brash challenger wouldn't be able to evade his deadly fists. But Clay danced away, stopping only to pile up points with hit-and-run combinations. A small cut opened above Liston's cheekbone, just beneath his left eye. Clay concentrated on the target. Suddenly the champ caught him with a long, arching left to the side of the jaw. "It rocked me back," Clay admitted afterward. But Liston was unable to follow up his advantage, probably because of the pain his left shoulder was causing him. The circumference of his left arm later swelled more than three inches because of the tendon he had ripped earlier.

By round four, Liston, who had confidently predicted a three-round contest, was slowing visibly. But, somehow, some of the liniment his corner men had been using to rub down his shoulder found its way from one of his gloves to Clay's forehead and dripped down into "Mighty Mouth's" eyes. "I can't see," Clay cried as the round ended. "I'm blind!" The pain was almost unbearable; Clay begged his trainer to stop the fight. But his trainer refused. He shoved Clay toward the center of the ring. Somehow, Clay survived round five, largely due to his astounding footwork and Liston's injury, which gravely impaired his offense.

Clay's eyes cleared as the bell rang for the sixth. For three solid minutes, he pounded Liston with a barrage of left-right combinations and uppercuts. The weary champ never emerged from his corner for round seven. Clay leapt into the air, ecstatic. Malcolm was equally jubilant, not only because Islam had apparently triumphed, but also because he had helped inspire the pugilistic victory he had never been able to achieve himself, just as he had helped Boise Philips defeat his opponent.

The victory party, which was held in Malcolm's motel suite, was a subdued affair; Clay, like Malcolm, was quiet and gentlemanly in private.

Clay was so tired that he took a cat nap on Malcolm's bed. Malcolm telephoned Alex Haley and told him what was going on. Clay, he said, was "in the next room, my bedroom." He seemed proud of the fact he was on good terms with the new champ, who publicly acknowledged, the next day, that he was indeed a Muslim. Malcolm accompanied Clay, who soon began using the name Muhammad Ali, to New York, where

Ali announced he might run for "Mayor of Harlem." During the following week, the two men appeared together frequently. They toured the United Nations and posed for photographs with African delegates. The resultant press coverage enabled Malcolm to stay in the news without uttering a word.

Yet since Ali, not Malcolm, was the hero of the hour, the relationship between the two celebrities had subtly changed. The Nation of Islam quickly capitalized upon the fact and publicly embraced the champ, who had suddenly replaced Malcolm as the leading symbol of black masculinity. For a while, every single issue of *Muhammad Speaks* ran material on Ali; the photographs of him were sometimes half a page large. Herbert Muhammad, who still ran the paper, eventually became Ali's manager. The result was a financial alliance that eventually helped Ali (who extolled Herbert's "keen business instincts") gross more than $27,000,000 in nine years. (Herbert got 30%.) Money changed hands in both directions. Ali made a large tax-deductible donation to the movement, then "borrowed" it back. He also made sizable donations to the "Herbert Muhammad Foundation"; one $49,000 transfer was made on the very last day of the fiscal year. The Nation, in turn, used Ali as its principal drawing card at the press conference it called to announce the opening of a drive to collect money for a multi-million-dollar hospital that was never built. Ali's father, who had opposed his conversion to Islam, told the *New York Times* that his son's Black Muslim associates (one of whom was Captain Joseph) were "a bunch of gangsters." "I raised him clean," Cassius Senior asserted. "He's got no reason to be ashamed of his name."

Ali, whose well-publicized relationship with Malcolm soon went the way of all political "friendships," supplanted him as the NOI's chief attraction virtually overnight. Consequently, there was no longer any compelling reason for Mr. Muhammad to reinstate Malcolm, who was no longer indispensable. Whether Malcolm, who reportedly made a number of unsuccessful attempts to win reinstatement, realized this at the time is difficult to tell. Other things had happened since December to make him realize that he would not be restored to his previous preeminent position. The NOI had leaked a story that Malcolm had openly defied Elijah Muhammad's authority by soliciting the support of unnamed Black Muslim officials. Mr. Muhammad didn't even bother to reply to the conciliatory letters Malcolm sent him. Nor did Malcolm have much luck getting through to him by phone; Elijah's underlings thwarted most of the attempts with or without his knowledge. Malcolm's apparent attempt to circumvent the Messenger's subordinates by trying to contact him through Heather proved equally unsuccessful. He wasn't even allowed to attend the annual Savior's Day Convention, which was held the day after Muhammad Ali trounced Liston.

What made it even more apparent that Elijah Muhammad had no intention of reinstating Malcolm were the death threats that began emanating from his subordinates. (There was no sense killing him if the movement intended to make use of his skills.) At first, the threats were not explicit; one NOI official who had been one of Malcolm's "most immediate" subordinates told his henchmen, "If you knew what the minister did, you'd go out and kill him yourself." Temple spokesmen began declaring that "hypocrites" should be slain. Then one of Malcolm's "close" former aides asked Langston X, a NOI member who had done demolition work, to wire Malcolm's automobile ignition with a bomb. Instead, Langston warned Malcolm of the plot. Malcolm and another disenchanted Muslim official later charged that Captain Joseph had been involved in the efforts to kill him.

"Only one man" could have sanctioned such efforts, Malcolm told Alex Haley. The realization, he said, nearly sent him "to Bellevue." But Malcolm did not flee into a world of make-believe, as Reginald and his mother had done. Instead, he mustered his strength and prevailed upon a friendly journalist to publish a hint that, unless he were restored to his former position by the first of March, he'd very likely return to center stage in a way that would "make his previous efforts pale by comparison." The *Amsterdam News* announced that he'd return to "the thick of things" after March 1, whether his suspension was lifted or not. Shortly thereafter, Elijah Muhammad notified Malcolm that it would remain in force indefinitely. Three days later, Malcolm announced he was leaving the Nation of Islam.

The Strength
to Continue Alone   43

Having liberated himself from the shackles of authority, Malcolm held two press conferences within five days:

> The microphones stuck up before me. The flash bulbs popped. The reporters . . . representing media that reached around the world, sat looking at me with their pencils and open notebooks.

He gave lip service to the ideal of separation, which he characterized as a long-range goal. In the short run, he declared, "Twenty-two million of our people who are still in America need better food, clothing, housing, education, and jobs right now." "I am prepared," he asserted, "to cooperate in local civil rights actions in the South and elsewhere, and shall do so." He said he hadn't participated in the civil rights struggle because Elijah Muhammad had forbidden him to do so.

Malcolm accompanied his declaration of independence from his mentor with assurances that he would not compete with him or provoke him. "I want it clearly understood," he declared, "that my advice to all Muslims is that they stay in the Nation of Islam under the spiritual guidance of the Honorable Elijah Muhammad. It is not my desire to encourage any of them to follow me." He told a New York television audience he had no intention of establishing a rival movement.

Yet when Malcolm showed up on March 12 at a press conference at the Park Sheraton Hotel, he was accompanied by several former members of the NOI—a fact suggesting that he intended to compete, just as he had competed, after careful preparation, against the other dancers at Roseland Ballroom and the other hustlers who had roamed Harlem's streets.

Despite his assertion that he didn't feel equipped to initiate a separate movement, Malcolm informed the reporters who were assembled at the Park Sheraton that he was going to organize his own Muslim Mosque. "I have no fear or doubts that I will be successful," he told Jimmy Booker. Yet Alex Haley and others noticed that he seemed uncharacteristically ill at ease. The day after he announced the establishment of his new, fledgling mosque, he went to Dr. Leona Turner because of the trouble he was having with his heart. It was beating a mile a minute. Dr. Turner found no evidence of any physical impairment. Neither did the other doctors who subsequently examined Malcolm's heart. He told Dr. Turner that he feared he was having, or was about to have, another "heart attack."

The fear, which may have been aroused by the fact that he occasionally had difficulty breathing, was understandable; several members of his family had heart conditions. His Aunt Sassie, whom one cousin described as "a mother to us all," had died of heart disease just two years earlier.

Malcolm tried his best to make it appear that his Muslim Mosque was not an attempt to steal the thunder—and the dues-paying members—of the Nation of Islam. He said he would preach the gospel of black nationalism the way Billy Graham preached the gospel of Christianity: without threatening existing churches or churchmen. In his effort to portray himself as a sort of black, Islamic Billy Graham, he told one woman who had followed him out of Temple Seven that she should consider herself a follower of "the Honorable Elijah Muhammad." He also discouraged a number of other disenchanted believers from leaving the temple. Charles 37X sensed that they might be more helpful to Malcolm inside it rather than outside it, not only as potential informants, but also as potential supporters of any attempt to wrest control of it. Charles was correct; within two weeks, six of Malcolm's men unsuccessfully attempted a coup at Temple Seven. The following day, in Massachusetts, Malcolm made several attempts to recruit members of the NOI's Boston temple.

Malcolm said the first order of business, now that he was free to do what he wished, would be a "house-by-house, block-by-block" voter registration drive. "I intend to mobilize the Negro's political strength not only in New York, but across the nation," he told reporters. He said he also intended to call a black nationalist convention. On five separate occasions, he asserted that he was going to organize a black political party. He even announced he might form a "black nationalist army." None of these projects ever materialized. For reasons that will become apparent, none of them were even started.*

---

* Ten days after Malcolm announced that he'd organize a "black nationalist party," he spoke at Harvard, where one faculty member pointed out that, historically, minor parties have fared badly in American politics. Malcolm replied: "I would not like to leave the impression that I have ever, in any way,

Despite Malcolm's assurance that he would cooperate in local civil rights campaigns, he declined to participate in a meaningful way in the civil rights struggles that were being waged in Harlem. Among them was Reverend Milton Galamison's brilliantly orchestrated campaign to end de facto racial segregation in New York City's 863 public schools, only three of which had black principals. Galamison's Citywide Committee for Integrated Schools organized an anti-segregation boycott that kept nearly half a million black and Puerto Rican pupils out of school. The boycott strategy was predicated on the fact that financial aid from New York State to New York City's school system was based upon school attendance.

The unwillingness of the New York City School Board to accede to the demands of the boycotters prompted Reverend Galamison to call a second boycott. This one, which was held several days after Malcolm's second press conference, was not nearly as successful as the first boycott, partly because the NAACP, the National Urban League, and most of the other prestigious civil rights groups that had supported the initial boycott withdrew their support after white New Yorkers threatened to withdraw their financial support from them if they continued to endorse Galamison's campaign. Their decision to forsake Galamison provided Malcolm with a perfect opportunity to make the leap from political rhetoric to political action. But except for verbal declarations of support for the second boycott, Malcolm restricted his response to a brief look-in at Galamison's Brooklyn headquarters. He sauntered inside, smiled, and talked with whoever would listen. He also posed for photographs with Galamison. But he would not join the boycotters and march to the Board of Education. He told Galamison he didn't want to burden him with more enemies. He gave the *New York Times* a different explanation:

> If I got in line, other believers in non-violence would join in, and when we met up with white non-violence believers, there might be violence.

Had Malcolm marched, it probably would have been interpreted as an endorsement of the concept of integration—an endorsement that

---

proposed a Negro party. Whoever entertains that thought is very much misinformed. We have never at any time advocated any kind of Negro party. The idea that I have been trying to convey is that black nationalism is our political philosophy. I didn't mention 'party.'" But after Malcolm left Harvard, he kept right on advocating a black party. At times, he hedged a bit by proclaiming his intention to establish such a party "if it's necessary." But on one occasion, he unequivocally declared, "I'll form a black political party."

would have further alienated what was left of his black nationalist, separatist following.

Hours before Galamison's marching legions converged on the Board of Education, Malcolm appeared in traffic court to contest a speeding ticket. He grinned as he claimed that a "prejudiced cop" had given it to him. The policeman had clocked him doing 55 MPH in a 40 MPH zone. Fifty-five miles per hour was uncharacteristically slow for Malcolm, who frequently zoomed along stretches of open highway at 100 miles per hour. When he stepped inside his navy blue Oldsmobile, he frequently turned the ignition key and started the car while he was still closing the door. He always seemed to be in a hurry and was constantly glancing at his watch. ("You won't find anybody more time-conscious than I am," he told Alex Haley.) He walked fast. He often talked fast. (On one occasion, he declared, with characteristic exaggeration, that he was incapable of talking slowly.)

But he was in no rush to engage in the rent strike that was gaining momentum in blighted sections of New York City, whose Building Commissioner told the press that more than 300,000 housing and building violations had been reported to his office the preceding year. *New York Times* reporter Homer Bigart visited one of the unheated Harlem tenements that had been cited for its failure to observe the housing code. Each night, he discovered, the building's inhabitants carried their mattresses into their kitchens and placed them near their gas ovens. If the family was too large to fit into the kitchen, some members slept on the floor of the nearest adjacent room, close to pans of steaming hot water that had been placed nearby to provide "warmth." Despite these measures, the temperature in one of the rooms of an apartment that Bigart visited sank to almost thirty degrees Fahrenheit. The week before his visit, two of the six children who inhabited the apartment had beaten a rat to death with a broom.

The leader of the rent strike, Jesse Gray, invited Malcolm to address one of his rallies. Malcolm did so. No evidence has been found that he did anything else on behalf of the rent strike. He insisted that he was keeping his political plans secret.

Soon after Malcolm's departure from the Nation of Islam, he began making conciliatory gestures to the Christian leadership of the civil rights movement. When he was asked at a gathering of church officials whether he was still down on Christianity, he replied with a smile, "I don't care what I said last year. That was last year. This is 1964." He told another group:

> I'm not out to fight other Negro leaders or organizations . . . . As of this minute, I've forgotten everything bad that the other leaders have

said about me, and I pray they can also forget the many bad things
I've said about them."

Late in March, he flew to Washington, where he watched the debate
on the 1964 Civil Rights Bill from the Senate gallery. Every so often, he
drifted out into the Senate corridors, where he held impromptu press
conferences. He told a representative of the *Herald-Tribune* that the
proceedings were a "con game." It was the kind of statement his militant
admirers loved. He asserted that passage of the bill would do "nothing
but build up the Negro for a big letdown." Perhaps he felt that America's
blacks would be disappointed the way he had been disappointed in
Mason, Michigan a quarter of a century earlier. "Even if the bill passes,"
he said, "it won't help the Negroes." (An earlier, similar remark
suggested that he meant it wouldn't help the blacks of the North.) Yet
his presence at the Senate proceedings constituted a subtle signal to black
moderates. He told one *New York Times* reporter he wanted the bill to
pass "exactly as is, with no changes."

Malcolm was not the only black leader who spoke to the press that
day in Washington. Martin Luther King—whose car, the previous
summer, had been pelted with eggs the day after Malcolm had publicly
suggested that Harlem might want to show the reverend doctor what it
thought of him—did too. As King left his Senate press conference,
Malcolm stepped out from another doorway into his path so that King
couldn't avoid him. Camera shutters clicked. The next day, the *Chicago
Sun-Times*, the *New York World Telegram and Sun*, and other dailies carried
a picture of Malcolm and King shaking hands. One of Malcolm's eyes
was half-closed, as if the camera had caught him winking.*

On the plane back to New York, Malcolm sat and chatted with
newsman Jules Loh. The conversation eventually turned to Malcolm's
boyhood and his father's premature death, which Malcolm said was the
result of foul play. Outwardly, he exhibited none of the doubt he had
expressed when he was younger about the theory that his father had
been a victim of political assassination.

In addition to the conciliatory overtures that Malcolm made to the civil
rights leaders he had portrayed as "parrots," he tried to repair his
relationship with Elijah Muhammad. Attributing the rift with Elijah to the
sycophants around him, Malcolm—who denied that he bore any respon-

---

* Perhaps this was when Malcolm reportedly told King that he was scaring
whites to death so that they would be more amenable to King's demands for
remedial legislation.

sibility for the break—kept mum about the Messenger's extra-marital exploits. He assured him, "You are still my leader and teacher . . . . I am still your brother and servant." He "frankly" maintained that Mr. Muhammad's teachings were "1,000 percent true."

Perhaps because of Malcolm's conciliatory gestures, some people who had followed him out of the Nation of Islam concluded that he wished to return to the fold. In an unguarded moment, Malcolm inadvertently admitted it himself to a CBS interviewer.

Elijah Muhammad was equally ambivalent about the break with Malcolm. When he first learned early in March that his errant "son" was leaving him, he shed tears. (Later, he denied it.) For some time thereafter, he became overwrought whenever Malcolm's name was mentioned in his presence. His voice sounded sad as he told the *New York Times* that the job of uplifting the black community "is absolutely divine work, guided divinely. Malcolm had that as long as he was with me. But otherwise, he does not have it." On another occasion, Elijah declared, "Brother Malcolm got to be a *big* man. I made him big. I was about to make him a *great* man."

But the Messenger's ambivalence about Malcolm did not prevent him from acting with political dispatch. Several days after Malcolm formally broke with the Nation of Islam, Elijah's dining room still resembled the war room of a head of state whose country had just been attacked. Messengers arrived and departed. They whispered things in Mr. Muhammad's ear. Less than three weeks later, he called a press conference in Chicago. Philbert was flown in from Lansing for the occasion. He later told an interviewer that, minutes before he went on the air, John Ali shoved a script in his hands and ordered him to read it.

"Ordinarily," Philbert began, "I would not suggest the airing of differences between brothers to outsiders." Breathlessly, he proceeded to read the prepared statement. He said his "wayward brother Malcolm" would "do anything" to grab headlines. Likening his "cunning" brother to Brutus, Judas, Benedict Arnold, and other turncoats, Philbert suggested that Malcolm might have succumbed to the same mental illness that had afflicted his mother, whom he said he loved.

Gingerly, the script turned to the subject of Mr. Muhammad's "personal affairs." Without naming or identifying the secretaries in question, Philbert said that he had been informed that Malcolm intended to use certain women to smear one or more unidentified influential Muslim functionaries:

> He has always prided himself on being a great user of people, especially women.

Philbert said he had already conferred with Wilfred, whose absence may have been due to a desire to disassociate himself from the proceedings. (Some of the people who later condemned Philbert for attacking Malcolm assumed he had been swayed not only by Elijah but also by envy. Few people knew how Malcolm had humiliated him years before by pretending he had made of whore of his wife.)

Referring to Malcolm's assertion that blacks should form rifle clubs for self-protection, Philbert told the press he didn't believe his brother intended to shoot it out with the white enemy. "An empty bag makes a lot of noise," he said.

Philbert's photograph and part of his statement were prominently displayed in the next issue of *Muhammad Speaks*. Accompanying the material was a cartoon showing "Little Red's" severed head bouncing along the ground toward a heap of discarded skulls. From its mouth emanated statements such as, "I split because no man wants to be Number Two."

Malcolm told the Associated Press that Philbert's remarks had been inspired by Chicago's fear that Malcolm was going to divulge the truth about the Nation of Islam and its leaders. Attributing his brother's attack to his need for a job (Philbert had a family to support), Malcolm said he was "not at all excited about it," despite the fact that he had a splitting headache. He had no ill feelings toward Philbert, he asserted. "We've been good friends all our lives." Yet the anger showed through. He portrayed Philbert as a minister without a congregation and his Lansing temple as "a complete failure," despite his earlier acknowledgement that it had been "doing fine." Philbert, like Wilfred, was highly intelligent and industrious. He, too, hoped the Nation of Islam could be saved from its corrupt leaders.

Publicly, Malcolm denied he felt any pain as a result of the attack by Philbert, who later acknowledged how much he regretted that he had allowed Chicago to use him. When an enterprising reporter tried to elicit Malcolm's feelings about his brother's attack, he brusquely replied, "When you're involved in a revolution, nothing is painful." He subsequently told an associate:

> Your enemies will never be the ones that will hurt you. It will be your old friends or [members of] your family.

Malcolm's first public rally after he officially broke with Elijah Muhammad was held in Harlem's Rockland Palace. He told his listeners that before Southern blacks succeeded in their dangerous attempt to exercise their constitutional right to cast their ballots, they would have to start packing bullets. For the next few weeks, Malcolm reiterated his "ballots or bullets" theme, which became a watchword in speech after speech. He may have obtained the idea for the catchy slogan from a movie he had seen in Boston years before. Entitled *Bullets or Ballots*, it was about a man who worries what will happen to the widow and children of a slain political martyr. The film's hero is outwardly a tough guy. Nearly everyone thinks he is a criminal. But he gives his life in an effort to combat corruption.

Paradoxically, the "ballots or bullets" theme strengthened Malcolm's position as the spokesman for black militants at the same time that it provided him with an opening to the political mainstream:

> Only two things bring you freedom—the ballot or the bullet. Only two things. Well, if you and I don't use the ballot . . . , we're going to be forced to use the bullet . . . . So let us try the ballot. And if the ballot doesn't work, we'll try something else. But let us try the ballot.

Malcolm tried to broaden his appeal to political moderates by leavening his rhetoric with the argument that America could have a bloodless revolution. But he balanced the statement, which elicited a gasp of surprise from one onlooker, with declarations that were designed to reassure his militant followers that he was not abandoning them. The miracle of it all was that the contradictory militant and moderate statements appeared in the same speeches. After assuring an audience at New York City's Militant Labor Forum that the days of nonviolence "are over," he declared, "America is the only country in history in a position to bring about a revolution without violence." "But," he promptly added, "America is not morally equipped to do so." In Michigan, he mingled dove-like statements and hawk-like images in the same paragraphs:

> Historically, revolutions are bloody . . . . You don't have a revolution in which you love your enemy . . . . Revolutions *overturn* systems! Revolutions *destroy* systems! A revolution is bloody. But America is in a unique position. She's the only country in history in a position, actually, to become involved in a *bloodless* revolution.

Without pausing, Malcolm suddenly reverted to bellicose imagery:

> The Russian Revolution was bloody. [The] Chinese Revolution was bloody. [The] French Revolution was bloody. [The] Cuban Revolution was bloody. And there was nothin' more bloody than the American Revolution."

"But today," Malcolm said as he shifted tack again, "this country can become involved in a revolution that won't take bloodshed. All she's got to do is [to] give the black man in this country everything that's due to him . . . . " "I hope that the white man can see this," he exclaimed as he made still another threatening about-face:

'Cause if you don't see it, you're finished . . . . You're gonna become involved in some action in which you don't have a chance. We don't care anything about your atomic bomb. It's useless.

The white man, he said, could not win a guerrilla-type war:

He's brave when he's got tanks. He's brave when he's got planes. He's brave when he's got bombs . . . . But you take that little man from Africa and Asia, turn him loose in the woods with a blade . . . . That's all he needs. All he needs is a blade. And when the sun . . . goes down and it's dark, it's even Stephen.

The warlike images obscured the fact that Malcolm was sending mixed messages. The "ballots or bullets" and "bloodless revolution" themes served as trial balloons that helped him gauge the strength of the political backlash that was being generated by his efforts to broaden his political appeal. They were fitting preludes to the "discoveries" he was about to make abroad.

POLITICAL ACTOR

44

Malcolm's break with the Nation of Islam won him many admirers but few real followers; the vast majority of believers remained in the movement. His unsuccessful attempts to woo many of his former NOI associates, even in New York, made it imperative for him to attract other adherents. But any effort to do so was likely to be impossible unless he disassociated himself from the doctrines of Elijah Muhammad, particularly the white devil theory. Shortly after the rift was formalized, Malcolm cautiously took an ambiguous step in that direction by declaring, "I do not say there are no sincere white people, but rather that I haven't met any."

His dilemma was compounded by the fact that it was politically inexpedient for him to renounce the doctrines he had been preaching for so many years. People would have begun to question not only his credibiity, but also his sincerity, which was one of his principal political assets.

The problem was how to shift political position without undermining his credibility. For some, the predicament would have been insoluble. But not for a gifted politician like Malcolm. He announced his intention to make a holy pilgrimage to Mecca. He said he also planned to tour Africa. He told the *Amsterdam News* he needed spiritual renewal.

He also needed to refurbish his pocketbook. Since the Nation of Islam was no longer footing his living and travel expenses, he had to subsist on lecture fees, magazine article royalties, and the tithes of a few committed followers. In short, he was virtually broke. Having burned his bridges to potential domestic sources of financial support, he had to look elsewhere. Saudi Arabia, with its commitment to Islam and its oil-rich sheiks, was a logical place to start.

Malcolm later acknowledged that he also needed to go to Mecca to have himself remade into "an authentic Muslim." But before he could go, certain obstacles had to be overcome. First, he had to find the money to get to

Saudi Arabia. Secondly, only bona fide Muslims are allowed to enter the Islamic Holy Land. When Malcolm applied for a visa at the Saudi consulate, he was told that no American Muslim convert could obtain one without the signed approval of Mahmoud Youssef Shawarbi, Director of the Federation of Islamic Associations in the United States and Canada. Dr. Shawarbi, an Egyptian scholar whose family had suffered under Nasser's regime, held the keys to Mecca, or at least one of the keys.

Malcolm telephoned Shawarbi, whom he had met before, for an appointment. According to Malcolm, Shawarbi handed him the requisite letter of introduction the very first day he came to his Riverside Drive office. But it didn't happen that way according to Shawarbi, who later described what transpired when Malcolm called on him. Malcolm didn't request a letter. Instead, he told him, "I want to learn about the real Islam." Shawarbi flipped open his Qu'ran and read a verse that James 67X had heard Malcolm recite many times before. The passage, loosely translated, read, "No man is a true believer until he wishes for his brother what he wishes for himself." Malcolm had used the verse in Temple Seven to argue that none of the Muslims in the Middle East would become true Muslims until they wanted for their Muslim brothers in America the benefits that they themselves enjoyed. But Shawarbi, whose skin was white, suggested that the passage meant that all Muslims are brothers regardless of color or race. Malcolm—who knew the Qu'ran as well as Shawarbi did, according to James 67X (who worked for both men)—jumped to his feet and asked him to repeat the verse. Shawarbi obliged. Suddenly, Malcolm began weeping. He was shaking. Apparently, he convinced Shawarbi that he had never heard the verse as easily as he had convinced the army psychiatrist he was crazy. After a few more sessions, during which Malcolm played the obeisant student, Shawarbi urged him to take a pilgrimage to Mecca. According to Shawarbi's associate Heshaam Jaaber, he saw in Malcolm someone who could articulate orthodox Islam to prospective American converts.

The financial obstacles to the *hajj* were overcome by the generosity of Ella, who, Philbert sensed, was vicariously trying to realize her own thwarted ambitions through Malcolm. ("I was going to run him for President in 1968," she later told an interviewer.) By this time, she was fairly well-off because of her real estate holdings, which included property in New York City as well as Boston. Eventually she purchased a brownstone on Striver's Row. (The attics and basements of a number of buildings that she owned in Boston became depositories for sizable quantities of china and silverware, according to Heshaam Jaaber, who lived in one of the buildings and checked on her tenants for her. He also noticed, as did another of Malcolm's associates, that one of her rental units was a brothel. A pimp patrolled the sidewalk outside.)

Ella, who had quit the Nation of Islam and was studying orthodox Islam, had actually been saving up for her own *hajj*. But when Malcolm, who later claimed that she "had never once really wavered" from his corner, visited her in Boston, she told him it was more important for him to go. For the entire length of the trip back to New York, he thought about how important a role she had played in his life. Twenty years before, she had pointed him the wrong way. Now she was pointing him the right way.

Malcolm, who had prided himself on his ability to con money from women, initially found it difficult to admit that he had borrowed $1,500 from Ella, who says she had also been buying him clothes. He told the *Amsterdam News* that, because he was a Muslim convert, the airfare to Egypt had been provided free. The other trip expenses, he said, had been defrayed by members of his congregation.

Without fanfare, Malcolm left for the Middle East on April 13. His autobiography, which says he "little" realized he'd return with a splash, says he feared that the State Department might try to impede his path. Moreover, it would have been a mistake for him to publicize his departure, only to discover later on that, despite Sahwarbi's letter of introduction, he couldn't get into Mecca.

After a brief stopover in Frankfurt, Germany, Malcolm boarded Middle East Airlines flight #788 for Cairo. He always tried to sit in the rear of the planes he traveled in. Despite his death-defying rhetoric, he apparently put great store in the fact that the two stewardesses who had been sitting in the tail of the airliner that had crashed outside Paris had survived because they had been thrown clear of the flaming wreckage.

In Cairo, Malcolm spent "two happy days" sightseeing. Then he boarded a plane for Jedda, Saudi Arabia. After it took off, he learned that another ticket holder had been "bumped" from the flight to make room for him. He later told Alex Haley that it made him feel very humble.

The plane landed at Jedda airport, where all Mecca-bound passengers are carefully scrutinized by the Saudi authorities. Malcolm handed an official his American passport. The official, who did not speak English, refused to let him proceed. An Egyptian judge and some of the people Malcolm had befriended in Cairo vainly tried to convince the official that Malcolm was a bona fide Muslim. But even Shawarbi's letter made no impression. Sadly, the judge, who spoke English, explained to Malcolm that he would have to appear before a court that would decide whether to accept his Islamic credentials. Since the court was not in session, they would have to proceed to Mecca without him. Reluctantly, Malcolm bid farewell to his friends. Shortly before dawn, he was taken to a large, multi-story dormitory and ushered into a room containing more than a dozen people, most of whom were asleep on rugs. After they awoke and said their morning prayers, they covered their respective rugs with tablecloths and made them into breakfast room tables. After they finished eating, they transformed them into living room sofas. Other rugs were used as classrooms or conference rooms.

The people in the room were friendly. One man invited Malcolm to join him and his wife for a meal. Malcolm, who shared his parents' reluctance to appear the beggar, politely declined. "I knew that it was an immense offer he was making," Malcolm later explained. "You don't have tea with a Muslim's wife." The youth who had boasted about stealing other men's women had come a long way.

An entire day passed. As Malcolm rested on his cot, he suddenly recalled that, during one of his excursions to the dormitory courtyard, he had noticed several officials seated at a table. On the table was a telephone.

He hurried downstairs. Fortunately, one of the officials knew some English. Malcolm showed him Shawarbi's letter and asked him if he would telephone Omar Azzam, whose Jedda phone number Shawarbi had given him before he had left New York. Dr. Azzam was an engineer. The Saudi government had borrowed him from the United Nations to direct the reconstruction of Mecca's religious shrines. Omar Azzam sped to the airport and secured Malcolm's release. His sister was the wife of the son of Crown Prince Faisal, Saudi Arabia's ruler.

Azzam brought Malcolm to his home. Though it was still early morning, his father, the Egyptian-born author of a book on Islam that Shawarbi had given Malcolm before his departure, was on hand to greet him.

Omar Azzam's father was Abdel Rahman Azzam. Before Nasser's Egyptian revolution had banned honorific titles, he had been called Azzam Pasha. In addition to being a respected scholar, he had also been a revolutionary. The British, who ruled Egypt at the time, had condemned him to death, but he eluded them by roaming the desert for eight years. He also fought the Italian troops who had occupied Libya. After Egypt won its independence, he ran for a seat in the country's parliament and became its youngest member. He helped Habib Bourgiba's Tunisian independence movement and supported the revolution in Algeria. He also played a key role establishing the Arab League and became its first Secretary General. Years later, his son Issam could not recall a single day that his father had spent with him when he was a boy.

Abdel Azzam, who was an accomplished orator, was impressed the first time he saw Malcolm perform on television. (At the time, he was working at United Nations headquarters in New York.) His colleagues advised him to steer clear of Malcolm to avoid offending the U.S. government. He kept his distance but retained his interest in the Black Muslims; he thought they might outgrow their racism. He foresaw the possibility that Malcolm might supplant the relatively conservative established leaders of the civil rights movement, just as Nasser had supplanted Naguib and Lenin had supplanted Kerensky. According to Issam, his aging father saw in Malcolm the young, defiant rebel he had been himself.

Malcolm was accorded the full measure of Arab hospitality by his hosts, who seemed embarrassed that he had been detained at the airport. Abdel Azzam even put him up in his own suite at the Jedda Palace Hotel; Malcolm's protests were of no avail. The suite had a porch that afforded a splendid view of the Red Sea city.

Overcome by the lavish reception, Malcolm prostrated himself on the floor and prayed. His autobiography, which devotes forty-three detail-studded pages to his April 1964 trip to the Middle East and only one short, unrevealing paragraph to his 1959 trip there, claims that he "first began to reappraise" Elijah Muhammad's white devil theory that morning, despite his earlier trip and the cordial relations he had maintained with Dr. Shawarbi and other fair-skinned Muslim scholars, diplomats, and officials.

Louis Lomax, who had followed Malcolm to the Middle East shortly after his 1959 trip and had interviewed officials who had received Malcolm there with open arms, was not fooled by his version of how he had discovered that whites could be human as well as Muslim. Nor were Philbert or Wallace Muhammad fooled. Nearly everyone else accepted Malcolm's assertion that the scales had suddenly fallen from his eyes that morning in Jedda. Even his wife was apparently fooled, for it would have been political suicide for him to admit that, despite his pronouncements about white devils, he had known for years that white-skinned people are no worse than anyone else.

The Azzams invited Malcolm to dine with them. He was deeply impressed with Omar's scholarly father, whose international outlook was a welcome contrast to the narrow, rigid outlook of the semi-illiterate Messenger. The elder Azzam, who was about seventy years old, behaved "as if he were my father," Malcolm later told Alex Haley. "I *felt* like he was my father."

The following morning, Malcolm appeared before the *hajj* court, accompanied by Prince Faisal's deputy chief of Protocol. The judge was Sheik Muhammad Harakan, whom Malcolm had met during his 1959 trip to Saudi Arabia. Harakan remembered Malcolm and asked him some questions. "I answered him as truly as I could," Malcolm subsequently told Alex Haley.

The *hajj* court, which seemed to understand that Faisal wanted it to grant Malcolm permission to enter Mecca, did so. Hours later, Faisal's deputy chief of protocol informed Malcolm that a car had been placed at his disposal for his trip to the Holy City. As the automobile sped along the highway connecting Jedda with Mecca, the guards that were posted at intervals took one look at the vehicle and the signals its driver was flashing and allowed it to proceed unhindered.

The steel and concrete hotels that dotted Mecca's hilly skyline were out of place among its ancient, teeming bazaars. Malcolm's driver stopped to pick up a waiting *mutawwif*, or guide. The *mutawwif* wore a long, nightshirt-like *gelibaya*, which shielded him from the sun's rays while allowing air to circulate around his body.

Malcolm's automobile parked near the Sacred Mosque. Removing his sandals, he performed the requisite ablutions and followed his *mutawwif*, who did not speak English, into the great mosque that houses the *kaa'ba*, the cube-like stone edifice that orthodox Muslims believe is the House of God. Embedded in the wall of the *kaa'ba*, encased in silver, sat the Black Stone, the *Hajar al-Aswad*. According to Islamic tradition, the stone is the surviving portion of the shrine that the patriarch Ibrahim [Abraham] and his son Ismail [Ishmael] had erected to venerate Allah, who had relented after commanding Ibrahim to sacrifice Ismail to prove his willingness to obey Him.

In the courtyard of the Sacred Mosque, which is surrounded by seven minarets that tower above its massive walls, Malcolm began the first of seven prescribed circumambulations of the *kaa'ba*. Tens of thousands of other pilgrims were doing the same thing; Malcolm couldn't even get close to the structure, which was covered by a gold-embossed silk cloth weighing nearly five thousand pounds. The seventh time around, he prostrated himself in prayer, his head on the ground. The *mutawwif* held back the surging crowd, so that it would not trample him.

Next, Malcolm drank from the 140-foot-deep Well of Zamzam, which, according to Islamic tradition, the archangel Gabriel revealed to Ibrahim's concubine Hadjar as she ran back and forth between the Hills *al-Safa* and *al-Marwah* in search of water for herself and Ismail. To commemorate her frantic search, Malcolm traversed the path she took seven times.

Having completed the *omra* portion of the pilgrimage, Malcolm stopped off in the village of Mina, a few miles southeast of Mecca, before proceeding further south and east to the Mount of Mercy, where the prophet Muhammad had preached his farewell sermon. To commemorate the historic event, more than a million pilgrims encamp in tents each year on the barren plain below the "mountain," which is only a couple of hundred feet high. Standing before their god, they pray from about noon—or, more precisely, the moment the sun reaches its zenith—until sunset, hoping, like their Christian and Jewish counterparts in other parts of the world, that their sins will be forgiven. The experience, which is the high point of the *hajj*, often brings tears to the hardest, most unfeeling believers.

It is unclear if Malcolm attended the Feast of the Sacrifice, which occurs in Mina the day after the great gathering on the plain. The Feast, at which pilgrims traditionally slaughter a sacrificial animal, commemorates Allah's willingness to accept an animal from Ibrahim instead of his son. Malcolm did participate in one more rite. The night before the Feast, each pilgrim gathers seven stones, or a multiple of seven. The following day, he hurls seven stones at the first of three pillars that are said to mark the places where the devil unsuccessfully tempted Ibrahim to defy Allah's authority. Those pilgrims who remain in Mina another day throw seven more stones at each of the three pillars. (The pillars represent the devil.) Some pilgrims stay in Mina two full days after the initial stoning, so that they can cast seven stones at the devil seven times. Though it is not completely clear how many times Earl Little's seventh child cast the seven stones, he seemed deeply moved by the pilgrimage, which greatly enhanced his credentials for his forthcoming struggle with his ex-mentor.

TAILORING THE
TEACHINGS

45

Prince Faisal's son informed Malcolm that he had been made a guest of state. Malcolm later admitted that he relished the privileges he had been accorded. Wherever he went, he was supplied with air-conditioned lodgings. Servants were at his beck and call. He said he "shamelessly" delighted in being transported around in his chauffeur-driven automobile.

Malcolm was even granted an audience with Faisal. Uncharacteristically, he found himself at a loss for words during the conference, which was his first with a head of state.* The customary photograph was taken, and it subsequently found its way into an American newspaper. The picture showed a rather boyish-looking Malcolm alongside the regal-looking, autocratic monarch, about whom Malcolm's autobiography has only good things to say. (Faisal's government was putting him up free.) The Prince criticized the Black Muslim movement. Malcolm replied that he had come to Saudi Arabia "to get an understanding of the true Islam." Whether Faisal was convinced is unclear; he pointed out that there was an abundance of material written in English about Islam, so that ignorance was no excuse.

Before leaving Saudi Arabia, Malcolm embarked on the most important letter-writing campaign of his career. He sent postcards or letters to practically everyone he knew. Most of the letters (which, he said, came straight from his heart) were virtual replicas of one another. He churned out so many pieces of mail that, on one occasion, he apparently forgot whom he had already written; the day after he mailed a postcard to C. Eric Lincoln, who had written a book about the Black Muslim movement,

---

* Faisal, at the time, was de facto head of state. Not long thereafter, he was made de jure head of state.

he sent him another that said essentially the same thing.

The letters Malcolm dispatched from abroad proclaimed his outwardly sudden conversion to orthodox Islam the way his letters from prison had proclaimed his conversion to Elijah Muhammad's version of Islam:

> During the past eleven days here in the Muslim world, I have eaten from the same plate, drunk from the same glass, and slept in the same bed (or on the same rug)—while praying to the *same* God—with fellow Muslims whose eyes were the bluest of blue, whose hair was the blondest of blond, and whose skin was the whitest of white.

These white Muslims, Malcolm said, had exhibited a spirit of brotherhood that he had previously believed was unattainable. He said he had therefore been forced to "rearrange" much of his thinking—the quotation marks around the verb "rearrange" were his. True Islam, he contended, precludes racism:

> . . . because people of all colors and races who accept its religious principles . . . also automatically accept each other as brothers and sisters, regardless of differences in complexion.

Malcolm knew the assertion was untrue; five years earlier, when orthodox Muslims had assailed the Black Muslim movement for teaching racial hatred, it was he who had pointed out that Muslim Arabs had been as guilty, historically, of enslaving black Africans as European Christians had been.

Malcolm mailed a long letter to the members of his nascent Muslim Mosque. Appended to the letter was a note directing them to duplicate and distribute it not only to the press but also to everyone who was anyone. James 67X, who had been appointed executive secretary of the mosque, was so unhinged by Malcolm's new position on whites that he pocketed the letter for several days before showing it to anyone else. Then, in accord with Malcolm's instructions, he finally forwarded copies to representatives of the media.

At the end of April, Malcolm left Saudi Arabia for Beirut, which, at the time, was still the commercial capital of the Middle East, as well as a lovely resort whose brightly colored high-rise hotels and apartment houses put their drab-looking American counterparts to shame. The libertine ways of the thriving Lebanese port, which is now a smoldering ruin, contrasted sharply with the puritanism of theocratic Arabia. Malcolm, who still had eyes for pretty women, was struck by what he characterized as the "moral weakness" of the younger Lebanese women, whose attire reflected decades of western, particularly French, influence.

His prudery, which may have helped him resist temptation, apparently extended to his own wife, whom he insisted should dress "modestly."

From Beirut, Malcolm began a three-week tour of Africa. Rumor had it that Faisal had arranged the financing of part of the journey, which took Malcolm back to Egypt and then to Nigeria, where he appeared on radio and television. He told a standing-room-only crowd at the University of Ibadan, Nigeria's oldest and largest institution of higher learning, that "the U.S. Peace Corps members are all espionage agents." During the question-and-answer period that followed his speech, a faculty member named O.R. Dathorne rose, described the racial discrimination he had suffered before he had emigrated to Africa, and questioned Malcolm's furious, dated emphasis on the institution of American slavery:

> I do believe there is a great deal of truth in what Mr. Malcolm X has said about the racial situation in America, and. . . the history of slavery. But I do not believe it is constructive or useful to focus our attention on past grievances. I want to say, with all due respect to Mr. Malcolm X, that I believe his position is fundamentally dishonest.

Dathorne's challenge elicited mutters, then roars. "Shut up! Shut up!" People hissed and booed. Suddenly, several people rushed the speaker's platform, grabbed the microphone, and threatened Dathorne, who planted his feet and gamely faced his adversaries. The chairman vainly attempted to restore order. Finally, one of Dathorne's associates persuaded him to leave the podium. Hecklers followed him outside, scooped up stones, and hurled them at him.

The Nigerian Muslim Students' Society made Malcolm an honorary member. They also named him "Omewale," which in Yoruba means "the child who has come home." Malcolm later told Alex Haley that he meant it when he told the students he had never received an honor that he had treasured more highly.

From Nigeria, he flew to Accra, Ghana, which boasted a small, vocal colony of black American expatriates that included Shirley Graham DuBois, W.E.B. DuBois's widow, and authors Maya Angelou and Julian Mayfield. Banding together into an ad hoc "Malcolm X Committee," they persuaded the Ghanaian authorities to give Malcolm a resounding welcome. The local press, which paid his hotel expenses despite his declared objections, turned out in force. For the next few days, Malcolm was treated like visiting royalty by diplomats, government ministers, and others. A party in his honor was given by Ghana's Defense Minister, who was so impressed with him that he was invited to address the national assembly—an honor usually reserved for visiting heads of state. Afterwards, Kwame Nkrumah himself granted Malcolm an audience. Before Malcolm entered Nkrumah's office, he was thoroughly searched. Despite his distaste for such procedures, which resembled the practices of the Nation of Islam, he later maintained that he "respected" the Osgayefo's indiscriminate security precautions. He lavishly praised the Ghanaian president, despite reports that their meeting was unproductive.

Malcolm's autobiographical account of his week-long stay in Ghana is replete with detailed descriptions of the parties, dinners, and other affairs that were given in his honor and the dignitaries who wined and dined him. He dropped the names of distinguished politicians the same way he had dropped the names of the famous jazz musicians who had performed at the Roseland Ballroom. The difference was that now the celebrities whose names he bandied about knew who he was and accorded him respect.

Malcolm spoke at the University of Ghana. During the question-and-answer session following his address, a student arose and said, "Mr. Malcolm X, what I don't understand is why you call yourself black. You look more like a white man than a Negro." Malcolm opened his mouth wide and emitted a long, loud laugh before acknowledging that he had been called "Red" when he was young. But he said "nobody" in the black community had ever accused him of being white. "I was accepted," he asserted.

Ghana, which Malcolm regarded as the fountainhead of pan-Africanism, afforded a suitable locale for a letter-writing gambit that enabled him to put more distance between himself and his separatist rhetoric. In a letter from Accra, he ambiguously asserted that even though America's blacks "might" remain in the United States physically, they should return to Africa philosophically and culturally. Later on, back in the United States, he amplified the theme, which gave considerable impetus to the flowering "Afro" movement. By coincidence, Muhammad Ali arrived in Ghana shortly before Malcolm left the country. Ali booked lodgings at the same hotel. Malcolm avoided him. But just as he and his companions were leaving the hotel for Accra's airport, he encountered Ali and his entourage. The champ turned and walked away, but Malcolm, who was sporting an African walking stick, followed him, calling, "Brother Muhammad. Brother Muhammad." Ali turned and faced Malcolm, who assured him he still loved him and that he was still "the greatest."

Ali looked hard at him, shook his head, and sadly replied, "You left the Honorable Elijah Muhammad. That was the wrong thing to do, Brother Malcolm."

Ali and his followers departed. Malcolm's shoulders sagged. His face was glum. "I've lost a lot," he said. "Almost too much."

Shortly thereafter, Malcolm sent Ali a telegram stating that, since so many black people adored him "blindly," he needed to make sure he'd never let his enemies—Malcolm didn't say who they were—exploit his reputation. When Ali was asked about the telegram, a copy of which found its way to the *New York Times* despite Malcolm's insistence that he wanted to avoid putting the champ on the spot, Ali characterized Malcolm as the irresponsible one. "Did you ever get a look at him?" he snapped:

> "Dressed in that funny white robe and wearing a beard, and walking with that cane that looked like a prophet's stick? Man, he's gone."

Ali, who sometimes sported a walking stick of his own, then turned to Herbert Muhammad, who had accompanied him to Africa, and said, "Nobody listens to Malcolm any more." On another occasion, he publicly ridiculed his former "spiritual adviser," whom he derisively nicknamed "Little Malcolm." The statement may have had something to do with the fact that Malcolm was spreading the word that Ali lacked confidence in himself, despite his cocky exterior.

A motorcade of diplomats went to Accra's airport to see Malcolm off. "*Five ambassadors*," he would later exclaim. After all, how many junior high school dropouts end up hobnobbing with diplomats and heads of state?

No sooner had Malcolm left Ghana when one of Nkrumah's aides, a white South African expatriate who was known for his opposition to apartheid, published a highly critical appraisal of Malcolm's views in the government-controlled *Ghanaian Times*. State Department officials concluded that Nkrumah was endeavoring to produce a thaw in his chilly relations with the U.S.; Ghana's new seven-year development plan was heavily dependent upon foreign aid.

After stopovers in Monrovia, Dakar, and Casablanca, Malcolm arrived in Algiers on May 19. It was his thirty-ninth birthday. Two days later, he disembarked at New York's Kennedy Airport, ostensibly unaware which passenger the throng of fifty or sixty reporters had come to interview. But according to James 67X, who had notified the newsmen about Malcolm's planned return, he expected them to be at the airport. They had to be there if they wanted to interview him before rival newsmen did at the formal press conference that had been scheduled for that evening. The latter—the biggest press conference Malcolm had ever hosted—was a fitting culmination to the public-relations campaign that had begun with his letter-writing campaign. The reporters gathered in a thick semicircle in front of him and fired away:

> Q: Do we correctly understand that you now do not think that all whites are evil?

A: *True* sir! My trip to Mecca has opened my eyes.

His trip to Mecca had enabled him to abandon the white devil theory without acknowledging that he had privately discarded it years earlier.

Another motive that had prompted Malcolm's trip became apparent when he told a journalist:

> I hope that once and for all my *hajj* to the holy city of Mecca has established our Muslim Mosque's authentic religious affiliation with the 750 million Muslims of the orthodox Islamic world.

Forty-eight hours later, Malcolm carried the battle of credentials to the enemy in Chicago and announced plans to establish a mosque there. (His representatives had already made attempts to woo away some of Mr. Muhammad's Chicago supporters). He conceded that he had allowed himself to make sweeping indictments of all whites:

> These generalizations have caused injuries to some whites who did not deserve them.

He said he no longer subscribed to a blanket indictment of the entire white race. "In the future," he promised, "I intend to be careful not to sentence anyone who has not been proven guilty."

After Malcolm returned from abroad, sporting a reddish, curly beard on his determined, dimpled chin, he began calling himself Malik El-Shabazz. It wasn't the first time he had used the name or other, similar Muslim names. Yet, physically and otherwise, he seemed like a new man. He no longer went to Dr. Turner with psychosomatic complaints. The zest he had exhibited before his break with Elijah Muhammad returned. He appeared elated about the respect and recognition he was finally obtaining.

Yet the political problems he faced were of sufficient magnitude to depress the most seasoned politician. The few dues-paying followers he reportedly had at the time were mainly people who had followed him out of the Nation of Islam. Most were anti-white and felt betrayed by Malcolm's renunciation of the white devil theory. "They must have given him some money," one discontented brother exclaimed. Others threatened him physically. "They won't let me turn the corner," he lamented. I'm caught in a trap!" Malcolm tried to resolve the political dilemma by walking what he characterized as a political tightrope and by telling each ideological camp what it wanted to hear. He made clear he was still a Muslim but held out his hand to non-Muslims by stressing that religion was a private matter that should not be allowed to divide one segment of the black community from another. Before church audiences, he played down his Islamic ties. He continued his effort to dissociate himself from Elijah Muhammad's separatism without explicitly repudiating separatist support or endorsing the concept of integration. He nimbly achieved this ideological feat by taking the position that neither integration nor separation was the proper goal for the American black. He said they were merely alternative means for achieving the real goal, which was the right to be treated as a human being. Though the argument was undeniably valid, it was also a skillful attempt to dodge the crucial question of which political approach—separation or integration—would most likely secure for America's blacks their long-denied human rights. His evasiveness enabled him to continue soliciting the support of blacks who rejected separation, without completely burning his separationist bridges.

Malcolm's gradual abandonment of separatism was accompanied by periodic redefinitions of "black nationalism," a term he used a lot. Prior to his break with Elijah Muhammad, he had used the concept to signify the establishment of a separate black nation. But as soon as he left the Nation of Islam, he redefined the term to mean not black separatism but the ability of America's blacks to control the politics, the economics, and the schools and other social institutions of their communities. (It was Malcolm who paved the way for the Black Power movement). Repeatedly, he declared that black nationalism "only" meant that blacks should have the power to manage and direct their own affairs; "no more." But sometimes, he neatly balanced the assertion with the separatist-sounding statement that the concept of black autonomy would "eventually lead to the complete physical independence of the black people in this country."

An event that prompted him to rethink his position still further had occurred just before his return from Africa. He was talking with the Algerian ambassador to Ghana, Taher Kaid. According to one account, Kaid inquired, "Brother Malcolm, what are your plans? What are you going to do?"

Malcolm's answer was evasive. Instead of discussing his plans for the voter registration drive he had announced he intended to organize, he launched into a long philosophical disquisition about black nationalism.

"Brother Malcolm," Kaid said, smiling gently, "that sort of leaves me out, doesn't it?"

"What do you mean?" Malcolm replied.

"Well," said Kaid, "I'm a Muslim brother and a revolutionary. But I'm not black—I'm Caucasian." The gentle rebuke evidently prompted Malcolm to realize that the politics of blackness might cut him off from potential sources of support from other "third world" countries. After he arrived back in the U.S., he shifted his emphasis from black nationalism to Afro-Americanism—a concept that was likely to repel neither Arab mullahs nor Chinese revolutionaries.

In a similar effort to open up new avenues of support, Malcolm continued to push his new, non-anti-white image:

> I don't speak against the sincere, well-meaning, good white people .
> . . . I have learned that not all white people are racists. I am speaking
> against . . . the white *racists*.

He acknowledged that many American whites supported their black fellow citizens in their struggle for full emancipation. He emphasized the difference between the good whites and the bad ones and repeatedly declared that people should be judged not by the color of their skin, but by their deeds.

As for his previous portrayals of whites as blue-eyed devils, he attributed them to the fact that he had been speaking for Elijah Muhammad at the time. He told one fair-skinned woman who had followed him out of the Nation of Islam:

> Sister, if we take Elijah's position that whites are devils because of
> the color of their skin, then you have some devil in you, don't you?
> What makes you different from a dark Italian?

The woman, who could easily have been mistaken for white, was tall and slim and wore her shiny black hair shoulder-length. She had recently resigned her position at the Chicago "University of Islam," partly because of her inability to stomach the movement's demonology, and partly because of her unwillingness to endure Elijah Muhammad's incessant advances. When she arrived in New York, she telephoned Malcolm, who asked her if he could meet her at her midtown Manhattan hotel rather than his Harlem office, which was invariably crowded with reporters and admirers.

Malcolm arrived at the hotel and sank down, exhausted, in a chair. He asked the young woman, whose name was Ethel Minor, whether she had anything for a bad headache. Despite the throngs that hovered around him, he seemed to need someone to talk to. He gazed at Ethel with his penetrating gaze, as if he were trying to decide whether or not he could trust her. (Perhaps he feared that Elijah Muhammad, with whom she had often dined, had "planted" her as a spy).

Time passed. Ethel said she needed to visit someone in Queens. Despite Malcolm's crushing schedule of public appearances, which he constantly cited as the reason he couldn't spend sufficient time with his family, he volunteered to drive her there. (The trip took quite a while by auto, for the hotel was located at 96th Street and West End Avenue, relatively far from any of the east-side bridges or tunnels that connect Manhattan with Queens).

They stopped for a bite to eat on the way. Malcolm made no advances. Nor did he make any the second time he chauffeured her to Queens.

He had enormous self-control. One evening, he unexpectedly dropped in at the home of his co-worker Sara Mitchell. "I don't want to talk," he reportedly told her. "I just want to sleep." Despite the double entendre and Sara's beauty (she later won a Harlem beauty contest), he made no advances. Instead, he curled up and fell asleep.

Malcolm's attempt to bury his racist image cost him dearly among those who had once constituted his chief source of support. He reportedly tried to retain their allegiance by arguing, after his return from the Middle East, that the real enemy was not the white man per se, but the white Jew. Yet on other occasions, he maintained that a number of Jews had become his "dearest friends" since his "conversion" to orthodox Islam.

Malcolm also attempted to retain the support of anti-white elements by making statements to the effect that his new-found tolerance for whites was strictly limited to those who adhered to the Islamic faith. And that, short of the unlikely possibility of a mass conversion to Islam, the existence of a relatively few good whites hadn't altered his conviction that, collectively, they were still a bad lot. Not all his former supporters accepted his explanation. At one Harlem gathering, one of them rose and declared, "We heard you changed, Malcolm. Why don't you tell us where you're at with them white folks?"

Malcolm's reply vividly illustrated his ability to appear all things to all people—a talent he had been perfecting ever since he had learned to behave one way with Lansing blacks and another with Mason whites; one way with the Roxbury blacks who lived on the Hill and another with the hoods who inhabited Lower Roxbury. He categorically denied he had changed, then promptly declared he had acquired a broader perspective. The white man, he said, can't help the color of his skin and has to be given a chance:

"He probably won't take it, the snake!"

He made other disparaging remarks about "whitey" despite his promise to be careful not to sentence anyone who had not been proven guilty. At times, he depicted whites as domineering and "ego-ridden." The accusations poignantly illustrated his tendency to paint his political enemies with brush strokes that betrayed his own imperfections. He claimed that Ralph Bunche's "international mouth" was always open. (Bunche had claimed that Malcolm was "mentally depraved.") He even scolded a number of unidentified political opponents for manipulating the press and for being political actors.

Like the letters he had sent to the prison authorities, Malcolm's utterances were alternately belligerent and conciliatory. He asserted he had "learned a lot" at a recent NAACP convention and described Martin Luther King, Jr. as "a friend" of his and "one of the foremost" black leaders. "I have no criticism of him whatsoever," he declared in one speech. But he hotly contested King's emphasis on nonviolence and periodically renewed his blistering attacks on "Uncle Toms," whom he accused of telling other people what they wanted to hear. He wouldn't even agree to permit a predominantly white audience to observe a moment of silence in honor of Reverend Bruce Klunder, the white Presbyterian minister who had been crushed to death beneath a bulldozer during a demonstration protesting the construction of an elementary school for Cleveland blacks. (CORE and other civil rights groups opposed the new school because it would have resulted in the resegregation of black pupils who were being bussed to integrated institutions). Malcolm explained:

> We're not going to stand up and applaud any contribution made by some individual white person when 22 million black people are dying every day.

Derisively, he continued, "What he did—good, good, great . . . . Hooray, hooray, hooray . . . ."

> It's time that some white people started dying in this thing. If you'll forgive me, . . . many more beside [Reverend Klunder] are going when the wagon comes.

Malcolm admitted that he said one thing in Harlem and another downtown. His remarkable ability to keep one foot in each political camp was facilitated by his extraordinary capacity for political ambiguity. An example of this was the way he rephrased his acknowledgement that his earlier condemnation of all whites had been unfair. "There might be some good ones," he told his black audience. "All of them might not be guilty." "But most of them are," he ominously added.

Malcolm, who repeatedly dismissed his contradictory pronouncements with allegations that he had been misquoted or misunderstood, proved particularly adept at fence-straddling when he was asked if he would accept communist support. He'd smile and declare, enigmatically, "The enemy of my enemy is my friend." He told one group of reporters that if he were held prisoner by a wolf, he'd accept help from anyone in order to attain release. When the newsmen pressed him about whether this meant he would accept communist help, Malcolm grinned and replied that he was only talking about a wolf.

In apparent hope of broadening his political following, Malcolm began a series of lectures at the Militant Labor Forum, which was run by the Socialist Workers Party, a mainly white, Trotskyite group that had detached itself from America's Communist Party, with which it sometimes cooperated. His flirtation with the radical left was, like most political marriages, an expedient that enabled each party to use the other. The Socialist Workers Party viewed America's blacks as "potentially the most revolutionary element of the population":

> They are designated by their whole historical past to be, under adequate leadership, the very vanguard of the proletarian revolution.

For the SWP, Malcolm was a means of entry into the black community. Its leaders hoped he'd draw thousands of blacks into their movement, as he had done for Elijah Muhammad's. In turn, the Militant Labor Forum enabled Malcolm to air his militant views before predominantly white audiences. (At Marxist functions, he played up social and economic issues and downplayed his religion). The Socialist Workers Party was also conveniently equipped with a ready-made propaganda organ, a newspaper called *The Militant*, the sale of which Malcolm facilitated at selected Harlem outlets. The newspaper gave him heavy coverage. The proceeds of the collections that were undertaken at the Forum whenever he spoke there went to him and helped him remain financially afloat.

Malcolm tailored his teachings accordingly with Marx-like predictions about the inevitability of a showdown between the exploiters and the exploited. "It is impossible for capitalism to survive," he told the *Young Socialist*. "It's only a matter of time, in my opinion, before it will collapse completely." In a document that he planned to submit to the United Nations, he (or the aide who drafted it) argued that "monopoly capital" was the "prime mover" in white America's attempts to keep black America subjugated. He told one leftist audience that it was "impossible" for white people to believe in capitalism without believing in racism.

Yet when Malcolm was asked what he thought about socialism, he evaded the question by responding with one of his own. "Is it good for black people?" he asked. His questioner said it seemed to be. "Then I'm for it," Malcolm casually replied. On another occasion, he conceded it was necessary for blacks to "consider" socialist solutions. But when he was asked what economic system he preferred, he answered, "I don't know." "But I'm flexible," he added. "Flexibility" was a word he used to describe his efforts to attract people who held divergent political views.

Yet Malcolm did not permit his socialist admirers to trap him into explicitly endorsing socialism. The most the representative of one socialist publication could get out of him was a crisp "no" in response to the question of whether the problems America's blacks faced could be solved under the existing socioeconomic system. When the interviewer pressed on and asked Malcolm what the answer to those problems was, he evasively asserted that the answer to the question was so obvious that the question answered itself. And when the question of socialism was raised by the associate editor of a leftist publication, Malcolm replied:

> Why speak of it. If you want someone to drink from a bottle, you never put the skull and crossbones on the label, for [he] won't drink.

Socialists seized upon such statements as evidence that Malcolm was one of them. He used a similar suggestive technique at the Militant Labor Forum, where he drove home the argument that the existing socioeconomic order "cannot produce freedom for the Afro-American" with a metaphor that Aesop himself might have envied:

> It's impossible for a chicken to produce a duck egg—even though they both belong to the same family of fowl. A chicken just doesn't have it within its system to produce a duck egg. It can't do it.

"Capitalism used to be like an eagle," he exclaimed on another occasion, "but now it's more like a vulture." He told other listeners:

> You can't operate a capitalistic system unless you are vulturistic.

His colorful metaphor made excellent copy. "This is the farthest I've ever gone," he chuckled as he reviewed the transcript of the interview in which he had made the statement about the eagle and the vulture. "They will go wild over this!"

Not all of Malcolm's remarks about socialism were uncritical. He observed that the concept of workers' solidarity had little applicability to America's race problem; working-class whites tended to be highly unsympathetic to the aspirations of working-class blacks.

Malcolm privately warned his assistants about the danger of leftist infiltration. On one occasion, he even reproached some communists publicly.

Yet Malcolm sat for numerous interviews with representatives of the political left. On one occasion, two members of the staff of the *Young Socialist* went to his office and tape-recorded an interview. When one of them returned a few days later with an edited version of the tape, he noticed a small stack of *Militants* lying on the receptionist's desk. A couple of dimes lay on top of the newspapers, which appeared to be for sale. Whether they had been placed there for his benefit is unclear; Malcolm never sold copies of *The Militant* at his office—or anywhere else, according to former associates. (Sometimes, he did distribute, free of charge, copies of *The Militant* containing his speeches.)

Malcolm, who asserted that he wasn't a politician, kept right on telling the socialists and everyone else what they wanted to hear. Black revolutionaries hailed him as their champion. Moderates applauded the reorientation that appeared to have stemmed from his recent pilgrimage to Mecca. Leftists were convinced he was becoming, or already was, a disciple of Karl Marx. In reality, he was a political chameleon.

THE POLITICS
OF MANHOOD
46

Whites were understandably frightened by Malcolm's utterances about rifle clubs, hand grenades, and molotov cocktails. "We need a Mau Mau," he repeatedly asserted. He threatened to send armed guerillas— "freedom fighters," he called them—into Mississippi, which he ominously defined as any place south of the Canadian border. He raised the spectre of a black rebel army that would purge the land of black and white enemies alike. "It's freedom for everybody or freedom for nobody," he said, citing the example of Patrick Henry and his war cry about liberty or death.

The rhetoric about violent revolution suited Malcolm well. Revolutionaries are tough and manly. Invariably, they get lots of attention from the authorities. Their utopian visions of a blissful new order have little in common with the hardship that characterizes their everyday existence. They are outsiders by choice, not by compulsion. Their endeavors on behalf of the masses suggest they have little interest in the selfish pursuits of ordinary citizens. And their preoccupation with political problems makes it easy for them to avoid looking into their own.

Revolutionaries are not required to succeed. Usually, they end up defeated or dead, martyrs to their chosen cause.

Malcolm's brilliantly articulated case against nonviolence severely jolted the proponents of that strategy, which had generally been regarded as the only feasible means of transforming U.S. race relations. The ancient Hebrews, he observed, didn't love their enemies; they smote them. Nor was the American Revolution nonviolent. If white Americans could use violence to liberate themselves from British tyranny, why couldn't black Americans use violence to liberate themselves from racial tyranny? Malcolm said they had nothing to lose but their chains.

Nonviolence wouldn't work for a number of reasons, he argued. Pointing out that it could succeed only if the power structure had a sense of right and wrong, he asserted that white America was impervious to the kind of moral suasion that was making it possible, even then, for the civil rights movement to garner the congressional support that brought about the historic 1964 Civil Rights Act. He maintained that the political authorities were as hypocritical and unyielding as some of the authority figures who had once ruled him.

Malcolm, who said he didn't believe that Jesus had opposed the use of force, felt that Martin Luther King, Jr.'s attempt to apply Gandhi's nonviolent tactics to the American scene couldn't succeed because:

> Gandhi was a big, dark elephant sitting on a little white mouse. King
> is a little black mouse sitting on top of top of a big white elephant.

Malcolm did not say whether the argument applied equally well to the use of violence, or whether such violence would cause more suffering in black America than it sought to remedy. He asserted it was unimportant that black freedom fighters would have to navigate in a white sea. Men of courage, he said, care nothing about the forces arrayed against them:

> The young generation don't want to hear anything about the odds
> [that] are against us. What do we care about odds?

It was the kind of declaration a youthful gambler might have uttered.

With characteristic verbal exaggeration, Malcolm buttressed his arguments by portraying whites as a bunch of unregenerate Ku Klux Klanners. He claimed that if American blacks didn't wake up, they might end up inside gas ovens, as Hitler's Jews had. He said that "not one iota of progress" had been made in race relations since the Civil War. Malcolm dismissed the 1954 Supreme Court school desegregation decision as sheer trickery. He would later characterize the 1964 Civil Rights Act, which outlawed discrimination in public accomodations and in federally assisted programs, the same way, as if he did not want to acknowledge the sweeping, historic changes that were occurring—changes that were undermining his arguments for political violence. Malcolm, whose genius lay in his ability to move crowds rather than in fashioning effective political solutions to intractable problems that could not be remedied overnight, insisted on "immediate" resolution of America's race problem. He admitted that he was impatient, politically and otherwise, and that he had been so ever since he could remember.

His impatience was reminiscent of the impulsive, delinquent behavior that had characterized his youth. But the differences between Malcolm the defiant, demanding criminal rebel and Malcolm the importunate political rebel far outweighed the similarities. Whereas the criminal Malcolm had repudiated the very idea of law, the political Malcolm assailed existing laws in an effort to establish more equitable ones. Instead of venting his spleen on innocent victims, he lashed out at injustice. His struggle to liberate himself inwardly by liberating his people politically afforded him the first constructive outlet he had ever had for his anger. At last, he was a rebel with a proper cause.

Despite Malcolm's conciliatory, if inconstant, overtures to Martin Luther King and the other leaders of the civil rights movement, he continued denouncing the philosophy of nonviolence. Only a fool, he declared, turns the other cheek to physical attack or sings "We Shall Overcome" when set upon by billy clubs or police dogs. Again and again he stressed that revolutions are violent affairs. They are not won by loving one's enemies, or praying for their redemption. Or by sit-ins:

> Anybody can sit. An old woman can sit. A coward can sit . . . . It takes a man to stand.

Malcolm's characterization of the proponents of nonviolence as womanish and "cowardly" was typical of his tendency to accuse his political enemies of the very things he had been accused of. The way he sometimes talked about Martin Luther King, one might have thought it was Martin rather than Malcolm who had tried so hard to live down the boyhood sissy reputation.

Subtly, Malcolm, who scolded his black listeners for being "afraid to bleed," transformed the debate about political violence, which was a question of strategy, into an issue of masculinity. Again and again, he maintained that willingness to employ violence is the crucial test of manhood. "You're going to have to fight!" he told one audience, with emphasis upon each and every word. His speeches, which equated nonviolence with defenselessness and cowardice, were filled with the kind of imagery that might have been more appropriate to a discussion of his short-lived boxing career. During one speech, he belligerently told an imaginary white opponent, "I'll bust you in your mouth!" Characterizing Martin Luther King as a chump instead of a champ, Malcolm said, "It's time to stop singing and start swinging."

He exhorted his followers to do in the political arena what he had been unable to do to Bill Peterson in the boxing arena, or to Hank Ross and others in the streets. His rapt listeners, who were unaware of his boyhood fear of combat and his efforts to conquer it by pitting himself against dangerous adversaries, had no way of fully understanding the significance of his assertion:

> What you and I have to start doing . . . I mean, . . . what you
> have to do . . . .

Nor did his audiences grasp the connection between his utterances about violence and his recurrent affirmations of his own manhood. "I'm man enough!" he gratuitously exclaimed. On another occasion, he told James Baldwin, "I don't have to say I'm a man." But apparently he did, for he kept on saying it and equating willingness to commit violence with virility. His furious opposition to the doctrine of nonviolence, which marked the beginning of what Calvin Hernton has aptly called the "politics of manhood," was another example of his continuing effort to resolve unfinished private business in the dog-eat-dog public realm.

Despite the savageness of Malcolm's rhetoric, his position on political violence was ambiguous. He reproached the press for depicting him as a bloodthirsty ghoul who wanted to slay all whites, but added:

> ". . . as if you could kill all the white people . . . ."

"Or as if [you] shouldn't," he ominously declared on another occasion. He stressed that blacks should never initiate violence first but should do so only when hostile whites forced them to employ the "active self-defense" he had been unable to fashion against his adversaries when he was young. But the ironic way he often said it made people feel that he really felt that blacks shouldn't have to wait to be attacked before striking back. And when Alex Haley, who apparently sensed Malcolm's penchant for political ambiguity, tried to probe his feelings about race riots, Malcolm noncommitally replied, "I don't know if I could start one; I don't know if I'd want to stop one." He told another questioner: "If you want to know what I'll do, figure out what you'll do. I'll do the same thing—only more of it." Partly, perhaps, to protect himself against possible prosecution, he cautioned blacks not to do anything illegal, even though violent measures would "be justified."

His fondness for ambiguity came in handy when he was asked about a bloody incident that had occurred in New York City while he was abroad. Six black teenagers had attacked a middle-aged white couple who owned a Harlem clothing store. The woman was stabbed to death. According to the *New York Post*, the six knife-wielding youths were part of an anti-white gang that was allegedly being trained by dissident Black Muslims. People blamed Malcolm's incendiary rhetoric for the emergence of the hate-gang, whose members described themselves as "blood brothers." When Malcolm was queried about the incident, he said, "It didn't make me sad at all!" He said that all blacks were his blood brothers.

The reply, which some interpreted to mean that he favored such bloodshed, helped convince many of his followers that he was prepared to lead them into battle. He told one militant audience, "I just want to give you a little briefing on guerilla warfare, because before you know it . . . ." There was no need to finish the sentence. The crowd went wild.

Yet Malcolm, who alternately admitted and denied that he wanted to stir people up, neither committed any political violence nor directed any of his subordinates to do so. On the contrary, whenever violence threatened, he skillfully defused it, just as he had defused the rage of the Los Angeles Muslims who had been awaiting permission to exact revenge for Ronald Stokes's death. When action-oriented brothers decided to take Malcolm up on his proposal to send guerillas south, he refused to countenance the endeavor. The brothers in question left his organization in disgust. Others wanted to "occupy" the white-owned businesses on 125th Street, Harlem's principal crosstown artery. Still others wanted to pursue a vendetta against Elijah Muhammad's legions and seize control of Temple Seven by force. Malcolm firmly discouraged all these illegal, impractical schemes. At the outdoor rallies at which he whipped up anti-white sentiment to fever pitch, he repeatedly admonished his black listeners not to attack or provoke the white policemen who were listening impassively. They were only doing their job, he told one audience. He told another:

> Maybe some of these blue-eyed devils in blue uniforms here are really black. If any of them smiles, it's 'cause . . . he's a brother.

Invariably, in such cases, one or more of the white cops would grin and the crowd would laugh good-naturedly. Such techniques enabled him to forestall potential violence before it erupted.

Malcolm protected white reporters who ventured into Harlem the same way. But, at one rally, he didn't rescue newsman Al Ellenberg until he had frightened him half to death. He told the nearly all-black audience:

> Now, there's a reporter who hasn't taken a note in a half an hour, but as soon as I start talking about the Jews, he's busy taking notes to prove that I'm anti-Semitic.

Behind the newspaperman, a voice snarled, "Kill the bastard! Kill them all!"

The young journalist smiled uneasily. "Look at him laugh," jeered Malcolm. "He's not really laughing; he's just laughing with his teeth." An ugly tension curled the edges of the crowd as Malcolm declared:

> The white man doesn't know how to laugh. He just shows his

teeth. But we know how to laugh. We laugh deep down, from the bottom up.

The audience laughed, deep down from the bottom up, and the threat subsided as quickly as it had appeared. With words, Malcolm protected the very whites he condemned.

Malcolm admitted he was afraid what would happen if violence erupted. He was so apprehensive about one menacing crowd that he mounted the hood of a car and persuaded the angry throng to disperse. Later, he emphatically denied that he'd jump atop a vehicle to stop a riot.

He also kept the lid on by leavening his rhetoric, which was sometimes accompanied by ironic smiles, with admonitions that blacks should rampage "intelligently." They shouldn't burn down their own houses, he said. He cautioned them to sit down and carefully analyze the likelihood of success or failure before embarking on the path of violence. Likening their predicament to that of a boxer in the ring, he said they must learn to throw their punches at the right time. A cocked fist, he observed, was more effective than a weak punch. Obliquely, he suggested what he had learned from bitter experience in the streets of Lansing, Boston, and Harlem: that the threat of violence was often more effective than the use of it, particularly when the threatening party had to lead from a position of weakness. The lesson was imperfectly understood by many of those who tried to follow in his footsteps.

Malcolm characterized himself as an oratorical Joe Louis. In his effort to perfect the difficult art of encouraging and discouraging violence simultaneously, he played the tough guy to the hilt, as he had done when he was young. Deftly, he led his followers to the brink but no further. Like a dove in a hawk's plumage, he gave his followers their revenge in fantasy, but not in reality.

Malcolm bluffed the white enemy the way he had bluffed other adversaries. He was so apprehensive that people would think he was bluffing that he instructed Alex Haley not to reveal that he had palmed the bullet during the Russian roulette game he had played to cow his burglary associates into following his orders.

In short, despite Malcolm's repeated insistence about his readiness to kill, his violence was purely verbal. It was an astute compromise between bloody impulse and guilty deed. The political Malcolm, like the criminal Malcolm, was not nearly as "bad" as he claimed.

Yet his impact was enormous. Single-handedly, he changed the terms of the debate about the means that could be used by black Americans to achieve the goal of equal opportunity. By frightening whites and by making many of them feel that Martin Luther King's nonviolent approach was a blessing in disguise, Malcolm helped create the political climate that spurred the passage of the civil rights bills of 1964 and 1965. In fact, without Malcolm's help, King and his associates might not have succeeded in their arduous campaign to lift the yoke of legally sanctioned racial oppression. Malcolm's voice helped save a complacent America from racial catastrophe.

But the effects of his efforts to uplift America's blacks were not all positive. His rhetoric was instrumental in creating the political climate that allowed Eartha Kitt to be booed offstage by blacks who refused to concede her right to marry a white man. Subsequently, one of Malcolm's admirers acknowledged:

> Malcolm X became the personification of that part of me that was not as selfless and loving as Martin Luther King, nor as agreeable as Roy Wilkins, or as studied as Whitney Young, nor as dignified as A. Philip Randolph.

Jesse Gray put it more bluntly and said, "[Malcolm] taught me to be mean and black, and [to] hate the white man."

VI

GROPING FOR DIRECTION

ANOTHER EVICTION

47

Two and a half weeks after Malcolm's return from abroad, he renewed his campaign to undermine Elijah Muhammad's religious credentials. On June 7, he told nearly five hundred listeners that Mr. Muhammad had fathered six illegitimate children. The revelation came in response to a question that appeared prearranged to the FBI agent who attended the gathering. Malcolm acknowledged that the Black Muslims were highly sensitive to such disclosures. He said the Nation of Islam would even murder to keep the embarrassing truth under wraps.

On June 8, Malcolm reiterated the charges to Mike Wallace of CBS News. As CBS cameramen recorded every word, he claimed that the only reason he had not publicized the information when he left the Nation was that he felt it would have shattered the moral discipline of Elijah's followers, many of whom would have reverted to their former ways. Malcolm did not say why he no longer felt this way. A slight smile appeared at the corner of his mouth when Wallace asked him if he feared what might happen to him as a result of his disclosure. The smile broadened as Malcolm replied: "Oh, yes. I probably am a dead man already." He added that if he were still an NOI member and ignorant of the truth about the Messenger, he'd kill Elijah's accuser himself.

Four days later, on June 12, Boston radio station WEEI broadcast an afternoon program called "Conversation Piece," during which Malcolm reaffirmed that Elijah Muhammad had been siring children out of wedlock. That evening, on a popular Boston radio talk show hosted by Jerry Williams, he re-echoed the theme. Two days afterward, he canceled another Boston appearance and returned to New York, where he issued the same charges again. His place in Boston was taken by his assistant Benjamin Goodman, who told a gathering that included representatives of CORE and the Urban League that Malcolm no longer believed in political separation. ("We have to be realistic," Malcolm told a New York audience. "Africa is a long way off and there's a lot of water in between.") Goodman said Malcolm believed that blacks should stay in the United States and strive to attain their rightful place in American society. The meeting was hosted by Ella, who notified the Boston Police, on June 17, that her son Rodnell was missing from home.

The police informed the FBI, which was told by an informant that Ella didn't seem particularly upset about the disappearance of her son, for whom she appeared to have aspirations that resembled those she had for Malcolm.

Throughout the month of June, Malcolm, who leavened his warlike statements with the kind of conciliatory ones he had made when he first left Elijah Muhammad, continued his media blitz against the Messenger. On June 20, his accusations were published in the *Philadelphia Tribune*, a black newspaper. On the 22nd, in New York, he reiterated the charges, which an associate repeated in Chicago on June 25. Malcolm even telephoned one newsman at three a.m. in an effort to persuade him to print the story. The consequences of all this were predictable. The day Benjamin Goodman took Malcolm's place in Boston, an automobile forced his car to stop in the Callahan Tunnel on the way to Logan Airport. Men brandishing knives emerged from the vehicle. "We're going to kill the so-and-so," one shouted. "You're not going to get out of here alive." Goodman, whose companion brandished a shotgun and forced the assailants to retreat, realized that they were after Malcolm, who was not in the blocked car.

Malcolm, who asserted that Elijah Muhammad was the one who wouldn't let sleeping dogs lie, knew he was a marked man; his efforts to discredit his former mentor had apparently begun to bear fruit. The active membership of the Boston mosque had declined from an estimated two hundred fifty to one hundred or less. Believers reportedly began quitting other NOI mosques in droves. Elijah's son Wallace later told Chicago's *American*, accurately or otherwise, that the Nation of Islam had lost about half its members.

Elijah's aides tried to salvage his reputation with rumors that it was Malcolm who had fathered the Messenger's secretaries' children. Malcolm's sex appeal lent credence to the rumors, as did Heather's and Robin's fondness for him. But the counter-propaganda was not very effective, so Elijah's spokesmen tried other approaches. At Temple Seven, the faithful were subjected to a harangue entitled "So What If He Is Not All Pure; Look What He Did For You And I." *Muhammad Speaks* suggested that Elijah was one of those great historical figures, like Moses and David, who brought deliverance to their people despite their flaws.

The war of words continued. In an open letter that apparently reflected Mr. Muhammad's feelings, one henchman wrote:

> But YOU, Malcolm, were treated like a SON by the Messenger . . . . He did more for you than your real parents ever could, or were inclined to do.

The death threats also continued, but not without qualification. At Temple Seven, for example, an official announced that Malcolm should be destroyed. The statement, which elicited tears from a number of listeners, was promptly contradicted by another official. Obediently, the first speaker trundled back to the podium and intimated that Malcolm would expire, instead, by committing suicide. Two days later, in the Richmond, Virginia mosque, a minister proclaimed that Malcolm should be killed for what he was doing to Mr. Muhammad. Subsequently, a spokesman warned in *Muhammad Speaks* that "grave consequences" would ensue from further attempts to spread "evil" talk about the Messenger. Yet, in the same issue, Elijah wrote:

> Hypocrites . . . are not to be killed, for Allah desires to make them examples for others by chastising them, like a parent does a child.

Whether the conflicting messages were the result of differences within the leadership or Muhammad's ambivalence about Malcolm—or both—is unclear. The Messenger's statement may have been an attempt to insulate himself against future prosecution by creating the impression that he was trying to restrain his vengeful subordinates. Or perhaps he hoped the death threats would be sufficient to deter Malcolm from further efforts to undermine his religious credentials.

Whatever the case, the New York police took no chances the day Malcolm appeared in court to try to prevent the Nation of Islam from evicting him from his modest brick home. Twenty uniformed policemen and twelve plainclothesmen were on hand for the hearing, as well as eight of Malcolm's own men. They surrounded him so completely that he could hardly be seen from the gallery of the courtroom, which the authorities judiciously chose for its small size. The shade on the window was kept drawn during the two-day trial so no one could draw a bead on him from the outside.

Malcolm's attorney was Percy Sutton, who had recently declared his candidacy for a seat in the New York State Assembly. It was common knowledge that Malcolm lacked sufficient money to pay Sutton. But there were other ways to compensate an aspiring Harlem politician. Malcolm sent his followers out into the streets to campaign for Sutton. His doorbell ringers garnered enough votes to enable him to win the following November. Sutton's defense of Malcolm also improved his image among

Harlem's militants, who might otherwise have branded the urbane, resourceful assemblyman an Uncle Tom.

The ironic thing about the trial was that Malcolm had set himself up for eviction by refusing Elijah Muhammad's repeated offers to have the title to the house put in his own name. Now that the offer had been withdrawn, he argued that Muhammad had promised him the house in return for the service he had rendered the Messenger's movement. His problem was that he couldn't prove it. Consequently, Percy Sutton was reduced to a weak, two-pronged defense. First, he alleged that though the deed to the property indicated that the owner was the Nation of Islam, the NOI had purchased it in trust for Malcolm. But Malcolm undermined this argument himself when he inadvertently acknowledged that the house really belonged to the Nation.

Sutton's second, fall-back defense was more complex but equally flimsy. He argued that even if the court decided that the NOI was legally the owner and that Malcolm was a tenant by virtue of the fact he had been minister of Temple Seven, the eviction was illegal because he had been deprived of his office improperly, without due process. In an effort to buttress the argument, Malcolm claimed that the press had misquoted him when it had announced he had quit the movement. He said he was still under suspension, and that he could not legally be removed as minister without a hearing before his congregation. Malcolm's suspension therefore became a legal issue. Gingerly, in stages, he told the court that the reason he had been silenced was not his impolitic remark about President Kennedy's assassination. The real reason, he said, had to do with Elijah's private life. "You are making it public now?" the opposing lawyer asked sharply. Malcolm drew back, perhaps because Captain Joseph and several dozen of his subordinates were sitting in the courtroom. But, despite Sutton's efforts to steer Malcolm clear of the subject of Elijah's sex life, Malcolm asserted that Muhammad had "nine wives." He tagged the disclosure onto the end of a response to a question that had nothing to do with the Messenger, whom he kept calling "the Honorable Elijah Muhammad."

Despite Malcolm's commanding presence, he was not his usual self. Words poured from his mouth in breathless, run-on sentences. Once or twice, he angrily jumped up and tried to interrupt opposing witnesses. "He was putting up more of a fight than the situation warranted," the presiding judge later recalled.

Legally speaking, the judge was correct; it was an open and shut case. But Malcolm's determination to stand fast, as his father had done in 1929, was not motivated by legal considerations. In the self-sufficient world of Black Muslims and former Black Muslims, it was embarrassing for a man to be unable to provide a home for his family. "A home is really the only thing I've ever provided Betty since we've been married," Malcolm told Alex Haley. "I can't keep on putting her through changes—all she's put up with."

Malcolm may also have been determined to put an end to the lengthy series of evictions that had plagued him since his boyhood. The list included his family's 1929 eviction from the Lansing farmhouse that had burned down; their eviction from three of the six acres his parents subsequently purchased south of town; his expulsions from Mrs. McDaniel's class, Pleasant Grove School, and Lincoln Community Center; his transfer from Mrs. Swerlein's home to two different boarding homes; his dismissal from various jobs; his ejection from Harlem by West Indian Archie; and his self-induced expulsions from the Norfolk Prison Colony and the Nation of Islam.

The atmosphere in the New York courtroom was tense. Malcolm's men and the NOI contingent sat on opposite sides of the gallery, glaring at each other across the aisle. The court stenographer was struck by the charged, eerie silence. Comic relief was provided by Judge Maurice Wahl, who compared the proceedings to "a Perry Mason case." Wahl had been chosen to preside at the trial because he was immune to the blandishments that often accompanied politically sensitive cases. A number of other judges had reportedly expressed reluctance to officiate. Evidently, they didn't want to incur the wrath of Elijah Muhammad—nor that of Malcolm, whose belligerent rhetoric apparently fooled them as much as it fooled nearly everyone else.

But Maurice Wahl took the assignment in stride. It was he who subsequently fined Adam Clayton Powell, Jr. $575,000 for signing away property in an attempt to avoid a $46,500 libel judgment. Back when Wahl had been the only Republican assistant district attorney in Manhattan, it was he who had put New York City's most notorious brothel-keeper, Polly Adler, in jail. Adler, whose memoirs were later published in a book entitled *A House Is Not a Home*, had been arrested eighteen times but never convicted. In vain, she offered Wahl a $25,000 bribe.

After Sutton and the opposing attorney submitted briefs, Wahl (who had pointed out that Malcolm's decision not to put the title in his own name had enabled him to avoid paying property taxes) made his decision, which was unfavorable to Malcolm. Unlike Leland Carr, the Michigan judge who had ordered the Littles to vacate their home "forthwith," Wahl gave Malcolm nearly five months to find another place to live—that is, unless the Nation of Islam, which was paying the mortgage, objected. The NOI did not. The gesture, if that is what it was, had no apparent effect on Malcolm, whose speeches were full of the fiery images that pervaded his incendiary rhetoric. Some of the images were of burning or burned-out homes:

> Sometimes, when a person's house is on fire and . . . someone comes in yelling, "Fire!", instead of the person who is awakened by the yell being thankful, they make the mistake of charging the one who awakened them with having set the fire.

Outwardly, the statement suggested that white America should be grateful for Malcolm's predictions of impending political upheaval and shouldn't blame him if it occurred. But the statement was also reminiscent of his father's behavior during the fire that had gutted his Lansing farmhouse after Judge Carr had ordered him to vacate it. Malcolm said:

> When you're inside another man's house and the furniture is his, [and also the] curtains [and] all those fine decorations, . . . you let him know that when he puts his hands on you, it's not only you he puts his hands on, it's his whole house. You'll burn it down.

He pounded his fist on the lectern and declared:

> You have to let them know that you have as much right in the house as they. And that if both of you can't set down in that house in peace, it's better for you to put it on fire. And burn it to the ground. Burn it to the ground!

Malcolm started to laugh as he described the leaping flames. Shortly after the eviction trial ended, he exclaimed, in the midst of a statement that was ostensibly directed at the white enemy, "You give us what we've got coming, or nobody is going to get anything!"

ADAM AND MALCOLM 48

Partly because it lacked the trappings of nationhood that Elijah Muhammad's movement boasted, the Muslim Mosque that Malcolm had founded never got off the ground. Consequently, Malcolm, who claimed he hadn't even bothered to try to recruit Muhammad's followers, decided to establish another organization. The new one, which was loosely modeled after The Organization of African Unity and Marcus Garvey's UNIA, was called the Organization of Afro-American Unity. The name reflected Malcolm's desire to forge strong, viable links between the blacks of America and those of Africa. In contrast to Muslim Mosque, Inc., which had been unsuccessful in attracting non-Muslim blacks (or many Muslim ones), the OAAU was entirely secular in character.

Malcolm scheduled his first OAAU rally for Sunday, June 28, the very day Elijah Muhammad held a rally of his own in Harlem. The timing may have been coincidental. (Malcolm customarily held his Harlem rallies on Sundays.) But the Nation of Islam, which had been advertising its Harlem conclave for more than a month, viewed the rival gathering as a direct challenge, despite Malcolm's uncompetitive exterior.

On June 28, hundreds of blacks lined up in the street outside the 9,000-seat armory where the NOI rally was being held. As they waited to be searched, a man suddenly tumbled out of the door. "He's one of Malcolm's men!" someone yelled. Believers swarmed over him as others locked arms to form cordons to hold back the police. "Kill him! Kill him!" chanted the crowd. The object of its venom was beaten nearly senseless, then dumped against a fence. Nearby, a man named Jesus Emmanuel, who described himself as the "blood son" of the black religious leader Father Divine, handed out leaflets portraying the biscuit-colored Messenger as a "mix-bred phony." His nose was smashed and two of his teeth were knocked loose.

No violence marred Malcolm's rally, which was devoted primarily to the

OAAU charter. Portions of the document, which had been drafted in consultation with Jesse Gray, Gloria Richardson, Albert Cleage, and other black militants, read like a Black Power manifesto. It stressed the need for blacks to control their own educational, cultural, economic, and political institutions. It promised a housing self-improvement program. It envisioned school boycotts, a program to assist unwed mothers, an orphanage, a home for the aged, a clinic for drug addicts, and "an all-out war on organized crime." The multifaceted organization Malcolm described was to be divided into various departments. There would be a department of political action. An economics department would create employment and business opportunities. Malcolm said the OAAU would have a youth group, a speaker's bureau, and a newspaper. He told one interviewer he'd call the paper *The Flaming Crescent* because "we want to set the world on fire."

Malcolm said he was the organization's chairman. "Anything that goes wrong—any failures—you can rest them right upon my shoulders," he said. His willingness to accept the responsibility he had shunned as a youthful delinquent was indicative of how far he had come during the intervening years. But he paid a heavy price for that willingness; one aide described him as a man with a burden.

Malcolm said whites would not be permitted to join either of his organizations. "The white man calls that racism," he declared. "Mind you, this is right." He said he was suspicious of people from all-white neighborhoods who hovered around blacks in an effort to prove they weren't prejudiced. He told Bembry that if whites were permitted to belong to black political organizations, black leaders would fail to emerge and black youngsters would lose the opportunity to identify with the right kinds of role models. Malcolm asked Bembry if he remembered asking him about his relationship with the Messenger. Bembry said he did. Sadly, Malcolm responded: "You look up to a man. You do nothing to make him lie to you."

Despite Malcolm's earlier announcements that he'd be willing to accept financial help from whites, he shifted tack and ruled such assistance out on the ground that white donors would end up exercising control behind the scenes:

> A man who tosses worms in the river isn't necessarily a friend of the fish.

His about-face on the issue cost him nothing; whites were no more likely to contribute money to the new Malcolm than to the old one. Moreover, his independent-sounding stance was politically appealing; it enabled him to argue that his organizations were not dependent on white dollars, as the NAACP, CORE, SCLC, and the Urban League were. But the lack of white contributors was not offset by the presence of black ones. Wealthy, conservative blacks were not about to jeopardize their hard-won position by supporting Malcolm. The same applied to established black institutions like the Christian churches, which were doing so much to assist the civil rights movement. The contributions Malcolm requested from OAAU members—two dollars to start and a dollar a week thereafter—were a tiny fraction of the sums the Nation of Islam exacted from its members. Malcolm raised the possibility of a larger contribution—ten dollars a week for six months. For a while, some Muslim Mosque members contributed ten dollars a week, or nearly that, but the majority of OAAU members didn't even contribute their weekly dollar. Malcolm did obtain modest sums from the collection buckets his assistants passed around at his rallies, which had a financial purpose as well as a political one. And speakers' honorariums continued to roll in as a result of his backbreaking schedule of speaking engagements. But the money he received was insufficient to enable him to adequately support his family and his organizations. Doubleday came to the rescue several times with sizable checks. Shortly after one payment, Malcolm told Haley, with a wry laugh, "It's evaporated. I don't know where." And he told the *Washington Sunday Star*, "We are scratching." Yet, he insisted in virtually the same breath that "true" revolutionaries didn't worry about money. His unconcerned facade, which was somewhat reminiscent of his father's, helped him hide the fact that he sometimes lacked enough money to pay the rent for the dilapidated Theresa Hotel office that served as his headquarters. On some occasions, he even had to borrow money to pay for the meeting halls where he held his rallies.

With the approach of the forthcoming November 1964 elections, the Freedom Now Party asked Malcolm if he would be its U.S. Senatorial candidate from the State of Michigan. Malcolm, who had publicly praised the all-black party without explicitly endorsing it, was silent for a moment. Then he laughed and said, "I'll let you know." James 67X, who sensed that Malcolm wanted to accept the offer, counseled him against running for office in a state where his political following was far smaller than it was in New York. Others offered similar advice. After pondering the offer of the fledgling party, which disintegrated after the election, Malcolm declined. At times, he took the position that, though he intended to run black militants for public office—or at least support them—he would not seek political office himself. He gave the impression that he had no desire for political power.

But he did not hide the fact that he enjoyed the power that stemmed from his ability to manipulate his audiences with emotion-laden words. And his maiden OAAU speech suggested he was quite interested in recouping, in the political realm, the power he had lacked as a youth in the personal realm:

> You and I want to create an organization that will give us so much power [that] we can sit down and do as we please.

Like another famous political rebel named Lenin, who had maintained that the central question was who dominated whom, Malcolm stressed the importance of political power; without it, he said, America's blacks would remain oppressed. He characterized the white power structure, and the adults who comprised it, as immoral and hypocritical. Likening white tyranny to parental tyranny and equating the urge to revolt with youth, he applauded the *Life Magazine* photograph of the nine-year-old Chinese girl who was about to pull the trigger of the pistol she was using to execute her bearded, anti-revolutionary father, who was kneeling before her. Malcolm recalled the apocryphal story of the revolutionary who had asked a crowd of three hundred people how many of them wanted freedom. All three hundred raised their hands. He asked how many of them were willing to kill anyone who obstructed their quest for liberty. Only about fifty responded affirmatively. He told the fifty:

> You wanted freedom and you said you'd kill anyone who'd get in your way. You see those 250? You get them first. Some of them are your own brothers and sisters and mothers and fathers . . . .They're the ones who stand in the way of your freedom!

Despite Malcolm's assertion that he had no desire for political office, he did not rule out a race against Adam Clayton Powell, Jr., who had been representing Harlem in Congress for two decades. Indeed, he had been toying with the idea of running for office since 1960, the year he told one F.B.I. informant that he could win a congressional race if he could persuade Harlem's non-voters to vote. Later, he declared that he'd be willing, under certain conditions, to consider running for mayor of New York City—a political plum that Powell and Percy Sutton were also eyeing. Powell's congressional seat, which was as safe as those of many of the southern Democrats who fought him tooth and nail, was another attractive alternative. "The man who gets into Congress from this district can stay there the rest of his life," Powell told a friend who asked him why he had resigned from the New York City Council to run for a seat in the House. (Powell was the first black to sit on the City Council.)

The newly elected Powell, one of two blacks in the 435-member House of Representatives, had earned his seat in Congress. During the Depression, he had led the successful fight to reinstate five black physicians who had been dismissed by white administrators from Harlem Hospital, which was known as "the butcher shop." The soup kitchen he ran in the basement of the Abyssinian Baptist Church fed thousands. The year after Powell replaced his father as the church's minister, he became co-chairman of the Coordinating Committee for Employment, which reinvigorated stalled attempts to force the white merchants on 125th Street to employ blacks. "Don't buy where you can't work!" chanted the pickets who patrolled the entrances to dozens of white-owned stores. The blacks who patronized the business establishments gradually began to honor the picket lines. The Uptown Chamber of Commerce, which represented most of the retail establishments, finally agreed that its member stores would reserve one-third of all nonmanagerial jobs for blacks.

The Coordinating Committee, which had no more than $300 in its treasury, also forced the New York Telephone Company to begin hiring black operators by flooding its switchboards with thousands of operator-assisted local calls that could have been dialed directly. The Committee, which announced that Harlemites might have to begin paying their phone bills in pennies, told the local power company, Consolidated Edison, to employ blacks unless it wanted Harlemites to declare every Tuesday a lightless night. Though Powell and his associates said they were opposed to violence, they warned that there "might be" some blacks who would resent seeing lights burning in store windows on lightless nights. Harlem's shopkeepers, who had to keep their stores well lit, got the point and demanded that Con Edison change its hiring policy. Reluctantly, Con Ed caved in.

The Committee's most spectacular victory occurred when it challenged the New York City Omnibus Company's refusal to hire black bus drivers or black mechanics. The ensuing Harlem bus boycott, which provided an instructive model for the Montgomery bus boycott, compelled the company to hire more than two hundred black drivers and mechanics.

After Powell became a city councilman, he induced New York's city colleges, which collectively employed more than two thousand teachers, to begin including blacks on the faculty. When he came to Washington in 1944, he ignored the time-honored tradition that freshman congressmen should be seen but not heard and introduced a bill calling for the establishment of a Fair Employment Practices Commission. He also refused to heed the unwritten rule that barred black congressmen from the congressional gymnasium, steam room, and barber shop. He directed his staff to eat in the House cafeteria whether they were hungry or not. A couple of years later, he succeeded in having black journalists admitted to the press gallery of the House of Representatives. Until the emergence of Malcolm and Martin Luther King, Jr., Powell—together with A. Philip Randolph—was the preeminent voice of black protest in the U.S. This was largely due to his ability to move crowds. He declared, "There isn't a single person who wouldn't love to be able to control people by the power of their words."

Unfortunately, success spoiled Congressman Powell. As time passed, his absenteeism from the House grew legendary. After he divorced his second wife, he married the lowest-paid member of his congressional staff, quadrupled her salary, and bundled her off to Puerto Rico, where her uncle, a contractor, built him a luxurious home. Powell told the press she was busy answering the letters he received from his Puerto Rican constituents. He did not say why she couldn't do it in Washington or in Harlem. When a reporter asked him what he thought of nepotism, he replied, "I think it's wonderful!"

The Caribbean villa was only one of several homes that were at the disposal of Powell, who told his constituents he lived in Harlem. One of the homes was in Westchester County. It boasted four bathrooms and two servants. Powell had a Jaguar and an Austin-Healey. He also had two boats. When he junketed abroad to European capitals at taxpayer expense, the ghetto-dwellers he claimed to represent accompanied him—vicariously. They enjoyed in fantasy what he enjoyed in reality.

Though Powell was hardly the only congressman who abused the congressional privilege to travel at public expense, he openly flouted his misuse of public funds:

> Next Sunday, Pan American luxury flight to Paris. [Audience laughs and applauds vigorously]. Paid for by Congress. [More laughter.] The United States delegate to the World Naval Conference in Geneva—all expenses paid. [More laughter. One man yells, "First class!" Powell replies]: "First class all the way. All the way. [More applause and laughter]. Sarsaparilla too.

He was equally contemptuous of the moral code clergymen are expected to adhere to. He seemed proud of his unwillingness to conceal his transgressions the way his father, who had admonished his parishioners to forgo liquor, had attempted to conceal his bottles of gin.

In 1958, a grand jury indicted Powell for income tax evasion. The indictment alleged, among other things, that he had improperly deducted as professional expenses forty percent of his fuel, light, and laundry bills, virtually all his clothing store and department store purchases, his large liquor bill, the cost of maintaining his boats, and his son's private school tuition. (Powell attributed this last item to the fact he had "always been in favor of federal aid to education.") Evidence indicated that, though Powell and his second wife had reported a joint income of $70,000 in 1951, they had paid less than $1,000 in income tax. The following year, their combined income was approximately $90,000, but they claimed a tax liability of only $700. At the trial, the prosecutor told the jury:

> [Powell] claimed $2,500 for living expenses in Washington for four days each week during a ten-month period. But he was only in the United States for eight months.

The lawyer Powell chose to defend him was Edward Bennett Williams, whose clients included Jimmy Hoffa, Senator Joe McCarthy, and underworld czar Frank Costello. Williams was a brilliant legal strategist. He was also a courtroom actor who manipulated the emotions of his audiences as skillfully as Malcolm did.

At the trial, Williams proved that the government had failed to inform the grand jury that had indicted Powell that he had inadvertently reported some income twice on one tax return. The amount of the error was greater than the amount the government claimed Powell had underreported. Williams emphasized that the authorities had never invited Powell to discuss the deductions it was challenging, as the Internal Revenue Service customarily does. Several times, he intimated that the government was out to get the independent-minded black congressman, who was such a thorn in the side of the Eisenhower Administration and its southern Democratic allies. Williams also pointed out that, before the Department of Justice brought the case to trial, it had sent a letter stating that Powell was the subject of criminal investigation to every important black newspaper, ostensibly for the purpose of ferreting out information. Williams, who had been in the forefront of the successful battle to admit blacks to the Washington D.C. Bar Association, asked the jury to ask itself whether the authorities had been conducting a criminal investigation against Powell or a political vendetta:

> I ask you to consider . . . whether he is on trial for political liquidation. I say that if you believe the latter, . . . you should give thundering notice. . . that there is no room for political trials in this land, [and] that an indictment is not a substitute for the ballot.

One of the spectators who watched Williams transform the playboy congressman into a political martyr was Malcolm, who attended the lengthy trial regularly.

The proceedings, which ended with a deadlocked jury, did not seem to diminish Powell's popularity in Harlem, where he was revered for precisely the opposite reasons Malcolm was revered. Whereas Malcolm was esteemed for his ability to rise above his criminal past and resist temptation, Powell was admired for his ability to get away with his skullduggery. The fact that he was a minister made the achievement that much more impressive.

Yet there were important similarities between the two pastor-politicians, both of whom were anathema to the leaders of the civil rights movement. Both exuded sex appeal. (Powell boasted about his women.) Both were gifted showmen and accomplished orators. Each, in his own way, voiced the aspirations of lower-class blacks and constituted living proof they were attainable.

The bad press Powell received from the white reporters and editors who ran America's major dailies helped him as much in Harlem as it helped Malcolm. The more the two men were criticized downtown by whites, the more convinced Harlemites became that they were their true spokesmen, even if their skin looked white or almost white.

Adam, who was even lighter-skinned than Malcolm was, had white ancestors. His father's father had been a slaveowner. His mother's mother, who had been the housekeeper and mistress of the beer baron Jacob Schaefer, had been part-white. Powell's blonde-haired, blue-eyed sister looked white. When he was young, his hair had also been blonde. When he was about twelve, a bunch of black boys beat him up because they thought he was white:

> The very next night, I had to go to Eighth Avenue to get something from the store for Mother. And a gang of white boys grabbed me and demanded, "What are you?" Remembering my . . . . beating of the preceding night, I answered, "Colored!" Whereupon I again was bloodied. On the third night [that I went out], another group of colored boys grabbed me on Seventh Avenue and asked the same question . . . . I said, "Mixed!"

"A Mick!" exclaimed one boy. Young Adam, who was accepted by neither camp, was sent home crying once again. Powell subsequently tried so hard to win white acceptance, as Malcolm had done in Mason, Michigan, that he succeeded, for a number of months, in convincing his classmates he was white. He also convinced Abraham Lincoln's elderly son Robert, who patronized the dining room of the summer resort where Powell was working. Whenever one of the black doormen placed his hand on the door of Robert's car to open it for him, the latter cracked him across the knuckles with his cane. So Powell was pressed into service. Each night, when Lincoln's car arrived, Adam placed his whitish hand on the door and opened it for him. Not once did the son of the Great Emancipator try to strike Powell. Years later, Dan Burley, who preceded James Hicks as managing editor of Harlem's *Amsterdam News*, pointed out that Powell looked so white:

> He constantly has to prove he's a Negro to Negroes.

Burley might have said the same about Malcolm.

The relationship between Malcolm and Powell became apparent when Tammany Hall, Manhattan's Democratic Party machine, unsuccessfully attempted to purge the irrepressible, flamboyant congressman. Two days after Carmine DeSapio announced that Powell was *persona non grata*, Powell attended an outdoor NAACP rally in Harlem. On the speaker's platform with him was DeSapio's yes-man uptown, Manhattan Borough President Hulan Jack, whom DeSapio wanted to oppose Powell in the forthcoming Democratic congressional primary. When Jack, who had snubbed a number of invitations to appear at Black Muslim rallies, rose to speak, Malcolm, who was still in the Nation of Islam at the time, gave a signal by walking through a nearby tavern door. People who had evidently been planted in the audience "spontaneously" booed Jack, who was visibly shaken. Others joined in. "Send that Uncle Tom back downtown!" one cried. Jack, who later accused Powell of orchestrating the proceedings, was hissed and booed for ten solid minutes. Finally, Powell stood up, silenced the crowd with a wave of his arm, and magnanimously offered his would-be challenger the microphone.

Powell, who was trying to make inroads among the new generation of militants, quietly courted Malcolm. In turn, Malcolm, who was viewed with suspicion by moderate blacks, made the most of the respectability that his association with the well-known congressman conferred upon him. Powell, who was adept at heading off potential challengers, referred to his young potential rival, whose brilliance he publicly acknowledged, as his "dear friend." He asserted they were "extremely close," notwithstanding their divergent views. Similarly, Malcolm, who shared political platforms with Powell, professed his friendship and gave several sermons in Powell's church. (For the occasion, he temporarily suspended his attacks on the Christian clergy). Malcolm also attended a number of Powell's political functions, and vice versa. An NBC television cameraman spotted him sitting attentively in the last row of the audience at one of the rallies staged by the successful congressman, who claimed that he was not a politician. When one of the deacons at Powell's church objected to his flirtation with Malcolm, Adam replied, "This cat and I are going to rule the world!"

But Powell began having political problems. The press raised a storm when, instead of staying in Washington to vote for the constitutional amendment barring payment of poll taxes as a prerequisite for voting in federal elections, he embarked for Europe on the Queen Mary during the summer of 1962, accompanied by two female members of his staff. The first was a pretty thirty-one-year-old brunette divorcee. The second, a twenty-one-year-old runner-up in a Miss Universe contest, had been Miss Ohio in 1960. When the trio, which was supposedly studying equal employment opportunities for women in the Common Market countries, arrived in London, they checked into a first-class hotel for a nine-day stay and went to the theater each evening in a limousine provided by the American embassy. (The embassy also furnished the tickets.) In Paris, they stayed at a fashionable hotel on the Place de la Concorde and went to the Lido. Moving on to Venice, they attended the film festival and toured the Grand Canal in a gondola. After a stop in Rome, they proceeded to Athens, then embarked on a six-day cruise of the Aegean Islands. Afterwards, the "Harlem globetrotter" and Miss Ohio flew to Madrid. The outcry at home was so unrelenting that he cut short his trip and returned home to his distraught-looking wife.

The flagrant manner in which Powell abused the right to travel at taxpayer expense made it difficult for his congressional associates to exercise their customary tolerance. Senator John J. Williams of Delaware disclosed that other federal agencies besides the State Department had been exceedingly generous to the Harlem congressman, who had become the chairman of the important House Committee on Education and Labor. The Department of Health, Education, and Welfare had made a grant of a quarter of a million dollars to Powell and his associates for the development of a nucleus of a domestic peace corps that had not yet been authorized by Congress. Part of the sum had been budgeted for the rental of space in a portion of the Abyssinian Baptist Church. The disclosures followed an announcement that the federal government had begun civil, as opposed to criminal, proceedings against Powell, who, according to the Internal Revenue Service, still owed the Treasury more than $40,000 in delinquent taxes and attendant penalties.

Late in 1962, Powell announced he would offer his resignation as minister of his prestigious church, many of whose members mobilized each election day to turn out the vote for him. The announcement—coupled with earlier declarations that he wanted to give up his House seat by 1964 and that he'd make "a fine successor" to Governor Muñoz-Marin of Puerto Rico—was interpreted as a hint that he had decided to relinquish control of his church-based Harlem political organization and the congressional seat it had assured him for two decades.

The tidings may have been welcome news to Malcolm, who had prophesied, wishfully or otherwise, that Harlem would stop sending Powell to Congress as soon as he stopped representing its inhabitants. Malcolm delivered the prediction from Powell's own pulpit. The time had not yet come when black politicians could acknowledge publicly that the wealthy, fun-loving congressman had not really represented the vast majority of his impoverished constituents for years.

Despite Powell's excellent relations with Harlem's Puerto Rican population—and despite his Puerto Rican wife, who was politically well connected—he was unable to make sufficient political headway in Puerto Rico. So he told the press he would not yield his House seat after all. Not long afterward, Malcolm, who kept saying he would "never" criticize Adam publicly, declared:

> It's hard to tell which direction Congressman Powell moves in. He moves in one direction one minute and another direction another minute.

When the congressman counterattacked, he did so with vigor, for he apparently knew that if anyone had enough charisma to effectively challenge him at the polls, it was Malcolm X.

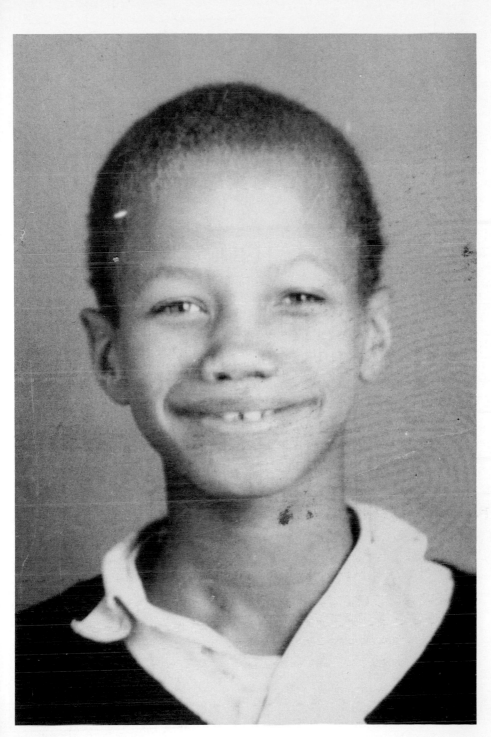

Young Malcolm.

Louise Little, Malcolm's mother.

Elementary school class picture.

Class picture, Pleasant Grove School, Grade 4 (1935-1936).

Enlarged details from Malcolm's class pictures.

"Big Red": the teenage Malcolm.

Malcolm carries his daughter, Ilyasah, as he enters a car at John F. Kennedy International Airport in New York on May 21, 1964, following his tour of the Middle East.

Malcolm, 39, is shown with Nobel Peace Prize winner Dr. Martin Luther King, in this 1964 photo.

Malcolm gestures as he addresses a Harlem rally in support of integration efforts in Birmingham, Ala.

Malcolm giving a speech.

Malcolm outside his home the day after it was ravaged by fire.

Malcolm's death.

WE WANT MALCOLM! 49

Robin, who had given birth to two of Elijah Muhammad's children, had moved from Chicago to Los Angeles, where she was expecting a third child. Faced with the prospect of another mouth to feed, she and Heather, who shared her apartment, went to Arizona to appeal for more money for their children. All they were receiving from the Messenger was $100 per month per child.

When the two women and their children showed up at Muhammad's Phoenix home, he refused to let them in. He would not even let the youngsters into the house to use the toilet; he made them use the bathroom in the cook's house. He cursed Robin and Heather. Robin replied that, after three pregnancies, the least he could do was to provide his surplus children with a roof over their heads.

Elijah was unmoved. He pulled some money out of his wallet and told Robin and Heather to take it or leave it. He warned them they would be killed if they revealed that he had fathered their children. If worse came to worse, he said, one or two of his sons would stand in his place and take the blame.

The women consulted some Phoenix lawyers. But, eventually, they decided to return to Los Angeles. Malcolm, who was in touch with them, sent James 67X to escort them back to California, ostensibly to protect them. But James was unarmed. He tried, on Malcolm's behalf, to obtain written statements from Robin and Heather that would confirm that Elijah, not Malcolm, had fathered their children. Malcolm also directed James to tell them that if Elijah passed away before his paternity was legally established, their children would not be able to claim part of his estate. Subsequent events would prove the assertion groundless.

Malcolm, who was unable to convince the two women to take their story to the Los Angeles *Herald-Dispatch*, also instructed James to give a letter to the newspaper's editor. When James telephoned Malcolm to report on his progress, Malcolm asked him whether the letter had been delivered. James said no. "Dammit, why not?" fumed Malcolm. It was the only time that James, who had not attempted to deliver the letter because it was Sunday, ever heard him swear.

Many of the newspaper editors and radio announcers to whom Malcolm had leaked the story of Elijah Muhammad's sex life advised him that, because of the danger of libel suits, they would air his charges only if the women in question initiated legal proceedings. So Malcolm prodded Heather and Robin to take legal action. The attorney they retained was Gladys Towles Root, whose flamboyance had attracted attention during the trial of Frank Sinatra, Jr.'s kidnappers.

Ms. Root wrote Elijah Muhammad on behalf of her two clients and expressed hope that the matter could be settled amicably. When it became apparent that the Messenger would not give ground, she filed two separate paternity suits—one on Heather's behalf, one on Robin's. They were filed less than a week after the *New York Post* published an open letter from Malcolm to Mr. Muhammad calling for an end to their feud. But Malcolm's conciliatory exterior, which he maintained even around Ms. Root, didn't impress the Nation of Islam, which made clear it regarded him as the cause of the lawsuits. Nor was the NOI leadership pleased by the national coverage United Press International and one television network accorded the litigation. One evening, Heather and Robin spied two men clambering up their back stairway. They quickly telephoned the police, who intervened before the men could harm them. Unwittingly, they had become pawns in Malcolm's attempt to destroy his well-protected rival by undermining his reputation. He insisted that his campaign to expose his former mentor was a matter of principle. "Do you really believe that?" asked Sharon 10X, who had been helping him since her teens. Malcolm didn't reply; he just stared at her. Philbert sensed that his campaign to discredit the Messenger was prompted not only by political considerations but also by feelings that harkened back to his youth. The sin he confronted Elijah with was the one with which he had never been able to confront his skirt-chasing father and lonely mother.

By coincidence, Malcolm was due to appear on "Hot Line," a late-night Chicago radio show, on July 2, the day Gladys Root filed the paternity suits. Shortly before his scheduled appearance, he telephoned "Hot Line's" host, Wesley South. He said his life had been threatened. He also told South that Chicago television station WBKB had cancelled an arrangement to videotape a show with him while he was in the Windy City. He did not explain why, nor did he say who had called off the taping session. He said that since WBKB was no longer planning to pay his travel expenses to Chicago, he preferred to cancel his trip. But, according to the television show's producers, Norman Ross and David McElroy, it was a low budget show that did not pay the travel expenses of the celebrities who appeared on it. And neither Ross nor McElroy nor anyone else had invited Malcolm to appear on it. The alleged cancellation enabled him to avoid the hazardous trip to Chicago without impairing his fearless image.

But it may have impaired his self-image. The evening after he had been scheduled to appear on "Hot Line," Malcolm went home and switched on the television set to watch the eleven o'clock news. The babysitter, who was keeping house for Betty while she was in the hospital recuperating from delivering their fourth child, had just finished preparing Malcolm's dinner. Again and again, he told her how impressed he was that someone so young could cook and care for children so well.

Malcolm had never asked the babysitter to watch the news with him. But that night he did. When she entered the living room, he rose from his chair, left the room, and fetched a rifle. He told the babysitter his car was parked across the street and that he wanted to move it closer to the house so that he could watch it. Ordinarily, he parked in front of the house, which was frequently staked out by the NOI. But that particular night, he had parked on the far side of the street. Later, the babysitter had difficulty understanding why. The street, which was lined with single-family residences, contained plenty of parking space; Malcolm usually had no difficulty parking right in front of his home. She also wondered why, if he was so concerned about the safety of his car, he had waited until almost midnight before going back outside to move it.

Malcolm, who had been having difficulty convincing the press and the police that his life was in danger, picked up the rifle and showed the babysitter how to operate it. Then he laid it on the divan, opened the door, and left it ajar as he walked outside. As he descended the front steps, the babysitter went to a window and peered out. From the left, she saw two figures running toward him, along the street. At first, she thought they were teenage boys; then she realized they were grown men. According to one report, they were brandishing knives. Malcolm spotted them, jumped into his car, locked the door, and drove off. Later, he said he had been trying to draw his pursuers—there were four, he told the Daily News—away from his home and children.

Malcolm circled the block, parked his car, and rushed back into the house. "Did you see that? Did you see that?" he breathlessly inquired.

The babysitter said she had and later told the police what she had seen. Years later, she said she couldn't understand why Malcolm had left the front door of the house ajar. "Unless he wanted me to see," she declared. The babysitter, whose father was one of Malcolm's devoted followers, also wondered out loud if his decision to venture outside so late was an attempt to dramatize the danger he faced. There was no way of knowing if he was trying to reaffirm his courage with the kind of death-defying behavior that had characterized his youthful criminality.

Shortly after the paternity suits were filed, the *Chicago Defender* disclosed that Elijah Muhammad's grandson, Hasan Sharrieff, had defected from the Nation of Islam. In an apparent attempt to embarrass his mother and his stepfather, Raymond, Hasan addressed his open letter of resignation to them. The letter, which depicted Elijah Muhammad as "a fake and a fraud," described how his "two-faced relatives" were embezzling hundreds of thousands of dollars of the money that was supposedly being collected for the movement's poor. Young Sharrieff, who said he had always felt closer to the rank and file than he had to unspecified members of his own family, declared, "It makes me want to retch!"

Hasan, who subsequently changed the spelling of his last name, was branded a supporter of Malcolm. So was Wallace Muhammad, whose eight-page denunciation of the NOI leadership was partly reproduced in the *Defender* two days after it began airing Hasan's charges. Wallace, who characterized his attack as mild, said he had tried hard, for some time, to explain away the corruption that pervaded the Nation of Islam. He said his morally lax relatives found lying easier than breathing:

> They are just as bad as the Belgian devils who once ruled the blacks of the Congo . . . . Perhaps they are as bad as the whites who now rule our people of South Africa. I say this because their crimes are against their own people.

Wallace was unsparing in his assessment of his father. He said the more he sought to help Elijah remedy his moral inadequacies, the worse his father treated him. One reporter subsequently asked him to characterize the Messenger's ultimate goal. Without hesitating, Wallace replied, ". . . to be the strongest black man on the face of the earth."

Most of the members of the Royal Family were incensed by Wallace's disclosures. (His middle initial "D," they said, stood for "deceitful.") Wallace told the press he had repeatedly been threatened by the Nation of Islam's officials. "They will kill!" he told one reporter. It was no revelation to Malcolm, who was blamed for Wallace's defection. The day after the *Defender* published Wallace's broadside, Malcolm quietly departed for London. He told Bembry, just before he left, that there are times when "something is about to happen," and that the best way to avoid it is to disappear.

A week after Malcolm's departure, a black youth named James Powell left home for school, accompanied by two friends. Powell, who had no father to teach him how to assert his budding manhood constructively, was a bully and belonged to a gang of toughs. At school, he was continually in trouble. Though he was only fifteen, he had already experienced at least four run-ins with the authorities. Two of them involved attempts to board a public conveyance without paying. The third time, he was taken into custody for breaking a car window. The fourth time, he was arrested for attempted robbery but was cleared of the charge.

Powell was carrying two knives that morning. He asked each of his companions to hold one of the weapons for him.

The three boys waited outside their school for classes to begin. Across the street from them other summer school students sat on the front stoop of an apartment house. The superintendent of the building, whose name was Lynch, was hosing down the adjacent sidewalk. He later testified that he had asked the students to move so that he could water some flowers without getting the youngsters wet. According to Lynch, they refused. The students subsequently testified that he had angrily exclaimed, "Dirty niggers! I'll wash you clean!"

At any rate, they got wet. They retaliated with garbage can lids and empty soda bottles. The sound of breaking glass attracted the attention of an off-duty white policeman named Thomas Gilligan, who happened to be in a nearby repair shop. Lieutenant Gilligan, who had won the New York Daily News' Hero Cop Award several years earlier, had also been awarded nineteen citations for meritorious service during his seventeen years on the police force. Some of them were for disarming armed suspects; others were for saving lives. He had rescued people from burning buildings. Though he had never killed anyone, he had wounded two men with his pistol. The first had reportedly tried to push him off a roof. The second had broken two of his fingers with the nozzle of a fire hose.

Gilligan later testified that as he emerged from the repair shop, he heard Powell yell, "Hit him! Hit him!" He saw Powell run toward the entrance to the apartment building into which Lynch had retreated. Gilligan didn't see Lynch, but he said he did see, in Powell's right hand, a knife. He said the blade, which Powell held close to his chest, was pointed downward.

Powell's companions later testified that, when he saw the melee across the street, he said, "I am going to cut that . . . ." He asked one companion for the knife he had given him. The boy pretended he didn't have it. Powell turned to the second boy and asked him for the other knife. The boy handed the weapon to Powell, who darted off in pursuit of Lynch. A bystander tried to grab Powell and restrain him but failed.

Gilligan, dressed in civilian clothes, later told interrogators that he pulled his pistol from his right trouser pocket and moved to a point opposite the entrance to the apartment house. He said he identified himself as a police officer and ordered Powell to come out of the building and drop the nine-inch-long knife, which had a three-and-a-half-inch-long blade.

Powell emerged. According to some witnesses, he held a knife in his right hand and his right arm was raised. Gilligan fired his revolver once. There was a pause; then he fired twice more. One bullet missed Powell. (Gilligan later testified it was a warning shot that Powell declined to heed.) The second tore through Powell's right forearm, near the wrist, then bore into his chest, cutting an artery above the heart. The third burrowed into his abdomen and out his back. Powell fell to the sidewalk, spit blood, and died.

At the inquest, the question was whether Powell's arm had been raised and, if so, why. That one bullet had passed through his right forearm and upper chest suggested that his right arm had been making, or had been poised for, a downward knife thrust. But many of the student eyewitnesses denied that Powell had been wielding a knife, or testified that they hadn't seen any. Ten of them said that, after Powell fell to the pavement, Gilligan fired two more bullets into him. Some claimed, further, that Gilligan fired the last two shots into Powell's back. But the autopsy proved that the two bullets that struck Powell entered his body from the front. The absence of any bullet marks on the newly cemented sidewalk negated the possibility that the slug that had pierced his abdomen and emerged from his back had been fired while he lay on the ground.

One of the witnesses who testified that Gilligan's first shot had felled Powell was shown photographs of the apartment entrance indicating that the first bullet had hit the building rather than Powell. The witness studied the photos and then said he wasn't sure what he had seen. Reflecting further, he admitted he hadn't witnessed the shooting at all. Some students who had claimed to have witnessed the shooting eventually acknowledged they had run for cover when the gunfire began, or that their view had been obstructed.

But there were witnesses whose view had apparently been unimpeded. An air-conditioning mechanic who had passed the apartment house when the shooting occurred testified that, from his elevated truck cab, he had seen Powell raise his knife and lunge at Gilligan twice. A bus driver who had been standing nearby also saw the knife. Corroborating testimony was supplied by one of the owners of the repair shop and by a workman who had been on a scaffold four buildings away. And two of the students conceded they had seen a knife on the ground after the shooting. A teacher who was passing by noticed it lying next to Powell's thigh, between his prostrate body and the apartment house. As she stood there, she saw someone kick the weapon to the curb. Another teacher retrieved it and gave it to the authorities. The blade was unsheathed. Gilligan, who received medical treatment, later testified that the knife had lacerated the arm he had used to parry one of Powell's lunges.

But the day after Powell was killed, this testimony was unavailable to the CORE officials who had been campaigning for the establishment of a civilian review board that would have jurisdiction over cases of alleged police brutality. CORE protestors paraded in front of Powell's school, chanting, "Killer cops must go!" As the demonstration ended, teenagers gathered around TV cameras and expressed their anger. Three of Malcolm's men appeared and urged the youths not to let anyone push them around.

The following day, CORE held a rally that had been scheduled to protest the disappearance of the three civil rights workers who had been abducted and murdered in Mississippi. But, instead of discussing the Mississippi incident, which was useless as an argument for a New York City civilian review board, the rally officials focused on the Powell incident. "This shooting of James Powell was murder!" cried CORE member Judith Howell, who said she was "scared of every cop out there." Howell finished her speech and relinquished the microphone to an official who reminded the crowd about the plea for a peaceful demonstration that had been made by the wife of Bronx CORE chairman Herbert Callender. "If I were Herb Callender's wife," Howell rejoined, "I'd have said, 'Let's go down to the precinct and take it apart brick by brick!'"

The CORE speakers were followed by a Baptist cleric who urged the crowd to march on the nearest police station, which was situated on 123rd Street. The station, the same one Malcolm's Muslims had besieged during the Johnson Hinton incident, was the headquarters of the twenty-eighth precinct, not Gilligan's precinct.

By ten o'clock that night, the crowd, which vilified the policemen who tried to contain it, had swelled to immense proportions. Police officials decided it was time to act. Working in squad-size flying wedges, the elite Tactical Patrol Force, whose well-disciplined members brandished their clubs yelling, "Charge!," plowed into the mob milling about the intersection of 123rd Street and Seventh Avenue. The part of the crowd that was pushed south on Seventh Avenue began setting rubbish afire and assaulting whites. The horde that swept north left a swath of shattered windows and looted stores that extended to 135th Street. Even the iron grillwork that Harlem storeowners had used for years to protect their doors and windows failed to deter the looters, some of whom pried apart the metal bars with crowbars. Others hooked chains to the metal gates and yanked them from their moorings with automobiles. Entire inventories disappeared into the streets. Policemen cornered one looter as he reached in to grab merchandise from a jewelry store window he had smashed with a brick. The patrolmen bundled

DISSENSION IN
THE RANKS
50

Malcolm had hoped that his Organization of Afro-American Unity would furnish him with the political credentials that would enable him to attend the July conference of the Organization of African Unity as an official delegate. But, despite his assertion that he "was met with open arms" in Cairo, where the conference was held, he was not permitted to address the OAU gathering; the U.S. government, which had been doling out considerable aid to Egypt and other OAU member-states, might not have taken the affront lightly.

Yet, if Malcolm's effort to win international recognition for his budding movement was not a total success, neither was it a total failure. According to the English-language *Arab Observer*—a semi-official publication that generally reflected the Nasser regime's views—Malcolm was made an accredited observer to the OAU conference, despite U.S. State Department's assertions to the contrary. The Egyptian government, which might have been embarrassed had it completely rebuffed a well-known, charismatic figure who claimed to represent twenty-two million African-Americans—many of whom were Muslim—provided Malcolm with a berth on Nasser's yacht Isis, where the leaders of the various African national liberation movements were quartered. Malcolm was also allowed to circulate among the OAU delegates who had been assigned rooms at various Cairo hotels. By way of contrast, the two U.S. Foreign Service officers who had been instructed to cover the conference for the State Department couldn't even get into the lobby of one hotel. From the outside looking in, they could see Malcolm conversing with diplomats and moving with prince-like ease among the assembled statesmen, whose dossiers he had compiled and studied before he had left the U.S.

Malcolm was also given leave to circulate a petition urging the OAU member-states to bring the issue of American racism before the United Nations—an objective he described as his number one priority. Various delegations expressed a desire to help, but not at the price of losing foreign aid or otherwise incurring the displeasure of the powerful United States. Malcolm, sensing their reluctance, lamented that Africa's leaders had freed themselves from European colonialism but had succumbed to the blandishments of American "dollarism." He also assailed the argument that Africa's newly emergent nations had more than enough problems of their own without incurring Uncle Sam's wrath. "Our problems are your problems," he declared. He asserted that Africa's blacks were obligated to come to the rescue of America's blacks. He conceded that he was "almost fanatically" drawn to the proposition that the Africans, whom he repeatedly characterized as the older brothers of their American counterparts, should defend their younger brothers across the sea.

The resolution on American racism that finally emerged from the OAU conference was not the ringing denunciation Malcolm pretended it was. Rather, it was a moderately phrased, balanced declaration that acknowledged "with satisfaction" the passage of the 1964 Civil Rights Act but expressed concern about continued evidence of racial discrimination. The innocuous resolution was not substantially stronger than a similar resolution that had been passed by the OAU the year before at Addis Ababa. Nevertheless, Washington apparently regarded it as enough of an achievement to ask the Justice Department to consider the possibility of prosecuting Malcolm for violating the Logan Act, which made it a crime for a private citizen to communicate with foreign powers for the purpose of thwarting the established policies of the U.S. government.

Malcolm's imaginative attempt to internationalize the struggle against white oppression, as Marcus Garvey and W. E. B. DuBois had tried to do, was reminiscent of the way he had invoked the assistance of imaginary Egyptian allies to persuade Warden O'Brien to give him a cell facing east. His effort to shift the focus from "civil rights" to "human rights" was predicated upon the provision of the United Nations Charter that proclaims "universal respect for, and observance of, human rights and fundamental freedoms for all, without distinction as to race." He pointed out that if the U.N. could claim jurisdiction over South African racism on the ground that it is not purely a domestic problem, then it could also claim jurisdiction over American racism. His grasp of the subtleties of the Charter attested to his legal skill. "I do believe I might have made a good lawyer," he told Alex Haley.

Malcolm apparently knew there was little the United Nations could do for America's blacks besides focusing international opinion on their plight. He virtually conceded the point in a message of "appreciation" to George Breitman, who had written an article entitled, "Going to the U.N. Can Help, But It's No Cure-All." But seeking votes from friendly governments was not the only reason Malcolm returned to Africa seven weeks after he left it. His highly publicized attempt to internationalize Black America's struggle for equal opportunity afforded a perfect cover for his unpublicized attempts to obtain abroad the financial support that was foreclosed to him at home.

Egypt gave Malcolm some financial assistance, according to heavily censored documents from the Central Intelligence Agency. Nasser's representatives in the U.S. were reportedly under orders to cultivate contacts in the black community, perhaps in hope of fostering the growth of a potential counterweight to Washington's powerful pro-Israeli lobby.

Malcolm's return to Africa was also an attempt to secure abroad the political support he lacked at home, where church-based groups like the Southern Christian Leadership Conference wouldn't have anything to do with him. Neither would "respectable" middle-class organizations like the NAACP and the Urban League. Malcolm was paying the price for his polemical attacks; he had alienated the only American organizations with which he had interests in common. He publicly acknowledged the problem:

> You can't build a power base here . . . . No, you have to have that base somewhere else. You can work here, but you'd better put your base somewhere else.

But obtaining political support abroad was no easier that it was at home. Malcolm tried to counter reports that his mission was a failure. "I found no doors closed to me," he told Cairo reporters. He claimed that several unnamed African states had "promised officially" to help the OAAU bring the issue of American racism before the U.N. He made much of the fact that he had been authorized to distribute a number of scholarships to Al-Azhar University and the University of Medina. Publicly, he boasted that his trip had been an "unqualified" success. He said he was "not at all doubtful of support" for his effort to persuade Africa's blacks to stand by their African-American counterparts. But he quickly added:

> I've learned that one cannot take things for granted and then cry when nothing materializes. We must learn that we are masters of our own destiny.

Privately, he admitted his discouragement to a number of associates.

Capitalizing on Arab hospitality, Malcolm lingered in Egypt the rest of July, all of August, and part of September. From Cairo, he traveled to Alexandria. He visited archaeological sites on the Nile and immersed himself in Egyptian history books. He also managed to stay in the news.* The Cairo press accorded him coverage almost daily.

One Egyptian journalist interviewed him in the popular Semiramis Hotel. When the reporter arrived and asked for Malcolm, the receptionist pointed to a tall man who was carrying a briefcase. The newsman, who assumed Malcolm was dark-skinned, took one look at the fair-skinned man and protested that he wanted Malcolm, not his secretary. Afterwards, he learned that he was not the only newspaperman who had been fooled by Malcolm's complexion; an Associated Press correspondent who had been sitting opposite them for more than an hour finally realized that the American celebrity he had been awaiting had been there all the time.

The first journalist, who worked for the prominent newspaper *Al Gumhuriya*, interviewed Malcolm twice. Malcolm told him that, prior to his conversion to Islam, he had been a mugger and a rapist. He said that whites had killed not only his father, but also four of his uncles. He also asserted that one of his own brothers had been knifed to death by a white man before his very eyes.

While Malcolm was in Egypt, United Press International reported that Elijah Muhammad's son Akbar, who had been billed as *Muhammad Speaks'* Egyptian correspondent, was about to follow his brother Wallace out of the Nation of Islam. The *Arab Observer* reported that Akbar was merely considering leaving the movement. Akbar, who was in Cairo studying at Al-Azhar, had written his father and demanded an explanation of the charges that had been leveled against him.

The news that Akbar was disenchanted came on the heels of a meeting he had held in Cairo with Malcolm, who wrote his subordinates on August 29 and said he might be killed before he could return to the United States. The statement may have been prompted by an incident that had occurred at the Nile Hilton. Shortly after dinner, Malcolm experienced intense abdominal pain. He was so ill that he was taken to the hospital, where his stomach was pumped. He maintained that he had been poisoned, just as he had maintained, in 1941, that Earl Junior had been poisoned. Malcolm seemed so convinced he had been the victim of a deliberate poisoning attempt (rather than dysentery or the

---

* He complained that the New York press had acted as if he had "ceased to exist" during his trip abroad the previous spring.

abdominal pain that had prompted him to consult Farrow Allen several months earlier) that when he later visited Philadelphia, he refused to eat the food at his hotel; instead, he asked one of his followers to bring him his food from someplace else. His fear of poisoning was the reason he didn't want doctors to innoculate his children. (His mother, in Kalamazoo State Hospital, would not even take medicine by mouth.)

Malcolm's fear of poison—a word he often used in place of the word "hate"—was somewhat difficult to reconcile with the frequency with which he had once imbibed harmful drugs. Right or wrong, he appeared convinced that others were doing to him what he had done, years earlier, to himself.

Part of Malcolm's August 29 letter to his associates addressed organizational problems that had been festering back home due to his lengthy absence, which many of his followers resented. Despite his pronouncements to the contrary, his OAAU was not faring any better than his Muslim Mosque, for the bond between leader and led was an intensely personal one that withered with distance. And, despite the audiences Malcolm's speeches and rallies attracted, his movement had few real members. At one point, approximately seventy-five names appeared on the membership rolls of the Muslim Mosque, but only about a dozen people attended its meetings with any regularity. The number that attended OAAU functions was larger, but not large. And if Malcolm's August 29 letter was any indication, the number was shrinking rather than growing—particularly when it came to the kind of committed workers he had taken for granted in the Nation of Islam. Except for the OAAU's Education Committee, its organizational machinery never even began functioning.

The members were incessantly squabbling about inconsequential things, such as whether the Muslim Mosque or the OAAU should pay the overdue bill for the telephone they jointly used. At picture-taking time, they elbowed each other so that they could appear as "close" to Malcolm as possible. The rivalry was nurtured by the fact that Malcolm kept his associates at arm's length. (He called Percy Sutton "Mr. Counselor." Sutton reciprocated with "Mr. Minister.") Rarely, if ever, did Malcolm display interest in the personal problems of his associates. "I knew him better than he knew me," Charles 37X lamented, years later.

Charles, who had received his education on the streets, was Malcolm's one-man intelligence arm. After Malcolm returned home from abroad, he suggested that Charles change his last name to Kenyatta, in honor of Jomo Kenyatta, who had been accused of directing the Mau Mau. Charles, who had been urging Malcolm to strike back at Elijah Muhammad's thugs, readily acceded. Perhaps because of the way he revered Malcolm, "the Big M," as Malcolm was sometimes affectionately called, seemed to trust him more than he trusted many of his other aides.

Charles distrusted the intellectuals Malcolm had allied himself with, and there was friction between him and James 67X, who not only was college-educated but also spoke Japanese, as well as some French and German. James had been urging Malcolm to refrain from provoking Elijah Muhammad. He was Malcolm's chief "man Friday." In time, he made himself almost as indispensable to Malcolm as Malcolm had been to Mr. Muhammad.

Friction also arose between James (who changed his last name to Shabazz) and Benjamin Goodman, who frequently spoke in Malcolm's place when he had to cancel speaking engagements. The apparent rivalry between Brother Benjamin, who was an able orator, and James harkened back to the days when they had been officials in Temple Seven.

Benjamin managed to stay aloof from most of the petty wrangling. But he was unhappy about Malcolm's departure from Black Muslim orthodoxy. Nor was he alone. Part of Malcolm's problem was that, intellectually, he had left most of his aides far behind.

He tried to fill the gap with a new breed of sophisticated, militant blacks, many of whom scorned the unpatrician backgrounds, the lack of schooling, and the doctrinaire attitude of the former NOI members. But what irritated the Old Guard the most was that many of the interlopers were women—not ones that were dominated, as Elijah Muhammad's female followers were, but strong, assertive women such as Lynn Shifflett, who later became one of America's first black female television newscasters. Shifflett, whom Malcolm made the nominal head of the OAAU despite his rhetoric about the weakness of women, was frequently at odds with James Shabazz, who remained nominally in charge of the Muslim Mosque.

Malcolm also continued relying upon Ella, who later asserted in an interview that Malcolm was so dependent upon her for advice that Betty told her, "Why, he can't even move unless he gets permission from you!" The friction between the two women may have been aggravated by the fact that Malcolm did not include Betty in many of his political activities or decisions. He was reportedly annoyed when he discovered she had been coming to his office and checking on things during his absence. (He may also have been annoyed when she left one of his rallies early without telling him, so that when he asked her to rise and take a bow, he was greeted with an embarrassing silence.)

The petty squabbling was not the only reason the OAAU and the Muslim Mosque failed to achieve anything in Malcolm's absence; he refused to delegate sufficient authority to enable his subordinates to accomplish anything. He forbade his feuding lieutenants to make public statements while he was gone. Nor did he leave anyone clearly in charge or designate clear channels of authority. After he returned, Ethel Minor asked him why. Quietly, Malcolm replied, "Sister, who would you have suggested that I leave in charge?" When Minor found herself struggling to come up with an answer, Malcolm's face broke into a smile.

One thing that may have contributed to Malcolm's inability to delegate authority was the perfectionism his mother had instilled in him. "Any time you want something done right," he told a former member of the Philadelphia temple, "do it yourself." As it became increasingly evident that the things he wanted done were not being done with the military-like dispatch to which he had become accustomed in the Nation of Islam, he seemed to grow even more impatient than before. The aide who kept him waiting learned to regret it. "If we were going somewhere and you were five minutes late," Benjamin Goodman later recalled, "He'd pour boiling water on you, even if we didn't have to make a scheduled train or plane." Another aide arrived two minutes late and spotted Malcolm eying him through the rear view mirror of his car. Malcolm just drove off and left him. Yet, if a woman kept him waiting, Malcolm, who was always punctual, would often tolerate her lateness.

His unwillingness to delegate the authority he had delegated so effectively in the Nation of Islam was also partly due to his inability to fully trust anyone, even the assistants he praised for their loyalty. "Experience has taught me," he wrote from Cairo, "never to take anyone . . . for granted." He underscored the fact that Gabriel Prosser and Denmark Vesey, who had organized abortive slave revolts, had been betrayed by Judas-like associates. His inveterate mistrust was reinforced by the fact that the movement he had labored so hard to build had turned not only its back on him but also its guns.

Malcolm exhibited little reluctance to exercise the authority he had labored so long to obtain. "He was a tyrant," one of his former aides recalls." Not all his former aides agree. But even those who do are quick to say that, no matter how severely Malcolm tongue-lashed his deferential assistants, he never did it in public. And, though he drove his subordinates almost as hard as he drove himself, he was often tolerant toward slow learners. Indeed, until he left the Nation of Islam, he was surrounded by his intellectual inferiors, whose presence may have bolstered his self-esteem nearly as much as the movement's racial doctrines had. By way of contrast, Martin Luther King, Jr. gathered about him a group of articulate, independent-minded co-workers who could make him see his mistakes. While King and his aides transformed their disagreements into a consensus that produced creative political solutions to pressing political problems, Malcolm permitted the disagreements to tear his stillborn movement apart.

Malcolm apparently struggled against his authoritarian proclivities; he stressed that the best way of encouraging people to produce was to make suggestions instead of giving orders. But, more often than not, he forgot to heed his own advice. With his aides, he seemed to vacillate between authoritarianism and anti-authoritarianism. Though he was indisputably the boss—some brothers affectionately called him "the chief"—he did not encourage bowing and scraping, nor did he seek out yes-men. What he demanded was loyalty and obedience. In some ways, his relationship with his subordinates resembled his youthful relationship with Reginald. He instructed and guided them. His strength enabled them to feel secure. In turn, they acknowledged his leadership and looked up to him.

Malcolm's unwillingness to delegate authority and his preference for speechmaking, as opposed to organizational work, were not the only things that hampered his efforts to build an effective political organization. For a man who had become accustomed to hobnobbing with statesmen, it might have been difficult for him to begin fishing for followers again in ghetto poolrooms. And even if he had delegated such tasks to subordinates and restricted his membership-building activities to periodic pep talks, he still had no clear-cut, concrete political program that was capable of attracting the legions of dedicated volunteers that King and others employed so effectively.

Malcolm told one journalist he was quite aware of how much time it took to get an organization rolling. Yet, in the very next breath, he contended he could get his followers properly organized "overnight." He tried to conceal his organizational weakness with announcements that he intended to establish branches in Philadelphia and Boston, and that he had already done so in Egypt. Despite his stated eagerness to accept responsibility for his failures, he tried, in his letter from Cairo, to shift the blame to his subordinates:

> I've stayed away this summer and given all those who want to show what they can do the opportunity to do so . . . . I'm going to be away for at least another month. During that time you can overlook the small differences that you have and make progress by working with each other, or you can be at odds and make no progress. You can make the Muslim Mosque and OAAU a success, or you can destroy both organizations. It's up to you.

"I've never sought to be anyone's leader," he declared. He even threatened, obliquely, to chuck his nascent movement and to start again from scratch. There wasn't much to chuck. He was "a general without an army," sneered Elijah Muhammad in *Muhammad Speaks.*

GOVERNMENT SURVEILLANCE

51

In September, Malcolm finally left Egypt and flew to Saudi Arabia, where Azzam Pasha tried to secure financing for the mosque Malcolm wanted to build in Harlem. The effort was unsuccessful; such a highly visible commitment by the Saudis would undoubtedly have offended Washington. But Malcolm apparently did succeed in obtaining enough financial help to enable him to announce that he was about to begin a lengthy tour of Africa, and that he would not return home until after the November elections. Despite his assertions to the contrary, the money probably came from Surrur Sabban, a wealthy black Saudi who was Secretary General of the Islamic World League. The League, which was dedicated to the propagation of Islam, supported various causes, financially and otherwise. Some of the people it supported were political exiles whom the Saudi government could not openly assist without displeasing the governments in question. One of them was a Muslim Brotherhood leader named Said Ramadan, who lived in Switzerland.

Surrur Sabban, who had close ties to the Saudi government, had reservations about the unorthodox doctrines of America's black-skinned Muslims. But instead of opposing them, he tried to reeducate them. Malcolm had several meetings with the prominent Muslim philanthropist, whose father had been the slave of a soap manufacturer named Sabban.

Malcolm's talks with Surrur Sabban were productive. Sabban arranged to have the League or one of its subsidiaries pay the expenses of a Sudanese teacher who was soon sent to the U.S. to assist Malcolm's Muslim Mosque. The League made Malcolm one of its official representatives. The rector of Al-Azhar University certified his Islamic credentials.

Having obtained the support of the Islamic authorities, Malcolm renewed his campaign against Elijah Muhammad, whom he described as a religious "faker." The attack followed the publication, in the *Saturday Evening Post*, of a condensation of Malcolm's forthcoming autobiography that made Elijah's private life common knowledge. *Muhammad Speaks* published rebuttals, including a "special memorandum from the desk" of the Messenger and a declaration by one of his ministers that he'd follow Muhammad "to the death." There was no need for the minister, who acknowledged that he had amassed "plenty" since he had assumed office, to specify whose death.

In subsequent issues of the Nation's newspaper, various spokesmen continued their efforts to defend Elijah and malign Malcolm. "He was no 'empire builder,'" proclaimed Captain Joseph and the NOI minister who was later implicated in the murder of Hamaas Abdul Khaalis's children. The two officials said it was really Mr. Muhammad who had "planted the seeds of Islam" in the dozens of mosques that had sprung up after Malcolm had joined the Nation of Islam.

Malcolm, who was busy trying to plant seeds of his own, was apparently aware of Saudi Arabia's desire to avoid antagonizing the U.S. government. He toned down his rhetoric while he was there and downplayed political themes, as opposed to religious ones. A U.S. embassy official who kept track of his activities noted that he seemed to have difficulty articulating what should be done to solve America's racial problem.

From Saudi Arabia, Malcolm went to oil-rich Kuwait. From there, he flew via Beirut and Khartoum to Addis Ababa, Ethiopia. By this time, it was October. He kept placating his Harlem followers, who longed for him to come back, with proclamations that his return to the States was imminent. The announcements, some of which were peppered with militant utterances, helped keep his name in the news.

In Ethiopia, as in Saudi Arabia, Malcolm's political rhetoric was low-key, perhaps because he wanted to avoid anything that might prompt Washington to put pressure on his Ethiopian hosts. At Addis Ababa's University College, he stressed the points of agreement between him and Martin Luther King, Jr. He said he differed with King not about goals but about the means that should be employed to achieve those goals. "The main difference," he declared, "is that he doesn't mind being beat up and I do."

From Ethiopia, Malcolm traveled to Nairobi, Kenya, where he made contact with a number of government officials. Then he went to Tanzania. In Dar-es-Salaam, the capital, he had a three-hour audience with President Nyerere. Later, Malcolm made quite a point of the private audiences he had been granted by the chief executives of several of the countries he had visited. His name-dropping was part of his continuing effort to enhance his self-esteem.

When Malcolm returned to Kenya from Dar-es-Salaam, he was accompanied by Jomo Kenyatta and Milton Obote. The American ambassador in Nairobi, William Attwood, received instructions to keep tabs on Malcolm. Attwood first saw him out at the race track, sitting in the President's box with Kenyatta and members of his cabinet. "I thought he was white," the ambassador later recalled:

> In fact, some of the Africans were a little put off by the color of his skin. They called him an albino.

Attwood's reaction to Malcolm's appearance was similar to that of Adam Clayton Powell, III, who was struck by the color of his eyes. "My goodness!" he said to himself. "How light they are." The fact that Malcolm's eyes looked darker in a photograph that appeared on the cover of the *Saturday Evening Post* attested to the way they appeared to change color. (Malcolm's face was bathed in golden sunlight in the *Post* photo. In other photos taken by the same photographer, the color of his eyes ranged from rich brown to a gray-like blue-green. Similar diversity of color appeared in photographs that were taken elsewhere by another photographer.)

Malcolm had grown accustomed to the constant surveillance back home. He never discussed business on the telephone; he correctly assumed that his phone was tapped. It was even risky to use pay phones. On one occasion, a man entered the phone booth that was adjacent to the one he was using. It was obvious to friends standing nearby that the other man was listening. He could have been one of the F.B.I. agents who monitored Malcolm's activities. Or he may have been a member of the New York City Police Department's "Bureau of Special Services," which kept him under close surveillance.

Outside the borders of the United States, State Department functionaries kept an eye on Malcolm. Usually, they ranked lower than Ambassador Attwood did. But at one point, one of Dean Rusk's assistants, Benjamin Read, asked the Central Intelligence Agency to help. The CIA official who visited Read's office to discuss the request reminded him that there were certain "inhibitions" about CIA surveillance of American citizens.* Nonchalantly, Read replied, "Malcolm X has, for all practical purposes, renounced his U.S. citizenship." The CIA later tried to cover its tracks by showing

---

* When Congress passed the National Security Act of 1947, it stipulated that the CIA was to have no police or law-enforcement powers, or any internal security functions.

reporter M.S. Handler, whose articles about Malcolm had appeared in the *New York Times*, a CIA log purporting to show that the Agency was not keeping Malcolm under surveillance. The man who spoke with Handler did not show him the Agency's other files on Malcolm.

The CIA tried to ascertain what funds Malcolm was receiving from abroad. Several military intelligence agencies also kept watch on him. So did the Secret Service, which may have been responding to the derogatory remarks Malcolm had made about Presidents Kennedy and Johnson. But the most intensive surveillance was conducted by the Federal Bureau of Investigation, which tried to exacerbate the feud between Malcolm and Elijah Muhammad. In addition, J. Edgar Hoover badgered his superiors in the Justice Department to institute legal proceedings against Malcolm. The "Department of Injustice," as Malcolm called it, considered several avenues of approach. The first involved the Smith Act, which made it a crime to teach or advocate the forceful overthrow of the U.S. government. But the Justice Department's Internal Security Division was stymied by the fact that Malcolm's rhetoric about rifle clubs—clubs that Malcolm said were constitutionally sanctioned by the Bill of Rights' right-to-bear-arms clause—was carefully couched in terms of individual or collective self-defense, as opposed to military initiatives against the state. And even if Malcolm's utterances could have been construed as advocating the forceful overthrow of the political establishment, no attempt had been made to translate those utterances into reality. No black nationalist army had been formed. No specific plans for it were in evidence. No guerrillas had been sent into Mississippi.

The head of the Internal Security Division pointed out that no rifle clubs had been established either. Consequently, Assistant Attorney General J. Walter Yeagley informed Hoover that he thought the available evidence was insufficient to warrant criminal proceedings against Malcolm, who told reporters he was not dumb enough to advocate armed revolt. Yeagley was equally pessimistic about the possibility of successful prosecution under the seditious conspiracy statute, which made it a crime for two or more people to conspire to defy or overthrow the government by force. Nor did the Justice Department, which may have been under orders to avoid any move that would antagonize the highly volatile black community, offer much hope of placing Malcolm's Muslim Mosque on the Attorney General's list of subversive organizations. The Department did, however, discuss the possibility of invoking the Foreign Agents Registration Act and requiring Malcolm to register as an agent of whatever foreign entities were assisting him financially. The Act, whose applicability to Malcolm was highly doubtful, provided criminal penalties for those who were obliged to register but didn't.

In an apparent effort to uncover additional evidence, Hoover subsequently suggested that the New York FBI office step up its surveillance. But Malcolm avoided prosecution despite the battalions of government sleuths and attorneys arrayed against him. From Kenya, he returned once more to Addis Ababa. Why he did is not entirely clear; at the time, there were no militant Ethiopian revolutionaries who could provide him with political or financial support. Haile Selassie, the Christian emperor who ruled the country with an iron hand, was not about to jeopardize his cozy relations with Washington for the likes of a Muslim rebel such as Malcolm X.

Malcolm told one Peace Corps volunteer that he had been traveling in Africa because he was disenchanted with the 1964 election campaign and the candidates it had spawned. He said he wanted to dissociate himself from it entirely. But, later, he hinted that he was prolonging his stay in Africa because of what awaited him back home. He said there were brothers in the street who would kill you for a dime. There were those who wouldn't even charge that much; they'd do it "for Allah" if one of their superiors told them to do so.

There were other reasons Malcolm stayed in Africa, which broadened his perspective the way his travels to Boston and Harlem had broadened his youthful perspective. One reason, Malcolm told friends, was the need to establish a dependable foreign source of income. Another was the regal reception he was accorded in Africa. "The Africans loved me," he later told Alex Haley. In similar, intensely personal language, he reiterated the same theme on another occasion. He said he felt more at home in Africa than he had ever felt in the United States. He called it "Mother Africa." His characterization of the "mother continent" as one that had had an "illicit honeymoon" with the European "lovers" that had exploited her was grimly reminiscent of the love affair his lonely, vulnerable mother had had with Butch's father.

The acceptance Malcolm won in Africa was probably a welcome respite from the hostile reception he was accorded by most Americans. Like his earlier attraction to the doctrine of racial separation, his Garvey-like withdrawal to a distant continent was partly a response to the rejection he simultaneously feared and courted.

Like his peripatetic father, Malcolm continued traveling. His five-day stay in Nigeria did not create the kind of stir his previous visit had. By early November, he was back in Ghana. From there, he went to Liberia and Guinea. He apologized for his absences from his family—absences that seemed to trouble him. And he preached about the need for men to spend enough time with their families. Yet he neglected his wife and children. Even when he was home, he was stingy with the amount of time he devoted to his family. He would withdraw into his attic study, or someone would hustle the children into the basement playroom, so that he could work without being distracted. One visitor was struck by the way the children, who missed Malcolm when he was away, seemed to vanish after they were ushered out of the living room. There was no noise. No toys were visible.

Yet Malcolm cared very much about his young ones. When they accompanied him to public functions, he was heedful of their needs. They'd come and grasp his hand or wrap a little arm around his tall leg. He'd bend down and smile or speak softly to them. He was similarly attentive to other people's children. On occasion, even reporters had to defer to them. Malcolm came down hard on parents who let their children run the streets till midnight with apartment keys strung around their neck. He stressed the plight of parentless youngsters, particularly those who were born out of wedlock or fatherless:

> You'll find many men who [will] . . . walk away from that woman like she didn't even exist and leave those children in the house without a second thought. [Malcolm's voice grows angry.] Without a second thought!

He told one audience, "Once you straighten out the parents, you straighten out the children." He had definite opinions about the way children should be raised. He said they should be educated and self-supporting, and that they should help their brothers and sisters.

Unlike his father, who had terrified youngsters, Malcolm was gentle with children, who readily took to him. Yet he was also a stern parent. He insisted that Betty be "very strict" with their oldest daughter, in whom he said he detected some of his own youthful traits. Mrs. Shabazz, who discussed her childrearing methods and her marriage in a number of published interviews, later characterized her oldest girl's childhood as "kind of hard and cruel." One of her friends asserted that she ran her home "like an army sergeant."

Yet Malcolm felt that Betty should be even stricter with their children. He was unable to break the authoritarian chain stretching, link by generational link, back through Louise Little to Jupiter, Mary Jane, and Gertrude Langdon—and, ultimately, back to slavery itself.

Malcolm's daughter Attallah was tall and slim, as he was. Her reddish skin, like his, was very fair. According to one photograph, her hair was rusty-red; according to others, it was sandy or ash-blonde. And her light-colored, greenish eyes seemed to change color, as Malcolm's did. In fact, the resemblance between Malcolm and Attallah was so striking that, when Malcolm Jarvis first saw her, he couldn't stop staring at her. "If she had been a boy," he later told an interviewer, "I'd have sworn it was a younger version of Malcolm himself!"

According to Betty, Malcolm was disturbed that Attallah was so light-skinned:

> We both wondered what in the world we'd done wrong for this little
> girl to come out looking like that.

Yet there is evidence he favored her. He even took her to the rallies at which he extolled the virtues of blackness. Though this may have been due to the fact that Attallah was his oldest child, it was reminiscent of the favoritism his father had accorded him. But if Malcolm was partial to Attallah, who frequently cried because of his lengthy absences,* she was apparently unsure of it, for she told her babysitter, who became her close friend, that she felt her sister Ilyasah was her father's favorite. "Yasah" was the dark-skinned baby daughter with whom Malcolm usually posed for photographs. She was constantly sitting in his lap. The apparent rivalry between her and Attallah, who was Malcolm's lightest-skinned child,** resembled the youthful rivalry between him and Philbert.

One reason Malcolm may have been partial to Ilyasah in certain ways was that she was boyish-looking. For a girl, she didn't have much hair. And her voice was rather husky. But she was not the only one of Malcolm's daughters who was named after a man. Attallah was named after Attillah the Hun. Qubilah, Malcolm's second daughter, was named after Qubilah Qhan.

That Malcolm defeminized his daughters with masculine names was not the only indication he longed for a son. He talked about having one who would bear his name and carry on his work after his death. At times, he predicted that his next child would be a boy; at other times, he prophesied that the boy would be his seventh child. He said he'd name him after Patrice Lumumba. "If it's a girl, Lamumbah." His third child, who turned out to be a girl, was named Gamilah Lamumbah.

There were interesting similarities between Malcolm and Lumumba.

---

* Attallah reportedly grieved more than the other children did when Malcolm died.

**Malcolm's fair-skinned twins were not born until after his death.

Before becoming a political rebel, the tall, slim, goateed Congolese leader had been a student rebel. He was expelled from school and later imprisoned for stealing. His voracious reading helped him overcome his lack of formal education. He even studied some law. His capacity for political invective rivaled Malcolm's, as did his ability to tailor his teachings to various audiences.

Malcolm said Lumumba was "the greatest black man who ever walked the African continent." It might have been more accurate to say "the greatest martyr," for Lumumba, who sensed he only had a short time to live, did not remain prime minister of the Congo (now Zaire) for long. Mutinies erupted in the army. One province seceded; so did part of another. Civil administration broke down almost completely. Foreign troops intervened at will. Then, less than three months after Lumumba assumed office, Joseph Kasavubu, the Congolese president, dismissed him. Vainly, Lumumba attempted to countermand Kasavubu's decree. The collapse of his government prompted him to flee from Leopoldville, where United Nations troops were protecting him, to Stanleyville, where forces loyal to him were in control. Lumumba admitted that the attempt to reach Stanleyville, which was hundreds of miles away, would probably fail. (Hostile troops were stationed along the way.) He told one associate:

> I shall probably be arrested, tortured, and killed. One of us must sacrifice himself if the Congolese people are to understand and accept the ideal we are fighting for. My death will hasten the liberation of the Congo.

He reportedly told another colleague to make sure that he did not become a martyr himself. Days later, he practically walked into the arms of his executioners. His martyrdom, which affected Malcolm deeply, obscured his failure to surmount the tremendous problems that had confronted his stillborn regime. And it assured him his place in history.

DETOUR TO SWITZERLAND 52

Malcolm might have been pleased had he known that Dean Rusk himself had prodded the American Embassy in Guinea to urge Harry Belafonte, who knew Sekou Toure, to ask the Guinean President to accord Malcolm a less cordial welcome. Despite Rusk's efforts, Malcolm spent three days as Toure's house guest. Then, in mid-November, he flew from Guinea to Algeria. But he didn't go directly; first, he detoured to Switzerland. He was there less than twelve hours.

When Malcolm left Algeria several days later, he again flew to Switzerland. Both his seatmates on the plane were Americans. One, a male, worked in Geneva; the other, a woman, kept eying his briefcase. Finally, she inquired, "May I ask you a personal question?" ("They always do," Malcolm told one audience.)

"What kind of last name do you have that begins with X?"

"That's it—X," Malcolm replied.

"X?"

"Yes."

The woman asked Malcolm's first name. She grew silent when he told her. Then, after a long pause, she asked in apparent disbelief, "You're not Malcolm X?"

With slight variations, Malcolm retold the story a number of times. He stressed how pleasantly he had passed the time with his white fellow-passengers. They weren't trying to be white, he told one group of listeners. "I certainly wasn't trying to make them think I wasn't black."

From Switzerland, where Malcolm met with Said Ramadan and his associates,* he traveled to Paris to deliver a speech. Afterwards, he was asked if he had a clearly defined political program. His response was devoid of specific recommendations. "I don't profess to be anybody's

---

* It is unclear during which trip to Switzerland Malcolm met with Ramadan, who later described the encounter as "quite a visit."

leader," he said. Yet he was clearly irked by the *New York Times* survey indicating that only six percent of the New York City blacks who had been polled considered him to be their most effective leader. (Nearly seventy-five percent said Martin Luther King was doing the best job). Malcolm told Alex Haley, "Brother, do you realize that some of history's greatest leaders never were recognized until they were safely in the ground?"

From Paris, Malcolm flew to New York. He arrived there twelve days after his mother was released, on probation, from Kalamazoo State Hospital. During the quarter century she had been there, she had reportedly had very few visitors. But Philbert, with Yvonne's encouragement, arranged for her release and assumed the responsibility of caring for her. Malcolm contributed what he could. The day before he left for Michigan for his first reunion with his mother in more than two decades, he joyfully related the news to Bembry. Then, looking happier than Bembry had ever seen him, he sat with his former mentor in silence, visibly overcome with emotion. For once, there was no need to talk.

After the reunion, Malcolm returned to New York and happily told Bembry that his mother, who has never fully recovered her faculties, was "completely lucid." He told Haley, "She has more of her teeth than those who were instrumental in sending her to the institution." It was quite an admission for a guy who had been called Toothless Blondie.

Malcolm stayed in the United States for exactly six days. Then, on November 30, he departed for Europe under the watchful eyes of FBI agents who tried to ascertain the identity of the organization that had paid for his plane ticket. The highlight of his trip, which may have included another quiet excursion to Switzerland, was a televised debate at Oxford University. The proposition at issue was: "Extremism in the Defense of Liberty Is No Vice; Moderation in the Pursuit of Justice Is No Virtue."

Malcolm took the affirmative. The negative was ably argued by a member of parliament named Humphry Berkeley, who asserted that Malcolm's approach to race was not fundamentally different from that of Prime Minister Hendrick Verwoerd of South Africa. Malcolm later confided to the author and film maker Lebert Bethune that he was so furious that it took a conscious effort on his part to keep from trembling. But his control didn't fail him. The audience, which was accustomed to hearing the finest debaters in the world, gave him a standing ovation.

He addressed two other groups in England—one in Manchester and one in Sheffield. The Nation of Islam apparently regarded the speeches, which were sponsored by Muslim organizations, as a continuation of Malcolm's efforts to undermine Elijah Muhammad's reputation and to project himself as the leader of the African-American community's Muslims. The day after Malcolm returned to the States, Raymond Sharrieff sent him the following telegram:

> Mr. Malcolm:
> We hereby officially warn you that the Nation of Islam shall no longer tolerate your scandalizing the name of our leader and teacher, the Honorable Elijah Muhammad, regardless of where such scandalizing is done.

More ominous warnings appeared the same week in *Muhammad Speaks*, which characterized Malcolm as an international "hobo" who roamed foreign lands to escape Mr. Muhammad's vengeance. The charge appeared in conjunction with a five page article written by Minister Louis X, who subsequently became minister of Temple Seven as well as the Messenger's National Spokesman. (After Malcolm, there were no more National Representatives who had the authority to act on the Messenger's behalf.) Louis, three of whose children married into Mr. Muhammad's family, did not spare his fallen predecessor, whom he accused of trying to see how many of Elijah's relatives he could induce to join his camp. Recalling Malcolm's meeting with Akbar Muhammad in Cairo, Louis asserted that if Akbar had known what was happening, he would have advised Malcolm to look for his head "on the sidewalk." Louis, whose oratorical prowess had been overshadowed by Malcolm's, challenged him to stay in the U.S. and "face the music." "Malcolm shall not escape," he wrote. "The die is set!" He contended that Malcolm was worthy of death. The only reason he was still alive, Louis said, was that the Messenger knew that Allah was on his side and had no need to resort to arms:

> He just allows his [enemies] . . . to come to their end—as he did his brother in 1935.

The remarkable thing about Louis's behavior was that he, like Captain Joseph and John Ali, was a former protege of Malcolm. He had served as an assistant minister at Temple Seven and had accompanied Malcolm on several nationwide speaking tours. "He learned well," says one former associate: "He listened to [Malcolm's] words carefully. He studied his style and learned how to fire up a crowd."

Louis, who later changed his name to Louis Farrakhan, had been Malcolm's confidant and best student. ("I am not afraid of death!" he claimed.) For a while, he had reportedly lived in Malcolm's home. He had been appointed minister of the Boston temple at Malcolm's suggestion and was regarded as one of "Malcolm's ministers." But he was ambitious.

When Elijah Muhammad jettisoned Malcolm, Louis turned against his mentor, just as Malcolm had turned against Lemuel Hassan. Malcolm, who emphasized the need for public figures to be alert to the motives of those who flocked around them ("I can hear sincerity," he told Alex Haley), frequently trusted the wrong people. Yet he claimed that the Uncle Toms were the ones who mistook their enemies for friends.

The week Louis's diatribe was published, Malcolm appeared in court a second time to contest a speeding ticket he had received nine months before. With the help of Percy Sutton's brother Oliver, who represented him at the hearing, he persuaded the judge—who was white—to rule in his favor despite opposing testimony by two police officers, both of whom were white. But the time and effort he devoted to the enterprise were disproportionate to its worth.

Despite his clockwatching, which made some people feel that Malcolm knew that his time was running out, he frittered away his time in other ways. He spent hours chatting aimlessly over the phone with Charles Wiley, the writer whom he had called "Mr. Lucifer" in 1957. The conversation rambled so much that Wiley was able to hold the telephone receiver to his ear with his shoulder while he quietly performed other tasks.

Three days after the traffic court hearing, Malcolm addressed the Domestic Peace Corps. The following day, he spoke at the Audubon Ballroom. Both speeches contained a theme that he repeatedly emphasized: that blacks should fight for their rights "by any means necessary." The phrase, which became another one of Malcolm's watchwords, underscored the pragmatism that prompted his efforts to tailor his teachings to different audiences. The catchy slogan implied he was willing to employ violence but did not commit him to use it.

During December, Malcolm gave his third speech at Harvard. During the question-and-answer period, a student asked:

> Sir, I would like to know the difference between a white racist and a black racist—besides the fact they are white and black.

Even Malcolm had difficulty answering this one. At first, he argued that black racists are usually the product of white racists. Then Malcolm, who told his future biographer Peter Goldman that it was easier for whites to hate than it was for blacks to hate,* tried to argue that the anti-white feeling that pervades the black community is not racism at all. He did not propose a more apt description.

---

* Goldman thought Malcolm was talking about harboring hate, not venting it.

Ella went to Harvard to hear Malcolm speak and later characterized his performance as "perfect—just perfect." She presented him with a homemade diploma she had prepared for the occasion. "Do you think I deserve it?" Malcolm asked, as if he had just been awarded an Ivy League doctorate.

Other New England universities invited him to speak. At one, a former Roxbury hustler walked up to the lectern after Malcolm had finished speaking. Malcolm took the man's proferred hand in both of his. He seemed so glad to see his old friend, who later recalled:

> Usually, when I saw him on television, he was a firebrand. But tonight, I had the feeling I was seeing the real Malcolm. There was sort of a sad look in his eyes. He seemed lonesome and friendless.

It was lonely at the top.

TRAPPED! 53

As Christmas approached, Alex Haley bought two dolls, one for each of Malcolm's two oldest daughters. He showed them to Malcolm first. As the mechanical dolls began to walk, a broad smile registered on Malcolm's face. Haley sensed that he appreciated the gifts. Later, Malcolm told him:

> You know, this isn't something I'm proud to say, but I don't think I've ever bought one gift for my children . . . I've always been too busy.

On another occasion, he told Haley, "I know that my shortcomings are many." He told black activist Gus Newport that he felt so guilty about what he had preached on Elijah Muhammad's behalf that he had consulted a psychiatrist. "He was just guilt ridden," Newport later told an interviewer.

He seemed less assured than Haley had ever seen him. He said the press was virtually ignoring the threats to his life. Haley had largely completed his manuscript of Malcolm's autobiography and presented him with a contract governing foreign publication rights. Haley signed it and offered the pen to Malcolm, who eyed it suspiciously and said, "I had better show this thing to my lawyer." Later, as the two men were driving through Harlem, Malcolm abruptly hauled out the contract and signed it. "I'll trust you," he said.

Selectively, in Haley's hotel room, Malcolm read aloud from his carefully kept diary and sketched the highlights of his recent trip to Africa. He said he was not disclosing the full contents of the diary (which disappeared after his death) because he was thinking of turning it into another book. Perhaps it was the one friend he confided in completely. Its attention never wavered. One could tell it everything. It revealed nothing and was fully trustworthy.

During the latter part of December, Malcolm was interviewed by

Claude Lewis of the *Herald-Tribune*. Lewis asked Malcolm where he was headed politically. "I have no idea," Malcolm replied. "So when you ask where I'm headed, what can I say?" There was a long pause as he toyed with his cup of coffee. Then he said, "Isn't anything wrong with that."

Portions of the Lewis interview sounded like a man composing his own obituary. "I'll never get old," Malcolm asserted. "I can't even see myself old," he added with a leaden chuckle.

Lewis asked him whether there was a new Malcolm. With a sharp, unmusical laugh, Malcolm responded:

> The white man asks the question, "Is there a new Malcolm X?" 'Cause what he has been demanding is, politically, a new me while there's not yet been a new him. Which means I'm supposed to change before white people change. As long as there's an old problem—the same old problem —I don't see how there can be a new Malcolm X.

Despite Malcolm's assertion that there was no new Malcolm, he tried to rid himself of his anti-Semitic image by citing "the great Jewish historical tradition" as an example of the way African-Americans, like American Jews, could forge cultural and emotional ties with their brethren across the sea. He also had a photograph taken of himself posing next to a life-sized advertisement depicting a black youth happily munching a sandwich made with Levy's rye bread. The difficulty he had in eradicating his anti-Semitic image was illustrated by an incident that occurred one day in a Jewish delicatessen. Malcolm's waitress, who was apparently Jewish, became so flustered when she realized who he was that she neglected to give him any silverware. Malcolm summoned her and said, "Young lady, I'm afraid you forgot to bring me some eating utensils."

The waitress started to fetch the silverware, but Malcolm stopped her. "You'd better not get any for me right now," he said, "I think I see a man over there who could be the manager . . . If he is and he sees you made a mistake, he might get angry with you."

Then he turned to his companions and borrowed some of their silverware. "I'll make out," he told the waitress. "Don't get in any trouble." He gave her a smile.

The chivalry may also have been prompted by Malcolm's desire to stress his new position on women, which was that they should be treated as equals. He expressed admiration for the women who were at the forefront of the struggle for Vietnamese independence. He told a former NOI member how much he regretted the way he had "spit acid at the sisters." Black men must learn not to boss their women around, he said. He was particularly critical of men who didn't respect their mothers.

Malcolm dropped his long-standing opposition to interracial marriage. He also acknowledged that he no longer believed in racial separation, either as an immediate goal or a long-range one. There were indications he was even beginning to question his religion. He disparaged Elijah Muhammad's assertion "that Islam is the right religion, the religion of God, and all of that." He bitterly told one group of listeners that if their religion hadn't benefited them any more than it had, they should "forget it." And when he was asked if he still believed in Islam, he frowned and parried the question with one of his own. Yet he told an associate, "I still believe in Allah—I must."

On some issues, it was impossible to discern what Malcolm (whom one television commentator nicknamed "Shifty") believed. He told a predominantly black audience that the white man was "tricky," but ambiguously added:

> When I say this, it's not a racist statement. Some of them might not
> be tricky, but all of them I've met are tricky.

His characterization of Martin Luther King (who called him "demagogic") was equally ambiguous. He said King was on the right track, but wasn't doing enough for America's blacks. And despite Malcolm's "new" position on Jews, he fueled anti-Semitic sentiment by suggesting that most of Harlem's slumlords were Jews who lived on the Grand Concourse.

He tried to mollify the "action"-oriented militants by inviting famous revolutionaries such as Che Guevara to address the OAAU. And when a former member of the Los Angeles mosque took him to task for the way he had deterred a violent response to the shooting of Ronald Stokes, Malcolm said that he was sorry the Nation of Islam had not "moved." He said he had been constrained by Elijah Muhammad. He buttressed his militant credentials with the announcement that:

> White people in the South are praying in the secrecy of their closets
> that King never dies. King is the best thing that ever happened to
> white folks. *For* white folks! As long as anybody can keep Negroes
> nonviolent, it helps white folks.

After King received the Nobel Peace Prize, Malcolm bitterly told Claude Lewis, "He got the Peace Prize; we got the problem." "I don't want the white man giving me medals," he added.

Like his pronouncements about King, Malcolm's declarations about whites illustrated his knack for political fence-straddling. On the one hand, he kept insisting he was not a racist. On the other, he kept castigating "whitey." One night, as he drove the babysitter home, his car narrowly missed a white pedestrian. "I should have run over him," he said. "I'm sorry I missed." Such statements made him a political pariah. He exhibited a wry sense of humor about the fact he was a political reject, at least outside the ghetto. After all, political rebels, like teen-age criminals, didn't care about social acceptance. Or did they? One person who saw through Malcolm's unconcerned facade was Ossie Davis, who told Peter Goldman, "He desperately wanted to belong!"

But the part of Malcolm that wanted to enter the political mainstream ran aground on the incendiary rhetoric that enabled him to stay in the limelight. As Goldman later pointed out, Malcolm had become the prisoner of the very newspaper clippings he had helped write. Yet the more he tried to broaden his political base, the more he antagonized many of his militant followers, particularly those on the political fringe. Out of the blue one day, as he was ostensibly talking about something else, he bluntly summarized his dilemma:

> So we're trapped. Trapped! Double-trapped! Triple-trapped! Any way we go, we find that we're trapped. And every kind of solution that someone comes up with is just another trap.

On another occasion, he elaborated:

> For Muslims, I'm too worldly; for other people, I'm too religious . .
> for militants, I'm too moderate; for moderates, I'm too militant.

He lamented how America's blacks, through no fault of their own, had felt trapped by their skin color. In language that was intensely personal, yet poignantly descriptive of the agony of being black in white America, he exclaimed:

> We hated our hair . . . . Yeah! We hated the color of our skin . . . . We hated ourselves. Our color became to us a chain . . . a prison, . . . not letting us go this way or that.

He seemed to be talking, not only about people who had dark skin, but also about people who resembled the Malcolm-like character he called "Mr. In-Between":

> You're not this and you're not that. [You're] Mr. In-Between . . . . Nobody want[s] ya 'cause you don't want yo'self . . . . Nobody wants Mr. In-Between . . . . They won't let ya be white and ya don't want'a be black.

During another speech, Malcolm pondered anew the tragic quandary of the unfortunates who are accepted by neither camp. Then he uttered a long, joyless laugh.

VII

DEATHWARD

ELIJAH SPEAKS 54

The first issue of *Muhammad Speaks* that appeared in 1965 contained the conciliatory pronouncement that disbelievers "are to be forgiven if they renounce hypocrisy." There was also a declaration that Allah "specifically chooses for his mercy whom he pleases." Yet, in the next issue, Elijah Muhammad dwelled at considerable length on the fate of "hypocrites." He singled out Malcolm, whom he called "the Chief Hypocrite," for particular criticism. "He has said everything imaginable against me," Muhammad declared. "I will never forget." Though he predicted "painful chastisement" for those who defied him, he admonished his followers not to kill them. The admonition was apparently necessary; one believer told Charles Kenyatta, "You fell in love with that red nigger, but we're going to kill him."

The January 15 issue of the Nation of Islam's newspaper suggested that the NOI leadership was divided about how to proceed on the Malcolm issue. In a column entitled "From The Messenger," the following passage appeared:

> You and I have arrived at a day of decision. We have come to the crossroads—the point where we must make a decision on what we shall do.

Identical language appeared in an accompanying editorial. That same week, Akbar Muhammad announced that he had quit the Nation of Islam. He said he could no longer abide his father's "concocted religious teachings, which are . . . in most cases diametrically opposed to Islam." Akbar, whom *Muhammad Speaks* dubbed the "Little Hypocrite," indicated that he sympathized with many of Malcolm's views. Eight days later, Malcolm, whom the NOI blamed for Akbar's defection, was reportedly attacked in front of his Queens home. He told one newsman there were three assailants. The number eventually grew to five or six. "I came out with my talking stick," he told the *Amsterdam News*. He told one questioner he had thrashed his attackers.

By this time, violent reprisals against dissidents had become established practice in the Nation of Islam. The preceding December, a number of Malcolm's Philadelphia followers had been assaulted by ten or fifteen members of Elijah Muhammad's Philadelphia temple. The same week, Leon 4X Ameer, who described himself, accurately or otherwise, as Malcolm's New England organizer, was clubbed to his knees in the lobby of Boston's Sherry Biltmore Hotel by the captain of Elijah's Boston temple and three other Black Muslims. An armed detective who happened to be in a shop inside the hotel dashed out and rescued Ameer. But, later the same night, another pack forced its way into his hotel room. Battering his face to a pulp, they fractured a number of his ribs and ruptured both his eardrums. The following day, he was discovered, unconscious, in the bathtub. He was rushed to Boston City Hospital, where he lay in a coma with a blood clot on the brain. He emerged from the hospital a semi-invalid.

Nevertheless, Ameer fared better than a NOI defector named Kenneth Morton, who had allegedly died the previous month as a result of a beating administered by members of the Messenger's New York temple. The unwillingness of the NOI leadership to brook any rivals was underscored by the shooting of Benjamin Brown, a defector who had been trying to establish his own mosque in the Bronx. Information that Brown, who was unaffiliated with Malcolm, later furnished the police enabled them to arrest three suspects, all of whom were members of Temple Seven. One was a karate-trained enforcer named Norman 3X Butler. The second, whose twelve-year-long criminal record included eight arrests and six convictions, was Thomas 15X Johnson. Both were Captain Joseph's lieutenants. When Malcolm was Temple Seven's minister, they had performed yeoman's service as his "security guards." But Malcolm (who reproached his security men for hovering too close when he was engaged in conversation) had apparently concluded that they were spying for Joseph.

Despite the military-like chain of command that prevailed in the Messenger's private army, the commanders often couched their orders in language that made them sound like suggestions. Elijah Muhammad, Jr., who reportedly ran the enforcement apparatus that was outwardly commanded by Raymond Sharrieff, told a gathering of "security" officials:

> That house [i.e., the one Malcolm's family was living in] is ours, and the nigger don't want to give it up. Well, all you have to do is [to] go out there and clap on the walls until the walls come tumbling down, and then cut the nigger's tongue out and put it in an envelope

and send it to me. And I'll stamp it "APPROVED" and give it to the Messenger.

Norman Butler, who apparently attended the gathering, later acknowledged that the statement was an attempt to foment murder by suggestion. A member of Temple Seven who defected to Malcolm told the *New York Post* that Joseph had privately made a similar suggestion.

The attacks on Brown, Ameer, and others underscored a late-January prediction by *Muhammad Speaks* that 1965 would be "a year in which the most outspoken opponents of the Honorable Elijah Muhammad will slink into ignoble silence." But Malcolm, who had vowed to tame the pseudo-Islamic monster that was devouring its own adherents, had no intention of keeping silent. The day before the NOI newspaper published its ominous prophecy, he flew to California, ostensibly to establish an OAAU chapter in Los Angeles and to "look after" Heather and Robin. But no organizational meeting was held. Instead, Malcolm escorted the two women to Gladys Towles Root's law office. Without being asked, he volunteered to testify in their behalf, presumably about Elijah Muhammad's admission that he had fathered a number of illegitimate children. Though he had never spent a day in law school—or even high school—he seemed thoroughly cognizant of the fact that, if the paternity suits ever came to trial, his testimony would likely prove decisive. (Uncorroborated, Heather's and Robin's story might not have been believed.)

The visit to Mrs. Root's office was the third or fourth Malcolm had made. "He was frightened," she later recalled. Malcolm, who asked her if she had inadvertently disclosed his involvement in the proceedings, had every reason to be apprehensive; everywhere he went in Los Angeles, he was hounded by Elijah's followers. The official in charge of the surveillance was apparently John Ali, who was on hand at Los Angeles airport when Malcolm arrived there. The minister and the captain of the Los Angeles mosque even showed up at the Statler Hilton, where Malcolm stopped briefly before meeting with Mrs. Root. In fact, Malcolm ran into the two men at the top of one of the hotel escalators. The mouth of one of them curled up at the side, almost like a dog baring its fangs. "They wanted to kill Malcolm . . . right there," his companion Hakim Jamal later recalled.

Malcolm just smiled. He stepped onto the escalator and fingered his beard as the moving stairway descended to the ground floor, where a squad of believers stood waiting. They stared at him and then upward at their NOI superiors, as if they were awaiting word to act. Malcolm was still smiling. As the escalator reached the lobby, he shoved Jamal toward the door of the hotel. "Keep moving," he declared. "Don't stop!" After he was out of immediate danger, he told an associate, "They know why I'm here . . . . They really want to get me."

The following day, on the way to the airport, two automobiles filled with NOI men gave chase. As one car tried to pull abreast, Malcolm grabbed a cane and poked it out the window, as if it were a rifle. The pursuing vehicle dropped back. Malcolm's car sped on to the airport, where other NOI men kept him under surveillance. Consequently, the police, who were also on hand, accompanied him to his plane through an underground passageway.

Hours later, when Malcolm arrived in Chicago, policemen were present. They escorted him to his hotel and took up residence in the room next to his. Malcolm had not requested the police protection and appeared suspicious of the motives of the officers. But after Sergeant Ed McClellan, whose men treated Malcolm with deference, explained that they were there to help, Malcolm warmed up considerably.

McClellan asked Malcolm if he would continue exposing himself to danger by appearing in public. "No matter what the cost!" Malcolm replied. Later, in response to a question that had nothing to do with success or failure, he told McClellan he was very pleased with his accomplishments.

During his stay in Chicago, he met a number of times with representatives of the Illinois Attorney General, who had requested the meetings to explore the possibility that Malcolm might be willing to testify in *Cooper v. Pate*, a case that had been dragging through the federal judiciary for more than two years. Cooper, a Stateville Penitentiary inmate, had sued the State of Illinois, partly because the prison had denied Black Muslim convicts permission to hold religious services. It had also denied them access to a Muslim chaplain. And Cooper had been unable to receive reading material that had been mailed to him. The material ranged from *Muhammad Speaks* to the *Pittsburgh Courier*. Officials would not even allow the Qu'ran into the prison, let alone the books that Cooper wanted to use to learn Arabic.

The U.S. District Court for the Northern District of Illinois summarily dismissed Cooper's petition for redress. The U.S. Court of Appeals affirmed the decision, arguing that the Black Muslim movement constituted a threat to racial peace in Stateville and that Elijah Muhammad's followers were not inclined to obey non-Muslim authority. (Elijah Muhammad enjoined his followers to obey the secular authorities unless their edicts conflicted with his teachings.) The U.S. Supreme Court reversed the appellate court's decision and remanded the case to the district court for trial.

The Illinois Attorney General's office contacted Malcolm. It was preparing to argue in court that the religious activities of the Nation of Islam were merely a facade. The argument dovetailed nicely with Malcolm's attempts to undermine Elijah Muhammad's religious credentials.

There are conflicting reports about whether Malcolm agreed to testify against Cooper and his associates, who were demanding the same religious freedom that Malcolm had demanded at Charlestown Prison. Two of the government officials assigned to the case thought he was eager to testify. Another thought he was reluctant to do so.

The ambivalence Malcolm apparently had about testifying may also have been due to the fact that, several years earlier, he had urged Elijah Muhammad to finance litigation designed to compel New York State to permit Islamic services at Attica Prison. In fact, he had testified in court on behalf of Attica's Muslims himself. Now he would have to decide whether to testify against the movement he had helped build.

While Malcolm was in Chicago, he was interviewed by the television talk-show host Irv Kupcinet, who asked how he felt about the argument that the Black Muslim movement was not a bona fide religion. Malcolm conceded that it might be a religion but said it was not the real Islam. As he prepared to leave the television station, he noticed one of Elijah Muhammad's followers in the lobby. Outside, a Volkswagen truck pulled out in front of the unmarked police car that had been waiting for him. Ten or more tough-looking black men began converging on it. The police kept back the attackers, who may have been prompted by reports that the Illinois Attorney General was scrutinizing the Nation of Islam's tax-exemptions. When Malcolm returned to his hotel, he spotted another swarm of NOI men. "Elijah seems to know every move I make," he told Sergeant McClellan. Moments later he added, "It's only going to be a matter of time before they catch up with me."

One of the people who visited Malcolm at his hotel that weekend was Wallace Muhammad, who later acknowledged that he had been seeking a way to return to his father's movement. Malcolm, who had good reason to be wary of the man who had been his chief rival for the succession to the Messenger's throne, threw all caution to the wind and told Wallace he was determined to expose his father. Within a week, Wallace contacted Elijah and told him that he'd had a change of heart. Whether he told his father what Malcolm had told him, we may never know.

Malcolm dug his own grave deeper by announcing, back in New York, that he planned to expose Elijah Muhammad's flirtation with the Ku Klux Klan, which, like the Nation of Islam, advocated racial separation. Five days later, *Muhammad Speaks* published the following statement by one of Elijah's "personal" secretaries:

Throughout the years, I have witnessed the birth and death of many
ministers.

The remainder of the article assailed Malcolm and defended Elijah.
Elsewhere in the same issue, another spokesman attacked Malcolm. He
predicted that the time was coming when the opposition would be dealt
a final, crushing blow. "Soon . . . you will see," he declared. In the
following issue (which devoted considerable space to Malcolm), he said
it was too late for Malcolm to retract all the bitter seeds he had sown.
On another page, the Messenger—who had reportedly proclaimed that
Malcolm was destroying himself—announced that the so-called Chief
Hypocrite had "stepped beyond the limits." "I am no more to suffer,"
he said. Malcolm apparently understood what he meant; he told Alex
Haley he wanted to read the manuscript of his autobiography one more
time because he didn't expect to read it in finished form. He also told
Haley, "Each day I live as if I am already dead."

WAITING IN THE WINGS 55

There were rumors that Elijah Muhammad wanted to deliver a speech at Tuskegee Institute. Tuskegee reportedly said no. It asked Malcolm instead.

During the first week of February, Malcolm flew to Alabama to make the speech. He had planned to depart the next morning. But Tuskegee students insisted that he change his plans and go to a town called Selma, which is located west of Tuskegee.

The events that were unfolding at Selma were the culmination of the decade of struggle that had begun with the Montgomery bus boycott and had ripened into the Birmingham campaign and the March on Washington. The ensuing 1964 Civil Rights Act had outlawed racial discrimination in hotels, theaters, restaurants, lavatories, and other public conveniences. But not even this epic piece of legislation, or the constitutional amendment barring the use of poll taxes in federal elections, had done much to enhance the ability of black southerners to vote, particularly in election contests involving state and local officials. This was partly due to intimidation and partly due to the inadequacy of legal provisions that had supposedly assured southern blacks access to the polls. In Selma, the birthplace of Alabama's first White Citizens Council, the Dallas County voting registrar's office was open only twice a month. When it was, its employees took long lunches. Prospective voters had to complete an application form containing more than fifty questions. They also had to read and correctly interpret various parts of the Constitution. As a result, the voting registrars seldom processed more than thirty application forms a month. The dilatory tactics were largely responsible for the fact that only 335 of the 15,115 black adults in Dallas county were registered to vote. But nearly 10,000 of the county's 14,400 eligible whites were listed on the voting rolls. Martin Luther King estimated that, at the rate Dallas County's blacks were being permitted to apply, it would take a hundred and three years to register them all.

The situation in Lowndes County, to the east, and Wilcox County, to the south, was even worse. The two counties were part of Alabama's Black Belt, eighty-five percent of whose black families subsisted on less than $3,000 a year. On one enormous Wilcox County plantation, six hundred black families toiled. They were paid not in U.S. currency but in octagonal tin coins that were redeemable only at the plantation commissary. Though eighty percent of the population of the two counties was black, not a single African-American was registered to vote in either one.

The chief reason King and his associates selected Dallas County, rather than Wilcox or Lowndes, as the locale for their campaign for effective voting rights legislation was Dallas County's chief "law enforcement" officer, Sheriff Jim Clark. The square-faced lawman was notorious for unprovoked brutality. The previous July, his deputies had attacked the newsmen and photographers who had been reporting attempts by blacks to implement the desegregation provisions of the 1964 Civil Rights Act. The virtual absence of violence in Albany, Georgia two and a half years before had been largely responsible for the failure of King's Albany campaign to generate the kind of press coverage that had attended such headline-creating events as the upheaval in Birmingham and the mob violence that had accompanied James Meredith's admission to the University of Mississippi. King, who acknowledged that protest marches were ineffective in mobilizing public opinion unless they provoked a violent reaction, told a group of supporters:

> We are here today to say to the white men that we will no longer let them use their clubs on us in dark corners. We are going to make them do it in the glaring light of television.

Though Clark's initial reaction was restrained, the spectacle of long lines of blacks ringing the green-walled courthouse that contained the voting registration office, as well as his own, seemed to make his blood boil. Finally, one day outside the courthouse, he made the mistake of shoving a tall, powerfully built SNCC advocate named Annie Lee Cooper. Muttering a curse, Mrs. Cooper whirled and slugged him. As Clark, who was a big man, staggered to his knees, she hit him again. Two deputies rushed her. One threw his arms around her from behind and tried to push her to the ground. But she stomped on his foot and jammed her elbow into his belly. Breaking loose from his grip, she turned her attention, once again, to the sheriff, who was still trying to regain his footing. She socked him once more. Finally, the three men grabbed her and wrestled her to the pavement. Mrs. Cooper wasn't through with Clark, however. She called him a scum and openly dared him to hit her. The sheriff raised his billy club and swung. But Cooper was ready; she grabbed the club and hung on. She even succeeded in knocking loose Clark's helmet. At last, he wrenched the club free and, with trembling hands, brought it down on her head with a resounding thump. A widely circulated photograph of the encounter aroused the nation against him and everything he represented, for Martin Luther King, who witnessed the melee from across the street, had learned the importance of photographers. Like Malcolm, he subtly manipulated the media. But he didn't do it the way Malcolm did. Instead, he used his undulating, rhythmic baritone to transform his courageous followers into willing martyrs.

King was in jail when Malcolm reluctantly arrived in Selma. His aides were not eager to let Malcolm speak to the youths who had gathered to pray before marching out to face Clark and his underlings. But a group of SNCC workers—some of whom resented the way SCLC was getting most of the credit for the voter registration drive SNCC had begun two years earlier—insisted that he be heard. SCLC yielded, partly to avert a rift with SNCC, partly because it was difficult to defend the proposition that those who had different opinions should be denied the freedom to speak. James Bevel and Andrew Young took Malcolm aside and urged him not to make any statements that might encourage violence. Yet, several weeks later, Young acknowledged that the civil rights movement had been "sustained more or less" by the white violence the movement's activities had provoked. He also admitted that Jim Clark and Bull Connor had been playing right into the movement's hands. One of the paradoxes of the Black Revolution was that, whereas Malcolm refrained from the violence his militant rhetoric encouraged, King and his aides courted violence despite their insistence on nonviolence.

With a smile, Malcolm listened to Young's and Bevel's entreaties. Before he mounted the speaker's platform, he told a SNCC worker, "Remember this—nobody puts words in my mouth!" Days earlier, he had made the same point to the Illinois officials who had been trying to persuade him to testify against the Nation of Islam.

"I don't advocate violence," Malcolm told the audience. But he said he didn't believe in nonviolence either. He told a journalist, "I am not for or against violence. I am for freedom, by whatever means necessary." He told Selma's blacks:

> Whites better be glad Martin Luther King is rallying the people, because other forces are waiting to take over if he fails.

It did not require a great deal of political sophistication to guess who the others were. Malcolm, who said he wanted to "give people an alternative to think about," told Coretta King he was trying to help her husband by presenting the white establishment with a less palatable alternative. (On another occasion, he looked a perceptive reporter in the eye and told him that the white power-structure would turn a deaf ear to the demands of the black moderates unless black extremists continued to threaten from the wings.) Yet it was clear that the alternative he was offering was intended not only for white ears but also for those of the followers of his eminent black rival, who expressed dismay when he learned that Malcolm had invaded his political turf.

Instead of joining the Selma campaign, Malcolm left Alabama in order to begin another speaking tour. One of the people who took him to task for his failure to register any concrete political gains before the civil rights revolution passed him by was his former idol, Jackie Robinson:

> Malcolm has big audiences, but no constructive program. He has big words, but no record on deeds in civil rights. He is terribly militant on soapboxes on streetcorners of Negro ghettos. Yet he has not faced police dogs in Birmingham, as Martin Luther King has done; nor gone to jail for freedom, as Roy Wilkins and James Farmer have done; nor led a March on Washington, as A. Philip Randolph did; nor brought about creative dialogue between business and civil rights leaders, as Whitney Young does daily.

But how could Malcolm participate in the civil rights movement without repudiating all the negative things he had said about nonviolent protest? If he marched or demonstrated, it would have impaired his credibility among many of his ghetto followers.

Had he marched, it would have destroyed his political uniqueness. He would have become just another civil rights leader. For a man who had striven so long to become Number One, such a fate would have been difficult to endure. He told the OAAU, before he went to Selma, that "we" do not want to duplicate what has already been done. "What we need to do," he declared, "[is to] shake the world!"

The question was how.

For the time being, Malcolm contented himself with verbal broadsides against political targets such as George Lincoln Rockwell, the fuehrer of the American Nazi Party. Rockwell, who had also been in Selma, had been outmaneuvered by National States Rights Party leader Jimmy George Robinson, who had stolen the show by luring Martin Luther King into a conversation that ended when he slugged King. Malcolm, who saw the incident on television, sent a telegram threatening "maximum physical retaliation" if anyone else was hurt. He gave the press a copy of the telegram, which one of his aides apparently sent to Rockwell instead of Robinson. But the press did not accord it prominence. About a week later, Malcolm told an interviewer that it was easy for outsiders to stand on the political sidelines making militant-sounding pronouncements. Outwardly, the remark was a critique of an ultra-leftist publication that had accused him of reaching an accommodation with the establishment. But perhaps it was also a self-critique. He told a group of Mississippi youths who had distinguished themselves in the civil rights struggle:

> How do you think I feel to have to tell you, "We, my generation, sat around like a knot on a wall while the whole world was fighting for its human rights . . . . What did we do, who preceded you? I'll tell you what we did: Nothing."

Malcolm said he wanted a "real" revolution, as opposed to what he characterized as James Baldwin's "pseudo-revolt." He intimated that Martin Luther King was the one who lacked a political program.

But the rapidly approaching culmination of the civil rights movement rendered such rhetoric increasingly immaterial. Malcolm's growing political irrelevance, which he tried to conceal with claims that he had been offered jobs by Nasser and Nkrumah, made it difficult for him to carve out a niche for himself in the rapidly changing political landscape. The alternative was to seek meaning in the personal realm. But, despite his assertions to the contrary, Malcolm never had been able to maintain close personal attachments.

Thus, despite his political genius, Malcolm had little reason for optimism. At times, he seemed terribly dejected. His shoes, which he had always taken such great care to shine, were unpolished and unkempt. Some associates sensed that he still regretted severing his ties with the Nation of Islam. One of them was Christine Johnson. "His heart was still with the movement," she later recalled. "He had given everything for the Nation. After he left it, he had nothing to live for. He didn't care whether he lived or died."

ANOTHER FIRE

During the eleven months that had elapsed since Malcolm had severed his relationship with the Nation of Islam, he had been abroad six months. Nevertheless, on Friday, February 5, the same day Martin Luther King and his associates renewed their carefully-planned Selma campaign, Malcolm left once again for Europe. Before he departed, he announced that he would reveal a bold, militant action-program at an OAAU rally February 15. Earlier, he had promised it for January.

On Monday, February 8, Malcolm addressed the Council of African Organizations in London. On Tuesday, while en route to Geneva, he flew to Paris to address the Federation of African Students. But at Orly Airport, he was detained by French immigration officials, whose superiors were reportedly upset by a speech he had given in Paris the previous November. The Interior Ministry announced that his presence in France, which has a sizable black population, was "undesirable."

The immigration authorities, who feared that Malcolm's presence might provoke the kind of racial disturbances that England was beginning to experience, would not even let him telephone the people who had planned to meet him at the airport. Nor would they allow him to call the American embassy. They hinted that the U.S. State Department had asked them to bar him from France. Malcolm admitted that he didn't know whether this was true. The likelihood was remote that de Gaulle's government, which was doing everything it could to stress its independence from the United States, had yielded to American pressure on an issue that didn't even involve the U.S.

Yet, as time passed, Malcolm appeared to put increasing stock in the thesis that he was the target of an international conspiracy. "This thing is bigger than Chicago," he told one associate. "I know what they can do and what they can't," he told another. Ella also subscribed to the thesis that he was the victim of an international plot.

The French authorities kept Malcolm under guard at the airport. After a while, Malcolm dug into his pocket, fished out an English penny, and handed it to one of the gendarmes. "Give that to de Gaulle," he said, "because the French government is worth less than a penny." The gendarme declined the coin. Malcolm flung it to the floor. Minutes later, he was bundled onto a plane back to England. Whether he managed to get to Geneva is unclear; he had scheduled a visit to the city's "Islamic Center," according to a cablegram the American Legation in Paris addressed to J. Edgar Hoover. (The quotation marks were the legation's.) The Center, which was headed by Said Ramadan, worked closely with Surrur Sabban's Islamic World League.* Ramadan and his associates urged the League and its Saudi backers to aid Malcolm financially.

Two days after Malcolm was barred from France, he spoke at the London School of Economics. He also gave a speech in Birmingham. Afterwards, the BBC invited him to accompany a team of reporters to a suburb of Birmingham named Smethwick, which was experiencing a large influx of "colored" immigrants.

Smethwick's whites were fleeing the town, which was seething with racial tension. The BBC unsuccessfully tried to arrange a face-to-face confrontation between Malcolm and a Conservative member of Parliament from Smethwick named Peter Griffiths, who had recently unseated a leading Labor Party M.P. with the help of anonymous leaflets that read, "If you want a nigger neighbour, vote Liberal or Labour." The refrain became so popular that it was reportedly taken up by children, who sang it in the streets.

Malcolm returned to New York on Saturday, February 13, the day after the Nation of Islam's lawyers petitioned the authorities to oust him from his home, which Judge Wahl had ordered him to vacate by January 31. Percy and Oliver Sutton had already begun a last-ditch effort to postpone the eviction date again. Judge Wahl scheduled a hearing for Monday, February 15.

At about 2:30 a.m. on the fourteenth— the same time of night the 1929 fire had occurred—a taxi driver drove by Malcolm's East Elmhurst home and saw something ablaze in a small tree that stood adjacent to two porch windows. The driver stopped, leaped from his cab, and beat out the flames

---

* When Surrur Sabban died, Muhammad Harakan, the Saudi jurist who had given Malcolm permission to enter Mecca, succeeded him as the League's Secretary General.

with his clipboard. No one else was in sight except his passenger, who drew his attention to flames emanating from a living-room window on the south side of the house—flames neither man had noticed when the taxi had approached the house from that direction. Both men rushed to the front door to warn the occupants. Inside, they heard yelling and glass breaking, but no one came to the front door. They decided to return to the cab and look for the nearest fire alarm box. As the cab driver re-entered his taxi, he spotted, in the rear yard, another fire—a blaze he hadn't seen when he had alighted from his cab to douse the first one. There was still no one else in sight.

When the fire engines reached the burning house, fireman John McLaughlin found Malcolm standing outside in a white robe and a black Russian hat. Fireman Kenneth Kopp was struck by the fact that he was smiling.*

By the time the firefighters forced the front door and doused the flames in the front part of the house, the curtains on the shattered living-room window had been devoured. Pieces of broken bottles—remnants of molotov cocktails—lay scattered throughout the house. The captain of one engine company was surprised to discover unburned gasoline in the bottom of a number of shattered bottles. (Usually, the gasoline is completely consumed when a molotov cocktail explodes.) The gasoline-soaked rag wick of one firebomb was found in Malcolm's bedroom. But the wick was not even scorched; whoever had tossed the bottle had apparently refrained from igniting the wick.

The remains of a small fire were discovered at the base of the drawn venetian blind that hung all the way to the bottom of a broken window in the children's bedroom. Upstairs in the smoke-filled attic, a fireman found Malcolm gasping for air. According to one report, he had returned to the house to retrieve the tape-recordings of some of his speeches. According to another, he was trying to retrieve his clothes. Later, he blamed the firemen for the fact his suits had been ruined. He claimed they did it deliberately.

Fireman Hugo Mazzu, who persuaded Malcolm to leave the attic after the other fireman had tried and failed to do so, continued searching the house to make sure no one was left inside. He was surprised to find so few books in the house. (Malcolm's appetite for

---

* So was Gordon Hall, a political adversary who was struck by televised photographs of Malcolm smiling as he boarded a plane for Detroit just hours after the fire. He was also smiling in a UPI photograph taken outside his charred home.

books was common knowledge.) The lack of books may have been due to the fact that Malcolm had removed some of them from the house before the fire.

A burned-out molotov cocktail whose glass neck contained the ash-like remains of its cloth wick was discovered in the back yard, near the window that had been broken in the children's bedroom. Due to the fact the firemen had removed all the windows and window-frames in order to make sure no hidden embers remained smoldering, it was difficult to tell whether the windows had been broken from the outside or inside. But there were clues. No window glass was found inside the children's bedroom. Yet glass from a window, a storm window, and the homemade molotov cocktail that had evidently shattered them was discovered in the back yard, outside the bedroom. Charred weeds formed a spreading, fan-shaped pattern that indicated that the fire-bomb had been thrown from the house into the yard, rather than vice versa.

Standing upright on a dresser, on the other side of the children's bedroom from the scorched area near the window, was a gasoline-filled bottle of Dewar's White Label Scotch. The device had no wick. Another unshattered, unexploded molotov cocktail was discovered in another part of the house. Had the assailants who had allegedly tossed the firebombs through the windows neglected to insert and light the fuses? Could a gasoline-filled bottle land unbroken and upright after penetrating a window, a storm window, and drawn venetian blinds?*

Malcolm prevailed on friends to house his family. He would not permit the police to question the children, who seemed unfazed by the night's events. Nor would he let Betty talk much. He told detective Ralph Aiello he had fired a pistol at the firebombers, as he said his father had done in 1929. But neither the cab driver nor anyone else the authorities questioned heard the shots. (Malcolm said his pistol had misfired.)

---

* Malcolm and Betty later maintained that a fireman or policeman—or someone dressed as one—had planted the incriminating evidence in the house after the fire engines had arrived on the scene. But fireman Hank Thoben, who had discovered the upright, gasoline-filled bottle in the children's bedroom, recalls that when he lifted the bottle from the smudge-coated dresser to examine it, there was a ring of smudge on the dresser top. (The dresser was coated with smudge from the smoke, but the circular spot where the bottle had been standing was free of smudge.) The absence of smudge beneath the bottle suggested that it had been placed atop the dresser before the fire, not after.

When Fire Department officials questioned him, he displayed none of the righteous indignation he had expressed the night of the fire. He was cool and collected; the answers flew from his mouth as soon as each question was asked. Percy Sutton, who accompanied him to the hearing, turned his back and buried his head in a newspaper.

The press also questioned Malcolm, who replied with a laugh when a reporter asked if he knew why his home had been set ablaze.* He had no fire insurance, so insurance had to be ruled out as a possible incentive. The fire marshall's office knew nothing about the 1929 fire, Malcolm's sensitivity to eviction, or his tendency to commit desperate acts in desperate situations. (He did not appear to have sufficient means to assure his family a place to live—unless, of course, the stage could be set for a public appeal.)

The Nation of Islam accused Malcolm of staging the incident in order to gain publicity and sympathy. It also suggested that the fire had been set in an effort to discredit Elijah Muhammad, and that it had been prompted by a desire for revenge. "We hope," a spokesman said, "it's not a case of if he can't have [the house], we can't either." (Rumors were circulating that Malcolm, who sometimes used the word "burn" to mean "punish," had vowed that the NOI would never get the house).

Had the authorities accepted the Nation's assessment and arrested Malcolm for suspected arson, it might have enhanced his political credentials, for Martin Luther King had demonstrated that being jailed was an effective road to political martyrdom and black leadership. Moreover, in captivity, Malcolm would have been nearly as safe from Elijah Muhammad's vengeance as he had been in Charlestown Prison from Bea's husband's. Perhaps that is why he looked one police official in the eye and told him that he owned a pistol. He told the fire marshall's office and the media the same thing. It was common knowledge that, because of his youthful criminal record, he lacked the requisite permit. But it was not common knowledge that, in 1929, the Michigan authorities had jailed his father on a gun-carrying charge when it had become apparent they were going to have trouble proving arson.** Was Malcolm contemplating a similar scenario? "I had the feeling he didn't care if he was arrested or not," Detective Aiello told an interviewer years later. Aiello recommended Malcolm's arrest. So did another police official. But they were over-ruled by their superiors, who may have feared that Malcolm's arrest

---

* Another published version of what happened says that Malcolm laughed in response to the question who had set the fire.
**Arson is frequently hard to prove because of the lack of witnesses and the difficulty of establishing a clear-cut motive.

would precipitate another Harlem riot.

A few hours after the fire engines departed, Malcolm flew to Detroit and told a gathering:

> I was in a house, last night, that was bombed. My own! But I d . . . [Malcolm stopped and changed the word "I" to "It."] It didn't destroy all my clothes.

Privately, he charged the Nation of Islam with responsibility for the fire. Initially, he limited his public response to a declaration that "supporters" of the movement might have set the blaze. But, on Monday, February 15, he placed the blame squarely on the Messenger's shoulders. He candidly admitted that he was "well aware" of what he was setting in motion. "Let the chips fall where they may," he declared.* His charges afforded a convenient excuse for his failure to unveil his much-heralded action-program, which, despite its ringing preamble, was not a program at all; for the most part, it was merely an elaborate restatement of the views he had been uttering for months.

Malcolm said that the bomb-throwers were so familiar with the layout of his home that he was "quite certain" they knew where each member of his family usually slept. But in his zeal to deny that he had set fire to his home, he blundered and claimed that he had known absolutely "nothing" about the eviction proceedings until he had heard over the radio that Judge Wahl had refused to grant him another extension.

Malcolm pulled out all the stops. He characterized the Nation of Islam as a "criminal organization" and described Elijah Muhammad as a senile old man interested in nothing but money and sex. He also depicted the Messenger, as well as Martin Luther King, as men who placed innocent children in the line of fire. He told his Harlem followers that he had neither compassion for such people nor desire to forgive them. "If anybody can find where I bombed my house," he said, "they can put a rifle bullet through my head." The invitation was hardly necessary. Someone in the audience exclaimed, "Get your hand out of my pocket!" The audience's attention was diverted. Not for several days would the incident's significance become apparent.

---

* Malcolm predicted that the program he had scheduled for the Audubon Ballroom the following Sunday, February 21, would be one of his "last." He said it twice.

POLITICAL MARTYR 57

After the fire, Malcolm, Betty, and their four children moved into the home of Tom Wallace, who lived nearby. Wallace, whose sister was actress Ruby Dee, had followed Malcolm out of Temple Seven. As a result, he had been waylaid and beaten by some of those who had stayed.

Malcolm and Betty occupied the bedroom of one of Wallace's sons, who discovered under his bed a piece of luggage containing some cash. Malcolm told Tom, who may have been unaware of his penchant for reverse psychology, that he had to take the money to Switzerland for an unnamed friend. But he confided to James 67X that he had received financial help from abroad. Despite his denunciations of welfare, he was largely dependent upon others for sustenance.

Leaving his family at Wallace's, Malcolm reportedly moved to a hotel. But his family stayed at Tom's. He said he made the move to minimize the likelihood that his wife and children would be subjected to NOI retaliation. But it was rumored that a bitter argument had arisen between him and Betty after the fire.

Again and again, Malcolm reiterated that he expected to die prematurely, as his father had. "It will be all over soon," he told one associate. He told another that he had been informed that the NOI wanted him dead by February 26, the day the movement's Savior's Day Convention was scheduled to begin.

He said he did not fear death. But Gladys Towles Root and others sensed that, beneath his fearless exterior, he feared it as much as we all do. He asked Root how he could protect himself. And he began preparing his followers for a retraction of his allegation that the Nation of Islam had firebombed his home.

There were other indications that he did not accept the idea of an early death with equanimity; for instance, the way he had canceled his scheduled Chicago appearance the day after Mrs. Root had filed the paternity suits against Elijah Muhammad. And his fear of poison, as well as his extended African safaris, which he tacitly acknowledged were partly prompted by the need to put distance between himself and Elijah's henchmen.

He bridled at shadows. One night as he walked to his car, an automobile backfired and emitted a loud "bang." Malcolm froze. His companions tactfully ignored the look that registered on his face. Others noticed how jittery he became when strangers approached and how he kept looking back over his shoulder. He made it a practice never to sit with his back to the front door. He said it was a lesson he had learned from his confrontation with West Indian Archie.

To discourage further attempts to wire his car ignition with explosives, Malcolm secured the hood of his Oldsmobile with a lock and chain. He also obtained an application form for a pistol permit. There are conflicting reports as to whether he filled it out; it was virtually impossible for a New Yorker who had committed a felony to obtain a pistol permit.

But it had become apparent that the political Malcolm, like the youthful criminal Malcolm, was provoking the very retaliation he dreaded. A case in point was his disclosure of Elijah Muhammad's secret contacts with the Ku Klux Klan. The disclosure (which was reminiscent of the way James Eason had disclosed Marcus Garvey's contacts with the Klan) focused on a 1961 meeting Malcolm had held on the Messenger's behalf with representatives of the Klan. Since the K.K.K. opposed racial mixing, Elijah had requested the meeting to enlist its aid in obtaining land that the Nation of Islam could use to implement its separatist doctrines. The Imperial Wizard, the Klan's top leader, had reportedly instructed his subordinates to talk with Elijah's representatives in hope of eliciting information that could be turned over to the federal government.

At the meeting, which was held in Atlanta, Malcolm told the Klan officials what they wanted to hear. Both their movement and his, he asserted, needed to fight the Catholics and the Jews. He asserted that Jews were running the civil rights movement and manipulating its black members. According to an F.B.I. informant who reported the results of the meeting to the Bureau, Malcolm said he could not understand why the Klan allowed Martin Luther King, Jr. to live.

Malcolm also disclosed that Elijah Muhammad had invited American Nazi Party leader George Lincoln Rockwell, who advocated racial separation, to address the NOI's 1962 national convention, where he was booed before the audience could be induced to allow him to speak.

As a result of his disclosures about the Messenger, Malcolm's youthful premonitions about death had become self-fulfilling prophecies. "Surely man is the most ardent contributor to his own doom," he had written years earlier:

> . . . Man is actually the tool of his own destruction, . . . laboring towards the completion of his own end.

When a *New York Times* reporter asked him why he expected to be killed, he replied, "Because I'm me."

Malcolm acknowledged that he sometimes deliberately invited death. "It's a time for martyrs!" he told one writer. Though he often ridiculed the nonviolent black demonstrators who martyrized themselves in their efforts to secure their civil rights, he lauded famous martyrs such as Socrates and Gandhi, and likened himself to Jesus and Samson:

> I am ready to pull down the white man's temple, knowing full well that I will be destroyed by the falling rubble.

Malcolm, who said he had no desire to be mourned, characterized death as a refuge. He attributed the threats to his life to predestined forces that were entirely beyond his control. "There's no way out; there's nothing I can do," he told Oliver Sutton. He told Percy Sutton the apocryphal story of the caliph Omar, who saw the face of Death approaching. So Omar, the ascetic Muslim convert who had popularized Islam the way St. Paul had popularized Christianity, asked for the fastest horse in the kingdom. For three days, he drove the horse in an effort to outrace his deadly caller. Each evening, as he came to a fork in the road, he carefully chose his route in an effort to throw his pursuer off the track. At the end of the third day, he selected his route and rode on—right into the arms of Death. "Omar, Omar, where have you been?" asked Death, who told him he had been waiting.

Not everyone was fooled by Malcolm's fatalistic exterior. "He wanted to die," an associate later recalled. "Malcolm *wanted* to die!"

Despite his gun-slinging rhetoric, the adult, political Malcolm was no more a killer than the youthful, criminal Malcolm had been. When one of his men proposed killing Elijah Muhammad before Muhammad could kill him, Malcolm angrily told him he was losing his religion. When his companion persisted, Malcolm said, "If someone killed him, it would make a martyr out of him."

The day before the Sunday, February 21 rally that Malcolm had scheduled at the Audubon Ballroom, he checked into the New York Hilton and had supper in the hotel's dining room. By coincidence, Judge Wahl was also there. He was struck by Malcolm's confident demeanor, which was so different from the way he had behaved during the trial.

But that evening when he met his aides, there were tears in his eyes. They were not the only tears he had shed that week; during a meeting with Ella, who had agreed to help him purchase a home, tears streamed down his face. It was the first time that Ella had seen him cry since Aunt Sassie's death. "I looked at his eyes," she later recalled. "They seemed blue."

Around ten that evening, a man named Talmadge Hayer, who later testified that he had been offered an undisclosed sum of money to assassinate Malcolm, materialized in the Hilton lobby with two companions and began asking bellmen what room he was in.

Hayer, alias Thomas Hagan, had been a member of the Nation of Islam's Newark, New Jersey, temple for some time. (He had hawked *Muhammad Speaks* so aggressively at one poolroom that the proprietor had to summon the police.) On occasion, he had served as a member of Elijah Muhammad's honor guard. According to Norman Butler, Hayer was also a member of an NOI "hit squad" that commuted to New York City from New Jersey. He was reportedly a familiar figure to the Passaic and Paterson police. In 1963, he had been arrested for possessing a small arsenal of stolen guns. The weapons were found in his basement. Hayer subsequently claimed that the person who had offered him the money to kill Malcolm was not an NOI member. He also asserted that he never took any of the money, even though it had prompted him to stalk Malcolm. Later, he changed his story. He told Peter Goldman that he had always ached to be someone "big." It went without saying that it would take someone "big" to kill Malcolm.

The Hilton bellmen did not tell Hayer or his companions what room Malcolm was in. Instead, they promptly notified the hotel security force, which kept the three men under surveillance until they left of their own accord. The same evening, Hayer went to the Audubon Ballroom. Earlier, Temple Seven had hosted an affair of its own there. (The February 16 gathering had been billed as an "annual class closing." But it was an uncommon time of year for such an affair, and according to several former NOI members, Temple Seven did not hold class closings.*) One police informant reported that some of the participants had exhibited keen interest in the exits. Whether the gathering was a disguised dress rehearsal for an assassination attempt is unclear; Hayer later acknowledged that he had participated in an assassination rehearsal, but he would not say when or where.

---

* Unlike the classes the Chicago Temple taught at the "University of Islam," those taught at Temple Seven, which had no school affiliated with it, were informal.

The New York police department's "Bureau of Special Services" (BOSS) knew that an attempt to assassinate Malcolm was imminent. Police spokesmen later emphasized that officials had repeatedly offered him round-the-clock protection. At least three of the offers had been made in the presence of witnesses.

But the police knew that Malcolm would likely refuse the offers. He was frank about his reluctance to accept protection. A man who had made his reputation defying the authorities could hardly acknowledge that he needed their help. (He may have quietly sanctioned police protection for his family; the night Hayer was discovered at the Hilton, squad cars patrolled the street outside Tom Wallace's home.)

Pride also deterred Malcolm from requesting protection, says Charles 37X. He had to consider the impact of a request for police protection on his fearless image. He was apparently so afraid to appear afraid that, despite the death threats, he wouldn't even request protection from his own men, who had to urge it on him.

Moreover, Malcolm, who had had so many run-ins with the police, didn't trust them. (The officers assigned to protect him were probably reporting his activities to their superiors.) "The police know I'm going to be dead by Tuesday," he told a friend. He told another that he had been marked for death by February 21.

Malcolm said police protection wouldn't work:

> Nobody can protect you from a Muslim but a Muslim—or someone trained in Muslim tactics.

But the fact that the police could not guarantee his life was not a convincing reason for stopping them from trying.

Malcolm's refusal to request police protection did not excuse New York City's failure to provide it. When he visited Chicago and Philadelphia, policemen stayed with him wherever he went. Malcolm, who hadn't requested their presence, thanked his protectors, just as he did when his own men guarded him. It might have been costly for the New York police to provide the security he needed for weeks or months at a time. However, they could have done it. But even though BOSS officials knew that Malcolm's life was in grave jeopardy, the police department declined to act unless he formally accepted its offer of protection. His refusal to do so took the police "off the hook," one official later asserted cavalierly.

The rally Malcolm had scheduled for Sunday, February 21 was the last one before the Savior's Day Convention that the Nation of Islam had scheduled for the following weekend. That morning at seven o'clock, some of the Hilton's employees were questioned by an unidentified black man about the location of Malcolm's room. Precisely at eight o'clock, Malcolm's phone rang. A voice intoned, "Wake up, brother!" Then the unknown caller hung up.

Malcolm telephoned Ella and told her about the call. Later she told the *Afro-American*:

> Malcolm knew he was going to die . . . . When he spoke to me that morning, [he] was so sure this was it.

At nine o'clock, Malcolm phoned Betty and told her about the call. (He seemed to turn to her for support that week, just as he had turned to her after Elijah Muhammad had silenced him.) He asked her if she would accompany the children to the rally that afternoon. Betty was surprised; the day before, Malcolm had forbidden her to attend the meeting. She was later asked whether the abrupt turnabout suggested that her husband had had a premonition that something was about to happen. "I have no idea," she replied. "But it was a very warm conversation," she said with a sad laugh.

Malcolm seemed to need warmth that day. Despite the spring-like weather, he put on a pair of long johns and a vest beneath his dark-brown suit.

At about one o'clock, he checked out of the Hilton, fetched his Oldsmobile from the hotel garage, and drove uptown to Harlem. But he did not drive all the way to the Audubon Ballroom, which was at 166th Street and Broadway. Instead, he parked his car at 146th Street and stood at a bus stop for a bus that would take him the rest of the way. Whether he feared that someone was waiting near the ballroom to ambush him near his easily identifiable car is unclear. Benjamin Brown, the Black Muslim defector who had been shot because of his attempt to establish an "unauthorized" mosque in the Bronx, had been ambushed in his car.

An automobile bearing New Jersey tags abruptly pulled up to the bus stop. The driver waved Malcolm over. Malcolm peered anxiously at the young man. Then he glanced into the back seat and saw one of his own men, Charles Blackwell. He grinned and got in.

At around one-thirty, another of Malcolm's aides arrived at the Audubon and noticed that several people were already seated up front near the stage. She attributed no significance to it at the time; some people always came early to Malcolm's rallies in the hope of obtaining front-row seats. By the time the security detail was finally posted at the front door, several dozen people were already inside the auditorium. Hayer was evidently one of them. Another was Thomas 15X Johnson, according to witnesses who later testified in court. One witness said he informed Malcolm's "security chief," Reuben Francis, that Johnson was in the hall.

Francis, who had reportedly been hired a few days earlier, was also told that Johnson was in the auditorium by a follower of Malcolm's named Brother Jamil, who also spotted Norman Butler and reported his presence. Butler, whose criminal record included three arrests and one conviction, was already under indictment for shooting Benjamin Brown. So was Johnson, who, according to the police, had admitted firing the shot that had felled Brown. (The rifle that had been used to shoot Brown was later discovered in Johnson's home.) Johnson did not hide his hatred for Malcolm, who, he would later claim, deserved to die. (There are disputed reports that Malcolm had suspended Johnson and Butler from Temple Seven for carrying weapons.)

It is unclear whether Francis interrogated Butler and Johnson. The slack security, which evidently accounted for the ability of the NOI triggermen to proceed unchallenged, was not merely the result of poor organization or lax discipline; Malcolm had instructed his men not to search anyone. The no-search policy had been standard procedure for months; Malcolm said he wanted to avoid the kind of fear-ridden atmosphere that pervaded the Nation of Islam. He felt that the frisking frightened away potential followers.

He seemed determined to trust the people who came to hear him. "If I can't be safe among my own kind, where can I be?" he had once asked. When Francis said it would be prudent to start searching, he replied, "Rather than have you brothers harm any of Elijah Muhammad's followers, I'd rather die."

Malcolm, who had asserted that the Uncle Toms were the ones who defended others better than they defended themselves, also refused to authorize his men to carry guns. He was afraid they might precipitate an ugly, politically embarrassing incident, such as the confrontation six of his followers had nearly provoked with members of Temple Seven. He was also concerned about the fact that Elijah Muhammad's men were constantly "dropping dimes" on his supporters. "Dropping a dime" meant telephoning the police, who frequently stopped and frisked Malcolm's followers to see if they were violating the gun registration laws. Since many of his men ignored the laws, the ranks were slowly being decimated. Yet some brothers continued carrying weapons. Malcolm's silent acquiescence poignantly attested to the part of him that yearned to stay alive.

Due to the constraints that made it difficult for Malcolm to rely on the police for protection, he made it a practice at the Audubon to ask the police to position themselves outside it; his own men, he asserted, were protection enough inside. The police department always, or almost always, acquiesced, just as it did at indoor NOI rallies. Sometimes, it had several dozen men on hand; at other times, there were merely a handful. On this particular day, the uniformed contingent contained twenty men. One of Malcolm's aides told the officer in charge that Malcolm wanted most of them moved to a less conspicuous place. The officer obliged and withdrew all but three of the twenty to the Columbia Presbyterian Medical Center, part of which was located across the street. One uniformed patrolman, Thomas Hoy, was stationed outside the front entrance of the Audubon. Two more were discreetly posted in the Rose Room, which adjoined the auditorium where Malcolm was scheduled to speak. They had a walkie-talkie and orders to call for help if anything untoward occurred.

With the police confined to the outer perimeter, the defense of the meeting hall itself was left to Malcolm's forces. It was hardly effective. A man who was denied admittance loitered near the entrance for a moment, then walked right past the very guard who had barred him. An NOI lieutenant with a Fruit of Islam pin gleaming in his lapel entered the auditorium without being challenged at all. Someone finally spotted him and asked him to step to the rear, where a couple of brothers questioned him. He told them he had been getting disillusioned with the Nation of Islam and its teachings. They asked him to put his pin in his pocket and allowed him to return to his seat without searching him or assigning anyone to keep an eye on him. (In an apparent effort to encourage NOI defectors to join the OAAU, Malcolm had given instructions that members of the Nation could be admitted to his meetings if they were watched.) Despite his entreaties to America's blacks to defend themselves by any means necessary, the defense he erected that day at the Audubon was no better than the defense he had erected against the Massachusetts prosecutor who had sent him to prison for nearly seven years.

Malcolm arrived at the Audubon at around two. "I don't feel right about this meeting," he told his associate Earl Grant. " I feel that I should not be here. Something is wrong." Grant asked him to cancel the meeting or let someone else speak in his place. Malcolm said he'd think about it.

Wearily, he trudged down one aisle of the sixty-yard-long auditorium to an anteroom adjoining the stage. Usually his presence lit the place. But not that afternoon. He looked like an old man.

Neither Grant nor Benjamin Goodman had ever seen Malcolm so upset. He became even more overwrought when he learned that none of the guests he had invited to share the platform were going to show up. Some had offered convenient excuses. One didn't even bother to send an excuse. Malcolm became testier and testier as each no-show report arrived.

Since Betty and the children had not yet arrived, Malcolm asked Grant to call Tom Wallace's house to make sure they were on their way. Someone else had been phoning Tom's home. The caller, whose voice sounded like Wallace Muhammad's, left a message requesting Malcolm to return the call. If he was telephoning to warn Malcolm, he failed to convey the fact to Tom*, who took the message.

Malcolm kept jumping up from his anteroom seat, pacing the floor and staring out at the empty chairs on the stage. Sara Mitchell asked him if it would be all right for Goodman to introduce him. Malcolm whirled and upbraided her for asking in front of Goodman, whom he asked to make the opening address. Malcolm slouched in his seat, his head bent, staring at the floor. Sheikh Ahmed Hassoun, the elderly Sudanese scholar who had been loaned to Malcolm at Surrur Sabban's request, stepped over and touched his shoulder in an effort to comfort him. "Get out of here," Malcolm snarled. Goodman later reported that it was the only time he had ever seen him lose his self-control.

Hassoun left the anteroom along with Goodman, who walked onstage and began warming up the audience. "I ought not to go out there at all today," Malcolm said.

Onstage, Benjamin was winding up his introduction:

"I present to you . . . a man who would give his life for you . . . ."

The audience, which numbered several hundred, applauded vigorously. At the anteroom door, Malcolm turned and looked back at Sara Mitchell. "You'll have to forgive me for raising my voice to you," he said. "I'm just about at my wit's end." She told him she understood. Malcolm's voice sounded far away as he wanly smiled and replied, "I

---

* Wallace Muhammad later acknowledged he was concerned that people would hold him partly responsible for what happened that day at the Audubon. After he succeeded his father as titular leader of the Nation of Islam, he lamented, "I never got a chance to get a hearing before Malcolm X."

wonder if anybody really understands."

It took enormous courage for Malcolm to venture out onto that auditorium stage feeling the way he did. As he stood alone before the audience, the applause became a standing ovation, then subsided. He greeted his listeners, "As salaam alaikum." Enthusiastically, they responded, "Wa alaikum as salaam."

Suddenly, a disturbance occurred in the audience; it resembled the one that had taken place the evening of February 15. Two men who were later identified, correctly or otherwise, as Talmadge Hayer and Norman 3X Butler stood and began to argue. "Get your hand out of my pocket," one of them said. The guards who had been posted in front of the stage, near the speaker's rostrum, moved toward the two men, leaving Malcolm unprotected. As they did, a smoke bomb, a homemade device consisting of a lighter-fluid-soaked sock stuffed with matches and combustible film, was detonated. Once again, the audience's attention was diverted.

The shotgun was apparently hidden beneath the jacket of the Black Muslim gunman who was later identified, accurately or otherwise, as Thomas 15X Johnson.* The stock of the gun had been shortened and both barrels had been sawed down from thirty inches to eight and a half.

The first barrel was fired at near-point-blank range. Shotgun pellets perforated Malcolm's chest, forming a pattern seven inches high and seven inches across.

Malcolm's hand clutched his chest; blood appeared on his shirt. His lean frame stiffened as he toppled over backward into two of the empty guest chairs. His head struck the stage with a thud.

The man with the shotgun took no chances and fired the second barrel. Simultaneously, Hayer and another pistol-wielding gunman charged the stage and began emptying their guns into Malcolm's motionless body. Members of the shrieking audience threw themselves on the floor to avoid the fusillade.

The three assassins—Hayer later said there were more—tried to escape. One apparently ducked into the women's lounge, from which there were two exits to the street. Hayer and his pistol-packing partner sprinted toward the stairway leading to the main exit, hurdling chairs and firing wildly at the pursuing mob. His confederate was felled by a body block that sent him spinning down the staircase. Hayer was floored by a chair hurled by a man named Gene Roberts, whose suitcoat had been nicked

---

* In *The Death and Life of Malcolm X*, Peter Goldman initially concluded that Hayer's accomplices were Butler and Johnson. Later, he changed his mind. The identity of the triggermen is still hotly debated.

by one of Hayer's bullets. Hayer got up and began limping. Then Reuben Francis shot him in the thigh. Hayer fell face down, rolled over on his back, and tried to shoot back, but his gun failed to fire. Somehow, he regained his footing, made it to the doorway, and started downstairs—half-hopping, half-sliding down the banister. He vaulted over the gunman who had been knocked down the stairs. The latter melted into the pack, which clawed at Hayer, who dropped his .45. The howling mob finally caught him. It would have dispatched him then and there had he not been rescued by the policemen who had been summoned by one of the two officers in the Rose Room.

Meanwhile, in the auditorium, Gene Roberts rushed to the stage and tried to revive Malcolm with artificial respiration. He found it was no use; a nurse had already tried in vain. Malcolm's ruddy features had grown ashy. They were frozen in a ghastly smile. Like Patrice Lumumba, he had become a martyr before the age of forty. And he would never be forgotten. Never!

Malcolm X, leader of the American Black Muslim Sect.

VIII

EPILOGUE

AMERICA'S LUMUMBA   58

Hours after the assassination, John Ali, who had evidently arrived in New York two days earlier, checked out of his Manhattan hotel and flew back to Chicago. Hayer subsequently denied a report that he had met with Ali the night before Malcolm was killed. Similarly, Butler, who made no attempt to hide his enmity for Malcolm after he and Johnson were arrested for murdering Malcolm, denied having met that night with Ali and Captain Joseph, whose antipathy for Malcolm was common knowledge. (Earlier that week, Malcolm had told a Harlem audience that he had rescued "Fat Joseph" from a garbage can.) Yet, under cross examination, Butler did not deny that he had chatted with Joseph on Sunday morning, a few hours before Malcolm's death. "Captain Joseph is a popular man right now," snapped one of Malcolm's men. He said that Joseph had just been made "number one on the hit parade."

Joseph, who later assisted Butler's lawyers in their unsuccessful effort to keep Butler from being sentenced to prison for Malcolm's murder, was eventually promoted to the highest echelons of the NOI leadership. He said his men had nothing to do with Malcolm's death or with the violence that had been unleashed against such dissidents as Benjamin Brown. Elijah Muhammad, who claimed he was "deeply shocked" by Malcolm's death, also asserted that he and his followers were innocent. He said that Talmadge Hayer was not his follower. But, years later, Hayer acknowledged that he was. He described the assassination as an act of reprisal for Malcolm's attempts to discredit Muhammad. Christine Johnson, who had been dismissed from the "University of Islam" because she had been unable to hide her belief that the Holy Apostle had ordered Malcolm's death, was told that he had trouble sleeping after the assassination. He wrote in *Muhammad Speaks*:

When you are dead, you are dead. I have proof of that. Do you have proof that you will come back?

His anxiety called to mind a passage from one of Aesop's fables that Malcolm had been fond of:

Even when you are dead, you can get even with an enemy.

In *Muhammad Speaks*, one of Malcolm's former protégés claimed that it was "preposterous" to blame "the peace-loving and law-abiding Muslims" for his death. The writer—the same one who had prophesied, three weeks earlier, that the enemy was about to receive a lethal blow—asserted that he had tried to induce Malcolm to stop attacking the Messenger:

I went out of my way to give Brother Malcolm my personal assurance that, as long as he stopped his unduly bitter criticism of the "Nation of Islam" and . . . Elijah Muhammad, no harm would ever come to him.

He said his last attempt to dissuade Malcolm had occurred at a chance October 1964 meeting in New York, during which he had recited the following admonition:

When you have agreed to follow one man, then, if another man comes forward intending to [disrupt your plans], . . . kill him.

He said he did not mean to imply that the doctrine had been invoked against Malcolm. But his statements conflicted with the fact that the alleged New York meeting never took place; Malcolm was in Africa at the time. His assertions were also at variance with the preceding issue of *Muhammad Speaks*, which included a pronouncement of death for "the architect" of "evil" and for anyone else who vilified "Allah." The belated death sentence was portrayed as an edict from Elijah Muhammad himself; the words "DEATH" and "MESSAGE" were both capitalized.

Indeed, *Muhammad Speaks* seemed so eager to convince its readers that the NOI was responsible for Malcolm's death that when non-Muslim newspapers began ruminating about the possibility that Malcolm might have been killed by a black Leninist fringe group called the Revolutionary Action Movement, the NOI paper published a denial by RAM's leader that it had anything to do with the assassination.

Speculation that Malcolm had been done in by some other group was fueled by James Farmer, who called a news conference and said he didn't believe the Black Muslims were responsible for Malcolm's death. He intimated that Malcolm, whom he claimed had been "deeply involved" in fighting Harlem drug merchants, had been killed at the behest of drug dealers. When Farmer was asked about a rumor that Malcolm had been slain by "reds" who had allegedly infiltrated one or both of his tiny, loosely knit organizations, he noncommittally replied, "I would not say it is impossible." Years later, Farmer tacitly conceded that such theories were nonsense. He said that the reason he had denied that the NOI was to blame was to avert the outbreak of open warfare between Malcolm's followers and Elijah Muhammad's. (Temple Seven was gutted by fire-bombs a day and a half after Malcolm was killed; the NOI's San Francisco mosque was damaged by fire a few hours later).

The ease with which the assassins had entered the Audubon Ballroom and done their deadly work gave rise to speculation that one of Malcolm's aides had been a double agent who had been planted in Malcolm's camp by the NOI.* It also prompted allegations that the police, the FBI, or the CIA, separately or jointly, had participated in the plot. Proponents of this view cited the fact that only one policeman had been visible outside the Audubon and that none had been visible inside. That Malcolm wanted it that way was accorded little, if any, weight.

The police conspiracy theory, which took some of the heat off the brothers who had been assigned to protect Malcolm, gained further credence when the press published reports that one of the assassins had been spirited away by the New York police. At least two newspapers disclosed how Patrolman Hoy, the lone rookie policeman who had been stationed outside the Audubon's front entrance, had collared an assassin, wrested him from his pursuers, and placed him in a police car. Press reports also described how police sergeant Alvin Aronoff and his partner, Louis Angelos, had arrived at the Audubon just as the pursuing mob was spilling out of the building. Aronoff fired a warning shot into the air to halt the angry crowd. Then, with help from other officers, he shoved Hayer into his patrol car. Since Aronoff and Angelos were debriefed at the stationhouse while Hoy was interviewed by journalists at the Audubon, no one realized, at the time, that Aronoff, Angelos, and Hoy were all talking about the same man. By the time the mistake was detected, a number of newspapers had already published accounts suggesting that a second assassin had been arrested at the Audubon. Later editions conveyed the correct information, which was that only one man had been caught and arrested at the scene of the crime. But the failure of the press to explain the discrepancies between the various reports gave rise to suspicion that the power structure was protecting

* "Elijah seems to know every move I make," Malcolm had lamented.

the "second suspect."

Some people maintained afterward that Malcolm had been targeted for assassination by an FBI operation called COINTELPRO. Billed as a "counterintelligence" operation, COINTELPRO was really an effort to discredit and disrupt political groups that J. Edgar Hoover and his aides considered subversive. Begun in the 1950s, when anti-communist hysteria was rife, it had gradually been broadened to include "black nationalist hate groups"—a category that, Hoover claimed, included Martin Luther King's Southern Christian Leadership Conference. But COINTELPRO's clandestine campaign against black nationalists did not begin until two and a half years after Malcolm's death.

The police conspiracy theory gained additional currency with the subsequent disclosure that one of the men who had been assigned to help protect Malcolm at the Audubon, Gene Roberts, was an undercover BOSS agent. Those who contended that this was evidence of police complicity were unimpressed by the fact that Roberts had challenged Hayer's pistol with a wooden chair and had narrowly missed being wounded or killed. They also minimized the fact that Roberts had tried to revive Malcolm with artificial respiration. Roberts, who had apparently liked and admired Malcolm, later embarrassed some of his superiors by corroborating reports that the policemen who had leisurely sauntered into the Audubon after the shooting had taken their time getting Malcolm to the hospital.* But he did not accuse anyone in the Police Department of participating in the assassination. Evidently, he knew the difference between police indifference to Malcolm's death and police complicity in it.

But the assumption persisted in certain quarters that there had to be a white man behind the scenes calling the tune. Yet, when Elijah Muhammad was asked about Malcolm's assassination, he didn't convey that impression. He and his spokesmen did nothing to dispel the impression that the assassination, which had been perpetrated in broad

---

* The police were not the only ones to blame for the delay in getting Malcolm to the nearby hospital emergency room. Due to the mob that tried to jam into the elevator leading to the surgical emergency room, it took about five minutes to close the elevator door. By the time Malcolm was wheeled into surgery, he had no pulse or blood pressure. Since his heart had been shredded by bullets, attempts to revive him with cardiac massage proved fruitless. One of the physicians, V. R. Back, was struck by the irony of the fact that the skin of the white surgeons who were trying to revive Malcolm was virtually the same color as Malcolm's.

daylight in front of hundreds of witnesses, had been intended as an object lesson to Muhammad's followers—a grim warning of what happened to those like Malcolm, Benjamin Brown, Leon Ameer, Aubrey Barnette, and others who defied the Messenger or threatened his vital interests.

The grief in Harlem was nearly universal; the estimates of the number of mourners who silently filed into the Unity Funeral Home ranged from fourteen thousand to thirty thousand. There was a peaceful look on Malcolm's face as he lay in his glass-covered coffin.

For his Islamic burial, he was wrapped in seven white linen shrouds. One woman threw herself on the casket. Ossie Davis, the noted actor, film director, and screenwriter, delivered the eulogy:

> Here, at this final hour, in this quiet place, Harlem has come to bid farewell to one of its brightest hopes—extinguished now, and gone from us forever.

Cries of assent reverberated as Davis declared, "Malcolm was our manhood, our living black manhood . . . . our own black shining prince." Other commentators described him as America's Lumumba. In death, the encomiums he received far exceeded those he had received in life.

He died without life insurance. One source reported that he had been unable to obtain it. According to another, he had regarded life insurance as a racket, perhaps because one of his father's life insurance policies had proved worthless.

New Yorkers and others contributed generously to Malcolm's family, just as Lansingites had contributed to Earl Little's. In fact, Betty, who was pregnant again, received checks from all over the United States. "Buy milk for Malcolm's babies," one donor wrote. A Committee of Concerned Mothers, consisting of well-known figures such as Ruby Dee and Juanita Poitier, raised more than $12,500 for Betty and her children in less than three months. (The money was raised to permit Malcolm's homeless family to make a down payment on a house). Before six months had elapsed, the announced goal was raised to $40,000. To raise the amount, Mrs. Poitier reportedly opened the doors of her eighteen-room house to more than a thousand guests, each of whom paid ten to fifty dollars to be entertained by luminaries such as Dizzy Gillespie and Abbey Lincoln.

Other committees sprang up. One, which solicited money for the future education of Malcolm's daughters, was established by a number of the black Christian clergymen he had pilloried while he was alive.

Another, headed by an admirer who had resigned his position at *Muhammad Speaks* after Malcolm was murdered, established a memorial to him. In addition, Said Ramadan invited Betty to Switzerland and then accompanied her to Saudi Arabia, where she participated in the *hajj* and was reportedly received by a member of the Saudi royal family. The trip, she later told one journalist, proved to be an "excellent" remedy for her uncertainty about how she'd manage. So did Malcolm's autobiography, which was rushed into print. Partly because of his assassination, the book became a bestseller. In addition to the large number of hardcover copies that were sold, more than two and a quarter million paperback copies were eventually sold. As administrator of Malcolm's estate, Betty shared the royalties with Alex Haley. A similar arrangement governed the movie rights, which brought a substantial sum. Dead, Malcolm did far more financially for his wife and children than he had been able to do when he was alive.

Freed from Malcolm's control, Betty, who was catapulted to national prominence by his assassination, blossomed. Like Louise Little, she maintained that her deceased husband, to whom she had been married seven years, had been a good one. She returned to school, obtained a doctorate, and became a public figure in her own right. "I'm not just Malcolm's widow," she proudly told a reporter. During the interview, she alluded to men who misuse women. Such abuse, she said, is spawned by unhappy childhood relationships with mothers or sisters. The reporter, a woman, asked her:

> Do you mean you think that if women had raised their sons properly
> in the past, there would be no need for a women's lib movement
> today?

Betty—who stressed, in another interview, that we are all shaped by what happens to us during our early, formative years—replied that it was precisely what she meant.

The assassination also propelled Ella into the limelight; she told the press she would serve as "caretaker head" of the OAAU until a successor could be chosen. She said she would choose the organization's leaders and have veto power over its decisions. Then she asserted that she had assumed the leadership herself. "I will serve in my brother's place," she declared. She claimed that everyone had concurred and that Malcolm had appointed her his successor the day before his assassination. But she was a leader without a following.

In Detroit, Wilfred was visibly shaken when he was told that Malcolm had been killed. He told his congregation, "No sense in getting emotional about this . . . . Once you are dead, your troubles are over." "It's those [who are] living that are in trouble," he cryptically added.

The press tried breaking through the curtain of silence the Nation of Islam drew about Wilfred. When reporters were finally permitted to interview him, he told them, "My brother is dead and there is nothing we can do to bring him back." Instead of attending Malcolm's funeral, he attended the Nation of Islam's annual Savior's Day Convention. According to a news report that was later disputed by a spokesman for the Littles, Ella was the only one of Malcolm's brothers and sisters who attended the funeral.

The convention was held in Chicago the same weekend the funeral was held in New York. Few, if any, of the NOI delegates came smiling. Nearly all of them were unusually quiet. During the opening day of the three-day conclave, which included demonstrations in the arts of strangling and stabbing one's opponents, Wallace Muhammad recanted his apostasy and pledged his fidelity to his father, whom he later succeeded as head of the movement.*

Wilfred came to the podium—reluctantly, if his subsequent resignation from the movement was any indication. He praised Elijah Muhammad for transforming Malcolm from a small-time, petty criminal into a prominent Muslim clergyman:

> In a short time, you saw a man who was no good become recognized nationally and internationally . . . , but he chose to go off on a reckless path. The recklessness of his path no doubt brought about his early death.

Philbert, whose wife and children, like Wilfred's, may have been dependent on what he received from the Nation's treasury, came to the microphone and denounced Malcolm for deviating from the party line. He described how he had vainly tried to dissuade him from provoking the Messenger. "No man," he said, "wants to see his own brother destroyed." He echoed Wilfred's feeling that, now that Malcolm was dead, there was nothing he could do. Later, back in Lansing, friends sensed his reluctance to talk about his brother's murder.

Elijah Muhammad addressed the rank-and-file from behind a wall of grim-looking guards who shielded his entire body except his head. The

---

* Malcolm's defiant example had given Wallace and other dissidents the courage to stand up to Elijah Muhammad and his henchmen. Now that he was dead, there was no one to inspire them.

ghost of Malcolm, who had defended his embattled followers better than he had defended himself, seemed to permeate the air. Elijah recalled earlier, happier days:

> In those days Malcolm was safe.

Even after he left the movement, he was given freedom, Muhammad asserted. "He went everywhere—Asia, Europe, Africa, even to Mecca— trying to make enemies for me."

> He criticized . . . he criticized . . . he criticized . . . .

"He turned his back on the man who taught him all he knew."

> He tried to make war against me.

The Messenger said that Malcolm had provoked his own death. Yet he kept denying that the Nation of Islam had been responsible for it. "We didn't want to kill Malcolm," he breathlessly contended. "And we didn't try to." His voice began growing strident; he started to cough violently. He warned:

> I am not going to let crackpots destroy the good things Allah sent to you and me.

Two days later, he told his assembled followers, "No man will be successful in opposing me."

No More Fear 59

Two weeks after Malcolm was assassinated, an event occurred that civil rights strategists had long been waiting for. The sky was gray and hazy as more than five hundred marchers set out from Selma, Alabama for Montgomery to petition Governor George Wallace to eliminate the procedural roadblocks that made it nearly impossible for the state's blacks to register to vote. As the column, accompanied by four ambulances, neared the Edmund Pettus Bridge, which spans the muddy Alabama River, it passed a large number of Sheriff Jim Clark's possemen, who stood lounging in the shadows.

Heading the column were SCLC's Hosea Williams and SNCC's John Lewis. As they came to the crest at the midpoint of the bridge, they saw the blue-helmeted state troopers standing shoulder to shoulder, blocking the entire width of the roadway. The troopers were massed several lines deep. Gas masks hung from their waists.

Behind the troopers, whose billy clubs were held ready, were several dozen more possemen, some of whom were on horseback. The marching column fell silent as it advanced toward the state policemen, who donned their protective masks. Their commander, Major Cloud, brusquely ordered the marchers to halt and disperse within two minutes. When Hosea Williams asked to speak with Cloud, who was already counting, he tersely replied, "There is no word to be had."

In vain, Williams repeated the request twice. Then, after about one of the two minutes had elapsed, Cloud barked, "Troopers, advance!"

Forming a wedge, the lawmen charged into the peaceful demonstrators. As the column dissolved in panic, the troopers began pursuing the fleeing marchers, flailing their clubs. Some of the marchers—those who could run fast—made it to safety. The older people didn't have a chance; one after another was clubbed to the pavement. As they screamed in pain, a cheer went up from the whites who were watching from the sidelines. "Get the SOB's!" "Kill them!" Their faces were distorted with hatred.

The troopers fell back, reformed their lines, grabbed their tear gas cannisters, and flipped off the safety rings. Meanwhile, some of the marchers who had eluded them began circling back to retrieve their fallen comrades, many of whom were unconscious. A number of those who were still conscious knelt to pray. They were still kneeling when the policemen struck again. Clouds of tear gas enveloped half of the bridge as the troopers charged right over their vomiting, helpless victims.

Yet the violence had only begun. Urged on by Sheriff Clark (who shouted, "Get those goddam niggers!"), the mounted possemen, armed with bullwhips and lengths of rubber tubing wrapped in barbed wire, rode into the melee with shrill "reb" yells. The blacks who attempted to flee were met, from the Selma side of the bridge, by the club-wielding possemen who had been waiting in the shadows. The carnage that ensued that "Bloody Sunday" was viewed on television by millions of Americans, many of whom were outraged still further by the beating and subsequent death of an out-of-town, thirty-eight year old clergyman named James Reeb.

The resulting torrent of indignation was soon translated into the congressional votes that made possible the 1965 Voting Rights Act, which broke the political back of Jim Crow.

There is nothing to suggest that Malcolm would have marched on Bloody Sunday had he lived. Yet, though he stayed aloof from the civil rights struggle, he was instrumental in fashioning the political climate that helped ensure its success. If his own fledgling organizations (which quickly withered after his death) were unsuccessful, he was still the foremost black American militant of the entire era—the spiritual progenitor of the militance that swept the black community during the 1960's.

Had Malcolm lived, he might have been New York City's first black mayor. Eventually, he might even have run for President, as Ella wanted him to do. Or perhaps he would have transformed his budding Organization of Afro-American Unity into an updated, mid-twentieth century version of Marcus Garvey's movement—one that might have effectively internationalized the struggle for black freedom.

But even if he hadn't, his place in history would have been assured. He made African-Americans feel proud of their color. In his effort to fashion a remedy for his self-hatred, he fashioned one for them.

Were it not for Malcolm, Islam never would have become a potent force in black America. What his future contributions would have been had he lived longer is anybody's guess. If prior behavior is any indication, he may have been preparing himself for some new, competitive political venture, just as he had diligently prepared himself for competition in the boxing ring, the dance hall, and the lecture hall. Eventually, I think he would have overcome his lack of political direction and whatever fear of failure hindered him from committing himself to a course of action that would have enabled him to re-utilize his enormous leadership potential. His ability to conquer his fear was part of his uniqueness, as was his talent for overcoming youthful handicaps that would have overwhelmed a man of lesser intelligence and determination. Malcolm's greatness was not his ego-boosting attempt to counteract white ethnocentrism with black ethnocentrism, but his enormous capacity for intellectual, moral, and political growth—the kind that made possible the transformation of the pseudo-masculine criminal Malcolm into the manly political Malcolm.

Another aspect of Malcolm's greatness was his extraordinary ability to transform youthful weakness into adult strength: the strength to practice the morality his father and Elijah Muhammad—both of whom Malcolm eclipsed—had merely preached; the strength to question his own beliefs; the strength to free himself of his financial and emotional dependence on Elijah and his herd-like movement. And the strength to confront death head-on.

Malcolm X fathered no legislation. He engineered no stunning Supreme Court victories or political campaigns. He scored no major electoral triumphs. Yet, because of the way he articulated his followers' grievances and anger, the impact he had upon the body politic was enormous. He mobilized black America's dormant rage and put it to work politically. He made clear the price that white America would have to pay if it did not accede to black America's legitimate demands. By transforming black fear into white fear, he irrevocably altered America's political landscape. His ability to conquer his fear—and to inspire his followers to conquer theirs—suited him uniquely to this vital historical task.

IX

NOTES AND BIBLIOGRAPHY

INTRODUCTION TO THE NOTES

I have inserted in the notes material that I could not fit into the narrative without transforming it into a tedious debate with other published works. The version of Malcolm's autobiography that I have referred to in the notes is the Grove Press paperback edition. Wherever possible, I have cited the edition of the newspaper in which a particular article appeared. (The *Afro-American* was published in different cities, and I could not always ascertain, from its archives, which editions contained a given article.)

Since the F.B.I. deleted the file and serial numbers from the F.B.I. records it sent me in 1978, I have cited the relevant documents by date and page number.*

In most cases, I have relied on the published transcripts of the tape-recordings of Malcolm's speeches. But wherever I have detected discrepancies between the transcript and the tape-recorded (or filmed) version, I have relied on the latter. Some tape-recordings have been copied so many times and have passed through so many hands that they have apparently been misdated or mislabeled in the process.

Due to the current state of U.S. copyright law, I have had to delete substantial amounts of material from certain chapters. Much of that material came from letters that Malcolm wrote from prison. Should the law change, some deleted material may be reinserted in subsequent editions of the book.

A number of my sources agreed to furnish information only if I guaranteed them confidentiality. I have therefore done so. The identity of each confidential source will be placed under seal in Harvard University's Houghton Library, and will be made available to scholars as soon as it is legally feasible.

---

* When the FBI later reprocessed its files on Malcolm during the 1980's, it restored the deletions.

ABBREVIATIONS USED IN THE NOTES

BAMN: George Breitman (editor), *By Any Means Necessary* (Pathfinder Press, 1970).

BMIA: C. Eric Lincoln, *The Black Muslims in America* (Beacon Press paperback, 1961).

BP: Bruce Perry (editor), *Malcolm X: The Last Speeches* (Pathfinder Press, 1989).

EOEM: Cook County (Illinois) Circuit Court, Probate Division. Probate File #75-P-4128, entitled "Estate of Elijah Muhammad."

EPPS: Archie Epps (editor), *The Speeches of Malcolm X at Harvard* (Morrow, 1968).

EWWS: Benjamin Goodman (editor), *The End of White World Supremacy* (Merlin House, 1971).

FBI: Federal Bureau of Investigation files on Malcolm X. (This abbreviation will not be used for FBI files on the Nation of Islam or Elijah Muhammad.)

FDL: Hakim A. Jamal, *From the Dead Level: Malcolm X and Me* (Warner paperback, 1973).

FR or 1965 Fire Department Report: Unpublished New York City Fire Department records of the February, 1965 fire that severely damaged Malcolm's home.

JHC: John Henrik Clarke (editor.), *Malcolm X: The Man and His Times* (Collier Books, 1969).

LYMX: George Brietman, *The Last Year of Malcolm X* (Schocken Books, 1968).

MX: *The Autobiography of Malcolm X* (Grove Press paperback, 1965). The autobiography, which was published after Malcolm's death, was written by Alex Haley.

NYT: *New York Times.*

PG: Peter Goldman, *The Death and Life of Malcolm X* (Harper & Row, 1973).

PR: Malcolm's Prison Record.

SPKS: George Breitman (editor), *Malcolm X Speaks* (Grove Press, 1965).

TKBM: Louis E. Lomax, *To Kill a Black Man* (Holloway House, 1968).

WWG: Louis Lomax, *When the Word Is Given . . .* (Signet Books, New American Library, 1963).

NOTES

Introductory Quotations

ii "TO UNDERSTAND. . . ANY PERSON, HIS WHOLE LIFE, FROM BIRTH, MUST BE REVIEWED": *MX*, p. 150.
"I WAS BORN IN TROUBLE": SPKS, p. 135.

1. Parental Demands

2 THE SEVENTH CHILD IS SPECIAL: "Seven has always been my favorite number," Malcolm tells us in his autobiography. According to him, the number seven was endowed with special qualities. (Letter dated Mar. 13, 1978 from confidential source to author; *MX*, p. 307.) So, his father maintained, was the seventh-born child. (Interviews: Ella Little, Mozelle Jackson, Mary Little, J. C. Little. [See also *MX*, p. 2, *NYT*, Mar. 16, 1965, p. 33.]) The idea that the seventh child is specially endowed appears frequently in African-American folklore as well as the folklore of other cultures, past and present. Sometimes, the idea is expressed in terms of the seventh male child; other times, it expressly includes any seventh-born child, male or female. See, for instance: Newbell Niles Puckett, *Folk Beliefs of the Southern Negro* (Negro Universities Press, 1969 reprint of original Dover Publications edition), pp. 138, 337. Richard M. Dorson, *Negro Folktales in Michigan* (Howard University Press, 1956), p. 113. E. & M. A. Radford, *Encyclopedia of Superstitions*, revised edition (Hutchinson of London, 1969), pp. 301-302. Maria Leach, ed., *Standard Dictionary of Folklore, Mythology, and Legend*, Vol. 2 (Funk & Wagnalls, 1950) p. 999. *The Philadelphia Inquirer*, Feb. 19, 1984, p. 13-I, column 6. *Popular Beliefs and Superstitions: A Compendium of American Folklore* (G. K. Hall & Co., 1981), pp. 49, 77, 78, 152, 276, 321, 1048, 1050, et al. The historical antecedents of these folk beliefs are discussed in *The Interpreter's Dictionary of the Bible* (Abingdon Press, 1962), Vol. 4, pp. 294-295. See also pp. 354-356 of the latter's Supplementary Volume, which describes how Old Testament genealogies were sometimes rewritten to make it appear as if the worthiest descendant of a given biblical figure had been the seventh descendant.

EARL'S TELEGRAM: Interview: Ella Little.

PHYSICAL SIMILARITY: Interviews: Mary Little, Ella Little, Clara Little, Mozelle Jackson.

EYE COLOR: Interviews: Yvonne Little, Ella Little, Mary Little, Philbert Little, Mozelle Jackson, John Breathour, John ("Buster") Doane, Geraldine Nelson, Al Lewis. See discussion of Malcolm's eye color that follows later in this chapter and the notes to this chapter. Please see the pertinent material in subsequent chapters.

HAIR COLOR: One of Malcolm's Lansing barbers, Roy Johnson, describes Malcolm's hair as "dark sandy," tinged with red. Some observers have stressed the blonde component; others have stressed the reddish component. (Interviews: Ella Little, Mary Allen, John Breathour, Katherine Gillion, Johnny Jones, Bobby Pointer, Clifford Walcott.) Malcolm himself deemphasized the blonde component, perhaps for political reasons. (*MX*, pp. 2, 104.)

GRANDPARENTS APPALLED ABOUT "ALBINO": Interview: Ella Little. Also interviews with Mary and Clara Little. "He looked almost like an albino," says Harold Hyman -- so much so that, when he was young, some of his brothers and sisters nicknamed him "Albino." (Interview: Philbert Little.)

LOUISA'S MOTHER DIES; HER CHILDREN ILLEGITIMATE: Interviews: Olive Orgias, Daphne Orgias, Margaret Williams, Louise Little. "I never knew my mother or father," Mrs. Little stated.

MARY JANE AND GERTRUDE RAISE LOUISA: Interviews: Malcolm Orgias, Hamburg E. D. Wells, Olive Orgias, Margaret Williams.

CHILDREARING METHODS: Interviews: Hamburg E. D. Wells, Olive Orgias, Daphne Orgias.

INDIFFERENT AND OFTEN ABSENT: Interview: Malcolm Orgias.

LOUISA BEATS YOUNGER CHILDREN: Interviews: Olive and Malcolm Orgias.

3 ECONOMIC LIABILITY: Interviews: Margaret Williams, Olive Orgias, Daphne Orgias.

LOUISA SENT AWAY; EMPTINESS AND LONELINESS; EMIGRATES: Interview: Louise Little. See also May 4, 1918 letter from Louise's uncle Edgerton to her uncle Joseph Orgias.

EARL MET AND MARRIED LOUISE IN MONTREAL, NOT PHILADELPHIA: Certificate of marriage, Montreal, May 10, 1919. May 6, 1946 letter from Medical Superintendent, Kalamazoo State Hospital to Charlestown State Prison. Interview: Mozelle Jackson.

EARLY LITTLE: Certificate of marriage between Early Little and Louise Norton, Montreal, May 10, 1919. Birth certificates of Malcolm & Hilda Little. CIA report dated 4/30/64. FBI report dated 11/17/59, p. 31. Interviews: Philbert Little, Malcolm Orgias. See also MX, p. 9.

HAIR: Interviews: Louise Little, Wilfred Little, Philbert Little, Yvonne Little, Reginald Little, Rose Little, Erwin Frederick Hoffman, M.D., Enos Major, Sr., Mr. & Mrs. Marvon Worthy, Allie Cooper, Bessie Springer, Tom Amiss.

MISTAKEN FOR WHITE: MX, p. 2. Interviews: Wilfred Little, Enos Major, Sr., Yvonne Little, Louise Little, Anna Stohrer. Stohrer recalls that Earl asked her, one day, "Mrs. Stohrer, do you know how we got this house right here among all these white people?" He proceeded to explain that when he had attempted to purchase it from its white owner, she had refused him because he was black. So he sent Louise. The owner didn't know that Louise was his wife. Nor did the owner realize that she was part-"colored." So she sold Louise the house, to the subsequent consternation of certain white neighbors.

BLUE EYES: Interviews: Louise Little, Mrs. Lloyd Hackenberg.

WALKED OUT: Interviews: Mary Little, John H. Johnson.

WIDOWER: Certificate of marriage, Montreal, May 10, 1919.

SHORTLY AFTER: Interviews: Mary Little, Philbert Little.

EDUCATIONAL GAP; PRETENSIONS; CONFLICT: MX, pp. 4, 7, 9. Interviews: Reginald Little, Hamburg E. D. Wells, Louise Little. May 6, 1946 letter from Medical Superintendent of Kalamazoo State Hospital to Charlestown State Prison.

ELECTED PRESIDENT; LOUISA JOINS: Ted Vincent, "The Garveyite Parents of Malcolm X," The Black Scholar (March/April, 1989), pp. 10-13. MX, p. 4.

4 INCIDENT NEVER OCCURRED: Interview: Louise Little. In a subsequent interview, Mrs. Little again denied that the alleged siege ever took place. Moreover, the account that Malcolm gave of the alleged incident in one published interview differs substantially from the account that appears in his autobiography. [MX, p. 1. Interview with Malcolm X in Kenneth B. Clark (ed.), The Negro Protest (Beacon Press, 1963), p. 19.]

ROSE LITTLE'S TESTIMONY: Interview: Rose Little. See starred footnote in text.

EARL AND WRIGHT LITTLE CONVICTED: Minute Book J, p. 198, Taylor County (Georgia) Superior Court docket records (October Term, 1915). According to one member of Earl's mother's family, "something traumatic" happened to Earl around this time -- so traumatic that he left Georgia for good. (Interview: Homer Gray.)

PROMINENT ROLE IN UNIA: The Negro World, May 7, 1927. Ted Vincent, "The Garveyite Parents of Malcolm X," The Black Scholar (March/April, 1989), pp. 10-13.

According to Reginald's birth certificate, he was born in Milwaukee on August 23, 1927.

TO ALBION; JIM LITTLE AND MOONSHINE: Interview: Philbert Little.

"CHINK": Interview: Philbert Little.

MADE FUN: Interview: Ella Little.

EYE COLOR: (Please see additional note on eye color, supra.) Former associates describe Malcolm's eyes as "funny-colored" or "odd-colored." (Interviews: Harold Hyman, Bob High.) "He didn't have colored people's eyes," says Maxine Kitchen. According to Eulalia Walker, "His eyes were the most noticeable part of his face. If they had been in a white face, maybe they wouldn't have looked so light. I remember looking at them because you don't usually see a black person with eyes like that." (Interviews: Maxine Kitchen; Eulalia Walker.) Still another observer, a white man who had ample opportunity to see Malcolm up close, recounts, "I remember him well. He was very light complected, with red hair and blue eyes. No -- I couldn't be right; blacks don't have blue eyes!" (Interview: Stephen Slack.) A number of African-Americans whom I interviewed evidently felt the same way and became evasive or irate at the suggestion that Malcolm's eyes were not brown.

The chief the difficulty in pinpointing the precise color of Malcolm's eyes at any given moment in time is due to the fact that the color of his eyes appeared to change, not only over time but also as the color of the surrounding light changed. (Interviews: Philbert Little, Yvonne Little, Attallah Little, Katherine Gillion, Geraldine Nelson, Jim Reed.) According to his sister Yvonne and half-sister Ella, his eyes were blue, at least when he was young. According to others, they were "kind of bluish" or light grayish-blue. (Interviews: Mary Little, Mozelle Jackson, Philbert Little, John Breathour.) Still others describe Malcolm's eyes as blue-green or green or greenish-gray or greenish blue-gray. (PG, p. 6. Interviews: Al Lewis, Eulalia Walker, Tom Wallace, Kenneth Collins, J. C. Little, John ("Buster") Doane.) Some say they were as "kind of gray" or hazel or hazel-brown, or a combination thereof. (Interviews: Ted Davenport, Billy Rose, Wilfred Little, Charlice Doane.) A number of law enforcement officials who kept tabs on Malcolm felt that his eyes were brown. (PR, report dated Feb. 28, 1946. FBI reports dated 3/18/53 and 7/29/59.) The Detroit Police characterized his eyes as "maroon." In the color photographs that are currently available, the eye color of the adult Malcolm ranges from brown to sort of a light bluish-gray, depending upon the color of the incident light. Similar color changes occurred not only in his mother's eyes but also in those of several paternal relatives, some of whom had blue eyes, at least initially. (Interviews: Clara Little, J. C. Little, Ella Little, Louise Little.)

"FREAK OF NATURE": Interview: Yvonne Little.

HATED WHITES: Interview: Betty Walker.

WHITES HAD DIFFERENT IMPRESSION: Interviews: Maxine Kitchen, Mrs. Samuel Woolcock, Mr. & Mrs. Marvon Worthy, Homer Gray. Ironically, the interviewees who had good things to say about Earl Little were white people. Nearly all the black interviewees disapproved of him.

GAVE WHITES PRODUCE: Interview: Pearl Reist.

SHUNNED BLACKS: Interviews: George Ross, Richard Jenkins. See also PR, preliminary record form, which suggests, inter alia, that Mr. Little purposely avoided living in black neighborhoods.

PARADED LIGHT-SKINNED MALCOLM: Interview: Philbert Little.

4 TOOK ONLY MALCOLM TO GARVEYITE GATHERINGS: MX, pp. 4, 6.

FAVORED LIGHT-SKINNED RELATIVES: Interview: Ella Little.

NOT AFRICAN-AMERICAN: Interview: Anna Stohrer.

WHITE "PRINCE": Interview: Clarence Seaton. Mrs. Little repeatedly asserted that she was of royal blood. (Petition for Admission -- Mentally Diseased [in] Ingham County Probate file #B-4398, entitled "Louise Little -- Insane"; interview: Betty Walker.) The fantasy that one is descended from royalty is frequently characteristic of children who have lost, or never known, their parents. (Edmund S. Conklin, "The Foster Child Fantasy," American Journal of Psychology, Vol. 31 [1920], p. 59.)

TRIED TO UNCURL HAIR: Interview: Anna Stohrer.

BOASTS ABOUT WHITE FRIENDS: Interviews: Anna Stohrer, William Stohrer.

"I CAN MAKE HIM LOOK ALMOST WHITE"; LOUISE FELT MALCOLM SUPERIOR BECAUSE OF LIGHT COMPLEXION: Interview: Anna Stohrer. Margaret Williams says that when Louise was young, she frquently acted superior to her darker-skinned Grenadian friends. And Ella has indicated that Louise favored her lighter children. (Interviews: Margaret Williams, Ella Little.)

BUT MALCOLM THOUGHT SHE FAVORED THE DARKER CHILDREN: MX, pp. 7-8.

Philbert, who apparently failed to perceive his mother's ambivalence about skin color, says his mother was more pro-black than his father had been.

2. Home Life

6 EARL'S BRUTALITY: *MX*, p. 4. Interviews: Philbert Little, Clara Little, Art Jones, Clifford Green. Margaret Lisco, a friend of the Littles, confirms that Earl was mean.

LOUISE FEARED EARL: Interviews: Allie Cooper, Charlice Doane, Betty Walker, Philbert Little.

OTHER PEOPLES' CHILDREN FEARED EARL: Interviews: Betty Jean Thiel, Betty Walker. Betty's father, Herb Walker, told her that Earl was full of "unnatural" hate.

ATTRIBUTED FAVORITISM TO LIGHT SKIN COLOR: *MX*, p. 4.

IRON HAND: *PR*: March 8, 1946 interview by Pete Donahue. Interviews: S. DeWitt Rathbun, Philbert Little, Charlice Doane, Watoga Doane, Katherine Gillion, Malcolm Orgias.

WITHOUT VISIBLE EVIDENCE OF AFFECTION: Allie Cooper, John ("Buster") Doane, Ray Bebee, Clarence Seaton, Bethel Seaton, Jean Seaton.

WHIPPED BY MOTHER: *MX*, p. 7. Interviews: Philbert Little, Wilfred Little, Louise Little, Malcolm Orgias.

VERBAL PROTESTS: *MX*, pp. 7-8, 15.

RESISTS BEING BATHED: Interviews: Philbert Little, Louise Little.

RESISTS BEING SENT OUTDOORS TO ACQUIRE A SUNTAN: Interview: Louise Little. *MX*, p. 8.

STAYED IN ANOTHER PART OF THE HOUSE: Interview: Louise Little.

SURLY: Interviews: Tom Amiss, Anna Stohrer, Katie Darling.

WOULDN'T SPEAK TO MOTHER: Interviews: Anna Stohrer, Louise Little.

"ALL WITCHY": Interview: Louise Little.

"I COULD KILL YOU": Interview: Rose Little.

7 FAVORITISM BRED RESENTMENT: Interviews: Reginald Little, Ella Little. According to Ella, the other children attributed the favoritism to Malcolm's light skin color. They apparently knew nothing about the significance of the fact that Malcolm was Earl Little's seventh child. Mr. Little reportedly wrote and told his father that the favoritism was causing resentment. His father reportedly wrote back and said that Malcolm had to fulfill his destiny.

RESENTS BROTHERS: *MX*, pp. 7-8. And see, on p. 19, how Malcolm compares his brothers with "Big Boy." Interviews: Arlington Cooper, Philbert Little, Wilfred Little. *Muhammad Speaks*, Sept. 25, 1964.

RIVALRY WITH PHILBERT: August 16, 1939 letter from social worker Maynard Allyn to Ingham County Probate Judge John McClellan. Interviews: Byron Delamarter, Tom Amiss, Sam Clay, Maxine Kitchen, Betty Walker, Bethel Seaton, Arlington Cooper, Philbert Little. *MX*, pp. 11, 17.

DARKEST BOY: Interviews: Stan Levandowski, Charlice Doane, Reginald Little, Louise Little, Clara Little, Hayward Howard, Yvonne Little, Chuck Lyons, Katie Darling, Maxine Kitchen, Ray Bebee, Bob Bebee, Philbert Little. Young Philbert cried when he was told that he was so dark that he could "swim up a tar river and leave a black path."

"MILKY": Interviews: Geraldine Grill, Robert Higdon, Harvey ("Junior") Miller, Frances Walter, Philbert Little.

MOTHER'S FAVORITE: Interview: Philbert Little.

PHILBERT DETERMINED: Interview: Philbert Little.

LOSES TOOTH; "TOOTHLESS BLONDIE": *PR*: Medical report dated Feb. 28, 1946. *Yale News*, Oct. 21, 1960. Interviews: Yvonne Little, Philbert Little, Norman Lyons, Frances Lone, John Doane, Esther Abrams, Marjorie Morrow.

DENIES NEGATIVE FEELINGS: *MX*, p. 19, particularly Malcolm's claim that "there was a feeling of brotherly union" between himself and Philbert, and that he "had nothing either against the babies, Yvonne, Wesley, and Robert". But Malcolm contradicts himself elsewhere on the same page where he says, "It was better, in a lot of ways, [living] at the Gohannas'

[home]. Big Boy and I shared his room together, and we hit it off nicely. He just wasn't the same as my blood brothers."

"VERY CLOSE": *MX*, p. 22. Also p. ll. Many years afterwards, when Philbert publicly castigated Malcolm at Elijah Muhammad's behest, Malcolm responded, inter alia, with the assertion that he and Philbert had been "good friends all our lives." (*New York Herald Tribune*, March 28, 1964.)

CLOSEST TO REGINALD: *MX*: pp. 11, 157. Interview with Leon Moffett, who was friendly with both Malcolm and Reginald.

IN REALITY, NOT CLOSE TO REGINALD: Interview: Reginald Little.

RELATIONSHIP WITH REGINALD: *MX*, pp.11-12.

"JACKLEG": It was common knowledge, in Lansing's African-American community, that Earl was a self-ordained preacher. See also Earl Little, Jr.'s description of his father in *PR*: July, 1930 Concord Reformatory report of conversation with Earl Junior.

"SO MANY RULES": *MX*, p. 4.

"FAILED TO OBSERVE": Interviews: Rose Little, Arthur Jones, Anna Stohrer, Mrs. Van D. Walker, Allie Cooper.

8 "NATURAL BORN WHOREMONGER": Interview: Arthur Jones (quoting his father Chester).

WORKS SPORADICALLY AND DOESN'T SUPPORT FAMILY: *PR*: July, 1930 Concord Reformatory report of conversation with Earl Little, Junior. Interviews: Rose Little, Allie Cooper, Bessie Springer, Anna Stohrer, Ray Riddle, Fred Green, Richard Jenkins, S. DeWitt Rathbun. Rathbun recalls how hard it was for him to get Louise to acknowledge that Earl didn't support his children. (But in a December 14, 1926 letter, she did tell Aunt Gertie that she was having difficulty raising her youngsters.)

ARISES LATE: Interview: William Stohrer.

CHILDREN GO HUNGRY WHILE EARL DINES: Interview: Anna Stohrer.

CHILDREN VIE FOR THE LEAVINGS: Interview: Philbert Little.

EARL RESENTS CHARITY: Interview: Allie Cooper.

EARL'S ASPIRATIONS: Interview: Allie Cooper.

TELLS CHILDREN TO MAKE SOMETHING OF THEMSELVES: Interview: Wilfred Little.

DRESS STORE: Interview: Mrs. Van D. Walker.

BUSINESSMAN: Interview: Charlice Doane. (Years later, during a discussion about the difficulty African-Americans have obtaining jobs, Mr. Little's daughter Ella talked about unemployed people who walk the streets carrying empty briefcases.)

EMPLOYMENT AGENCY: Interviews: Mrs. Van D. Walker, John Tyler. The woman who owned the house in which Earl had established his agency told Mrs. Walker, "I'm mad at the way he sends people around to work when there aren't any jobs."

UNABLE TO SECURE FINANCING: Interview: Allie Cooper.

"MONEY'S NO PROBLEM": Interview: Mrs. Van D. Walker.

9 RESTRICTIVE DEED: Deed #324-57, dated March 2, 1928. Recorded March 5, 1928 in Ingham County Courthouse.

EVICTED FROM HOME: Capital View Land Co. and James W. Nicoll, plaintiffs, vs. Earl Little, Louise Little, and Cora I. Way, defendants; Ingham County Circuit Court, Chancery Docket #14215, 1929.

SHOOK FIST: According to Wilfred, Earl had mixed feelings about religion. On occasion, he would even argue against it, or at least certain aspects of it. (Interview: Allie Cooper.)

WARNED NOT TO SLEEP UPSTAIRS: Interview: Philbert Little.

THE 1929 FIRE: Michigan State Police Special Report #2155 concerning the November 8, 1929 fire. Interview: Ernie Wolfe. *The State Journal* [Lansing], November 9 and November 11, 1929. *MX*, pp. 3, 4. Years later, during an interview, Malcolm characterized his father as "a clergyman, a Christian." "And it was Christians who burned the home," he abruptly added. (Kenneth B. Clark, ed., *The Negro Protest* [Beacon Press, 1963], p. 19.)

10 PISTOL: In *MX*, p. 4, Malcolm mentions the pistol and says that the authorities would not issue his father a permit for it.

WERE THE EVICTION AND THE FIRE CONNECTED?: Interview: Betty Walker. In Michigan State Police Report #2155, supra., see the transcript of Earl Little's interrogation. The transcript contains Earl Little's signature. (The word "Nicoll's" may have been mistyped "Nichols" by the stenographer who typed the transcript.)

ARSON CHARGE DISMISSED: The arson charge was dismissed Feb. 26, 1930, according to State Police Report #2155. According to one former Ingham County deputy sheriff, arson is usually hard to prove because of the lack of witnesses and the difficulty of proving criminal intent.

APPARENTLY QUIT JOB: Payroll records, H. D. Christman Co., Lansing.

CONTRIBUTIONS ENABLE EARL TO SURVIVE: Interviews: Clara Busby, Wilfred Little.

11 DISPUTED REPORTS ABOUT BEING ON WELFARE: Malcolm's autobiography asserts that, while his father was alive, his family was "much better off" than most of the black families that lived in Lansing. (*MX*, pp. 5-6.) But Mrs. O. F. Poindexter, who used to work for the Ingham County Welfare Department, recalls reading departmental documents indicating that Mr. Little was dependent on public assistance. Allie Cooper also got the feeling he was, perhaps because she witnessed his violent verbal response to a suggestion that he was dependent on charity.

ACCIDENTS FEIGNED?: Interviews: Norman Lyons, Robert Lyons.

CAR TURNS OVER: Interviews: Philbert Little, Wilfred Little.

HERBERT COMMITS SUICIDE: Interviews: Clara Gray, Samantha Gray, Howard Riley, Mary Little, Ella Little, Clara Little, Ella Little.

OSCAR KILLED BY POLICE: Allegheny County (Pa.) Coroner's Report dated August 29, 1929. The supporting documents include a signed affidavit from the police officer whom Oscar Little shot and wounded in the shoulder and in the hip. Interviews: Clara Gray, Samantha Gray, Howard Riley, Clara Little, J.C. Little, Reginald Little.

JOHN SHOTGUNNED: Interviews: Howard Riley, Clara Gray, Samantha Gray, Mary Little, Ella Little, Clara Little, J. C. Little.

JAMES SHOT: *Albion Evening Recorder*, September 27, 28, 29, 1934. Interviews: Clara Little, Reginald Little, J. C. Little.

AGAIN EMBROILED IN LITIGATION: Ingham County Circuit Court (sitting in Chancery). In the Matter of the Petition of Oramel B. Fuller, Auditor General of the State of Michigan, for the Sale of Certain Lands Delinquent for Taxes . . . . Docket #14569. (The relevant portion of the proceedings began in April, 1930.)

BEGAN KINDERGARTEN 1931: School record, Pleasant Grove Elementaru School.

OLIVE HICKS: Interviews: Olive Hicks, Philbert Little, Katie Darling, Phyllis Davis, Geraldine Grill, Maxine Kitchen.

12 "EARLY! EARLY!, IF YOU GO, YOU WON'T COME BACK!": Interview: Philbert Little. Also *MX*, pp. 9-10.

ON VERGE OF LEAVING: Interview: Anna Stohrer.

EARL LITTLE'S DEATH: Death certificate dated Sept. 28, 1931. Coroner's Report (undated). Sept. 28-29, 1931 State Police Report by Trooper Laurence J. Baril. June 4, 1973 and June 14, 1973 letters from Baril to author. Interview: Laurence Baril. *The State Journal*, Sept. 29, 1931. (The newspaper article suggests that Mr. Little had left the first trolley to retrieve his coat as well as his changepurse.) Also see *The State Journal*, Jan. 24, 1963.

FRIENDS GET THE IMPRESSION THAT EARL'S DEATH WAS ACCIDENTAL: Interviews: Bob Bebee, Ray Bebee, Harold Cramer, Irene Cooley, Phyllis Davis, Chester Grill, Ken Palmer. Also interview with S. DeWitt Rathbun. Years later, in prison, Malcolm said that his father's death had been accidental. (*PR*: Feb. 2, 1946 report by case worker John Rockett; March 8, 1946 report by social worker Pete Donahue.)

LEANING, AS HE GROWS OLDER, TOWARD THEORY WHITES KILLED FATHER: Interviews: Clara Little, Mary Little, Howard Bannister, Leon Moffett, Lawrence Pointer, Jean Seaton, Clarence Seaton.

SKULL NOT CRUSHED; EARL WAS CONSCIOUS AND TOLD BARIL HOW THE ACCIDENT HAD OCCURRED: June 4, 1973 and June 14, 1973 letters from Trooper Laurence J. Baril to author. Interview: Laurence Baril. The death certificate makes no mention of any injury to Earl Little's head or skull. Baril's written report and oral testimony indicate that

Mr. Little was still conscious when Baril found him.

BLACK LEGION BLAMED: *MX*, pp. 3, 9, 10, 15.

WAS THE BLACK LEGION RESPONSIBLE?: Ingham County was not included in a 1936 *New York Times* list of Michigan counties in which Black Legion activity had been reported within "the past few years." *New York Times*, May 27, 1936, pp. 1ff. Also letters of Aug. 12, 1981 and Sept. 22, 1981 from Director of Michigan State Police to author. Letter dated August 12, 1981 from Lansing Police Department to author. Letter dated October 29, 1981 from Michigan State Library to author. Interviews: Allie Cooper, Ray Riddle, Clarence Seaton, Mrs. Celia Howard, Betty Jones, Clara Busby. (When I questioned Busby about the Black Legion, she exclaimed, before I even had a chance to ask her about Malcolm's father, "Earl Little was not killed by any Black Legion. He was killed by a streetcar.")

Moreover, it is unclear if the Black Legion was founded before or after Earl's September, 1931 death. See Will Lissner's confusing article in the *New York Times*, May 31, 1936, Section IV, page 6E; Morris Janowitz, "Black Legions on the March," in Daniel Aaron, ed., *America in Crisis* (Alfred A. Knopf, 1952), p. 305; *New York Times*, Sept. 2, 1936, p. 9; George Morris, *The Black Legion Rides* (Workers Library Publishers, 1936), p. 29; Michael S. Clinansmith, "The Black Legion: Hooded Americanism in Michigan," *Michigan History* (Vol. LV, No. 3) Fall, 1971, p. 255.

IRATE HUSBAND?: Interview: Ray Riddle.

13 ALLEGED SUICIDE: *MX*, p. 11.

"DON'T TELL ANYONE. . . . HE WAS A GOOD MAN.": Interview: Anna Stohrer. Louise told her neighbor Pearl Reist the same thing.

UNPAID BILLS: *Estate of Earl Little*, Ingham County Probate File A-8783. Interview: Anna Stohrer.

DID NOT LAMENT: Interview: Clifford Green.

THE KNIFE INCIDENT: June 2, 1973 letter from Anna Stohrer to author. Interviews: Anna Stohrer, Betty Stohrer, William Stohrer. Former probate court worker Merle Parker reports that welfare officials sent a young man to Mrs. Little's home to interview her. The man returned and reported, with a laugh, that he had been having a nice chat until, suddenly, Mrs. Little arose and picked up a large butcher knife. Though she laid it on a table and made no threatening gestures, the instrument made him so nervous that he decided to leave. Subsequently, Dr. Erwin Frederick Hoffman visited Mrs. Little at her home. She kept her butcher knife in her hand until the doctor, whose subsequent report noted her delusions of persecution, departed. He also reported, "She is extremely suspicious of everyone. She claims people talk about her when on the street. . . . The patient is suffering from a paranoid condition." (Physician's appraisal, Petition for Admission to a State Hospital, Ingham County Probate File #B-4398.) Mrs. Little was eventually committed to the Kalamazoo State Hospital, whose medical superintendent later reported that she was suffering from paranoid delusions. (May 6, 1946 letter from Medical Superintendent, Kalamazoo State Hospital, to Charlestown State Prison.)

Louise's delusions of persecution were also apparent to Anna Stohrer, who reported that she had been riding with Mrs. Little in her beat-up automobile when it stalled at one of Lansing's principal downtown intersections. Cars behind began honking. The drivers of other blocked cars honked their horns. After Mrs. Little got the car moving again, she turned to Anna and said, "You know, if I had been alone, I know those white people would have run me down." (Interview: Anna Stohrer.)

LOUISE'S PREMONITION: The psychological aspects of premonitions are discussed in Mortimer Ostow & Ben-Ami Scharfstein, *The Need to Believe* (International Universities Press, 1954), pp. 109-110. Many, perhaps all, premonitions are believed to be defense mechanisms against forbidden wishes. The wish in question is disguised. The person says to himself, "I don't want the event in question to occur; I merely *expect* it to occur."

MALCOLM SHARED MOTHER'S PREMONITION: See *MX*, p. 9, where Malcolm indirectly acknowledges that his father's death did not catch him "completely off guard." His belief in the efficacy of prophecy later manifested itself during a conversation with Mary Little, who told him to be careful with his pistol because it could go off. Malcolm replied, "Don't say such things, because if you do, they will happen." (Interview: Mary Little) See also *MX*, p. 365, where Malcolm talks about one of his wishful premonitions, then proceeds to deny the wishful element. A similar denial appears on p. 184 of his autobiography.

Malcolm's belief in the efficacy of prophecy may have been strengthened by an incident that had occurred as Louise and her children were sitting around the table. She predicted that one of the children would be hit by a car. Shortly thereafter, Wilfred stepped out in front of a passing car and was hit by it. (Interviews: Philbert Little, Wilfred Little.)]

GUILTY CONSCIENCE?: Numerous observers have written about the guilt that children often feel when a parent dies. (The worse the parent, the greater the buried hostility and resultant guilt.) See, for example, Margaret L. Meiss, "The Oedipal Problem of a Fatherless Child," *The Psychoanalytic Study of the Child* (Vol. 7, 1952), pp. 216 ff. Robert A. Furman, "Death of a Six-Year-Old's Mother during his Analysis," Ibid. (Vol. 19, 1964), p. 394. Adele E. Scharl, "Regression and Restitution in Object Loss," Ibid. (Vol. 16, 1961), pp. 472-473.

14 POLICEMAN: Interviews: Byron Delamarter, Philbert Little.

WOULDN'T TALK ABOUT FATHER: *MX*, p. 32. One day, as Malcolm, Philbert, and their boyhood friend John Breathour were walking to a movie theater, Philbert started to ask John whether he remembered the streetcar tracks where Earl Little had been fatally injured. Abruptly, Malcolm pulled Philbert aside and told him to drop the subject. Years later, Breathour recalled, "I would ask Malcolm about his dad. He'd reply, 'I don't want to talk about it.'" All he would say to Phyllis Davis about it was that his father had been run over by a streetcar. "He just didn't want to talk about it," says Davis. "He wanted to drop the subject." (Interviews: John Breathour, Phyllis Davis, Philbert Little, Chuck Lyons, Ken Palmer.)

UNPROTECTED AND AFRAID: Interviews: Reginald Little, John Elton Bembry. See *MX*, p. 11, where Malcolm describes how Earl Little's death left his children without any protector. Also see Jill Barbara Menes Miller, "Children's Reactions to the Death of a Parent: A Review of the Psychoanalytic Literature," *Journal of the American Psychoanalytic Association* (Vol. 19, 1971), pp. 697-719.

REFUSES TO EAT; HAS DIFFICULTY SLEEPING: Interview: Louise Little.

"ONLY DEAD PEOPLE STRETCH OUT.": Interview: Louise Little. "From early childhood, Malcolm had an unnatural fear of death," Philbert recalled during one interview. "He was always afraid of death." (See *MX*, p. 2, where Malcolm says, "It has *always* been my belief that I, too, will die by violence." See also *MX*, p. 378: "I *never* have felt that I would live to become an old man." Also see *JHC*, p. 91. "I *never* expected to die of old age." [Italics added].

3. Boyhood Fears

15 FEARS DARKNESS; WIGGLES BENEATH BROTHERS: Interview: Philbert Little.

TAUNTED FOR HIS FEAR OF COMBAT; "AFRAID TO BLEED": Interviews: Reginald Little, Philbert Little, Elaine Flynn, Sam Clay, "Vince," Louise Little, confidential source. In this and later chapters, note how Malcolm defends other people—and America's blacks—better than he defends himself.

STICK OR BOTTLE: Interviews: Ray Bebee, Philbert Little, Pearl Merchant.

CONVINCING BLUSTER: Interviews: Geraldine Grill, Malcolm Jarvis. Also see chapter 10.

THROUGH INTERMEDIARIES; NO CONFRONTATION: Interview: Margaret Shreve.

WEAKER OR SMALLER; TWO AGAINST ONE: Interviews: Mildred Thurston, Daryl Thurston, Kenneth Kimmel, Maury Baldwin, Dick Letts, Hayward Howard. Yet when Malcolm's mother was around, he treated one favorite victim "real nice." Years later, the victim said that he suspected that Malcolm's mother had been strict with him. (Interview: confidential source.)

UNDERDOGS: Ethel Helmeker, Malcolm's fourth grade teacher, reports that he "seemed to be expecting hurt, as if he were an underdog."

TO THE RESCUE: Interview: Harvey ("Junior") Miller.

DEFENDS BREATHOUR: Interview: John Breathour.

PHILBERT DEFENDS MALCOLM: Interviews: Sam Clay, Philbert Little.

16 ON TOM'S BACK: Interview: Tom Simmon. See *MX*, p. 11.

ORES WHITNEY DEFENDS MALCOLM: Interview: Katie Darling.

RELATIONSHIP BETWEEN ORES AND MALCOLM: Interviews: Robert Higdon, Katie

Darling, Helen Bywater, Maury Baldwin, Phyllis Ostrom. Ores Whitney's impish smile appears in one of his class pictures.

SUCCESSFULLY DEFENDS BOB BEBEE AND OTHERS: Interviews: Bob Bebee, Ray Bebee.

"SNOWFLAKE"; "CHINAMAN"; "ESKIMO": Interviews: Elaine Flynn, Bob Bebee, Lloyd Price, Louise Little, Ray Bebee.

GRINS: Interview: Frances Walter.

"THEY DON'T KNOW MY NAME AT SCHOOL": Interview: Louise Little.

HATED HIS NEITHER-WHITE-NOR-BLACK SKIN COLOR: Interview:Jean_____.

RELATIONSHIP WITH JEAN: Interview: Jean _____.

SETS ONE COMBATANT AGAINST ANOTHER: Interview: Jean _____.

RELATIONSHIP WITH BETTY: Interview: Betty Jean Thiel.

17 UNHAPPY: Interviews: Betty Jean Thiel, Reginald Little. Also see *MX*, chapter 1 and p. 391.

UNHAPPY LAUGHTER: Interviews: Reginald Little, Chuck Lyons, Mary Little. Reginald says that Malcolm laughed the heartiest about the things that were most painful to him. Mary reports that, on one occasion, he laughed about the fact that his father had not even noticed when he had fallen out of a moving car. See also the original unedited tape-recording of Malcolm's 11/10/63 "Message to the Grass Roots," in which he laughs after discussing his father's death.

LEADER AND FOLLOWER: Interview: Betty Jean Thiel.

4. Hunger

18 AUTOMOTIVE PRODUCTION: The figures cited are for nationwide production of cars, trucks, and busses. Willis F. Dunbar, *Michigan: A History of the Wolverine State* (Grand Rapids, Michigan: William B. Eerdmans, 1965), p. 571.

IMPACT OF GREAT DEPRESSION: See, inter alia, Sister Maria Heyda, "The Automotive Industry and the Great Depression, 1929-1939," paper delivered at Michigan State University, Jan. 19, 1980, pp. 88, 105, et al. Jess Gilbert & Craig Harris, "Unemployment, Primary Production & Population in the Upper Peninsula of Michigan in the Great Depression," paper delivered at Michigan State University, Jan. 19, 1980, p. 25. Polk Laffoon IV, "A Memorable Time, A Terrible Time," *Detroit Free Press*, October 21, 1979. Frances McDonald's *Reminiscences* in The Michigan State University Archives & Historical Collections.

EFFECT OF JOB DISCRIMINATION: *MX*, p. 12.

19 DECLINES SCARF: Interview: Howard Cramer.

SHOES: Interviews: Katherine Gillion, Katie Darling, Helen Bywater. Next-door-neighbor John Doane, Sr., accompanied Malcolm and his mother to the shoe store one day. When the salesman asked Malcolm whether the shoes [or sneakers] fit, Malcolm just smiled. He would not answer the question.

"FARMERS": Interview: Jean Seaton. Reginald Little, Ted Davenport, and Clifford Green all confirm the fact that many Lansing blacks looked down on the Littles because they were so poor.

INSISTENCE ON CLEANLINESS: Interviews: Katherine Marling, Helen Bywater, Anna Stohrer, Mrs. Samuel Woolcock, Enos Major, Sr., Charlice Doane.

HUNGER: *MX*, p. 13.

OFF IN A CORNER; RESEMBLING CAT FOOD: Interviews: Katie Darling, Mildred Thurston, Emerson Parker. "He kept hiding his lunch," Parker recalls. "He didn't want me to see what he was eating."

ODOR CAUSED BY LEEK SANDWICHES: Interviews: Howard Cramer, Katie Darling, Mildred Thurston.

WHITE CLASSMATES HELP: Interviews: Emerson Parker, Betty Jean Thiel, Irene Cooley.

FORBIDS CHILDREN TO "EMBARRASS" WHITES: Interviews: Joyce Tellier, Philbert Little.

20 LETS FOOD SIT, THEN WOLFS IT DOWN: Interview: Katie Darling.

AMBIVALENCE ABOUT ACCEPTING CHRISTMAS GIFT: Interviews: Helen Bywater, John Breathour.

NEGATIVE FEELINGS ABOUT SANTA CLAUS AND CHRISTMAS: Interviews: Wilfred Little, Philbert Little, Gloria Strother.

FATHER RESENTED CHARITY: Interview: Allie Cooper. (See chapter 2.)

MOTHER ASHAMED TO ACCEPT CHARITY: MX, pp. 12-14, 17. Interviews: Ernestine Artz, Charlice Doane, Allie Cooper, Katherine Marling, Enos Major, Sr., Katherine Gillion.

NEGATIVE RESPONSE: Interviews: Katherine Marling, Mrs. Celia Howard, Mrs. Samuel Woolcock.

INSISTS ON REPAYING: Interview: Clarence Seaton.

MISSING BUTTONS: Interview: Geraldine Grill.

PRIVATELY COMPLAINS ABOUT PAUCITY OF PUBLIC ASSISTANCE: Interviews: Ernestine Artz, Charlice Doane, Watoga Doane.

"POOR COMMISSIONER": "He was a regular Simon Legree," reports social worker Katherine Marling. "A cruel old man. He was so abusive that people would almost go hungry before going to him for assistance."

CAR VS. STOVE: Interview: confidential source.

CAR MEANS A LOT: Interviews: Louise Little, Philbert Little, Jean Seaton, Reginald Little.

RELUCTANT TO ACCEPT FREE FOOD: MX, pp. 13, 17.

21 TURNS TO JOB-LIKE RELIGION: Interviews: Clarence Seaton, Bethel Seaton, Wilfred Little. Also see Doctrinal Beliefs of the Church of God (Seventh Day), 1978 ed., (Denver: Bible Advocate Press).

SAYS HE LOVES HIS MOTHER: MX, p. 18.

GROWING REBELLION: MX, pp. 17, 18. Interview: Reginald Little.

UNPUNCTUAL; WON'T DO CHORES: Interviews: Katherine Gillion, Bob Bebee, Rose Little, Allie Cooper, Charlice Doane, Philbert Little, Wilfred Little, Rose Little, Anna Stohrer.

PRODS YOUNGER CHILDREN: Interview: Charlice Doane.

PRESSURE INTENSIFIES: MX, p. 17. Interviews: Reginald Little, Charlice Doane.

HAIR GRAYS; FACE EXPRESSIONLESS; UNAPPROACHABLE: Interviews: Mrs. Clyde Byrd, Katherine Marling, Clarice Doane, Ray Bebee, Geraldine Grill.

INTEREST IN CHILDREN EBBS: Interview: Reginald Little. Also MX, p. 19. Louise's neglect of her children, which grew progressively worse, is described in a subsequent petition for admission to Kalamazoo State Hospital and the accompanying physicians' statements. These documents appear in Ingham County Probate Court file B-4398, entitled "Louise Little Insane." See also May 6, 1946 letter from Kalamazoo State Hospital to Charlestown State Prison and March 27, 1946 memo by social worker John Herstrom, both of which appear in Malcolm's prison record. Looking back years later, Reginald recalled that his mother finally became unable to command obedience. (See MX, p. 18.) "She was no longer a mother," he said.

RUDDERLESS: Interviews: Reginald Little, Wilfred Little.

MALCOLM WITHDRAWS: Increasingly, he stayed away from home. (MX, pp. 14-15. Interviews: Katherine Gillion, Maxine Kitchen, Reginald Little, Wilfred Little, Philbert Little.

STEALS FROM MOTHER'S PURSE: Interview: Philbert Little.

ACKNOWLEDGES THE LESSER OFFENSE: MX, pp. 14-15, 17. Interviews: Clifford Green, James Elton Bembry.

STEALING ELICITS ATTENTION: MX, p. 15. See Franz Alexander & Shelton T. Selesnick, The History of Psychiatry (Harper & Row, 1966), p. 355.

PROUD OF SELF-RESTRAINT: MX, p. 15.

NEIGHBORS HEAR CRIES: MX, pp. 7, 15.

AMMUNITION FOR ACCUSATIONS Of MATERNAL NEGLECT: MX, p. 17. (Also see p. 18, where Malcolm says, "As much trouble and worry as I caused my mother. . . .")

5. Educational Authority

22 LOUISE WANTS CHILDREN TO SUCCEED: Interviews: Rose Little, Reginald Little, Philbert Little, Jean Seaton, Dorothy Collins, Clara Busby. Busby sensed that Louise was

determined that her children "weren't going to be washerwomen for white folks."

WEST INDIAN SUCCESS IMPERATIVES: Louise's Grenadian niece Daphne Orgias says that these success imperatives are very strong among Grenada's middle and upper classes. (The Langdons were middle-class.) See also *MX*, pp. 40-41, where Malcolm describes the West Indian strivers who were called "black Jews."

PUSHED HARD: Interviews: Rose Little, Louise Little, Enos Major, Sr., Mrs. Pearl Gardner, Clarence Seaton, Anna Stohrer, J. C. Little, Richard Jenkins.

MISTAKES IMPERMISSIBLE: Interviews: Reginald Little, Philbert Little. Helen Bywater reports that when Malcolm's sister Hilda invited her to his home, Louise would ask how well Hilda had done that day in school, and whether she had gotten anything wrong. If Hilda replied in the affirmative, Mrs. Little would say, "That's too bad." Bywater never heard Louise compliment Hilda for what she did right. (See *MX*, p. 29, where Malcolm says that one reason he disliked mathematics is that a single mistake made a successful outcome impossible.)

WITH A STRAP: Interviews: Louise Little, Hamburg E. D. Wells. Laughing softly as she recalled the pain, Mrs. Little told me, "When the teacher lashed me, he woke me up. He made me feel. When you feel the sting of the lash, it enables you to feel."

AUTOCRATIC TEACHER: Interviews: Margaret Shreve, Helen Bywater, Maxine Kitchen, Phyllis Davis, John Breathour, Betty Jean Thiel, Marion Simmon, Frances Walter.

ARTHUR DELAMARTER: Interviews: Dale Gardner, Katie Darling, Margaret Long, Olive Hicks, Tom Simmon, Maxine Kitchen, Elaine Flynn, Tom Amiss, et al.

23   DRAGS FEET WHEN WORK IS ASSIGNED: Interview: Olive Roosenraad.

DOODLES; DAYDREAMS; INATTENTIVE: Interviews: Bob Bebee, Barbara Hyde; Phyllis Davis; Emerson Parker; Katie Darling; Dale Gardner; Margaret Shreve. Reginald sensed that Malcolm's daydreams were about the things he wanted but couldn't have. (Interview: Reginald Little.)

TENDS TO QUIT WHEN FACED WITH DIFFICULTY: Interviews: Olive Roosenraad, Tom Amiss.

DOESN'T SEEM TO CARE: Interviews with Geraldine Gill, Bob Bebee, and Malcolm's second-semester, sixth-grade teacher.

CRAVES ATTENTION: In an August 17, 1939 memorandum to the Ingham County Probate Court, social worker Maynard Allyn wrote, "[Malcolm] seems to want to be the center of attraction wherever he is, which makes one feel that his conduct is more an attention-getting [device] than vicious." (Ingham County Probate file #4053.) Interviews: Sam Clay, Philbert Little.

WANTS TO BE FIRST: Interviews: Phyllis Davis, Ethel Helmeker, Elsie Taylor, John Breathour, Helen Bywater.

DISLIKED WOMEN: Interview: Cecille Jacobson.

TRIED PULLING HAIR: Interview: Frances Walter.

VENTS FRUSTRATION ON YOUNGER FEMALES: Interviews: Margaret Shreve, Howard Cramer, Elaine Flynn, Dale Gardner, Maxine Kitchen.

ATTENTIVE TO HELEN: Interview: Helen Bywater.

CARRIED GIRLS ACROSS RAIN PUDDLES: Interview: Elaine Flynn.

24   CARRIED THEIR SHOES: Interview: Maxine Kitchen.

TAUNTED FOR BEING "SISSIFIED": Interview: Katie Darling.

SECOND-SEMESTER TEACHER: Interviews with Olive Roosenraad and the teacher in question.

RIDICULES PENMANSHIP: Interview: Maury Baldwin. Baldwin characterized this particular teacher as the worst one he had ever had. Several years ago, she was interviewed at a school. A student approached her and asked her a question. Her response was unsympathetic. Though she seemed to believe in the importance of learning and appeared very proud of the innovations she had made in the curriculum, she seemed lacking in warmth. She appeared to regard corporal punishment favorably. At the end of the interview, she asked whether a teacher like herself could have been partly responsible for the rebellious behavior Malcolm had exhibited after he had left Pleasant Grove.

AMUSES CLASSMATES AT TEACHER'S EXPENSE: Interviews: Maury Baldwin, Maxine Kitchen.

REFUSES TO COMPLETE THEMES: Interviews with Ethel Helmeker and the teacher in question.

MALCOLM REFUSES TO BE EVICTED: Interview: Maury Baldwin.

HAD TO REPEAT THE SEMESTER: Malcolm's school record. Interviews: Ken Mead, Robert Higdon, Ray Bebee, and the teacher who flunked Malcolm. See MX, p. 35, where Malcolm makes a point of the fact he passed the following year and didn't have to repeat seventh grade.

PREGNANT: May 6, 1946 letter from Medical Superintendent, Kalamazoo State Hospital to Charlestown State Prison. Interviews: Reginald Little, Philbert Little, Wilfred Little, Robert Little, Yvonne Little.

LOUISE WITHDRAWS AND NEGLECTS HER CHILDREN: Interviews: Reginald Little, Jean Seaton, Philbert Little, Art Jones, Fred Green, Anna Stohrer, Enos Major, Sr., Marion Simmon. Louise's neglect of her children, which had been growing progressively worse, is described in a subsequent petition for admission to Kalamazoo State Hospital and the accompanying statements by E. F. Hoffman, M.D. and George R. Clinton, M.D. These documents appear in Ingham County Probate File B-4398, entitled "Louise Little — Insane." In MX, pp. 18-22, Malcolm describes his mother's emotional collapse, attributing it partly to the fact she was jilted by the unborn child's father and partly to uncaring white officials. But he does not mention the unwanted child.

25   A SENSE OF DREAD: MX, pp. 18-19.

BREAK-IN AT LEVANDOWSKI'S: Interview: Reginald Little.

6. The Long, Hard Road to Manhood

26   NO MAN TO GUIDE OR ADVISE:Reginald Little emphasized the emotional impact of the lack of a competent male role model.

TAGGED ALONG: Interviews: Clifford Green, James Davis, Sr., Dick Letts. In MX, p. 79, Malcolm acknowledges that he envied the older boys.

EXPECTED HIM TO PERFORM: Interview: Clifford Green.

EAGER YET RELUCTANT TO PARTICIPATE: Interviews: Johnny Davis, Jr., Ted Davenport, Maxine Kitchen, Dick Turbin.

COMPETITIVE: Interviews: Howard Cramer, Hayward Howard, Ethel Helmeker, confidential source. Rose Little reports that when Malcolm was very young, he'd curse if he lost a game of marbles.

PLAYING BASEBALL; RELATIONSHIP WITH DICK: Interview: Dick Turbin.

27   CONDEMNS ERRORS: Interview: Robert Corbin.

BERATES HIMSELF: Interview: Dick Turbin.

FEAR OF BEING INJURED: Interviews: Carl ("Sonny") Simmon; Clifford Green.

COMPETES AT SOCCER; KICKS OPPONENTS: Interviews: Harvey ("Junior") Miller, Robert Higdon, Howard Cramer, Maury Baldwin, Tom Simmon.

COMPASSIONATE: Interviews: Louis Lee, Helen Bywater, Bob Bebee.

FRITZ: Interview: Dick Turbin.

28   OUTWARDLY INDIFFERENT TO GIRLS: Interviews: Helen Bywater, Maxine Kitchen, Nada Bowen. Jewel Harris and Bethel Seaton report that Malcolm later acted the same way toward African-American girls.

GRINNED IN APPROVAL: Interview: Frances Walter.

EYED BETTY GIRVEN: Interview: confidential source.

MALCOLM AND BETTY: Interviews: Betty Girven, Maury Baldwin, Tom Simmon.

CONQUESTS: Interviews: Margaret Shreve, Glenn Snyder, Oceola Jackson, Arlington Cooper, confidential source.

HAS SEX: Interview: Bob Bebee. Rumors of the incident later began to spread. When Maxine Kitchen teased the young woman about having a black boyfriend, she grew violently angry.

(Interviews: Maxine Kitchen, Elaine Flynn, James Harmon.)

ROBERT: Interviews: Bob Bebee, Philbert Little, Geraldine Grill, Katie Darling.

29 INCIDENT IN THE WOODS; FELLATIO: Interviews: Bob Bebee, Ray Bebee.

7. To Leave or Not to Leave?

30 "BUTCH BORN": May 6, 1946 letter from medical superintendent, Kalamazoo State Hospital to Charlestown State Prison. The information has been confirmed by several members of the Little family, including "Butch."

HERB WALKER BOARDS AT MALCOLM'S HOME: Interviews: Betty Walker, Eulalia Walker, Clarence Seaton, Jean Seaton, Reginald Little, Mr. & Mrs. Marvon Worthy, Dick Turbin, Louise Little.

QUESTIONS PARENTAGE; CONCEIVED IN INIQUITY; FATHER A WHITE RAPIST: Interviews: Jean _____, Louise Little. (Jean is certain that Malcolm was talking about his own father, not his mother's white father.)

HIS CONCEPTION INSTRUMENTAL IN CAUSING MOTHER'S EMOTIONAL DECLINE: Interview: Jean _____.

BEGINS SEVENTH GRADE: Malcolm remained at Pleasant Grove for only a few weeks; by late October, he had transferred to West Junior High. See seventh grade transcript in Malcolm's school record. Also "School History" summary in Malcolm's prison record, and social worker Maynard Allyn's August 16, 1939 letter to the Ingham County Probate Court.

OLIVE ROOSENRAAD: Interviews: Barbara Hyde, Max Cunningham, Bob Worthy, Cecille Jacobson, Olive Roosenraad.

REACTION TO ROOSENRAAD AND HYDE: Interviews: Olive Roosenraad, Barbara Hyde. Nada Bowen, who was probably the most understanding, warmest elementary school teacher that Malcolm had, observed in retrospect, years later, that despite his unwillingness to request help, he must have needed it badly.

31 SHUT HIMSELF OFF: Interview: Barbara Hyde.

EXPELLED FROM PLEASANT GROVE: The school expulsion described on MX, p. 25 is chronologically in error and occurred at Pleasant Grove, not at West Junior High School. Interview: Olive Roosenraad. See also the "School History" summary in Malcolm's prison record. Also see social worker Maynard Allyn's August 16, 1939 letter to the Ingham County Probate Court.

INSISTED HE DID NOT WANT TO LEAVE: MX, pp. 17-20, particularly p. 19.

WANTS TO GO TO BIG CITY AND MAKE MONEY: Interviews: Katherine Gillion, Art Jones, Philbert Little, Bob High, Bobby Pointer. Looking back years later, Philbert observed that there was good reason for Malcolm to want to leave home. He had no father. His mother was rapidly declining. Most of the welfare officials were cold and uncaring, partly because the Littles were black. There was no one on whom he could rely.

PRETENDS, BUT LOOKS DEADLY SERIOUS: Interviews: Arlington Cooper, Katherine Gillion.

PREFERS REFORM SCHOOL: Interview: Philbert Little.

PASTED CAR: Interview: Philbert Little.

ARLINGTON AND ALLIE COOPER: Interview: Arlington Cooper.

INABILITY TO PROVIDE LOVE: Interviews: Allie Cooper, Mrs. Celia Howard.

HACKLES ROSE: MX, p. 31. Interview: Maynard Allyn.

"WITHOUT HESITATION": MX, p. 22.

TRANSFER TO WEST JR. HIGH: School record. See above note about Malcolm's expulsion from Pleasant Grove.

32 LONER: MX, p. 20. Interviews: Lewis Clark, Howard Bannister.

FOR A FEE: The fee was four dollars a week. (Ingham County Probate file #4058.)

PLOT: MX, pp. 17-22.

TO ENABLE HIM TO CONTINUE HIS SCHOOLING: August 16, 1939 letter from social worker Maynard Allyn to Ingham County Probate Court. See also letter in Malcolm's prison record from West Junior High School to Charlestown Prison.

BETTER AT THE GOHANNAS': *MX*, pp. 14, 19-20. Interviews: Bessie Springer, Ed ("Dave" or "Big Boy") Roper, Dick Letts, Philbert Little, Richard Jenkins, Pearl Merchant, Jr.

SEEMS TO DOUBT WHETHER THEY LIKE HIM: See first full paragraph in *MX*, p. 19.

"FAIRLY WELL": August 16, 1939 letter from social worker Maynard Allyn to Ingham County Probate Court.

STEALING CONTINUED: Interview: Loren Keeney.

HEADACHES: Interview: Ed ("Dave" or "Big Boy") Roper.

DISPUTED REPORTS OF CONFLICTS: Interviews: Bessie Springer, Ed Roper.

STRAITLACED: Interviews: Geraldine Nelson, Ernestine Artz.

SNOOPED: Interview: Geraldine Nelson.

RELIGIOUS FERVOR; "NICE"; LIKED THEM: *MX*, pp. 14, 19-20.

"VERY LITTLE RESPECT": *MX*, p. 5.

NICELY; "JUST WASN'T THE SAME": *MX*, p. 19.

NOT CLOSE: Interview: Ed Roper.

STAYED CLOSE TO SHORE: Interview: Ed Roper.

33 IMPATIENT: Interview: Ed Roper. *MX*, p. 20.

DELIGHTED IN OUTWITTING COMPETITORS: Interviews: Reginald Little, Byron Delamarter, Ed Roper, Albert ("Junior") Clark, Godfrey Joiner. See also Louis Lomax, *To Kill a Black Man* (Holloway House, 1968), p. 27.

CLAIMED MOTHER LET HIM HAVE RIFLE; YET SHE WAS PETRIFIED OF GUNS: MX, p. 20. Interviews: Dick Turbin, Louise Little.

CARELESS WITH SAFETY OFF: Interview: Philbert Little.

VERY TALKATIVE: Interviews: Pearl Merchant, Jr., Ted Davenport, Johnny Davis, Jr., Katherine Gillion, Dick Lyon. Lyon later observed, "Either Malcolm wouldn't say anything or you couldn't shut him up."

OPINIONATED; BECOMES ANGRY IF AUTHORITY IS QUESTIONED: Interviews: Margaret Shreve, Albert ("Junior") Clark, Cyril McGuire, Hayward Howard. Interview: confidential source.

TOLD TO LEAVE: Interview: Ed Roper.

BARRED FROM LINCOLN CENTER: Interviews: Hugh Bronson, Philbert Little, Ed Roper.

FINGERNAILS INTO NECK; THREATENED TO KILL; EVICTED MALCOLM; SUMMONED POLICE: Interviews: Retha Fowler, Philbert Little, Ted Davenport.

"MADE THE ORDEAL EASIER": *MX*, p. 20.

WIDOW'S PENSION TERMINATED: Ingham County Probate Court Index, p. 489. Entry dated September 30, 1938. The relevant details, which were evidently recorded in Ingham County Probate File #2846, are no longer available because the file has disappeared. Interviews: Walter Levandowski, Sr., Mrs. Celia Howard, Yvonne Little.

MENTAL BREAKDOWN: Interviews: Bertha Dresser, John ("Buster") Doane, Charlice Doane, Watoga Doane, Jean Seaton, Mrs. Lloyd Hackenberg.

MALCOLM BLAMES WHITE SOCIAL WORKERS: *MX*, pp. 17-22. Interview: Clara Little.

34 RELUCTANT TO ADMIT SHE WAS MENTALLY ILL: In *MX*, pp. 33-34, Malcolm states that, after one visit to the state mental hospital where his mother was incarcerated, he felt as if he "had visited with someone who had some kind of physical illness that had just lingered on." Interviews: Robert Little, Pearl Merchant, Jr.

RELUCTANT TO ADMIT THAT THE CAUSE WAS ASCERTAINABLE: *MX*, p. 21.

ACKNOWLEDGED THAT HE CONTRIBUTED TO MOTHER'S BREAKDOWN: *MX*, pp. 11, 17, 18. Cora Spencer, "A Psychological Evaluation of the Political Perspectives of Malcolm X," unpublished term paper, p. 12.

COMMITTED: Aug. 27, 1979 letter from Kalamazoo Regional Psychiatric Hospital to author. Also see Ingham County Probate File B-4398, entitled "Louise Little — Insane."

TEARS: Interviews: Elaine Flynn, Maury Baldwin.

FIRST FIGHT WITH BILL PETERSON: Interviews: Reginald Little, Philbert Little, Pearl

Merchant, Jr., Katie Darling, confidential source. (Malcolm's version appears on *MX*, pp. 23-24.) In later chapters, as well as chapter 3, note how Malcolm defends other people — and America's blacks — better than he defends himself.

35 TRYING TO SHORE UP SELF-ESTEEM: Interview: Reginald Little. In an April 18, 1977 letter to the author, J. Prescott Adams, who assisted Malcolm in his study of the Bible when Malcolm was in prison, wrote, "Malcolm had a great ego that he was feeding."

SEWELL HENRY INCIDENT: *MX*, pp. 24-25. Interviews: Jill Leyton, Ted Davenport.

REMAINS AT WEST JR. HIGH AND SQUEAKS THROUGH SEVENTH GRADE: Malcolm's school record indicates that he completed seventh grade at West Jr. High, which he attended until mid-June, 1939.

RETURNS HOME: August 16, 1939 letter from social worker Maynard Allyn to Ingham County Probate Court. Interviews: Arlington Cooper, Maynard Allyn.

WILFRED STRUGGLES TO SUPPORT FAMILY; NO TIME FOR FATHERING: August 16, 1939 letter, supra. Interviews: Reginald Little, Arlington Cooper, Sam Clay, Ray Bebee.

"SECOND MOTHER": *MX*, p. 19. Interviews: Dorothy Collins, Wilfred Little, Kenneth Collins, Katherine Gillion, Ed Roper, Anna Stohrer, Betty Jones.

ELPRESSED CONCERN: Interview: Arlington Cooper.

LOVED HILDA: Interview: Malcolm Jarvis. (According to Reginald Little, J. C. Little, and Godfrey Joiner, Malcolm admired his older sister.)

LEFT ALL THE WORK TO HILDA: Interview: Arlington Cooper.

DISOBEYED HILDA: Interviews: Reginald Little, Katherine Gillion, Dick Letts. Also see summary of testimony given at the Probate Court hearing held in August, 1939 to determine whether Malcolm should be sent to the Ingham County juvenile home.

SCHOOLWORK; CLEANLINESS: Interview: Philbert Little. Dorothy Collins, Clara Little, and Katherine Gillion report that cleanliness was very important to Hilda. (See *MX*, p. 32.)

DICTATORIAL: Interview: Reginald Little.

DARKEN SKIN: Interview: Philbert Little.

SECRETLY FAVORED MALCOLM: Interview: Reginald Little.

SLEPT HOME VERY LITTLE: August 16, 1939 letter from Maynard Allyn to Ingham County Probate Court.

IT WASN'T JUST THE LONELINESS: Interviews: Arlington Cooper, Pearl Merchant, Jr.

NO ONE CARED: August 16, 1939 letter from Maynard Allyn to Ingham County Probate Court.

REQUESTED MOVE TO COUNTY JUVENILE HOME: *Ibid.*

ALLYN'S RECOMMENDATIONS: August 17, 1939 memo from Maynard Allyn to Judge McClellan. August 16, 1939 letter from Maynard Allyn to Ingham County Probate Court. Interview: Maynard Allyn.

McCLELLAN GRANTS REQUEST: Court order dated August 25, 1939 [in] Ingham County Probate and Juvenile Court file #4053.

SHED NO TEARS: *MX*, p. 25.

ONLY TOO GLAD: *MX*, p. 25, makes it appear as if Malcolm was sent to the Mason, Michigan juvenile home from the Gohannas', and that the Gohannas and "Big Boy" cried as they watched Malcolm leave. But Big Boy does not recall the incident. And Maynard Allyn's August 16, 1939 letter to the Ingham County Probate Court makes clear that, some time before Malcolm moved to Mason, he left the Gohannas' and returned to live in his family home, where he spent part of the summer of 1939. Allyn, who never met the Gohannas, picked Malcolm up at the Littles' home and took him to Mason in his car. (Interviews: Maynard Allyn, Ed Roper.)

8. Chameleon

36 EX-SLAVE HANGED: *Mason Area Centennial Historical Program* (published in Mason, Michigan in June, 1965 by the Mason Printing Co.), p. 8.

"MA" SWERLEIN: *MX*, p. 26. Interviews: Martha Thayer, Reginald Little, Mrs. Richard

Mills, Gwynneth Shultis, Forrest Dwain Shultis, Vera Hoover. Martha Thayer reports that Lois Swerlein became so attached to one of her young charges that she finally adopted him. Children were very fond of her. After she resigned her position because of fragile health, things began to go downhill at the detention home. Late at night, pajama-clad children would be seen running across the fields, fleeing the place.

NO EXCEPTION: Former Ingham County Probate Court worker Merle Parker reports that Malcolm liked Mrs. Swerlein. And Marie Lyons recalled that years later when Malcolm returned to Michigan from the east coast, he frequently expressed a desire to visit Mrs. Swerlein.

APPETITE IMPROVED; PUT ON WEIGHT: Interviews: Ed Roper; confidential source.

EXTRA CHORES: Interview: Louise Lathrop.

37 UNSURE: *MX*, p. 26.

INCORRECTLY ASSERTED: Interview: Clifford Walcott. (Cf. *MX*, p. 28.)

FREE TO COME AND GO: Interview: Lucille Lathrop.

TOLD HE WOULD BE SENT: *MX*, pp. 25, 28.

RECORDS MAKE NO MENTION: Court order dated August 25, 1939 [in] Ingham County Probate & Juvenile Court file #4053. Also social worker Maynard Allyn's August 16, 1939 letter to the court.

DIDN'T WANT TO LEAVE JUVENILE HOME: *MX*, p. 28.

MALCOLM ATTRIBUTED: *MX*, p. 28.

SMILED ON: *MX*, pp. 26, 28.

RANKED THIRD: My comparison of Malcolm's grades with those of his eighth grade classmates was made possible by Kenneth J. Mead, who arranged for me to obtain access to the relevant school records. The records show that Malcolm was correct when he reported that only two members of his eighth grade class obtained better grades than he did. One was Jim Cotton. The other was Dewey Doane (not Audrey Slagh, as *MX*, p. 35 contends).

But Malcolm apparently told Nat Hentoff that he had been first in his class. (Nat Hentoff, "Elijah in the Wilderness," *The Reporter*, August 4, 1960, p. 39.)

MRS. SWERLEIN WANTED HIM TO DO WELL: Interview: Lucille Lathrop.

AD-LIBBING: Interview: Edna Mae Hamlin.

GREIN: *MX*, p. 29. Interviews: Forrest Dwain Shultis, Ken Palmer, Shirly Feight.

POLITICIAN: Interviews: Jim Cotton, Rollin Dart.

38 MALCOLM'S EXPLANATION OF HIS ELECTION: *MX*, p. 31.

CLASSMATES LIKED HIM: In a portion of Malcolm's prison record summarizing his experience at Mason Jr. High School, there is a brief notation that states, "Liked by classmates." Numerous ex-classmates confirm this assessment. (Interviews: Herb Fox, Don Oesterle, Joyce Dolbee, Louis Lee, Katherine Curtis, Forrest Dwain Shultis, Hazel Fairbotham, Colleen Schaft.)

DEFENDS "FARMER": Interview: Harold Lavis.

KEEPS ORDER: Interview: Viva Riker.

INVARIABLY GENTLEMANLY: Interviews: Gwynneth Shultis, Chuck Lyons, Ruby Thomas, Virginia Colby, et al.

GOOD DANCER: Betty Kennedy, Joyce Dolbee. Edna Mae Hamlin, Vera Hoover, Philbert Little, Jean Seaton, Art Jones, James Davis, Sr., Marjorie Morrow, and others attest to the fact that Malcolm was a good dancer. Yet his autobiography repeatedly asserts that he "couldn't dance." (*MX*, pp. 27, 57, 79.) Perhaps he felt that if he couldn't be the "greatest" dancer (*MX*, pp. 59, 64), he was no dancer at all. (Years later, he apparently felt the same way about his position as a political leader.)

SIDEWALK SOLOS: Interview: Vera Hoover.

LEARNED NOT TO ASK WHITE GIRLS TO DANCE: *MX*, pp. 29-30, 31. Interviews: Betty Kennedy, Audrey Slagh.

"YOUR ANCESTORS EITHER": Interview: Don Dachman.

"A WALL": *MX*, p. 30.

THOUGHT HIM COLD: Information supplied to Robert Lyons by several of the girls in

Malcolm's eighth-grade class.

BETTY KENNEDY: Interviews: Betty Kennedy, Don Oesterle, Edna Mae Hamlin, Robert Lyons.

AUDREY SLAGH: Audrey was the girl who had nominated Malcolm for class president. (*MX*, p. 392.) Interviews: Audrey Slagh, Clifford Walcott, Betty Kennedy, Ella Little, confidential source.

39 AUDREY'S FATHER: Audrey's father died February 9, 1940. Interviews: Audrey Slagh, Shirley Feight, Edna Mae Hamlin, Betty Kennedy, confidential source.

"FELT SOMEWHAT RESPONSIBLE": Interview: confidential source.

DIDN'T SHARE: Interview: Audrey Slagh.

CONVERSATION WITH RALPH TAYLOR ABOUT EARL LITTLE'S DEATH: Interview: Ralph Taylor.

"ONLY VAGUELY": *MX*, p. 29.

WISHED HE WAS WHITE: *MX*, pp. 31, 54.

BOASTED HE WAS LIGHTEST CHILD: Interview: Louise Lathrop.

TAILORED HIS BEHAVIOR: Interviews: Bob High, J. C. Little, Malcolm Jarvis, confidential source.

AMONG SERIOUS MINDED, INTELLIGENT BLACKS: Interviews: Jim Reed, Arlington Cooper, Jean Seaton, Yvonne Little, Luther Jermany, Lionel Beane, Phyllis Ashby Scott.

WHITE WOMAN MOLESTED: Petition for Investigation by peace officer William Knapp, dated May 8, 1939. Maynard Allyn's August 16, 1939 letter to the county court says that "it was definitely established that Malcolm did not touch the woman." See Ingham County Probate and Juvenile Court file #4053.

EASILY LED BY OLDER BOYS: Malcolm tagged after the older boys. (*MX*, p. 42. Interviews: Dick Letts, Phil Jackson.) Maynard Allyn's August 16, 1939 letter to the county court says Malcolm was "easily led" by the [older] boys who had molested the white woman.

ENVIED AND IMITATED: See, for example, *MX*, p. 23, where Malcolm acknowledges his envy for his older brother Philbert, whose success in the boxing ring Malcolm tried to duplicate.

YOUNGER BOYS SOUGHT HIS LEADERSHIP: *MX*, p. 42.

INFURIATED ABOUT "RED": Interviews: Dick Letts, Katherine Gillion, Philbert Little, Pearl Merchant, Jr., Arlene Seaton,

PREFERS "HARPY": Interviews: Lucille Lathrop, Ken Palmer, Vivian Shaffer. Malcolm's campaign for class president included signs saying, "Harpy for President."

MOUTHING OFF: Interviews: Reginald Little, Edna Mae Hamlin, Philbert Little.

40 VULTURE-LIKE FEMALES: J.E. Zimmerman, *Dictionary of Classical Mythology* (Harper, 1964), p. 117. *Larousse Encyclopedia of Mythology* (Prometheus Press, 1960), p. 166. Gertrude Jobes, *Dictionary of Mythology, Folklore, and Symbols* (Scarecrow Press, 1961), Vol. 1, p. 728. Michael Grant and John Hazel, *Gods and Mortals in Classical Mythology* (Merriam Webster, 1973), p. 195. *Webster's Third New International Dictionary* (G. & C. Merriam Co., 1976), p. 1035. Interviews: James Davis, Sr., Zelma Holman.

CONSIDERED "FEMININE"; SEEN WEARING A DRESS: Interview: confidential source. Some of Malcolm's friends used the word "harpy" to describe ugly women. (Interview: Carlton Barnette.)

"MADAME HARPY": Interviews: Reginald Little, Zelma Holman, James Davis, Sr.

"MADAME": Interview: Clifford Green.

CONSIDERED UNATHLETIC: Interviews: Oceola Jackson, Clifford Green.

FEAR OF PHYSICAL ENCOUNTER; "SISSY!": Interviews: Reginald Little, Philbert Little, Clifford Green, Ted Davenport, "Vince," confidential source. Also see chapters 3, 13, and 18.

FOUGHT TO CONTROL HIS ANGER: Interviews: Ed Roper, Chuck Lyons, Phil Jackson, John Elton Bembry, et al. "I suspect," says Arlene Seaton, "that Malcolm was carrying inside what Philbert expressed openly with his combativeness." And Godfrey Joiner says that Malcolm later hid his anger so well in prison that it was difficult to tell when he was angry.

But Joiner could often tell by looking into his eyes. Malcolm told him that a person who loses his self-control and shows his anger is weak.

SOUNDLY THRASHED: Interviews: Dick Letts, Clifford Green.

ACTED UNINTERESTED: Interviews: Cecelia McGee, Mamie Breedlove, Art Jones, Ed Roper, Reginald Little. Also see *MX*, p. 27.

BLUSH OR RETREAT INTO THE NEAREST CORNER: Interview: Bethel Seaton.

ANGRY: Interview: Cecelia McGee.

ZELMA: Interview: Zelma Holman.

JEAN SEATON: Interviews: Bethel Seaton, Clarence Seaton, Arlene Seaton, Jean Seaton, Pearl Merchant, Jr.

REJECTED BY LANSING BLACKS: Interviews: Pearl Merchant, Jr., Reginald Little, Dick Letts.

STOOD AROUND: Interview: Willie MacDonald.

EDGE OF THE CROWD; A LONELY-LOOKING, UNCOMMUNICATIVE, FORGOTTEN YOUNGSTER: Interviews: Cecelia McGee, Willie MacDonald, Regina Booker, Leon Moffett, Pearl Merchant, Jr., Arlington Cooper, Howard Bannister.

9. Dashed Hopes

41   ELLA UNWANTED CHILD: Interview: Mary Little.

SHE SAW HIM ONLY ONCE MORE: Interview: Ella Little.

SARAH RAISED ELLA: Interviews: Ella Little, Mary Little.

SEVENTH CHILD: Interviews: Mozelle Jackson, Ella Little, J. C. Little, Mary Little.

ELLA GROOMS MALCOLM: Interview: Ella Little.

THREATENS TO SCALD; QUICK RIGHT: Interview: Philbert Little.

MALCOLM IMPRESSED; ELLA PRAISES HIM: *MX*, pp. 32-33.

THE CONTRAST: *MX*, pp. 32-24.

"JET BLACK": *MX*, p. 33. Article by Dick Schaap in *New York Herald Tribune*, Feb. 22, 1965.

42   NEITHER EARL NOR ELLA WAS THAT DARK: Interviews: Kenneth Collins, Dorothy Collins, Mary Little, Clara Little, J. C. Little, Philbert Little, Ella Little.

KAMINSKA AMD MALCOLM: Tape-recorded interview with Bill Campbell, radio station WCAU (Ed Harvey Show), Philadelphia, April 10, 1964. *MX*, pp. 35-37. Interviews: Clifford Walcott, Rollin Dart, Herb Fox, Vivian Shaffer, Beatrice Walline, Rodney Felton. The incident with Kaminska, who was Malcolm's eighth-grade advisor, occurred during eighth grade, not during seventh grade, which Malcolm spent at West Junior High.

ATTEMPT TO REASSURE: Interview: Jim Cotton.

"GAVE UP": *PG*, p. 29.

SCHOOLWORK: See Malcolm's school record.

43   BASKETBALL: June 26, 1974 letter from editor of the *Ingham County News* to author. *MX*, pp. 23, 29. Interviews: Shirley Feight, Don Oesterle. *Michigan State News* (East Lansing), Feb. 15, 1973, p. 7.

FOOTBALL: June 26, 1974 letter, supra. Interviews: Bernard Show, Bill Gordon Dawson, Richard Diehl, Malburne Curtis.

BOXING; RE-ENTER GOLDEN GLOVES: Interview: Hank Fries.

"DO WHAT YOU FEAR TO DO": Interview: Malcolm Jarvis. Malcolm X also frequently quoted Shakespeare's "Screw your courage to the sticking place!" (Interview: Philbert Little.)

OUTWARDLY INDIFFERENT: Interview: Hank Fries.

HAD PREVIOUSLY LAMENTED: Interview: Audrey Slagh.

NONCOMPLIANCE: "Malcolm X Life Story Triggers Recollection of Mason Stay," *Ingham County News*, undated clipping. Interviews: Elsie Taylor, Kendal Merlau, Clifford Walcott, Helen Bentley, Dick Lyon.

OUSTED FROM BAND PRACTICE: Interviews: Chuck Seeley, Edna Mae Hamlin.

EVICTED FROM SCHOOL DANCE: Interviews: Clifford Walcott, Richard Brown.

BITTER AND WITHDRAWN: *MX*, p. 37. Interviews: Jim Cotton, Katie Randall, Richard Brown, Kendal Merlau, Pearl Merchant, Jr., Jean Seaton, Arlene Seaton.

"GOING TO EXPLODE": Interview: Maynard Allyn.

IMPATIENT: *MX*, pp. 195-196.

SEEMED LIKE A MONTH: *MX*, p. 34. Malcolm's autobiography intimates that he had to sit in the back of the Greyhound bus because he wasn't white. But the Greyhound busses connecting Michigan with Massachusetts were not racially segregated, according to an August 13, 1974 letter from Greyhound Bus Lines to the author.

44 BLACKS VS IRISH: Oscar Handlin, *Boston's Immigrants* (Belknap Press, 1979), pp. 52-53, 69-70, 204-205, 320, 357.

ONLY SIX: Stephan Thernstrom, *The Other Bostonians* (Harvard University Press, 1973), pp. 179, 194.

MORE THAN HALF: Ibid., pp. 197-198.

"A LONG WAYS BACK": Charles H. Trout, *Boston, The Great Depression, and The New Deal* (Oxford University Press, 1977), pp. 20, 326.

UNABLE TO TELL: *MX*, p. 35.

INABILITY TO TRUST WOMEN: *MX*, pp. 67-68, 91, 225-226, 389.

APPARENTLY ATTEMPTED TO DENY HIS SECOND-CLASS POSITION: In *MX*, p. 31, Malcolm asserts that, before he went to live with them, Mr. and Mrs. Lyons treated him as though he "was one of their children." He says that their feeling toward him "was the same warm feeling" that he says he got when he went into Lansing to visit the Gohannas and his brothers and sisters.

MALCOLM DOLED OUT SUNDAY FUNNIES, AS WILFRED HAD: Interviews: Chuck Lyons, Philbert Little.

NICE PEOPLE, BUT DIDN'T LIKE LIVING WITH THEM: Interview: Lucille Lathrop.

NO IDEA: Interview: Chuck Lyons.

LAUGHED AT JOKES: Interview: Robert Lyons.

45 CHRISTMAS PRESENTS: Interview: Marie Lyons, Chuck Lyons.

REPAY: Interviews: Reginald Little, Ed Roper.

BARBELL INCIDENT: Interviews: Norman Lyons, Robert Lyons.

HAD TO GET ALONG: Interview: Thomas V. Wallace.

AUTOCRATIC: Interviews: Chuck Lyons, Norman Lyons.

SAT ALONE IN BALCONY: Interview: Elsie Taylor.

HELD RESPONSIBLE: Interview: Norman Lyons.

SEVERELY JEOPARDIZED: Interviews: Kendal Merlau, Clifford Walcott, Ilene Lassen.

MALCOLM'S DETERMINATION: Interview: Chuck Lyons.

JUNE PALMER: Interviews: Barbara Wallace, Edna Mae Hamlin, confidential source.

SCHOOL ADMINISTRATORS PETITION COURT: "Malcolm X Life Story Triggers Recollections of Mason Stay," *Ingham County News*, undated clipping. Interview: Clifford Walcott.

SHORT STAY WITH GRAYSON FAMILY: Interview: Louise Lathrop. See also Malcolm's school record, which indicates that he was living on Rogers Street with the Graysons, not on Elm Street with the Lyonses, when he left Michigan for Boston in February 1941.

DID NOT TELL ELLA WHY: *MX*, p. 38.

NO ONE IN MICHIGAN SEEMED TO WANT HIM: Interview: Retha Fowler. (Louise Little says that, after she was sent to Kalamazoo State Hospital, Malcolm "didn't know what home to go to.")

10. A Home at Last

48 "NO TOMORROW": *MX*, p. 39.

ELLA MYTHOLOGIZES EARL: Interview: Ella Little.

DAILY PEP TALKS: Interview: Ella Little.

LAWYER: In *MX*, p. 61, Malcolm discusses his youthful desire to be a lawyer and his feeling that Ella would have even taken in laundry to help him obtain a professional degree.

PRESIDENT: Interviews: Heshaam Jaaber, Ella Little.

"DIDN'T WANT TO DISAPPOINT": *MX*, p. 42. See also p. 46, where Malcolm denies that he cared about what Ella thought about the job he had selected.

ELLA'S AMBITIONS THWARTED: *MX*, p. 139. Also p. 40, where Malcolm includes Ella among the "Southern strivers and scramblers." See also Archie Epps, *The Speeches of Malcolm X at Harvard* (William Morrow, 1968), p. 21.

UNEDUCATED: In 1936, Ella told court-appointed investigators that she had graduated Girls' High School, Boston, at the age of sixteen after being double-promoted twice. But Boston school officials cannot find any evidence that Ella ever attended the school. (Undated response from Boston School Committee to November 21, 1986 inquiry by author.)

TRIED TO PLEASE: In *MX*, p. 59, Malcolm describes how he reluctantly accepted the job at the Townsend Drugstore in order to please Ella. Interview: Ella Little. See also *MX*, p. 42.

PERFECTIONISTIC: "I told him [i.e.,Malcolm] on several occasions that if he was going to be a lawyer, I wanted him to be the best," Ella later declared. Describing his Dec. 16, 1964 address at Harvard Law School, she said, "That speech was perfect. He was perfect. There was no doubt in my mind." (Interview: Ella Little.)

"RIPPED HIM APART": "One of the things I give myself credit for in Malcolm's life is that I gave him self-confidence," Ella asserted during our first, lengthy interview, which was conducted face-to-face. "I use this [approach] on Brother Small here. When he gets low in spirit, I rip him apart!" (Interview: Ella Little.) Sharon 10X describes how Ella publicly ridiculed her son Rodnell, years later, when he failed to meet her expectations. (Interview: Sharon 10X.)

WITH A BRICK: Interview: Ella Little.

RULED EVERYONE ELSE: In *MX*, pp. 39, 319, Malcolm describes Ella as a domineering woman "whose every instinct was to run everything and everybody she had to do with—including me." "She had broken the spirits of three husbands." Two of them, Kenneth Collins and Frank Johnson, report that she was very domineering. So do Clara Little and author Louis Lomax [*To Kill a Black Man* (Holloway House, 1968,) pp. 26-27.) "As a rule," Ella told me in 1976, "I have very good control over my own family. . . . We can't control everybody." She said she "never hesitated to chastise Malcolm," and that he considered her word to be law. The kind of parent-substitute she was is suggested in *MX*, p. 44, where Malcolm's friend "Shorty" tells him that a sister who gives him free bed and board "couldn't be all bad."

AGAIN AND AGAIN: Interview: Mary Little.

SHE DEMANDED: Interviews: Phil Jackson, Lawson Riley, Mary Little.

REFUSED TO ALLOW PARTIES: Interview: Kenneth Collins.

LAVISHLY: Interviews: J. C. Little, Kenneth Collins.

YIELDED, AT FIRST: Interviews: Kenneth Collins, J. C. Little. Also see *MX*, p. 59.

DIDN'T WANT TO UPSET: *MX*, p. 42.

LOVED: Interviews: Clara Little, Malcolm Jarvis, C. Eric Lincoln.

PRIVATELY COMPLAINED: Interviews: Kenneth Collins, Mary Little. See also *MX*, p. 44, where "Shorty" assures Malcolm that a sister who gives him free bed and board "couldn't be all bad."

BEGAN TO REBEL: Interviews: Mary Little, confidential source.

WRITTEN CONFESSIONS: Interviews: Ella Little, Kenneth Collins.

REFUSED TO LEND A HAND: Interview: Kenneth Collins.

49 SHOT HORSE; CRIED: Interview: J. C. Little.

RESTRICT HIS CONTACTS: *MX*, pp. 42-43.

RESENTED PRETENSIONS: *MX*, pp. 40-41, 43.

HILL BOYS UNAWARE: "I couldn't stand those Hill characters," Malcolm says in *MX*, p. 59. See also *MX*, p. 65, where Malcolm characterizes the inhabitants of the Hill as "stuck-up." Yet he spent a great deal of time with youthful members of the so-called Four Hundred, some of whom he appeared to like very much. (Interviews: Malcolm Jarvis, Austin Norman.)

Neither Mr. Norman nor Johnny Jones detected any negative feelings on Malcolm's part toward Hill people. "If he had them," Norman told me, "he kept them to himself."

FOLLOWED OLDER ONES: Interview: Phil Jackson. See *MX*, p. 42.

"WHAT DID YOU SAY?"; BLUFFS OPPONENTS: Interviews: Johnny Jones, Larry Nesblitt, Robert Corbin. See Malcolm's description of another attempted bluff on *MX*, pp. 124-125.

SNICKERED; FARM BOY: Interview: Viola Thacker. See also *MX*, p. 39.

SPURNED: Interviews: Ruth Lane, Gloria Strother, Malcolm Jarvis.

MORE RELAXED; FELT ACCEPTED: *MX*, pp. 43, 51. "It all felt so good because I was accepted," Malcolm says on page 51.

DIDN'T GO IN: *MX*, p. 43.

50 FICTIONAL COMPOSITE: Perhaps for legal reasons, Malcolm's autobiography combined a number of real-life people into a single, fictional autobiographical character called "Shorty." The identity of the first person—the former Lansingite whom Malcolm met at the pool hall—is unclear. The second is Malcolm Jarvis. According to Arnold Perl, who produced a filmed documentary about Malcolm, there was a third person. If so, I have been unable to ascertain who he is.

"ALL BAD": *MX*, p. 44.

SMOKING MARIJUANA: *MX*, pp. 51, 56.

ORIGINS OF ZOOT SUIT: "Zoot Suit Originated in Georgia; Bus Boy Ordered First One in '40," *New York Times*, June 11, 1943.

"PROFILING"; CONSPICUOUSLY JANGLED: *FDL*, p. 17. Interviews: Lawson Riley, Gloria Strother, Alton Cousins, J. C. Little.

CONKS: *MX*, pp. 52-54.

51 ATTENTION-GETTING BEHAVIOR: Malcolm and his friend John Richmond were the first to wear zoot suits on the Hill. According to Malcolm Jarvis, they became the talk of Upper Roxbury. "I would say he craved attention," Lionel Beane says. George P-4P37agrees with Beane's assessment. And Gloria Strother says, "I'm just surmising, but I think that if [Malcolm] felt rejected or ignored, he would try to gain attention, like a little kid does when it is ignored. He would gain attention one way or another."

ENSURED HIS REJECTION; SNUBBED; GIRLS REPELLED: Interviews: Viola Thacker, Gloria Strother, Ruth Lane, Malcolm Jarvis, Austin Norman.

BOASTS HE'LL DATE GIRLS, BUT DOESN'T ASK THEM OUT; HE APPEARS UNINTERESTED IN THEM: Interviews: Mozelle Jackson, Viola Thacker. Hugh ("Chico") Holmes and several others got the feeling that Malcolm was uninterested in girls. But years later, Malcolm told a journalist, "In those days, I was very interested in little girls." (Hans J. Massaquoi, "Mystery of Malcolm X," *Ebony* [Vol. 19, Sept., 1964].) Malcolm Jarvis and Oceola Jackson concur. And J. C. Little says, "Even if [Malcolm] was crazy about a girl, . . . he never showed any emotion. He could be bubbling over for some girl, but she'd never know it."

GIRL IN COFFIN: Interview: Mozelle Jackson.

JOHN RICHMOND: Little is known about John Richmond, who is deceased. For a while, he worked on the railroad, as Malcolm did. He reportedly admired Malcolm's hipster ways. Eventually, he became a drug addict. Interviews: Johnny Jones, Austin Norman, Malcolm Jarvis, Lionel Beane, "Paddy" Thorne.

INDIFFERENT TOWARD MARGARET RICHMOND UNTIL SOMEONE STEALS HER AWAY: Interviews: Malcolm Jarvis, confidential source.

RESPONSE TO COLEMAN: Confidential source.

LIKED GLORIA BEST: Interviews: Viola Thacker, Herbert Craigwell, Malcolm Jarvis, Lionel Beane, confidential source.

52 PURSUED GLORIA HESITANTLY: Interview: Gloria Strother.

THEY'D BE LUCKY TO SEE HIM BY TEN: Interview: J. C. Little.

WOMEN DIDN'T SPURN HIM; HE SPURNED THEM: Interview: Vivian Mann.

"SHE'S MY OLD LADY": Interview: Gloria Strother.

NEVER EVEN TRIED TO TOUCH HER: Interview: Gloria Strother.

NEVER EXPRESSED ANGER: Gloria Strother.

NO COMMUNICATION: "I guess we didn't communicate," Gloria lamented years later.
LOVE AT A DISTANCE: In a February 14, 1978 letter to the author, Gloria poignantly recalled how Malcolm had kept her at a distance. Also see, in *JHC*, p. 132, Malcolm's widow's comment about the way he held people at a distance.

11. White Woman

53 DEFIED ELLA'S EFFORTS TO KEEP HIM IN SCHOOL: Hans J. Massaquoi, "Mystery of Malcolm X," *Ebony* (Vol. 19, Sept., 1964). Interview: Ella Little. PR: Prison social worker Calvin Peterson's report of his May 17, 1946 interview of Ella. "For Ella to have been able to guide Malcolm in the direction she wanted him to go," Reginald says, "she would have had to understand the things which had hurt him. Malcolm wasn't the kind to communicate the things which had hurt him."

SUCCESS PRECLUDED: Lawson Riley reports that, when Malcolm first came to Boston, he was bitter about school. It had nothing for him, he told Gloria Strother. Years later, as he was describing the meager job opportunities that were available to American blacks prior to World War II, he said, "We knew what our position was going to be even before we graduated from school." (Unedited, tape-recorded version of Dec. 12, 1964 speech at HARYOU ACT rally.)

NOT WHAT ELLA HAD IN MIND: *MX*, p. 46.

GOOD TEACHER: *MX*, pp. 46-49.

PROSTITUTES: *MX*, p. 49.

"GREATEST": *MX*, pp. 59, 64.

"CLOSE": *MX*, pp. 110. See also pp. 28, 77, 103.

NOT REALLY HIS FRIENDS: Interviews: Sy Oliver, Sonny Greer. Lionel Hampton's wife Gladys reports that Malcolm was "sort of underfoot." ("Like It Is," WABC-TV, New York City, Feb. 22, 1969.) See *MX*, p. 94, where Malcolm criticizes someone else for being "underfoot."

54 TAUNTED: Interview: Johnny Jones.

THOROUGH PREPARATION: *MX*, pp. 56-57. Interview: Ella Little.

MODEL EMPLOYEE: Interview: George Landon,

INSUFFERABLE: *MX*, pp. 59-60. Interview: Ella Little.

55 LAURA RESEMBLES MALCOLM'S MOTHER: Interview: Ella Little.

NO IDEA WHAT WAS ABOUT TO HAPPEN: *MX*, p. 65. But see *MX*, p. 9, where Malcolm states: "When something is about to happen, I can feel something, sense something. I have never known something to happen that has caught me completely off guard — except once. And that was when, years later, I discovered facts I couldn't believe about a man who, up until that discovery, I would gladly have given my life for."

56 AUTOBIOGRAPHICAL VERSION OF HOW MALCOLM MET BEA: *MX*, pp. 67-68.

BLAMED HIMSELF: *MX*, p. 68.

TWO DECADES LATER, THE GUILT STILL TORMENTED HIM: *MX*, pp. 63-64, 68, 414. "Everybody feels guilty," Malcolm declared less than a month before he was assassinated. (*Malcolm X on Afro-American History* [Pathfinder Press, 1970], p. 40.)

AT THE TIC TOC CLUB, HE APPROACHED HER, NOT VICE VERSA: Interview: Larry Neblett. PR: March 8, 1946 memorandum.

ASPIRING NIGHTCLUB DANCER: Brookline Police report, Jan. 15, 1946.

ELEGANT CLOTHES; ACCESS TO MONEY: Interview: Malcolm Jarvis.

BEA BOUGHT MALCOLM CLOTHES: Interview: Ella Little

"STATUS SYMBOL OF THE FIRST ORDER": *MX*, p. 67.

"PARADED"; "SEEMED TO ENJOY": *MX*, pp. 67-68. Interview: John Elton Bembry.

BEA CAME TO HIM: Malcolm describes white women who use black men to satisfy their lust—"particularly 'taboo' lust"—in *MX*, pp. 95-96. And in *MX*, p. 55, he wryly says, "Any white woman with a black man isn't thinking about his hair."

DIDN'T KNOW WHAT SEX WAS: Interview: Walter McLaughlin.

STUD: See *MX*, pp. 67, 95-96, 99-100.

DOWN THE STAIRS: Interview: Ella Little. (After communication between Ella and me ended, she reportedly told another interviewer that she threw Malcolm down the stairs. But Malcolm was too big for her to control physically. In any event, her statements say a lot about the kind of surrogate mother she was.)

LIKE A VIPER: *MX*, p. 69.

57 CUT A SWATH; NEARLY HAD A CORONARY: Interviews: Ella Little, J. C. Little. See Malcolm's comment about Samson and Delilah in *MX*, p. 226. (Also see *MX*, p. 55, where Malcolm says, "Any white woman with a black man isn't thinking about his hair.")

MILKY SUBSTANCE: Interview: Ella Little. Aristotle was one of the first to record the fact that males sometimes lactate. Reuben D. Rohn, "Galactorrhea in the Adolescent," *Journal of Adolescent Health Care* (Vol. 5, No. 1), Jan., 1984. James Wyngaarden, editor, *Cecil, Textbook of Medicine* (seventeenth edition: W. B. Saunders, 1985), p. 1398. *Williams Textbook of Endocrinology* (seventh edition: W. B. Saunders, 1985), p. 416. "A Young Man with Visual Defect and Galactorrhea," *Hospital Practice* (August, 1982), pp. 122D-122V. J. K. Kulsky, P. E. Hartmann, and D. H. Gutteridge, "Composition of Breast Fluid of a Man with Galactorrhea and Hyperprolactinaemia," *The Journal of Clinical Endocrinology and Metabolism* (Vol. 52, No. 3), March, 1981, pp. 581-582.

The effect of marijuana on breast development and lactation is discussed in: John Harmon and Menelaos A. Aliapoulios, "Gynecomastia in Marijuana Users," *The New England Journal of Medicine* (Vol. 287, No. 18), Nov. 2, 1972, p. 936. "Hyperprolactinaemia in Patients with Suspected Cannabis-Induced Gynaecomastia," *The Lancet*, Feb. 2, 1980, p. 255. John W. Harmon and Menelaos A. Aliapoulios, "Marijuana-Induced Gynecomastia: Clinical and Laboratory Experience," *Surgical Forum* (Vol. 25), 1974, pp. 423-425. Robert F. Ryan and Martin L. Pernoll, "Virginal Hypertrophy," *Plastic and Reconstructive Surgery* (Vol. 75, No. 5), May, 1985, pp. 737-742, especially pp. 740, 742. August 22, 1990 letter to author from University of Pennsylvania endocrinologist Professor Thomas Moshang, Jr.

SENT TO GROCERY STORE WITHOUT MONEY: Interviews: Mary Little, Malcolm Orgias. Rodnell Collins, the son of Ella and Kenneth Collins, subsequently told Kenneth that, when Rodnell became old enough, Ella tried to force him to steal from grocery stores.

SHE STOLE FOOD HERSELF; HER HUSBAND WOULD NOT ACCOMPANY HER TO THE MARKET: Interview: Kenneth Collins. For Ella's larceny convictions, see Suffolk County Superior Court [transacting criminal business], docket entries #1916 (1938), #5318 (1942), #109, 110, 112, 113 (1947), #927 (1959).

VALUE OF STOLEN MERCHANDISE NEGLIGIBLE: Interview: Kenneth Collins. In 1942, Ella was convicted for stealing a twenty-nine cent can of tomatoes, a fifty-nine cent can of wax, $2.18 worth of butter, eighty-five cents worth of "tenderetts," thirty-five cents worth of cold cuts, twenty-nine cents worth of hamburger, thirty-nine cents worth of sausage, seventy cents worth of frankfurters, and forty-six cents worth of candy. (Suffolk County Superior Court [transacting criminal business], docket entry #5318, 1942.)

For a description of some of Ella's assets, see certificate of surety dated July 1, 1946, Suffolk County Superior Court criminal docket entry #110 (1947) and *PR*: report of social worker Calvin Peterson's May 17, 1946 interview of Ella. Kenneth Collins estimates that Ella's assets during the early 1940's were approximately two-thirds of the amount cited in the certificate of surety.

IT WASN'T THE LOOT THAT PROMPTED HER STEALING: According to Kenneth Collins, one judge characterized Ella as a compulsive thief who derived pleasure from the act of thievery itself.

ELLA'S MOTHER: A July 1930 Massachusetts Reformatory report on Earl Jr.'s background describes Ella as a "bad character" who took after her mother, Daisy Mason. According to the report, Daisy had loose morals and had "several run-ins with the police for bootlegging and lotteries."

LAWLESSNESS PERVADED FAMILY: "No one in this family was a criminal," Ella asserted during one telephone interview. But see chapters 1, 2, and the rest of chapter 11. Also see June 18, 1975 letter from the *Albion Evening Recorder* to the author. The letter describes the police and court record of Malcolm's uncle James ("Bud") Little.

CRIMINAL RECORD: The following court docket entries refer to criminal proceedings, appellate and otherwise, that Ella has been involved in. They are grouped according to which court the proceedings occurred in, and then chronologically: Boston Municipal Court:

Docket entries #2739 (G-1930), #2003 (G-1931), #2830 (1950), #891-892 (1957). Domestic Relations Criminal Docket entry #278 (1957). Docket entries #2176-2177 (1960), #4065-4066 (1960), #4926 (1961), #2171-2172 (1962), #2176 (1964), #3964 (1973).

Suffolk County Superior Court: Docket entries #4460 (1936), #1916 (1938), #9209 (1938), #5316-5318 (1942), #109-110, 112-113 (1947). Domestic Relations criminal docket entry #2230 (1957). Docket entries #2700-2701 (1957), #5010 (1957), #925-930 (1959), #908-909 (1961).

Roxbury Municipal Court: Docket entries #1455 (1939), #746 (1945), #13557 (1957), #13701-13703 (1959).

MONTH IN JAIL: Interviews: Kenneth Collins, John Brassil. And during one telephone interview, Ella repeatedly substituted the words "Charles Street jail" for the words "Charlestown State Prison." She served her 30-day sentence at the former institution. She entered it Jan. 7, 1947 and was discharged Feb. 5, 1947. The sentence was for her conviction for larceny and assault and battery. See Suffolk County Superior Court criminal docket entries #109, 110, 112, 113 (1947).

EARL JUNIOR'S CRIMINAL RECORD: Earl Jr.'s criminal record is summarized in Malcolm's prison record.

NIGHTCLUB ENTERTAINER; "JIMMY CARLTON": Interviews: Clara Little, Mozelle Jackson, Mary Little, Ella Little. PR. Archie Epps, The Speeches of Malcolm X at Harvard (Morrow, 1968), pp. 21-22. MX, p. 34 spells the last name of Earl Junior's stage name "Carleton," with an "e." But the last name of Malcolm's stage name, which was virtually a duplicate of Earl Junior's, was spelled "Carlton." (FBI correlation summary dated August 22, 1961. Malcolm Jarvis, Myself and I (Carlton Press, 1979), p. 32. PR: March, 1946 interview.) So it is likely that the correct spelling of the last name of Earl Junior's stage name was "Carlton."

"SOMEDAY, I'M GOING TO BE LIKE EARL!": Interview: J. C. Little.

12. Success or Failure?

58 EARL JUNIOR DIED OF TUBERCULOSIS: Death certificate dated June 3, 1941.

GRIEF-STRICKEN: Interview: Ella Little.

POISONED: PR: March, 1946 interview.

$18/WEEK: PR: employment history (March, 1946).

"I'LL MAKE IT": FDL, p. 16. Reginald says that Malcolm had "always wanted to be somebody, but he never thought he'd make it."

QUIT NEW HAVEN RAILROAD: PR: employment history. Dec. 6, 1974 letter from Railroad Retirement Board to author.

BIGGER FISH TO FRY: Years later, in an Aug. 5, 1949 letter to Bazely Perry, Malcolm acknowledged that he had been ambitious when he was young. Interviews: Phyllis Ashby Scott, Lawson Riley, Hugh ("Chico") Holmes, Hank Fries, Enos Major, Sr., Jean Seaton, Mrs. Mildred Mitchell, Allie Cooper, Jim Reed. Also see MX, p. 183.

LAWYER: MX, pp. 35-37, 183. Interview: Mary Little. Louis Lomax, To Kill a Black Man (Holloway House, 1968), p. 26.

DANCER; ACTOR; ENTERTAINER: (See chapter 18.) When Malcolm entered Charlestown State Prison in 1946, he listed his occupation as "show business" and gave the name "Rhythm Red." He had already described himself to the Lansing police as a dancer. Apparently, he was referring to the dancing he had done at Lansing and Manhattan nightclubs. He told one prison official that he had been a part-time drummer at Small's Paradise and that he had also been a nightclub master of ceremonies. (See PR: employment history.) Years later, Lionel Hampton recalled, "[Malcolm] always came around the band. He wanted to be an M.C. He wanted to sing or wanted to dance. He wanted to go out in front and entertain the people. He wanted to be on the stage." ("Like It Is," WABC-TV, New York, Feb. 22, 1969.)

MAKE A NAME FOR HIMSELF: April 18, 1977 letter from J. Prescott Adams to author. Interviews: Jean Seaton, Pearl Merchant, Jr., Johnny Davis, Jr., Mrs. Mildred Mitchell.

MONEY: Interviews: Katherine Gillion, Jean Seaton, Oceola Jackson, Robert Foggie, Luther Jermany, Phyllis Ashby Scott, Allie Cooper, Godfrey Joiner.

CADILLAC: Interviews: John McIlvaine, Lawson Riley.

LIMITLESS: "We'd be talking about what we were going to do when we grew up," recalls a teenage friend. "His goals were limitless; ours conformed more to reality." Confidential source.

CONQUER THE WORLD: Interviews: Reginald Little, Gloria Strother.

AFRAID OF FAILURE: "He always wanted to be somebody," says Reginald, "but he never thought he'd make it. He always felt he'd never quite make it. . . . He felt like a failure." Interview: Reginald Little.

59 "SLAVE": *MX*, pp. 44-45, 139.

RAN THROUGH SEVERAL JOBS: *PR*: employment history. *MX*, pp. 69, 160.

CASCO BAY SHIPYARD; PORTLAND WAS TOO DEAD: Interviews: J. C. Little, Johnny Jones, Ella Little.

CHRISTMAS GIFTS: Interview: Ella Little.

DIDN'T NEED ANYTHING: Interview: J. C. Little.

CHRISTMAS A HOAX: Interview: Gloria Strother.

RETURNS TO NEW HAVEN RAILROAD: *PR*: employment history. Dec. 6, 1974 letter from Railroad Retirement Board to author.

"SANDWICH RED" SUPPLANTS RIVAL: *MX*, pp. 72, 75, 77.

60 HE LAMENTED: *MX*, p. 75.

SEEMED TO PREFER: Interview: Ken Collins.

INTO THE POCKETS: Confidential source.

JUMPS INTO BAY: Interview: Alton Cousins.

"I JUST WANT PEOPLE TO NOTICE": Interview: Alton Cousins.

"HE LIKED EVERYBODY, EVEN ME": *MX*, p. 78.

LIKED MALCOLM; LENT A PATERNAL EAR; VOLUNTEERED FOR EXTRA DUTIES: Interview: Alton Cousins.

TOSSED OUT SAILORS: Interview: Alton Cousins.

61 CLAIMS PAPPY PROTECTED HIS JOB AND FAVORED HIM: *MX*, pp. 77-78.

MALCOLM WAS MISTAKEN: Interview: Alton Cousins.

AGAIN QUIT NEW HAVEN RAILROAD: *PR*: employment history. Dec. 6, 1974 letter from Railroad Retirement Board to author.

JOBS PLENTIFUL: *MX*, p. 78.

"I WANT TO HAVE A LITTLE FUN": Interview: John McIlvaine. Reginald says that Malcolm was despondent when he wasn't having fun.

13. The Return

62 FROM JOB TO JOB AND CITY TO CITY: See Chapters 13-19. With varying degrees of accuracy, Malcolm's prison record describes his travels between late 1942 and late 1945. See, for instance, the early 1946 report of the interview conducted by John F. Rockett in Dedham jail. The material in the prison record describing Malcolm's travels must be read in conjunction with other relevant material, particularly the information his former employers have furnished me.

RETURNED TO LANSING: According to Michigan police records, Malcolm applied for a job with Oldsmobile on Nov. 17, 1942. Evidently he was not hired; he started work at Shaw's jewelry store, Lansing, on Nov. 25.

SPORTING BOSTON ACCENT: Interviews: Howard Bannister, Katherine Gillion, confidential source. Cf. *MX*, pp. 59, 60.

COULDN'T BELIEVE: *MX*, p. 78.

LORDING IT OVER: Interviews: Dick Letts, Geraldine Nelson. Nelson says, "He seemed to act superior to everyone else. He strutted like a rooster."

CENTER OF ATTENTION: *MX*, p. 79.

"HALF-SENSED": *MX*, p. 79.

IRENE COOLEY, TOO: Interview: Irene Cooley.

"DO YOU REMEMBER ME?": Interview: Elaine Flynn.

MALCOLM VISITS BETTY: Interview: Betty Girven.

63 APOLOGIZES TO TELLIER SISTERS: Interviews: Joyce and Lorraine Tellier.

CONQUESTS: Interviews: Hayward Howard, Howard Bannister, Dick Letts, confidential sources.

ANNE THE BARMAID: Interviews: Malcolm Jarvis, John Elton Bembry.

MALCOLM AND WELDON: Interviews: Howard Bannister, Ann Lee Bannister, confidential source.

MALCOLM AND GERALDINE: Interview: Geraldine Nelson.

64 MOVES TO FLINT: Malcolm began working at A/C Sparkplug in Flint on December 28, 1942, according to the firm's personnel records.

WEST INDIAN DESCENT; NOTIFY HOWARD'S MOTHER: A/C Sparkplug's personnel office supplied this information.

SENSITIVE TO COLD: Interviews: Reginald Little, Tom Amiss, Louise Little, Philbert Little, Ella Little, Malcolm Jarvis. *U. S. News and World Report*, March 30, 1964, p. 39.

THIN, STYLISH COAT OR NO COAT: Interviews: Howard Bannister, Bill and Mary Jane Downs, J. C. Little, confidential source.

"TO LOOK GOOD": Interview: J. C. Little.

"IN DEFIANCE"; SISSIES PULLED THEIR COAT COLLARS UP": Confidential source.

MALCOLM AND BLANCHE: Interviews: Willie MacDonald, Ann Lee Bannister, Howard Bannister, Jim Reed, confidential source.

"REALLY WANTED": *MX*, p. 30.

COMPETES FOR OTHER MEN'S WOMEN: Interviews: Howard Bannister, confidential source.

NO BIG THING TO CUCKOLD: Interviews: Herbert Craigwell, Malcolm Jarvis. Reginald recalls how Malcolm would boast about his conquests by acting as if someone else's conquests were comparatively insignificant.

WOMAN-THEFT A PERSONAL CHALLENGE: Confidential source.

TO A PULP; MALCOLM ROARED: Interview: Phil Jackson.

65 THE FIGHT WITH HANK ROSS: Interview with the man whose name has been changed to Hank Ross. Recalling another, earlier fight that Malcolm had had with someone else, Clifford Green told an interviewer, "He didn't put up his dukes. When he got in a fight, he didn't fight." (Interview: Clifford Green.)

In later chapters, as well as chapters 3 and 8, contrast how Malcolm defends other people—and America's blacks—better than he defends himself.

NEW HAVEN RAILROAD: PR: employment history. See also Dec. 6, 1974 letter from Railroad Retirement Board to author.

LEAVING GLORIA FOR HER OWN GOOD: Interview: Gloria Strother.

A DESPERATE ATTEMPT TO AVOID ANTICIPATED REJECTION: "He had hurt me so many times," Gloria told an interviewer years later. "I never knew that I could hurt him."

"NEVER WEAR YOUR HEART ON YOUR SLEEVE": Interview: Malcolm Jarvis. "I don't think he wanted anyone to see any tender spot," says Mary Bibbs. "He didn't wear his feelings on his shoulder."

REACTION OUTWARDLY COLD: Interview: John Little.

14. School for the Unschooled

66 SEVENTEEN DAYS AFTER: PR: employment history.

"IT WAS INEVITABLE": *MX*, p. 78. See note below describing the relevant chronological errors in Malcolm's autobiography.

PRISON RECORD SUGGESTS: PR: employment history. According to Lionel Beane, "Paddy" Thorne, and Willard Chandler, there was such an unwritten rule, despite the denials of former white employees. The employment history section of Malcolm's prison record attributes his final departure from the New Haven Railroad to defiance of this rule. But it is not entirely clear whether the information in the record came from Malcolm or, if it did, whether it was accurate.

INTERVIEWED AND HIRED BY CHARLIE SMALL: *MX*, p. 80, says that Malcolm began working at Small's Paradise in 1942, just after he ceased working for the Seaboard Railroad. But Railroad Retirement Board records show that Malcolm didn't begin working for the Seaboard Railroad until February 1944. They also show that the only railroad he worked for during 1942 was the New Haven. According to his prison record, the New Haven was the first railroad he was fired from. He left the New Haven March 18, 1943, when he was seventeen years old. According to his prison record, he worked at Small's Paradise no more than two months. *MX*, p. 96 says that he stopped working at Small's before mid-1943. (My attempts to obtain access to Small's personnel records were repeatedly rebuffed.)

OBSERVED BY EVERY DRINKING ESTABLISHMENT: *MX*, p. 96.

VIRTUALLY INDISPENSABLE: *MX*, p. 81,

67   INGRATIATING BEHAVIOR PAID OFF: *MX*, pp. 80-81.

MALCOLM EMPHATICALLY DENIED THAT FEWCLOTHES WAS BEGGING: *MX*, p. 89.

SEEMED TO EMPATHIZE: *MX*, pp. 90, 117.

LEARNED TO SENSE WHICH PEOPLE WERE POLICEMEN: *MX*, pp. 86, 98.

UNCANNY: Interview: Malcolm Jarvis.

68   "PATERNAL": *MX*, p. 86.

LIKE A SPONGE: *MX*, p. 83.

SCHOOLROOM: In his autobiography, Malcolm repeatedly characterizes what he was being taught as his schooling or education. (*MX*, pp. 81, 83, 85, 91.)

SCHOOLED AT CREOLE PETE'S: Interview: Pete Robertson. (Malcolm's autobiography changed Creole Pete to "Creole Bill," perhaps for legal reasons.)

TRUSTED PROSTITUTES MORE: *MX*, pp. 91, 226. Interview: Bob High.

SEX EDUCATION: "It was in this [prostitute-filled] house that I learned more about women than I ever did in any other single place. It was these working prostitutes who schooled me to things that every wife and every husband should know." (*MX*, p. 91.)

ENTIRELY VERBAL: Interview: John Elton Bembry.

"THE CLAP": According to Malcolm's prison record, he contracted a case of gonorrhea in New York City in 1942 and was treated by a Dr. Carrington, whose office was located at 795 St. Nicholas Avenue. He later told a friend, "You're not a man until you've had the clap!" (Confidential source.)

SAID HE PREFERRED TO SLEEP WITH WOMEN WHO CARED FOR HIM: Interview: John Elton Bembry.

69   THE TRYST HAD NOT GONE WELL: Confidential source.

SELF-INDUCED OUSTER: *MX*, pp. 80, 96-97.

15. Addict

70   MALCOLM CLOTHES-CONSCIOUS: Malcolm's perfectionism was apparent in the way he dressed. (Interviews: Gloria Strother, Reginald Little, confidential source.)

SAMMY McKNIGHT: Interview: Malcolm Jarvis. *MX*, pp. 97-100.

BEFORE HE COULD "GRADUATE": *MX*, p. 98.

71   ORALLY: *PR*: Response by Malcolm to interviewer's question, March 8, 1946. [The relationship between drug addiction and so-called "oral," or maternal, deprivation has been studied for decades. See, for example, Abraham Wikler & Robert Rasor, "Psychiatric Aspects of Drug Addiction," *American Journal of Medicine* (Vol. 14, 1953), p. 567. Robert Rasor, "Neurotic Addicts: Personality Characteristics & Hospital Treatment," in Paul H. Hoch & Joseph Zubin (eds.), *Problems of Addiction & Habituation* (Grune & Stratton, 1958), pp. 8-9.]

LIKE FOOD: *MX*, p. 138.

FEAR OF INJECTION: *PR*: "Preliminary Record," March 8, 1946. Also mentioned in 1949 prison psychiatrist's report. *FDL*, pp. 54, 56.

MOVIE IN WHICH VACCINATION CAUSES AFRICANS TO DIE: Interview: Ella Little.

OCCASIONALLY USED STRONGER DRUGS: *PR*: "Preliminary Record," March 8, 1946.

MX, pp. 123, 130, 153.

MARIJUANA PRIMARILY; COCAINE SECONDARILY: *PR*: "Preliminary Record," March 8, 1946. Interviews: John Elton Bembry, Malcolm Jarvis, Luther Jermany. *MX*, pp. 78, 99, 123, 134, 139, 146-147.

LESS ESTRANGED: Interview: John Elton Bembry.

IMAGINARY CONVERSATIONS: *MX*, p. 134.

DIDN'T NEED PEOPLE: Malcolm tried very hard to show that he didn't need women or anyone else, according to Howard Cramer, Emily Seaton, Cecelia McGee, and Pearl Merchant, Jr.

GAMBLING: *MX*, pp. 51, 60, 84, 108, 109-110, 117, 136. Interviews: John K. Terry, Johnny McIlvaine, Malcolm Jarvis, Larry Neblett, "Vince," Johnny Davis, Jr., Robert Foggie, Pearl Merchant, Jr.

72 POVERTY: *MX*, pp. 90, 102, 117, 127, 136, 139. Interviews: Philbert Little, Reginald Little, Harold Vaughan, "Vince."

ADMITTED IT WAS FOOLISH TO GAMBLE: Interview: Howard Bannister.

HIDDEN MOTIVES: See Charlotte Olmsted, *Heads I Win, Tails You Lose* (Macmillan, 1962), p. 25. See also *Psychoanalytic Quarterly* (Vol. 23, 1954), p. 152, which contains an abstract of Edward E. Harkavy's "The Psychoanalysis of a Gambler," a paper delivered at the March 10, 1953 meeting of the New York Psychoanalytic Society.

BIG SPENDER: *MX*, pp. 110, 145. Interviews: Johnny McIlvaine, Malcolm Jarvis, Howard Bannister, Larry Neblett, Bob High, Stanley Allen, Junius Thomas Vaughan.

LOANED LAST TEN AND BORROWED FIVE: Interview: Malcolm Jarvis.

PAWNED HIS SUIT: Interview: Howard Bannister. Jarvis and a confidential source attest to the generous side of Malcolm's nature.

ADDICTED TO MOVIES: *MX*, pp. 42, 99, 110. Interviews: Reginald Little, Robert Foggie. Foggie says Malcolm would go to a movie at 9:30 a.m. "to kill his morning."

HE'D EMERGE A COP. . . . A BOW-LEGGED COWBOY: Interview: Philbert Little.

STORMY WEATHER; CABIN IN THE SKY; CASABLANCA: *MX*, p. 99.

JOHNNY EAGER: Interview: Reginald Little.

TOOK GREAT PRECAUTION AGAINST ARREST: *MX*, pp. 100-102.

73 FOOLED THE POLICE ; *MX*, pp. 109, 145.

1943 HARLEM RIOT: Dominic Capeci, Jr., *The Harlem Riot of 1943* (Temple University Press, 1977), pp. 99-103, 120, 124, 177. *New York Times*, August 2-3, 1943. *Time*, Aug. 9, 1943, p. 19. *Newsweek*, Aug. 9, 1943, pp. 48-50. *New Republic*, Aug. 10, 1943, pp. 221-222. *Life*, Aug. 16, 1943, p. 32. *MX*, pp. 113-114. Neil Hickey & Ed Edwin, *Adam Clayton Powell and the Politics of Race* (New York: Fleet Publication Corp., 1965), pp. 78-81.

IN DEBT: *MX*, p. 102.

NEW YORK CENTRAL: Dec. 6, 1974 letter from Railroad Retirement Board to author. *PR*: employment history.

FIRED: Ibid.

ORDERS TO REPORT: Nov. 21, 1974 letter to author from New York City Director, Selective Service.

SCARED; PREFERRED TO BE LIVE COWARD THAN DEAD HERO: *MX*, p. 104. Interview: Reginald Little. In a subsequent July 26, 1946 letter to the Charlestown State Prison authorities, Mrs. Swerlein's friend Mrs. Leo Kelly wrote: "Some of the boys have told me. . . . how afraid he [Malcolm] was that the war would last long enough to get him . . . [T]hey say he practically shed tears for fear that would happen."

74 AT THE INDUCTION CENTER; MALCOLM VS. THE PSYCHIATRIST: *MX*, pp. 104-107.

"SEXUAL PERVERSION": Report by FBI's New York office dated Jan. 28, 1955. A similar, unclearly dated 1955 report from the same office states: "Selective Service records of Local Board 59, NYC, reflect that on 10/25/43, the subject was found mentally disqualified for military service for the following reasons: psychopathic personality; inadequate [sic]; sexual perversion; psychiatric rejection."

16. Romance with Finance

75 LITTLE ALTERNATIVE BUT TO FEED HIM: Interview: "Vince." Also see *MX*, p. 14.

LOANED HIM MONEY: Interview: Luther Jermany.

MONEY IS THE TEST WHETHER A WOMAN CARES: Interview: Malcolm Jarvis.

PILLAR OF SUPPORT; MILKED HER DRY: *MX*, pp. 68, 135. Interviews: Malcolm Jarvis, Kenneth Collins.

ONE MUST EXPLOIT IN ORDER TO AVOID BEING EXPLOITED: *MX*, p. 135.

BEA MARRIES IN EARLY 1944: Certificate of marriage consummated Feb. 22, 1944.

SEX WITH BLACKS: *MX*, P. 95.

HANGS AROUND BARS; PICKS UP WOMEN: *PR*: Record of initial interview. Interview: Luther Jermany.

SEEMS TO PREFER WHITE ONES: Interviews: Arlington Cooper, Mary Little, Johnny Jones, Albert ("Junior") Clark.

76 "BUSINESS EXECUTIVE" ACT: Interview: Malcolm Jarvis.

"ROMANCE WITHOUT FINANCE" DIDN'T INTEREST HIM: Interviews: Malcolm Jarvis, Larry Neblett, Robert Foggie, Jim Reed, Kenneth Collins, Johnny Davis, Jr., Mary Little, Cornelia Williams. See also *MX*, p. 27, where Malcolm emphasizes his unwillingness to "squander" his money on females.

JEWISH GIRLFRIEND: Interviews: J. C. Little, Ken Collins, Reginald Little, confidential source.

MORE INTERESTED IN HER BOOKS: Interviews: Johnny Davis, Jr., confidential source. (The latter reports that Malcolm was reading all the time.)

EVEN READS THE BIBLE: Interview: Luther Jermany.

"BITCHES": Interviews: Johnny Davis, Jr., Jim Reed, Esther Abrams, Charles Pritchett.

PHYSICAL ABUSE: "I would feel evil and slap her around," Malcolm says on *MX*, p. 135. Godfrey Joiner reports that Malcolm said that he treated his women roughly.

WOMEN ARE WEAK: *MX*, pp. 92-93.

MEN MUST RULE WOMEN: *MX*, pp 92-93, 135.

"ANYTHING": Confidential source. They'd suck his penis, he later told Godfrey Joiner.

NO INTEREST: *MX*, p. 98.

PIMP; CHAIN OF WHITE WOMEN: Interviews: Stanley Allen, Howard Bannister, Philbert Little, Leon Moffett, Austin Norman, Willard Chandler, Godfrey Joiner, and two confidential sources. (See also Mike Wallace's "The Hate that Hate Produced," which was televised in July, 1959.)

REFUSED TO REVEAL WHEREABOUTS: Confidential source.

"SOMEONE YOU KNOW": Confidential source.

CLAIMED PHILBERT'S WIFE HAD BEEN WHORING FOR HIM: Interview: Philbert Little.

77 RELATIONSHIP WITH PHILBERT'S ESTRANGED WIFE: Interview with confidential source.

WILLIE MAE JONES: Two confidential sources. (A third confidential source confirms that Willie Mae Jones was homosexual.) According to Malcolm's prison record, he apparently carried his memories of Willie with him to prison; when a prison official asked him about a female relative nicknamed "Mae Willie," Malcolm called her "Willie Mae."

"HELL, WITH ALL THESE LITTLE 'GIRLS' HERE, I'M GOING TO MAKE SOME MONEY.": Confidential source. Years later, in a speech describing his youthful waywardness, Malcolm lamented, "The rent is high. You got no money. You turn to dope, liquor, sex." (*Chicago Defender*, June 19, 1963.) Subsequently, out of the blue, Ella repeatedly told an interviewer that Malcolm had never explained what a homosexual is. (Interview: Ella Little.)

An additional, unconfirmed report of Malcolm's homosexual activity appears in the tape-recorded July 30, 1990 conversation between the author and Mark Brown, who has been conducting research on Malcolm independently.

Also see Chapters 17 and 18.

WITHERSPOON INCIDENT: Interviews: Johnny Davis, Jr., and two confidential sources.

FINANCIAL MOTIVE FOR HOMOSEXUAL ENCOUNTERS: Interviews: Malcolm Jarvis and three confidential sources. Also see Chapters 17 and 18.

17. Part-time Hustler

79 SEABOARD RAILROAD: Employee Registration Card dated Feb. 12, 1944, U.S. Railroad Retirement Board. (Malcolm began working for the Seaboard Railroad after, not before, his 1943 dismissal from Small's Paradise and his rejection by the draft board.)

CONFRONTATION WITH SOLDIER: MX, p. 77.

ATLANTIC COAST RAILROAD: Employee Registration Card dated March 8, 1944, U.S. Railroad Retirement Board. MX, pp. 102-103.

FREE OF CHARGE: MX, pp. 102-103.

80 CAREER AS ITINERANT DOPE SALESMAN DIDN'T LAST LONG: The end, which is described in MX, p. 108, apparently came before October 20, 1944, for Malcolm began working at Sears Roebuck's Brookline, Mass. warehouse on that date and was arrested in Boston on November 29. (See next chapter.) In fact, the end may have come as early as July, 1944, for Malcolm's prison record indicates that he worked from July to September, part-time or otherwise, at a Manhattan establishment called The Lobster Pond.

ROBBERY: MX, pp. 83, 109, 114-115, 385. Interview: John Elton Bembry.

CANDY STORES AND THE LIKE: MX, p. 109. Interview: Luther Jermany.

ALLEGED BANK ROBBERY: Interview: Tom Wallace. Also see New York Herald Tribune, Feb. 22, 1965, p. 5. Then see PG, pp. 30-31 and the material that follows later in this chapter and Chapter 20.

ALLEGED MURDER: New York Amsterdam News, Apr. 20, 1957, p. 4.

COCAINE: MX, pp. 109, 129, 134.

FOOLS POLICEMEN: MX, p. 109.

HORTENSE: Interview: Malcolm Jarvis.

CONFRONTATION WITH HORTENSE; SAMMY PULLS A GUN: MX, pp. 114-115. Interview: Malcolm Jarvis.

NEVER AGAIN ABLE TO TRUST SAMMY: MX, pp. 114-115. Interview: Reginald Little.

ONLY PERSON HE COULD TRUST: MX, p. 115.

"LIKED" REGINALD: MX, p. 104.

81 IN DIRECT PROPORTION: MX, pp. 112-113.

"GOT VERY CLOSE": MX, p. 110.

REGINALD DISAGREES: Interview: Reginald Little.

NEVER KNEW WHAT HE WAS THINKING: Interviews: Katherine Gillion, Carlton Barnette, Luther Jermany, Jim Reed, J. C. Little, Dick Letts, confidential source.

OFF IN ANOTHER WORLD: Interviews: Ted Davenport, confidential source.

"REPUTATION": MX, pp. 116, 136. But see PG, pp. 30-31.

HE DIDN'T EXPLAIN: MX, p. 116.

GANGLEADER; "LIEUTENANT": Confidential source.

FELONS WORKING FOR HIM; BRIBED POLICE: BMIA, p. 191. Playboy, May, 1963, p. 60. Chicago Daily News, Aug. 21, 1962.

EXAGGERATED HIS IMMORALITY: Interviews: Philbert Little, Ted Poston.

PROUD HE WASN'T A HYPOCRITE: MX, p. 15.

"IN ACTION"; TOES TO FOREHEAD: Interview: Malcolm Jarvis.

82 "EAT PUSSY": Confidential source. One of Malcolm's barbers remembers Malcolm saying, "I'd sure like to eat her!" as an attractive woman passed by the barbershop window.

LOBSTER POND: PR: employment history. According to the Lansing Police Department, Malcolm said he was a dancer when he was arrested in Michigan in 1945 and was asked to state his occupation.

DRUMS: PR: Social worker John T. Herstom's report of July 23, 1946.

JACK CARLTON: PR: initial interview sheet. FBI, correlation summary dated 8/22/61.

CARLTON BELL DONALDSON: Interviews: Hakim Jamal, Johnny McIlvaine, Malcolm Jarvis.

SECRETIVE: But when Malcolm entered Charleston Prison in 1946, he stated that his occupation was "show business."

CONFIDED HIS AMBITION: "He spoke of being a movie star," recalls Allie Cooper. "But he didn't know how to go about accomplishing it."

OUT FRONT, ON STAGE, ENTERTAINING: Lionel Hampton later told an interviewer: "[Malcolm] wanted to be be a M.C. He wanted to sing or wanted to dance. He wanted to go out in front and entertain the people. He wanted to be on the stage." (Gil Noble interviewing Lionel Hampton on WABC-TV's "Like It Is," Feb. 22, 1969 [page 4 of transcript].)

MAKING MOVIES: Interview: Allie Cooper.

UNSTABLE AND NEUROTIC, BUT A "GOOD BOY": PR: employment history.

SEARS ROEBUCK: PR: employment history.

"PSYCHOLOGICALLY UNSUITED": MX, p. 262.

MARGARET RICHMOND: Interview: Malcolm Jarvis.

PAUL LENNON HAZY ABOUT MALCOLM'S DUTIES: In his reply to an inquiry from Charlestown State Prison, Lennon said that since he had employed Malcolm temporarily, it was "obviously impossible to answer more fully." (PR: employment history.)

83 MASSAGE ALL OVER WITH POWDER: Interview: Malcolm Jarvis. Written response by Malcolm Jarvis to author's inquiry about the powdering expeditions at Paul Lennon's.

OLD ENOUGH TO BE MALCOLM'S FATHER: Later, after Malcolm went to prison, he told one interviewer that Paul Lennon was one of three individuals who were "interested" in him. (PR: initial interview sheet.) The death certificate for Mr. Lennon indicates that he was born on March 25, 1888; Malcolm's father was born on July 29, 1890, according to his death certificate and the records of the Massachusetts Bureau of Identification. But, according to Malcolm's birth certificate and Michigan State Police Special Report #2155 (1929), Earl Little may have been born in 1889 instead of 1890.

SOMEONE ELSE: MX, p. 140.

HE DESCRIBED THE PROCEEDINGS TO JARVIS: Interview: Malcolm Jarvis. In a 1963 speech describing his youthful delinquency, Malcolm lamented: "The rent is high. You got no money. You turn to dope, liquor, sex." (Chicago Defender, June 19, 1963.) In another speech, he suggested that one way to handle the white enemy is to "rock him to sleep; send him to bed." (Phonograph record entitled "Malcolm X Speaks to the People in Harlem," Up Front Records, record #UPF-152.) And in a speech opposing integration Malcolm said, "If you try n' cuddle up to [the white man], he condemns you. If you lay down flat on the sidewalk and say, 'Walk on me, Mr. White Folk,' he's still not satisfied; he says, 'Roll over on your other side, nigger. Get over on your back.' You just can't please him. You just can't satisfy him. Why, you're out of yo' mind tryin' to make love to a white man." (The Wisdom of Malcolm X, Mo' Soul Records, record #MS-8001.)

Years later, Jarvis wrote, "People like Paul Lennerd [sic], the queer, always liked to see a new face on the scene every now and then. After meeting Paul Lennerd and participating ina few of the [powdering] parties, Malcolm confided in me about the affair. As I look back in the years, I believe today that Malcolm's idea in telling me all this was to get me to join the party as a new face on the scene, and make a few easy dollars on the side while doing so. . . . It was the practice of Mr. —or Mrs. (smile)—Lennard to pay for your time if it was satisfying. " [Malcolm Jarvis' undated, written response to author's written inquiry.]

"GREATEST URGE": MX, p. 92.

18. More Humiliation

84 ROOMED AT ELLA'S: PR: Case worker Calvin Peterson's 1947 report on Malcolm's Nov. 29, 1944 arrest.

GRACE AND SASSIE LIVED WITH ELLA: Interview: Ella Little.

STEALS FUR COAT: PR, particularly Calvin Peterson's 1947 report on Malcolm's Nov. 29, 1944 arrest.

ATTRIBUTED TO ELLA'S INFLUENCE: Interview: Mary Little.

ELLA SUMMONED THE POLICE: Interviews: Mary Little, William Dorsey.

ELLA LATER DENIED THAT SHE CALLED POLICE: Interview: Ella Little.

ELLA THREATENS QUESTIONER: Telephone interview: Ella Little.

SUSPENDED SENTENCE: *PR*, particularly Calvin Peterson's 1947 report on Malcolm's Nov. 29, 1944 arrest.

TEMPORARY NIGHTCLUB JOB ENDED: *PR*: employment history.

RETURN TO MICHIGAN: *PR*: particularly employment history and report by case worker John F. Rockett of 1946 interview in Dedham jail. See also *MX*, pp. 122-123, which describes an additional reason for Malcolm's wintertime return to Michigan, despite his sensitivity to the cold.

CONSERVATIVE APPAREL: The evolution of Malcolm from flashy dresser to conservative dresser is described in *MX*, pp. 72-73, 104, 136.

"IN SHOWS": Interview: Elaine Flynn.

HOLLYWOOD MOVIES: Interview: Irene Cooley.

"IN BUSINESSS": The former schoolmate was Belva Otis, who later married Jim Cotton. (Interview: Jim Cotton.)

MADISON AVENUE: Interview: June Tellier.

SPIRITS SEEEMED LOW: Confidential source.

"A MAN NEVER RISES SO HIGH . . .": Interview: Malcolm Jarvis.

85   CORAL GABLES: *PR*: employment history. The employment records of the Reo Motors truck factory, where Malcolm briefly worked in July, 1945, indicate that he remained at his Coral Gables job only two weeks. Interviews: Elaine Flynn, Johnny Davis, Jr.

MAYFAIR BALLROOM: Lansing, Michigan police record. *PR*: employment history. Interview: Marion Simmon.

RHYTHM RED: *PR*: employment history. Interview: Alvin ("Shorty") Williams. *FBI*, correlation summary dated 8/22/61.

STEALING: Richard Jenkins reports that Malcolm engaged in shoplifting.

FEMALE WRESTLER: Confidential source.

SCAR: Office of Chief Medical Examiner, New York City, Autopsy report #1686, Feb. 22, 1965. Malcolm's FBI record says there were three scars. Johnny Davis, Jr. says that Malcolm had to use a cane for a while. When Malcolm was asked what had caused the scar, he laughed and said it had been an accident.

RELATIONSHIP WITH JIMMY WILLIAMS: Interview: "Vince." (On Malcolm's July 6, 1945 application for employment at Reo Motors, Inc., he listed Mr. Williams as a reference.)

JIMMY WILLIAMS WAS HOMOSEXUAL: Interviews: "Vince" and confidential source. "Vince" reports that Malcolm lived with Jimmy Williams for a number of months.

"VINCE" CONFRONTS MALCOLM: Interview: "Vince."

ROBS THE MAN WHO PUT HIM UP: May 11, 1946 memo prepared for Charlestown State Prison by 13th precinct, Detroit Police Dept. Information prepared March 12, 1945 by Office of the Prosecuting Attorney, Wayne County, Michigan. Interview: "Vince."

ARRESTED IN LANSING MARCH 17, 1945: Detroit Police Record (I.D. #74831). Nov. 19, 1975 letter to author from Chief of Police, Lansing, Michigan. Warrant #39931, issued 3/14/45 by the Recorder's Court for the City of Detroit.

POLICE CONFRONT MALCOLM WITH MERCHANDISE: May 11, 1946 memo prepared for Charlestown State Prison by 13th precinct, Detroit Police Dept.

RELEASED ON BOND: Interview: Wilfred Little. According to Malcolm's prison record, he was released from jail on bond March 26, 1945. See also Jan. 15, 1946 letter from Bureau of Criminal Investigation, Boston Police Dept., to Chief of Detectives, Detroit Police Dept.; May 11, 1946 memo prepared for Charlestown Prison by 13th precinct, Detroit Police Dept.

PLAYED UP "BAD" REPUTATION: Interviews: Philbert Little, Esther Abrams, Dick Letts, Betty Walker, confidential source. Years later, Malcolm continued to stress how bad he had allegedly been. (See, for example, *MX*, p. 379 and the rest of this and the next chapter.)

BOSTON COPS STILL AFTER HIM: Interview: Jean Seaton.

"DONE TIME": Interviews: Chuck Lyons, Dick Letts, Jean Seaton.

WITHOUT A CONSCIENCE: Hans J. Massaquoi, "Mystery of Malcolm X," *Ebony* (Vol. 19), Sept., 1964. *MX*, p. 391.

PERSONIFICATION OF EVIL: *MX*, p. 170.

PREDATORY ANIMAL: Hans J. Massaquoi, supra. *MX*, pp. 75, 102, 134, et al.

VULTURE: *MX*, pp. 102, 109, 262.

86 CONCEALS MISDEEDS FROM ALLIE COOPER: Interview: Allie Cooper.

"IF I DON'T HUSTLE, SOMEONE ELSE WILL": Interview: Jean Seaton.

BATHS: Interview: "Vince." Lucille Lathrop reports that Malcolm also took a lot of baths when he lived in Mason at the county juvenile home.

PHYSICAL AND MORAL CLEANLINESS: See, for instance, *WWG*, p. 23 and undated clipping from the *Philadelphia Tribune*. After Malcolm's conversion to Islam, he told his barber Roy Johnson that people should educate themselves and keep themselves clean. Johnson thought that Malcolm meant physically clean.

"SORDID" PAST: *MX*, p. 150.

JIMMY WILLIAMS HADN'T GIVEN UP: *PR*: employment history. Jimmy Williams later informed the authorities at Charlestown State Prison that Malcolm had worked at Capitol Bedding "on and off" from April 2, 1945 until July 5, 1945. He indicated that Malcolm did not work hard while he was employed there.

REO: Reo Motors, Inc.'s employment record of Malcolm Little.

RETURNED TO HARLEM: Malcolm stayed in Lansing until August, 1945, according to case worker John F. Rockett's report of the interview that occurred in 1946 in Dedham jail. Malcolm returned to Harlem the same month, according to *MX*, pp. 124-125 and *Current Biography*, 1947, p. 545, which indicate that he was back in Harlem in August, the month Jackie Robinson joined the Brooklyn Dodgers.

MALCOLM AND HYMIE: *MX*, pp. 123-124.

87 TRIES TO BLUFF: *MX*, pp. 124-125.

CONFRONTATION WITH ARCHIE: *MX*, pp. 116-117, 125-131.

88 ANOTHER CONFRONTATION: *MX*, p. 131. On p. 132, Malcolm depicts his adversary as "scared."

CLAIMED HE WOULD HAVE SHOT HIM: *MX*, p. 131.

EMPHASIZED HIS READINESS TO KILL: *MX*, pp. 22, 131, 132, 138.

GAVE AWAY HIS GUN: *MX*, p. 131.

89 JARVIS PHONES: Written response by Jarvis to author's inquiry. (Cf. *MX*, p. 132, which conveys the impression that Sammy had called Jarvis.)

THE TRIP BACK TO BOSTON: Written response by Jarvis to author's inquiry. Cf. *MX*, pp. 132-133, where Malcolm allegedly calls Jarvis (who didn't grow up in Lansing, as *MX*, p. 44 says "Shorty" did) "Homeboy."

RUN OUT OF HARLEM: *MX*, p. 217.

19. Tough Guy

90 "STILL LIKED": *MX* p. 138.

JARVIS PUT HIM UP: *MX*, p. 134. Interviews: Malcolm Jarvis, J. C. Little. (Part of Malcolm's prison record suggests that he was living at Ella's. But other parts of it suggest that no matter where Malcolm was living, he would assert that he was living c/o Ella or some other brother or sister.)

STARVED FOR MOTHERLY AFFECTION: *Malcolm L. Jarvis, Myself and I* (Carleton Press, 1979), pp. 4-8. Also see pp. 57, 60.

MISTREATS BEA: *MX*, p. 135.

"NOTHING TO DO": *MX*, p. 135.

OUTWITS GEORGE HOLT: *MX*, pp. 136-138, 139. (In Malcolm's autobiography, George Holt's name has been changed to "John Hughes.")

91 "IF I AIN'T GONNA GAMBLE TONIGHT, NOBODY'S GONNA GAMBLE!": Interview: Malcolm Jarvis. See *MX*, p. 138 for what may be its version of this incident.

FLASHED GUNS: Interviews: Lionel Beane, Robert Foggie, Bob High, Johnny Jones. The Belmont, Mass. police files on Malcolm and *MX*, pp. 138, 146 confirm that Malcolm habitually carried guns.

HE WOULD EXPOSE GUN HOLSTER OR "ACCIDENTALLY" DROP A PISTOL: Interview: Malcolm Jarvis.

THE SECOND GEORGE RAFT: Interview: Larry Neblett.

SWAGGERED: Interview: Bobby Pointer.

IN SEARCH OF IRISHMEN OR JEWS: Interviews: Larry Neblett, Joe Stokes. Years later, Malcolm said that the white man was the one who ganged up on his adversaries: "You look at that man and you know he's nuthin' but a coward. . . . If he wasn't a coward, he wouldn't gang up on you." (Filmed Warner Brothers documentary entitled *Malcolm X*.)

DID NOT PURSUE THE MATTER: Confidential source.

"BOLDEST COWARD": Interview: Reginald Little.

CONFRONTATION WITH SEAMAN: *MX*, p. 138.

"CRAZY ENOUGH TO KILL HIM": *MX*, p. 138.

A CAREFULLY CALCULATED CRAZINESS: Interview: Malcolm Jarvis. Also see, in *MX*, p. 143: "They thought I was crazy. They were afraid of me."

After Malcolm went to prison, he wrote Shirley Johnson and told her that he had never had any trouble making people think he was loony. (Excerpt from June 29, 1950 letter to Shirley Johnson.)

TRIGGER-HAPPY: *MX*, p. 138. Interview: Malcolm Jarvis.

92 "I'LL BELIEVE THEM, EVEN THOUGH I DON'T WANT TO": Interview: Mary Little.

"DELIBERATELY" RISKED DEATH: *MX*, p. 138.

93 CONFRONTATION WITH PLAINCLOTHES POLICEMAN: *MX*, pp. 145-146. Interview: Malcolm Jarvis. According to Jarvis, the telephone rang, not as the detective walked through the doorway, as Malcolm's autobiography asserts, but while the detective (whose name wasn't Turner) was lounging at the bar.

CONFRONTATION WITH YATES: Interview: Malcolm Jarvis.

CONFRONTATION WITH WHITE PATROLMAN: Interview: Malcolm Jarvis.

"TOUGH GUY WITH A TEAR IN HIS EYE": Interviews: John K. Terry, Herbert Craigwell. Archie Epps makes the same point on pp. 26-27 of his introduction to *The Speeches of Malcolm X at Harvard* (William Morrow, 1968).

20. Burglar

94 ABOUT THREE WEEKS BEFORE CHRISTMAS: Norfolk County Superior Court, criminal docket #21550-#21553, 1946. Middlesex County Superior court, criminal docket #31752-#31756, 1946. "The Christmas season was Santa Claus for us," Malcolm says in *MX*, p. 144.

THERE WOULD BE NO WITNESSES; THE LIKELIHOOD THAT ONE WOULD HAVE TO MAIM OR KILL WOULD BE MINIMAL: *MX*, p. 140.

HIGHLY PROFESSIONAL: *MX*, p. 142.

AMATEURISH AND UNPLANNED: Interview: Malcolm Jarvis.

THE FIRST BREAK-IN: *PR*: "Subject's Version of Crime."

"FAMILY UNIT": *MX*, p. 141.

WOULD SUPPLY THE LAWYERS AND CONNECTIONS: Interview; Malcolm Jarvis.

JARVIS COERCED: According to Malcolm's prison record, both Malcolms later told the Massachusetts authorities that Malcolm had coerced Jarvis into participating in the burglaries, at least initially. Interview: Malcolm Jarvis. (Compare the version of events offered in *MX*, pp. 139-143.)

95 TO ENFORCE HIS AUTHORITY: "He had to be the boss in everything he did," Jarvis later told an interviewer. (Interview: Malcolm Jarvis.) Also see *MX*, pp. 142-143.

RUSSIAN ROULETTE; PALMED THE BULLET: *MX*, pp. 142-143, 416.

UNHAPPY ABOUT SONNY'S SUGGESTIVE REMARKS; KEEPS JARVIS AWAY FROM

JOYCE: Interview: Malcolm Jarvis.

BURGLARY TECHNIQUES USED: *PR*: preliminary record. Interviews: Malcolm Jarvis, Charles Pritchett. The method that was used to gain entrance to the houses is described not only in the records of the Massachusetts Bureau of Identification but also in Malcolm's prison record. (Compare the version of events given in *MX*, pp. 140-144.)

NO GLASS CUTTER OR LOCKPICK; DIDN'T KNOW HOW TO PICK A LOCK: Interview: Malcolm Jarvis. (Compare the version of events given in *MX*, pp. 149, 169.)

WORE GLOVES: Sept. 1, 1975 letter from Detective Stephen J. Slack to author. Interview: Malcolm Jarvis.

HE REMOVED HIS GLOVES: Interview: Malcolm Jarvis.

REPORTEDLY FOUND FINGERPRINTS: Interviews: M. Arthur Gordon, Esq., Stephen Slack, Malcolm Jarvis.

LEFT FLASHLIGHT BEHIND; THE BATTERIES MAY HAVE CONTAINED FINGERPRINTS: Sept. 1, 1975 letter, supra.

96   PAUL LENNON'S HOME: *MX*, p. 143. But, according to what Malcolm later told the prison authorities, the burglary at Lennon's was not his first, as *MX*, p. 143 asserts.

DREW HIS GUN: Interview: Malcolm Jarvis.

FOOLS THE POLICE AGAIN: *MX*, pp. 144-145. Interview: Malcolm Jarvis.

"DOWN TO A SCIENCE": *MX*, p. 143.

SLEEPING VICTIMS: *MX*, p. 144.

IMPORTANCE OF MINIMIZING THE RISK: *MX*, p. 140.

DURING EARLY EVENING: Interview: Malcolm Jarvis. Written response from Jarvis to author's inquiry. Note the apparent contradiction between *MX*'s assertion that the burglars entered the bedrooms of their sleeping victims and the statement, further down page 144, that "if . . . there was no answer when one of the girls rang the bell, we would take the chance and go in." Also note the first six words of the the last paragraph on p. 143: "If the people weren't at home . . . "

COMPULSIVE: *New York Amsterdam News*, April 20, 1957.

REVENGE MECHANISM: See H. M. Tiebout, "Delinquency: Problems in the Causation of Stealing," *Journal of American Psychiatry* (Vol. 4, 1930), pp. 822-823. Hedwig Schwarz, "Dorothy: The Psycho-Analysis of a Case of Stealing," *British Journal of Delinquency* (Vol. 1, 1950), p. 32. Franz Alexander & William Healy, *Roots of Crime* (Patterson Smith, 1969), p. 288. Edmund Bergler, "Mechanisms of Criminosis," *Journal of Criminal Psychopathology* (Vol. 5, Oct., 1943), pp. 223-224.

INDIGENCE: July 28, 1947 petition to the prison authorities requesting transfer to Norfolk Prison Colony.

REGINALD SAW THROUGH HIS EXCUSE: Interview: Reginald Little.

"STAND ON THEIR OWN FEET": Movietone News film clip #185-76, May 16, 1963.

THE DESIRE TO BE SUPPORTED AND TAKEN CARE OF: See Franz Alexander & William Healy, *Roots of Crime* (Patterson Smith, 1969), pp. 286-287. Edmund Bergler, "Mechanisms of Criminosis," *Journal of Criminal Psychopathology* (Vol. 5, Oct., 1943), p. 219.

97   "BAD" RATHER THAN AN ACKNOWLEDGED FAILURE: See Seymour Halleck, *Psychiatry and the Dilemmas of Crime* (Harper & Row and Hoeber Medical Books, 1967), pp. 78-79.

A REPUDIATION: Erik Erikson's concept of "negative identity" is certainly applicable.

AN AFFIRMATION: Years later, over the phone, Ella told the author: "[Malcolm] didn't come from a criminal element. No one in this family was a criminal!"

21. Self-caught

98   I COULD HAVE HIT YOUR TIRES: Interview: Malcolm Jarvis.

TWO DAYS BEFORE CHRISTMAS: *PR*: "Subject's version of crime."

PROVOKE A CONFRONTATION: *MX*, pp. 148-149. That Malcolm was aware how provocative his behavior was is indicated by his assertion that being cuckolded by a black man is an "automatic red murder flag to the white man." (*MX*, p. 135.)

AT THE CAMBRIDGE APARTMENT: *MX*, pp. 148-149.

SUCCESS: *MX*, pp. 143-147. (Twice on page 145, for instance, Malcolm's autobiography says that his burglary operation was doing "fine.")

SEVERAL WEEKS: Norfolk County Superior Court, criminal docket #21550-21553, 1946. Middlesex County Superior Court, criminal docket #31752-31756, 1946.

ONLY A FRACTION: *MX*, p. 144.

HIDING THE REST; SEED MONEY FOR LEGITIMATE BUSINESS: *PR*: "Subject's Version of Crime." More than once during a burglary, Jarvis caught Malcolm trying to sneak a piece of stolen jewelry into his pocket without telling his fellow burglars about it. (Interview: Malcolm Jarvis.) See also *MX*, p. 389, where Malcolm admits that he doesn't entirely trust himself.

99 PROFESSED DETERMINATION *MX*, pp. 100-102, 140-141.

"INEVITABLE: *MX*, p. 146.

ON, OR WITHIN A FEW DAYS OF, THE SEVENTH ANNIVERSARY OF HIS MOTHER'S INCARCERATION: Malcolm was arrested in Boston on January 12, 1946, according to the records of the Milton, Mass. police, the Brookline, Mass. police, and the Bureau of Identification of the Masssachusetts Dept. of Public Safety. According to Malcolm's autobiography, the arrest was precipitated by a broken stolen watch that he had taken to a jewelry shop for repair "about two days" earlier; i.e., around January 10. (*MX*, p. 148. Interview: Alex Haley.) In all likelihood, the date was slightly earlier than January 10, because by January 10 Detective Stephen Slack had already been informed by material that had been mailed or delivered to Boston Police Headquarters that Malcolm was the proprietor of the watch. (See the complaint Slack swore out against Malcolm Jan. 10, 1946 in Norfolk County Superior Court.) Taken together, the complaint, *MX*, p. 148, Malcolm's prison record, and Detective Slack's testimony suggest that Malcolm placed the stolen watch in the jewelry store some time between January 5 and January 9, the seventh anniverary of the date his mother was officially declared insane and legally [not physically] committed to Kalamazoo State Hospital.

Years after Malcolm's release from prison, he told a Massachusetts audience, "He that leads into captivity shall go into captivity." (Louis E. Lomax, *When the Word Is Given* [NAL: A Signet Book, 1963], p. 123.) Outwardly, Malcolm was talking about the white enemy. But, as *MX*, p. 287 makes clear, he was thinking of other things as he stood at the speaker's podium:

"I happened to glance through a window. Abruptly, I realized that I was looking in the direction of the apartment house that was my old burglary gang's hideout. It rocked me like a tidal wave. Scenes from my once-depraved life [f]lashed through my mind."

HE KNEW VERY WELL: *MX*, p. 141. Malcolm knew this from experience; when he was arrested the previous spring in Michigan for stealing Douglas Haynes's property, the police confronted him with the stolen merchandise he had placed in a pawnshop under his own name.

HE WAS EQUALLY AWARE OF THE NEED TO REMOVE IDENTIFYING MARKS: *MX*, p. 142.

FOR A SINGLE DOLLAR, HE PAWNED A WEDDING BAND THAT WAS CLEARLY STAMPED WITH ITS OWNER'S INITIALS: Interview: Stephen Slack.

EASILY-IDENTIFIABLE, DIAMOND-STUDDED MAN'S WATCH: Interview: Malcolm Jarvis. *MX*, p. 148.

SUPPLIED HIS REAL NAME AND ELLA'S ADDRESS: Interview: Stephen Slack.

STANLEY SLACK STAKED OUT THE SHOP: Interview: Stephen Slack.

ARRESTED JANUARY 12, 1946: Records of the Milton, Mass. police, the Brookline, Mass. police, and the Bureau of Identification of the Massachusetts Department of Public Safety.

CONVICTION IN MICHIGAN VIRTUALLY A FOREGONE CONCLUSION: For instance, according to the May 11, 1946 memo the Detroit police subsequently prepared for the Charlestown Prison authorities, police officers had retrieved from Malcolm's family's home four of the articles he had stolen from Douglas Haynes. They had also recovered a coat belonging to Haynes that Malcolm had placed in a pawnshop under his own name. (See also Warrant #39931, issued March 14, 1945 by the Recorder's Court for the City of Detroit. Also see the January 15, 1946 letter from the Deputy Superintendent, Bureau of Criminal

Investigation, Boston Police Dept. to the Chief of Detectives, Detroit Police Dept.)

KILL WITHOUT COMPUNCTION: *MX*, pp. 22, 130, 131, 132, 138.

DID NOT DRAW HIS GUN AND SHOOT: *MX*, pp. 148-149.

BEA'S HUSBAND HAD REPORTEDLY BEEN GUNNING FOR HIM: *MX*, p. 149.

ADMITTED HIS ROLE: Brookline, Mass. police record. Belmont, Mass. police report. Prison record. Interview: Stephen Slack.

IMPLICATED FELLOW BURGLARS: *PR*: Preliminary Record, dated March 8, 1946. Belmont, Mass. police report. Framingham Women's Reformatory records on Beatrice Bazarian. Confidential interview with one of the Bookline, Mass. detectives who investigated the burglaries. Judge Eisenstadt handed down the suspended sentence on January 15, 1946. Bea and Joyce were apparently arrested later the same day. Whether they or Malcolm implicated Jarvis is unclear from available records, which are somewhat contradictory.

100 LATER ASSERTED THAT THE WOMEN HAD INFORMED ON SONNY: *MX*, p. 149.

FRIENDLESS, SCARED KID: Interview: Stephen Slack.

SMOKED WITHOUT STOPPING: Interview: Stephen Slack. *MX*, p. 139. Feb. 15, 1960 speech at Boston University. Interviews: Malcolm Jarvis, Lionel Beane.

SHE REFUSED: Interview: J. C. Little.

THE FEBRUARY, 1946 TRIAL: Since the burglaries had occurred in two different counties, there were two separate trials. The first took place in Middlesex County Superior Court on February 27, 1946. The second took place in Norfolk County Superior Court several weeks later. The sentences handed down at the second trial did not prolong Malcolm's lengthy stay in prison because they ran concurrently with the sentences that had been handed down at the first trial.

SEATING ARRANGEMENTS AT TRIAL: Interviews: Walter H. McLaughlin, Esq., Malcolm Jarvis, Ella Little. (The prisoner's cage is mentioned in *Malcolm Jarvis, Myself and I* (Carlton Press, 1979), p. 34. Compare the version in *MX*, p. 150.)

"THE BASTARDS"; "STRUNG UP BY NOW"; MASK OF STONE; HIS MOUTH CURLED: Interview: Malcolm Jarvis.

EVEN TRIED TO PIN: Interviews: M. Arthur Gordon, Esq., Malcolm Jarvis.

LESS COMMITTED: *MX*, p. 150. During a chat with the author, one defense attorney later characterized the two black defendants as "schvartzas." Another portrayed them as minor Al Capones.

NO LAWYER: Contrary to what is asserted in *MX*, p. 150, Malcolm had no lawyer. (Interviews: Malcolm Jarvis, Kenneth Collins, Ella Little, M. Arthur Gordon.) Jarvis had a paid attorney, not a court-appointed one. The female defendants also had lawyers. But Malcolm told Kenneth Collins that, since the case against him was air-tight, a lawyer would be useless. (His prison record confirms that he had no attorney. Not until 1958 did Massachusetts require its Superior Courts to furnish counsel for indigent defendants in noncapital felony proceedings.)

ELLA WANTED HIM TO GO TO PRISON: Interview: Ella Little. Ella told me she wanted to tie Malcolm down so that she could "help" him. "I thought he'd get a light sentence," she said. Both J. C. Little and Heshaam Jaaber confirm that Ella thought Malcolm should be in jail; in jail there was discipline, just as there was in the army. (See *MX*, p. 70, where Malcolm says, without explaining why, that Ella "would have loved nothing better" than for him to join the army. Also see Chapter 28.)

BEA'S TESTIMONY: Interview: Ella Little. (Instead of testifying directly, Bea reportedly made these allegations to the District Attorney, who read her self-serving statement to the court.)

NO DEFENSE: Interviews: Ella Little, Malcolm Jarvis. Malcolm's Brookline, Mass. police record indicates that, except for Malcolm's decision to initially plead not guilty in court, he put up no defense prior to trial either.

101 BOTH MALCOLMS CHANGE THEIR PLEA: Interview: Malcolm Jarvis. *Malcolm Jarvis, Myself and I* (Carlton Press, 1979), p. 33. The relevant Middlesex Superior Court documents (criminal docket #31752-31756, 1946) indicate that, despite Malcolm's earlier confession to the police, he pleaded not guilty when he was arraigned before Middlesex County Superior Court on Feb. 8, 1946. But on Feb. 27 [during the trial], he revised his plea and pleaded guilty. He also pleaded guilty on April 10, when he was tried at Norfolk County Superior Court for four additional counts of burglary. (Norfolk County Superior Court, criminal docket #21550-21553, 1946).

JARVIS'S REACTION: Interviews: Malcolm Jarvis, M. Arthur Gordon. *Malcolm Jarvis, Myself and I* (Carlton Press, 1979), pp. 13, 34-35. MX, p. 151. (Since Jarvis had been charged by the Middlesex County authorities with five counts of burglary, and since Judge Buttrick sentenced him to 8-10 years for each count, Jarvis thought he was being sentenced to forty or fifty years in prison.)

SAME SENTENCE: Middlesex County Superior Court, docket #31752-31756, 1946.

BUTTRICK MADE NO BONES: *Malcolm Jarvis, Myself and I* (Carlton Press, 1979), p. 34. Interview: Malcolm Jarvis.

ENTIRELY TO THE JUDGE'S BIGOTRY: MX, p. 150. PR: Sept. 26, 1949 memo by Dr. Weisman, prison psychiatrist. Hans J. Massaquoi, "Mystery of Malcolm X," *Ebony* (Vol. 19), Sept., 1964. *Malcolm Jarvis, Myself and I* (Carlton Press, 1979), p. 34. Interview: Malcolm Jarvis.

PREVIOUS ARRESTS AND SUSPENDED SENTENCES: In MX, p. 150, Malcolm characterizes himself as "a first offender." Not even Jarvis knew that he'd had previous run-ins with the police. (*Malcolm Jarvis, Myself and I*, supra., p. 33.)

EVEN ELLA WAS UNAWARE: MX, pp. 191-192 indicates that Ella had no idea Malcolm had a police record in Detroit. Nor did her husband Ken Collins or Malcolm's cousin J. C. Little know about it. (Interviews: Ken Collins, J. C. Little.)

NEARLY STARTED A RIOT: Interview: Charles Pritchett (who was later told what had happened).

SAT IN THE CAGE AND SMILED: Interview: Ella Little. A photograph taken by the Massachusetts authorities the day after the trial shows Malcolm wearing a sardonic smile. (PR: mug shot dated Feb. 28, 1946.) A week later, when Pete Donahue interviewed him in Charlestown State Prison, he was still smiling. (PR: Preliminary Record, March 8, 1946. Also see Chapter Twenty-Four's discussion of Malcolm's ambivalent feelings about being in prison.)

22. Convict

104   SAME SARDONIC SMILE: Photograph taken at Charlestown Prison, Feb. 28, 1946, the day after Malcolm was sentenced by Judge Buttrick. A week later, when Pete Donahue interviewed him at Charlestown, he still had a sardonic smile on his face. (PR: Preliminary Record, March 8, 1946.)

HEART FLUTTERING: PR: medical report dated Feb. 28, 1946. Malcolm Jarvis confirms that he and Malcolm received medical examinations as soon as they arrived at Charlestown State Prison.

RATS AND LICE: The warden's report of Dec. 31, 1946 asserts, "There have been no serious rat or vermin problems." But Malcolm Jarvis and George Conway remember the white lice. They were about half an inch long, with sharp, pointed tails. "They'd crawl over the inmates as they slept," Jarvis recalls. "I mashed many of them myself."

SOLITARY CONFINEMENT FIRST DAY: Middlesex County Superior Court, criminal docket #31752-31756, 1946. Interview: Malcolm Jarvis.

105   ELLA REFUSED TO ANSWER: PR: summary of case worker Calvin Peterson's May 17, 1946 interview of Ella.

"DEVOTED"; "MISSIONARIES": PR: interview, March 8, 1946. (Cedric J. Robinson has perceptively observed that Malcolm's autobiography portrays both his parents as heroic, martyr-like victims. See Cedric J. Robinson, "Malcolm Little as a Charismatic Leader" [paper delivered at the 1970 annual meeting of the American Political Science Association], p. 14.)

FINANCIAL CONDITION "GOOD"; STUDYING LAW: PR: interview, March 8, 1946.

FATHER'S DEATH ACCIDENTAL: PR: interview, March 8, 1946.

MOTHER WHITE: PR: interview, March 8, 1946. Also May 6, 1946 report by case worker John F. Rockett. Malcolm's insistence that his mother was white prompted prison social worker John T. Herstrom to write Kalamazoo State Hospital, on July 29, 1946, and ask "if [Malcolm's] mother is a white woman, as he claims." The hospital's August 7, 1946 reply stated that she was "colored."

MOTHER LIVING IN LANSING: PR: May 6, 1946 report by case worker John F. Rockett. Also caseworker Calvin Peterson's earlier report on Malcolm's Nov. 29, 1944 arrest. Also see Ingham County Probate file B-4556.

RESENTED PROBING QUESTIONS: Interviews: John Elton Bembry, Malcolm Jarvis.

EVERY FOUL NAME: MX, p. 152. According to Malcolm Jarvis, the therapist was a psychiatrist, not a psychologist. (Malcolm's prison record contains reports from a number of psychiatrists.)

LOSING HIS MIND: PR: Social worker John T. Herstom's July 23, 1946 summary of Malcolm's conversation with prison psychiatrist.

"FRIENDLY": PR: interview, March 8, 1946.

DID NOT DISCLOSE SIXTH GRADE FAILURE: Ibid.

"BUSINESS"; "BARTENDER AND DRUMMER": PR: employment history.

FULLY SELF-SUPPORTING: PR: interview, March 8, 1946. When the Belmont, Mass. police interviewed Malcolm, he claimed that he had financed his week-long, December 1945 spending spree in New York. But after he arrived at Charlestown State Prison, he admitted that Bea had paid his way.

DENIED HE HAD EVER BEEN DEPENDENT ON DRUGS: PR: Malcolm made a number of conflicting statements about his use of drugs and their effect on him. He told Jarvis that one reason he had been partial to marijuana is that it is not habit-forming. Whether he meant physically or psychologically, or both, is unclear. Years later he acknowledged, or at least asserted, that he had been addicted to one or more drugs. (MX, pp. 123, 127, 134, 138, 139, 146-147. Chicago Tribune, Feb. 13, 1964. New York Amsterdam News, April 20, 1957.)

EXAGGERATIONS: See, for instance, BMIA, p. 191, where Malcolm claims that he went to prison several times.

BIG-TIME HOOD: Interview: Godfrey Joiner. See also PR: 9/5/47 disciplinary report.

106 HOW MANY WOMEN HE HAD CONQUERED: Interviews: Charles Pritchett, Godfrey Joiner, Gloria Strother.

IMAGINATION DO THE REST: Interview: Reginald Little.

A WOMAN'S SLIP: Interview: Godfrey Joiner.

SO FULL OF INSTRUCTIONS; "MR. KNOW-HOW": Interviews: John Elton Bembry, Malcolm Jarvis.

"GREEN-EYED MONSTER: Interview: Malcolm Jarvis.

SEEMED TO RELISH HIS DEVILISH IMAGE: Interview: John Elton Bembry.

TOUGH, REFRACTORY CONVICT: MX, p. 153.

ADDRESSED BY NAME, NOT BY NUMBER: Interview: Malcolm Jarvis.

PRISON RECORD CONTAINS NO EVIDENCE MALCOLM SPENT MORE THAN HIS FIRST DAY IN SOLITARY CONFINEMENT: In late September 1950 — long after Malcolm had converted to Islam and had become a model prisoner — he told the Massachusetts Commissioner of Correction that he had never been in solitary confinement, even though he had been in jail for nearly five years. (Sept. 27, 1950 petition to Mass. Commissioner of Corrections.) The rest of Malcolm's prison record — particularly a March 23, 1950 disciplinary report and a letter the Massachusetts Supervisor of Parole wrote the Michigan authorities — supports this assertion. It contains no evidence he was ever deprived of any of the "good time" that was automatically awarded to reasonably well-behaved convicts and deducted from their sentences. It contains no evidence he spent any time in solitary other than the traditional first day there. The record does, however, indicate that in March and November 1946 he was placed "in detention" for shirking his prison duties. (See Charlestown Prison work report #1059, dated November 12, 1946.) "Detention" was often called "isolation." It meant not that one was in solitary confinement but merely that one was isolated from the general prison population and denied access to movies, the prison yard, and so forth. Prisoners in detention were not kept alone in special cells. They received the same things to eat as the rest of the prison population did. In contrast, those in solitary confinement were kept in lightless cells behind solid steel doors. They were denied mattresses and ate only bread and water. (Interviews: Tom Mulchern, Anthony Paul Meleski, Don Myers. Also interviews with Charles Pritchett and Malcolm Jarvis.)

Had Malcolm spent as much time in solitary as his autobiography claims, he never would have been allowed to transfer, in 1948, to Norfolk Prison Colony, the model prison that was then so selective, according to Anthony Meleski, the social worker who screened the prisoners who applied for admission to Norfolk. Meleski recalls that when he interviewed Malcolm, he was impressed with him.

See note, infra., entitled "But He Was Not a Real Troublemaker."

MINOR DISCIPLINARY INFRACTIONS: *PR*: Charlestown Prison work report #1059, dated Nov. 12, 1946. Discipline report dated Sept. 5, 1947. Interview: Charles Pritchett.

PASSIVE RESISTANCE: *PR*: A pardon [application] summary dated Dec. 19, 1950 states, "[During] the last half of the year 1946 he was reported not inclined to do any work." Similar comments appear throughout his prison record.

BUT HE WAS NOT A REAL TROUBLEMAKER: *PR*: Interviews: Charles Willhauck, Charles Scafati, Malcolm Jarvis, Charles Pritchett, Albert Thompson. By virtue of his position as Assistant Deputy Warden, Albert Thompson was in charge of prisoner discipline. He reports that many prisoners tried to convince their fellow convicts they were tough by pretending that they had been in solitary confinement.

A DEFIANT KID: Interview: Charles Pritchett.

CURIOUSLY OPTIMISTIC; REFUSED TO BELIEVE; INSISTED THAT THE DISTRICT ATTORNEY HAD FORCED HER: Interviews: Al Lewis, Ella Little, confidential source.

107 MALCOLM'S SENTENCE COMPARED WITH AVERAGE SENTENCE: "Burglary Sentences in 1945," memorandum prepared at the author's request by Arthur Isberg, Counsel, Massachusetts Dept. of Correction.

HE BROKE DOWN; THE TEARS STREAMED DOWN HIS FACE: Interview: J. C. Little.

LATER CONTENDED THAT BEA HAD TURNED HIM IN TO THE POLICE: Interview: Mozelle Jackson. Malcolm told John Elton Bembry that the reason he had taken the easily-identifiable stolen watch to Al Beeman's jewelry store was that he wanted to fix it and give it to Bea. But, according to Stephen Slack and Malcolm Jarvis, it was a man's watch.

MALCOLM CONFRONTS BEA AT SECOND TRIAL: Interview: J. C. Little. (Since all four defendants pleaded guilty, the second trial was apparently limited to the issue of what sentences should be imposed; the quoted exchange between Malcolm and Bea may have occurred while the court was considering what sentence to give Bea.)

108 INITIALLY SOUGHT THE COMPANY OF WHITE CONVICTS: *MX*, p. 182.

LAUGHED ASIDE; SENSED THE HURT: Interview: Malcolm Jarvis.

COMMANDED ATTENTION AND RESPECT ENTIRELY WITH WORDS: *MX*, pp. 153-154. Years later, Malcolm acknowledged that he had envied Bembry's ability to do so. (*MX*, p. 171.)

MALCOLM CONFRONTS BEMBRY: Interview: John Elton Bembry.

NOT THE KIND OF ADVICE HE HAD BEEN LOOKING FOR: *MX*, p. 154.

HE PLIED HIM WITH QUESTIONS: Interview: John Elton Bembry.

HIS SUBSEQUENT ASSERTION THAT HE COULDN'T READ WAS UNFOUNDED: Interviews: Wilfred Little, Malcolm Jarvis, Johnny Davis, Jr., Luther Jermany, Ella Little, confidential source. The latter reports that, even during the period that Malcolm was hustling, he was reading all the time.

109 LACK OF CONFIDENCE: Interview: Ella Little.

BEMBRY GAVE IT TO HIM; "SMART, BAD NIGGER": Interview: John Elton Bembry.

FOND OF AESOP'S FABLES; IN ORDER TO UNDERSTAND MALCOLM, ONE SHOULD VISUALIZE HIM AS THE FOX: Interview: Malcolm Jarvis.

JUST A LOVE STORY: Interview: John Elton Bembry.

UNABLE TO COMPREHEND: Interview: John Elton Bembry.

110 "THAT BITCH WAS NUTS"; BEMBRY ASSURED MALCOLM; THE SINGLE MOST UPLIFTING THING; REMOVED A VERY HEAVY BURDEN: Interview: John Elton Bembry.

23. Convert

111 RECORDING BETS: Interview: Heywood Hampton.

SNEAKING MONEY INTO PRISON: Interview: Malcolm Jarvis.

JANUARY, 1947 TRANSFER TO CONCORD: *PR*: transfer summary. The records of the Bureau of Identification of the Massachusetts Dept. of Public Safety confirm that Malcolm was transferred to Concord Reformatory on January 10, 1947.

"LIKE A BABY": Interview: Ella Little.

FREQUENT FIGHTS; TOUGH PLACE: Interview: Heywood Hampton.

FORTY PERCENT RETURNED TO JAIL; COMPLETE FAILURE: Massachusetts House of Representatives Report No. 2087 (1939), p. 23. Massachusetts Senate Report No. 750 (June, 1955), p. 41.

112 LACERATION ON CHIN: *PR*: Concord Reformatory medical record entries dated Feb. 11, 13, 17, 1947. Malcolm told Godfrey Joiner that he preferred Charlestown to Concord. (Interview: Godfrey Joiner.)

"SHIV": *PR*: Report dated April 9, 1947. Prison guard Arthur Roach recalls the rumor about the "shiv." He does not know whether the rumor was true.

"NO JOKING": Interview: Arthur Roach.

PETTY OFFENSES; REFUSING TO DO CHORES: Interview: Richard Colleton. *PR*: Reports dated 3/6/47, 9/4/47, and 12/18/47. All three reports complain that Malcolm shirked his prison duties and did poor work.

SNEAK TO FRONT OF LINE: Interview: Heywood Hampton.

STOMACH DISTRESS: While Malcolm was at Concord, he sought medical help for stomach trouble twice during a period of four weeks. He also had considerable trouble with his stomach at Charlestown and Norfolk. After he left prison, the problem periodically recurred. (*PR*: record of medical treatment dispensed at Concord Reformatory. Interviews: Philip Picard, Robert B. Moore, Clifford Hyman, confidential source.)

HEADACHES: *PR*: May 4, 1951 report by prison psychiatrist. Intervews: Malcolm Jarvis, confidential source.

COMPARING BRAIN TO AN ACHING MUSCLE: Page 221 of the original, unedited, longer manuscript that was later published as *FDL*.

PLACEBO TREATMENT: *PR*: Medical report dated Jan. 10, 1947 (the day Malcolm was transferred from Charlestown to Concord).

PENIS: *PR*: Medical entry dated Feb. 26, 1948.

BLOOD IN URINE: *PR*: "Transfer summary" dated March 23, 1950. See record of admissions to prison hospital, Norfolk Prison Colony. (Also see, inter alia, Karl Menninger, "Psychological Factors in Urological Disease," *Psychoanalytic Quarterly* (Vol. 5, 1936), particularly pp. 497 ff. Also William Guy & Michael H. P. Finn's discussion of possible symbolic factors in *Psychoanalytic Review* (Vol. 41, 1954), p. 357.)

HEMORRHOIDS: *PR*: "Transfer summary" dated 3/23/50. Also record of admissions to prison hospital, Norfolk Prison Colony. Interviews: Malcolm Jarvis, Howard Cramer. (Cramer learned about Malcolm's hermorrhoid problem from someone else.) Malcolm's prison record indicates that his hermorrhoid problem recurred after he was paroled from prison.

CONSTIPATION; LAXATIVES: Interview: Malcolm Jarvis. Malcolm said that watermelon, which he loved to eat, was a good laxative. (Interview: Clifford Hyman.)

MATERNAL BEATINGS: Anna Stohrer.

LAX ABOUT CHANGING DIAPERS: Interview: John Doane.

REACHED DOWN TO WIPE CHAIR, THEN SMELLED HER HAND: Interviews: Betty Walker, Mrs. Lloyd Hackenberg.

"THE CLINIC FIXED THEM; THEY DID NOT MESS": Interview: Louise Little. "I had no diapers to wash," Mrs. Little asserted.

113 VERY PROUD: *MX*, p. 156.

VASQUEZTELEZ: Interview: Arthur Roach.

"UNTIL I PROVE UNWORTHY": Petition requesting transfer to Norfolk Prison Colony. Approximate date June, 1946.

"I HAVE NO ONE TO HATE BUT MYSELF": *PR*: July 28, 1947 petition for transfer to Norfolk Prison Colony.

NORFOLK ACCEPTED ONLY THE BEST-BEHAVED PRISONERS: Dec. 31, 1946 report to Commissioner of Correction from Warden Lanagan, p. 4.

CONCORD WAS NOT OVERCROWDED: June 23, 1977 response by Massachusetts Department of Correction to author's inquiry whether Concord Reformatory's 1,040-inmate capacity was fully utilized when Malcolm was transferred from Concord to Norfolk Prison Colony.

114 INTEREST IN JESUS; SIMILARITIES BETWEEN CHRIST AND MUHAMMAD; MAKE A NAME; "A GREAT EGO THAT HE WAS FEEDING": April 18, 1977 letter from J. Prescott Adams to author. Interview: J. Prescott Adams.

SETTLE DOWN AND MAKE SOMETHING OF HIMSELF: PR: Memorandum dated 1/20/49. Interview: Heywood Hampton.

STUDY LAW: Interview: Ella Little.

DISCUSSED THE POSSIBILITY: Interviews: Saladin Matthews, J. C. Little, Ella Little. See also MX, pp. 183, 269-270, 379.

POLITICAL SCIENCE: Interview: J. C. Little.

ROBESON; ANDERSON: Interview: Malcolm Jarvis.

JACKIE ROBINSON: MX: p. 155. Also pp. 124-125.

JOE LOUIS: Interview: Malcolm Jarvis.

BOISIE PHILIPS: Interview: Malcolm Jarvis.

115 BERTHA LITTLE: Interviews: Philbert Little, Wilfred Little.

MALCOLM'S REACTION TO BERTHA'S DEATH: Interview: Ella Little.

116 DECISIVE IMPACT: Interviews: Heywood Hampton, Malcolm Jarvis.

ALLEVIATE THEIR GUILT: In MX, pp. 163 and 170, Malcolm acknowledges the "enormity" of the guilt he felt. Some of his prison letters vividly convey his sense of guilt. See undated letter to Bazely Perry and prison censor's copy of excerpt of Feb. 10, 1949 letter to Wilfred Little.

APPARENT DATE OF RELIGIOUS CONVERSION: There have been some undocumented, published assertions that Malcolm's religious conversion occurred in 1947 while he was in Concord Reformatory. But Malcolm's autobiography places it at Norfolk Prison Colony, as do Godfrey Joiner and George Power, Malcolm's house officer at Norfolk. Moreover, Charles Pritchett recalls that when he left Norfolk in November 1948, Malcolm had not yet embraced Islam, even though he and Pritchett had discussed religion a number of times. And the earliest available prison record entry suggesting that Malcolm had definitely converted to Islam is dated March 10, 1949.

INTENSE CONFLICT; TOOK A WEEK TO BEND KNEES; BUT HIS NEED FOR ATONEMENT DROVE HIM BACK DOWN: MX, pp. 163, 169-170.

24. Student, Teacher, and Budding Orator

Author's note: The three undated letters to Bazely Perry were all probably written in 1949.

117 TOOK SUNBATHS; TWITTED JARVIS: Interview: Malcolm Jarvis.

SHAVED HEAD: PR: Report of psychiatrist Henry M. Baker, M. D. Also see MX, p. 258.

TO UNINTENTIONALLY LOSE ONE'S HAIR IS TO LOSE ONE'S STRENGTH; SAMSON AND DELILAH: Interview: Malcolm Jarvis. (Also see MX, p. 226.)

STOPPED ATTENDING PRISON SCHOOL: A prison report dated Jan. 4, 1950 says Malcolm finally stopped attending prison school at his own request. "I would have liked him to stay in school," officer George F. Magraw wrote. A summary of Malcolm's formal prison education record appears in a prison transfer summary dated March 23, 1950.

"HUNGER-STRICKEN SOUL": Undated letter to Bazely Perry. (See author's note, supra.)

PREFERRED THE HERMIT-LIKE EXISTENCE: See, inter alia, MX, pp. 170, 173.

118 IN PUBLIC, BROOKED NO ARGUMENT AND JEALOUSLY PRESERVED HIS NEW-FOUND AUTHORITY: Interview: Malcolm Jarvis. Also interviews with Margaret Shreve,

Albert ("Junior") Clark, Cyril McGuire, Hayward Howard.

INTELLECTUAL HUMILITY: August 2, 1949 letter to Bazely Perry.

PONTIFICATING ABOUT GENIUS: The theme of genius reappears over and over in the surviving notes that Jarvis diligently took during Malcolm's prison lectures.

"A GREAT MAN IS ALWAYS WILLING TO BE LITTLE": Notes Jarvis took during Malcolm's prison lectures. Interview: Malcolm Jarvis. (Sometimes, Malcolm used the word "small" instead of the word "little.")

119 DEFENDS JARVIS: Interview: Malcolm Jarvis.

OMAR KHALIL'S VISIT: Interviews: Bazely Perry, Malcolm Jarvis.

HAD TO SKIP TOWN: Interview: Malcolm Jarvis.

HAND-WRITTEN FACSIMILIES: Interview: Malcolm Jarvis.

120 "I WRITE TO ALL OF YOU . . . . FOR I THINK OF YOU ALL AS ONE": Undated letter to Bazely Perry. (See author's note supra.)

ELEVATED, BIBLICAL LANGUAGE: Collectively, the relevant portions of the letters to Bazely Perry.

"FORTUNATE": Undated, mid-1950 petition to the Massachusetts Commissioner of Correction. Years later, Malcolm told a group of followers that jail was a good place to be. (FBI, Nov. 17, 1959, p. 49.)

"DO NOT PICTURE US AS BEING IN PRISON": July 25, 1949 letter to Bazely Perry. Similar language appears in one of Malcolm's undated letters to Bazely Perry.

"I WAS IN PRISON BEFORE ENTERING HERE. . . . THE KEY TO MY FREEDOM": Undated letter to Bazely Perry. (See author's note, supra.)

MORE CONTENTED IN JAIL: August 2, 1949 letter to Bazely Perry. And in MX, p. 173, Malcolm says that, until he went to jail, he "never had been so truly free" in his life.

LIBERATED FROM THE NAGGING TYRANNY OF A GUILTY CONSCIENCE: MX, pp. 163, 170. Charles Pritchett says, "I never thought he felt his punishment was unjust."

VIRTUALLY ACKNOWLEDGED HE HAD GOTTEN WHAT HE HAD DESERVED: PR: Prison censor's copy of excerpt of Feb. 10, 1949 letter to Wilfred.

"WHEN ONE COMMITS A CRIME, HE SHOULD BE PUT IN JAIL": The Daily Pennsylvanian, Jan. 28, 1963.

"DISTRACTIONS": August 2, 1949 letter to Bazely Perry. In his July 15, 1949 letter to Bazely Perry, Malcolm described the temptations as "ensnaring."

PHYSICAL RESTRAINT FREED HIM FROM THE NECESSITY OF MORAL SELF-RESTRAINT: In MX, p. 65, Malcolm broadly hints that he wishes he had been restrained from hurting Laura.

HAD ENABLED HIM TO RECAPTURE THE CONTENTMENT HE SAID HE HAD KNOWN AS A CHILD: August 5. 1949 letter to Bazely Perry.

"COWARDS DON'T GO TO JAIL": New York Herald Tribune, March 12, 1960. Harry L. Ashmore, The Other Side of Jordan (W. W. Norton, 1960), p. 49. Years later, Malcolm told a group of listeners, "When you're a man, you're not afraid to go to jail." (Record album entitled The Wisdom of Malcolm X, Mo' Soul Records, album #MS-8001.)

BECOMING BITTER: Prison censor's copy of excerpt of Feb. 10, 1949 letter to Wilfred.

MIGHT NEVER BE READY: Prison censor's copy of excerpt of Feb. 10, 1949 letter to Philbert.

"I WANT TO GET OUT OF HERE": Prison censor's copy of excerpt of Feb. 10, 1949 letter to Wilfred. (The letter Malcolm wrote the same day to Philbert said the same thing. See also March 19, 1950 letter to Gloria Strother, MX, p. 155, and the pardon summary in Malcolm's prison record.)

121 ILL-DISGUISED PLEA: Prison censor's copy of excerpt of Feb. 10, 1949 letter to Philbert.

"BUT I WOULD NOT LET HIM": Ibid.

"THE FATHER": July 15, 1949 and July 25, 1949 letters to Bazely Perry.

"THE SON": Undated letter to Bazely Perry. (See author's note, supra.)

"DIVINE OBEDIENCE": 1960 Boston University speech.

CARED FOR HIS "CHILDREN": July 15, 1949 letter to Bazely Perry.

THOSE WHO OBEYED HAD NOTHING TO FEAR: Undated letter to Bazely Perry. (See author's note, supra.)

GOD-LIKE: July 15, 1949 letter to Bazely Perry.

WHITES WERE "UNNATURAL": August 2, 1949 letter to Bazely Perry.

"FREAK OF NATURE": July 15, 1949 letter to Bazely Perry. On page 94 of Malcolm Jarvis, *Myself and I* (Carleton Press, 1979), Jarvis also characterizes whites as "freaks of nature."

"LEPROUS WHITE SKIN": Jarvis's copy of undated letter from Malcolm to unknown recipient.

"HIS NEAREST RELATIVE, THE PIG": Jarvis's copy of undated letter from Malcolm to unknown recipient. Malcolm said that whites were pigs themselves. (Interviews: Joseph LeBlanc, Gloria Strother.)

WHITE "SWINE": Undated letter to Bazely Perry. (See author's note, supra.)

"LOVE THE FILTH IN WHICH THEY WALLOW": August 2, 1949 letter to Bazely Perry.

"MAN IS WHAT HE EATS"; WALKING GERMS: Undated letter to Bazely Perry. (See author's note, supra.)

122 HOT WEATHER ACTIVATES THE GERMS AND KILLS THEM: Jarvis's copy of undated letter from Malcolm to unknown recipient. Undated letter to Bazely Perry. (See author's note, supra.)

"TRUTH": See, for example, Sept. 7, 1949 letter to Bazely Perry; June 6, 1950 petition to Massachusetts Commissioner of Correction.

"YOU'RE STILL IN A HOLE. . . . I'M OUT IN THE SUNSHINE": Note from John Elton Bembry to author.

"BLINDING LIGHT": *MX*, p. 164.

VERBALLY EQUATED BLINDNESS WITH IGNORANCE: Undated letter to Bazely Perry. Debate with Louis Lomax, May 23, 1964.

EQUATED BLINDNESS WITH SUBMISSIVENESS: *MX*, p. 183.

EXHILARATING: *MX*, pp. 184-185.

LOVED MATCHING WITS: Interview: Malcolm Jarvis.

123 IN CHARGE; DID ALL THE TALKING; NEVER LOST HIS POISE, THOUGH HE SOMETIMES LOST HIS TEMPER: Interview: Malcolm Jarvis.

PUT GROWING EXPERTISE TO WORK: Interview: John Little.

"DEVOTE MY LIFE TO HURTING YOU PEOPLE": Interview: Malcolm Jarvis.

25. Prison Philosopher

Author's note: The three undated letters to Bazely Perry were all probably written in 1949.

124 MIND OVER MATTER; THE MIND COULD CONTROL THE BODY: Interview: Malcolm Jarvis.

ONE COULD CONTROL OTHERS: Interview: Oliver Sutton.

NO KNEE JERK; PR: May 4, 1959 report by Henry M. Baker, M.D.

"IN ONE'S HEAD, NOT BETWEEN ONE'S LEGS": Interview: Malcolm Jarvis.

TEMPTRESSES: Interview: Malcolm Jarvis.

UNFLATTERING REMARKS: Clifford Hyman

WOMEN RUN THE WORLD: July 15, 1949 letter to Bazely Perry. See also *New York Amsterdam News*, May 18, 1957, where Malcolm says, "The hand that rocks the cradle rules the world."

STARVED FOR AFFECTION: *Malcolm L. Jarvis, Myself and I* (Carlton Press, 1979), pp. 5-8, especially p. 7, where Jarvis describes his "yearning for motherly love."

MOTHER AND SISTER: Note from Malcolm Jarvis to author.

COULDN'T UNDERSTAND WHY: *MX*, p. 119-120.

OCCASIONALLY ENDORSED PURSUIT OF LOVE AND MARRIAGE: Interview: Malcolm

Jarvis.

MARRIAGE OF OPPOSITES; DUALISTIC PHILOSOPHY: Interview: Malcolm Jarvis. Also Malcolm L. Jarvis, *Myself and I* (Carlton Press, 1979), pp. 48, 52, and interview with Jay V. Thomas.

125 TOO CONTENT: Interview: Malcolm Jarvis.

BE HAPPY: Interview: Viola Thacker.

LIVE FOR TODAY: August 5, 1949 letter to Bazely Perry.

"AH, . . . HOW I WEEP AS I THINK BACK": August 5, 1949 letter to Bazely Perry.

GOOD CAUSE TO WEEP: See, for example, the first two chapters and p. 391 of *MX*.

RELUCTANT TO DISCUSS: Interview: Malcolm Jarvis.

GREW ANGRY: Interview: John Elton Bembry.

"EXTREMELY PAINFUL"; "NEVER PERMITTED US TO . . . BE CHERISHED BY OUR PARENTS": Undated letter from Malcolm Jarvis to author.

FATHER HAD NEVER TAUGHT HIM ANYTHING OF VALUE: Interview: Benjamin Goodman. (Much later, in a January 1965 speech, Malcolm said, "Everything a child knows before he gets to school is learned from his mother, not his father. And if it never goes to school, whatever native intelligence it has, it got it primarily from its mother, not its father."

POEM ABOUT MONKEYS: The author of the poem, which is entitled *The Three Monkeys*, is apparently unknown.

126 WROTE POETRY: For legal reasons, I have deleted examples of Malcolm's poems, among other things.

CHIEF CONTRIBUTORS: Undated letter to Bazely Perry. (See author's note, supra.)

ONE IS ONLY HASTENING ONE'S OWN SELF-DESTRUCTION: April 18, 1950 petition to Massachusetts Commissioner of Correction.

TALKS ABOUT DEATH, BUT DOESN'T FEAR IT: Interview: Malcolm Jarvis.

"CRIME IS PREVENTED IN THE HIGH CHAIR": Interview: Malcolm Jarvis. Also see Malcolm Jarvis, *Myself and I* (Carlton Press, 1979), p. 110.

"KICKED ABOUT ": *MX*, p. 183. (Malcolm verbally equates being a child with being kicked.)

PSYCHOLOGY BOOKS: Interview: Malcolm Jarvis.

FEAR OF BEING A BORE; DETERMINED TO BE HIMSELF: Feb. 10 and Feb. 23, 1950 letters to Gloria Strother.

TRANSFORM FAULTS INTO ASSETS: Interview: Malcolm Jarvis.

"DON'T QUIT": The author of this moving poem is apparently unknown.

127 ASCERTAIN WHAT KIND OF LEADER WOULD APPEAL TO AMERICA'S BLACKS: Interview: John Elton Bembry.

REBELS AND TYRANTS: *FBI*, Jan. 3, 1961, p. 1 and May 17, 1961, p. 20. *MX*, pp. 176, 243, 389. Interviews: Malcolm Jarvis, Saladin Matthews.

RIDICULED DEMOCRACY; DEMOCRACY MEANS RULE BY WHITE DEMONS: Undated letter to Bazely Perry. (See author's note, supra.) See also Archie Epps (editor), *The Speeches of Malcolm X at Harvard* (William Morrow, 1968), pp. 134-135 and Eugene Victor Wolfenstein, *The Victims of Democracy* (University of California Press, 1981).

ISRAEL AND AZRAEL: Undated letter to Bazely Perry. (See author's note, supra.)

HOLLYWOOD AND BIG BUSINESS; TRUMAN AND EISENHOWER: Interview: Malcolm Jarvis. In one of his undated letters to Bazely Perry, Malcolm wrote that the Jewish star "is the ruling factor everywhere."

128 "MOVIES FROM HEAVEN": Interview: Louise Little.

THE APPARITION: *MX*, pp. 186-189.

FARD LOOKED WHITE: *Insight*, Nov. 11, 1985, p. 9. In prison, Malcolm told Jarvis that Fard was six feet tall and jet black. Later, he backtracked somewhat and asserted that Fard was "half black and half white." (*MX*, p. 167.)

NO EMPATHY: *MX*, p. 187.

COLD-SHOULDERED BY FAMILY: Interview: Philbert Little. *MX*, p. 189.

COURTING GLORIA: Interview: Gloria Strother.

"REGINALD'S DEAD!": Interview: Malcolm Jarvis.

REGINALD HOSPITALIZED: Available records indicate that Reginald was admitted to Massachusetts's Taunton State Hospital February 19, 1954 and discharged December 21, 1957. In 1970, Taunton was informed by Michigan's Kalamazoo State Hospital that Reginald was a patient there.

PARTLY RESPONSIBLE: *MX*, pp. 17, 18, 187-189, 295. Cora Spencer, "A Psychological Evaluation of the Political Perspectives of Malcolm X," unpublished paper, p. 12.

26. Second Try

Author's note: Though this chapter has been truncated for legal reasons, I hope the deleted material can some day be restored.

129 NO VISITORS: Interview: Malcolm Jarvis.

JACKIE MASSIE: Interviews: Malcolm Jarvis, Ella Little. Malcolm's prison record confirms that Jackie Massie visited him regularly for a period of time.

LOW OPINION: *PR*: Memo dated Feb. 10, 1949.

SHABBY: *PR*: A July 15, 1948 memo by H. R. Dow indicates that Jackie frequently complained about Malcolm's erratic behavior. An earlier memo describes a letter in which she threatened to end her relationship with him.

130 "THAT WAS THE TEST": February 22, 1950 letter to Gloria Strother.

"I WOULD NOT BE SATISFIED"; "CRAVE YOUR UNDIVIDED ATTENTION"; URGES WEEKLY VISITS: Feb. 10, 1950 letter to Gloria Strother. (Malcolm misspelled the word "undivided.")

"I DIED INSIDE": Interview: Gloria Strother.

ATTRIBUTES SARCASM TO SENSE OF HUMOR: Feb. 10, 1950 letter to Gloria Strother.

GLORIA'S FEBRUARY 23, 1950 VISIT: Interview: Gloria Strother.

DISTANT: Years later, in a Feb. 14, 1978 letter to the author, Gloria poignantly recalled how Malcolm had kept her at a distance.

"DEAREST GLO"; "CONCOCTING A PLAN"; "ITS CLUTCHES"; "HESITATINGLY"; BORE: February 23, 1950 letter to Gloria Strother. (Malcolm misspelled the words "conniving" and "principal.")

131 BEGGED FORGIVENESS; "ALWAYS ON MY MIND AND FOREVER IN MY HEART"; ONE DAY, SHE'D SEE; MUCH TO TELL; "PLEASE DON'T HAVE ME EXPECTING YOU IN VAIN": February 26, 1950 letter to Gloria Strother.

NEVER VISITED AGAIN: Interview: Gloria Strother.

"QUITE A STRANGER"; RENEWED HIS PLEA; ADMITTED HE LOVED HER: March 19, 1950 letter to Gloria Strother.

DIDN'T BELIEVE IT: Interview: Gloria Strother.

27. J.C.

132 REFUSES TYPHOID INOCULATION: *PR*: March 20, 1950 letter from Deputy Warden Edward Grennan to Commissioner of Correction Elliott McDowell. Ella Little and Malcolm Jarvis confirm that Malcolm knew that he'd be expelled from Norfolk if he refused to take the typhoid shot. (Despite his fear of inoculation, he had already taken at least three typhoid shots since he had entered prison, according to a prison medical report dated March 31, 1948.)

WOULD LATER BLAME PRISON ADMINISTRATION: *MX*, p. 189.

HAD RUN OUT OF CONVERTS; REPORTEDLY FELT THE NEED TO SPREAD THE GOSPEL ELSEWHERE: Interviews: Anthony Meleski, Wilfred Little.

DID IT EASE THE PAIN OF BEING REJECTED?: When I informed Gloria that Malcolm's final plea for her return was written the same day he initiated the meeting that prompted his martyr-like return to Charlestown, she asked whether I thought he had been depressed. CHEERFUL: Interview with Malcolm Jarvis, who followed Malcolm back to Charlestown State Prison from Norfolk Prison.

"THEY'RE TRYING TO BREAK ME": Interview: confidential source.

STARVE HIM: Interview: confidential source.

ATE BARELY ENOUGH TO KEEP HEALTHY; BREAD AND CHEESE; VITAMIN DEFICIENCY: Interviews: Clement Brunelli, Dorothy Collins, Malcolm Jarvis, Godfrey Joiner. *Ebony* (June, 1969), p. 176.

MARRYING JACKIE MASSIE OUT OF OBLIGATION: Interviews: Ella Little, Malcolm Jarvis.

133 SENT BY GOD; "NAILS OF DEATH"; "CROWN OF THORNS" Undated petition to Massachusetts Commissioner of Correction (probably written June 1950 or shortly before). Undated letter to Bazely Perry.

"J. C."; JACK CARLTON: Malcolm Jarvis, *Myself and I* (Carlton Press, 1979), pp. 32-35.

STOOD FOR JESUS CHRIST: Interview: Charles Pritchett.

"JUSTICE CRUSHED": July 22, 1949 letter to Bazely Perry. Interview: Malcolm Jarvis. Malcolm Jarvis, *Myself and I* (Carlton Press, 1979), p. 62.

TALKED ABOUT JESUS CHRIST: April 18, 1977 letter from J. Prescott Adams to author. *MX*, pp. 190, 242, 389, 395. Undated, tape-recorded speech at Brandeis University.

"RETURN AGAIN IN THE FLESH": July 22, 1949 letter to Bazely Perry.

RIPPED OUT MATERIAL: *MX*, p. 395.

QUOTED ST. LUKE: Louis E. Lomax, *When the Word Is Given* (Signet Books paperback edition), p. 164.

"THE CHILDREN SHALL RISE UP AGAINST THEIR PARENTS": Interview: Malcolm Jarvis. *St. Matthew*, 10:21.

DIDN'T BELIEVE IN CHRISTMAS: Interview: Malcolm Jarvis. See Chapters Four and Twelve.

CELL FACING EAST: The incident did not occur at Norfolk Prison, as one writer has reported. It occurred at Charlestown in April 1950 about a month after Malcolm's March 23, 1950 transfer there from Norfolk. See Jarvis's handwritten copy of unavailable April 20, 1950 *Boston Post* article. Also the *Springfield Morning Union*, April 21, 1950. Interviews: George Conway, Don Myers, Henry Crawford, Malcolm Jarvis, Charlie Grand, Joe Rull.

134 WARDEN'S REPORT IGNORES MUSLIMS: See, for instance, pages 5-6 of Dec. 31, 1952 annual report by Charlestown State Prison Warden John J. O'Brien.

"YOU BLACK BASTARD"; DRILLED TWO HOLES THROUGH THE OFFICER WITH HIS EYES: Interview: George Conway (who was the guard who witnessed the incident, not the guard who was involved in it.)

TAILORED HIS REBELLION: In his Sept. 27, 1950, Dec. 13, 1950, and June 6, 1951 petitions to the Massachusetts Commissioner of Correction, Malcolm emphasized that, except for the beard he had grown, he had not violated any of the prison rules. Also interviews: Al Lewis, Malcolm Jarvis.

SIX, EIGHT, AND TEN-PAGE LETTERS: *PR*: Memorandum discussing the letter-length issue.

PROMISED THERE WOULD BE NO TROUBLE: Interview: Clement Brunelli

135 SAID HE WASN'T CONCERNED; "I'VE ALWAYS BEEN A COMMUNIST"; JAPANESE ARMY: *PR*: Copy of June 29, 1950 letter to Shirley Johnson.

FEIGNING MADNESS: Ibid. Malcolm Jarvis confirms that Malcolm feigned madness.

BRIDGEWATER: See Malcolm Jarvis, *Myself and I* (Carlton Press, 1979), pp. 57-58.

KNEW LETTERS WERE BEING MONITORED: *MX*, p. 171.

"I MUST ADMIT I WAS CRAZY": *PR*: Copy of undated letter to Doris X. Jones.

"IF MY MOTHER WAS WEARING THE DEVIL'S UNIFORM, SHE WOULD HAVE TO DIE TOO": *PR*: Partly-typewritten copy of Nov. 29, 1950 letter to J. C. Little. In the copy of the letter that is in Malcolm's prison record, the words "my mother" are underlined. It is unclear if the underlining was done by Malcolm or by the prison official who copied the letter.

28. To Be Or Not To Be Free?

138 HAD CONVERTED AS MANY AS HE WAS GOING TO: Interview: Tom Connally.

"WHICH RULE DID I BREAK?"; "AN INJUSTICE"; SHIFTED TACK; "WITHOUT MAL-ICE": Sept. 27, 1950 petition to Massachusetts Commissioner of Correction.

COMMISSIONER DENIED REQUEST FOR RETRANSFER: *PR*: In an October 3, 1950 communique, Commissioner Elliott McDowell instructed Warden O'Brien to tell Malcolm his requested retransfer to Norfolk Prison was deemed "inadvisable."

THREATENING STATEMENTS: April 18, June 6, and Dec. 13, 1950 petitions to Massachusetts Commissioner of Correction.

"KINDNESS"; "WITH A SMILE"; "A MAN WITH A HEART": June 26, 1950 petition to Warden John O'Brien. (Malcolm was initially eligible for parole on June 26, 1951, according to a letter that one of O'Brien's predecessors sent the Detroit authorities on June 11, 1946.)

"ALL WITHIN MY OWN MIND"; "I MYSELF HAVE BEEN AGAINST MYSELF": Dec. 26, 1950 petition to Massachusetts Commissioner of Correction.

139 "SELF-INFLICTED WRONGS"; "THE ONE WHO WAS MAINLY RESPONSIBLE FOR ALL OF MY TROUBLES . . . MYSELF": Copy of Jan. 9, 1951 petition to unspecified public official, reproduced in *FBI*, March 16, 1954, pp. 8-9.

MALCOLM DENIED PAROLE: *FBI*, March 16, 1954, p. 5. Also *FBI* report dated Feb. 17, 1953. (A number of FBI reports confuse the date Malcolm was first eligible for parole with the date the parole board met to consider his application for parole.) Interview: Malcolm Jarvis.

ASSERTS JARVIS WAS THE ONE WHO HAD DIFFICULTY: *MX*, p. 191. Interview: Malcolm Jarvis.

ELLA DID NOT EVEN ASK: Interview: Malcolm Jarvis.

ELLA HAD ASKED PRISON AUTHORITIES NOT TO PAROLE MALCOLM; SHE FEARED PEOPLE WOULD LINK HIS PREVIOUS CRIMINAL ACTIVITY WITH HER: Interview: Heshaam Jaaber. (Compare Malcolm's version in *MX*, p. 317.)

SHE COULD "DO MORE" WITH HIM IF HE WERE BEHIND BARS: Interview: Ella Little. "My problem was to tie him down so I could help him," Ella told me years later. "I knew I could do more with him in prison than in college."

"I'D HAVE RATHER SEEN HIM DEAD THAN MARRY JACKIE": Interview: Ella Little.

TELL THE PAROLE BOARD WHAT IT WANTS TO HEAR: Interview: Wilfred Little. Later on, Malcolm perfected the technique of telling each listener or group of listeners what it wanted to hear. (See chapters entitled "Chameleon" and "Tailoring the Teachings.")

PRISONERS REBEL: The rebellion is described in the *Boston Post*, July 23, 29, and Nov. 23, 1952; *Boston Herald*, July 23, 24, & Nov. 23, 1952, and the *Boston Globe*, July 23, 1952. Malcolm was released from prison Aug. 7, 1952.

140 DID NOT PARTICIPATE: Malcolm's prison record mentions no participation. Had he participated, his parole probably would have been revoked. All those who participated in the rebellion were placed in solitary confinement for ten days.

"I NEVER LOOKED BACK": *MX*, p. 191.

REFUSAL TO REGISTER FOR THE DRAFT NEARLY RESULTED IN HIS REINCARCERA-TION: *MX*, pp. 202-203. Nov. 21, 1974 letter from Director, New York City office, Selective Service System to author. *FBI*: March 18, 1953 report from FBI's Detroit office. Interview with Malcolm's parole officer.

MALCOLM AND SELECTIVE SERVICE: Selective Service classified Malcolm 1-A on April 15, 1953, 1-O on May 6, 1953, and 4-F on June 3, 1953, according to a Sept. 5, 1975 letter to the author from the Executive Secretary of the Livonia, Michigan draft board. Also see the June 16, 1978 letter to the author from the Office of the Director, National Headquarters, Selective Service System. Also see *FBI*: "Succinct Resume of Case," compiled by New York FBI office (date unclear). (*MX*, p. 203 tells only part of the story. And see *MX*, p. 262, where Malcolm describes himself as "an army reject.")

141 INCOME AND OTHER DISPARITIES. U.S. Census Bureau, *Historical Statistics of the United States. Negro Year Book*, 1952, p. 204. Richard Kluger, *Simple Justice* (Knopf, 1976), p. 327.

INKSTER FURNITURE STORE: The furniture store was located at 8940 Oakland Ave., Inskster, Michigan, not in the Detroit ghetto, as *MX*, p. 192 maintains. Interview: Wilfred Little.

VISITS MOTHER AT KALAMAZOO STATE HOSPITAL: *MX*, p. 21. Mrs. Lloyd Hackenberg, who worked at Kalamazoo State Hospital, recalls how unapproachable Malcolm's mother was when Malcolm visited her in 1952.

142 MOVED BY THE RESPECT: *MX*, pp. 194-195.

FATHERLY: Interviews with one of Elijah Muhammad's former mistresses, as well as Chauncey Eskridge and Sharon 10X.

BABIES: Muhammad Ali, *The Greatest* (Random House, 1975), p. 210.

BALDWIN'S STEPFATHER; BALDWIN'S FEELINGS ABOUT ELIJAH MUHAMMAD: James Baldwin, *Notes of A Native Son* (Bantam Books, 1968), pp. 72, 90. "Blood of the Lamb: The Ordeal of James Baldwin," in Calvin Hernton, *White Papers for White Americans* (Doubleday, 1966), pp. 109-113. W. J. Weatherby, *James Baldwin: Artist on Fire* (Donald I. Fine: 1989), pp. 6-10, 197-200. "James Baldwin: The Price of the Ticket," Philadelphia, WHYY-TV, August 14, 1989.

"A FATHER TO EVERYBODY": Interview with one of Muhammad's former mistresses, who later wrote, "I trusted him without reservation, as you would trust your father." (Undated letter from the woman to her attorney.)

FATHERLY FACADE: *MX*, pp. 197, 209. March 25, 1945 statement by Elijah Muhammad to Parole Board, cited in April 23, 1945 Parole Progress report.

143 VIRTUALLY ABANDONED HIS FAMILY: *MX*, pp. 197, 209.

DICTATORIAL AND CRUEL: John Facenda interviewing Elijah's son Wallace Muhammad, WCAU-TV, Channel 10, Philadelphia, Nov. 12, 1978. J. Gallagher interviewing Wallace, *Chicago Tribune* (4th star final ed.), Feb. 21, 1977. Undated statement by Wallace Muhammad in Gladys Towles Root's files. Interview: Philbert Little.

HAD BEEN A GARVEYITE: Ted Vincent, *Black Power and the Garvey Movement* (Ramparts Press, 1975), p. 222.

CHILDREN HAD TO BE SACRIFICED: John Facenda interviewing Wallace Muhammad, WCAU-TV, Channel 10, Philadelphia, Nov. 12, 1978.

ARRESTED FOR REFUSING TO SEND HIS CHILDREN TO SCHOOL: *Chicago Sun-Times*, fEB. 26, 1975. Elijah Muhammad, *Message to the Blackman in America* (Muhammad Mosque of Islam No. 2, 1965), pp. 179, 213-214.

IMPRISONED FOR REFUSING TO REGISTER FOR THE DRAFT: Criminal Docket #70284, U.S. District Court for the District of Columbia. Record of 1942-1943 Court Commitment of "Gulam Bogans" in Elijah Muhammad's parole record. *MX*, pp. 164, 209-210.

HIDING UNDER BED: *Chicago Tribune*, Sept. 22, 1942 (2 star final edition), p. 9.

"IN BONDAGE": *WWG*, p. 103. *MX*, p. 196. According to Elijah Muhammad's parole record, he portrayed himself as a martyr in prison.

ALLEGEDLY OVERAGE: *Message to the Blackman in America*, supra., p. 179. (Elijah Muhammad was born October 7, 1897, according to his criminal record, his death certificate, *FBI* correlation summary dated April 9, 1969, and Edward Peeks, *The Long Struggle for Black Power* [Charles Scribner's Sons, 1971], p. 262.)

ELIJAH MUHAMMAD'S ALIASES: *FBI* correlation summary dated 4/9/69, p. 2.

MOTHER'S VISION: *MX*, p. 205.

FORD LOOKS WHITE; SELLS DOPE; IMPRISONED FOR SELLING HEROIN: "Waiting for 'The New Mecca,'" *Insight* (Nov. 11, 1985), p. 9. Ben Holman, *Daily News*, July 8, 1962. John Facenda interviewing Wallace Muhammad, WCAU-TV, Channel 10, Philadelphia, Nov. 12, 1978. Malcolm told Jarvis, in prison, that Fard was jet black. Later, he backtracked somewhat and asserted that Fard was "half black and half white." (*MX*, p. 167.)

CONFLICTING CLAIMS ABOUT HIS ETHNIC BACKGROUND: "Waiting for 'The New Mecca,'" supra., pp. 8-9. Arna Bontemps & Jack Conroy, *Anyplace But Here* (Hill & Wang, 1966), p. 217. Alfred Balk & Alex Haley, "Black Merchants of Hate," *Saturday Evening Post*, Jan. 26, 1963, p. 72. *MX*, p. 206. *WWG*, p. 41.

DESCRIBES MOTHER AS WHITE: John Facenda interviewing Wallace Muhammad, WCAU-

TV, Channel 10, Philadelphia, Nov. 12, 1978.

FORD'S ALIASES: *WWG*, p. 41.

FROM MECCA; MEMBER OF THE PROPHET MUHAMMAD'S TRIBE: *WWG*, p. 41. *Anyplace But Here*, supra., p. 217. *MX*, p. 207.

144 EACH BROTHER HAD BEEN SIRED BY A DIFFERENT FATHER: *Anyplace But Here*, supra., p. 219.

ARRESTED IN DETROIT IN 1933: "Waiting for 'The New Mecca'", supra., p. 9. The *Philadelphia Inquirer*, March 26, 1972. The sacrificial killing is described in *Anyplace But Here*, supra., p. 222.

ACCORDING TO ELIJAH MUHAMMAD, FORD WAS LATER ARRESTED IN CHICAGO: *Message to the Blackman in America*, supra., pp. 24-25.

MISSION COMPLETED; APPOINTED ELIJAH MUHAMMAD: Interview: Osman Sharrieff.

ALLEGEDLY DEPORTED: *Anyplace But Here*, supra., p. 222. Edward Peeks, *The Long Struggle for Black Power* (Charles Scribner's Sons, 1971), p. 258. Elijah Muhammad claimed that Ford had been deported from Detroit via airplane. (Ben Holman, *Daily News*, August 18, 1962.) Yet Ford told a former girlfriend he had made plans to leave the country by ship. ("Waiting for 'The New Mecca'," supra., p. 9. See also *WWG*, p. 47.)

"RETURNED TO ALLAH": "Waiting for 'The New Mecca'," supra., p. 9.

POSSIBILITY OF FOUL PLAY: C. Eric Lincoln, writing in *New York Journal American*, March 7, 1965, p. 12L. Interview: Osman Sharrieff. *WWG*, p. 47. According to Elijah Muhammad, white people were the murderers. (*WWG*, p. 56.)

ELIJAH MUHAMMAD BOASTED THAT HE KNEW WHERE FARD [i.e., FORD] WAS: Undated, unidentified magazine article in the library archives of the *Philadelphia Inquirer*.

AFRAID OF ASSASSINATION: *MX*, p. 248.

MOVED TO CHICAGO: *Anyplace But Here*, supra., pp. 223-224. Interview: Osman Sharrieff. One reason for Elijah Muhammad's move to Chicago was his unwillingness to obey a court order that gave him six months to enroll his children in an accredited school. (*Message to the Blackman in America*, supra., p. 179.)

NOT A SINGLE WHITE WOULD BE LEFT ALIVE; ELDERLY BLACKS WOULD REGAIN THEIR POTENCY: Undated statement by Wallace Muhammad, supra.

DEIFIES FARD [i.e., FORD]; ELIJAH BECOMES ALLAH'S MESSENGER: "My father," says Elijah Muhammad's son Wallace, "knew that he would need a stronger title than First Minister if he were to control . . . the members of The Lost-Found Nation of Islam, as his teacher had. Consequently, he began presenting the new God concept by telling the Muslims that Mr. Fard [had been] . . . more than a prophet [and] that he [had been] Allah in . . . person. . . . His new teachings were that Allah chose him to lead the seventeen million so-called Negroes. Thus, by pushing Mr. Fard's position up from prophet to God, he raised his own from First Minister to Holy Apostle, and finally the Messenger of Allah." (Undated statement by Wallace Muhammad, supra.)

STILL IN COMMUNICATION WITH ALLAH: Undated, unidentified magazine article in the library archives of the *Philadelphia Inquirer*.

PARALLEL WITH JOB: *MX*, p. 197.

145 STREETS PAVED WITH GOLD: John Facenda interviewing Wallace Muhammad, WCAU-TV, Philadelphia, Nov. 12, 1978.

USUALLY LOW KEY: Interviews: Betty Walker, Mary Smylor, Milton Henry, Jewel Harris, Kenneth Collins, confidential source.

NO RESENTMENT: Interviews: Louis Jackson, Howard Bannister.

"WE'RE GOING TO KILL ALL YOU YELLOW NIGGERS!": Interview: Ray Riddle. Page 5 of an FBI report dated May 23, 1955 states that Malcolm "became very incensed" when only two members of one audience indicated willingness to join the NOI. He said that were it not for Allah's mercy, he'd take their heads himself.

MASKING ANGER: Malcolm acknowledges the anger in *MX*, pp. 199, 201.

BOWED AND PROMISED: Interview: Barbara Trevigne.

LINCOLN-MERCURY: Malcolm worked at Lincoln-Mercury's Wayne, Mich. assembly plant from Jan. 14 until Jan. 21, 1953, according to a Sept. 8, 1975 letter from Ford Motor Co. to the author. (See note entitled "GARBAGE TRUCK FACTORY," infra.)

PRODDED: Interview: Tony Agrieste.

GARBAGE TRUCK FACTORY: Notwithstanding the chronology set forth in *MX*, Malcolm worked at the Gar Wood truck factory after, not before, he worked at Lincoln-Mercury. (See note entitled "LINCOLN-MERCURY," supra.) According to *MX*, pp. 202-203, and a March 18, 1953 report from the FBI's Detroit office, he was at Gar Wood in February 1953, when FBI agents questioned him about his failure to register for the draft. According to *MX*, pp. 202-203, he went to his draft board and registered immediately after he was interrogated. According to a Sept. 5, 1975 letter from the Livonia, Michigan draft board to the author, Malcolm registered on Feb. 20, 1953.

146   PUBLICLY PRAISES LEMUEL HASSAN: Interview: Lemuel Hassan.

ONE OF LEMUEL HASSAN'S ASSISTANT MINISTERS: *MX*, p. 201. FBI report dated June 8, 1953. (Lemuel Hassan and Philbert Little confirm that, contrary to *MX*, p. 201, Malcolm was not the only assistant minister; he was one of several.)

"NEVER OCCURRED"; FELT UNQUALIFIED; "IN THE LOWLIEST CAPACITY": *MX*, p. 200.

"GOING TO REACH THE TOP"; RIGHT-HAND MAN": Interview: Johnny Davis, Jr.

"SEVENTH AND LAST PROPHET": June 6, 1950 petition to Massachusetts Commissioner of Correction.

GRAB BROOM AND SWEEP FLOOR: *MX*, p. 204.

LIKE HIS SEVENTH SON: *Chicago Tribune*, Feb. 24, 1969 (4-star final edition). *MX*, pp. 204, 252, 298. *Muhammad Speaks*, July 3, 1964, p. 9. *WWG*, p. 179. *PG*, p. 47.

ELIJAH MUHAMMAD ACKNOWLEDGED THAT HE FELT FATHERLY TOWARD MAL-COLM: Interview: "Robin."

ELIJAH CALLED MALCOLM "SON": *MX*, pp. 298-299.

SELDOM IN EVIDENCE: *MX*, p. 204.

ELIJAH MUHAMMAD'S OWN CHILDREN HAD LESS ACCESS: Interviews: Wilfred Little, Charles 37X.

SEEMED TO CARE MORE FOR MALCOLM: Interviews: Christine Johnson, Wilfred Little, Sharon 10X. When the author asked Elijah Muhammad's son Akbar, over the phone, whether Elijah had loved Malcolm more than he had loved his own children, there was a discernible pause before Akbar replied, "No comment!" (Interview: Akbar Muhammad.)

NOT REARED PROPERLY: Handwritten March 25, 1945 petition from Elijah Muhammad to U.S. Board of Parole. See also *MX*, p. 197, where Elijah claims he was "deprived of a father's love for his family."

"NERVOUS BREAKDOWN": Handwritten March 25, 1945 petition from Elijah Muhammad to U.S. Board of Parole.

ADEPT AT PENETRATING FACADES: See, inter alia, *MX*, p. 304.

THE IMAGE OF THE LOVING FATHER: Interviews: Philbert and Robert Little. Years later, Malcolm's widow told a writer, "Remember that Malcolm never had a father from the time he was six years old. . . . So that this need for a father image probably had a lot to do with his profound faith in Elijah Muhammad." (*JHC*, p. 139.)

29. Ascetic

147   LEMUEL RECOMMENDED: Interview: Lemuel Hassan.

HAD FULFILLED PAROLE OBLIGATION: Malcolm was discharged from parole in May, 1953.

DIDN'T EVEN MENTION ISLAM: *MX*, p. 215.

TRIES TO CONVERT HIS FRIENDS AND RELATIVES: Interviews: Lionel Beane, J. C. Little, Malcolm Jarvis, Gloria Strother, Clara Little.

"DIDN'T BOTHER": *MX*, p. 213.

ACKNOWLEDGES ANGER: *MX*, p. 199.

NOT ONLY AT THE PEOPLE WHO REJECTED HIS OVERTURES: Godfrey Joiner recalls, "Malcolm suggested I get a Qu'ran. I said, 'I don't need a Qu'ran.' We still remained friends.

. . . But I think he resented [my] not accepting Islam."

ALSO ANGRY AT HIMSELF: *MX*, p. 218. Interview: J. C. Little.

CALLED ON GLORIA: "After Malcolm became a Muslim," Gloria says, "he was a different person."

"I'M GOING TO BUILD A TEMPLE": Interview: Vivian Mann.

ORGANIZES BOSTON TEMPLE IN ABOUT THREE MONTHS: *MX*, pp. 212-215.

JARVIS VS. ELIJAH MUHAMMAD: Interview: Malcolm Jarvis.

148 VIEWS RELIGIOUS MOVIES: Interview: J. C. Little.

"SO AS NOT TO PROHIBIT CONCENTRATION"; "TO PREVENT TEMPTATION": *New York Herald Tribune*, June 30, 1963.

POT-BELLIED STOVE: Interview: Tom Wallace.

"SLUGGISHNESS": Interviews: Saladin Matthews, Clifford Hyman, Benjamin Goodman, Malcolm Jarvis.

THE DANGERS OF OBESITY: Interview: Benjamin Goodman.

"BACK INTO THE PIT": Sept. 27, 1950 petition to the Massachusetts Commissioner of Correction.

SOMETIMES RELUCTANT TO DISCUSS CRIMINAL PAST: Interview: Roy Johnson. Also see pp. 233-236 of the unedited, pre-publication manuscript of *FDL*.

"IT SOUNDS AS IF I HAVE DONE SOME CRIME!": *MX*, p. 367.

ASCRIBED PRISON STAY TO RELIGIOUS PERSECUTION: *FBI*, Sept. 7, 1954, p. 3.

BEHAVED AS IF HE HAD NEVER BEEN IN PRISON: Interview: Betty Walker.

"WE GAIN STRENGTH FROM THE TEMPTATIONS WE RESIST": Interview: Malcolm Jarvis.

149 MALCOLM AND HEATHER: Interviews with Malcolm's former fiancee and her ex-guardian Dorothy Young. Also interviews with Philbert Little, Wilfred Little, Ella Little, and "Robin."

"HE DIDN'T TRUST ANYBODY": Interview with Malcolm's former fiancee. Bessie Springer, Bob Bebee, and Ethel Helmeker concur. See *MX*, p. 389.

ADMITTED THAT THE EXAMPLE ELLA HAD SET HAD PROFOUNDLY INFLUENCED HIS YOUTHFUL DESCENT INTO CRIME: Interview with Malcolm's former fiancee.

"ELLA RUINED MALCOLM": Interview: Mary Little.

QUIETLY ENGAGED: Interviews with Malcolm's former fiancee, and "Robin," and a confidential source. The engagement was later mentioned in the *New York Amsterdam News*, the *California Eagle*, the *Herald-Dispatch*, and *The Chicago Crusader*. To protect the privacy of Malcolm's former fiancee, the dates of the relevant articles have purposely been omitted.

151 "WEAKNESS": "He didn't want anyone to see his weakness," says Malcolm's former fiancee, who points out that he used the word "weakness" quite a bit, particularly when discussing male-female relationships. (See *MX*, p. 131, where Malcolm describes how Sammy the Pimp was "weak" for Hortense.)

ELLA ADVISED MALCOLM AGAINST MARRYING HEATHER; "WEAKNESS"; WOULD HAVE DIVERTED MALCOLM: Interview: Ella Little.

CONNIVING: Interview with Malcolm's former fiancee.

WESLEY LOVED HEATHER: Interviews with Malcolm's former fiancee, Dorothy Young, and Philbert Little. When Malcolm finally realized that Wesley was seriously interested in Heather, he told her she should marry him. (Interview with Malcolm's former fiancee.) fiancee, the dates of the relevant articles have purposely been omitted.

30. In Search of a Leader

152 CHECKING WATCH: Muhammad Abdul Baasit, "The Malcolm X They Didn't Know," *Showcase* (Vol. 17, No. 1), undated, p. 4. Baasit confuses the relevant dates. (See note entitled "ACTING MINISTER," infra.)

ACTING MINISTER: According to memos dated April 30, 1951 and Nov. 18, 1954 from the Philadelphia FBI office, Malcolm became Acting Minister of the Philadelphia temple in March 1954. See also *MX*, p. 215, which erroneously leaves the impression there was no NOI presence in Philadelphia until Malcolm's arrival.

CLOTHES TOO LARGE: *WWG*, p. 21. Photograph in *New York Amsterdam News*, May 24, 1958. Also film entitled "Malcolm X: Struggle for Freedom." Interviews: Wilfred Little, Robert 35X, Benjamin Goodman, Christine Johnson.

PRECAUTIONS ABOUT FOOD: Baasit, supra., p. 8.

"YOU WOULDN'T EAT IT": Interview: Sharon 10X. See also Betty Shabazz, "The Legacy of My Husband, Malcolm X," *Ebony* (June, 1969), p. 176.

TOO MANY CHEMICALS: Interview: Harold Hyman.

RETURN TO SCHOOL; LAWYER; INTERNATIONAL LAW; STUDY OF HUMAN BEHAVIOR: *MX*, pp. 269-270, 379-380. (Also p. 183.) Interviews: Saladin Matthews, Gene Roberts.

ERIC HOFFER'S OBSERVATION: Eric Hoffer, *The True Believer* (Perennial Library, Harper & Row, 1951).

BY THE END OF MAY, 1954: *MX*, p. 215 and note entitled "ACTING MINISTER," supra.

153 "BUT I LOVE MY WIFE": Interview: Ulyssees X.

UPTOWN VS. DOWNTOWN: William Stringfellow, *My People Is the Enemy* (Holt, Rinehart, & Winston, 1964), pp. 4ff. Also Robert Caro, *The Power Broker* (Knopf, 1974), p. 510.

156 3,871 RESIDENTS IN ONE HARLEM BLOCK: Neil Hickey & Ed Edwin, *Adam Clayton Powell and the Politics of Race* (New York: Fleet Publishing Co., 1965), p. 60.

THE RISE AND FALL OF HARLEM: Gilbert Osofsky, *Harlem: The Making of a Ghetto* (Harper, 1966), pp. 71-153. Also James Weldon Johnson, *Black Manhattan* (Knopf, 1930), pp. 148-152 et seq. *The Power Broker*, supra., pp. 352-358, 444-447, 452. Book review of August Heckscher's *When La Guardia Was Mayor* in *Philadelphia Inquirer*, Jan. 21, 1979. *New York Times*, June 10, 1982.

NOT FOND OF BLACKS; ONLY ONE PLAYGROUND BUILT IN HARLEM; VERY FEW BLACKS VENTURED NEAR; HARLEM BENEFITED LEAST; NOT A SINGLE RECREATIONAL FACILITY; ADORNED WITH IMITATION MONKEYS; "SLAVE MARKET": *The Power Broker*, supra., pp. 242, 318-319, 490, 491, 509-514, 525-561 (especially 557-560), 578, 579, 736, 834, 1086 (note), & 1101.

31. Building the Nation

160 WHEN MALCOLM SAW HOW SUCCESSFUL PETE HAD BECOME: Interview: Pete Robertson.

TAXI: *MX*, pp. 129, 216. "If he didn't have a car, he'd take a cab, not a bus or subway," recalls Charles 37X. "I can't imagine him on a subway," says Sharon 10X.

161 "I REPRESENT THE BLACK MAN'S GOD"; "WE MAY NOT TAKE YOU ANYWAY!": Interview: John Elton Bembry.

"LOOK AT HIS WALL STREET!": *MX*, pp. 220-221.

"DIRTY"; "STINKING"; "LEPROUS-LOOKING": *FBI*, April 30, 1958, p. 130 (containing a copy of an article Malcolm wrote in the Nov. 21, 1957 issue of the *Herald-Dispatch*.) *FBI*, April 23, 1957, p. 26. It is unclear whether the date of the latter report was actually 1957.

"QUEEN-MOTHERS: *New York Amsterdam News*, May 4, 1957. *Herald-Dispatch*, Dec. 3, 1957, reprinted in *FBI*, April 30, 1958, p. 117.

DESCENDED FROM PRINCES AND KINGS: See, inter alia, *Malcolm X on Afro-American History* (Pathfinder Press, 1970), p. 40.

ISLAM OLDEST RELIGION ON EARTH: *FBI*, May 19, 1959, p. 38.

162 MUSA: *FBI*, May 19, 1959, pp. 15, 42. Elijah Muhammad, *Message to the Blackman* (Muhammad Mosque No. 2, 1965.) On one occasion, Malcolm asserted that Columbus had been half-black. (*Playboy*, May 1963, p. 58.)

SUMERIANS; EGYPTIANS; MOORS; CARTHAGINIANS: *Malcolm X on Afro-American History*, supra., pp. 19-24, 27.

NECESSARY "OVERDOSE": *PG*, p. 69.

BEETHOVEN AND HAYDN: *Playboy*, May, 1963, p. 58.

"EATING UP THEIR MOTHERS AND FATHERS": *PG*, p. 69.

FRUIT OF ISLAM: See Chapter 34 for the widely-held misconception that the Fruit of Islam was the Nation of Islam's paramilitary arm.

FEARLESS "FRUITS": *FBI*, May 23, 1955, p. 11.

REMAINED IN CHARGE OF PHILADELPHIA MOSQUE: *FBI*, Jan. 28, 1955, pp. 1-4; April 12, 1955; Jan. 31, 1956, p. 3; April 23, 1957, p. 3. Malcolm lectured at the Philadelphia temple each Wednesday (*MX*, p. 222.)

"I'D BETTER NOT HEAR ANYONE MENTIONING MY NAME IN CRITICISM...": *FBI*, Jan. 31, 1956, p. 10.

FUND-RAISING: *FBI*, April 23, 1957, pp. 29. 57, 63, 68.

163   "L.T.E.": It is unclear if anyone noticed that the abbreviation "L.T.E." contained half the letters in Malcolm's last name.

"HARDEST WORKING MINISTER: *FBI*, May 17, 1962, p. 3.

"ONE MILLION DOLLAR" CAMPAIGN: *FBI*, April 30, 1958, pp. 74-75, citing *Herald-Dispatch*, Aug. 8, 1957.

"YOU CAN'T ADVANCE WITHOUT FINANCE: *FBI*, May 19, 1959, p. 12.

EAST COAST REPRESENTATIVE: Interview: Philbert Little. Also see, inter alia, *FBI*, April 23, 1957, pp. 11-12.

EACH TEMPLE REPORTED TO MALCOLM: "We all reported to him," says Philbert, who was one of Elijah Muhammad's ministers. *BMIA*, p. 198. *FBI*, May 19, 1959, pp. 5, 45. (Also see p. 17.)

IF A MAN WANTED HIS CHILDREN TO RESPECT HIM, HE SHOULD SUPPORT THEM: Interview: Philbert Little.

NUMBER OF TEMPLES: Trial transcript, L & T case #4845, Queens Civil Court, 1964 Special Term (Part I), p. 129. E. U. Essien-Udom, *Black Nationalism* (University of Chicago Press, 1962), p. 70, citing the *Herald-Dispatch*, Dec. 19, 1959. Peter and Mort Bergman, *The Chronological History of the Negro in America* (New American Library, 1969), p. 574.

"THANK ALLAH FOR MY BROTHER MINISTER MALCOLM:" Arna Bontemps and Jack Conroy, *Anyplace But Here* (Hill & Wang, 1966), p. 232.

COMPARED HIS RELIGIOUS CONVERSION TO ST. PAUL'S, BUT FIRMLY DISCLAIMED ANY INTENTION OF LIKENING HIMSELF TO HIM: *MX*, p. 163. Years later, Malcolm told an associate, "Some ministers are evangelists. Others are pastors. But rarely is one minister both — like Paul." Then he smiled. (Interview: confidential source. In an October 30, 1978 letter to the author, the source writes, "Malcolm saw himself as . . . Paul, as Omar.")

OMAR: In an October 30, 1978 letter to the author, a confidential source writes, "Malcolm saw himself . . . as Paul, as Omar." For material about Omar, see, inter alia, Hamid Ali, *Omar, The Empire Builder* (Pakistan Press Syndicate, 1961). *Shorter Encyclopedia of Islam* (Cornell University Press, 1953), pp. 600-601. Thomas Patrick Hughes, *A Dictionary of Islam*, pp. 652-654.

164   "THIS ISN'T ALABAMA OR GEORGIA": Different versions of the quoted statement appear in *PG*, p. 55; the *New York Amsterdam News*, May 4, 1957; *Johnson Hinton v. The City of New York, Ralph Plaissance, and Michael Dolan*, New York Supreme Court, Appellate Division, 1st Dept., Index #5742/1958, pp. 967-968, 978. (According to *PG*, p. 56, numerous versions of the Johnson Hinton incident circulated.)

JOHNSON HINTON'S NAME: *EWWS*, pp. 2-6, *PG*, p. 56, and others assert that the man's name was Hinton Johnson. However, according to the relevant court records and other sources, his name was Johnson Hinton. (*Johnson Hinton v. The City of New York, Ralph Plaissance, and Michael Dolan*, New York Supreme Court, Appellate Division, 1st Dept., Index #5742/1958. April 7, 1958 report to the New York City Bureau of Law & Adjustment by the examiner who interrogated Patrolman Michael Dolan. *13 Appellate Division Reports*, 2d Series, First Dept. (March 21, 1961), pp. 475-477. *New York Times*, April 29, 1957. *New York Amsterdam News*, July 1, 1961. *MX*, p. 233. *WWG*, pp. 27-30. PBS film documentary "I Remember Harlem." Interview with Edward Jacko, Esq., who represented Hinton in court.

JOHNSON HINTON INCIDENT: *Johnson Hinton v. The City of New York*, supra. *New York Amsterdam News*, May 4, 1957 and Jan. 26, 1963. *New York Times*, April 29, 1957. *PG*, pp. 55-59. *EWWS*, pp. 2-7. *WWG*, pp. 27-30. *MX*, pp. 233-235, 309. April 7, 1958 report to the New York City Bureau of Law & Adjustment by the examiner who interrogated Patrolman

Michael Dolan. PBS interview of James Hicks that was broadcast in Part 4 of the PBS television series entitled "I Remember Harlem." Interviews: James Hicks, Walter Arm, Edward Jacko.

166 WOULD NOT APPEAR EN MASSE: *EWWS*, p. 4.

NO INTENTION OF FOMENTING VIOLENCE: *New York Amsterdam News*, May 4, 1957. *EWWS*, pp. 5-6.

HARD TIME KEEPING THE PEACE: *FBI*, April 30, 1958, pp. 7, 36.

HINTON COMPENSATED: *New York Amsterdam News*, July 1, 1961, p. 1. (*MX*, p. 234 confuses the jury's $75,000 award with the final $70,000 award, which was the result of a negotiated settlement that followed New York City's decision to appeal the jury's verdict.)

POLITICAL IMPACT OF HINTON INCIDENT: *MX*, p. 309.

WIRED THE MASSACHUSETTS AUTHORITIES FOR INFORMATION: According to the records of the Massachusetts Bureau of Identification, the New York Police Department, on April 30, 1958, asked the Massachusetts authorities for Malcolm's criminal record. The following day, the Massachusetts authorities sent a summary of it to New York.

GOOSE PIMPLES: Charles W. Wiley, "Who Was Malcolm X?" *National Review*, March 23, 1965, p. 239. Interview: Charles W. Wiley.

32. Two More Bettys

167 NATIONAL REPRESENTATIVE: *FBI*, May 20, 1964, p. 2. Interview: Charles 37X. See also *Muhammad Speaks*, Feb. 4, 1963.

LEARNING NEWSPAPER TRADE: *MX*, p. 237.

EDITORIAL ALLIANCE: *BMIA*, pp. 129-132.

LOUIS LOMAX HELPED FOUND *MUHAMMAD SPEAKS*: *FDL*, p. 196. Aubrey Barnett, Lomax's widow, and others confirm that Lomax, an experienced journalist, did the bulk of the writing. (In *MX*, pp. 237-238, 264, Malcolm says he founded *Muhammad Speaks*. In *BAMN*, p. 5, he says that the initial editions were written "entirely" by him. But in *BAMN*, p. 62, he says, "I and another person started [*Muhammad Speaks*] myself in my basement.")

TASKMASTER: *FDL*, pp. 188-190.

OBEDIENTLY DESISTED: Interview with Malcolm's boss.

SURPRISED THAT SHE HAD REMEMBERED; INTELLIGENT, "WONDERFUL" HUSBAND: Undated letter from Malcolm to the woman in question, who prefers to remain anonymous. Interviews with her and two others who know her husband.

PRIVATELY CRITICIZES LEMUEL; LEMUEL IS REMOVED; MALCOLM IS MADE ASSISTANT MINISTER; WILFRED LATER BECOMES MINISTER: *FBI*, April 30, 1958, pp. 23, 32, 131. *PG*, p. 47. *New York Amsterdam News*, Oct. 26, 1957. *MX*, p. 230. Interviews: Lemuel Hassan, Philbert Little. (Lemuel apparently had no idea that Malcolm had criticized his performance.)

168 REPROACHED WOMEN: Interview: Harold Hyman. *FBI*, January 31, 1956, p. 25. *MX*, pp. 225-226.

"TRICKY"; "DECEITFUL": *MX*, p. 226. *FBI*, April 23, 1957, p. 37.

"HALF-NAKED"; BODY LANGUAGE: *FBI*, Jan. 31, 1956, pp. 13, 18. Interview with "Heather."

BUNCH OF PROSTITUTES: *FBI*, Jan. 31, 1956, p. 10.

"HAIR FIVE DIFFERENT SHADES": *FBI*, Jan. 31, 1956, p. 25.

SOME SISTERS COMPLAINED: *MX*, p. 225.

PURPOSE NOT TO CRITICIZE; WOMEN WHO DOMINATE THEIR MEN DESTROY THEM: *FBI*, April 23, 1957, p. 43.

"YOUR OWN MOTHER WILL LIE TO YOU": Interview: Harold Hyman.

"NO WONDER OUR CHILDREN DO NOT RESPECT THEIR PARENTS": *FBI*, April 23, 1957, pp. 37-38.

"DON'T EVER MENTION MY MOTHER!": Interview: Harold Hyman.

TO BOLSTER MALE EGOS BY DENIGRATING FEMALES: Interview: Sharon 10X.

169 "THE CLOSEST THING TO A DEVIL IS A WOMAN: Interviews: Ulysses X, Sharon 10X.

"THE WOMAN WHO MARRIES HIM WILL HAVE TO BE AN ANGEL": Interview: Harold Hyman.

UNINTERESTED IN MARRIAGE: *MX*, pp. 225, 226. Also see *JHC*, p. 133. Interviews: Godfrey Joiner, Ella Little, Charles 37X.

MARRIED TO HIS WORK: *New York Amsterdam News*, April 20, 1957.

THREE OR FOUR HOURS' SLEEP: *Village Voice*, Feb. 25, 1965. *MX*, p. 174. (Also see p. 387.) Interview: Harold Hyman.

TELEPHONE AT ONE OR FIVE IN THE MORNING: Interview: Dorothy Young.

WENT WITHOUT MEALS AND WORKED AROUND THE CLOCK: Interviews: Saladin Matthews, Harold Hyman.

ATTRIBUTED TO FEAR OF WOMEN: Interview: Philbert Little.

SONS WHO COULD CARRY ON HIS WORK; ATTILLAH AND QUBILAH: Interview: Malcolm Jarvis.

"BETTER TO MARRY THAN TO BURN": Corinithians, Chapter 7, Verses 1, 2, 8, 9, particularly Verse 9. Though scholars differ as to what St. Paul meant by the word "burn," Malcolm interpreted it to mean "burn in hell for sex out of wedlock." (Interview: confidential source.)

"MALCOLM WANTED TO GET MARRIED": Interview with one of Bettye's brothers.

MALCOLM ASKED BETTYE TO MARRY HIM: Interview with another of Bettye's brothers.

170 TIME TO THINK IT OVER; WHILE MALCOLM WAS STILL AWAITING BETTYE'S DECISION: Interview with one of Bettye's brothers.

"HEART ATTACK": *FBI*, April 30, 1958, pp. 1, 131-132. (In the FBI report, the term "heart attack" is in quotation marks. Harold Hyman had the impression that Malcolm had been hospitalized for exhaustion.)

THE DOCTOR FOUND NOTHING WRONG WITH HIS HEART: Interview with sources that had access to the relevant Sydenham Hospital records.

ELLA HOSPITALIZED WITH "HEART ATTACK": Interview: Ella Little. (Malcolm thought that Ella had heart trouble, according to *PR*: interview, March 8, 1946.)

SHE UNDERWENT SURGERY FOR SOMETHING ELSE: Interviews: Mary Little, Dorothy Young, Ella Little. Ella's hospitalization occurred during November, 1957. "She had no heart problem," says Dorothy Young.

HER ILLNESS KEPT HER OUT OF JAIL: Interviews: Ken Collins, Violet Houze.

CONVICTED OF ASSAULT: Suffolk County Superior Court, 1957, docket #5010. Interviews: Violet Houze, Kenneth Collins.

NO LONGER LIVING WITH THIRD HUSBAND: When Kenneth Collins told Malcolm that he had left Ella, Malcolm replied, "I'm glad to see you got out. Just because she's my half-sister doesn't mean she's so great. I don't see how you stayed with her this long." (Interview: Kenneth Collins.)

ALSO CONVICTED OF ASSAULTING HER THIRD HUSBAND: Kenneth Collins recalls that, when he left Ella, she told him, "I'll see you dead if you don't come back to me." The authorities officially made note of Ella's penchant for violence and sent her to the Massachusetts Mental Health Center for psychiatric observation. She was subsequently convicted, in Boston Municipal Court, for assaulting Kenneth Collins and sentenced to three months in jail. Her attorney filed an appeal in *Suffolk County Superior Court*. On April 1, 1957, the case was dismissed for want of prosecution. (*Boston Municipal Court*, 1957, domestic relations criminal docket #278. Jan. 3, 1957 letter to the Municipal Court from the Assistant Medical Director of its medical service. *Suffolk County Superior Court*, 1957, domestic relations docket #2230. Interview: Kenneth Collins.)

DECIDED NOT TO CONTEST THE APPEAL; FEARED THAT RODNELL WOULD HAVE NO HOME: Interview: Kenneth Collins.

COLLINS'S FRIEND AGREED NOT TO CHALLENGE THE APPEAL: Interview: Violet Houze. *Suffolk County Superior Court*, 1957, docket #5010.

DID NOT EXPECT TO SURVIVE; IMPERATIVE TO FIND RODNELL ANOTHER HOME; WILFRED WOULD BE TOO "EASY": Interview: Ella Little.

BROWBEAT HIM IN PUBLIC: Interview: Sharon 10X.

ACCUMULATED QUITE A CRIMINAL RECORD: Dorothy Young reports that Ella encouraged Rodnell to steal, just as she had encouraged Malcolm to steal. (See Chap. 11.) "Ella ruined Rodnell," she says. For a period lasting eight years, he was continually in court for stealing and similar offenses. He was convicted at least five times. *Suffolk County Superior Court*: 1961, docket #202-206; 1964, docket #12284 and #12821; 1967, docket #26958-26961 and #30564-30565. *Boston Municipal Court*: 1964, complaint #2306; 1966, docket #5677; 1969, dockets #5109-5110, 5112, 5114, 5343-5345, and 5351-5354.

WOULD MARRY ONLY IF HE WANTED TO: *MX*, PP. 229-230.

"I GUESS I'M GOING TO HAVE TO GET MARRIED"; "I CAN ALWAYS GET A DIVORCE": Interview: Ella Little.

171   "SOMEWHAT AKIN TO RESPECT, OR MAYBE EVEN FEAR": *JHC*, p. 132.

HE HAD GIVEN NO INDICATION: *MX*, pp. 226-227, 228.

BETTY REASSURED HIM SHE KNEW HIS INTEREST WAS PURELY BROTHERLY: *JHC*, pp. 132-133.

"NEVER KID ABOUT": *JHC*, p. 133.

172   SHE SENSED HE WAS LEERY OF MARRIAGE: *JHC*, pp. 133-134.

HE BECAME SO ALARMED THAT HE BEGAN AVOIDING BETTY: *MX*, p. 229.

WEIGHING THE ADVANTAGES: *MX*, p. 229.

"IT COULD BE ANY SISTER IN ANY TEMPLE": *MX*, p. 229.

OUTLAWS: *MX*, p. 229.

ONE HALF THE GROOM'S AGE PLUS SEVEN: *MX*, p. 229.

THEIR MARRIAGE CERTIFICATE: Marriage certificate, Jan. 14, 1958, Ingham County, Michigan. Also see affidavit for license to marry, Jan. 14, 1958, Ingham County. The affidavit contains Betty's signature.

INCONSISTENT BIRTHDATES: On one driver's license application, the date May 28, 1934 appears as Betty Shabazz's [Betty Sanders's] birthdate. It is the same birthdate that appears on the papers that are on file at the New York State Division of Professional Licensing, which issued her nursing license. But, on one automobile registration application, Betty stated that her birthdate was June 23, 1934. On one voting registration application, she declared it was May 28, 1936. The same 1936 birthdate appears in *Who's Who Among Black Americans* (1977-78 ed.). *The Negro Almanac* (1976 ed.) also gives 1936 as the year of her birth.

Yet in 1963, Betty told an interviewer she was 28. In 1965, she told a different interviewer she was still 28. And in 1969, two published articles (at least one of which was the result of an interview with her) reported she was 32. If so, she could not have been 23 when she married Malcolm, as her marriage license application asserts.

(See marriage license and signed marriage license application dated Jan. 14, 1958, Ingham County, Mich. Signed driver's license application, N.Y. State Dept. of Motor Vehicles [date unclear]. Nursing license #141226, N.Y. State, 1958. Signed voter registration application #C197625, Westchester County, N.Y., Aug. 13, 1971. *The Negro Almanac*, 1976, p. 1014. *Who's Who In Black America*, 1977-78, p. 802. Jan. 23, 1980 letter from the publisher of the latter volume confirming that the birthdate appearing in it was supplied to it by Betty Shabazz or her representative. *New York Herald Tribune*, June 30, 1963, p. 6. Statement by Betty Shabazz to N.Y. City Fire Marshall's Office, Feb., 1965. Fletcher Knebel, "A Visit with the Widow of Malcolm X," *Look*, March 4, 1969, p. 75. *Newsweek*, Nov. 3, 1969, p. 16. *The Philadelphia Inquirer Daily Magazine*, May 12, 1988, p. 1.)

"THAT WAS ABOUT IT": *JHC*, pp. 133-134.

SEEMED RELUCTANT: *Herald Tribune*, June 30, 1963.

TOLD MALCOLM NOTHING: *MX*, pp. 228-229. Betty's foster parents were strict. (Fletcher Knebel, "A Visit with the Widow of Malcolm X," *Look*, March 4, 1969, p. 75.)

"I THINK MALCOLM WAS A VERY HAPPY CHILD UNTIL HE WAS SIX": *Chicago Daily News*, May 22, 1972. When Betty was asked to describe Malcolm's childhood, she said nothing that was not already public knowledge. ("A Tribute to Malcolm," a film produced by the National Educational TV and Radio Center.)

NEVER REALLY COURTED; "JUST FRIENDS": *JHC*, pp. 132-133.

NOT A SINGLE WORD OF ENDEARMENT: In *MX*, p. 229, Malcolm says, "There had never been one *personal* word spoken between us."

AFRAID SHE WOULD REJECT HIM; "TOO MUCH EXPERIENCE": *MX*, p. 229.

173 NEVER DID GET BACK IN TOUCH WITH BETTYE: Interview: confidential source.

JANUARY 12, 1958: *MX*, p. 230 says it was the Sunday before Malcolm's January 14, 1958 wedding. The Sunday before the wedding was January 12.

MEMORIZED "MOST NUMBERS," BUT HAD MADE IT A POINT NOT TO MEMORIZE BETTY'S: *MX*, p. 230.

LONG-DISTANCE PROPOSAL: *MX*, p. 230.

"ROMANCE STUFF": *MX*, p. 229.

"JUST LIKE I KNEW SHE WOULD": *MX*, p. 230.

"DIDN'T HAVE A WHOLE LOT OF TIME": *MX*, p. 231.

"WITHOUT A WHOLE LOT OF MESS AND WAITING": *MX*, p. 231.

HURRIED WEDDING: *MX*, pp. 230-231.

NOT ONE FRIEND OR FAMILY MEMBER: *MX*, p. 231. Interview: Philbert Little.

WHISKED HER OUT; "ALL OF THAT HOLLYWOOD STUFF": *MX*, p. 231.

BETTYE HAD BEEN WAITING; "I DIDN'T KNOW"; MALCOLM CRIED: Interview with one of Bettye's brothers.

ACKNOWLEDGED THAT HE WASN'T IN LOVE WITH HIS WIFE: "I guess by now I will say I love Betty," Malcolm told Alex Haley years later. (*MX*, p. 232. Also see *MX*, p. 226.)

"I GUESS HE GOT LONELY": Fletcher Knebel, "A Visit with the Widow of Malcolm X," *Look*, March 4, 1969, p. 75.

33. Into the Limelight

175 "LIKE THE RAPIST ASKING THE RAPED": *MX*, p. 241.

STRESSED IMPORTANCE OF PUBLIC RELATIONS: *MX*, p. 345.

HAD TO "BITE THEIR WAY INTO PRINT": Stan Bernard, "Contact," New York City radio station WINS, Feb. 18, 1985.

CULTIVATED THE PRESS: Mike Wallace speaking (on page 76 of the filmscript for the Warner Brothers film documentary "Malcolm X.")

DROPPED IN TO SEE ONE OF THE EDITORS: Interview: Mildred O'Neill.

"THE REPORTERS . . . WERE LOOKING FOR SENSATIONALISM. . . . AND I GAVE IT TO THEM.": *Village Voice*, Feb. 25, 1965. Interview: Claude Lewis.

"I REJOICE WHEN A WHITE MAN DIES!": *New York World-Telegram*, July 3, 1964. *Boston Globe*, evening edition, July 3, 1964.

EPITOME OF CORDIALITY: *New York Herald Tribune*, July 21, 1962, March 22, 1964, Feb. 22, 1965. *Village Voice*, Feb. 22, 1965. Interviews: Saladin Matthews, Harold Hyman. White visitors to Temple Seven were treated cordially.

MALCOLM MEETS "MR. LUCIFER": Interview: Charles W. Wiley.

JACK MALLON MARVELED: Interview: Jack Mallon.

HOLLYWOOD ACTOR: He performed like an actor on stage, according to Jack Mallon, Harold Hyman, and Gertrude Wilson. Kenneth Clark reports that Malcolm seemed to have the "ability to turn on the proper amount of emotion, resentment, and indignation, as needed." (*JHC*, p. 148.) Also see *MX*, pp. 105-106.

COMPLAINED ABOUT "BAD" PUBLICITY: See, for example, *SPKS*, pp. 91-93. *MX*, p. 242, 243; *JHC*, p. 308; *EPPS*, pp. 162-163.

"PENCIL-SCRATCHERS"; MISQUOTING HIM: *BAMN*, p. 138. *MX*, p. 243.

THE VERY IMAGE HE WANTED TO CREATE: Shortly before his death, Malcolm acknowledged that the fiendish image he had helped the media create was "useful." (*Village Voice*, Feb. 22, 1965.)

JUST AS LONG AS YOU KEEP PRINTING MY NAME: Interview: Wilfred Little.

MANIPULATED THE PRESS: Interviews: Claude Lewis, Reggie Le Vong. (Also see *Village Voice*, Feb. 22, 1965.) Malcolm asserted that white people were the ones who manipulated the press. ("The Last Message," phonograph record #LP-1300 [New York: Discus Hablands Records]. *New York Amsterdam News*, November 17, 1962. *SPKS*, pp. 91-93. *MX*, pp. 242, 243.)

STUDIED BILLY GRAHAM'S TECHNIQUES: "Ballots or Bullets," phonograph record #100 (Philadelphia: Jamie/Guyden Distributing Corp.) *Afro-American*, Feb. 23, 1965. *PG*, p. 138. *FBI*, April 8, 1963, p. 5.

LIKE A HAWK: *New York Post*, April 10, 1964. *PG*, p. 15. Interviews: Robert Little, Sharon 10X. Also see *MX*, pp. 213, 282-283, 310, 395.

176 LEAPED TO ITS FEET: *WWG*, pp. 21-22.

STUDIED THE WRITINGS OF CICERO: Interview: confidential source.

"THEY WOULD HAVE EATEN THEM WHEN THEY WERE YOUNG AND TENDER": *BP*, p. 147.

NOVACAINE; "YOU SUFFER — PEACEFULLY": Phonograph record entitled "Malcolm X: Grass Roots Speech" (Paul Winley Records; stereo record #134). Also see *SPKS*, p. 12. The discrepancy between the version in *SPKS* and the version quoted here (which seems more faithful to the phonograph record) is that Malcolm apparently started out to say "he squirts," but changed it to "they squirt."

"I'M JUST, UHM, ANALYZING IT": Tape-recording of January 23, 1963 speech at Michigan State University. The February 22, 1965 *New York Herald Tribune* made note of the ironic smile that frequently appeared on Malcolm's face.

BOTH BELONG TO THE DOG FAMILY: Phonograph record entitled "Ballots or Bullets," phonograph record #100 (Philadelphia: Jamie/Guyden Distributing Corp).

"REPTILES"; "STRINGY, DOG-LIKE HAIR": Phonograph record album entitled "The Wisdom of Malcolm X" (Mo'Soul Records: record album #MS-8001).

177 LIONS AND LEOPARDS: *WWG*, p. 58.

LAUGHS HEARTILY ABOUT HIS ENTERTAINING EXAGGERATIONS: Interview: Lawrence Henry. Also see *MX*, p. 38.

RUSSIA AN AMERICAN SATELLITE: *SPKS*, p. 120. *BP*, p. 113. Tape-recording of January, 1965 speech entitled "Prospects for Freedom in 1965."

NEW YORK STATE VS. MISSISSIPPI: James Wechsler, "The Cult of Malcolm X," *Progressive* (Vol. 28), June, 1964, pp. 24-28.

THE IMPORTANCE OF ADAPTING ONE'S ORATORY TO EACH SET OF LISTENERS: *MX*, pp. 219, 221. "I tailored the teachings," Malcolm says in *MX*, p. 219.

USED "PSYCHIC RADAR" AND FASHIONED HIS PRESENTATION ACCORDINGLY: *MX*, pp. 282-283. Interviews: Edward Jacko, Robert Little, Clifford Hyman, confidential source.

BLACK MAN'S RELIGION: *MX*, p. 220.

EMPHATICALLY DENIED IT: Tape-recorded comment made during question & answer period following Jan. 23, 1963 speech at Michigan State University,

DESCENDANTS OF THE MOON-PEOPLE: *FBI*, Jan. 31, 1956, p. 23.

BLACK ATHLETES: "Anything that they've let us do, we do it better than they," Malcolm told one African cultural organization." (*BAMN*, pp. 120-121.)

"YOU ARE BETTER THAN THE WHITE MAN"; "YOUR SKIN LOOK[S] LIKE GOLD BESIDE HIS": Television documentary entitled "Eyes on the Prize," broadcast on Channel 39, Allentown, Pa., Jan. 15, 1990. Also see *BAMN*, pp. 120-121.

"EAT THEM UP!": *BAMN*, p. 150.

"THE BLACK MAN WILL BE THE DOMINANT MAN": *BAMN*, pp. 117-118.

THE WHITES WOULD ONE DAY BE THE SLAVES: *FBI*, May 19, 1959, p. 7.

PREACHERS KILLED AND CHURCHES BURNED: *FBI*, May 19, 1959, p. 37. Also see *FBI*, Jan. 28, 1955, p. 1.

EVEN THE CHILDREN: *FBI*, Nov. 18, 1954, p. 7.

178 REFRAIN FROM VIOLENCE BECAUSE WHITES WILL DESTROY THEMSELVES: *FBI*, May 19, 1959, p. 43.

ILL AT EASE: Pat Robinson, Philbert Little, and Alex Haley sensed Malcolm's sensitivity about his lack of formal educational credentials. He told Robinson, "I always wanted to be educated, but I never made it." On another occasion, he included himself among the "ignorant." (*FBI*, April 30, 1958, p. 100.)

EXCUSED HIMSELF BEFORE DINNER AND WENT HOME: Interview: confidential source. (The banquet is described in *FBI*, Nov. 19, 1958, p. 27.)

PRACTICALLY HAD TO HOLD HIS HAND: Ibid.

VISIBLY NERVOUS AT HARVARD LAW; DEROGATORY REMARKS ABOUT HIMSELF: Interview: Leon Friedman, Esq.

GREATEST SHORTCOMING: *MX*, p. 379. "I am not educated." (*SPKS*, p. 20.) "I'm not a student of much of anything." (*SPKS*, p. 25.) "I'll tell anybody that I'm not a college graduate . . . . When you hear me talk, you know I'm not a college graduate." (Printed insert accompanying record album entitled "The Wisdom of Malcolm X" [Mo' Soul Records: Album #MS-8001.])

At Harvard Law School, Malcolm asserted that he was "way up on" his audience of future Harvard lawyers. Then he paused and emphatically added the words "in religion." (Tape recording of Dec., 1964 speech at Harvard Law School Forum. The pause and the comment that followed it were edited out of the version of the speech reproduced in *EPPS*, p. 164.)

"BOOKS": *MX*, p. 179.

THE NERVOUSNESS HE EXHIBITED: (Interviews: Leona A. Turner and two confidential sources.) Sometimes, he'd plunge his big hand into his pocket. Or he'd wipe his forehead or fidget with his glasses. (June 8, 1964 interview by Mike Wallace. Interviews: Hakim Jamal, Gene Roberts.)

RELISHED PROFESSORIAL ROLE: Interviews: Pat Robinson, Jim Campbell, Howard Bannister. Kenneth Clark got the feeling that Malcolm would have liked to have been a college professor. (Interview: Kenneth Clark.)

RARELY LET THEM FORGET: Interviews: Sharon 10X, Benjamin Goodman. Also see *WWG*, p. 23.

STUDIED DEBATING TECHNIQUES: *MX*, p. 269.

LOADED QUESTION; STOCK ANSWER: Interview: Godfrey Joiner. *MX*, p. 284.

179 "IF HE IS NOT A DEVIL, LET HIM PROVE IT": *WWG*, p. 172.

A MIRACLE: *MX*, p. 247.

BY ARGUING THE OPPOSING POSITION: Interview: Robert Little.

AT HOME, REVIEWED PLAYBACKS: *JHC*, p. 135. *PG*, p. 14.

VERBAL BATTLEFIELD; INTELLECTUAL BULLETS: *MX*, p. 282. Also see p. 379.

HIS ADVERSARIES LEARNED NOT TO DEBATE HIM: *PG*, pp. 16-17. Interview: Charles W. Wiley. *WWG*, p. 153. Lewis Baldwin, "A Reassessment of the Relationship between Malcolm X and Martin Luther King, Jr.," *The Western Journal of Black Studies* (Vol. 13, No. 2), 1989, pp. 105-106. Also see the Feb. 11, 1961 issue of the *Pittsburgh Courier*, which describes how Malcolm bested historian Arthur Schlesinger, Jr., in a brief, decisive exchange.

TAILORED HIS SPEECHES: Interviews: Edward Jacko, James 67X, Robert Little, Clifford Hyman. *MX*, pp. 219, 221.

WHITES SMELLED BAD: Phonograph record album entitled "The Wisdom of Malcolm X" (Mo' Soul Records: record album #MS-8001).

CONVINCED ONE ASSOCIATE: Interview: confidential source.

IMPATIENT WITH LONG-WINDED INTRODUCTIONS: *EWWS*, p. 14.

A WAVE OF THE HAND; "CUT THAT OUT!"; "I DON'T WANT TO HEAR THAT!": WCBS interviews dated August 18, 1959 and March 15, 1964. Tape-recording of May 1, 1962 speech entitled "The Crisis of Racism." "Like It Is," WABC-TV, 2/22/69, et al.

ENJOYED THE ADULATION: Interview: Robert 35X. (Also see *MX*, p. 316.)

COLLECTED PRESS CLIPPINGS: *MX*, p. 353.

"DID YOU SEE THIS?": Interview: Hayward Howard.

WATCH HIMSELF ON TV: "He used to sit by the TV set and watch himself, and you could see how much he liked it," one associate later told biographer Peter Goldman. (*PG*, p. 14.)

"EVERY GRATIFICATION: *MX*, p. 289.

180   BIG, HAPPY FAMILY: In the May 9, 1963 edition of the Washington, D. C., *Evening Star*, Malcolm likens part or all of the Nation of Islam to "a family." On p. 236 of the original, lengthy manuscript that was later shortened and published as *FDL*, he tells an associate, "Your family will be those brothers and sisters who have accepted Islam and the teachings of the Messenger." (Also see *MX*, pp. 194-195 and E. Victor Wolfenstein, *Personality and Politics* [Dickenson Publishing Co., 1969], p. 62.)

"PERMANENT LODGERS": September 7, 1949 letter to Bazely Perry.

"HOUSE OF ALLAH": Undated letter to Bazely Perry.

34. Fear Transformed

181   MOTHER-WIT: *Malcolm X on Afro-American History* (Pathfinder Press, 1970), p. 35.

"ON THE TOILET": *SPKS*, p. 9. (Also see *BAMN*, p. 138, inter alia.) Malcolm told a Harlem street crowd that integration meant: "You'll have a chance to go to the toilet with white folks. Why, you're out of your mind! [The] only way I want to go to the toilet with him is if I can flush him down with the rest of that stuff. Flush him right down the drain with the rest of his kind." (James Cone, *Martin & Malcolm in America: A Dream or a Nightmare* (Orbis Books, 1991), p. 116.)

SOUGHT-AFTER SPEAKER: *MX*, p. 281.

A HOST OF DIFFERENT SMILES: *FDL*, pp. 119, 162, 163, 182, 187, 235. *LYMX*, pp. 99, 136, 137. *PG*, pp. 6-7. George Plimpton, "Miami Notebook: Cassius Clay & Malcolm X," *Harper's Magazine* (June, 1964). *New York Herald Tribune*, Feb. 22, 1965. Interview: Gene Roberts.

INGRATIATING SMILE: *MX*, p. 413. Hans J. Massaquoi, "Mystery of Malcolm X," *Ebony* (Vol. 19, Sept., 1964).

SMILE FOR PHOTOGRAPHERS: See photograph on back cover of paperback edition of *FDL*.

CONDESCENDING SMILE FOR DEBATING OPPONENTS: Nat Hentoff, "Elijah in the Wilderness," *The Reporter* (Aug. 4, 1960), p. 38. Interviews: Charles W. Wiley, Saladin Matthews, Godfrey Joiner, Bob High.

BITTERSWEET SMILE: Recall the smile on Malcolm's face when he was sentenced to prison by Judge Buttrick. Also *PR*: interview dated March 8, 1946. Also *PG*, pp. 24-25, where Malcolm laughs joylessly and says, over and over, that one must laugh at painful things in order to endure them.

SMILE CONCEALED ANGER: Interview: Malcolm Jarvis.

"EVERY TIME I SMILE, IT DOESN'T MEAN I AM HAPPY": Interview: John Thimas. Malcolm complained to Al Lewis about the way whites erroneously assume blacks are happy because they are "always grinning." See also *MX*, pp. 344-345.

ANGER IN VOICE: *MX*, p. 241. Interview: Louis Mechaux. For relevant examples, see, inter alia, phonograph record entitled "The Last Message" (Afro-American Record Club: LP-1300); GOAL Show radio broadcast, April 18, 1964.

EYES FLASHED: Interview: Herb Craigwell.

VEINS BULGED; FACE FLUSHED RED; BACK OF EARS: *MX*, pp. 388, 394, 406. *PG*, p. 13. *TKBM*, p. 98. Interviews: Alex Haley, Aubrey Barnette, Tom Wallace, Saladin Matthews, and others. Matthews says, "[Malcolm] was an angry man. He had veins that would stand out on the side of his neck, and they'd turn blue."

ANGRIEST NEGRO: *MX*, pp. 366, 397.

DENIED HE WAS ANIMATED BY HATRED: *TKBM*, p. 73. *The Village Voice*, Feb. 25, 1965. *SPKS*, p. 106. Louis Lomax, *The Negro Revolt* (Harper & Row, 1962), p. 172. *MX*, p. 381. Undated tape-recorded speech, Lemberg Center for the Study of Violence, Brandeis University. Also see *JHC*, p. 202 and the note entitled "inadvertently acknowledges his hatred," infra.

"I DON'T HAVE ANY HATE": *SPKS*, p. 145.

INADVERTENTLY ACKNOWLEDGES THE HATRED: In his eagerness to deny that he hated the U.S. government or the F.B.I., Malcolm said, "It is incorrect to clarify that as hate." And see Pierre Berton, *Voices from the Sixties* (Doubleday, 1967), p. 34, where Malcolm acknowledges that hatred pervades Elijah Muhammad's movement and then tries to explain it away. Also see "Pro and Con," radio station WMCA, March 3, 1960, reproduced in *FBI*,

March 18, 1960, pp. 5-6.

EXPLICITLY ACKNOWLEDGES THE HATRED: "I have so much hate in me against whites," Malcolm told Malcolm Jarvis. He made the hatred "abundantly clear" to Hans J. Massaquoi ("Mystery of Malcolm X," *Ebony* [Vol. 19, Sept., 1964]). He told one group of listeners, "If we don't hate the white man, then you don't know what you're talking about." (C. Eric Lincoln papers in Trevor Arnette Collection, Robert W. Woodruff Library.) And he told a reporter, "The hostility is good." He said it was time "we" stopped "turning the hate against ourselves." (*SPKS*, p. 208.)

See *FBI*, May 17, 1960, p. 54, where Malcolm tells whatever government spies are listening that they can tell their superiors that the Nation of Islam does teach its members to hate whites.

182 TOLD JULES LOH THE HATRED HAD ORIGINATED BEFORE HE WAS BORN: January 7, 1975 letter from Jules Loh to author.

ACKNOWLEDGED THAT HATRED WAS TAUGHT AT TEMPLE SEVEN: *FBI*, May 17, 1960, p. 54.

TOLD CONGREGATION THEY SHOULD HATE WHITES: *FBI*, May 19, 1959, p. 44.

HAD TO BE HATED IN ORDER TO BE DEFEATED: May 14, 1964 airgram #A-715 from American embassy in Lagos to U.S. Dept. of State, citing May 10, 1964 article published in Lagos, Nigeria's *Sunday Express*. On Dec. 18, 1987, the author sent a letter to the *Express* requesting a copy of the original article, but he never received a reply.

"NOT ALL HATE": *FBI*, April 23, 1957, p. 39.

CARDINAL RULE: *MX*, p. 284. "He might be furious," Alex Haley later told an interviewer. "But you'd never know it, oftentime." (Terry Gross, "Fresh Air," Philadelphia radio station WHYY-FM, March 15, 1985.)

TOTAL CONTROL: Interviews: James Hicks, M. S. Handler, Gertrude Wilson, John Elton Bembry, Godfrey Joiner, Herbert Craigwell, Lionel Beane, Charles 37X. "One certainly does not get the impression of spontaneity," said the psychologist Kenneth Clark. (Kenneth Clark, *The Negro Protest* [Beacon Press, 1963], p. 17.)

"WE WANT TO GET OUT OF CONTROL: *SPKS*, p. 119.

"HOSTILITY IS GOOD": *SPKS*, p. 208.

NEIGHBORHOOD ALL BLACK: *MX*, p. 232. (Reggie Le Vong used to kid Malcolm about his white neighbors.)

LIVING IN HARLEM: Tape recording of a November, 1963 speech. (The tape recording was apparently misdated and mislabeled, so it is unclear which November speech was recorded on this tape.)

"Harlem is the only place for me," Malcolm told the *Afro-American*. (*Afro-American*, August 3-6, 1963.)

HAD LIVED IN EAST ELMHURST SINCE HE HAD MOVED TO NEW YORK: *PG*, pp. 54-55. (This has been confirmed by several of Malcolm's associates as well as court and FBI records.)

NEIGHBORS UPSET: Interview: Reggie Le Vong.

EXAGGERATED YOUTHFUL CRIMINALITY: See Part II of this book; *PG*, pp. 30-31; and the April 20, 1957 issue of the *New York Amsterdam News*, where Malcolm claims that he had even committed murder.

"I'M THE MAN YOU THINK YOU ARE": *SPKS*, p. 197.

183 FOND OF BIG WORDS: Lerone Bennett, Jr., *What Manner of Man?* (Johnson Publishing Co.: 3rd rev. ed., 1968), p. 17. Robert M. Bleiweiss (ed.), *Marching to Freedom: The Life of Martin Luther King, Jr.* (American Education Publications, 1968), p. 38. Jim Bishop, *The Days of Martin Luther King, Jr.* (Putnam, 1971), p. 91.

SUCCESS-ORIENTED, TYRANNICAL FATHERS: Stephen Oates, *Let the Trumpet Sound: The Life of Martin Luther King, Jr.* (Harper & Row, 1982), pp. 4, 6-8. David Garrow, *Bearing the Cross* (Morrow, 1986), p. 34. Martin Luther King, Sr. (with Clayton Riley), *Daddy King* (Morrow, 1980), p. 130. Lerone Bennett, Jr., *What Manner of Man?* (Johnson Publishing Co., 3rd rev. ed., 1968), p. 18. Lawrence Dunbar Reddick, *Crusader Without Violence* (Harper, 1959), pp. 60, 75. Jim Bishop, *The Days of Martin Luther King, Jr.* (Putnam, 1971), pp. 110, 98-99, 90. David Lewis, *King: A Biography* (Praeger, 1970), p. 13.

WORRIED THAT PEOPLE WOULD THINK HE WAS SEEKING MARTYRDOM: Martin Luther King, Jr., "Suffering and Faith," *Christian Century*, Apr. 27, 1960, p. 510.

STUDENT JUMPS FROM BALCONY: *TKBM*, p. 64.

"TELLING THE TRUTH": *Life*, May 31, 1963, pp. 29-30.

SOME THINGS ARE BETTER LEFT UNSAID: Interview: Robert 35X.

184 OUTWARDLY CRAVE FREEDOM BUT INWARDLY FEAR IT: Eric Hoffer, *The True Believer* (Harper & Row: Perennial Library, 1966). Erich Fromm, *Escape from Freedom* (Holt, Rinehart, & Winston, 1941).

ATTENDANCE SOMETIMES EXCEEDED 10,000: *Chicago Daily News*, August 15, 1962. *MX*, p. 248. TV documentary entitled "The Hate that Hate Produced," broadcast July, 1959 by Mike Wallace.

ATTENDANCE FIGURES SOMEWHAT MISLEADING: Aubrey Barnette, "The Black Muslims Are a Fraud," *Saturday Evening Post*, Feb. 27, 1965.

OBLIGED OR STRONGLY PRODDED TO ATTEND: *FBI*, May 19, 1959, p. 44.

PACK INDIVIDUAL TEMPLES; LARGE TURNOUTS NECESSARY: *FBI*, date unclear, p. 32. Confidential source.

REPORTEDLY MALCOLM'S IDEA: Interview: Benjamin Goodman. *PG*, p. 87.

"HELP THE CAUSE, BROTHER"; BUCKETS EMPTIED AND PASSED AGAIN: *Chicago Daily News*, August 15, 1962. *Chicago Sun Times*, Feb. 27, 1961. *MX*, 256-257.

185 FUND-RAISING BY MALCOLM AND JOHN: *Chicago Sun Times*, Feb. 27, 1961.

SUMS COLLECTED "ALWAYS" EQUAL OR EXCEED EXPENSES: *MX*, p. 257.

ERRONEOUS BELIEF THE FRUIT OF ISLAM WAS A PARAMILITARY FORCE: Tape-recorded answer to question put to Malcolm after Jan. 23, 1963 address at Michigan State University. *Muhammad Speaks*, special (undated) 1961 issue, p. 28. Aubrey Barnette, supra., p. 25.

AS SALAAM ALAIKUM, ETC.: These Arabic greetings are incorrectly quoted in *MX*, p. 253.

"MISSIONED": *WWG*, pp. 104, 106.

CHOSEN BY GOD HIMSELF; DIRECTLY FROM HIS MOUTH: *WWG*, p. 102.

ELIJAH MUHAMMAD'S CONFLICTING CLAIMS ABOUT HIS EDUCATION: *Chicago Daily News*, Feb. 28, 1974. *MX*, p. 205. Elijah Muhammad's parole record (U.S. Bureau of Prisons). *New York Post*, Feb. 28, 1965. *Chicago Tribune*, Oct. 6, 1942.

"ALL YOU HAVE TO DO IS LISTEN": *WWG*, p. 103.

"ABSOLUTE CURE: *WWG*, p. 102-103.

186 DRILLED A SHAFT INTO THE EARTH THOUSANDS OF MILES DEEP: *WWG*, p. 99. Also see, inter alia, Elijah Muhammad, *Message to the Blackman in America* (Muhammad Mosque of Islam No. 2, 1965).

AARON: Interview: James 67X.

RALLY IN PHILADELPHIA ARENA: Elijah Muhammad made the speech, which lasted two hours and fifty minutes, on Sept. 29, 1963.

35. Marital Martyr

187 MARRIAGE - DIVORCE METAPHOR: *Life*, March 20, 1964, pp. 40-40A.

PARENT-CHILD METAPHOR: *Muhammad Speaks*, Sept. 15, 1962, p. 14. *Afro-American*, date unclear. Also see the following two notes.

MOTHER AND CHILD MUST BE SEPARATED: *MX*, p. 246.

SOMETIMES PRECIPITATED THE MOTHER'S DEATH: *WWG*, pp. 149-151. Also see *MX*, p. 246, where Malcolm says, "When the time of birth arrives, the child must be separated [from its mother], or it will *destroy* its mother and itself."

"I KNOW FROM PERSONAL EXPERIENCE. I TRIED HARD ENOUGH.": *MX*, p. 31.

188 "YOU CAN'T PLEASE THE WHITE MAN. . . . YOU CAN'T SATISFY HIM. WHY, YOU'RE OUT OF YOUR MIND TRYING TO MAKE LOVE TO A WHITE MAN.": Record album entitled "The Wisdom of Malcolm X," Mo' Soul Records, record album #MS-8001.

RACIAL FREAKS: *MX*, p. 277.

BLACKS HAVE NO INTEREST IN HAVING SEX WITH WHITES: *MX*, p. 273.

"WE DON'T WANT TO SLEEP NEXT TO THAT OLD PALE THING. NO, WE CAN DO WITHOUT HIM.": Warner Brothers film documentary entitled "Malcolm X." Also see: "Who Killed Malcolm X," KERA-TV, Dallas, Texas, Feb. 22, 1972. "Like It Is," WABC-TV, New York City, Feb. 22, 1969. Grove Press film entitled "Malcolm X Speaks." Also see the *Chicago Defender*, June 19, 1963, where Malcolm talks about teen-age "fairies," recounts the sins of his youth, and says, "The rent is high. You got no money. You turn to dope, liquor, sex."

"IT'S NO JOKING MATTER. I'M A MARRIED MAN NOW: Interview: Ella Little.

SAYS ELIJAH MUHAMMAD PRODDED HIM TO GET MARRIED: Interview: Charles 37X.

ACKNOWLEDGES THAT ELIJAH MUHAMMAD HAD URGED HIM TO STAY SINGLE: *MX*, p. 226.

DOMINEERING HUSBAND: In addition to the material that follows in this chapter, see Fletcher Knebel, "A Visit with the Widow of Malcolm X," *Look*, March 4, 1969, p. 75. *Philadelphia Inquirer Daily Magazine*, May 12, 1988. (Additional, suggestive statements about who called the shots appear in *MX*, p. 339 and *JHC*, pp. 134, 143.)

STRICTURES: Fletcher Knebel, supra., p. 75.

"TRAUMATIC": *The Philadelphia Inquirer Daily Magazine*, May 12, 1988.

CONDITIONED BY A LIFETIME OF DISCIPLINE: Fletcher Knebel, supra., p. 75. Interview: Fletcher Knebel. Also see *MX*, p. 228.

SHE LET HIM SPEAK FOR HER: *New York Herald Tribune*, June 30, 1963.

"DADDY": *JHC*, p. 134.

"GIRL": Betty Shabazz, "The Legacy of My Husband Malcolm X," *Ebony*, June, 1969.

ONCE A WEEK: *Ebony*, June, 1969, pp. 177-178.

189   NEVER TOOK HER TRAVELING: *Journal-American*, Feb. 23, 1965. (Also see *MX*, p. 233.)

ONLY ONE MOVIE: *Ebony*, June, 1969, pp. 177-178.

RAISED BY REAL-ESTATE-OWNING FAMILY THAT HAD HIRED HELP AND TWO CARS: *Chicago Today*, May 16, 1971.

UNLIMITED ACCESS: *MX*, p. 290.

$150 PER WEEK: Page 188 of trial transcript, Landlord & Tenant case #4845, Queens Civil Court, 1964 Special Term (Part I.)

NO NEST EGG: *MX*, p. 291.

CHECKS MADE OUT TO THE NATION RATHER THAN TO HIMSELF: Interview: Aubrey Barnette.

EACH MONDAY MORNING: Interview: Confidential source

HE WARNED ABOUT LEADERS WHO TOOK ADVANTAGE: *MX*, p. 291.

WORDS HE WOULD LIVE TO REGRET: *JHC*, p. 138. *MX*, p. 291. *PG*, p. 196. Interview: Philbert Little. Though Malcolm refused to put the title to his home in his own name, he admonished his followers, "You should own your own home." (*FBI*, Apr. 23 [year unclear], p. 38.) THE DEMANDS OF THE MOVEMENT: *MX*, p. 233.

BUT NOT THE LOVE LETTER: *JHC*, p. 135.

NEVER SAW HIM HUG OR KISS: Interview with the babysitter, who wants her name withheld. Also see *MX*, p. 231.

"THE ONLY WOMAN" HE EVER THOUGHT ABOUT LOVING: *MX*, p. 232.

RIDICULED WOMEN WHO EXPECTED "KISSING AND HUGGING," WHICH HE CHARACTERIZED AS HOLLYWOOD-CREATED WANTS: *MX*, 231. Also see p. 229.

AT TIMES, HE SLEPT IN THE ATTIC; UNFOLDED MORE OFTEN THAN NOT: Interviews: Charles 37X, confidential source. (*PG*, p. 191, erroneously conveys the impression that Malcolm just took naps there.

190   BANISHING HER FROM HIS BED UNTIL SHE SUBMITS: Interview: Charles 37X. See Yusuf Ali's translations of *The Qu'ran*, 4:34.

WOULD BE TEMPTED: Interviews: Clifford Hyman, Charles 37X.

VISIBLY TROUBLED: *JHC*, p. 136.

MISTRUST: *MX*, p. 389.

"SHE CLAIMS": *MX*, pp. 231-232.

NEGLECTED TO TELL SOME OF HIS FRIENDS HIMSELF: Interview: Harold Vaughan. "He didn't talk about his family," says Harold Hyman.

"SEVENTY-FIVE PERCENT": *MX*, p. 389.

MORE THAN HE TRUSTED MOST WOMEN: *MX*, p. 389.

ONE OF FOUR: *MX*, p. 232.

DIFFICULT TO CONFIDE: "Betty didn't know what Malcolm was thinking," says Lawrence Henry. The day after Malcolm's assassination, she was asked whether Malcolm had expected to be killed so soon. "I have no idea whether he expected it this soon or not," she replied. (Filmed ABC interview, Feb. 22, 1965.) Nor did she readily confide in him. (*MX*, p. 228.)

INSISTED HE LOVED BETTY: *MX*, dedication page, et al.

"I GUESS BY NOW I WILL SAY I LOVE BETTY": *MX*, p. 232.

HE ASSERTED HE HAD TO LOVE HER: *MX*, p. 421.

AS LONG AS SHE RAISED THEIR CHILDREN PROPERLY: Filmed ABC interview, Feb. 23, 1965. *New York Journal-American*, Feb. 23, 1965.

ADMITTED HE WAS NOT EASY TO LIVE WITH: *MX*, p. 233.

TEARS: Interview: confidential source.

TRIED HARD TO PLEASE HIM: Interview: confidential source. Also see *JHC*, p. 143.

THE FACADE OF THE HAPPY HOUSEHOLD: *New York Journal-American*, Feb. 23, 1965. *New York Amsterdam News*, March 13, 1965. *JHC*, pp. 134-135, 138, 143. *Ebony* (June, 1969), p. 176.

THE UNHAPPINESS SHOWED THROUGH: Interviews: Pat Robinson and confidential source.

TACITLY, SHE ACKNOWLEDGED IT HERSELF: She said that, whenever she became pregnant, Malcolm treated her "with such tender care and consideration" that she "was just plain happy." (*JHC*, p. 137.)

MUHAMMAD'S FOLLOWERS TAUGHT TO OBEY THE LAW: *New York Amsterdam News*, August 19, 1961. Feb. 3, 1963 interview on radio station WMAL, Washington, D.C. *FBI*, May 19, 1959, p. 9.

191 "SUBMISSIVENESS": *Boston Advertiser*, May 6, 1962.

192 BACK AT TEMPLE TWENTY-SEVEN; SHARPENING KNIVES; PRACTICING KARATE CHOPS; "WE ARE GOING TO SELL NEWSPAPERS"; "BE SURE YOU PAY FOR THEM RIGHT NOW"; SOLITARY WHITE VICTIMS, SOME OF WHOM DID NOT SURVIVE: *FDL*, pp. 192-198.

MALCOLM CREATED THE IMPRESSION HE WAS GOING TO ORGANIZE THE OPENING SKIRMISH: *TKBM*, p. 97. *PG*, pp. 97-98.

193 "I'M GOING OUT THERE TO DIE!": Interview: Louis Michaux.

MALCOLM WAS LIVID; HE ORDERED A STOP TO THE BLOODSHED: *FDL*, p. 197.

MALCOLM, WHO HAD KNOWN STOKES, CRIED: *PG*, pp. 97, 98. Interview: Kenneth Clark. Also see *FDL*, pp. 150, 152, 197.

STOKES WOULD BE AVENGED, NOT BY MORTALS, BUT BY ALLAH: *Los Angeles Times*, May 15, 1962. *Muhammad Speaks*, July, 1962. *FDL*, pp. 197-200

VIOLENCE ENDED, EXCEPT FOR "LITTLE DEATHS" HERE AND THERE: *FDL*, pp. 197-198.

MANIPULATED EMOTIONS OF HIS VOLATILE AUDIENCES: *PG*, pp. 97-98. *FDL*, p. 199. *New York Post*, April 10, 1964.

194 QUIETED THE INCIPIENT MOB: Warner Brothers film documentary entitled "Malcolm X."

FAILED TO DISTINGUISH BETWEEN WHAT HE SAID AND WHAT HE ACTUALLY DID: In addition to the Warner Brothers film documentary, supra., see *MX*, p. 395 and *PG*, p. 98.

36. The Enemy in the Mirror

195 CASTIGATED BLACK PREACHERS FOR SPONGING OFF THEIR FOLLOWERS: One associate says he got the feeling Malcolm felt that most Christian preachers were parasites

who lived off their followers. (Interview: Milton Henry.)

RESEMBLED HIS FATHER: Malcolm characterized Christian clergymen as adulterers. (*FBI*, April 23, 1957, p. 57.)

CRIMINALS IN DISGUISE: Malcolm described Christian clergymen as racketeers, and said that they were better hustlers than he had been. Interview: Eugene Callender. *Afro-American* (Baltimore edition), August 3, 1963, August 6, 1963. *FBI*, April 30, 1958, p. 114.

INGRATIATE THEMSELVES WITH WHITES: *BMIA*, p. 79.

"TOURING CARS": *New York Amsterdam News*, May 25. 1957. *WWG*, p. 137. *TKBM*, p. 81. Elijah Muhammad also used the phrase "touring car of Christianity." Whether he borrowed the phrase from Malcolm is unclear.

"IN THE DITCH": *WWG*, p. 137. *FBI*, April 30, 1958, p. 91.

"BASTARD BABIES": *New York Amsterdam News*, April 27, 1957. *FBI*, April 30, 1958, p. 130.

"FAVORITE SUBJECT": *MX*, p. 200. (Also see p. 153.)

LOST CONTROL: *MX*, pp. 219-220.

AN EDUCATOR: Interview: Ernie Wolf.

196   BRAINS FROZEN; "ICE-BOXES"; "ICE-MAKERS": *FDL*, pp. 161-164. *MX*, pp. 159, 160. Interviews: Malcolm Jarvis, Godfrey Joiner, Al Lewis, Harold Hyman, confidential source.

ANTI-SEMITIC STATEMENTS: "Malcolm was raging about Jews," recalls Gertrude Wilson. *FBI*, April 30, 1958, pp. 6, 118-123. *FBI*, June 24, 1964, citing James A. Wechsler, "The Cult of Malcolm X," *Progressive* (Vol. 28, June, 1964), pp. 24-28. Also see *New York Herald Tribune*, June 30, 1963; *MX*, p. 283; and the relevant material in the text and infra.

MODEL AND PRECEDENT: The *Chicago Crusader*, March 19, 1960. Also see *MX*, p. 278.

ACHIEVEMENTS OF JEWISH INTELLECTUALS: *MX*, pp. 277-278.

SENSE OF CORPORATE IDENTITY; "THE BIGGEST DIFFERENCE": *SPKS*, p. 198. *New York Times*, 5/24/64. *FBI*, March 9, 1964, p. 2.

GRATUITOUS JIBES: *MX*, pp. 59, 122, 148, 160, 192, 283. Original, unedited, uncut tape-recording of entire Nov. 10, 1963 "Message to the Grass Roots" speech. *BAMN*, p. 4. *FBI*, April 30, 1958, p. 6.

CONTROL ALL OF HARLEM'S LIQUOR STORES: New York *Herald Tribune*, June 30, 1963. Also see *MX*, p. 122.

"YIDS": Interview: Malcolm Jarvis.

THE WORST OF THE WHITE DEVILS: *FBI*, Nov. 17, 1959, p. 12.

SATAN'S STAR: Undated letter to Bazely Perry.

JESSE JAMES: *FBI*, April 30, 1958, pp. 118-123, particularly the statement on p. 122, which must be read in the context of the rest of the material on pp. 118-123.

THE MORE HOSTILITY JEWS COULD DEFLECT FROM THEMSELVES: *MX*, pp. 283, 372.

NO SYMPATHY FOR SOVIET JEWS: *SPKS*, p. 55. (Also see p. 153, where Malcolm claims he cannot pronounce the word "pogrom." "It's not my word," he says.)

GREEDY: See, for instance: *FBI*, May 17, 1960, pp. 5-6, 17. *Playboy*, May, 1963, p. 57. *MX*, pp. 148, 283, 395.

"BOUGHT" ATLANTIC CITY AND MIAMI BEACH": Question-and-answer session following Jan. 23, 1963 speech at Michigan State University. *Playboy*, May, 1963, p. 57.

"WHEN THERE'S SOMETHING WORTH OWNING, THE JEW'S GOT IT ": *Playboy*, May, 1963, p. 57.

GOLDBERG, GOLDSTEIN, GREENBERG: Record album entitled "The Wisdom of Malcolm X," Mo' Soul Records, album #MS-8001.

197   A CONVENIENT SYMBOL: Interview: Gertrude Wilson.

INTELLECTUALS; THE AVERAGE JEW IS SMARTER: *FBI*, Nov. 17, 1959, p. 12. *MX*, pp. 277, 278. *Malcolm X on Afro-American History* (Pathfinder Press, 1970), p. 25.

DEFENSIVE: *MX*, pp. 372-373, 395. *New York Post*, April 10, 1964.

"OH, YES. BUT TRUTH IS TRUTH": *MX*, pp. 372-373.

NOT AS BAD: Phonograph record entitled "The Last Message" (Discus Hablands LP #1300).

EVEN WHITE BABIES: Original, unedited manuscript of *FDL*, p. 216.

EVEN IF CERTAIN WHITES WERE INNOCENT, WHITES WERE GUILTY COLLEC-TIVELY: *MX*, p. 266. *WWG*, p. 171.

WHITE SNAKES: See, for example, *TKBM*, pp. 54, 73-74; television documentary entitled "The Hate that Hate Produced" (1959); and the original, unedited, uncut tape-recording of the entire Nov. 10, 1963 "Message to the Grass Roots." (The projective element becomes apparent in *MX*, pp. 69, 106-107, 148, & 152, where Malcolm likens himself to a snake and acknowledges that he was treated "like a viper.")

DENIED HE WAS PREJUDICED: See, for instance, *SPKS*, pp. 145, 162; *BAMN*, p. 170; *TKBM*, pp. 73-74; *Village Voice*, Feb. 25, 1965; Louis Lomax, *The Negro Revolt* (Harper, 1962), p. 172

"IT IS INCORRECT TO CLARIFY THAT AS HATE: *JHC*, p. 202. (Malcolm had apparently intended to say, "It is incorrect to classify that as hate.")

PRIDED HIMSELF: Interview: John Elton Bembry. Also see *MX*, pp. 153, 154.

BLUE AND GREEN EYED: Though Malcolm habitually employed the phrase "blue-eyed devil," he occasionally used the phrase "green-eyed devil." (*FBI*, June 18, 1964, p. 13.)

WHITES ARE COWARDS: *BAMN*, p. 184. Warner Brothers film documentary "Malcolm X." Film entitled "A Tribute to Malcolm" (National Educational TV and Radio Center). Also see Malcolm's contrasting portraits of white and black warriors on the phonograph record "Ballots or Bullets" (First Amendment Records; record #100) and on the Jan. 17, 1965 tape-recording of "The History of the *Afro-American*."

198 MASKED THEIR HATRED WITH GRINS: *MX*, p. 352.

SOLELY THE RESULT OF WHITE BIGOTRY: *New York Times*, May 8, 1964. Also *SPKS*, p. 195-196.

WHITES DESPISE THEIR PARENTS: Interview: Malcolm Jarvis.

DOPE-PEDDLING BEAST: *WWG*, p. 22.

THIEVES AND CRIMINALS: See, inter alia: *JHC*, pp. 160, 165. October 11, 1963 speech at Berkeley. Unclearly dated FBI report, p. 38. (According to the report, Malcolm made the statement in Brooklyn on January 27, 1959.) *SPKS*, pp. 53, 93. May 1, 1962 tape-recorded speech entitled "Crisis of Racism."

VULTURES: *Chicago Defender*, June 19, 1963. *MX*, p. 18. *FBI*, Jan. 31, 1956, p. 33. Also see *MX*, p. 262, where Malcolm characterizes himself as as a vulture.

SELF-HATRED: Malcolm asserted that the black proponents of racial integration were the ones who hated themselves. (*MX*, p. 272.)

RACIAL STEREOTYPES BETRAY THE SELF-IMAGE OF THOSE WHO EMPLOY THEM: *EPPS*, p. 165.

JUDGE NOT, LEST YE BE JUDGED: Interview: Malcolm Jarvis.

DISSENSION IN, AND BREAKUP OF, HIS BOYHOOD HOME: *MX*, pp. 13, 21. Also see p. 159.

ATTRIBUTED YOUTHFUL CRIMINALITY ENTIRELY TO WHITE OPPRESSION: *JHC*, p. 172. *MX*, p. 391. *WWG*, pp. 23-24. *Washington Daily News*, May 9, 1963. *New York Times*, Feb. 22, 1965.

"THE WHITE MAN MAKES YOU A DRUG ADDICT": TV documentary entitled "Eyes on the Prize," broadcast Jan. 15, 1990 on Channel 39, Allentown, Pa. "Like It Is," WABC-TV, Feb. 22, 1969. Also see *WWG*, pp. 23-24 and *Sepia*, (Vol. 13) May, 1964, pp. 60-61.

GAMBLING HABIT THE FAULT OF THE WHITES WHO HAD MANUFACTURED THE DICE: Original, unedited manuscript of the book that was later published as *FDL*, pp. 250-251. "Like It Is," WABC-TV, Feb. 22, 1969.

WHITES ARE ENTIRELY RESPONSIBLE: Louis Lomax, *The Negro Revolt* (Harper & Row), p. 172. *TKBM*, p. 74. Broadcast commemorating Malcolm X's birthday, WHYY-FM, Philadelphia, May 19, 1976.

RESPONSIBLE FOR UNWANTED BLACK CHILDREN: Malcolm pointed out that the relevant childrearing practices were a holdover from slavery. "We've got to get rid of [them]," he declared. "But you're never going to get rid of [them] until you get rid of the cause, and, man, you know who the cause is." *Malcolm X on Afro-American History* (Pathfinder Press, 1970), p. 42.

WHITES ARE TO BLAME FOR THE FACT MANY BLACKS HATE THEIR PARENTS: Original, unedited manuscript of the book that was later published as *FDL*, p. 166.

STILL LONGED TO BE PART OF THE DOMINANT WHITE MAJORITY: Malcolm told one group of listeners:

"We don't even want to be what we actually are. We want to be somebody else. We want to be someone else. We want to be something else. "(*JHC*, p. 314.)

199 HIS INSISTENCE HE HAD NO DESIRE TO BE ANYTHING BUT BLACK: "I certainly wasn't trying to make them think I wasn't black," Malcolm asserted. (*JHC*, p. 308.)

HATED "EVERY DROP OF BLACK BLOOD" *New York Post Daily Magazine*, April 7, 1964. *Newsweek*, March 8, 1965, p. 25. *PG*, p. 11. Interview: Peter Goldman. (Sigmund Freud's *The Psychopathology of Everyday Life* discusses the psychological dynamics of slips of the tongue.)

"THAT'S AN INTERESTING SLIP"; "I SAY IT AS A PSYCHOLOGIST": *JHC*, p. 159. Interview: Kenneth Clark.

OTHER SLIPS OF THE TONGUE: Malcolm said that an "Uncle Tom", ". . . . thinks that he's black 'cause God cursed him. He's not black 'cause God cursed him. He's black because — rather, he's cursed because he's out of his mind."

He maintained that blacks shouldn't overestimate the contribution of whites who had sacrificed their lives for the cause of black freedom because: "Any time you find white people who help you just so you can say you're a good white man, . . . "(*BP*, p. 33; *BAMN*, pp. 98-99.)

SAYS BLACK MILITANCY IS NOT SYNONYMOUS WITH "WHITE SUPREMACY": Tape recording, "The Crisis of Racism," May 1, 1962. Malcolm also substituted the word "white" for the word "black" on the January 14, 1965 WCAU radio show "Talk of Philadelphia." He was not the only member of his family who did so; during a number of interviews with his mother and his two oldest brothers, they did too.

"ON THEIR INTELLIGENCE PLANE": *JHC*, p. 200. Also see p. 201, where Malcolm deplores the lack of programs designed to "show Negroes how to act in a higher society." Also pp. 199-200, where an FBI agent tells him that education is the only thing that will persuade whites to accept blacks as equals. Malcolm agrees and says that Elijah Muhammad is the only leader who is educating America's blacks. The FBI agent replies that he meant whites had to be educated, not blacks.

"MESSED UP THE WHOLE COUNTRY": *JHC*, pp. 331-332.

AMBIVALENCE ABOUT SKIN COLOR: E. B. Bovell, "Psychological Considerations of Color Conflicts Among Negroes," *Psychoanalytic Review* (Vol. 30, 1943), pp. 447-459. E. B. Brody, "Color and Identity Conflict in Young Boys: Observations of Negro Mothers and Sons in Urban Baltimore," *Psychiatry* (Vol. 26, 1963), pp. 188-201. Kenneth Bancroft Clark, *Prejudice and Your Child* (Beacon Press, 1963), pp. 22-24, 37, 42-44, 49, 168. S. C. Drake & H.R. Cayton, *Black Metropolis* (Harcourt Brace, 1945), pp. 496-497, 503. A. Kardiner & L. Ovesey, *The Mark of Oppression* (World Publishing Co., 1967), pp. 286, 294-295, 304, 310, 314, 365. Richard Kluger, *Simple Justice* (Knopf, 1976), pp. 317-318, 321-322. J.D. Teicher, "Some Observations on Identity Problems in Children of Negro-White Marriages," *Journal of Nervous and Mental Diseases* (Vol. 146, 1968), pp. 249-256. M. J. Radke & H. G. Trager, "Children's Perceptions on the Social Roles of Negroes and Whites," *Journal of Psychology* (Vol. 29, 1950), pp. 3-33. H.J. Myers & L. Yochelson, "Color Denial in the Negro," *Psychiatry* (Vol. 11, 1948), pp. 39-46.

HIS ABILITY TO TRANSFORM HIS OWN PERSONAL STRUGGLE FOR IDENTITY INTO A UNIVERSAL ONE: "Great leaders become great and . . . become leaders precisely because they themselves have experienced the identity struggle of their people in . . . a most personal and a most representative way."—Erik Erikson

37. None Are White!

202 BLUE-EYED, BLONDE-HAIRED PATERNAL GRANDMOTHER WAS PART-WHITE: Interviews: Mary Little, Clara Little, Louise Little, Ella Little, Howard Riley.

THREE CHILDREN OUT OF WEDLOCK: Interviews: Olive Orgias, Daphne Orgias, Margaret Williams.

RAPED: *MX*, pp. 2, 201-202. *Chicago Defender*, June 19, 1963. *Playboy*, May, 1963, p. 60. *Ebony*, April, 1965, p. 44. Interview: Pete Robertson.

NO EVIDENCE HAS BEEN FOUND: Interviews: Malcolm Orgias, Olive Orgias, Louise

NO EVIDENCE HAS BEEN FOUND: Interviews: Malcolm Orgias, Olive Orgias, Louise Little, Daphne Orgias. "I heard no grounds for the assertion it was a rape," Philbert says. "Malcolm was the one who told me my maternal grandmother had been raped."

A REDHEAD: In *MX*, p. 201, Malcolm claims that his mother's father was "red-headed." Yet in the very same paragraph, he says she had never seen him. In *MX*, p. 2, he also says she had never seen him.

CLAIMS HIS MATERNAL GRANDFATHER'S NAME WAS MALCOLM: *PR*: interview dated 3/8/46.

NEVER LAID EYES ON HIM: *MX*, pp. 2, 201.

NO ONE SEEMS TO KNOW WHAT HIS NAME WAS: Interviews: Malcolm Orgias, Daphne Orgias, Olive Orgias, Wilfred Little, Philbert Little. When Louise married Earl Little in Montreal in May 1919, she said her father's first name was John. Her father-in-law's name was John. Her mother's first name happened to be the same as her mother-in-law's. Did she call her father John because it was her father-in-law's name? (See marriage certificate, Montreal, May 10, 1959.)

TALKED ABOUT RAPE: *MX*, pp. 2, 162, 201-202, 212, 218, 241. *WWG*, pp. 170-171. *Life*, May 31, 1963, p. 31. *Ebony*, April, 1965, p. 44. *FBI*, Jan. 28, 1955, pp. 4-5; Jan. 31, 1956, pp. 6, 23; April 30, 1958, pp. 110; et. al.

"THINK OF IT!": *MX*, p. 202.

"I SAID HE'S AFTER YOUR MOTHER!": Original, unedited, uncut tape-recording of Nov. 10, 1963 "Message to the Grass Roots."

NO RIGHT TO CALL THEMSELVES MEN; REAL MEN EXHIBIT TENDERNESS, ETC.: Interview: John Elton Bembry.

"DO YOU REALLY HATE ME?": Interview: James Hicks.

203 A "WHITE MAN'S NIGGER": Interview: John Elton Bembry.

"BLACK BODY WITH A WHITE HEAD": *TKBM*, pp. 74, 79. Television documentary entitled "The Hate that Hate Produced" (1959). Also see *MX*, p. 244.

"STOOGES": *FBI*, Aug. 6, 1963, p. 10A. Also see *FBI*, Nov. 15, 1963, p. 26.

GRUDGING ADMIRATION: *MX*, pp. 399, 401. Interview: Johnny Davis, Jr.

"CHUMP": *TKBM*, p. 99. *WWG*, pp. 74, 86.

SUSPENDERS DRAGGED THE GROUND WITH UNIVERSITY DEGREES: *MX*, p. 181.

"NINCOMPOOPS WITH PH.D.'S": Interview: M. S. Handler. Years later, recalling a meeting with Malcolm, Harold Cruse told an interviewer, "We didn't hit it off. Malcolm didn't like intellectuals." (Interview: Harold Cruse.)

"DOCTOR": *SPKS*, pp. 180, 181, 186, 190-193. Phonograph record entitled "Malcolm X Speaks to the People in Harlem" (Up Front Records; record # UPF-152). Oct., 1961 Howard University speech. *MX*, p. 243. *BAMN*, p. 31.

"NIGGER!": *MX*, p. 284.

CRITICIZES BLACK LAW STUDENTS AND LAWYERS: Phonograph record entitled "The Last Message" (Discus Hablands; record #LP-1300). "Malcolm X Speaks to the People in Harlem," supra. *MX*, p. 284.

"THEY WISH THEY HAD WHITE SKINS": *New York Herald Tribune*, June 30, 1963.

WHITE HEARTS: *New York Herald Tribune*, June 30, 1963. *FBI*, Nov. 15, 1963, p. 12.

LIVING IN WHITE NEIGHBORHOODS: Tape-recorded Jan. 23, 1963 speech at Michigan State University. Also see tape-recording of Feb. 16, 1965 speech at Corn Hill Methodist Church, Rochester, N.Y.

DEPENDENCE ON WHITE CONTRIBUTIONS: *SPKS*, p. 223. Press conference, Lansing, Mich., Jan. 23, 1963.

"MASOCHISTS": *Harper's Magazine* (Vol. 228), June, 1964, p. 59. Also see *SPKS*, p. 223.

"PASSSIVE": *SPKS*, p. 12.

"ANEMIC": *Muhammad Speaks*, Sept. 15, 1962.

OBSEQUIOUS: See *MX*, p. 272, for instance.

MARRYING WHITE WOMEN: *New York Herald Tribune*, June 30, 1963. *WWG*, p. 170. Michigan State University, Jan. 23, 1963. *JHC*, pp. 284.

"A HOMO": *JHC*, p. 201. Also see *PG*, pp. 104-105 and Malcolm's June 6, 1950 petition to the Massachusetts Commissioner of Correction. (The sexual preferences of the leader that Malcolm assailed in *JHC*, p. 201 are discussed in Taylor Branch, *Parting the Waters* (Simon & Schuster, 1988), pp. 172-173, 846-847; David Garrow, *Bearing the Cross* (William Morrow, 1986), p. 280; *PG*, pp. 104-105; and interview: Milton Galamison.

204 "A BED PARTNER"; "THEY'RE SLEEPING TOGETHER": *BAMN*, pp. 147-148. Still another repetition, somewhat reworded, appears in the unedited, uncut tape-recording of the January 7, 1965 speech entitled "Prospects for Freedom in 1965."

ADMITTED HE DID NOT BELIEVE EVERYTHING HE SAID PUBLICLY: *TKBM*, p. 93. Interview: Oliver Sutton. After Malcolm left the Nation of Islam, he publicly acknowledged that, when he was Elijah's spokesman, he had kept his own views to himself and had propagated the Messenger's. (Dec. 2, 1964 broadcast, Les Crane Show, reprinted in *BP*, p. 86.)

GOD DIDN'T WORK MIRACLES; HUMAN BEINGS WOULD HAVE TO DO IT: *FDL*, p. 194.

"MEN FOUGHT IN THE BATTLE OF JERICHO": Interview: Hakim Jamal.

RHETORIC ABOUT POLITICAL SEPARATION: *FBI*, Nov. 16, 1962, p. 3. Also see the 1960 Boston University speech in which Malcolm not only emphasized that the separatism he was advocating was Elijah Muhammad's, but also encouraged his listeners to question it. (In 1960, Malcolm made two speeches at Boston University. Since one of the resultant tape-recordings may have been misdated, it is unclear which speech of the two speeches is the relevant one.)

BECOMING INCREASINGLY DIFFICULT: Interview: Charles 37X.

MECHANICAL AND UNCONVINCING: Warner Brothers film documentary entitled "Malcolm X." Jesse Walker, former managing editor of the *New York Amsterdam News*, later told an interviewer, "Sometimes, before Malcolm's break with Elijah Muhammad, I got the feeling his . . . rhetoric was mechanical — like a preacher preaching in church because he had to."

QUESTIONED WHETHER A NATION WITHIN A NATION COULD SURVIVE: *WWG*, p. 125. In a 1960 Boston University speech, Malcolm said the same thing, almost word for word. (In 1960, Malcolm made two speeches at Boston University. Since one of the resultant tape-recordings may have been misdated, it is unclear which of the two speeches is the relevant one.)

MALCOLM QUICKLY CHANGED THE WORD "HE" TO "WE": 1960 Boston University speech. (Malcolm made two speeches at Boston University in 1960. Since one of the resultant tape-recordings may have been misdated, it is unclear which of the two speeches is the relevant one.)

"MOSES NEVER TOLD THE JEWS": *New York Times*, March 12, 1963, p. 27.

ASKED THE ATTENDING NEWSMAN NOT TO TURN ON HIS CAMERA: Lansing, Mich. press conference, June 22, 1963.

"GOOD TALKING POINT": Interview: Harold Vaughan.

ACCORDING TO LOMAX, THE MESSENGER PRIVATELY AGREED: *WWG*, p. 79. See also Arna Bontemps & Jack Conroy, *Anyplace But Here* (Hill & Wang, 1966), p. 235. Also "Malcolm X, The Black Vigilante" [in] Pierre Berton, *Voices from the Sixties* (Doubleday, 1967).

HE'D EXCHANGE KNOWING GLANCES: Interview: Charles 37X.

SINCE THE AGE OF SIX; MEN WHO HAD NEVER SMILED: *PG*, pp. 42-43.

THE "MOTHER PLANE": *PG*, pp. 42-44. *FBI*, Nov. 17, 1960, p. 13. Elijah Muhammad, *Message to the Blackman in America* (Muhammad Mosque of Islam #2, 1965).

205 THE SMILE, WHICH SOMETIMES ASSUMED AN IRONIC QUALITY, . . .: Interview: Charles Keil. *New York Herald Tribune*, Feb. 22, 1965. The *New York Herald Tribune* article described "the slight smile, the ironic smile, that mocked his words, even when he was making the most outrageous statements."

"YOU KNOW YOU DON'T BELIEVE THAT": Interview: Christine Johnson.

"THE WISDOM OR FOLLY": *WWG*, pp. 114, 154.

MALCOLM ANNOUNCED HIS INTENTION TO VISIT MECCA HIMSELF: "Malcolm X Off to Tour Middle East," *New York Amsterdam News*, July 11, 1959. *FBI*, Nov. 17, 1959, pp.

33-34, citing the *Pittsburgh Courier*, July 11, 1959 and the aforementioned *New York Amsterdam News* article. The *Pittsburgh Courier*, Aug. 15, 1959, magazine section. *FBI*, July 24, 1959, p. 3. Interview: Ulysses X.

HE SCHEDULED HIS TRIP TO COINCIDE WITH THE *HAJJ*: According to one CIA report (the date of which is unclear), the authorities issued Malcolm a passport on May 27, 1959, after he had indicated that he intended "to attend annual Sacred Moslem Pilgrimage Rites at Holy City of Mecca (Saudi Arabia), 9 June to 16 June 1959." *FBI*, July 27, 1959, p. 1 and *FBI*, Nov. 17, 1959, pp. 31-34.

DIDN'T GO TO MIDDLE EAST UNTIL HAJJ HAD ENDED: *New York Amsterdam News*, July 11, 1959. Tape-recording of Ed Harvey Show, broadcast by Philadelphia radio station WCAU on Sept. 26, 1962.

"THE HATE THAT HATE PRODUCED": The five-part program was televised July 13-17, 1959.

"MIGHT" GO TO MECCA: According to *FBI*, August 22, 1961, p. 23, the statement was made in the Buffalo, N.Y., temple on July 20, 1959.

DESPITE PRONOUNCEMENTS FROM NEW YORK THAT HE WAS ALREADY THERE: Temple 7C, the Brooklyn temple, announced on July 7, 1959, that Malcolm was in Mecca. (*FBI*, Nov. 17, 1959, p. 33.) *FBI*, July 21, 1959, p. 1. See also *FBI*, July 24, 1959, p. 3 and Part 4 of the televised documentary "The Hate that Hate Produced."

SAID HE WAS AUTHORIZED TO ENTER MECCA: *WWG*, p. 62.

LEAVING SAUDI ARABIA WITHOUT VISITING THE HOLY CITY: *FBI*, July 24, 1959, p. 3. *New York Post*, May 22, 1964. Sept. 29, 1964 State Department airgram from American Embassy, Jedda, to Washington. The *Pittsburgh Courier*, August 15, 1959, magazine section. Interview: Philbert Little.

"WOULD BREAK THE AVERAGE MUSLIM'S HEART": The *Pittsburgh Courier*, August 15, 1959, magazine section.

GASTROINTESTINAL AILMENT: The *Pittsburgh Courier*, August 5, 1959, magazine section. See also *FBI*, July 24, 1959, p. 3; *FBI* July 29, 1959, p. 1; *FBI*, Nov. 17, 1959, p. 35. Interview: Ulysses X.

HE HAD REPORTEDLY RECOVERED BEFORE HE HAD ARRIVED IN JEDDA: Confidential source of information.

CLAIMED THAT HE HAD TO CANCEL HIS TRIP TO MAKE A TOUR OF AFRICA: The *Pittsburgh Courier*, August 15, 1959, magazine section.

206 IN TIME FOR THE HARLEM RALLY: *FBI*, July 29, 1959, p. 1. Interview: Philbert Little. Confidential source. But the *New York Amsterdam News* of July 11, 1959 indicates that, when Malcolm departed for the Middle East, his itinerary included both a trip to Mecca and a return date that would enable him to attend the July 26, 1959 Harlem rally.

BUT HE RETURNED HOME AT LEAST TWO DAYS BEFORE THE HARLEM RALLY: *FBI*, Nov. 17, 1959, p. 23.

ALLEGEDLY NEVER ON ITINERARY: Interview: Akbar Muhammad.

ELIJAH'S DISPLEASED: Interview: Mike Wallace.

RUMORS THAT ELIJAH HAD INSTRUCTED MALCOLM TO BYPASS MECCA: Interview: Ulysses X.

DIDN'T WANT TO UPSTAGE: *WWG*, p. 62. Interview: Christine Johnson. *BMIA*, p. 192. Confidential source.

OUTWARDLY "IN CHARGE": *WWG*, p. 62. *MX*, p. 286.

REMAIN ON GUARD: *FBI*, May 17, 1960, p. 37.

"NONE ARE WHITE"; "NINETY-NINE PERCENT"; "RIGHT AT HOME": The *Pittsburgh Courier*, August 15, 1959, magazine section. *BMIA*, p. 225. Also see *JHC*, p. 166, where Malcolm describes Islam's 725 million adherents as "non-white."

NASSER A BLACK MAN: *TKBM*, p. 95.

PRIVATE ACKNOWLEDGEMENTS: *TKBM*, p. 95. *PG*, p. 160. March 6, 1981 letter from James 67X to author. Interviews: Philbert Little, confidential source.

HE EVEN SAID SO PUBLICLY: *TKBM*, pp. 94-95. *WWG*, p. 61. *New York Amsterdam News*, Nov. 24, 1962.

HE TOLD PHILBERT: Interview: Philbert Little.

COMPLIMENTED NEW CONVERT: Interview: Malik Hakim.

PRAISED ANOTHER MEMBER: Interview: Saladin Matthews.

207 MAINTAINED EXCELLENT RELATIONS: *WWG*, pp. 62-63. *New York Journal-American*, Feb. 24, 1965. In 1960, Malcolm invited white-skinned Mahmoud Youssef Shawarbi to Temple Seven, where Shawarbi minimized his philosophical differences with the Nation of Islam. (James Cone, *Martin & Malcolm in America* [Orbis Books, 1991], pp. 163-164.)

SOUNDED MECHANICAL: Interview: Jesse Walker.

"TEACHES US THAT GOD TAUGHT HIM": *FBI*, April 8, 1963, p. 3.

REMARKS SUGGESTING THE TEACHING WAS ELIJAH'S, NOT MALCOLM'S: Tape-recording of Ed Harvey Show, broadcast by Philadelphia station WCAU on Sept. 26, 1962. *FBI*, May 17, 1960, p. 47.

THE MESSENGER'S ATTTEMPTS TO TONE DOWN HIS MINISTERS' PRONOUNCEMENTS: Sometimes, Malcolm reluctantly toned down his rhetoric. (*MX*, p. 293.) According to *FBI*, May 22, 1964, p. 5, et al, Elijah Muhammad had been advised by counsel to tone down the NOI's rhetoric. According to Chauncey Eskridge, Philbert Little, and p. 83 of *TKBM*, Mr. Muhammad specifically warned Malcolm against making provocative statements.

BUT ELIJAH MUHAMMAD DIDN'T: *TKBM*, p. 83. Interviews: Chauncey Eskridge, Philbert Little. *FBI*, March 15, 1965, pp. 49-50, quoting a statement by Muhammad Ali that was broadcast by Chicago talk show host Irv Kupcinet a week after Malcolm was assassinated.

ELIJAH WAS ALSO UPSET ABOUT MALCOLM'S EFFORTS TO INDUCE THE NOI TO ABANDON ITS POLICY OF POLITICAL NONINVOLEMENT: *BAMN*, pp. 158-159. *MX*, p. 289. *New York Times*, Nov. 8, 1964. *PG*, pp. 105-106.

210 JEREMIAH X ANNOUNCED THAT MALCOLM WOULD SOON ARRIVE IN BIRMINGHAM: *New York Herald Tribune*, May 15, 1963.

DISCLAIMED KNOWLEDGE; ONLY IF DIRECTED BY ELIJAH MUHAMMAD OR INVITED BY JEREMIAH: *FBI*, May 15, 1963, p. 2. *FBI*, Nov. 15, 1963, p. 26.

BEGAN TO SUSPECT: See inaccurate version of events described in *EPPS*, p. 75.

211 POLITICAL ACTIVITY COULD INDUCE THE GOVERNMENT: Malcolm briefly alludes to this point in *BP*, p. 174.

MALCOLM CHAFED: *BAMN*, pp. 158-159. *MX*, p. 289. *PG*, pp. 105-106. *Sepia*, May 1964, p. 59. CBC interview, June 0, 1964. Interviews. John Elton Dembry, Saladin Matthews, "Heather."

RIDICULES MARCH ON WASHINGTON: Neil Hickey and Ed Edwin, *Adam Clayton Powell and the Politics of Race* (Fleet Publication Corp., 1965), pp. 10-11. *EWWS*, pp. 141-146. *MX*, pp. 278-281.

"WHAT I TELL THE PRESS IS SOMETHING ELSE" : *PG*, p. 107.

CIRCUS: *EWWS*, p. 144. *MX*, p. 280.

TOO HAPPY: Phonograph record entitled "Malcolm X Speaking" (Ethnic Records, #E-1265).

FORBIDDEN TO VOTE: *TKBM*, p. 138. Also see *New York Times*, May 12, 1963.

"NOT POLITICALLY INCLINED": 1963 address to NAACP.

EMBARRASSING; HAD BEEN TRYING TO NUDGE THE NATION OF ISLAM: *TKBM*, pp. 98-99.

BOYCOTT HARLEM STORES: *FBI*, July 13, 1959, p. 1.

THE MESSENGER MADE MALCOLM APOLOGIZE PUBLICLY: The *Pittsburgh Courier*, Feb. 14, 1959. *FBI*, May 19, 1959, citing article in the Feb. 7, 1959 issue of the New Jersey *Herald News*.

MALCOLM KEPT PRESSING MR. MUHAMMAD: *TKBM*, pp. 98-99. Also see *FBI*, Nov. 15, 1963, p. 27.

THE MESSENGER INSTRUCTED HIM NOT TO RAISE THE SUBJECT AGAIN; MALCOLM OBEYED: *FBI*, Nov. 15, 1963, p. 27. *TKBM*, pp. 98-99.

HOSPITAL EMPLOYEES' UNION: Undated 1977 letter to author from Executive Sec'y., Hospital Union Local #1199. *Muhammad Speaks*, Jan. 31, 1963; Nov. 22, 1963. *FBI*, Nov. 16,

1962, p. 23; Aug. 6, 1963, p. 17. July 22, 1962 entry in the file the New York Police Department's Bureau of Special Services kept on Malcolm. Interview: Mo Foner. Also *New York Amsterdam News*, Jan. 24, 1959.

212   ENGLEWOOD SCHOOL SYSTEM: *New York Times*, Aug. 6 & 7, 1962.

MALCOLM LATER WITHDREW: *New York Herald Tribune*, Aug. 8, 1962. *New York Times*, Aug. 23, 1962.

"NEVER INVOLVED": *New York Times*, Aug. 6, 1962.

BROOKLYN CONSTRUCTION SITE: *New York Herald Tribune*, July 23, 1963. *New York Amsterdam News*, Feb. 27, 1965. *TKBM*, pp. 98-99. Interview: Milton Galamison.

SEALTEST: *Muhammad Speaks*, Oct. 15, 1962.

"A WORKING RELATIONSHIP": *FBI*, Nov. 7, 1961, pp. 20-23.

"UNITY RALLY": Phonograph record entitled "Malcolm X Speaks to the People in Harlem" (Up Front Records; record #UPF-152). *New York Times*, Aug. 11, 1963.

ELIJAH MUHAMMAD FORBADE HIM TO ASSIST OTHER BLACK ORGANIZATIONS: Elijah forbade Malcolm from doing so on or before June 13, 1963, according to an uncensored version of *FBI*, Nov. 15, 1963, p. 27.

REPORTED IN THE *AMSTERDAM NEWS*: *New York Amsterdam News*, July 6, 1963. Also see July 20, 1963 issue.

"IT'S A LIE"; "ANY DIFFERENCE WITH HIM IS MAJOR"; "WANT TO SEE SOME ACTION": *TKBM*, pp. 104-105. Also see *WWG*, p. 179, which contains a portion of Malcolm's tape-recorded response. Pages 209-210 of the *original hardcover* edition of *WWG* contains his complete response.

38. Under Guise of Religion

213   RESENTED MALCOLM: *FBI*, May 16, 1963, p. 21; Nov. 19, 1958, p. 11; Nov. 15, 1963, p. 15. Also "Correlation Summary" of the FBI's files on Elijah Muhammad, April 9, 1969, p. 41. Interview: Wilfred Little. Also see *PG*, p. 412 and *MX*, pp. 198, 264-265, 290, 292.

ORDERED THEM AROUND: *FBI*, May 16, 1963, pp. 6, 21.

MALCOLM'S MINISTERS: *FBI*, Nov. 17, 1961, p. 9; Aug. 6, 1963, p. 5; April 30, 1958, pp. 23, 32. *MX*, p. 293.

FUND RAISING DRIVE: *MX*, pp. 204, 263-264. *JHC*, p. 138.

ULTIMATELY PROVED FATAL: *JHC*, p. 138.

214   ACCUSED OF TAKING CREDIT: *MX*, p. 290.

TOOK OVER NEWSPAPER COLUMNS: *MX*, p. 237. *BMIA*, pp. 129-130. *PG*, p. 61. *FDL*, pp. 189-190. (See, for instance, the August 3, 1957 issue of the *New York Amsterdam News*.)

LESS COVERAGE; TRIED TO DISCOURAGE: *MX*, p. 292.

ENVIED MALCOLM'S POPULARITY ON COLLEGE CAMPUSES: *New York Times*, March 9, 1964. *MX*, pp. 284-285.

REPORTEDLY UPSET: Interview: Philbert Little.

DEDICATION AND ROYALTIES: *MX*, 386-387. The dedication was changed after Malcolm left Elijah Muhammad's movement and switched publishers.

NEITHER LOMAX NOR ALEX HALEY: *TKBM*, p. 55. Interview: Alex Haley.

215   WHO WAS STRUCK BY MALCOLM'S ABILITY TO SAY ONE THING WHILE HE WAS PONDERING ANOTHER: *MX*, p. 390.

"IF SHE DOESN'T, SHE AT LEAST PRETENDS": *MX*, p. 390.

"YOU CAN NEVER FULLY TRUST ANY WOMAN: *MX*, p. 389.

HIS TALKING ABOUT HIS MOTHER TRIGGERED SOMETHING: *MX*, pp. 389-391.

NEXT TO COLLEGE: *MX*, pp. 391-392.

"THE BEST THING THAT COULD EVER HAVE HAPPENED: Undated petition from Malcolm to the Massachusettts Commissioner of Corrections. (The letter was written around mid-1950.) Also see *FBI*, Nov. 17, 1959, p. 49.

"I DON'T WANT . . TO MAKE IT SOUND": *MX*, p. 392.

216 "DON'T PRINT THAT": *MX*, pp. 394-395.

"THE SEVENTH SON OF A SEVENTH SON": March 13, 1978 and May 17, 1978 letters from James 67X to author. (The material in the letters was subsequently verified via interview.)

"THEY KNOW I'M AROUND" : Interview: John Elton Bembry.

"FINGERS ON A GIANT HAND": Interview: John Elton Bembry.

JOHN WAS MALCOLM'S ENEMY: *TKBM*, pp. 102-105. Interviews: Wilfred Little, James 67X, and two confidential sources. See the relevant material that follows in this and subsequent chapters.

STARTED AS MALCOLM'S PROTEGE: Interviews: Lemuel Hassan, Wilfred Little, Philbert Little, Harold Hyman. (Also see *FBI*, Aug. 22, 1961, p. 13 and the Patterson, N.J. *Morning Call*, Feb. 22, 1965.)

JOHN ALI: *Chicago Defender*, July 7, 1964, Feb. 11, 1964. Interviews: Christine Johnson, Philbert Little. Malcolm later told a Philadelphia radio audience that John was using his position to get as much money as he could. (*FBI*, Jan. 20, 1965, p. 59.) Also see *New York Times*, Feb. 26, 1976.

217 JOHN VS. ULYSSES: Interview: Ulysses X.

MALCOLM AND JOSEPH: Interviews with Ulysses X and the woman who rebuffed Joseph.

REMOVED JOSEPH AS CAPTAIN: See *FBI*, August 22, 1961, pp. 11-12.

CAPTAINS MADE DIRECTLY RESPONSIBLE TO CHICAGO: *New York Amsterdam News*, March 21, 1964. *PG*, p. 110. *WWG*, pp. 70-71. Interviews: Aubrey Barnette, Philbert Little, John Thimas.

MALCOLM TRIED TO HAVE JOSEPH REMOVED AGAIN: *New York Amsterdam News*, March 21, 1964. *PG*, p. 110.

ROUTINELY SUBJECTED TO CORPORAL PUNISHMENT: Interviews: Tom Wallace, Charles 37X, Lemuel Hassan. But in cases where the offender had stolen money from a temple or had publicly challenged or defied Elijah Muhammad or Malcolm, Malcolm tacitly authorized corporal punishment. The orders for such punishment were not given directly; the official in charge would merely suggest what should be done. The process of suggestion was called "dropping seeds." (Interviews: Philbert Little, Harold Hyman, confidential source.)

218 CHILDREN WHO HAD TO BE DISCIPLINED PHYSICALLY: Undated statement by Wallace Muhammad. (The statement was found in the files of Gladys Towles Root, Esq.) "Like It Is," WABC-TV, Jan. 6, 1980.

CONSIDERED HIMSELF IN CHARGE: Interviews: Sharon 10X, James 67X.

IN THE RED: Trial transcript, Landlord & Tenant case #4845, Queens Civil Court (1964 Special Term, Part I), p. 194. *FBI*, April 23, 1957, pp. 17-18. *Chicago Defender*, Feb. 11, 1964.

"EVERYTHING SHOULD BE PERFECT HERE": *FBI*, April 23, 1957, pp. 17-18.

MONEY WAS THE PRIME OBJECTIVE: *JHC*, p. 140. *New York Post*, Feb. 28, 1965. *Chicago Defender*, Feb. 11, 1964. Undated statement by Wallace Muhammad. (The statement was found in the files of Gladys Towles Root, Esq.)

"THE BLACK MUSLIMS ARE A FRAUD": *Saturday Evening Post*, Feb. 27, 1965, pp. 23-29. Also see *Chicago Defender*, July 6, 1964.

219 "BEFORE THESE FOOLS . . . WAKE UP": Interview: James 67X. In a July 27, 1964 letter, the daughter's husband (who was accused of corruption in a July 7, 1964 *Chicago Defender* article) also characterized Elijah Muhammad's followers as fools.

OTHER BUSINESSES: Addendum to Internal Revenue Service form #1023 filed in 1967 by Muhammad's Temple #2. *Chicago Daily News*, Aug. 15, 1962; Aug. 23 & 24, 1975. *Saturday Evening Post*, supra. *Chicago Defender*, Feb. 6, 1969. *Chicago Tribune*, Feb. 26, 1975. *Muhammad Speaks*, Feb. 26, 1965, April 2, 1965. *WWG*, p. 69.

SUBSTITUTED "PROFIT" FOR THE WORD "PROPHET": April 9, 1969 *FBI* correlation summary on Elijah Muhammad. (The correlation summary contains all his known aliases.)

PAID HIGHER PRICES: *Chicago Defender*, July 6, 1964.

SUBSTANDARD WAGES: Undated statement by Wallace Muhammad. (The statement was found in the files of Gladys Towles Root, Esq.) *Chicago Defender*, Feb. 22, 1972. *New York Times*, Aug. 8, 1976. "Like It Is," WABC-TV, Jan. 6, 1980.

"NOT FOR PROFIT": *Bilalian News*, Jan. 23, 1976, p. 2.

QU'RAN FRANCHISE: *Saturday Evening Post*, supra. Confidential source.

RUN PRIMARILY FOR THE BENEFIT OF THE MUHAMMADS AND THEIR BUSINESS ASSOCIATES: Lease for 79th Street dressmaking shop executed August 7, 1962 by lessees Raymond & Ethel Sharrieff. Lease for State Street bakery executed May 24, 1966 by lessee Raymond Sharrieff. Lease for 71st Street bakery executed Feb. 1, 1967 by lessee John Hassan. Annual Report #D 5157-703-5 filed Jan., 1979 by Shabazz Bakery with Illinois Secretary of State. *Chicago Defender*, July 7, 1964. Interview: Christine Johnson.

NATHANIEL MUHAMMAD CALLS HIMSELF "PROPRIETOR": *Muhammad Speaks*, April 2, 1965.

ELIJAH HAD USED HIS FOLLOWERS CONTRIBUTIONS TO PURCHASE AND OPERATE BUSINESSES IN HIS OWN NAME: October 30, 1980 statement by Nathaniel Muhammad.

"INTERTWINED": *EOEM*: Statement by Sidley & Austin, Esqs., concerning ownership of NOI property. Also Wallace Muhammad's statement on "Like It Is," WABC-TV, Jan. 6, 1980.

CLAIMED THEIR FINANCIAL INTERESTS WERE SYNONYMOUS: *EOEM*: "Petition of Administrator to Resign," notarized May 10, 1979.

220 SECRECY: *New York Times*, Dec. 5, 1963. *Chicago Daily News*, June 16, 1975.

NO BOOKS: Aug. 11, 1967 letter to Internal Revenue Service from Brozan & Holman, Esqs. *New York Times*, Feb. 26, 1976. *EOEM*: "Reply to Petitioners' Response to First Pacific's Motion for Summary Judgment."

NOT UNTIL THE RIFT BECAME IRREPARABLE: *New York Journal-American*, Feb. 28, 1965. *Muhammad Speaks*, Sept. 11, 1964.

TAXES: Application for exemption from federal income tax filed 1967 by Muhammad's Temple #2. Dec. 22. 1960 letter from Illinois Dept. of Revenue to John Hassan.

ALL BUT ONE DECLINED TO RESPOND; HERBERT ASSERTED THAT HE RECEIVED NO COMPENSATION: Addendum to Internal Revenue Service form #1023 filed 1967 by Muhammad's Temple #2.

THE CLAIM THAT THE BUSINESSES WERE OWNED BY A NON-PROFIT RELIGIOUS ORGANIZATION: Application for exemption from federal income tax filed 1967 by Muhammad's Temple #2. Trial transcript, Landlord & Tenant Case #4845, supra., p. 221.

PAID NO INCOME TAX: *Chicago Sun-Times*, April 27, 1963; June 12, 1963. *Chicago Tribune* (1-star final edition), June 12, 1963.

TAX BENEFITS WOULD HAVE BEEN JEOPARDIZED: See Temple #2's negative answers to questions 8(f) and 8(g) on 1967 application for exemption from federal income tax. (The questions concern political activity.) Dec. 22, 1960 letter from Illinois Dept. of Revenue to John Hassan. (Also see *Chicago Defender*, Feb. 11, 1964.)

FLIRTATION WITH BILLIE SOL ESTES" *Muhammad Speaks*, July 19, 1963.

WIELDED HIS POWER BEHIND THE SCENES: *Chicago Tribune*, Feb. 26, Feb. 27, Mar. 2, 1975. Muhammad Ali (with Richard Durham), *The Greatest* (Random House, 1975), acknowledgement section, third page.

"ASSISTANT EDITOR": *Chicago's American*, Sept. 15, 1964. (For tax and other purposes, *Muhammad Speaks* listed Temple #2, not Herbert, as the publisher.)

SEVEN THOUSAND COPIES: *New York Amsterdam News*, Jan. 16, 1965.

MANDATORY QUOTAS: *New York Times*, Dec. 6, 1973; Feb. 26, 1976.

221 TWO HUNDRED COPIES: *Saturday Evening Post*, supra.

THREE HUNDRED COPIES: *Chicago Tribune*, Feb. 22, 1977; March 19, 1978. *Chicago Defender*, July 6 & 7, 1964.

ELEVEN CENTS PER COPY: *Chicago Defender*, July 6, 1964. In certain temples, the NOI leadership confiscated the portion of the sale price that the NOI vendors were supposed to keep for themselves. (*Saturday Evening Post*, supra.)

ENDED UP IN CLOSESTS OR CELLARS: *PG*, p. 82.

NIGHTTIME RIDE; WORKED OVER: *Saturday Evening Post*, supra. *PG*, p. 109. Also see *Chicago Defender*, July 6, 1964.

SURPASSED $100,000 A WEEK: Interview: Joe Ferstl.

MORE THAN FORTY-FIVE MILLION DOLLARS: *Chicago Daily News,* June 16, 1975.

SPOKESMEN WOULD CITE LARGER FIGURES: *Chicago Tribune,* March 2, 1975. *PG,* p. 394.

TWENTY-SIX MILLION POUNDS: *Bilalian News,* Jan. 23, 1976.

"I WOULD PREFER ANY LITTLE OLD CAR"; DIDN'T WANT IT TO APPEAR: *Chicago Sun-Times,* Feb. 26, 1975.

INVITED WHITE "DEVILS" TO HIS DINNER TABLE TO DISCUSS BUSINESS: Interview: Joe Ferstl. John Facenda interviewing Wallace Muhammad on Philadelphia television station WCAU-TV, Nov. 12, 1978.

REAL ESTATE PURCHASES: Muhammad's Temple No. 2, "Schedule of Real Estate Owned," Dec. 31, 1966. See other documents listing real estate holdings in *EOEM.* Also *New York Times,* Dec. 5, 1963. *Time,* March 7, 1969. *Chicago Daily News,* Aug. 23-24, 1975. *Bilalian News,* Oct. 6, 1978.

222 "REALLY-ESTATE": June 3, 1964 letter from Elijah Muhammad to Lucille Karriem.

PLACED TITLE IN HIS OWN NAME; BECAME PART OF HIS ESTATE: Oct. 30, 1980 statement by Nathaniel Muhammad. *EOEM:* Petitions to sell real estate dated Feb. 27, 1979 and "1981." See other relevant documents in *EOEM;* for instance, p. 6 of "Reply to Intervenors'-Respondents' Response to Motion for Summary Judgment of the First Pacific Bank of Chicago," which indicates that Elijah Muhammad repeatedly told one National Secretary that he was the "safekeeper" of the movement's funds.

TWO TIGHTLY-CONTROLLED FIRMS: The two firms were Progressive Land Developers, Inc., and United Dynamics, Inc.

REALLY FAMILY-OWNED CORPORATIONS: October 30, 1980 statement by Nathaniel Muhammad.

MALCOLM CLAIMED THAT SHE WAS THE REAL POWER: Malcolm told James 67X that Elijah Muhammad had lamented the fact that Ethel had been born female. (Interview: James 67X.)

SUPERVISED BY SHARRIEFF, HERBERT MUHAMMAD, JOHN ALI, AND ELIJAH MUHAMMAD: Bank checks #1787, 1788, 1789, & 1791, signed July 27, 1964 by Herbert Muhammad and Raymond Sharrieff. July 27, 1964 letter from Raymond Sharrieff to Lucille Karriem. Addendum to Internal Revenue Service form #1023 filed 1967 by Muhammad's Temple #2. Muhammad Ali, *The Greatest,* (Random House, 1975), p. 207. (Also see p. 206.) *MX,* p. 387. William Brashler, "Black on Black," *New York Magazine,* June 9, 1975, pp. 46, 49. *Chicago Tribune,* June 12, 1975, Feb. 27, 1975. Interviews: Louis Lerner, Harold Hyman, Christine Johnson, Philbert Little, Lemuel Hassan, John Thimas, Joe Ferstl.

DEEDED TO ELIJAH MUHAMMAD & SONS: EOEM: Sidey and Austin's petition for payment of attorney's fees, p. 4. Also see Progressive Land Developer, Inc.'s "Petition for Direction of Disposition of Proceeds in the Sale of Land." (The 100-acre figure cited in the second petition may be an approximation. To minimize the discrepancy between the farm's actual size and its alleged size, which the NOI said was a thousand acres, I have used the 120-acre figure.)

PRETENDED IT WAS A THOUSAND-ACRE FARM: *Chicago Tribune,* Jan. 26, 1969. *Time,* March 7, 1969.

"PUFFERY": *Chicago Tribune,* Dec. 8, 1969.

"YOUR SUPERMARKET"; "YOUR FISH HOUSE": Financial statement from undated *Bilalian News* clipping. *Time,* March 7, 1969. *New York Times,* August 8, 1976. Interview: Christine Johnson. Among the other relevant sources is the Chicago telephone directory.

OFFICIALS AMASSED ENOUGH MONEY TO BUY PROSPEROUS FARMS NEARBY: *New York Times,* August 8, 1976.

EMBEZZLEMENT PUBLICLY ACKNOWLEDGED: *Chicago Defender,* July 7, 1964. *Philadelphia Daily News,* March 1, 1976.

MAKE UP THE DEFICITS: *Chicago Tribune,* 3/19/78 (five star final ed.). Interviews: Philbert Little, "Robin."

CAPTIVE MARKET: *Chicago Defender,* July 6, 1964.

THE CONSTANT APPEALS FOR MONEY: Judith Stein, *The World of Marcus Garvey*

(Louisiana State University Press, 1986), p. 182. (Also see Ted Vincent, infra., p. 203.)

"A LOSS IN MONEY, BUT A GAIN IN SOUL": Ted Vincent, *Black Power and the Garvey Movement* (Ramparts Press, 1965), p. 202.

223 APPORTIONMENT OF COLLECTED FUNDS: Photograph of "Muhammad's Mosque Charity Slip" that appeared in an undated *New York Amsterdam News* clipping. The slip was actually a receipt for Brother Leon 4X's $15.00 weekly contribution to his temple. See also *Chicago Tribune*, Feb. 21, 1977 (4th star final ed.). Transcript of Irv Kupcinet's Feb. 28, 1965 interview of Aubrey Barnette (reprinted in *FBI*, April 1, 1965). Interviews: Tom Wallace, Sharon 10X, Philbert Little, confidential source.

MORE THAN THREE MILLION DOLLARS: *EOEM*: See documents relating to First Pacific Bank of Chicago savings account #20-198-7, which was called "The Honorable Elijah Muhammad's Poor Fund." Also see "Like It Is," WABC-TV, Jan. 6, 1980 and *New York Times*, Feb. 18, 1982. The latter indicates that, over the years, nearly $19 million passed through the account.

STOKES'S WIDOW AND CHILD RECEIVED NOTHING: Transcript of Irv Kupcinet's Feb. 28, 1965 interview of Aubrey Barnette, supra. (The transcript indicates that Stokes was sometimes called Wallace rather than Ronald.)

BROTHERS WHO DIED PENNILESS: *Chicago Defender*, July 7 & 8, 1964. Also see the letter from a former Muslim that appears in one of the Sept., 1964 issues of the *Chicago Defender*.

"NUMBER TWO POOR IS MAKING NUMBER ONE RICH": Interview: Sharon 10X.

"MY CHECKING ACCOUNT": *EOEM*: "Response to the Motion of First Pacific Bank for Summary Judgment on Count I of the Petition for Recovery Citation," pp. 3-4.

OBLIGED TO TITHE; SAVIOR'S DAY "GIFT": Grand jury testimony by Benjamin Goodman, March 3, 1965, pp. 465-467. *FBI*, Jan. 31, 1956, p. 5; May 17, 1960, pp. 4, 31. (Peter Goldman was told the amount required for the Savior's Day gift was $200 [*PG*, p. 82.]) In addition to the Savior's Day gift, each NOI member who attended the annual Savior's Day Convention had to pay for his or her busfare, hotel room, and the tithes that were repeatedly solicited at the convention. (Interviews: Charles 37X, Christine Johnson.)

EXPENSIVE PRESENTS TO HIS CHILDREN: *EOEM*: Testimony of Emmanuel Muhammad before Cook County Probate Court, Oct. 13, 1978. (Also see Oct. 30, 1980 statement by Nathaniel Muhammad.)

THREE-YEAR ECONOMIC PLAN: *Muhammad Speaks*, Sept. 11, 1964; Feb. 5 & April 2, 1965.

TWENTY-MILLION-DOLLAR ISLAMIC CENTER: *New York Amsterdam News*, August 3, 1957. *Chicago Defender*, July 26, 1960. *Muhammad Speaks*, Sept., 1960. *MX*, 263. *FBI* correlation file on Elijah Muhmmad, April 9, 1969, p. 27, citing 1959 newspaper articles that discussed plans for the announced Center.

"FIVE (5)+ CHILD": *Bilalian News*, Sept. 8, 1978, Nov. 3, 1978.

224 ISLAMIC CENTER NEVER MATERIALIZED; NO ACCOUNTING GIVEN; "SEED PLANTERS": *Saturday Evening Post*, Feb. 27, 1965, supra. Arno Bontemps & Jack Conroy, *Anyplace But Here* (Hill & Wang, 1966), pp. 229-230. *Chicago Tribune*, Aug. 10 & 24, Sept. 9, & Nov. 30[?], 1960.

RENEWED ITS APPEALS: *Muhammad Speaks*, April 2, 1965. *Chicago Tribune*, July 3, 1966. Years later, the movement bought, for four million dollars instead of twenty million, a church and school belonging to the Greek Orthodox Church. It converted the enormous church, which was located on Chicago's south side, into a mosque and used part of the property as its new national headquarters. But it built no hospital or library. (See, inter alia, *Chicago Tribune*, July 23, 1971 [4-star final]).

HOSPITAL: *Chicago Defender*, June 6, 1972. *Chicago Sun-Times*, Feb. 11, 1973; Feb. 28, 1974. *Chicago Daily News*, Feb. 28, 1974; May 21, 1974; June 6, 1974.

NURSING HOME: *Chicago Tribune*, June 16, 1975 (4-star final ed.).

FOR THE MENTALLY ILL; FACTORIES: *FBI*, April 30, 1958, pp. 88-89. *Chicago Tribune*, June 16, 1975 (4-star final).

CONSULTED LAWYER: Interview: Chauncey Eskridge, Esq.

REAL ESTATE IN ARIZONA AND MEXICO: See the relevant documents in *EOEM*.

$150,000 JEWEL-STUDDED FEZ: Don Atyeo and Felix Dennis, *The Holy Warrior, Muhammad Ali* (Simon and Schuster: Fireside Books, 1975), p. 54. The fez was embroidered with gold.

(*New York Times*, Feb. 27, 1964.)

DENOUNCED THE "ROBBERS": *Sepia*, Nov., 1959, p. 26.

MORE THAN THREE AND A QUARTER MILLION IN BANK DEPOSITS: *New York Times*, Feb. 18, 1982 and the relevant documents in *EOEM*.

RESORT TO CRIMINALITY TO MEET CHICAGO'S DEMANDS FOR MONEY: *Chicago Tribune*, March 2, 1975. *Philadelphia Daily News*, July 28, 1978. *New York Times*, Dec. 6, 1973. The *Philadelphia Inquirer*, Oct. 27, 1973.

MARRIAGE WITH PHILADELPHIA'S "BLACK MAFIA": The *Philadelphia Inquirer's Today Magazine*, Aug. 12, 1973. *Philadelphia Magazine*, Nov. 1973, pp. 124ff. The *Philadelphia Inquirer*, July 27, 1975. The *Sunday Bulletin*, Feb. 1, 1976. The *Evening Bulletin*, Jan. 25, 1977. *Philadelphia Daily News*, July 28, 1978 and Sept. 13, 1978. Interview: James Nicholson.

225 BROKE HER JAW IN FOUR PLACES: *Chicago Defender*, October 13-19, 1962. *New York Amsterdam News*, Oct. 20, 1962. *Chicago Sun-Times*, Nov. 27 & 28, 1962. Undated clipping from archives of *Chicago Defender*.

ARRESTED FOR ARMED ROBBERY: Dec. 12, 1979 letter from Chicago Department of Police to author. *Chicago Tribune*, Feb. 6 and/or Feb. 7, 1965.

REPORTEDLY ON DOPE; THREATENED THE LIFE OF THE ROBBERY VICTIM: Interview: Christine Johnson (who was told by other members of the Chicago temple). *Chicago Tribune*, Feb. 6 and/or Feb. 7, 1965.

TWO FOR DRAFT EVASION: July 3, 1980 letter to author from Federal Correctional Institution, Milan, Michigan, plus other documents furnished by the U.S. Bureau of Prisons. *Chicago's American*, Sept. 21, 1959; Sept. 15, 1964. *Chicago Tribune*, August 16, 1957; March 24, 1960; April 7, 1960; April 29, 1960; March 22, 1961; Oct. 10, 1961; Nov. 1, 1961; Nov. 2, 1961; Nov. 11, 1961; Feb. 21, 1977. *Chicago Sun-Times*, March 2, 1975.

ONE FOR SELLING DOPE: U.S. District Court for the Western District of Missouri, Docket #75CR220-W-4 (1975-1976). *Bilalian News*, Dec. 26, 1975. Undated 1976 reply from *Kansas City Star* to author's Feb. 27, 1976 inquiry. *New York Times*, Feb. 26, 1976.

TWO OF THE MESSENGER'S GRANDSONS WERE ALSO ARRESTED ON DRUG CHARGES; EXTREMELY WEALTHY PARENTS: Interview: Christine Johnson. *Chicago Tribune*, Aug. 6, 1970 (4-star final).

HATED HIM BECAUSE: Interview: Christine Johnson.

"HE WAS EVERYTHING JOHN WASN'T!": Interview: confidential source.

HE DID IT RIGHT ON THE SPEAKER'S PLATFORM: Interview: Harold Hyman.

OUTWARDLY PRAISED SHARRIEFF: *FBI*, May 17, 1960, p. 4.

39. Loyalty or Rivalry?

226 WELL AWARE: *FBI*, April 30, 1958, pp. 45, 99.

TORTURE HIM FOR A NUMBER OF DAYS: *FBI*, April 23, 1957, p. 64.

"ONE OF THOSE OLD BLUE-EYED THINGS": Phonograph record entitled "Malcolm X Speaks to the People in Harlem" (Up Front Records, record #UPF-152).

THE F.B.I. SENSED THE FRICTION: *FBI*, May 19, 1959, pp. 5-6. Also see Oba T'Shaka, *The Political Legacy of Malcolm X* (Third World Press, 1983), p. 218.

227 "HE WANTED TO BE TOP MAN IN ANYTHING HE DID": Interview: Malcolm Jarvis. See *Chicago's American*, Feb. 24, 1965, where Elijah Muhammad says that Malcolm "wanted to be the boss."

ENCOURAGED RANK AND FILE TO ASPIRE: *FBI*, April 23, 1957, p. 39.

"SECOND FIDDLE": Interview: James 67X.

"*ALL* MUSLIMS ARE NUMBER TWO: *MX*, p. 291.

"HOT SEAT": 1963 press conference at Michigan State University.

JAMES EASON ASSASSINATED: See chapter entitled "Violence as Racial Politics: The Murder of James Eason" in Judith Stein, *The World of Marcus Garvey* (Louisiana State University Press, 1986), pp. 171-185. Also see, inter alia, Theodore G. Vincent, *Black Power and the Garvey Movement* (The Ramparts Press, 1975), pp. 120, 196-200.

HAVING TROUBLE WITH HIS AIDES: See, for instance, *Muhammad Speaks*, Jan. 15, 1965.

KHAALIS DENOUNCES ELIJAH MUHAMMAD; KHAALIS'S WIFE AND CHILDREN MURDERED; *The Washington Post*, Jan. 23, Jan. 24, and Feb. 2, 1973. *Chicago Tribune*, Jan. 21, 1973, July 21, 1974.

MALCOLM POSED THE GREATEST POTENTIAL THREAT: *FBI*, August 6, 1963, p. 5.

"GREATEST": *MX*, p. 297. Also see pp. 64, 417. "Malcolm wanted to be great." (Interview with "Robin.")

"DANGEROUS": *MX*, p. 297.

TAKE OVER AND BUILD AN EMPIRE; "DIDN'T ANGER" HIM: *MX*, p. 290.

SEND HIM TO CAIRO: *PG*, p. 111.

228   NO POLITICAL ASPIRATIONS: Tape-recording of broadcast from New York City radio station WLIB, July 12, 1964.

TURNED DOWN INVITATIONS: *MX*, p. 293. *FBI*, Nov. 16, 1962, p. 1. Elijah Muhammad told Malcolm he was moving around the country too much. (*FBI*, 11/15/63, p. 16.)

"USE MR. MUHAMMAD'S PICTURE": *MX*, p. 291.

"I DIDN'T CARE WHAT THEY SAID ABOUT ME." *MX*, p. 267.

WILLINGNESS TO SACRIFICE HIMSELF: *Sepia*, Nov., 1959, p. 26. *MX*, pp. 210, 287, 305.

"I WOULD HAVE HURLED MYSELF": *MX*, p. 287.

"ANY FOOL . . . IS WELCOME TO TRY TO ATTACK HIM": *New York Amsterdam News*, Aug. 26, 1961, pp. 1, 35.

"THEN WHO IS?" :*New York Amsterdam News*, June 16, 1962.

LACK OF SLEEP: *MX*, p. 225.

"SELFLESS": *MX*, p. 292.

"FOR AS MUCH AS FIVE MINUTES": *MX*, p. 306.

IT WAS MALCOLM: Interviews: Philbert Little, Lemuel Hassan, Wilfred Little. Hans J. Massaquoi, "Mystery of Malcolm X," *Ebony* (Vol. 19), Sept., 1964.

POOR SUBSTITUTE: *MX*, p. 264.

ILYASAH NAMED AFTER ELIJAH: *PG*, p. 48.

229   "HONORBUBBLE": *PG*, p. 48.

PRIVATELY DISAGREED: Interviews: Edward Jacko, Toni Ardelle Killings, Louis Michaux.

"I AM NOTHING"; CHARLIE MCCARTHY AND EDGAR BERGEN: *WWG*, pp. 80-81.

MALCOLM'S NEED TO BOLSTER HIS SELF-ESTEEM: Interview: Reginald Little. J. Prescott Adams, the Jehovah's Witness who taught Malcolm about the Bible in Norfolk Prison, writes, "While [he was] studying with me, I realized that Malcolm had a great ego that he was feeding." (April 18, 1977 letter from J. Prescott Adams to author.) Also note the name-dropping that pervades Malcolm's autobiography.

STOOP TO CONQUER: Interview: Malcolm Jarvis.

OVERHAULED AND CLEANSED HIS HEART: *JHC*, p. 139.

"NO MAN ON EARTH TODAY IS HIS EQUAL": *Playboy*, May 1963, p. 60.

DOUBLE-EDGED SWORD: Interview: Philbert Little.

SUBTLY UNDERMINED: "Malcolm's way of undermining you was to compare you to an ideal," says Philbert Little.

ELIJAH MUHAMMAD CONDEMNED MALCOLM BEHIND HIS BACK: *MX*, p. 297.

JARRING QUESTIONS AT YALE: *WWG*, pp. 154-157.

230   "PROFESSING TO SPEAK FOR BLACK PEOPLE BY REPRESENTING THE HONORABLE ELIJAH MUHAMMAD": *BP*, p. 27.

"MENTALLY BLIND, DEAF AND DUMB, AND AS IGNORANT"; "HE TELLS US CONSTANTLY"; "AUTHORED BY GOD"; "THE ILLITERATE ONE": *FBI*, April 30, 1958, p. 100, quoting the relevant part of the August 29, 1957 issue of the *Herald-Dispatch*. An accurate translation of the passage about "the unlettered Prophet" is found in A. Yusef Ali, *The Glorious Qu'ran*, Sura 7, Verse 157.

AS FAR BACK AS 1955: *MX*, p. 295.

REGINALD UNWELCOME: *MX*, p. 295.

HE NEVER SAW MALCOLM AGAIN; HIS PENT-UP RESENTMENT: Interview: Reginald Little.

231 SEX WITH ROBIN; AFTERWARDS, ELIJAH ASSERTED . . .: Two undated, written reports from "Robin" to Gladys Towles Root, her attorney.

SAID THE SAME THING TO "HEATHER"; AISHAH; DIVINELY INSPIRED: Written June 10, 1964 report from "Heather" to Gladys Towles Root, Esq.

GOOD "SEED": Undated statement by Wallace Muhammad, who cites "Minister Louis" as his source. (Wallace's statement was found in Gladys Towles Root's files.)

SIRED MORE THAN A DOZEN CHILDREN OUT OF WEDLOCK: *EOEM*: "Amended Order Declaring Heirship," filed Dec. 1, 1978.

WERE SUPPORTED BY THE TITHES OF THE FAITHFUL: Cancelled checks #1787, #1788, #1789, and #1791, drawn by Muhammad's Temple #2 on the American National Bank & Trust Co. of Chicago. (The checks were dated July 27, 1964.) July 27, 1964 letter from NOI treasurer Raymond Sharrieff to "Robin." *The California Eagle*, July 16, 1964. Undated, written reports from "Robin" and "Heather" to Gladys Towles Root, Esq.

"THE NATION OF ISLAM" Undated *Herald-Dispatch* clipping.

HOMES FOR SEVERAL OF HIS OTHER MISTRESSES: Typed, unsigned, June 3, 1964 letter from Elijah Muhammad to "Robin." Handwritten, unsigned, undated letter from Elijah Muhammad to "Robin." *EOEM*: Emmanuel Muhammad's testimony, pp. 8, 11, 17, 19-20, 22-23. *FBI* correlation file on Elijah Muhammad, 4/9/69, p. 46.

"I SIMPLY REFUSED TO BELIEVE": *MX*, p. 295. Also see *JHC*, p. 139.

MALCOLM PRETENDED; "I SLID OVER ADMITTING": *MX*, p. 296.

CONTENDED THAT HE DIDN'T ADMIT THE TRUTH TO HIMSELF UNTIL LATE 1962 OR 1963: *MX*, pp. 294-299. "It was not a case of my knowing all the time, because I didn't," Malcolm told a Harlem audience on Feb. 15, 1965. (*BP*, p. 116.)

232 BUT ONE OF HIS FORMER MUSLIM ASSOCIATES LATER ASSERTED THAT MALCOLM HAD LEARNED ABOUT IT IN 1957: Undated tape-recorded speech by Muslim minister Don Muhammad.

AFTER TWO OF THE MESSENGER'S SECRETARIES BECAME PREGNANT AND GAVE BIRTH: "Contact," radio station WINS talk show with Stan Bernard, Feb. 18, 1965. *Egyptian Gazette*, August 17, 1964.

FOUR MORE SECRETARIES PREGNANT BY 1959 OR 1960: *Egyptian Gazette*, August 17, 1964. *EOEM*: March 7, 1979 "Application for Award," p. 1, plus pp. 6, 9-10 of Emmanuel Muhammad's testimony. Court documents filed by Gladys Towles Root for two former secretaries who initiated paternity suits indicate that they became pregnant in 1959, as does "Robin's" undated, handwritten report to Ms. Root.

The documents indicate that "Robin" gave birth to one of Elijah Muhammad's daughters on Jan. 17, 1960. Malcolm's ex-fiancee "Heather" gave birth to another on March 30, 1960. Before the year had ended, at least one more former secretary had given birth to a child who had been fathered by the Messenger.

MALCOLM WAS WITH ELIJAH MUHAMMAD WHEN TWO OF HIS FORMER SECRETARIES, ACCOMPANIED BY THEIR ILLEGITIMATE CHILDREN, PAID THE MESSENGER A SURPRISE VISIT: "Like It Is," WABC-TV, Jan. 6, 1980. (Also see *Los Angeles Sentinel*, July 9, 1964.)

HAD TRIED TO ENLIST SECRETARY AS AN INFORMANT: Interview with "Robin."

TO IMPROVE THE MOVEMENT'S "IMAGE": Interview: James 67X. (The irony is even more apparent here.)

"STRONGER" MEN: Interview: Charles 37X. (The irony in the statement should have been apparent.)

"WEAK": *MX*, p. 131.

BY 1960, PHILBERT KNEW: Interview: Philbert Little.

REPORTEDLY WHITE: Interview: Christine Johnson.

ALLAH HAD ORDAINED IT; DAVID AND BATHSHEBA: Interview: Philbert Little.

"NEVER" BIT HIS TONGUE: *MX*, p. 273.

HAD BEEN HOLDING HIS TONGUE FOR YEARS: "He acted as if he had just found out about the babies," says Philbert, who emphasizes that though Malcolm's version of events is partly true, "the chronology is way off." (Interview: Philbert Little.)

40. Submit or Rebel?

233 WALLACE MUHAMMAD NAMED AFTER FARD; NO AFTERBIRTH; DESTINED AND GROOMED TO SUCCEED ELIJAH MUHAMMAD: *Chicago Sun-Times*, March 2, 1975. *Chicago Tribune*, Feb. 21, 1977. Undated, typewritten statement by Wallace Delaney Muhammad. (The statement was found in Gladys Towles Root's files.) John Facenda interviews Wallace Muhammad, WCAU-TV (Philadelphia), Nov. 12, 1978. The *Philadelphia Inquirer*, July 27, 1975. *Philadelphia Daily News*, Feb. 27, 1975. Interviews: Lemuel Hassan, Philbert Little, Charles 37X.

REFUSED TO PAY HIS TUITION: *Chicago Tribune*, Feb. 21, 1977. John Facenda interviews Wallace Muhammad, *supra*.

WALLACE WENT TO PRISON: *Chicago Tribune*, Aug. 16, 1957, March 24, 1960, April 7, 1960, April 29, 1960, March 22, 1961, Oct. 10, 1961, Nov. 1, 1961, Nov. 2, 1961, Nov. 4, 1961. *Chicago's American*, Sept. 21. 1959, Sept. 15, 1964. *Chicago Sun-Times*, March 2, 1975.

EMMANUEL WENT TO PRISON: July 3, 1980 letter to author from Federal Correction Institution, Milan, Michigan.

CONSIDERED SPECIAL: *Chicago Tribune*, Feb. 21, 1977.

"NOT LIKE THE REST"; BEST SON: Interviews: Philbert Little, Christine Johnson, confidential source.

F.B.I. TRIED HARD TO AGGRAVATE THE DIFFERENCES: Oba T'Shaka, *The Political Legacy of Malcolm X* (Third World Press, 1983), p. 218.

RESPECTED ONE ANOTHER: "Like It Is," WABC-TV, Jan. 6, 1980. Interviews: Charles 37X, confidential source.

"EXCEPTIONAL CLOSENESS AND TRUST": *MX*, p. 297.

234 WALLACE WOULD LATER DISPUTE CLAIM: "Like It Is," *supra*.

"HE WANTED TO BE THE BOSS" :*Chicago's American*, Feb. 24, 1965. Elijah Muhammad said he had known for "a long time" that Malcolm wanted to be the boss. (Jan. 27, 1964 report on Nation of Islam by FBI's Phoenix office.)

"HE IS INSANE FOR LEADERSHIP": *Muhammad Speaks*, Jan. 15, 1965. Also in Elijah Muhammad, *Message to the Blackman in America* (Muhammad's Mosque No. 2), p. 263.

"DESPERATELY"; ENLISTED WALLACE'S HELP: *MX*, pp. 296-298.

NIGHTMARES IN WHICH HE COULD SEE THE HEADLINES: *MX*, p. 296. Behind the conscious fear, an unconscious wish often lurks. See, inter alia, Sigmund Freud, *The Interpretation of Dreams* (Buccaneer Books, 1983); *The Psychopathology of Everyday Life* (W. W. Norton, 1971).

MALCOLM WROTE; MEETING IN PHOENIX; "SUCH A GOOD UNDERSTANDING"; "I HAVE TO FULFILL ALL OF THOSE THINGS": *MX*, pp. 297-299.

TRANSFERRED TO WASHINGTON: *Afro-American* (Washington edition), April 30, 1963. *The Evening Star* (Washington), May 1, 1963. May 1, 1963 press release in archives of the *Philadelphia Tribune*. *New York Herald Tribune*, May 5, 1963. *Washington Post*, Oct. 21, 1963. *Chicago Defender*, Nov. 5, 1963.

WOULD CONTINUE AS LEADER IN HARLEM: *New York Times*, May 10, 1963, May 11, 1963. *FBI*, May 23, 1963, pp. 2, 3.

INTERIM WASHINGTON MINISTER UNTIL A PERMANENT ONE IS SELECTED: *FBI*, May 13, 1963, p. 3; May 15, 1963, p. 2; May 23, 1963 file on NOI, pp. 1-3; Nov. 15, 1963, pp. 3, 4. *Washington Post*, Oct. 21, 1963. Interviews: Dolphin Thompson, Charles 37X, Benjamin Goodman, confidential source.

TOLD WASHINGTON PRESS CORPS HE WOULD EVENTUALLY LEAVE NEW YORK AND MOVE TO WASHINGTON: *Washington Daily News*, May 10, 1963.

IN DANGER OF REMOVAL HIMSELF: *The Evening Star* (Washington, D.C.), May 9, 1963.

235 TO SPREAD TEACHINGS, TO REORGANIZE WASHINGTON MOSQUE, AND "TO HELP

FIGHT JUVENILE DELINQUENCY": *Afro-American* (Washington edition), April 30, 1963. *Washington Post*, May 1, 1963. May 13, 1963 F.B.I. transcript of May 12, 1963 broadcast of Washington D.C. radio station WUST's program "Focus."

DEPRIVE HIM OF HIS POWER BASE: One F.B.I. analyst told his superiors,"A full time assignment to Washington, D.C. for Malcolm X would hinder his activities and be...a demotion." (*FBI*, May 13, 1963, p. 3.)

APPARENTLY MAINTAINED CONTROL; TEMPLE SEVEN'S MEMBERS CONTINUED TO REGARD MALCOLM AS THEIR MINISTER: Interviews: Tom Wallace, Sharon 10X, Charles 37X. *New York Times*, May 10, 1963, May 11, 1963. *Washington Post*, Oct. 21, 1963. *Chicago Defender*, Nov. 5, 1963. *FBI*, May 15, 1963, p. 2; May 23, 1963, p. 2. (Though Malcolm apparently retained control of Temple #7 until the following December, he let other officials conduct services there, perhaps because he had to conduct services in the Washington temple.)

SHUTTLED BACK AND FORTH: *The Evening Star* (Washington), May 1, 1963. *Washington Daily News*, May 9 & 10, 1963. *FBI*, May 15, 1963, p. 2; May 23, 1963, p. 3. Interviews: Sharon 10X, Charles 37X, Philbert Little, Dolphin Thompson. Also see the *Chicago Defender*, Dec. 5, 1963, which briefly describes how Malcolm rushed back to Temple Seven from Washington.

TRYING TO INNOCULATE: *MX*, p. 299.

DID NOT BELIEVE IN INNOCULATION: Interview: Leona A. Turner, M.D. Perhaps because of his former drug habit, Malcolm was apprehensive about injecting "poison" into the bloodstream. (Interviews: Tom Wallace, Wilfred Little.) Though he didn't try to forbid his followers from having their children innoculated, he emphasized that Muslims don't take "injurious things" into their bodies. (*FBI*, 1/31/56, p. 4. *MX*, p. 161.)

FELT BETRAYED: *PG*, p. 202-203. *MX*, p. 305. Interviews: "Heather," Christine Johnson.

LETTER OF APOLOGY: *FBI*, Nov. 15, 1963, p. 16.

VOTER REGISTRATION DRIVE: *New York Amsterdam News*, June 15, 1963. Also see *WWG*, p. 180.

MIGHT INITIATE: *Muhammad Speaks*, March 18, 1963. Also see *WWG*, p. 180.

236   "UNITED BLACK FRONT"; AND A BLADE: *New York Times*, Aug. 11, 1963.

"HE WILL FOLLOW ME UNTIL HE DIES": *MX*, pp. 293-294. (The author, who attended the rally, clearly recalls the shock the declaration produced.)

LOST JOB TEMPLE NUMBER FOUR: *Washington Post*, Oct. 21, 1963.

DISPEL RUMORS; NEW RESIDENT MINISTER FOUND: *Chicago Defender*, Nov. 5, 1963, Dec. 5, 1963. *The St. Louis Argus*, Nov. 8, 1963. *Jet*, Nov., 21, 1963, p. 52.

"JUST TOO MUCH FOR HIM": *Jet*, Nov. 21, 1963, p. 52.

BLACK POLITICAL PARTY: *FBI*, June 18, 1964, p. 14.

PROBABLY WOULD HAVE HANDLED SITUATION DIFFERENTLY: *FBI*, June 18, 1964, pp. 10, 11. (The incident in Flint is described in *Muhammad Speaks*, Dec. 30, 1963.)

237   MESSAGE TO THE GRASS ROOTS; "REVOLUTION IS BLOODY": Tape-recording of 11/10/63 "Message to the Grass Roots." *SPKS*, pp. 4-9. *FBI*, June 18, 1964. *Chicago Defender*, Nov. 21, 1963.

ERRONEOUS PRESS REPORT: *Chicago Defender*, Nov. 21, 1963.

"EVERYTHING IS HYPOCRISY": *New York Herald Tribune*, June 5, 1963. Kenneth B. Clark (ed.), *The Negro Protest* (Beacon Press, 1963), p. 22.

238   "SLAVE": *WWG*, p. 179.

"FEEL"; "PERFECT FREEDOM": *MX*, p. 252. *WWG*, p. 129.

DIFFICULT TO LEAVE: See the March 11, 1964 telegram Malcolm sent Elijah Muhammad. (A copy of the telegram found its way to the files of the *New York Amsterdam News*.)

BY-LAWS: Article II, Section 3 stated that membership could also be terminated via "exclusion" but did not explain the difference between exclusion and dismissal, which was written "dismission." See also *Chicago Defender*, July 6, 1964, where an ousted NOI member said there was no such thing as voluntary withdrawal from the NOI. "It's like the Mafia!" he explained.

"I LOVED THE NATION AND MR. MUHAMMAD": *MX*, p. 292.

HOPING TO PURIFY THE NOI: *TKBM*, p. 102.

RUINED BY "NIGGERS": *MX*, p. 411.

41. Silenced

239 "THE OLD DEVIL IS DEAD!": Interview: Sharon 10X.

TALKING ABOUT ONE WHILE HE WAS THINKING ABOUT ANOTHER?: Alex Haley emphasizes how Malcolm "could be talking about one thing and thinking of something else." (*MX*, p. 390.)

USED THE WORD "OLD" TO DESCRIBE AN AUTHORITY FIGURE WHO WAS NEARLY TEN YEARS YOUNGER THAN HE WAS: Three times in one paragraph, Malcolm uses the word "old" to dsecribe Oscar Ronald Dathorne, who was born Nov. 19, 1934, according to the Directory of American Scholars. (*MX*, pp. 350-351.)

"ALMOST LIKE A GOD": *New York Amsterdam News*, May 18, 1957. *FBI*, April 30, 1958, p. 102, reprinting *Herald Dispatch*, Sept. 5, 1957. Also see *WWG*, p. 159.

A PRISON WARDEN; A DEPUTY WARDEN; A "SCREW": *Newsday*, June 5, 1963. Kenneth B. Clark (ed.), *The Negro Protest* (Beacon Press, 1963), p. 24. *FBI*, Nov. 17, 1960, p. 12; Nov. 15, 1963, p. 19.

PREVIOUS ATTACKS ON PRESIDENT KENNEDY: *New York Herald Tribune*, June 30, 1963. (Also June 16, 1963.) *Washington Post*, May 13, 1963. *New York Times*, May 17 and June 30, 1963. *SPKS*, pp. 170-171. *Afro-American* [L.C. edition], August 3, 1963. "Like It Is," WABC-TV, Feb. 22, 1969. Tape recording of question & answer period following Jan. 23, 1963 addresss at Michigan State University. Also see Taylor Branch, *Parting the Waters* (Simon and Schuster, 1988), p. 344. Simeon Booker, *Black Man's America* (Prentice Hall, 1964), Chapt. 2. Richard Kluger, *Simple Justice* (Knopf, 1976), pp. 735, 755-756. Arthur Schlesinger, *A Thousand Days* (Houghton Mifflin, 1965), pp. 929, 930-931, 938.

240 "K.K.K.: *Afro-American* [L. C. edition], August 3, 1963.

NOVEMBER 22 SPEECH; OBLIQUE REFERENCE; PEOPLE REAP WHAT THEY SOW; TWO DIRECTIVES: *MX*, p. 300. *TKBM*, p. 123. *EWWS*, p. 21. Interviews: Sharon 10X, Philbert Little.

APPREHENSIVE; HAD TYPED OUT DEC. 1 SPEECH BEFOREHAND: Interview: Sharon 10X. *EWWS*, p. 20. Leona Turner recalls Malcolm voicing concern that he was saying things he wasn't supposed to say.

"LET THEM STAY"; WORD FOR WORD: Interview: James 67X.

241 DECEMBER 1 SPEECH AT MANHATTAN CENTER: *EWWS*, pp. 121-148.

INEVITABLE: *MX*, pp. 300-301.

"WITHOUT A SECOND THOUGHT": *MX*, p. 301.

SHED THE RESTRAINT: Interviews: Pat Robinson, Sharon 10X, Robert 35X.

"CHICKENS COMING HOME TO ROOST": *New York Times*, Dec. 2, 1963, Dec. 5, 1963. *Chicago Defender*, Dec. 5, 1963. *MX*, pp. 300-301. Interviews: Robert 35X, Sharon 10X, Charles 37X, Pat Robinson.

Philbert recalls that, contrary to *MX*, p. 9, the animal his father had beheaded hours before his death was a chicken, not a rabbit. If Philbert's recollection is accurate, it suggests that Malcolm may have had still another authority figure in mind when he made his famous "chickens roost" statement. (See *MX*, p. 390, which emphasizes Malcolm's ability to talk about one thing while he is thinking about something else.)

HUGE GRIN: Interviews: Pat Robinson, Sharon 10X.

BUT THE NOI OFFICIALS ON THE STAGE DIDN'T LAUGH: Interview: Pat Robinson.

242 ANOTHER PREMONITION: *MX*, p. 301.

TELEPHONED DECEMBER 4; "PUBLIC SPEECHING"; INCLUDED SERMONS: FBI reports on the Nation of Islam dated Dec. 4, 1963 (pp. 1-7) and Dec. 5, 1963 (pp. 2, 5). Also *MX*, p. 302.

"I WILL DECIDE": *New York Times*, Dec. 5, 1963.

F.B.I. LEARNS THAT MALCOLM HAD BEEN SILENCED INDEFINITELY : F.B.I. report on the Nation of Islam dated Jan. 23, 1964, p. 5. Also see the F.B.I. report on the Nation of

Islam dated Dec. 13, 1963, pp. 3-5. Malcolm told reporter Ted Poston that he had been silenced indefinitely. (*New York Post*, Dec. 5, 1963.) Also see the *Afro-American*, Dec. 14, 1963 and *Muhammad Speaks*, Dec. 20, 1963.

TOLD OTHERS THAT HE EXPECTED TO BE REINSTATED "WITHIN NINETY DAYS ": *MX*, pp. 302, 304. Also see p. 150 of trial transcript, Landlord & tenant case #4845, Queens Civil Court, 1964 Special Term, Part I.

MALCOLM SAYS HE'S STILL IN CHARGE OF TEMPLE SEVEN: *New York Post*, Dec. 5, 1963. *New York Times*, Dec. 6, 1963.

ALREADY CHOSEN A NEW MINISTER FOR TEMPLE SEVEN; REMOVAL ONLY A MATTER OF TIME: *New York Times*, Dec. 6, 1963.

NECK REDDISH; HALEY AND OTHERS COULD FEEL MALCOLM'S RAGE: *MX*, p. 406. Interviews: Malik Hakim, Leona Turner, Clifford Hyman.

OTHERS FOOLED BY HIS CONTRITE FACADE, WHICH ASTOUNDED THE F.B.I.: Interview: Benjamin Goodman. *JHC*, pp. 189-195, 201-202. *FBI* reports dated Feb. 12, 1964, June 18, 1964, and Jan. 20, 1965 indicate that Malcolm was interviewed by the Federal Bureau of Investigation Feb. 4, 1964, not May 29, 1964, as page 182 of *JHC* asserts. On pages 203-204, *JHC* itself makes clear that the interview occurred before the February 25, 1964 Clay - Liston fight, not after.

OUTWARDLY CONTRITE: *MX*, pp. 302, 406.

243 "ANYTHING THAT MR. MUHAMMAD DOES IS ALL RIGHT WITH ME": *New York Times*, Dec. 5, 1963.

FORBIDDEN "TO SPEAK IN PUBLIC": *New York Amsterdam News*, Dec. 14, 1963. *New York Times*, Dec. 5, 1963. *Muhammad Speaks*, April 10, 1964. *Afro-American*, Dec. 14, 1963. *PG*, p. 131. Interviews: Christine Johnson, Sharon 10X, Philbert Little.

FORBIDDEN TO GRANT INTERVIEWS: *New York Post*, Dec. 5, 1963. *MX*, p. 302.

MAKING STATEMENTS TO REPORTERS OVER THE TELEPHONE: *MX*, pp. 302, 406. See, inter alia, *New York Post*, Dec. 5, 1963. *New York Journal-American*, Dec. 5, 1963. *New York Times*, Dec. 5, 1963, Dec. 6, 1963. *New York Amsterdam News*, Dec. 7, 1963.

"I'M IN COMPLETE SUBMISSION": *MX*, p. 406.

REMAINS IN THE NEWS: See: *New York Amsterdam News*, Dec. 14, 1963; Jan. 4, 1964; Feb. 1, 1964; Feb. 15, 1964; Feb. 22, 1964. *Chicago Defender*, Feb. 11, 1964. *New York Times*, Feb. 26, 1964.

MICHAUX'S TELEGRAM: *New York Amsterdam News*, Feb. 29, 1964.

SUGGESTIVE LETTERS: *New York Amsterdam News*, Feb. 22, 1964.

LEAKS TO JIMMY BOOKER: *New York Amsterdam News*, Feb. 15, 1964, Feb. 22, 1964. Interview: Jimmy Booker.

INVITES LOMAX; I'M THINKING ABOUT MAKING A MOVE ON MY OWN: *TKBM*, p. 128.

"IT'S HARD TO MAKE A ROOSTER STOP CROWING ONCE THE SUN HAS RISEN": *New York Times Magazine Section*, March 22, 1964. Jan. 7, 1975 letter to author from Jules Loh.

WEAKNESS FOR SPEAKER'S PLATFORMS: *SPKS*, p. 65. Interview: Robert 35X.

NO LONGER MINISTER: FBI report on the Nation of Islam, Jan. 27, 1964, p. 4. Interviews: Sharon 10X, Philbert Little.

244 ISOLATED: *PG*, pp. 125-126.

CRIED: *PG*, p. 120. Interview: Philbert Little.

"EMOTIONAL SHOCK"; "BLEEDING INSIDE": *MX*, pp. 303, 304. Also see p. 294.

SEVERE HEADACHES; BRAIN TUMOR; THE CAUSE WAS NOT PHYSIOLOGICAL; "YOU DON'T NEED HIM"; DIDN'T HURT ANYMORE: Interview: Leona Turner, M.D.

NOTHING WRONG PHYSICALLY; CRAMPING WAS PSYCHOSOMATIC: Interview: Farrow Allen, M.D. Malcolm had trouble keeping down his food. (Oba T'Shaka, *The Political Legacy of Malcolm X* (Third World Press, 1983), p. 233.)

DEPRESSED; SLUMPED; BROKEN: Interviews: Tom Wallace, Ella Little, Charles 37X, confidential source.

BETTY SAID NOTHING: *MX*, p. 305.

REPORTEDLY CONTINUED ATTENDING: Interviews: Tom Wallace, Charles 37X, Sharon 10X, and two confidential sources. "They began teaching at the mosque how all hypocrites should be destroyed," Betty later recalled (*JHC*, p. 140).

MRS. SHABAZZ DECLINED: Dec. 29, 1971 letter from her attorney Clifford Alexander, Jr., to author. Sept. 3, 1977 letter to Betty Shabazz. Also see January 28, 1980 letter from James Griggs to the author and the author's March 1 response.

42. Another Boxer

245 CLAY'S FATHER ARRESTED TWICE; BEAT WIFE; Don Atyeo & Felix Dennis, *The Holy Warrior: Muhammad Ali* (Fireside Books, 1975), p. 10.

"WE WERE NOT TO BE STRUCK": Muhammad Ali with Richard Durham, *The Greatest* (Random House, 1975), p. 40.

ACKNOWLEDGED CORPORAL PUNISHMENT: *The Greatest, supra.*, pp. 47, 79. Also Atyeo & Dennis, *supra.*, p. 10.

LOOSENED TWO OF MOTHER'S TEETH: George Sullivan, *The Cassius Clay Story* (Fleet Publications, 1964), p. 7. Atyeo & Dennis, *supra.*, p. 9. *The Greatest, supra.*, p. 47.

SAID HE LOVED HER: *The Greatest, supra.*, p. 159. Atyeo & Dennis, *supra.*, p. 10.

WASN'T "NICE" BABY: *The Greatest, supra.*, p. 33.

HARD TIME CONTROLLING HIM: Atyeo & Dennis, *supra.*, p. 10.

WORRIED ABOUT GANG: *The Greatest, supra.*, pp. 34, 46.

DERAILED TRAIN: *The Greatest, supra.*, p. 35.

"PRETTY"; "BEAUTY": *The Greatest, supra.*, p. 37. (Note, on p. 40 of Atyeo & Dennis, how Cassius taunted Liston as being "too pretty to be a fighter.")

THWARTED ASPIRATIONS: Atyeo & Dennis, *supra.*, p. 10.

ANOTHER JOE LOUIS: *The Greatest, supra.*, pp. 39-40, 46.

ALREADY DREAMING: Sullivan, *supra.*, p. 12. *The Greatest, supra.*, p. 50. Atyeo & Dennis, *supra.*, pp. 12-13.

246 ONLY VACATION: *MX*, pp. 304, 407.

SENT THEM BACK TO NEW YORK: *FBI*, Jan. 21, 1964, p. 1.

MEANT "NOTHING"; "A SMALL CORNER OF MY MIND"; SCENES FROM THE PAST; "A LIE"; PHYSICAL VS. PSYCHOLOGICAL DIVORCE: *MX*, pp. 304-305.

MALCOLM HAD GIVEN SIMILAR ADVICE TO BOISIE PHILLIPS: Interview: Malcolm Jarvis.

247 SLUGGISH TICKET SALES; CLAY-MCDONALD COMPROMISE; MALCOLM HELPS OUT: *The Greatest, supra.*, pp. 101-105, 203. Atyeo & Dennis, *supra.*, pp. 41, 52-53. Sullivan, *supra.*, pp. 68, 82, 90-91. *New York Times*, Feb. 27, 1964. *New York Amsterdam News*, Jan. 25, 1964, March 7, 1964. *Philadelphia Daily News*, Feb. 25, 1965. *FBI*, April 20, 1964, citing undated articles in the *Miami Herald*, *Louisville Times*, and the *New York Herald Tribune*. Interview: Harold Conrad.

"SCARED TO DEATH": *The Greatest, supra.*, pp. 109-110.

248 "IN THE NEXT ROOM, MY BEDROOM"; HE SEEMED PROUD: *MX*, pp. 407-408. James D. Wilson, who had performed some dental work on Earl Little years before, was vacationing in the same Miami motel complex that Clay and Malcolm were in. Wilson recalls that Malcolm seemed very proud of his friendship with Muhammad Ali. "He did seem to push this point," he says.

249 "MAYOR OF HARLEM": *New York Amsterdam News*, March 7, 1964.

ACCOMPANIED MUHAMMAD ALI TO NEW YORK; APPEARED TOGETHER; ENABLED MALCOLM TO STAY IN THE NEWS: Sullivan, *supra.*, pp. 88-89, 100-101. Atyeo & Dennis, *supra.*, p. 53. *New York Herald Tribune*, March 2, 1964. *New York Times*, March 2 and March 5, 1964. *New York Amsterdam News*, March 7 and March 14, 1964. Interview: Bob High.

MORE THAN TWENTY-SEVEN MILLION DOLLARS: Pages 178, 183, and sections entitled "Professional Fight Record" and "Acknowledgement" in *The Greatest, supra. Chicago Tribune*, Feb. 21, 1966; Nov. 16, 1967; July 26, 1978. *New York Herald Tribune*, Jan. 9, 1966. *Chicago's*

American, Feb. 24, 1966. *Philadelphia Daily News*, Feb. 26, 1976.

IN BOTH DIRECTIONS: Interview: Daniel Nagle.

"BORROWED" IT BACK: *Chicago Today*, March 3, 1971. Also see *The Greatest*, p. 218.

DONATIONS TO HERBERT MUHAMMAD FOUNDATION: Information accompanying Internal Revenue Service Form #990, filed by Herbert Muhammad Foundation for 1976 tax year.

MONEY FOR HOSPITAL: *Chicago Sun-Times*, Feb. 28, 1974. See chapter 38.

OPPOSED ALI'S CONVERSION: *The Greatest*, *supra.*, p. 118. Sullivan, *supra.*, p. 91.

"A BUNCH OF GANGSTERS"; "I RAISED HIM CLEAN"; "NO REASON TO BE ASHAMED": *New York Times*, Feb. 23, 1965. Also see Atyeo & Dennis, *supra.*, p. 58.

REPORTEDLY MADE UNSUCCESSFUL ATTEMPTS: *PG*, pp. 128-131. *New York Post*, Feb. 26, 1965. Undated tape-recorded speech by Muslim minister Don Muhammad. (How accurate these reports are is unclear.)

STORY LEAKED BY NOI: *Newark Star-Ledger*, Feb. 22, 1964. Interviews: Charles 37X, Philbert Little.

ATTEMPTS TO PHONE ELIJAH MUHAMMAD: Interviews: Christine Johnson, "Heather."

NOT ALLOWED TO ATTEND CONVENTION: *New York Times*, Feb. 27, 1964; March 9, 1964. Also see *New York Amsterdam News*, Feb. 15, 1964.

250 "YOU'D GO OUT AND KILL HIM YOURSELF": *MX*, pp. 302-303. PG, pp. 126-127.

"HYPOCRITES" SHOULD BE SLAIN: *JHC*, p. 140.

CAR BOMB: *MX*, pp. 308-309. Interview: Sharon 10X.

ALLEGATIONS OF JOSEPH'S INVOLVEMENT: *New York Amsterdam News*, March 21, 1964. *New York Post Daily Magazine*, Feb. 23, 1965. (Also see *MX*, pp. 408-409 and Jan. 7, 1975 letter from Jules Loh to author.)

"ONLY ONE MAN": *MX*, p. 303.

NEARLY SENT HIM TO A MENTAL HOSPITAL: "It nearly sent me to Bellevue," Malcolm says in *MX*, p. 294. As Cedric J. Robinson has observed, Malcolm seemed afraid of succumbing to mental illness, as Reginald and his mother had done. (Cedric J. Robinson, "Malcolm Little as a Charismatic Leader," paper delivered at 66th annual meeting of the American Political Science Association, Sept., 1970, p. 13. *MX*, pp. 295, 303.)

MARCH 1 DEADLINE: *New York Times*, Feb. 26, 1964. *New York Amsterdam News*, Feb. 22, 1964. *FBI*, March 3, 1964, p. 2. Malcolm told "Heather" he could not submit to Elijah Muhammad any longer. (Interview with "Heather.")

ELIJAH MUHAMMAD NOTIFIED MALCOLM: *New York Amsterdam News*, March 14, 1964. Also see *New York Times*, March 9, 1964.

43. The Strength To Continue Alone

251 MICROPHONES AND FLASH BULBS: *MX*, p. 316.

UNCOMPETITIVE EXTERIOR: *New York Times*, March 9 and 13, 1964. *Chicago Tribune*, March 9, 1964. *Chicago Defender*, March 10, 1964. *Boston Globe* (P.M. edition), March 9, 1964. *SPKS*, pp. 18-22. *BAMN*, pp. 5-6. *New York Times Magazine*, March 22, 1964, p. 105. *EPPS*, p. 140. Bob Kennedy Talk Show (station WBZ, Boston), cited in FBI report dated April 3, 1964, p. 6.

NO INTENTION OF ESTABLISHING A RIVAL MOVEMENT: *FBI*, March 11, 1964 (page number not indicated), citing March 9, 1964 broadcast of WHDT-TV news program "The World at Ten."

ACCOMPANIED BY SEVERAL FORMER MEMBERS OF NOI: *New York Times*, March 13, 1964. Malcolm brought at least four former members of Temple Seven with him, according to *FBI*, March 13, 1964, p. 10.

DIDN'T FEEL EQUIPPED: Film entitled "A Tribute to Malcolm" (produced by National Educational Television and Radio Center).

"I HAVE NO FEAR OR DOUBTS THAT I WILL BE SUCCESSFUL": *New York Amsterdam News*, March 14, 1964. "As long as I am a true believer, as the holy Qur'an says, Allah will bless me with success," Malcolm declared on March 8. (Unidentified, undated clipping in the files of the *New York Amsterdam News*.)

252   ILL AT EASE: "Malcolm X for Rifle Clubs for Negroes," CBS newsfilm dated March 15, 1964. *MX*, p. 410.

HEART BEATING A MILE A MINUTE; FEARED HEART ATTACK; NO PHYSICAL IMPAIRMENT: Interview: Leona Turner. A prison medical report dated Jan.10, 1947 states, "Heart -- no evidence of disease. Heart size normal." Even on the day Malcolm died, his heart appeared normal except for a multitude of gunshot wounds, according to the autopsy report.

DIFFICULTY BREATHING, ON OCCASION: Interviews: Malik Hakim, Lawson Riley.

AUNT SASSIE DIES; OTHER FAMILY MEMBERS REPORT HEART CONDITIONS: City of Boston, Registry Division, death certificate #8854, dated Feb. 19, 1962. Interview: J. C. Little. Philbert reports that he had a heart attack around 1980. Wilfred reportedly had a heart murmur. Ella frequently complained of heart trouble, real or imaginary. (Interview: Philbert Little. See chapter 32.)

BLACK, ISLAMIC BILLY GRAHAM: *New York Times*, April 3, 1964. *TKBM*, pp. 138-139. *SPKS*, pp. 40-41. *Afro-American*, Feb. 23, 1965.

DISCOURAGES PEOPLE FROM LEAVING TEMPLE SEVEN: Interviews: Sharon 10X, Charles 37X. *New York Amsterdam News*, March 14, 1964. *PG*, p. 192.

ATTEMPTED COUP AT TEMPLE SEVEN: *FBI*, March 27, 1964, p. 1.

ATTEMPTS TO RECRUIT MEMBERS OF NOI'S BOSTON TEMPLE: *FBI*, April 3, 1964, pp. 2-3; April 20, 1964, p. 9.

VOTER REGISTRATION DRIVE: *New York Times*, March 23, 1964. *New York Herald Tribune*, March 30, 1964. *New York Post*, March 30, 1964. *New York Amsterdam News*, April 4, 1964. *Chicago Defender*, July 17, 1964. *Sepia*, Oct., 1964, p. 45.

BLACK NATIONALIST CONVENTION: *New York Herald Tribune*, March 23, 1964. *New York Amsterdam News*, March 28, 1964. *LYMX*, p. 74. *SPKS*, pp. 23, 41.

BLACK POLITICAL PARTY: *New York Times*, March 9, 1964, March 14, 1964. *New York Herald Tribune*, March 23, 1964. *U.S. News & World Report*, March 30, 1964, p. 39. *SPKS*, p. 47.

BLACK NATIONALIST ARMY: *New York Herald Tribune*, March 23, 1964. *New York Times*, March 23, 1964; April 3, 1964. *SPKS*, p. 41.253

253   MIXED MESSAGES ABOUT BLACK NATIONALIST PARTY: *EPPS*, pp. 146-147, 156-157. *New York Times*, March 23, 1964. *U.S. News & World Report*, March 30, 1964, p. 39. *SPKS*, p. 41.

GALAMISON'S SCHOOL BOYCOTTS: Unpublished manuscript provided by Milton A. Galamison. Interview: Milton Galamison. Fred C. Shapiro & James W. Sullivan, *Race Riots: 1964* (Thomas Y. Crowell, 1964), pp. 122-125. *Boston Advertiser*, March 15, 1964. *New York Times*, March 13, 15, 16, 17, and 23, 1964; April 3, 1964.

VERBAL DECLARATIONS: *New York Times*, March 17, 1964. *New York Amsterdam News*, Jan. 27, 1965. *PG*, pp. 144-145, 386. Unpublished manuscript provided by Milton A. Galamison.

DIDN'T WANT TO BURDEN HIM: Interview: Milton Galamison. *PG*, pp. 144-145.

"IF I GOT IN LINE, . . . ": *New York Times*, March 16, 1964.

254   TRAFFIC COURT: *New York Times* , March 16 & 17, 1964. *New York Herald Tribune*, May 20, 1964. *New York Journal-American*, May 20, 1964. *FBI*, Jan. 20, 1965, p. 2.

DRIVES DANGEROUSLY FAST : Interviews: Malcolm Jarvis, "Heather," Saladin Matthews, Robert 35X, Bill Downs. "I drive by my watch, not my speedometer," Malcolm said. (*MX*, p. 192.) Before the interstate highway connecting Lansing with Detroit was built, he boasted he could cover the eighty-five mile distance in fifty minutes. (See also *FBI*, June 21, 1963, p. 1, which describes how Malcolm was stopped by a policeman for driving eighty-seven miles per hour in a fifty-mile-per-hour speed zone.)

TIME-CONSCIOUS; IN A HURRY: *MX*, pp. 192, 385. "Especially after Malcolm came out of prison, he felt a lot of time had been stolen from him. It was almost as if he knew he had limited time," says Philbert Little. Interviews: Philbert Little, Saladin Matthews, Geraldine Nelson, John Elton Bembry, Benjamin Goodman, Art Jones, Reginald Little, Wilfred Little, Sharon 10X.

SAYS HE'S INCAPABLE OF TALKING SLOWLY: "Like It Is," WABC-TV, Feb. 22, 1969.

300,000 VIOLATIONS: *NYT*, July 15, 1964.

HOMER BIGART'S REPORT ON HOUSING CONDITIONS: *NYT*, Jan. 1, 1964.

ADDRESSES RENT STRIKE RALLY: *NYT*, March 16, 1964.

KEEPING POLITICAL PLANS SECRET: *BAMN*, pp. 10, 23-24. *SPKS*, p. 21.

"I DON'T CARE WHAT I SAID LAST YEAR": *NYT*, April 7, 1964.

"I'VE FORGOTTEN EVERYTHING": *SPKS*, p. 20.

255 SENATE DEBATE A "CON GAME"; SAID THE BILL WOULDN'T HELP: *New York Herald Tribune*, March 27, 1964. *NYT*, March 27, 1964; June 20, 1964. *FBI*, March 13, 1964, p. 10; June 18, 1964, unnumbered page; Jan. 14, 1965, p. 8; Jan. 20, 1965, p. 4.

"EXACTLY AS IS, WITH NO CHANGES": *NYT*, March 27, 1964.

PELTED WITH EGGS: Lewis V. Baldwin, "A Reassessment of the Relationship Between Malcolm X and Martin Luther King, Jr.," *The Western Journal of Black Studies* (Vol. 13, No. 2), 1989, p. 105.

MALCOLM BRIEFLY MEETS MARTIN IN SENATE GALLERY: *New York World Telegram*, March 27, 1964. *Chicago Sun-Times*, March 27, 1964. *PG*, p. 95 (note). Also see photograph in *PG* and Lewis V. Baldwin, "Malcolm X and Martin Luther King, Jr.: What They Thought About Each Other," *Islamic Studies* (Vol. 25, No. 4), Winter, 1986, p. 397.

REPORTEDLY TOLD KING: According to Alfred Duckett, King told Duckett that Malcolm told King, "I'm out there making the enemy scared to death so they'll have to come to you." Alfred Duckett, "Death in the Family: A Memory of Malcolm," *Malcolm X: A Tribute* (Steppingstones: Winter, 1983), p. 44.

FATHER'S DEATH: January 7, 1975 letter from Jules Loh to author. On two separate occasions, Malcolm maintained that his father had been lynched. (*FBI*, Jan. 31, 1956, p. 12. Tape-recording of Nov. 10, 1963 "Message to the Grass Roots.") Yet, about a month before Malcolm delivered his "Message to the Grass Roots," he asked his friend Howard Bannister if Howard's father knew something about Earl Little's death. Malcolm said it had bothered him all these years and that he wished to learn more about it. (Interview: Howard Bannister.)

"PARROTS": October, 1961 speech at Howard University. *MX*, p. 284.

TRIED TO REPAIR RELATIONSHIP: *Life*, March 20, 1964, p. 40. *JHC*, p. 32. *SPKS*, pp. 18-19. *BAMN*, pp. 3-5. *EPPS*, p. 140.

ATTRIBUTED BREAK TO SYCOPHANTS: *BAMN*, p. 4. CBS newsfilm dated June 8, 1964.

DENIED HE BORE ANY RESPONSIBILITY: Talk show moderated by Bill Campbell, WCAU (Philadelphia), April 10, 1964.

256 STILL MY LEADER; STILL YOUR SERVANT: March 11, 1964 telegram from Malcolm to Elijah Muhammad.

"1,000 PERCENT TRUE": *JHC*, p. 191.

RETURN TO THE FOLD: Interviews: Charles 37X, Christine Johnson, Robert 35X, confidential source. That Malcolm waited from December 1963 until March 1964 to formally split with Elijah Muhammad suggests he was reluctant to leave the Nation of Islam. (Also see *Muhammad Speaks*, Feb. 12, 1965, the *New York Post*, Feb. 26, 1965, and Betty Shabazz's statement in *JHC*, pp. 141-142.)

INADVERTENTLY ADMITTED IT HIMSELF: Mike Wallace interviewing Malcolm, CBS newsfilm, June 8, 1964.

ELIJAH SHED TEARS: March 11, 1964 telegram from Malcolm to Elijah Muhammad. *New York Amsterdam News*, March 14, 1964. Interview: confidential source.

DENIES WEEPING: *NYT Magazine*, March 22, 1964, p. 106.

OVERWROUGHT: *MX*, p. 409.

"DIVINELY GUIDED": *NYT Magazine*, March 22, 1964, p. 106.

"I MADE HIM BIG.": *MX*, pp. 409-410.

RESEMBLED WAR ROOM: Interview: confidential source.

SHOVED A PREPARED SCRIPT: Interview: Philbert Little. In Philadelphia two weeks later, during an April 10, 1964 WCAU talk show moderated by Bill Campbell, Malcolm said that a prepared script had been placed in Philbert's hands. See *PG*, p. 140.

PHILBERT ASSAILS MALCOLM: *Chicago Sun-Times*, March 27, 1964. *Chicago Daily News*, March 27, 1964. *Chicago Defender* for the week Mar. 28 to Apr. 3, 1964. ABC newsfilm dated

March 26, 1964. *Herald Tribune*, March 28, 1964. *New York Post*, March 29, 1964. *FBI*, March 27, 1964, pp. 1-3. *Muhammad Speaks*, April 10, 1964. Warner Brothers film documentary entitled "Malcolm X."

257   "EMPTY BAG": Undated, unidentified clipping in the files of the *New York Amsterdam News*.

"LITTLE RED'S" SEVERED HEAD: *Muhammad Speaks*, April 10, 1964.

MALCOLM'S RESPONSE TO PHILBERT'S ATTACK: *Chicago Tribune*, March 28, 1964. *Chicago Sun-Times*, March 28, 1964. *New York Herald Tribune*, March 28, 1964. *New York Post*, March 29, 1964. *PG*, p. 140. Radio talk show moderated by Bill Campbell, WCAU (Philadelphia), April 10, 1964.

"GOOD FRIENDS": *New York Herald Tribune*, March 28, 1964.

"COMPLETE FAILURE": *New York Herald Tribune*, March 28, 1964. *New York Post*, April 10, 1964.

LANSING TEMPLE "DOING FINE": *FBI*, Jan. 31, 1956, p. 20.

DENIED HE FELT PAIN: *New York Post*, April 10, 1964. *PG*, pp. 140, 200.

LATER ACKNOWLEDGED REGRET: Interview: Philbert Little.

"NOTHING IS PAINFUL": *New York Post*, April 10, 1964. *PG*, p. 140.

THE PEOPLE WHO WILL HURT YOU: *FDL*, p. 151.

FIRST RALLY: *NYT*, March 23, 1964.

258   A MOVIE HE HAD SEEN: Interview: J. C. Little. (In one speech, Malcolm apparently started to say, "the bullet or the ballot," but caught himself and changed it to "the ballot or the bullet." [Phonograph record entitled "Ballots or Bullets," First Amendment Records, Jamie/Guyden Distributing Corp.])

"BUT LET US TRY THE BALLOT": *BAMN*, p. 89.

GASP OF SURPRISE: Phonograph record entitled "Ballots or Bullets," *supra*.

AT MILITANT LABOR FORUM: *SPKS*, pp. 49, 56-57.

MINGLED DOVE-LIKE AND HAWK-LIKE IMAGES IN SAME PARAGRAPHS; "REVOLUTIONS ARE BLOODY"; "BLOODLESS REVOLUTION": Phonograph record entitled "Ballots or Bullets," *supra*.

44. Political Actor

260   HAVEN'T MET ANY: *NYT*, April 3, 1964.

SPIRITUAL RENEWAL: *New York Amsterdam News*, April 18, 1964. John Elton Bembry got the feeling that Malcolm's trip to Mecca had been prompted by a need to reaffirm his religious faith. (Interview: John Elton Bembry.)

VIRTUALLY BROKE: *PG*, p. 165. *FBI*, Jan. 20, 1965, p. 35; March 8, 1965, p. 3. Charis Waddy, *The Muslim Mind* (Longman, 1976), p. 108. (Also see Mike Wallace interviewing Malcolm, CBS newsfilm, 6/8/64.)

HE HAD TO LOOK ELSEWHERE: Malcolm said he had to go abroad to establish a reliable source of income. (*FBI*, March 8, 1965, p. 3.)

REMADE HIMSELF INTO "AN AUTHENTIC MUSLIM": *BP*, pp. 129-130.

261   SHAWARBI TUTORS MALCOLM; MALCOLM HAD RECITED THE PASSAGE MANY TIMES BEFORE; MALCOLM BEGAN WEEPING: *PG*, pp. 163-165. May 20, 1979 letter from James 67X to author. Interview: James 67X. Cf. *MX*, p. 320.

SHAWARBI'S AIM: Interview: Heshaam Jaaber.

"I WAS GOING TO RUN HIM FOR PRESIDENT IN 1968": Interview: Ella Little. Ella also told Heshaam Jaaber that she envisioned Malcolm as President.

262   BROTHEL: Interviews: Heshaam Jaaber, confidential source.

"HAD NEVER ONCE REALLY WAVERED": *MX*, p. 317.

HOW IMPORTANT A ROLE ELLA HAD PLAYED: *MX*, p. 319 and Part II of this book. "He would never make an important decision without consulting me," Ella told an interviewer years later. (Interview: Ella Little.)

BORROWED $1500 FROM ELLA: *MX*, p. 430. Interviews: 35X, confidential source. (The airfare cost $1300.80, according to *FBI*, April 24, 1964, pp. 1-2.)

BUYING HIM CLOTHES: Interview: Ella Little.

PROVIDED FREE; DEFRAYED BY CONGREGATION: *New York Amsterdam News*, April 18, 1964.

"LITTLE" REALIZED: *MX*, p. 320.

STOPOVER IN FRANKFURT: *MX*, pp. 320-322 gives the impression that the Muslim whom Malcolm went sightseeing with in Frankfurt was someone he met by chance on the plane. But *FBI*, April 24, 1964, pp. 1-2 and *FBI*, June 18, 1964, pp. 62 and 64 indicate that the man was an Egyptian official who was traveling with Malcolm. James 67X concurs. (Interview: James 67X.) Whether the official helped Malcolm get a seat on the plane from Cairo to Jedda is unclear. (See *MX*, p. 323 and the April 24 and June 18, 1964 FBI files.)

TRIED TO OBTAIN SEAT IN REAR: Interviews: Charles 37X and two confidential sources.

"TWO HAPPY DAYS": *MX*, p. 321.

"BUMPED": The FBI was told that, during the Hajj season, the only way an American Muslim could get a seat on a plane from Cairo to Jedda was with the help of the Egyptian government. Whether the Egyptian official who had accompanied Malcolm to Cairo helped him get a seat is unclear. (*FBI*, April 24, 1964, p. 2; June 18, 1964, p. 64. *MX*, pp. 320-323.)

VERY HUMBLE: *MX*, p. 323. See similar statements in *MX*, pp. 336, 341.

263 ABDEL RAHMAN AZZAM: There are several ways of translating Azzam Pasha's name from Arabic to English. (*MX*, pp. 320, 332.) But when Azzam Pasha signed his name in English, he spelled it Abdel Rahman Azzam. (Interview: Issam Azzam.)

AZZAM PASHA: Interview: Issam Azzam. (Also see *MX*, p. 332 and Charis Waddy, *The Muslim Mind* (Longman, 1976), p. 107.)

264 "FIRST BEGAN TO REAPPRAISE": *MX*, pp. 333-334. "Like It Is," WABC-TV, Feb. 22, 1969 (pp. 29-30 of written transcript).

DESPITE THE CORDIAL RELATIONS HE HAD MAINTAINED WITH DR. SHAWARBI AND OTHER FAIR-SKINNED MUSLIMS: *WWG*, pp. 62-63. In 1960, for instance, Shawarbi had addressed a large audience in Malcolm's Temple No. 7.

LOMAX WAS NOT FOOLED: *TKBM*, pp. 93-96. *WWG*, pp. 62-63.

NEITHER WALLACE NOR PHILBERT WERE FOOLED: John Facenda interviewing Wallace Muhammad, WCAU-TV (Philaelphia), Nov. 12, 1978. Interview: Philbert Little.

EVEN HIS WIFE: *Pittsburgh Courier* (national edition), March 6, 1965. *JHC*, p. 141. *MX*, p. 339. Also filmed ABC News interview with "Betty X," Feb. 23, 1965.

HE HAD KNOWN FOR YEARS: *TKBM*, pp. 93-96. *PG*, pp. 160-161. (When a group of white-skinned Muslim Arabs took Malcolm to task for espousing Elijah Muhammad's white devil theory, he replied that it was necessary to teach that whites were devils in order to "wake up the deaf, dumb, and blind American Negro." [*TKBM*, pp. 93-96.])

"I FELT LIKE HE WAS MY FATHER": *MX*, p. 335. (Emphasis Malcolm's.) Also see *MX*, p. 332, where Malcolm says Azzam Pasha embraced him as if he were "a long-lost child."

ACCOMPANIED BY DEPUTY CHIEF OF PROTOCOL: Press release of April 19, 1964 letter from Jedda. *MX*, pp. 335, 341.

HARAKAN: "Harakan" is the correct spelling, according to Herman Eilts, who was the U.S. ambassador to Saudi Arabia in 1964.

265 "I ANSWERED HIM AS TRULY AS I COULD": Press release of April 19, 1964 letter from Jedda. *MX*, p. 335.

THE COURT SEEMED TO UNDERSTAND: Azzam Pasha got the feeling that Faisal had sent the *hajj* court a message. (Charis Waddy, *The Muslim Mind* (Longman, 1976), p. 107.) Moreover, it would have been hard for Harakan to overlook the significance of the fact that Faisal's deputy chief of protocol had escorted Malcolm to the court. (*MX*, p. 341). Malcolm later told Christine Johnson that Faisal had facilitated his journey to Mecca.

THE RITUALS EACH PILGRIM PERFORMS DURING THE HAJJ: *MX*, pp. 336-340. Also see the following sources, which spell the relevant Arabic words differently than Malcolm's autobiography does: "The Hajj: Special Issue," *Aramco World Magazine*, Nov.-Dec., 1974. David Edwin Long, *The Hajj Today* (State University of New York Press, 1979). *Shorter Encyclopedia of Islam* (section on Hajj). D. Lewis, et al, eds., *The Encyclopedia of Islam*. *National Geographic* (Vol. 154, No. 5), Nov., 1978, pp. 581-607. *Encyclopedia Britannica*, 1967.

45. Tailoring the Teachings

267 GUEST OF STATE; "SHAMELESSLY": *MX*, pp. 341-343. Sept. 29, 1964 airgram from U.S. Embassy, Jedda, to U.S. State Department.

AUDIENCE WITH FAISAL: *MX*, pp. 347-348. Malcolm's autobiography says that Faisal also told him there was "no reason for sincere people to allow themselves to be misled."

LETTER-WRITING CAMPAIGN: *MX*, pp. 338-339, 412. *PG*, p. 168. Letters and postcards from El-Hajj Malik El-Shabazz to Howard Bannister, Christine Johnson, C. Eric Lincoln, M. S. Handler, and others. Interview: James Hicks.

LETTERS TO C. ERIC LINCOLN: May 19, 1964 and May 20, 1964 postcards from El-Hajj Malik El-Shabazz to C. Eric Lincoln.

268 OUTWARDLY SUDDEN CONVERSION: "I learned the truth in Mecca," Malcolm asserts in *MX*, p. 375.

"REARRANGE": *NYT*, May 8, 1964. Also see *FBI*, 1/20/65, p. 17 and *MX*, p. 340.

TRUE ISLAM PRECLUDES RACISM: *SPKS*, p. 60.

POINTED OUT THAT MUSLIM ARABS HAD ENSLAVED BLACK AFRICANS: *TKBM*, pp. 94-95. "Arabs sold slaves," Malcolm said. [*Malcolm X on Afro-American History* (Pathfinder Press, 1970), p. 39.]

LETTER FOR THE PRESS; POCKETED THE LETTER: Interview: Sharon 10X. *MX*, p. 339.

STILL HAD EYES FOR PRETTY WOMEN: *MX*, pp. 353, 354, 358.

"MORAL WEAKNESS": *MX*, pp. 348-349.

WOMEN SHOULD DRESS "MODESTLY": *Ebony* (June, 1969), p. 181.

269 "ALL ESPIONAGE AGENTS": *New York Journal American*, July 25, 1964. Malcolm later denied that he had made the statement. (May 14, 1964 airgram from American Embassy, Lagos to U.S. Dept. of State.)

DATHORNE'S CHALLENGE: Dathorne was not chased off campus, as *MX*, pp. 350-351 asserts. Abram V. Martin, "Apartheit and Malcolm X," *The New Leader* (June 22, 1964), pp. 8-9. May 12, 1964 telegram from American Consulate, Ibadan, to U.S. Dept. of State. *New York Amsterdam News*, March 20, 1965. Interview: O. R. Dathorne. Feb. 11, 1979 letter from Abram Martin to author. March 26, 1979 letter from E. U. Essien-Udom to author. (Professor Essien-Udom reports that, to the best of his knowledge, there is no truth in *MX*'s assertion that Dr. Dathorne challenged Malcolm at the behest of an unnamed "white-influenced" agency with which Dathorne was allegedly seeking employment.)

270 DISTASTE FOR NOI-LIKE SECURITY PRECAUTIONS: See chapter 57.

SAID HE "RESPECTED" NKRUMAH'S INDISCRIMINATE SECURITY PRECAUTIONS: *MX*, p. 356.

LAVISHLY PRAISED NKRUMAH DESPITE DISAPPOINTING RECEPTION: *PG*, pp. 176, 177. Additional praise appears in *MX*, pp. 356-357.

NAME-DROPPING: *PG*, p. 88. *MX*, pp. 353-359, et al. *BP*, p. 155. Interview: Frank Ford.

"YOU LOOK MORE LIKE A WHITE MAN THAN A NEGRO"; "NOBODY"; "I WAS ACCEPTED.": Maya Angelou, *All God's Children Need Traveling Shoes* (Random House, 1986), pp. 136-138. (Angelou's book asserts that Malcolm spoke at "Legon University." What she apparently meant was the University of Ghana at Legon. [See *JHC*, p. 223 and *PG*, p. 176.])

FOUNTAINHEAD OF PAN-AFRICANISM: *MX*, p. 352.

LETTER-WRITING GAMBIT: Floyd Barbour (ed.), *The Black Power Revolt* (Porter Sargent, 1968), p. 244. *SPKS*, pp. 62-63.

AMPLIFIED THE THEME: *BAMN*, pp. 145-146.

ENCOUNTERS MUHAMMAD ALI: Maya Angelou, *supra.*, pp. 142-146. *MX*, p. 359. *PG*, p. 178.

MALCOLM'S TELEGRAM AND CLAY'S RESPONSE: *New York Post*, May 18, 1964. *MX*, pp. 358, 359. *NYT*, May 18, 1964.

271 "LITTLE MALCOLM": Interviews: Irv Kupcinet, Raymond Hightower.

LACKED CONFIDENCE: Interview: Anas Mahmoud Luqman.

"FIVE AMBASSADORS": *MX*, p. 360. Maya Angelou, *supra.*, pp. 142-146. (According to

Angelou, seven ambassadors, not five, went to the airport to see Malcolm off.)

GHANAIAN TIMES CRITICIZES MALCOLM: *JHC*, pp. 224-225. *NYT*, May 21, 1964.

OSTENSIBLY UNAWARE: *MX*, p. 360. Note Malcolm's inclusion of the word "honestly" in his disclaimer. (*MX*, p. 360. Also see *NYT*, May 22, 1964 and *PG*, p. 182.)

272 "MY TRIP TO MECCA HAS OPENED MY EYES" *MX*, pp. 412-413.

ESTABLISHED AFFILIATION WITH ORTHODOX ISLAM: *MX*, p. 361.

PLANS TO ESTABLISH A MOSQUE IN CHICAGO: *Chicago Tribune*, May 23, 1964.

ATTEMPTS TO WOO AWAY: *FBI*, Jan. 20, 1965, p. 75.

"THESE GENERALIZATIONS"; NO LONGER SUBSCRIBE TO A BLANKET INDICTMENT OF ALL WHITES; "I INTEND TO BE CAREFUL": Pages 1-2 of transcript of Malcolm's May 23, 1964 Chicago debate with Louis Lomax. *NYT*, May 24, 1964. Floyd Barbour, ed., *The Black Power Revolt* (Porter Sergeant, 1968), p. 240. Also see *MX*, p. 362 and *SPKS*, p. 58. (The phrase "to some white people" in *SPKS*, p. 58 should be "to some whites," according to the original transcript of Malcolm's speech.)

BEARD: *Chicago Daily News*, May 22, 1964. *New York Post*, May 22, 1964. *New York Amsterdam News*, May 30, 1964. *MX*, pp. 337, 412, 413. "Eyes on the Prize," WLVT-TV, Allentown, Pa., Jan. 15, 1990.

WASN'T THE FIRST TIME: *FBI*, May 4, 1953, p. 6. *New York Amsterdam News*, July 11, 1959. *EWWS*, p. 13. Also see the records of the Bureau of Identification of the Massachusetts Department of Public Safety.

NO MORE PSYCHOSOMATIC COMPLAINTS: Interview: Leona Turner.

ZEST RETURNED; ELATED: Interviews: Tom Wallace, Leona Turner, Pat Robinson. (Note how frequently the theme "respect and recognition" appears in Malcolm's speeches.)

"THEY MUST HAVE GIVEN HIM SOME MONEY"; PHYSICALLY THREATENED: *PG*, pp. 182-184. *Afro-American* (Magazine Section), Feb. 19, 1966. Interviews: Robert 35X, confidential source.

"THEY WON'T LET ME TURN THE CORNER. I'M CAUGHT IN A TRAP!" : *MX*, p. 424. Also see *PG*, pp. 224-225, where Malcolm smiles and reminds James Farmer that if a political leader makes too sharp a turn, "he turns alone."

POLITICAL TIGHTROPE: *Brother Malcolm* (a pamphlet published May, 1965 by the Malcolm X Memorial Committee), p. 17.

TELLING EACH CAMP WHAT IT WANTED TO HEAR: Interview: Edward Jacko. "I tailored the teachings," Malcolm later told Alex Haley. (*MX*, p. 219. Also see p. 221.)

RELIGION A PRIVATE MATTER: *BAMN*, p. 180. "Ballots or Bullets," a phonograph record produced by First Amendment Records (Jamie/Guyden, distributor).

273 BEFORE CHURCH GROUPS, PLAYS DOWN ISLAMIC TIES: Interview: Robert Little.

EFFORTS TO DISASSOCIATE HIMSELF FROM SEPARATISM WITHOUT REPUDIATING SEPARATIST SUPPORT: *BAMN*, pp. 104-105. *PG*, p. 188. *LYMX*, pp. 57-64. *SPKS*, p. 63. Transcript of May 23, 1964 Chicago debate with Louis Lomax, p. 4. *FBI*, June 18, 1964, p. 1; July 2, 1964, page number unclear. Interview: Benjamin Goodman.

WITHOUT BURNING HIS SEPARATIONIST BRIDGES: "Ballots or Bullets" record, *supra*. Phonograph record entitled "Malcolm X Speaks to the People in Harlem" (Up Front Records; record #UPF-152.)

REDEFINES "BLACK NATIONALISM": *LYMX*, pp. 57-68. *SPKS*, pp. 19-21, 38-41. (Compare with pp. 9-10). *TKBM*, p. 139.

"ONLY"; "NO MORE": Phonograph record entitled "Malcolm X Speaking" (Ethnic Records; record #E-1265). *SPKS*, p. 38.

"THE COMPLETE PHYSICAL INDEPENDENCE OF THE BLACK PEOPLE IN THIS COUNTRY": "Malcolm X Speaking," *supra*.

SHIFT FROM BLACK NATIONALISM TO AFRO-AMERICANISM: *SPKS*, pp. 212-213. *LYMX*, pp. 64-66. *JHC*, p. 263. Also see *PG*, pp. 179-181.

274 NEW, NON-ANTI-WHITE IMAGE: *MX*, p. 367. *Life*, March 5, 1965, p. 28. Arna Bontemps & Jack Conroy, *Anyplace But Here* (Hill & Wang, 1966), p. 28. CBS newsfilm of June 8, 1964 interview. *FBI*, July 2, 1964, p. 3. *BAMN*, p. 78. *JHC*, pp. 206-207. Tape recording of Jan. 28, 1965 broadcast by New York City radio station WBAI-FM.

HAD BEEN SPEAKING FOR ELIJAH MUHAMMAD: CBS newsfilm of July 2, 1964 interview.

ETHEL MINOR: Interview: confidential source. (Also see *FBI*, July 23, 1964, pp. 1-2 and *Muhammad Speaks*, Jan. 15, 1963 and April 15, 1963.)

275   HE HAD ENORMOUS SELF-CONTROL: "When Malcolm was in Cairo," says Milton Henry, "plenty of women ran up to him and tried to seduce him. He wouldn't yield. And I mean a lot of girls tried to make him." (Interview: Milton Henry.) Mr. Henry told a reporter, "When [Malcolm and I] were in Cairo together, there were so many pretty girls, but he acted like they weren't even there." (*New York Amsterdam News*, March 13, 1965.)

SARA MITCHELL: Interview: Pat Robinson. (I was unable to locate Sara Mitchell.)

ATTEMPT TO BURY RACIST IMAGE: "I'm not a racist." (*SPKS*, p. 96. *BAMN*, p. 152.) Also see *PG*, p. 227.

THE REAL ENEMY IS THE JEW: Interview: Brother Jamil.

JEWS "DEAREST FRIENDS": *NYT*, October 4, 1964. *MX*, p. 375.

LIMITED TO ISLAMIC WHITES: *FBI*, Jan. 20, 1965, p. 17.

COLLECTIVELY STILL A BAD LOT: *PG*, p. 183.

DENIED HE HAD CHANGED, THEN DECLARED HE HAD ACQUIRED A BROADER PERSPECTIVE; HAS TO BE GIVEN A CHANCE, BUT PROBABLY WON'T TAKE IT: *SPKS*, p. 213. *PG*, p. 226.

"WHITEY": *BAMN*, p. 56.

"DOMINEERING, EGO-RIDDEN WHITES: *MX*, p. 274.

BUNCHE'S "INTERNATIONAL MOUTH" ALWAYS OPEN: *Chicago Defender*, April 25, 1963. *Playboy* (May, 1963), p. 56.

MANIPULATING THE PRESS: Phonograph record entitled "The Last Message" (Discus Hablands LP #1300).

POLITICAL ACTORS: Tape recording of Jan. 23, 1963 speech at Michigan State University. *EWWS*, pp. 145-146. *SPKS*, p. 17.

276   DESCRIBES KING AS "A FRIEND": December, 1964 newspaper clipping, a copy of which appears in the FBI files on Malcolm. It is unclear what newspaper the article was published in. (It may have been the *New York Herald Tribune*.)

"I HAVE NO CRITICISM OF HIM WHATSOEVER": "Malcolm X Speaks to the People in Harlem" (Up Front Records; phonograph record #UPF-152.)

THE "UNCLE TOMS" ARE THE ONES WHO TELL PEOPLE WHAT THEY WANT TO HEAR: Page 11 of undated transcript of undated Black Muslim meeting. (C. Eric Lincoln Collection, Atlanta University Center Library.) Tape-recording of question and answer session following 1960 speech at Boston University. (In 1960, Malcolm made two speeches at Boston University. Since one of the resultant tape-recordings may have been misdated, it is unclear which speech is the relevant one.)

REVEREND KLUNDER'S DEATH: *BAMN*, pp. 25, 28. *New York Amsterdam News*, April 11, 1964. *NYT*, April 7-10, 1964.

"I SAY ONE THING IN HARLEM AND ANOTHER DOWNTOWN.": *PG*, p. 224.

CAPACITY FOR POLITICAL AMBIGUITY: Interview: Sharon 10X.

"ALL OF THEM MIGHT NOT BE GUILTY. BUT MOST OF THEM ARE.": *BAMN*, pp. 54, 55. Also see *JHC*, pp. 327, 302-303 and *PG*, p. 185.

MISQUOTED OR MISUNDERSTOOD: *The Record* [Bergen, N.J.], June 16, 1964.

"THE ENEMY OF MY ENEMY IS MY FRIEND": *Ibid.*, June 17, 1964. *PG*, p. 189.

ONLY TALKING ABOUT A WOLF: *Esquire*, October, 1964.

277   RELATIONSHIP BETWEEN MALCOLM AND SOCIALIST WORKERS PARTY: *LYMX*, pp. 33-34. George Breitman, *Malcolm X: The Man and His Ideas* (Merit Publishers, 1969), pp. 17-18. *Village Voice*, May 29, 1990. *PG*, pp. 233-235. (Also see pp. 161-162, 189.) Interviews: two confidential sources.

PLAYED UP ECONOMIC ISSUES: Interview: Robert Little.

MARX-LIKE PREDICTION ABOUT THE INEVITABILITY OF A SHOWDOWN: *LYMX*, p. 38.

"IT IS IMPOSSIBLE FOR CAPITALISM TO SURVIVE"; "ONLY A MATTER OF TIME":

BAMN, pp. 165-166.

"MONOPOLY CAPITAL" WAS THE "PRIME MOVER": *JHC*, p. 348.

"IMPOSSIBLE" TO BELIEVE IN CAPITALISM WITHOUT BELIEVING IN RACISM: *SPKS*, p. 69. *JHC*, pp. 251-253.

"THEN I'M FOR IT": *PG*, pp. 234-235.

"I'M FLEXIBLE.": *SPKS*, p. 69. Also see *MX*, p. 428.

"FLEXIBILITY": *MX*, pp. 420-421.

278 "NO"; THE QUESTION ANSWERED ITSELF: *BAMN*, p. 12.

SKULL AND CROSSBONES: *The Liberator* (May, 1965), p. 13. *TKBM*, p. 173.

CHICKEN EGG VS. DUCK EGG: *SPKS*, pp. 68-69.

EAGLE VS. VULTURE: *BAMN*, pp. 165-166.

"VULTURISTIC": *SPKS*, p. 121. Also *SPKS*, p. 70, *JHC*, p. 261, and the unedited tape-recording of the Jan. 28, 1965 interview by representatives of the Young Socialist Alliance.

"THIS IS THE FARTHEST I'VE EVER GONE. THEY WILL GO WILD OVER THIS.": *LYMX*, pp. 38, 138.

LITTLE APPLICABILITY: *BAMN*, pp. 12-13. *FBI*, June 18, 1964 (page number unclear).

DANGER OF LEFTIST INFILTRATION: *FBI*, Jan. 20, 1965, p. 29. The unclearly written report says the FBI was informed that OAAU members "must be careful of communist and socialist groups trying to infiltrate the organization. Persons from these latter groups would be permitted to join the OAAU, but would not be allowed to hold positions of membership." [Perhaps the person who typed the report meant "responsibility" or "authority" instead of "membership."] Also note that when Malcolm was in the Nation of Islam, he delayed the ordination of a prospective NOI minister because of rumors the man was communist or homosexual or both. (*PG*, p. 108.)

PUBLICLY REPROACHED SOME COMMUNISTS: *BP*, p. 113.

APPEARED TO BE FOR SALE: *LYMX*, pp. 137-138.

279 NEVER SOLD COPIES OF *THE MILITANT*: Interviews: Sharon 10X, Charles 37X, James 67X.

ASSERTED HE WASN'T A POLITICIAN: "I am not a politician," Malcolm asserted. "I'm not even a student of politics." (*EPPS*, p. 134.) Similar statements appear in *EPPS*, p. 156; *SPKS*, p. 25; and a May 1, 1962 speech entitled "The Crisis of Racism."

WHAT THEY WANTED TO HEAR: Interviews: Edward Jacko, Saladin Matthews. "Tell him just what he wants to hear," Malcolm advised one audience. ("Malcolm X Speaks to the People in Harlem" [Up Front Records; phonograph record #UPF-152.]) See *PG*, p. 221.

CHAMELEON: Suggesting that Malcolm was keeping his real beliefs to himself, Dick Schaap wrote in the March 22, 1964 issue of the *New York Herald Tribune*: "It is impossible to take Malcolm X's words seriously -- unless you are willing to accept, at various times, both sides of every question. Sooner or later, he works both sides." Art Carter wrote in the Feb. 22, 1965 issue of the *Afro-American*: "Malcolm X . . . . often contradicted himself and many times appeared to be talking out of both sides of his mouth." In the 2/25/65 *Village Voice*, Malcolm acknowledged the need "to play" each audience differently.

46. The Politics of Manhood

280 "IT'S FREEDOM FOR EVERYBODY OR FREEDOM FOR NOBODY": Phonograph record entitled "Ballots or Bullets," (First Amendment Records: Jamie/Guyden Distributing Corp.).

281 DIDN'T BELIEVE JESUS HAD OPPOSED THE USE OF FORCE: *TKBM*, p. 208.

MICE AND ELEPHANTS: *Life*, May 31, 1963, p. 78.

"WHAT DO WE CARE ABOUT ODDS?": "Ballots or Bullets" record, *supra*. Also see *BAMN*, p. 154; *SPKS*, p. 68; *JHC*, pp. 215-216; tape-recording of April 8, 1964 speech sponsored by Militant Labor Forum.

MIGHT END UP INSIDE GAS OVENS: Phonograph record entitled "The Last Message" (Discus Hablands LP#1300.)

"NOT ONE IOTA OF PROGRESS": *SPKS*, p. 52. Tape recording of April 8, 1964 speech, *supra*.

TRICKERY: *MX*, pp. 242-243. Also see *SPKS*, p. 53.

1964 CIVIL RIGHTS ACT: *BAMN*, pp. 78-80.

IMPATIENT: *MX*, pp. 34, 195-196. Tape recording of Jan. 7, 1965 speech sponsored by the Militant Labor Forum. *SPKS*, p. 33. *BAMN*, pp. 82, 119. Interview: Benjamin Goodman.

282 "AN OLD WOMAN CAN SIT. A COWARD CAN SIT. IT TAKES A MAN TO STAND.": Tape-recording of "Malcolm X: A Retrospective" (broadcast March 30, 1965 by New York City radio station WBAI).

WOMANISH: "Malcolm X: A Retrospective," *supra. BP*, p. 126. Malcolm also described nonviolence as "unmanning." James Cone, *Martin & Malcolm in America* (Orbis Books, 1991), p. 107.

"COWARDLY": *BP*, p. 40. James Cone, *supra.*, p. 176. "Malcolm X: A Retrospective," *supra*. Tape-recording of Jan. 23, 1963 speech at Michigan State University.

THE WAY HE SOMETIMES TALKED ABOUT KING: *BP*, p. 40. Tape-recording of Jan. 23, 1963 speech at Michigan State University.

"AFRAID TO BLEED": *SPKS*, p. 7. The second time Malcolm said it, he placed considerable emphasis on the word "afraid." (Phonograph record entitled "Malcolm X: Grass Roots Speech," Paul Winley Records, stereo record #134.)

THE TEST OF MANHOOD IS WILLINGNESS TO COMMIT VIOLENCE: As Malcolm was describing the "Simbas" who had taken up arms against the Congolese government, he said, "They are men. They are men – the proof of which is that they are dying to get their freedom." (*BAMN*, p. 149.) "I don't mean one-way dying," he explained to another groups of listeners. "Dying must be reciprocal. . . . [There must be] some dying on both sides." (*BAMN*, p. 84.) He characterized nonviolent protest as "boyish" and "unmanning." (*New York Times Magazine*, March 22, 1964, p. 104. James Cone, *Martin & Malcolm in America* (Orbis Books, 1991, p. 107. Also see *SPKS*, p. 67 and "Like It Is," WABC-TV, Feb. 22, 1969.)

"YOU'RE GOING TO HAVE TO FIGHT!": *BAMN*, p. 154. (Also see "The Wit and Wisdom of Malcolm X," Douglas Record Company.)

"I'LL BUST YOU IN YOUR MOUTH!" Tape-recording of May 1, 1962 speech entitled "The Crisis of Racism."

CHUMP INSTEAD OF A CHAMP: *WWG*, p. 86. Don Atyeo & Felix Dennis, *The Holy Warrior: Muhammad Ali* (Fireside Books, 1975), pp. 39-42.

"IT'S TIME TO STOP SINGING AND START SWINGING": Phonograph record entitled "Ballots or Bullets," *supra*.

283 "I MEAN, . . . WHAT YOU HAVE TO DO": Phonograph record entitled "The Last Message," *supra*.

"I'M MAN ENOUGH!": Filmed CBS interview, June 8, 1964. *TKBM*, p. 230. Malcolm's affirmation of his manhood had nothing to do with the subjects being discussed. It was another example of his extraordinary ability to talk about one thing while he was thinking about something else. (*MX*, p. 390.)

"I DON'T HAVE TO SAY I'M A MAN.": *New Statesman*, June 12, 1964, pp. 901-902.

KEPT ON SAYING IT: Filmed CBS interview, July 8, 1964. *SPKS*, p. 197. *MX*, p. 428.

AMBIGUOUS: Alex Haley writes that Malcolm "relished" making ambiguous statements. (*MX*, pp. 395-396. Also see *MX*, p. 350.)

THE "POLITICS OF MANHOOD": Jan. 13, 1981 and March 6, 1981 letters from Calvin Hernton to author.

"AS IF YOU COULD KILL ALL THE WHITE PEOPLE": *EPPS*, p. 163. See similar statement on phonograph record entitled "By Any Means Necessary" (Douglas Records: record #Z30743).

"OR AS IF [YOU] SHOULDN'T": *SPKS*, p. 92.

"ACTIVE SELF-DEFENSE": *Boston Globe* (P.M. edition), March 9, 1964.

BUT THE IRONIC WAY HE SAID IT OFTEN CONVEYED THE OPPOSITE IMPRESSION: Malcolm's audience laughed and applauded when he said that though his followers were nonviolent, they were encouraged – for purposes of self-defense – to study judo, karate, and "everything else you should learn that will show you how to break a white man's neck." (*NYT*, Dec. 2, 1963.) Another audience laughed when he sarcastically told it, "I don't believe in violence. Uh, that's why I want to stop it." (Phonograph record entitled "The Last Message" [Discus Hablands LP #1300].)

"I DON'T KNOW": *MX*, pp. 395-396.

"I'LL DO THE SAME THING − ONLY MORE OF IT": *SPKS*, pp. 197-198.

PERHAPS TO PROTECT HIMSELF AGAINST PROSECUTION: Referring to Robert Williams, who had been deported to Cuba for violating the law, Malcolm said, "When someone in front of you makes a mistake, you should learn and benefit from those mistakes." (*BAMN*, p. 29.)

VIOLENCE WOULD "BE JUSTIFIED" : *SPKS*, p. 43. "And we don't do anything illegal," he sarcastically added. ("The Wisdom of Malcolm X" [Mo' Soul Records; record #MS-8001]).

BLOOD BROTHERS: *New York Post*, May 8, 10, 1964. *SPKS*, pp. 64-66. *MX*, p. 350.

284 BRIEFING ON GUERILLA WARFARE"; THE CROWD WENT WILD: Warner Brothers film documentary entitled "Malcolm X." Phonograph record entitled "Malcolm X: By Any Means Necessary" (Douglas Communication Corp.; record #Z-30743.)

ALTERNATELY ADMITTED AND DENIED THAT HE WAS TRYING TO STIR PEOPLE UP: *PG*, p. 17. Warner Brothers film documentary entitled "Malcolm X." Also see unedited tape-recording of April 8, 1964 speech entitled "The Black Revolution."

NEITHER COMMITTED POLITICAL VIOLENCE NOR DIRECTED HIS FOLLOWERS TO DO SO: "No, no," Malcolm declared when asked if he were directing his followers to "take action" against his enemies. (*BP*, p. 136.) Also see: Bill Moyers interviewing Andrew Young, TV Channel 12 (Philadelphia), April 2, 1978. *PG*, pp. 93, 204-205. *FBI*, Feb. 2, 1965, p. 2.

REFUSED TO SEND ACTION-ORIENTED MEN SOUTH; THE BROTHERS LEFT MALCOLM'S ORGANIZATION: Interview: Benjamin Goodman. Also *FBI*, Jan. 20, 1965, pp. 13-14.

OPPOSED "OCCUPATION" OF WHITE-OWNED BUSINESSES: Interview: James Hicks.

REFUSED TO COUNTENANCE SEIZURE OF TEMPLE SEVEN: Interview: Robert 35X.

"EVEN I PREFER BALLOTS TO BULLETS": *PG*, p. 224.

"IF ANY OF THEM SMILES, IT'S 'CAUSE . . . HE'S A BROTHER.": *PG*, pp. 22, 204-205. "Who Killed Malcolm X?" Channel 13 TV, Dallas, Tex., Feb. 22, 1972. Warner Brothers film documentary entitled "Malcolm X." "Like It Is." WABC-TV, Feb. 22, 1969. *New York Journal-American*, March 16, 1964. Also see phonograph record entitled "Malcolm X Speaks to the People in Harlem" (Up Front Records; record #UPF-152.)

PROTECTED WHITE REPORTERS: Interview: Ken Gross.

"KILL THE BASTARD!"; "BUT WE KNOW HOW TO LAUGH": *New York Post*, April 10, 1964. *PG*, p. 15. *MX*, p. 395.

285 AFRAID WHAT WOULD HAPPEN; MOUNTED THE HOOD OF A CAR; PERSUADED THE THRONG TO DISPERSE: *MX*, pp. 311-312. *TKBM*, pp. 136-137.

DENIED HE'D JUMP ATOP A VEHICLE TO STOP A RIOT: *PG*, p. 206.

IRONIC SMILES: *New York Herald Tribune*, Feb. 22, 1965. Warner Brothers film documentary entitled "Malcolm X."

RAMPAGE "INTELLIGENTLY": *SPKS*, p. 94.

THEY SHOULDN'T BURN DOWN THEIR OWN HOUSES: *PG*, p. 204.

THROW PUNCHES AT THE RIGHT TIME: The tape-recording containing this material is labeled "Nov. 7, 1963 speech at CCNY." But the recording may have been mislabeled and misdated.

COCKED FIST; THREATENING VIOLENCE VS. USING VIOLENCE: *PG*, pp. 65, 194, 227. "Only violence, or a real threat of it, will get results," Malcolm told Marlene Nadle. (*Village Voice*, Feb. 25, 1965.) Pages 77, 149 of his autobiography strongly suggest that he felt that attempts to implement the threat would be counterproductive.

ORATORICAL JOE LOUIS: *MX*, p. 350.

BRINKMANSHIP: *PG*, pp. 153, 227. Recall how, many years earlier, Malcolm had terrorized the owners of the bicycles he had "borrowed" by riding as close as possible to their owners without running them down.

INSTRUCTED ALEX HALEY NOT TO REVEAL THAT HE HAD BEEN BLUFFING: *MX*, pp. 142-143, 415-416.

ASSERTED READINESS TO KILL: *MX*, pp. 22, 130, 131, 138.

VIOLENCE PURELY VERBAL: *PG*, p. 227.

ASTUTE COMPROMISE: Cora Spencer, "A Psychological Evaluation of the Political Perspectives of Malcolm X" (unpublished paper; Jan., 1970), p. 13. (Cora was the student who kindled my interest in Malcolm X.)

286   EARTHA KITT: *BP*, p. 34. May 17, 1979 letter from Calvin Hernton to author. Calvin Hernton, "The Negro Male" in Doris Y. Wilkinson & Ronald C. Taylor (eds.), *The Black Male in America* (Nelson-Hall, 1977), p. 253.

"THE PERSONIFICATION OF THAT PART OF ME . . . ": *New York Amsterdam News*, Feb. 27, 1965.

"TAUGHT ME TO BE MEAN AND . . . [TO] HATE": Undated clipping in the files of the *New York Amsterdam News*.

47. Another Eviction

288   CAMPAIGN RENEWED: In addition to the sources cited below, see: Undated U.S. Secret Service file on Malcolm, section entitled "Origin & History," p. 2. *FBI*, June 8, 1964, p. 1; June 9, 1964, p. 1; July 2, 1964, p. 2. *MX*, p. 421. *Boston Herald*, Feb. 22, 1965. Aubrey Barnette, "The Black Muslims are a Fraud," *Saturday Evening Post*, Feb. 27, 1965.

ILLEGITIMATE CHILDREN; PREARRANGED QUESTION; WOULD EVEN MURDER: *FBI*, Jan. 20, 1965, pp. 3, 4, 22. Also *FBI*, June 9, 1964, p. 1.

CHARGES REITERATED; "OH, YES. I PROBABLY AM A DEAD MAN ALREADY.": CBS newsfilm, June 8, 1964.

AIRED CHARGES IN BOSTON: *FBI*, June 12, 1964, p. 3; Jan. 20, 1965, pp. 22-23, 60. Also see *FBI*, June 22, 24, & 26, 1964.

NO LONGER BELIEVED IN POLITICAL SEPARATION; "WE HAVE TO BE REALISTIC"; "AFRICA IS A LONG WAY OFF": *FBI*, June 18, 1964, pp. 1-2. PG, p. 148. *LYMX*, pp. 62-64.

289   RODNELL MISSING; ELLA NOT PARTICULARLY UPSET: *FBI*, June 18, 1964, pp. 1, 5.

ASPIRATIONS: Interview: Heshaam Jaaber.

CONCILIATORY STATEMENTS: *NYT*, June 27, 1964.

ON JUNE 20, JUNE 22, & JUNE 25: *The Philadelphia Tribune*, June 20, 1964. *FBI*, Jan. 20, 1965, pp. 23, 61, 62; July 2, 1964, p. 2.

TELEPHONES NEWSMAN AT THREE A.M.: *PG*, p. 130. Interview: Claude Lewis.

CALLAHAN TUNNEL INCIDENT: *Boston Globe*, June 15, 1964. *New York World-Telegram*, June 18, 1964. *New York Herald Tribune*, June 18, 1964. *The Philadelphia Tribune*, June 20, 1964. *PG*, p. 194. *MX*, p. 422.

ASSERTED THAT ELIJAH WAS THE ONE WHO WOULDN'T LET SLEEPING DOGS LIE: *New York Herald Tribune*, June 16, 1964. *BP*, pp. 117-118.

MARKED MAN: *MX*, p. 411.

NOI LOSING MEMBERS: *Chicago Defender*, July 9, 1964. *Chicago's American*, Sept. 15, 1964. *FBI*, June 18, 1964, p. 4. Aubrey Barnett, *supra*. Interview: Christine Johnson.

MALCOLM ACCUSED: *Egyptian Gazette*, August 17, 1964. *FDL*, pp. 206-207. Interview: Sharon 10X.

"SO WHAT IF HE IS NOT ALL PURE" *FBI*, Jan. 20, 1965, p. 71.

GREAT DESPITE MORAL LAPSES: *Muhammad Speaks*, August 14, 1964.

290   "HE DID MORE FOR YOU THAN YOUR REAL PARENTS EVER COULD": *Muhammad Speaks*, July 3, 1964.

MIXED MESSAGES AT TEMPLE SEVEN: *FBI*, Jan. 20, 1965, p. 71.

SHOULD BE KILLED: *FBI*, Jan. 20, 1965, p. 75.

"GRAVE CONSEQUENCES": *Muhammad Speaks*, July 31, 1964.

"NOT TO BE KILLED"; "LIKE A PARENT DOES A CHILD": *Ibid*. Also *PG*, p. 203.

SECURITY PRECAUTIONS: *New York World-Telegram*, June 18, 1964. *New York Herald Tribune*, June 16, 1964. *PG*, p. 195. *MX*, p. 421.

DOORBELL RINGERS HELP SUTTON WIN: Interviews: Oliver Sutton, Percy Sutton. *PG*, p. 152.

291 HAD SET HIMSELF UP: *JHC*, p. 138. Also *PG*, p. 196. Though Malcolm refused to put the title to his home in his own name, he admonished his followers, "You should own your own home." (*FBI*, Apr. 23 [year unclear], p. 38.)

INADVERTENTLY ACKNOWLEDGED: Trial transcript, Landlord & Tenant Case #4845, Queens Civil Court, 1964 Special Term, Part I, p. 211.

SUTTON'S FALL-BACK DEFENSE AND MALCOLM'S TESTIMONY: Trial transcript, *supra.*, pp. 157, 159, 165, 181, 201, 205, 218. *PG*, pp. 194-198.

NOT HIS USUAL SELF; ANGRILY TRIED TO INTERRUPT; "MORE OF A FIGHT THAN THE SITUATION WARRANTED": *New York World Telegram*, June 18, 1964. Trial transcript, *supra.*, pp. 146, 165. *PG*, p. 195. Interviews: Morris Sayburn, Maurice Wahl.

292 ARRESTED EIGHTEEN TIMES; $25,000 BRIBE: May 2, 1979 letter from Judge Wahl to author. Interview: Maurice Wahl.

WAHL'S DECISION: Judgment & stay of execution, officially filed and dated Sept. 2, 1964. (Landlord & Tenant Case #4845, *supra.*)

IMAGES OF BURNING OR BURNED-OUT HOMES: Slightly more than a week after the NOI first demanded that Malcolm vacate his home, he made the statements reproduced in *EPPS*, pp. 136-137 and *BAMN*, p. 12. In addition to the sources cited below, see *SPKS*, p. 45; the film entitled "A Tribute to Malcolm"; *PG*, p. 204; & Maya Angelou, *All God's Children Need Traveling Shoes* (Random House, 1986), p. 136.

293 INSTEAD OF THE PERSON BEING THANKFUL, HE MAKES THE MISTAKE OF CHARGING THE ONE WHO AWAKENED HIM WITH HAVING SET THE FIRE: On another level, the statement was also Malcolm's way of saying that Elijah Muhammad should have thanked him for alerting him to the damage Elijah's extra-marital affairs were doing to his reputation, and should not have blamed him for it. (Unedited tape-recording of April 8, 1964 speech at Palm Gardens. The published version of the speech, which appears in *SPKS*, p. 45, is slightly inaccurate.)

RECALLED HIS FATHER'S BEHAVIOR: In the Feb. 22, 1965 *Philadelphia Daily News*, Malcolm said his father was "a clergyman, a Christian, and it was Christians who burned our homes."

"YOU'LL BURN IT DOWN": *SPKS*, p. 103.

"YOU HAVE AS MUCH RIGHT IN THE HOUSE AS THEY"; BURN IT TO THE GROUND!": Unedited tape-recording of Jan. 7, 1965 speech sponsored by the Militant Labor Forum. (The portion of the speech quoted in this chapter was deleted when part of the speech was later published in *SPKS*.)

"YOU GIVE US WHAT WE'VE GOT COMING, OR NOBODY IS GOING TO GET ANYTHING": *BAMN*, p. 100. (See similar statement in *BAMN*, p. 22 and see *MX*, p. 390, where Alex Haley underscores the way Malcolm "could be talking about one thing and thinking of something else."

48. Adam and Malcolm

294 CLAIMED HE HADN'T EVEN BOTHERED: *New York Post Daily Magazine*, Feb. 23, 1965.

FOR MORE THAN A MONTH: *Muhammad Speaks*, May 22, 1964. *PG*, pp. 199-200.

A CHALLENGE: Louis X later described Elijah's June 28 rally as a victory for the NOI in the contest for the allegiance of New York City's Muslims. (*Muhammad Speaks*, Dec. 4, 1964.)

VIOLENT BEHAVIOR: *PG*, pp. 201-202.

295 BLACK POWER: *New York Journal-American*, July 1, 1964. *BAMN*, p. 34. *LYMX*, pp. 105-111. *PG*, pp. 189-190.

OAAU CHARTER: *LYMX*, pp. 105-111. *The Record* (Bergen, N.J.), July 1, 1964. *BAMN*, pp. 45-48, 52.

"WE WANT TO SET THE WORLD ON FIRE": *BAMN*, pp. 5, 60, 62. *FBI*, Jan. 20, 1965, p. 5.

"ANY FAILURES"; "REST THEM RIGHT UPON MY SHOULDERS": *BAMN*, p. 60. Anthony Meleski reports that, whenever the Muslims at Norfolk Prison made demands of the prison administration, Malcolm volunteered to take the blame. Meleski says it was Malcolm's way of showing that he was in charge. (Interview: Anthony Meleski.)

A MAN WITH A BURDEN: Interview: Benjamin Goodman.

"MIND YOU, THIS IS RIGHT.": *Malcolm X on Afro-American History* (Pathfinder Press, 1970), p. 11.

"YOU DO NOTHING TO MAKE HIM LIE TO YOU": Interview: John Elton Bembry.

EARLIER PRONOUNCEMENTS: *NYT*, March 13, 1964. *SPKS*, p. 21. *BAMN*, p. 7.

SHIFTED TACK AND RULED OUT ASSISTANCE FROM WHITES: *BAMN*, p. 58. *LYMX*, p. 109. Also see *MX*, p. 377.

"ISN'T NECESSARILY A FRIEND": *Playboy*, May, 1963, p. 57.

296 OAAU DUES: *Journal-American* (New York), July 1, 1964. *BAMN*, pp. 58-59.

POSSIBILITY OF LARGER CONTRIBUTION: *FBI*, Jan. 20, 1965, pp. 4-5.

MAJORITY DIDN'T EVEN CONTRIBUTE WEEKLY DOLLAR: Confidential source.

INSUFFICIENT FUNDS: Malcolm smiled as he told newsmen he was practically "unsupported." (Newsfilm of June 8, 1964 CBS interview.)

DOUBLEDAY: Doubleday sent the money to Alex Haley's literary agent Paul Reynolds, who deducted his commission and sent Malcolm his portion of the remainder. (Jan. 14, 1980 phone call from Doubleday to author.)

"IT'S EVAPORATED.": *MX*, p. 420.

"WE ARE SCRATCHING"; "TRUE" REVOLUTIONARIES DON'T WORRY ABOUT MONEY: *FBI*, Jan. 20, 1965, citing June 14, 1964 edition of Washington, D.C. *Sunday Star*.

HAD TO BORROW: *PG*, p. 222. Interviews: two confidential sources.

"I'LL LET YOU KNOW"; MALCOLM DECLINED THE OFFER: Interviews: Milton Henry, Harold Hyman. *BAMN*, pp. 14-15. Also see *EPPS*, p. 159.

WOULD NOT SEEK OFFICE: New York *Herald Tribune*, April 23, 1963. *U.S. News & World Report*, March 30, 1964, p. 39. Bill Campbell's radio show "Talk of Philadelphia," WCAU, April 10, 1964. *FBI*, March 13, 1964; June 18, 1964.

297 THE POWER OF WORDS *PG*, p. 35. "He liked power," Robin says.

298 MANIPULATE AUDIENCES: *New York Post*, April 10, 1965. *Village Voice*, Feb. 25, 1965.

"SO MUCH POWER [THAT] WE CAN . . . DO AS WE PLEASE": *BAMN*, p. 64. (Recall Malcolm's earlier threat that, once he and his former Muslim associates obtained power, they would settle accounts with all the "yellow niggers.")

WHO WOULD DOMINATE WHOM: Nathan Leites, *The Study of Bolshevism* (The Free Press, 1953), cited in Lucian Pye, *Mao Tse-tung: The Man in the Leader* (Basic Books, 1976), p. 63.

IMPORTANCE OF POLITICAL POWER: *State News* (Michigan State University), Feb. 21, 1969. *BAMN*, p. 64. Also see the emphasis Malcolm places on power in the tape-recorded, unedited version of the speech he made on Dec. 12, 1964.

IMMORAL AND HYPOCRITICAL: Malcolm's autobiography stresses the immorality and hypocrisy of the white power structure. (Also see, inter alia, *SPKS*, pp. 25, 26; *BAMN*, p. 47, and the phonograph records entitled "Ballots or Bullets" and "Malcolm X Talks to Young People.") For Malcolm's critique of the adults who comprise the power structure, see the unedited, tape-recorded version of the Jan. 18, 1965 interview the Young Socialist conducted.

LIKENED POLITICAL TYRANNY TO PARENTAL TYRANNY: "Beat me, Daddy!" (*BAMN*, p. 42.)

EQUATED THE IMPULSE TO REVOLT WITH YOUTH: *BAMN*, pp. 142, 164-165. (Also see *EPPS*, pp. 143, 156.)

APPLAUDED LIFE PHOTOGRAPH: *SPKS*, p. 8.

"YOUR OWN BROTHERS AND SISTERS AND MOTHERS AND FATHERS . . . . THEY'RE THE ONES WHO STAND IN THE WAY": *SPKS*, p. 134.

DID NOT RULE OUT RACE AGAINST POWELL: New York *Herald Tribune*, April 22, 1963. *WWG*, p. 180. *BMIA*, p. 192.

TOYING WITH THE IDEA SINCE 1960; COULD WIN IF . . .: *WWG*, p. 84. *FBI*, Nov. 17, 1960, cover pages P* and B and pages 17-18. Also *FBI*, August 6, 1963, p. 5 and *Boston Herald*, Feb. 28, 1965.

RUN FOR MAYOR: George Breitman, *Malcolm X: The Man and His Ideas* (Merit Publishers, 1969), p. 15.

"CAN STAY THERE THE REST OF HIS LIFE": *Look*, May 7, 1962, p. 35. Claude Lewis, *Adam Clayton Powell* (Gold Medal Books, 1963), p. 50. Neil Hickey & Ed Edwin, *Adam Clayton Powell and the Politics of Race* (Fleet Publication Corp., 1965), p. 83.

"CONTROL PEOPLE BY THE POWER OF THEIR WORDS": NBC-TV's "White Paper" on Adam Clayton Powell, March 12, 1964.

"I THINK IT'S WONDERFUL": Claude Lewis, supra., p. 72.

THEY ENJOYED IN FANTASY WHAT HE ENJOYED IN REALITY: Claude Lewis, supra., pp. 87-88. David Hapgood, *The Purge that Failed: Tammany vs. Powell* (McGraw Hill, 1959), p. 6. Kent Weeks, *Adam Clayton Powell and the Supreme Court* (Dunellen, 1971), chapter one.

"PAID FOR BY CONGRESS . . . FIRST CLASS ALL THE WAY": NBC-TV's "White Paper" on Adam Clayton Powell, March 12, 1964.

CONCEAL HIS BOTTLES OF GIN: Claude Lewis, supra., pp. 14-15. On page 30 of his autobiography *Adam by Adam* (Dial Press, 1971), Powell says, "The church was a fraud, my father the leading perpetrator."

NO ONE COULD ACCUSE HIM OF BEING A HYPOCRITE: Adam Clayton Powell, Jr., *Adam by Adam: The Autobiography of Adam Clayton Powell, Jr.*, (Dial Press, 1971), p. 235. MX, p. 15.

"I'VE ALWAYS BEEN IN FAVOR OF FEDERAL AID TO EDUCATION": Claude Lewis, supra., p. 63.

ACCUSED OF INCOME TAX EVASION: Neil Hickey and Ed Edwin, supra., pp. 168-170.

"THERE IS NO ROOM FOR POLITICAL TRIALS IN THIS LAND: *New York Times*, April 20, 1960. Neil Hickey and Ed Edwin, supra., p. 173.

MALCOLM ATTENDED THE LENGTHY TRIAL REGULARLY: Neil Hickey and Ed Edwin, supra., p. 170.

CRITICISM BY WHITES HELPED POWELL IN HARLEM: David Hapgood, supra., p. 28. Neil Hickey and Ed Edwin, supra., p. 114. Biographer Claude Lewis recalls that no other congressman had such uniformly bad press. (Claude Lewis, supra., p. 9.)

POWELL'S SKIN COLOR: "Adam Powell Looks white," Malcolm told a Michigan audience. (Transcript of tape recorded question-and-answer session following Jan. 23, 1963 addresss at Michigan State University.) NBC-TV "White Paper" on Adam Clayton Powell, March 12, 1964. Also see the relevant sources below.

WHITE ANCESTORS; SISTER LOOKED WHITE: *Adam by Adam*, supra., pp. 2-4, 14, 28. *Look*, May 7, 1963, p. 32. New York *Amsterdam News*, April 27, 1963. Neil Hickey and Ed Edwin, supra., pp. 2-3, 35-36.

BLONDE HAIR WHEN HE HAD BEEN YOUNG: *Adam by Adam*, supra., pp. 23, 28.

REPEATEDLY BEATEN BECAUSE OF SKIN COLOR: *Adam by Adam*, supra., p. 24. NBC-TV "White Paper" on Adam Clayton Powell, March 12, 1964. Neil Hickey and Ed Edwin, supra., p. 33.

CONVINCED CLASSMATES HE WAS WHITE: *Look*, May 7, 1963. Current Biography, 1942, p. 676. *Adam by Adam*, supra., p. 32. David Hapgood, supra., p. 7. Claude Lewis, supra., pp. 6, 7, 40. Neil Hickey and Ed Edwin, supra., pp. 2, 35.

ROBERT LINCOLN AND ADAM POWELL: *Adam by Adam*, supra., p. 33.

"HE CONSTANTLY HAS TO PROVE HE'S A NEGRO TO NEGROES": David Hapgood, supra., p. 4.

MALCOLM WALKED THROUGH THE DOOR; JACK BOOED OFF THE SPEAKER'S PLATFORM: Neil Hickey and Ed Edwin, supra., pp. 134-135, 139, 141. David Hapgood, supra., pp. 8-21. Television documentary entitled "The Hate that Hate Produced" (1959). *NYT*, May 16-20, 1958.

ADAM COURTED MALCOLM: Interview: Adam Clayton Powell, III. "The Hate that Hate Produced," supra.

ADEPT AT HEADING OFF POTENTIAL CHALLENGERS: Interview: Chuck Stone.

"DEAR FRIEND"; "EXTREMELY CLOSE": *Adam by Adam*, supra., p. 243. "The Hate that Hate Produced," supra. *Chicago Defender*, March 25, 1963. Interview: Chuck Stone. Also see Neil Hickey and Ed Edwin, supra., p. 6 and *PG*, p. 221. Tom Torpor wrote in the June 16, 1964 issue of the Bergen, N.J. *Record* that Adam's "friendship" with Malcolm was a "careful" one.

MALCOLM PROFESSED FRIENDSHIP: New York *Journal-American*, March 12, 1964. *PG*, p. 135.

SERMONS IN POWELL'S CHURCH: New York *Amsterdam News*, June 15, 1957, April 28, 1962. *FBI*, April 30, 1958, pp. 74-75, citing *Herald Dispatch*, August 8, 1957. "The Hate that Hate Produced, supra. *FBI*, 5/17/62, p. 24. New York *Herald Tribune*, June 24, 1963. Neil Hickey and Ed Edwin, supra., p. 9.

ATTENDED EACH OTHER'S POLITICAL FUNCTIONS: New York *Amsterdam News*, June 29, 1963, April 4, 1964. Interview: Jimmy Booker.

SITTING ATTENTIVELY IN THE LAST ROW: NBC-TV "White Paper" on Adam Clayton Powell.

"THIS CAT AND I ARE GOING TO RULE THE WORLD": Interview: Adam Clayton Powell, III.

RETIRE AS MINISTER AND RELINQUISH CONGRESSIONAL SEAT: *New York Times*, July 21, 1960.

MALCOLM DELIVERED THE PREDICTION FROM POWELL'S OWN PULPIT: New York *Amsterdam News*, April 28, 1962.

WOULD "NEVER" CRITICIZE ADAM PUBLICLY: *BAMN*, p. 93. Neil Hickey and Ed Edwin, supra., p. 166.

"HE MOVES IN ONE DIRECTION ONE MINUTE AND ANOTHER DIRECTION AN-OTHER MINUTE": *Chicago Tribune*, June 10, 1963. *NYT*, June 10, 1963. Also see Claude Lewis, supra., p. 33.

COUNTERATTACKED: New York *Herald Tribune*, March 14, 1964.

IF ANYONE COULD EFFECTIVELY CHALLENGE POWELL, IT WAS MALCOLM X: New York *Herald Tribune*, April 22, 1963. *PG*, pp. 134-135. Interview: Lawrence Henry.

49. We Want Malcolm!

305 ELIJAH'S EXTRA CHILDREN: *Los Angeles Times*, July 3, 1964. *MX*, p. 295.

$100 PER MONTH PER CHILD: *Chicago Tribune*, Feb 25. 1965.

TRIP TO PHOENIX; WOULD NOT LET CHILDREN USE TOILET; THE WOMEN WOULD BE KILLED: Undated memoranda from "Robin" and "Heather" to Gladys Towles Root, Esq. Interview: "Robin."

ATTEMPT TO OBTAIN WRITTEN STATEMENTS; "DAMMIT, WHY NOT?": Interview: James 67X.

306 WOULD AIR CHARGES ONLY IF WOMEN INITIATED LEGAL PROCEEDINGS: *FBI* correlation summary on Elijah Muhammad, April 9, 1969, p. 36. Also see tape-recording of Feb. 18, 1965 WINS talk show "Contact," where Malcolm assures moderator Stan Bernard that he's not going to make any accusation over the air because he understands the libel laws.

PRODDED HEATHER AND ROBIN TO TAKE LEGAL ACTION: *PG*, pp. 112, 193. Interviews: "Heather," "Robin," confidential source.

SETTLE AMICABLY: June 12, 1964 letter from Gladys Towles Root to Elijah Muhammad.

FILED SUIT: *Chicago Tribune*, July 4, 1964, Feb. 25, 1965. *Los Angeles Times*, Feb. 25, 1965. *MX*, p. 295. *PG*, pp. 203-204.

OPEN LETTER: *New York Post*, June 26, 1964. *PG*, p. 200.

CONCILIATORY EXTERIOR: To conceal his real motive, Malcolm initially told Ms. Root he was acting as an "intermediary" in an attempt to fashion an out-of-court settlement that would provide the two women with sufficient income without embarrassing Elijah Muhammad publicly. (*Chicago Tribune*, Feb. 25, 1965. *Los Angeles Times*, Feb. 25, 1965. Interviews: Gladys Towles Root, "Heather.")

CHIEF INSTIGATOR: *Chicago Defender*, July 6, 1964. *Herald-Dispatch*, July 16, 1964. *Muhammad Speaks*, April 10, 1964; Dec. 4, 1964. Interview: Peter Goldman.

NATIONAL COVERAGE: *Chicago Defender*, July 14, 1964. The *California Eagle*, July 16, 1964. May 1, 1980 letter from "Robin" to author.

TWO MEN CLAMBERING UP BACK STAIRWAY: Interviews: "Robin," "Heather." March 23, 1979 letter from "Robin" to author.

A MATTER OF PRINCIPLE; "DO YOU REALLY BELIEVE THAT?": Interview: Sharon 10X.

FEELINGS THAT HARKENED BACK TO HIS YOUTH: Interview: Philbert Little.

CANCELS CHICAGO TRIP: Interviews: Wesley South, David McElroy, Norman Ross. The FBI and its informant were apparently fooled too. (*FBI*, July 2, 1964, pp. 2-3.) Malcolm's decision to forego the trip to Chicago may also have been influenced by the July 1, 1964 birth of his daughter Gamilah Lamumbah.)

307 VENTURES OUT LATE AT NIGHT; THE BABYSITTER HAD DIFFICULTY UNDERSTANDING WHY: Confidential interview with the babysitter. Interview: Tom Wallace. *FBI*, Jan. 20, 1965, p. 73. (Malcolm told the police the attack had occurred as he was returning home in his car.) New York City Fire Dept. report on the Feb. 13, 1965 fire. Also see the inaccurate versions of the July 3, 1964 incident that are recorded in the *New York Daily News* of Feb. 15, 1965 and *PG*, p. 204.)

308 HASAN SHARRIEFF'S OPEN LETTER: *Chicago Defender*, July 6-9, 1964. *Sepia* (Oct., 1964), p. 45.

WALLACE MUHAMMAD DENOUNCES NOI: *Chicago Defender*, July 8, 1964. Undated statement by Wallace Muhammad. (The statement was found in Gladys Towles Root's files.) *Chicago's American*, Sept. 15, 1964. *FBI*, Feb. 17, 1965, p. 2. *PG*, pp. 192-193. *Chicago Sun-Times*, March 2, 1975. Also see *FDL*, p. 206.

"TO BE THE STRONGEST BLACK MAN ON THE FACE OF THE EARTH": *Chicago's American*, Sept. 15, 1964. (Also see John Facenda interviewing Wallace Muhammad on WCAU-TV, Philadelphia, Nov. 12, 1978.)

"DECEITFUL": *Chicago's American*, Sept. 15, 1964. Also see *Muhammad Speaks*, Sept. 25, 1964.

"THEY WILL KILL": *Chicago Defender*, July 8, 1964.

MALCOLM BLAMED: *PG*, p. 247. Also see *Muhammad Speaks*, March 12, 1965, which blames Malcolm for the "confusion and discord" in the Nation of Islam.

CONVERSATION WITH BEMBRY: Interview: John Elton Bembry.

309 GILLIGAN KILLS JAMES POWELL; HARLEM RIOT ENSUES: The material on James Powell, Lieutenant Gilligan, and the Harlem riot has been distilled primarily from Fred C. Shapiro and James W. Sullivan, *Race Riots: New York, 1964* (Thomas Y. Crowell, 1964). Shapiro and Sullivan covered the riot for the *New York Herald Tribune*. (See *NYT*, Sept. 27, 1964 for James Powell's background.)

312 JAMES FARMER'S ACCUSATIONS: *Race Riots: New York, 1964*, supra., pp. 70-73.

313 NEITHER CONDONED NOR CONDEMNED THE VIOLENCE: *NYT*, July 21, 1964. *Race Riots: New York, 1964*, supra., p. 67.

"LET'S GET WHITEY"; "LET'S KILL WHITEY!": *Race Riots: New York, 1964*, supra., pp. 142-143.

THREAT TO KNIFE JIMMY BRESLIN: Ibid., pp. 69-70.

314 "WE'RE GONNA KILL EVERY ONE OF YOU WHITE BASTARDS": *Ibid.*, pp. 171-172.

"WE WANT MALCOLM!": *PG*, p. 205.

50. Dissension in the Ranks

315 "MET WITH OPEN ARMS": *JHC*, p. 299.

NOT PERMITTED TO ADDRESS OAU MEETING: *Egyptian Gazette*, August 17, 1964. *PG*, p. 207. *JHC* erroneously portrays Malcolm's petition as a speech. (*JHC*, p. 288.)

ACCREDITED OBSERVER: *Arab Observer*, August 24, 1964. *NYT*, July 10, 1964; July 14, 1964. *PG*, pp. 206-208. *SPKS*, pp. 72, 78-79. July 1, 1981 letter from U.S. Embassy, Cairo, to author. Interviews: Donald Bergus; Muhammad Haqqui.

STATE DEPARTMENT ASSERTIONS TO THE CONTRARY: Sept., 1964 letter from Acting Assistant Secretary for Congressional Relations Robert E. Lee to Congressman Charles C. Diggs, Jr. Also see *NYT*, August 13, 1964.

CONVERSING WITH DIPLOMATS: *PG*, pp. 206-208. *BAMN*, p. 141. *SPKS*, p. 79.

COMPILED DOSSIERS: Interview: C. Eric Lincoln.

316 CIRCULATES PETITON: *PG*, p. 207.

NUMBER ONE PRIORITY: *FBI*, Jan. 20, 1965, p. 101.

"OUR PROBLEMS ARE YOUR PROBLEMS": July 17, 1964 press release containing Malcolm's petition to the OAU. Also *TKBM*, pp. 148-158 and *JHC*, pp. 288-293.

ELDER AFRICAN BROTHERS; "ALMOST FANATICALLY": Phonograph record entitled "The Last Message" (Discus Habands LP #1300.) *SPKS*, pp. 73, 77, 160. *TKBM*, p. 150. *JHC*, pp. 289-292. Michigan State University speech, Jan. 23, 1963. *FBI*, Sept. 17, 1964, pp. 2-3.

NOT THE RINGING DENUNCIATION: *PG*, p. 209 and *SPKS*, p. 84. Cf. *Egyptian Gazette*, August 17, 1964 and *SPKS*, p. 79.

JUSTICE DEPARTMENT CONSIDERS PROSECUTING, CITING LOGAN ACT: *FBI*, Sept. 11, 1964, pp. 1-2; Sept. 17, 1964, p. 1. Also *PG*, pp. 211, 212, 218 and *NYT*, August 13, 1964. (The following chapter discusses the other legal approaches the Department of Justice's Criminal Division considered.)

AS DU BOIS HAD TRIED TO DO: Taylor Branch, *Parting the Waters: America in the King Years, 1954-63* (Simon & Schuster, 1988), p. 293.

"I DO BELIEVE I MIGHT HAVE MADE A GOOD LAWYER": *MX*, p. 379.

317 VIRTUALLY CONCEDED THE POINT: *LYMX*, p. 159. *The Militant*, May 25, 1964. Malcolm conveyed the message orally. (Interview: George Breitman.)

OBTAIN FINANCIAL SUPPORT: *FBI*, March 8, 1965, pp. 3-4; Jan. 20, 1965, p. 35. *TKBM*, pp. 176-177. Charis Waddy, *The Muslim Mind* (Longman, 1976), p. 108. Also *Sepia* (Oct., 1964), pp. 43-44.

EGYPTIAN ASSISTANCE: Feb. 16, 1965 CIA memo entitled "Egyptian Funding of Malcolm X." Feb. 19, 1965 memo from CIA to FBI. Feb. 23, 1965 CIA memo from Richard Helms to FBI. *FBI*, March 8, 1965, pp. 3-4. (Also see March 3, 1965 airgram from Counselor for Political Affairs, U.S. Embassy, Cairo, to U.S. Dept. of State.)

UNDER INSTRUCTIONS TO CULTIVATE CONTACTS: Confidential written source.

"YOU CAN'T BUILD A POWER BASE HERE": *SPKS*, p. 129.

"I FOUND NO DOORS CLOSED TO ME": *JHC*, p. 299. *SPKS*, p. 86. *PG*, pp. 217-218. *BAMN*, p. 144.

"PROMISED OFFICIALLY": *SPKS*, pp. 84, 86. *NYT*, August 13, 1964. Malcolm's assertion that unnamed African countries would support his attempt to have U.S. racism condemned by the U.N. was reminiscent of similar assertions he had made after he had returned from Africa the previous May. (*FBI*, June 18, 1964, p. 65.)

SCHOLARSHIPS: *FDL*, pp. 222-223. *FBI*, Jan. 20, 1965, p. 47.

"UNQUALIFIED" SUCCESS: *SPKS*, p. 84. *BAMN*, p. 110. *FBI*, Jan. 20, 1965, p. 44. Also see *PG*, p. 209.

"NOT AT ALL DOUBTFUL OF SUPPORT"; "ONE CANNOT TAKE THINGS FOR GRANTED": *BAMN*, p. 110.

PRIVATELY ADMITTED DISCOURAGEMENT: *PG*, p. 241.

318 "CEASED TO EXIST": *The Record* (Bergen, N.J.), June 16, 1964.

STAYED IN THE NEWS: August 28, 1964 and Nov. 7, 1964 airgrams from U.S. embassy, Cairo, to U.S. Dept. of State.

MUGGER AND RAPIST; BROTHER KNIFED TO DEATH BY WHITE MAN: Al Gumhuriya, Feb. 24, 1965 (reproduced in March 3, 1965 airgram from U.S. Embassy, Cairo, to U.S. Dept. of State.)

NEWS REPORTS ABOUT AKBAR MUHAMMAD: *Arab Observer*, August 24, 1964. *Chicago Defender*, August 17, 1964. *NYT*, Jan. 15, 1965. Interview: Akbar Muhammad (Some U.S. newspapers erroneously reported that the impending rupture had already occurred.)

CONVINCED HE HAD BEEN POISONED: *PG*, p. 211. Eric Norden, "The Murder of Malcolm X," *The Realist* (Feb., 1967), pp. 9-10. George Brietman, Herman Porter, & Baxter Smith, *The Assassination of Malcolm X* (Pathfinder Press, 1976), pp. 83-84.

Without citing any source, Norden's article asserts that the excruciating abdominal pain that caused Malcolm to be taken to the hospital to have his stomach pumped occurred July 23,

1964, the day before he "was to deliver his speech to the [OAU] Summit Conference." But, despite Norden's assertions to the contrary, Malcolm neither delivered a speech at the conference nor was authorized to do so. Moreover, according to biographer Peter Goldman, the stomach-pumping incident occurred some time between July 17 and July 21, while the OAU Conference was in session. Also see Oba T'Shaka, *The Political Legacy of Malcolm X*, p. 233, which, like Farrow Allen's testimony, indicates that Malcolm had been having considerable trouble with his digestive system.

319 HE REFUSED TO EAT THE FOOD AT HIS HOTEL: Interview: Clifford Hyman.

EQUATED INNOCULATION WITH BEING POISONED: Interview: Tom Wallace.

MOTHER REFUSED TO TAKE MEDICINE BY MOUTH: Interview: Mrs. Lloyd Hackenberg.

A WORD HE OFTEN USED IN PLACE OF THE WORD "HATE": For example, see *FBI*, May 19, 1959, p. 33. (Also see *MX*, p. 297.)

ORGANIZATIONAL PROBLEMS FESTERING; LENGTHY ABSENCE RESENTED: *BAMN*, pp. 110-112. *PG*, pp. 191, 222, 240, 242-246. *MX*, pp. 419-420. Ethel N. Minor, editor's preface to Stokely Carmichael, *Stokely Speaks* (Random House, 1971), p. xiii. *NYT*, Feb. 25, 1965. *FBI*, Jan. 20, 1965, p. 13.

INTENSELY PERSONAL BOND: Interviews: John Thimas, Robert 35X Smith. Also see *FBI*, 1/20/65, p. 30.

FEW REAL MEMBERS: *Boston Herald*, Feb. 28, 1965. *New York Amsterdam News*, March 28, 1964. *FBI*, June 18, 1964, p. 2.

MUSLIM MOSQUE MEMBERSHIP: *FBI*, Jan. 20, 1965, pp. 7, 9. Peter Goldman, *The Death and Life of Malcolm X*, second edition (University of Illinois Press, 1979), pp. 192, 432. Interview: confidential source.

OAAU MEMBERSHIP: Second edition of *The Death and Life of Malcolm X*, supra., p. 432. *FBI*, Jan. 20, 1965, p. 29. Also see *MX*, p. 420.

SHRINKING: *BAMN*, p. 111.

NEVER BEGAN FUNCTIONING: *FBI*, Jan. 20, 1965, p. 14. Interviews: Sharon 10X and two confidential sources.

PETTY SQUABBLING: Second edition of *The Death and Life of Malcolm X*, supra., pp. 243, 432. *FBI*, Aug. 13, 1964, p. 2.

ELBOWED EACH OTHER: Interviews: Benjamin Goodman, confidential source.

ARMS LENGTH: Interviews: Benjamin Goodman, Toni Ardelle Killings, Aubrey Barnette, John Thimas, Hakim Jamal, Percy Sutton.

"I KNEW HIM BETTER THAN HE KNEW ME": Interview: Charles 37X.

STRIKE BACK: Interview: confidential source.

320 "THE BIG M": Interview: Robert 35X.

JAMES VS. BENJAMIN: See *PG*, p. 243, for instance.

BENJAMIN UNHAPPY: *PG*, pp. 245-246. Interviews: Benjamin Goodman, confidential source.

MEN VS. WOMEN; SHABAZZ VS. SHIFFLETT: *PG*, p. 245. Interviews: Sharon 10X and two confidential sources.

RELYING ON ELLA: Interviews: Toni Ardelle Killings, John Elton Bembry, Ella Little, Johnny Jones. (Also see *MX*, p. 415.)

"HE CAN'T EVEN MOVE": Interview: Ella Little.

FRICTION BETWEEN THE TWO WOMEN: *NYT*, May 20, 1966. Interviews: Ella Little, Wilfred Little, and two confidential sources.

DID NOT INCLUDE BETTY: Interviews: Lawrence Henry, Sharon 10X, confidential source. *NYT*, March 2, 1965. Mrs. Shabazz acknowledged, after Malcolm's death, that she had never traveled with him and that she hadn't realized how popular he was. She conveyed the impression that she'd had little idea of what he had really been thinking. (ABC newsfilm, Feb. 22 & 23, 1965. *Journal-American*, Feb. 23, 1965.) Cf. the relevant assertion in Stewart Kampel, "Menace or Messiah," *Memories* (February/March, 1989), p. 88.

REPORTEDLY ANNOYED: Interviews: Sharon 10X, confidential source.

EMBARRASSED SILENCE: *PG*, pp. 146-147.

WOULD NOT DELEGATE AUTHORITY: Interviews: Harold Hyman, Benjamin Goodman, confidential source. Albert Cleage and George Brietman, *Myths About Malcolm X* (Pathfinder Press, 1968), p. 12. *WWG*, p. 81. *TKBM*, pp. 102-103. *PG*, pp. 244, 245.

321 PERFECTIONIST: Interviews: Leon Moffett, Alex Haley, Saladin Matthews, Charles 37X, Benjamin Goodman. *MX*, pp. 29, 141.

"DO IT YOURSELF": Interview: Harold Hyman. Also interview with Jean Seaton.

IMPATIENT: Interviews: Benjamin Goodman, Saladin Matthews, Clifford Hyman, James Hicks, confidential source. *MX*, p. 421.

TOLERATED A WOMAN'S LATENESS: Interview: Toni Ardelle Killings.

INABILITY TO TRUST: Interviews: Benjamin Goodman, Toni Ardell Killings, Harold Hyman, Charles 37X. *MX*, p. 389. *BAMN*, p. 110. In *MX*, p. 339, Malcolm praises his loyal assistants. But in *The Revolutionary Personality* (Princeton University Press, 1967), E. Victor Wolfenstein points out that rebel leaders typically expect their followers to betray them. The expectation is sometimes a psychological projection of their own hostility toward authority.

PROSSER AND VESEY: Interview: John Elton Bembry. *The Negro Almanac*, fifth edition, (Gale Research, 1989), pp. 1444, 1446. Robert S. Starobin (ed.), *Denmark Vessey: The Slave Conspiracy of 1822* (Prentice Hall, 1970), pp. 11-12.

"HE WAS A TYRANT": Interview: Ulysses X. "I loved him, but didn't like him," says Ulysses. "He worked so hard for the Nation."

NOT ALL HIS FORMER AIDES AGREE: Interviews: Jim Campbell, confidential source.

BUT THOSE WHO DO [AGREE]: Interview: confidential source. "He would show [his subordinates] his anger in a hurry," recalls Aubrey Barnette. Saladin Matthews says, "He would come down very harsh."

NEVER REPRIMANDED THEM IN PUBLIC: Interview: Robert 35X.

DROVE HIS SUBORDINATES HARD: Interviews: Clifford Hyman, Benjamin Goodman, Saladin Matthews, Philbert Little, Charles 37X, confidential source.

TOLERANT TOWARD SLOW LEARNERS: Interviews: Harold Hyman, confidential source.

KING'S RELATIONSHIP WITH HIS CO-WORKERS: Stephen B. Oates, *Let the Trumpet Sound* (Harper & Row, 1982), pp. 286-289.

SUGGESTIONS, NOT ORDERS: Interviews: Harold Hyman, Malcolm Jarvis.

SEEMED TO VACILLATE: Interview: Charles 37X. Benjamin Goodman says, "Sometimes he made you feel you were on an equal basis; sometimes on a leader-follower basis."

THE BOSS: Interview: confidential source.

"THE CHIEF": Interview: Robert 35X.

DISCOURAGED BOWING AND SCRAPING AND YES-MEN: Interviews: Saladin Matthews, Harold Hyman, John Thimas, Ulysses X, confidential source.

QUITE AWARE HOW MUCH TIME; "OVERNIGHT": *JET*, April 2, 1964.

TRIED TO CONCEAL ORGANIZATIONAL WEAKNESS: *JHC*, pp. 36-38. *FBI*, Dec. 30, 1964, p. 2. *FBI*, Jan. 20, 1965, pp. 5, 44-47, citing Sept. 14 & Sept. 28, 1964 issues of mimeographed newsletter entitled the OAAU Backlash. "You should all learn how to organize," Malcolm told one group of admirers. (*JHC*, p. 231.)

"IT'S UP TO YOU"; "I'VE NEVER SOUGHT TO BE ANYONE'S LEADER"; OBLIQUELY THREATENS TO START AGAIN FROM SCRATCH: *BAMN*, pp. 111-112.

"A GENERAL WITHOUT AN ARMY": *Muhammad Speaks*, Sept. 11, 1964.

51. Government Surveillance

323 AZZAM PASHA TRIED TO SECURE FINANCING FOR MALCOLM'S MOSQUE: Charis Waddy, *The Muslim Mind* (Longman, 1976), p. 108. Rumors spread that the Saudis were going to build Malcolm a million dollar mosque and recognize him as the head of America's Muslims. (Interview: Christine Johnson.)

UNSUCCESSFUL: Interview: Issam Azzam.

SURRUR SABBAN: Sept. 29, 1964 airgram from U.S. Embassy, Jedda, to U.S. Dept. of State. Interviews: Issam Azzam, Heshaam Jaaber, Donald Bergus. (Also see *NYT*, Oct. 11, 1964.)

PAY EXPENSES OF SUDANESE TEACHER: Nov., 1981 letter from confidential source. *FBI*, March 8, 1965, p. 3.

OFFICIAL REPRESENTATIVE: *NYT*, Oct. 11, 1964. *PG*, p. 210. An informant told the *FBI* that Malcolm received a salary as the League's official representative. (*FBI*, March 8, 1965, p. 4.)

324 RELIGIOUS "FAKER": *NYT*, Oct. 4 & 11, 1964. *FBI*, Oct. 5, 1964, p. 1; Nov. 25, 1964, p. 3.

"SPECIAL MEMORANDUM"; "TO THE DEATH"; "PLENTY": *Muhammad Speaks*, Sept. 11 & 25, 1964.

NO EMPIRE BUILDER; "PLANTED THE SEEDS OF ISLAM": *Muhammad Speaks*, Sept. 25, 1964; Oct. 9, 1964; Oct. 23, 1964; Nov. 20, 1964.

SEEMED TO BE HAVING DIFFICULTY: Sept. 29, 1964 airgram from U.S. Embassy, Jedda, to U.S. Dept. of State.

FROM KUWAIT VIA BEIRUT AND KHARTOUM TO ADDIS ABABA: Sept. 22, 1964 telegram from U.S. Embassy, Jedda, to U.S. Dept. of State. Sept. 27, 1964 postcards from Malcolm to Mary Kochiyama and C. Eric Lincoln. *BAMN*, pp. 137, 141-142. *FBI*, Oct. 1, 1964, p. 1. Oct. 6, 1964 airgram from U.S. Embassy, Addis Ababa to U.S. Dept. of State.

SAYS RETURN IMMINENT: *FBI*, July 24, 1964, p. 1; July 30, 1964, p. 2; July 31, 1964, p. 1; Sept. 29, 1964, p. 1; Oct. 9, 1964, p. 1; Oct. 23, 1964, p. 1.

FIRST VISIT TO ETHIOPIA; LOW-KEY: Oct. 6, 1964 airgram from U.S. Embassy, Addis Ababa to U.S. Dept. of State, p. 1.

"HE DOESN'T MIND BEING BEAT UP AND I DO": Oct. 6, 1964 airgram from U.S. Embasssy to U.S. Dept. of State, p. 2.

FROM ETHIOPIA TO KENYA TO TANZANIA: Oct. 6, 1964 postcard from Malcolm to Christine Johnson. Oct. 12 & 13, 1964 telegrams from U.S. Embassy, Dar-es-Salaam, to U.S. Dept. of State. Oct. 22, 1964 telegram from U.S. Embassy, Nairobi, to U.S. Dept. of State. Oct. 27, 1964 letter from Ass't. Atty. General Walter Yeagley to Office of New York State Attorney General. *BAMN*, pp. 142-144. *FBI*, Jan. 20, 1965, p. 119.

325 NAME DROPPING: *BAMN*, pp. 144-145, 161. *MX*, p. 370.

EFFORT TO ENHANCE SELF-ESTEEM: Years later, his brother Reginald emphasized how Malcolm struggled to boost his self-esteem. (Interview: Reginald Little.) "Malcolm had a great ego that he was feeding," writes J. Prescott Adams. (April 18, 1977 letter from Adams to author.)

BACK TO KENYA: Oct. 19, 20, & 22, 1964 telegrams from U.S. Ambassador, Kenya, to U.S. Dept. of State. *BAMN*, pp. 142-145. October 18, 1964 letter from Nairobi, Kenya to M.S. Handler.

"I THOUGHT HE WAS WHITE"; "CALLED HIM AN ALBINO": *PG*, p. 214.

"HOW LIGHT THEY ARE": Interview: Adam Clayton Powell, III.

EYE COLOR: Interview: Adam Clayton Powell, III. See the detailed discussion of Malcolm's eye color in the notes to Chapter One. Also see the photographs by John Launois and Lawrence Henry. (When I asked Lawrence Henry what color Malcolm's eyes were, he refused to answer the question and promptly terminated the conversation and the interview. He would not show me any of his photographs of Malcolm. What portion of them were later moved to the Schomburg Library is unclear.)

CONSTANT SURVEILLANCE: July 10, 1964 CIA memo to "Headquarters." Aug. 14, 1964 CIA memo to Richard Helms. Sept. 10, 1964 airgram from U.S. Dept. of State to the American embassies in Jedda, Cairo, Beirut, Algiers, & Rabat. *FBI*, Aug. 22, 1961, pp. 15, 16, 19. *MX*, pp. 371-372, 418, 419. *JHC*, p. 184. *PG*, pp. 211, 212, 214, 256-262. *TKBM*, p. 177. Interview: Harold Hyman.

PHONE TAPPED: U.S. Senate, Final Report of the Select Committee to Study Governmental Operations with respect to Intelligence Activities (Senate Report #94-755, 1976), Book II, p. 63. *JHC*, p. 92. Second edition of Peter Goldman, *The Death and Life of Malcolm X* (University of Illinois Press, 1979), p. 431.

MAN LISTENING FROM ADJACENT PHONE BOOTH: Interview: confidential source.

"BOSS": *PG*, pp. 258-262.

"HAS . . . RENOUNCED HIS U.S. CITIZENSHIP": August 11, 1964 CIA memo from undisclosed official to Richard Helms, p. 3.

CIA TRIED TO COVER ITS TRACKS: Interview: M.S. Handler.

326 CIA TRIED TO ASCERTAIN WHAT FUNDS MALCOLM WAS RECEIVING FROM ABROAD: August 11, 1964 CIA memo, supra.

MILITARY INTELLIGENCE: June 8, 1964 memorandum from F. J. Baumgardner to W. C. Sullivan. June 9, 1964 memo from J. Edgar Hoover to Chief, U.S. Secret Service.

SECRET SERVICE: Undated, censored Secret Service reports on Malcolm. June 9, 1964 memo from J. Edgar Hoover to Chief, U.S. Secret Service.

FBI EXACERBATES MALCOLM'S FEUD WITH ELIJAH MUHAMMAD: Goldman, supra., pp. 410, 429-430.

HOOVER BADGERS JUSTICE DEPARTMENT: Ibid., p. 431. George Breitman, Herman Porter, & Baxter Smith, *The Assassination of Malcolm X* (Pathfinder Press, 1976), p. 11.

"DEPARTMENT OF INJUSTICE": Phonograph record entitled "Malcolm X Speaks to the People in Harlem" (Up Front Records; record #UPF-152).

POSSIBILITY OF PROSECUTING MALCOLM UNDER THE SMITH ACT: Sept. 11, 1964 memo from J. Walter Yeagley, Assistant Attorney General, Internal Security Division, U.S. Dept. of Justice, to J. Edgar Hoover. April 30, 1979 letter from Criminal Division, U.S. Dept. of Justice, to author. Goldman, supra., p. 431. Breitman, Porter and Smith, *supra., p. 11.*

NOT DUMB ENOUGH TO ADVOCATE ARMED REVOLT: *PG*, p. 135.

SEDITIOUS CONSPIRACY STATUTE: Sept. 11, 1964 memo from J. Walter Yeagley to J. Edgar Hoover.

ATTORNEY GENERAL'S LIST: Sept. 3, 1964 memo from J. Walter Yeagley, Assistant Attorney General, Internal Security Division, U.S. Dept. of Justice, to FBI Director. April 30, 1979 letter from Criminal Division, U.S. Dept. of Justice, to author. Goldman, supra., p. 431.

FOREIGN AGENTS REGISTRATION ACT: Sept. 28, 1964 memo from J. Walter Yeagley, Assistant Attorney General, to FBI Director. Title 22, U.S.Code, Sections 611-620.

327 SUGGESTED: Dec. 3, 1964 letter from FBI Director to FBI's New York office. Also see Goldman, supra., p. 431.

BATALLIONS OF GOVERNMENT AGENTS: Even the Internal Revenue Service got into the act, according to *TKBM*, p. 183 and a rumor that appeared in the Sept 24, 1964 *Chicago Daily News*.

MALCOLM RETURNED TO ETHIOPIA: November 6, 1964 airgram from American Embassy, Addis Ababa to U.S. Dept. of State.

WANTED TO DISASSOCIATE HIMSELF: Interview: Nick Cordasco.

RETRIBUTION THAT AWAITED BACK HOME: *PG*, p. 220. Al Gumhuriya, Feb. 24, 1965, reprinted in March 3, 1965 airgram from American Embassy, Cairo, to U.S. Dept. of State.

ESTABLISH DEPENDABLE SOURCE OF INCOME: *FBI*, March 8, 1965, pp. 3-4. *FBI*, Jan. 20, 1965, p. 35. *TKBM*, pp. 176-177. Charis Waddy, *The Muslim Mind* (Longman, 1976), p. 108. *Sepia* (Oct., 1964), pp. 43-44.

"THE AFRICANS LOVED ME": *MX*, p. 419. Also see the incidents described in *PG*, p. 176 and *JHC*, p. 222-223.

REITERATED SAME THEME IN INTENSELY PERSONAL LANGUAGE: *SPKS*, p. 61. *BAMN*, p. 144.

FELT MORE AT HOME IN AFRICA: *NYT*, May 13, 1964. Also see *PG*, p. 176. Archie Epps points out that the image of "going home" was, for Malcolm, a very personal image. (*EPPS*, pp. 92-93.) He characterized Africa as a happy homeland. (Phonograph record entitled "Malcolm X Speaks to the People in Harlem [Up Front Records; record #UPF-152.] Also see *The Militant*, April 6, 1964 and *EPPS*, pp. 140, 169.)

"MOTHER AFRICA": Malcolm used the terms "Mother Africa," "mother continent," and "motherland" interchangably. See, for instance, *JHC*, pp. 295-298, 301; *MX*, p. 353; *BAMN*, p. 136; *SPKS*, p. 124; and Malcolm's Feb. 15, 1965 speech at the Audubon Ballroom.

ILLICIT HONEYMOON WITH EUROPEAN LOVERS: *JHC*, p. 297.

APOLOGIZED FOR ABSENCES, WHICH SEEMED TO TROUBLE HIM; NEGLECTED WIFE AND CHILDREN: *PG*, pp. 146-147. *TKBM*, p. 230. *MX*, p. 423 and dedication page. Interviews: John Elton Bembry, Robert Little, and confidential source. Years later, Malcolm's widow acknowledged that he had been concerned about his absences, which had been quite painful for his oldest three daughters. ("Like It Is," WABC-TV, Feb. 22, 1969; *JHC*, p. 134.) But on another occasion she asserted he was "a devoted family man." (*New York Amsterdam News*, March 13, 1965.)

328 WITHDRAW INTO ATTIC; CHILDREN HUSTLED INTO BASEMENT PLAYROOM: Interview: confidential source.

CHILDREN MISSED MALCOLM: "Like It Is," WABC-TV, Feb. 22, 1969.

CHILDREN SEEMED TO VANISH; NO NOISE; NO TOYS: Interview: Joe McCormack.

CARES ABOUT HIS CHILDREN: Interviews: Robert 35X, C. Eric Lincoln, Elizabeth Gethers.

OTHER PEOPLE'S CHILDREN: Interviews: Christine Johnson, Harold Hyman, Josephine English, Evelyn Smith Clark.

EVEN REPORTERS HAD TO DEFER: *PG*, p. 163.

KEYS AROUND NECK: *MX*, p. 271.

PLIGHT OF PARENTLESS CHILDREN; "WITHOUT A SECOND THOUGHT!": *Malcolm X on Afro-American History* (Pathfinder Press, 1970), p. 42. The anger is apparent in the tape-recording of the speech. *FBI*, Jan. 31, 1956, p. 7. *New York Amsterdam News*, June 1, 1957, et al.

"STRAIGHTEN OUT THE PARENTS ": The tape recording containing this material was labeled Nov. 7, 1963 speech at CCNY. But the recording may have been mislabeled. See *Ebony* (June, 1969), p. 176 and *JHC*, p. 179 for additional examples of Malcolm's emphasis on the need for parents to set good examples for their children.

DEFINITE OPINIONS: *Ebony* (June, 1969), p. 176.

CHILDREN SHOULD BE EDUCATED, SELF-SUPPORTING, ETC.: *JHC*, p. 136.

GENTLE WITH CHILDREN: Interviews: Tom Wallace, Jr., Attallah Shabazz. *JHC*, p. 136.

CHILDREN READILY TOOK TO HIM: Interviews: Tom Wallace, Jr., Christine Johnson.

STERN; "VERY STRICT": *JHC*, p. 136. "Like It Is," WABC-TV, Feb. 22, 1969. Interviews: Josephine English, Robert 35X.

HER CHILDREARING METHODS: *JHC*, pp. 132-143. *Ebony* (June, 1969), p. 176. "Like It Is," WABC-TV, Feb. 22, 1969. *Malcolm X: A Tribute* (Steppingstone press: Winter, 1963), p. 7.

"KIND OF HARD AND CRUEL": *JHC*, p. 136.

"LIKE AN ARMY SERGEANT": "Like It Is," WABC-TV, Feb. 22, 1969. "Soul," KERA-TV, Dallas, May 17, 1972. (Also see the second paragraph of the relevant article in *The Philadelphia Inquirer Daily Magazine*, May 12, 1988, p. 1-F.)

EVEN STRICTER: "Like It Is," WABC-TV, Feb. 22, 1969.

329 GREENISH EYES SEEMED TO CHANGE COLOR: Interviews: Philbert Little, Attallah Shabazz, confidential source.

"A YOUNGER VERSION": Interview: Malcolm Jarvis. As a child, Attallah looked just like Malcolm, says Tom Wallace. Another former member of Temple Seven says she was "the spitting image" of Malcolm. (Interview: confidential source.)

"WE BOTH WONDERED WHAT IN THE WORLD WE'D DONE WRONG": *JHC*, p. 136.

FAVORED HER: Interview: confidential source. When I telephoned Attallah Shabazz on Feb. 22, 1980, she asked why I wanted to know what she looked like. I said I wanted to know whether physical resemblance was the reason Malcolm had favored her. "I don't think that's why he favored me," she replied. She said it was because they had similar personalities. Haltingly, she added that she didn't think he had neglected her younger sisters.

TOOK HER TO THE RALLIES AT WHICH HE EXTOLLED BLACKNESS: "Today," NBC-TV, Feb 5, 1989. Interview: Attallah Shabazz.

REMINISCENT OF FAVORITISM: *MX*, p. 6.

FREQUENTLY CRIED: Interview: confidential source.

ATTALLAH GRIEVED MORE: *JHC*, pp. 142-143.

SHE FELT ILYASAH WAS MALCOLM'S FAVORITE, IN PHOTOS, IN HIS LAP: Interviews: Tom Wallace, Charles 37X, Ella Little, confidential source.

LONGED FOR A SON: *MX*, p. 424. *The Philadelphia Inquirer*, May 30, 1972. Interviews: John Elton Bembry, Charles 37X, Benjamin Goodman, Harold Hyman, Sharon 10X.

THE NEXT CHILD: *MX*, p. 424.

THE SEVENTH CHILD: *JHC*, p. 137.

WOULD NAME CHILD AFTER LUMUMBA: *BAMN*, pp. 64-65. (According to a October 6, 1982 letter from the Chief Clerk of the Queens County court that probated Malcolm's estate, the spelling of the names of his first four daughters is: "Attallah," "Quibilah," "Ilyasah," and "Gamilah Lamumbah." But I have been informed by a member of the family that "Qubilah" is the spelling that Malcolm's second oldest daughter uses.)

PATRICE LUMUMBA: Alan P. Merriam, *Congo: Background of a Conflict* (Northwestern University Press, 1961), p. 154. July 27, 1960 news dispatch from Leopoldville to The *Philadelphia Inquirer*. *New York Herald Tribune*, June 25, 1960; Sept. 7, 1960. The *Philadelphia Inquirer*, August 23, 1960. *London Times*, Feb. 14, 1961. Patrice Lumumba, *Congo: My Country*, foreword, p. xi. *Newsweek*, August 1, 1960. *NYT*, Feb. 11, 1961. Thomas Kanza, *The Rise & Fall of Patrice Lumumba: Conflict in the Congo* (Schenkman & G. K. Hall, 1979), pp. 122, 167, 169.

330 LUMUMBA'S ABILITY TO TAILOR HIS TEACHINGS: Lumumba's contradictory utterances are underscored in the New York *Herald Tribune*, Sept. 7, 1960; Feb. 14, 1961; and The *Philadelphia Inquirer*, Aug. 29, 1960; Feb. 14, 1961.

"THE GREATEST BLACK MAN WHO EVER WALKED THE AFRICAN CONTINENT": *BAMN*, p. 64.

SENSED HE ONLY HAD A SHORT TIME TO LIVE: Thomas Kanza, supra., p. 167.

"I SHALL PROBABLY BE ARRESTED, TORTURED, AND KILLED. . . . MY DEATH WILL HASTEN THE LIBERATION OF THE CONGO": Thomas Kanza, supra., p. 312.

CAUTIONED COLLEAGUE NOT TO BECOME A MARTYR HIMSELF: G. Heinz and H. Donnay, *Lumumba: The Last Fifty Days* (Grove Press, 1969), p. 31.

INTO THE ARMS OF HIS EXECUTIONERS: Thomas Kanza, supra., pp. 317-319. *Lumumba: The Last Fifty Days*, supra., pp. 36-39. Also p. xix of foreword to *Congo: My Country*, supra.

AFFECTED MALCOLM DEEPLY: *New York Post Daily Magazine*, April 10, 1964. *PG*, p. 162. *BAMN*, pp. 64-65, 148.

52. Detour to Switzerland

331 DEAN RUSK HIMSELF: Nov. 6, 1964 telegram from Dean Rusk to U.S. Embassy, Conakry.

TOURE'S HOUSE GUEST: *BAMN*, p. 145.

SWITZERLAND: *BAMN*, p. 144. *TKBM*, pp. 181-182. Also see *FBI*, Feb. 9, 1965, p. 1. Ella Little recalls rumors that Malcolm had a secret Swiss bank account. But Malcolm suggested that the detour to Switzerland was accidental. He said he had intended to fly directly from Guinea to Algeria but missed his flight because the airline had misinformed him about the plane's departure time. (*BAMN*, p. 144.) Whether the statement was designed to mislead the government agents who were trailing him is unclear.

HE AGAIN FLEW TO SWITZERLAND: *SPKS*, p. 91. *FBI*, Nov. 25, 1964, p. 2. *TKBM*, p. 181. Also see *FBI*, Feb. 9, 1965, p. 1.

VARIATIONS ON "YOU'RE NOT MALCOLM X?" STORY: See, for example, *SPKS*, pp. 91-92; *EPPS*, p. 162; *FDL*, pp. 215-216.

MET WITH SAID RAMADAN: Interview: Said Ramadan.

332 "I DON'T PROFESS TO BE ANYBODY'S LEADER": *BAMN*, p. 116.

CLEARLY IRKED; "SOME OF HISTORY'S GREATEST LEADERS: *MX*, p. 417.

VERY FEW VISITORS: Interview: Mrs. Lloyd Hackenberg.

MOTHER RELEASED; MALCOLM CONTRIBUTED: *MX*, pp. 21, 393. Interviews: Philbert Little, Robert Little, Albert ("Junior") Clark. In an earlier effort to obtain his mother's release from the hospital, Malcolm had visited her former neighbor, Enos Major, and had asked if he could supply any information about the events leading to her commitment. After she was released, Malcolm contributed financially to her upkeep. (Interviews: Enos Major; Philbert Little.)

VISIBLY OVERCOME BY EMOTION: Interview: John Elton Bembry.

FBI WATCHING: *FBI*, Nov. 30, 1964, p. 1; Dec. 1, 1964, pp. 1-2; Jan. 20, 1965, pp. 126-128.

DEBATE AT OXFORD; CONSCIOUS EFFORT; HIS CONTROL DIDN'T FAIL: *JHC*, pp. 232-233. *Daily Telegraph* [London], Dec. 4, 1964.

SPOKE IN MANCHESTER AND SHEFFIELD: *London Times*, Feb. 12, 1965.

333 SHARRIEFF'S TELEGRAM: *Afro-American*, 5-star edition, Feb. 23, 1965. *FBI*, Dec. 15, 1964, p. 1.

INTERNATIONAL "HOBO": *Muhammad Speaks*, Dec. 4, 1964.

MINISTER LOUIS; "MALCOLM SHALL NOT ESCAPE"; "THE DIE IS SET"; "AS HE DID HIS BROTHER": *Muhammad Speaks*, Dec. 4, 1964. *Philadelphia Daily News*, Feb. 26, 1975. *Chicago Tribune*, Feb. 26, 1975. *EOEM*: Emmanuel Muhammad's testimony, p. 14. *Insight*, Nov. 11, 1985, pp. 20-25.

LOUIS, WHO HAD BEEN MALCOLM'S PROTEGE, TURNED AGAINST HIM: *Chicago Sun-Times*, Sept. 7, 1976. *New York Amsterdam News*, Nov. 16, 1985. *BMIA*, pp. 193, 198. *Insight*, Nov. 11, 1985, pp. 21-22. Interviews: Philbert Little, Sharon 10X, Charles 37X, Lemuel Hassan, Raymond Hightower, and two confidential sources.

"HE LEARNED WELL": *Insight*, Nov. 11, 1985, p. 21.

334 REPORTEDLY LIVED IN MALCOLM'S HOUSE: *New York Amsterdam News*, Nov. 16, 1985.

EMPHASIZED THE NEED TO BE ALERT TO OTHERS' MOTIVES: *MX*, pp. 304, 333. Interviewees Anas Mahmoud Luqman and Tom Wallace emphasized that Malcolm had the capacity to see through people.

"I CAN HEAR SINCERITY": *MX*, p. 400.

SAYS UNCLE TOMS ARE THE ONES WHO MISTAKE THEIR ENEMIES FOR FRIENDS: *BP*, p. 39.

CONTESTS SPEEDING TICKET: File maintained on Malcolm by New York City Police Dept.'s Bureau of Special Services (BOSS), p. 12. *New York Post*, Dec. 9, 1964. *New York Daily News*, Dec. 10, 1964. *New York Herald Tribune*, Dec. 10, 1964. Interview: Judge William Brennan.

CLOCKWATCHING: Asked to comment, for two minutes, on the Vietnamese conflict, Malcolm replied, "It's a shame -- that's one second -- it is, it's a shame." (*SPKS*, p. 218.)

TIME RUNNING OUT: Interviews: Philbert Little, Wilfred Little.

CHATTING AIMLESSLY: Interview: Charles Wiley.

"I WOULD LIKE TO KNOW THE DIFFERENCE"; EVEN MALCOLM HAD DIFFICULTY ANSWERING: *EPPS*, p. 181.

EASIER FOR WHITES TO HATE THAN IT IS FOR BLACKS: *PG*, p. 7. Interview: Peter Goldman.

335 "PERFECT -- JUST PERFECT"; "DO YOU THINK I DESERVE IT?": Interview: Ella Little.

"I HAD THE FEELING I WAS SEEING THE REAL MALCOLM"; HE SEEMED FRIENDLESS: Interview: Al Lewis. Arlington Cooper, who had been far more attuned to Malcolm's feelings than the majority of his teen-age friends had been, later asked, "Even with all his followers, didn't Malcolm feel alone?" (Interview: Arlington Cooper.)

53. Trapped!

336 "TOO BUSY": *MX*, p. 423.

"SHORTCOMINGS": *MX*, p. 379.

FELT SO GUILTY THAT HE CONSULTED A PSYCHIATRIST: *Democrat and Chronicle* (Rochester, N.Y.), August 19, 1989.

"HE WAS JUST GUILT RIDDEN": Interview: Gus Newport. In one letter, Malcolm wrote, "I shall never rest until I have undone the harm I did to so many well-meaning, innocent Negroes." (Sept. 22, 1964 letter from Mecca, quoted in *NYT*, Oct. 4, 1964.)

"I'LL TRUST YOU.": *MX*, pp. 422-423.

DIARY: *TKBM*, p. 173. *MX*, pp. 334, 419. Interview: John Elton Bembry. "He who writes to himself writes to an eternal public," Malcolm told Malcolm Jarvis.

337 "I HAVE NO IDEA"; "ISN'T ANYTHING WRONG WITH THAT": *PG*, p. 222. *NYT*, Feb. 22, 1965. *Newsweek*, March 3, 1969, p. 27. "He was groping, I sensed, for direction," says Richard

Friedman, who interviewed Malcolm shortly after Claude Lewis did. "He seemed [to be] searching for answers," reports Pat Robinson. (Interviews: Richard Friedman, Pat Robinson.)

"I'LL NEVER GET OLD"; "I DON'T SEE HOW THERE CAN BE A NEW MALCOLM X": *PG*, pp. 236-238. The *Philadelphia Inquirer*, March 14 & 15, 1964.

"THE GREAT JEWISH HISTORICAL TRADITION": *New York Amsterdam News*, Oct. 17, 1964.

AS AN EXAMPLE: *NYT*, May 24, 1964. *New York Amsterdam News*, May 23, 1964, March 27, 1965.

LEVY'S RYE BREAD: *LYMX*, pp. 98-99.

WAITRESS IN JEWISH DELICATESSEN: *FDL*, p. 223.

NEW POSITION ON WOMEN: *BAMN*, p. 179. *FDL*, p. 221. "Malcolm X: Struggle for Freedom" (Grove Press film). *JHC*, p. 90. Interviews: Pat Robinson, Malik Hakim, Saladin Matthews, Sharon 10X.

"SPIT ACID AT THE SISTERS": *FDL*, p. 221.

CRITICAL OF MEN WHO DIDN'T RESPECT THEIR MOTHERS: Interview: Pat Robinson.

338 DROPPED OPPOSITION TO RACIAL INTERMARRIAGE: *MX*, p. 424. *BAMN*, p. 118. *PG*, pp. 72, 225. *TKBM*, p. 142. Pierre Berton, *Voices from the Sixties* (Doubleday, 1967), pp. 39-40.

NO LONGER BELIEVED IN RACIAL SEPARATION: *Voices from the Sixties*, supra., p. 40.

DISPARAGED ASSERTION "THAT ISLAM IS THE RIGHT RELIGION . . . AND ALL OF THAT": "The Editors Speak," WLIB radio, New York City, 1964 (precise date unclear).

"FORGET IT": Phonograph record entitled "Ballots or Bullets" (First Amendment Records; record #100), distributed by Jamie/Guyden. *SPKS*, p. 180.

FROWNED AND PARRIED: *FDL*, p. 222.

"I STILL BELIEVE IN ALLAH--I MUST": *FDL*, p. 217.

"SHIFTY": Interview: Raymond Hightower.

"TRICKY"; "IT'S NOT A RACIST STATEMENT": *Malcolm X on Afro-American History* (Pathfinder Press, 1970), p. 20.

"DEMAGOGIC": Lewis B. Baldwin, "Malcolm X and Martin Luther King, Jr.: What They Thought About Each Other," *Islamic Studies* (Winter, 1986), p. 403.

RIGHT TRACK, BUT NOT DOING ENOUGH: *FBI*, Feb. 18, 1965, p. 2.

MOST SLUMLORDS ARE JEWS: *SPKS*, pp. 204-206. Malcolm told James 67X that, when he was abroad and he wanted something from his Arab hosts, he adopted an anti-Israeli stance. (Interview: James 67X.)

SAID HE WAS SORRY; HAD BEEN CONSTRAINED: *FDL*, pp. 210, 216-217.

"KING IS THE BEST THING THAT EVER HAPPENED TO WHITE FOLKS": *PG*, p. 230.

"HE GOT THE PEACE PRIZE; WE GOT THE PROBLEM": *PG*, p. 17.

"WHITEY": *BP*, p. 147. Malcolm also used the word "honkies." (Audiotape entitled "The Wit and Wisdom of Malcolm X.")

339 "I SHOULD HAVE RUN OVER HIM": Interview: confidential source.

WRY SENSE OF HUMOR: Interview: Tom Decker.

"HE DESPERATELY WANTED TO BELONG": *PG*, p. 144.

PRISONER: *PG*, p. 242.

"TRAPPED": Phonograph record entitled "Ballots or Bullets," supra. (Outwardly, Malcolm was talking about a purely economic trap. But see *MX*, p. 390, which underscores Malcolm's habit of talking about one thing and thinking of another.)

"TOO MODERATE . . . TOO MILITANT": *Brother Malcolm* (Malcolm X Memorial Committee: May, 1965), p. 17.

TRAPPED BY AFRICAN FEATURES: *EPPS*, p. 168. *BP*, pp. 166-167. *SPKS*, p. 169.

"OUR SKIN BECAME A TRAP, A PRISON": *EPPS*, p. 168. I am indebted to Beverly Harris, who helped me see how Malcolm was trapped by his skin color, on the one hand, and by conflicting parental and cultural demands on the other.

"WE HATED OURSELVES"; "OUR COLOR BECAME . . . A PRISON, . . . NOT LETTING US GO THIS WAY OR THAT": Phonograph record entitled "By Any Means Necessary," Douglas Communications Corp. (The version appearing in *SPKS*, p. 169 contains minor errors.)

"MR. IN-BETWEEN": Record album entitled "The Wisdom of Malcolm X" (Mo' Soul Records; record album #MS-8001).

A LONG, JOYLESS LAUGH: Program commemorating Malcolm X, broadcast by WHYY-FM, Philadelphia, May, 19, 1976.

54. Elijah Speaks

341 CONCILIATORY STATEMENTS: *Muhammad Speaks*, Jan. 1, 1965.

"CHIEF HYPOCRITE"; "I WILL NEVER FORGET": *Muhammad Speaks*, Jan. 15, 1965. *PG*, p. 248.

"WE'RE GOING TO KILL HIM": *PG*, p. 149.

"WE MUST MAKE A DECISION": *Muhammad Speaks*, Jan. 15, 1965.

AKBAR QUITS NOI AND INDICATES SYMPATHY FOR MALCOLM'S VIEWS: *NYT*, Jan. 15, 1965. Interview: Akbar Muhammad. Also *New York Amsterdam News*, Jan. 30, 1965 and *New York Post Daily Magazine*, Feb. 23, 1965.

MALCOLM BLAMED: *PG*, p. 247. Also see *Muhammad Speaks*, Dec. 4, 1964.

ATTACKED; THREE ASSAILANTS: *New York Amsterdam News*, Feb. 6, 1965. A slightly different version appears in *PG*, p. 250. *BP*, p. 118. *Malcolm X on Afro-American History* (Pathfinder Press, 1970), p. 47. Interview: Gladys Towles Root.

FIVE OR SIX ASSAILANTS: Malcolm's statement to the officials who investigated the cause of the Feb., 1965 fire that damaged his home.

"TALKING STICK": *New York Amsterdam News*, Feb. 6, 1965.

342 THRASHED ATTACKERS: *PG*, p. 250.

VIOLENT REPRISALS: *The Philadelphia Tribune*, June 20, 1964. *Chicago Defender*, July 9, 1964. *Chicago Sun-Times*, June 8, 1969; Jan. 13, 1972. *PG*, pp. 248-251. *NYT*, Feb. 22, 1965. *New York Amsterdam News*, Jan. 16, 1965. *FBI*, Jan. 19, 1965, pp. 1-3. See relevant sources cited below.

LEON AMEER: *Boston Sunday Herald*, March 14, 1965. *New York Amsterdam News*, Jan. 16, 1965. *NYT*, Feb. 22, 1965. *Chicago Sun-Times*, March 14, 1965. *New York Herald Tribune*, March 14, 1965. *PG*, p. 249.

KENNETH MORTON: *New York Amsterdam News*, Nov. 14, 1964; Jan. 16, 1965; Feb. 27, 1965. *NYT*, Feb. 22, 1965.

BENJAMIN BROWN: *New York Amsterdam News*, Jan. 16, 1965. *NYT*, Feb. 22, 1965. *New York Post*, Feb. 26, 1965. *New York Journal-American*, Feb. 26, 1965. *New York Daily News*, Feb. 27, 1965. Second edition of Peter Goldman, *The Death and Life of Malcolm X* (University of Illinois Press, 1979), pp. 249-250, 419-420.

JOHNSON'S RECORD: New York City police record of Thomas Johnson. *NYT*, March 2, 1966. *New York Herald Tribune*, March 3, 1966. *New York Post*, Feb. 26, 1965. *New York Daily News*, Feb. 27, 1965. *PG*, pp. 250, 346.

BOTH WERE JOSEPH'S LIEUTENANTS: *New York Journal-American*, Feb. 26, 1965. *New York Herald Tribune*, Feb. 26, 1966. *NYT*, 3/2/66. In 1973, Peter Goldman wrote that Johnson was merely "a nominee for NOI lieutenant." But in 1979, he confirmed Leon Ameer's and Butler's wife's testimony that Johnson had already achieved the rank of lieutenant under Captain Joseph. (*New York Times Magazine*, August 19, 1979; cf. *PG*, p. 250.)

"SECURITY GUARDS": Deposition of Benjamin Goodman, The People of the State of New York vs. Muhammad Abdul Aziz (Norman 3X Butler) and Khalil Islam (Thomas 15X Johnson), Supreme Court of the State of New York, May 15, 1978, p. 1. Interview: confidential source. *New York Times Magazine, Aug. 19, 1979.*

COMMANDS IN THE FORM OF SUGGESTIONS: Goldman, supra., pp. 126, 413.

343 "CUT THE NIGGER'S TONGUE OUT"; "SEND IT TO ME"; "I'LL STAMP IT 'APPROVED' AND GIVE IT TO THE MESSENGER"; MURDER BY SUGGESTION: *New York Times Magazine*, August, 19, 1979. Also see the second edition of Peter Goldman, supra., pp. 413-414. *BP*, pp. 136-137. *New York Herald Tribune*, Feb. 23, 1965.

JOSEPH MADE SIMILAR SUGGESTION: *New York Post Daily Magazine*, Feb. 23, 1965. Also see Malcolm's accusation in the *New York Amsterdam News*, March 21, 1964, p. 50. And see page 12 of the August 22, 1961 FBI report that says: "On 7/22/56 he was excommunicated from the [NOI] for . . . threatening the life of Malcolm X. . . . Joseph X had also been replaced for failing to report [material deleted] "allegations" to Malcolm immediately."

"IGNOBLE SILENCE": *Muhammad Speaks*, Jan. 29, 1965.

VOWED TO TAME: Sept. 22, 1964 letter from Mecca, quoted in *NYT*, Oct. 4, 1964. *JHC*, p. 140. Interview: confidential source

ESCORTED TWO WOMEN; VOLUNTEERED TO TESTIFY: *New York Journal-American*, Feb. 28, 1965. *FDL*, pp. 209-229, 235. *Los Angeles Times*, Feb. 25, 1965. *Chicago Tribune*, Feb. 25, 1965. *PG*, pp. 193-194, 250-251. *TKBM*, pp. 184-186. *MX*, pp. 424-425. Interviews: Gladys Towles Root, "Heather," "Robin."

THOROUGHLY COGNIZANT: *TKBM*, p. 186. *FDL*, p. 235. Interview: Gladys Towles Root.

"HE WAS FRIGHTENED"; HE ASKED WHETHER ROOT HAD DISCLOSED HIS INVOLVEMENT: Interview: Gladys Towles Root.

HOUNDED: *FDL*, pp. 209-229. *PG*, pp. 250-251. *TKBM*, p. 184. *MX*, pp. 424-425. Earlier that month, FBI wiretappers overheard Elijah Muhammad talking on the phone about an NOI minister who had acknowledged the similarity between the Messenger and a number of his illegitimate "birdies." Elijah said someone had better close his eyes. (FBI file on the Nation of Islam, Jan. 27, 1964, pp. 4-8.)

JOHN ALI AT L.A. AIRPORT: *FDL*, pp. 211-213, 228.

"THEY WANTED TO KILL"; "THEY KNOW WHY I'M HERE"; "THEY REALLY WANT TO GET ME": *FDL*, pp. 224-227.

344 ON THE WAY TO THE AIRPORT: *The Morning Call* [Paterson, N.J.], Feb. 25, 1965. *MX*, p. 425. *TKBM*, p. 184. *PG*, p. 251.

"NO MATTER WHAT THE COST"; VERY PLEASED WITH ACCOMPLISHMENTS: *MX*, pp. 425-426. *PG*, p. 251. *FBI*, Jan. 29, 965, p. 1. Interview: Ed McClellan.

COOPER V. PATE: Feb. 13, 1976 letter from Tom Decker, Esq., to author. Thomas Cooper vs. Frank J. Pate, 324 F. 2d 165 (1963). June 7, 1965 opinion by Judge Austin in Thomas Cooper vs. Frank J. Pate, U.S. District Court, Northern District of Illinois, Eastern Division. *FBI*, Feb. 15, 1965, p. 1; Feb. 17, 1965, p. 1. *Chicago Defender*, June 8, 1965. Interviews: Richard Friedman, Tom Decker.

345 CONFLICTING REPORTS: *Chicago Sun-Times*, April 5, 1965. *FBI*, Feb. 17, 1965, pp. 1-2; Feb. 18, 1965, p. 1. Dec. 28, 1981 letter from Richard Friedman to author. Interviews: Richard Friedman, Tom Decker.

THOUGHT HE WAS EAGER: Dec. 28, 1981 letter from Richard Friedman to author. Interviews: Richard Friedman, Tom Decker.

THOUGHT HE WAS RELUCTANT: *FBI*, Feb. 18, 1965, p. 1.

HAD URGED; HAD TESTIFIED: Interview: Edward Jacko. Undated, unidentified clipping in *Chicago Defender* archives. Undated *New York Amsterdam News* clipping.

IRV KUPCINET INTERVIEW: The unedited version of Malcolm's remarks appears in *FBI*, March 15, 1965, p. 46. The edited version appears in *FBI*, Feb. 4, 1965, p. 7.

TOUGH-LOOKING MEN: Interview: Tom Decker. *Chicago Sun-Times*, April 5, 1965. *FBI*, Jan. 31, 1965, p. 1; Feb. 18, 1965, pp. 2-3. *BP*, p. 119.

REPORTS CONCERNING NOI TAX EXEMPTIONS: Undated *New York Journal-American* article by Sam Crowther. *PG*, p. 251. Interview: Richard Friedman. According to one member of the Illinois Attorney General's staff, Chicago or Cook County officials, not the state Attorney General, were reconsidering a number of the NOI's tax exemptions. (Feb. 13, 1976 letter from Tom Decker, Esq., to author.)

"A MATTER OF TIME": *MX*, pp. 425-426. Also *PG*, p. 251 and *TKBM*, p. 185.

WALLACE VISITED MALCOLM: FBI file on Wallace Muhammad, Feb. 17, 1965, pp. 1-3. Interviews: Ed McClellan, confidential source.

SEEKING A WAY: *Chicago's American*, Feb. 25, 1965. Also see *Chicago Tribune*, March 2, 1975 (4-star final).

DETERMINED TO EXPOSE ELIJAH MUHAMMAD: Interview: confidential source. "Malcolm is destroying himself," Elijah Muhammad reportedly declared. (*MX*, p. 410.)

CHANGE OF HEART: *Chicago's American*, Feb. 25, 1965.

PLANNED TO EXPOSE SECRET FLIRTATION WITH THE KKK: *FBI*, Feb. 2, 1965, pp. 1-3.

Pittsburgh Courier, Feb. 13, 1965.

346 "BIRTH AND DEATH"; "SOON . . . YOU WILL SEE": *Muhammad Speaks*, Feb. 5, 1965. TOO LATE TO RETRACT; "STEPPED BEYOND THE LIMITS"; "I AM NO MORE TO SUFFER": *Muhammad Speaks*, Feb. 12, 1965.

DIDN'T EXPECT TO READ BOOK IN FINISHED FORM: *MX*, p. 426.

"AS IF I AM ALREADY DEAD": *MX*, p. 381.

55. Waiting in the Wings

347 TUSKEGEE REPORTEDLY PREFERS MALCOLM: Interview: confidential source.

HAD PLANNED TO DEPART: *FBI*, Feb. 3, 1965, p. 1.

STUDENTS INSISTED HE GO TO SELMA: *JHC*, p. 208. *BP*, p. 120.

THE SITUATION IN DALLAS COUNTY: Charles E. Fager, *Selma, 1965: The Town Where the South Was Changed* (Scribner's, 1974), pp. 8-9. *Pittsburgh Courier*, Feb. 13, 1965. *Congressional Quarterly Almanac*, 1965, p. 538. David Garrow, *Protest at Selma* (Yale University Press, 1978), pp. 34, 40. Stephen B. Oates, *Let the Trumpet Sound* (Harper & Row, 1982), p. 326.

THE SITUATION IN LOWNDES AND WILCOX COUNTIES: Fager, supra., pp. 31, 80. *Pittsburgh Courier*, Feb. 13, 1965.

348 THE CHIEF REASON KING SELECTED SELMA, ALA.: Garrow, supra., pp. 1-3, 40, 42, 111, 220-236, especially pp. 222-227. *TKBM*, pp. 85-86. Fager, supra., pp. 19, 31, 34. *PG*, p. 93. Taylor Branch, *Parting the Waters* (Simon and Schuster, 1988), p. 608. David Garrow, *Bearing the Cross* (William Morrow, 1986), pp. 239-240, 248, 360, 379. James Forman, *The Making of Black Revolutionaries* (Macmillan, 1972), pp. 311-312. *PG*, p. 93. King's biographer David Garrow has written: "King and the SCLC consciously had decided to attempt to elicit violent behavior from their . . . opponents. Such an intent governed the choice of Selma and Jim Clark." (David Garrow, *Protest at Selma*, supra., p. 227.)

KING ACKNOWLEDGED THAT MARCHES WERE INEFFECTIVE UNLESS THEY PROVOKED A VIOLENT REACTION: In the *Saturday Review*, April 3, 1965, pp. 16-17, King acknowledged that the plight of Southern blacks would only be alleviated if it were dramatized by violent attacks by whites against peacefully demonstrating blacks. But, on the following page, he claimed that he had no idea the Alabama authorities would behave so brutally.

NO LONGER IN DARK CORNERS; IN THE GLARING LIGHT OF TELEVISION: *Protest at Selma*, supra., p. 111. Also see Fager, supra., p. 34.

349 KING SUBTLY MANIPULATED THE MEDIA: Protest at Selma, supra., pp. 1-3, 111, 220-236, especially pp. 222-227. Bearing the Cross, supra., pp. 239-240, 248, 264. Howard Hubbard, "Five Long Hot Summers," *The Public Interest* (Summer, 1968; Vol. 12), p. 7. *TKBM*, pp. 85-86. (Also see *Parting the Waters*, supra., p. 608.) "There never was any more skillful manipulation of the news media than there was in Birmingham," Wyatt Walker bluntly admitted. Andrew Young seconded the point and said, "We were consciously using the mass media to try to get across to the nation what our message was. . . . You had to bring [the injustice] out in[to] the open." (*Bearing the Cross*, p. 264.)

RELUCTANTLY ARRIVED: The reluctance, which Malcolm tacitly acknowledges in *JHC*, p. 208 and in *BP*, p. 120 was due to the fact that he had made plans to fly from New York to England immediately after his appearance at Tuskegee. (*FBI*, Feb. 3, 1965, p. 1.) But Malcolm hid his reluctance, if Charles Fager, supra., pp. 56-57. is any indication.

DISAGREEMENT WHETHER MALCOLM SHOULD BE ALLOWED TO SPEAK; YOUNG AND BEVEL URGE MALCOLM: *PG*, pp. 230-231. *BP*, pp. 145-146. *Jet*, March 11, 1965. Fager, supra., p. 57. Also see *Protest at Selma*, supra., pp. 30-34.

YOUNG ACKNOWLEDGED THE MOVEMENT HAD BEEN SUSTAINED BY VIOLENCE: *Protest at Selma*, supra., p. 230. Jan Howard, "The Provocation of Violence: A Civil Rights Tactic?" *Dissent*, Jan.-Feb., 1966 (Vol. 13, No. 1), p. 98.

KING AND HIS AIDES ACTIVELY COURTED VIOLENCE: Jan Howard, "The Provocation of Violence: A Civil Rights Tactic?" *Dissent*, Jan.-Feb., 1966 (Vol. 13, No. 1), pp. 94-99. Howard Hubbard, "Five Long Hot Summers and How They Grew," *The Public Interest*, Summer, 1968 (No. 12), pp. 3-10. *Protest at Selma*, supra., pp. 1-3, 40, 42, 111, 220-236, especially pp. 222-227. *TKBM*, pp. 85-86. Fager, supra., pp. 31, 34. *PG*, p. 93. *Parting the Waters*, supra., p. 608. *Bearing the Cross*, supra., pp. 225-229, 239-240, 248, 263-264, 360, 379. Ralph Abernathy, *And the Walls Came Tumbling Down* (Harper Perennial paperback, 1990), pp. 225-227, 243-244, 259-261, 282, 286, 300-303, 308, 319-320, 344.

When white policemen employed violence against some of Birmingham, Alabama's black inhabitants, two of King's close associates told SNCC's James Forman, "We've got a movement. We've got a movement. We had some police brutality. They brought out the dogs. We've got a movement!" The two aides, Wyatt Walker and Dorothy Cotton, were jumping up and down with glee. (James Forman, *The Making of Black Revolutionaries* [Macmillan, 1972], pp. 311-312.) King's biographer David Garrow later wrote: "King accurately believed that nothing could be more effective in activating support among the national audience for the movement and its goal of equal suffrage than scenes of peaceful demonstrators, seeking their birthright as American citizens, being violently attacked by southern whites. . . . King and the SCLC consciously had decided to attempt to elicit violent behavior from their . . . opponents." (*Protest at Selma*, supra., pp. 223, 227.)

WITH A SMILE; "NOBODY PUTS WORDS IN MY MOUTH!": *Jet*, March 11, 1965.

HAD MADE THE SAME POINT: Transcript of Jan. 30, 1965 tape-recording of "Kup Show," reprinted *FBI*, Feb. 4, 1965, p. 5. (The attorneys were with Malcolm in the television studio when he made the statement.)

"I DON'T ADVOCATE VIOLENCE": *Jet*, March 11, 1965.

DIDN'T BELIEVE IN NONVIOLENCE EITHER: *PG*, p. 231.

"NOT FOR OR AGAINST VIOLENCE": *U.S. News & World Report*, March 30, 1964, p. 39.

OTHER FORCES ARE WAITING: *Jet*, March 11, 1965. Also *New York Post*, Feb. 4, 1965 and *PG*, pp. 231-232.

"AN ALTERNATIVE TO THINK ABOUT": *Jet*, March 11, 1965.

TRYING TO HELP: Coretta King, *My Life with Martin Luther King, Jr.* (Holt, Rinehart, & Winston, 1969), pp. 255-256. *Jet*, March 11, 1965. *PG*, p. 232. (Also see *BP*, p. 120.) Malcolm told Coretta King that, in the long run, he could better help her husband by attacking him instead of praising him. (James Cone, *Martin & Malcolm & America* [Orbis Books, 1991], p. 267.)

350 EXTREMISTS MADE MODERATES LIKE KING MORE PALATABLE TO WHITES: *The Reporter*, August 4, 1960, p. 40. Also see *SPKS*, p. 172 and Lewis V. Baldwin, "A Reassessment of the Relationship Between Malcolm X and Martin Luther King, Jr.," *The Western Journal of Black Studies* (Vol. 13, No. 2), 1989, p. 106.

HIS TURF: Oates, supra., p. 341. James Cone, supra., p. 267.

"BIG WORDS, BUT NO RECORD ON DEEDS": *New York Herald Tribune*, April 26, 1964. Also see *New York Amsterdam News*, Nov. 16, 1963. Similar criticism of Malcolm appeared in *Yale Review* (Winter, 1967), p. 170; *TKBM*, pp. 136, 155; *PG*, p. 8; *MX*, p. 420; *New York Post*, April 10, 1964; *New York Herald Tribune*, Feb. 22, 1965.

JUST ANOTHER CIVIL RIGHTS LEADER: Five days before he was killed, Malcolm described himself as "a little insignificant American Negro." (*BP*, p. 152.)

"SHAKE THE WORLD": *Malcolm X on Afro-American History* (Pathfinder Press, 1970), p. 43.

ROCKWELL, ROBINSON, AND MALCOLM'S TELEGRAM: *Malcolm X on Afro-American History*, supra., pp. 43-44. *Bearing the Cross*, p. 379. *New York Amsterdam News*, Jan. 23, 1965. Fager, supra., pp. 26-29. *BP*, pp. 119-120.

351 EASY FOR OUTSIDERS TO STAND ON SIDELINES MAKING MILITANT PRONOUNCE-MENTS: *LYMX*, p. 35.

"I'LL TELL YOU WHAT WE DID: NOTHING": *SPKS*, p. 145.

"REAL" REVOLUTION, AS OPPOSED TO "PSEUDO-REVOLT": *Egyptian Gazette*, August 17, 1964.

KING WAS THE ONE WHO LACKED A PROGRAM: *BP*, p. 120.

NASSER AND NKRUMAH: Undated *New York Journal-American* clipping.

UNABLE TO MAINTAIN CLOSE PERSONAL ATTACHMENTS: *PG*, p. 19. Interview: Reginald Little.

DEJECTED; SHOES UNKEMPT; "NOTHING TO LIVE FOR"; "HE DIDN'T CARE WHETHER HE LIVED OR DIED": Interviews: Christine Johnson, Tom Decker, Charles 37X.

56. Another Fire

352 DEPARTED FOR EUROPE THE SAME DAY: *FBI*, Feb. 5, 1965, p. 1; Feb. 9, 1965, pp. 1-2. Also see Charles E. Fager, *Selma, 1965: The Town Where the South Was Changed* (Scribner's 1974), pp. 58-59.

ACTION-PROGRAM: *LYMX*, pp. 66, 78. *New York Amsterdam News*, Feb. 13, 1965.

PREVIOUSLY PROMISED: *Malcolm X on Afro-American History* (Pathfinder Press, 1970), p. 38. Also see *PG*, p. 244, which says that the program had first been promised for December.

LONDON: *JHC*, pp. 205, 209. Also see *London Times*, Feb. 10, 1965.

EN ROUTE TO GENEVA: Feb. 11, 1965 cablegram from American Legation, Paris to the FBI Director and the American Legation, Bern. *FBI*, Feb. 5, 1965, p. 1; Feb. 9, 1965, p. 1; Feb. 9, 1965, pp. 1-2. (There are two relevant FBI documents dated February 9. Both originated in the Bureau's New York office and were addressed to the FBI Director.) Also see *TKBM*, p. 181.

BARRED FROM FRANCE: France's refusal to admit Malcolm is described in the *London Times*, Feb. 10, 1965; the European Edition of the *Herald Tribune*, Feb. 10, 1965; the International Edition of the *New York Times*, Feb. 10 & 11, 1965; the Feb. 11, 1965 cablegram from the American Legation, Paris, supra.; and in *JHC*, pp. 205-208, *BAMN*, pp. 168-170, and *PG*, pp. 253-255.

INTERNATIONAL CONSPIRACY: *MX*, pp. 430-431, 433. *PG*, p. 267. Interview: Jim Campbell. Ella later asserted that she was the one who had convinced Malcolm he was the target of an international conspiracy. (Interview: Ella Little.) On occasion, he playfully pronounced the word "con-spire-acy." (Tape-recording of April 8, 1964 speech entitled "The Black Revolution.")

353 SCHEDULED VISIT TO GENEVA "ISLAMIC CENTER": Feb. 11, 1965 cablegram from American Legation, Paris, to the FBI Director and the American Legation, Bern.

SAID RAMADAN URGED THE LEAGUE TO AID MALCOLM: Interview: Said Ramadan.

LONDON SCHOOL OF ECONOMICS: *London Times*, Feb. 10 & 12, 1965.

BIRMINGHAM, SMETHWICK, AND PETER GRIFFITHS: *London Times*, Feb. 12, Feb. 15, and Feb. 19, 1965. (Also see *London Times*, Oct. 7, 1964; Oct. 13, 1964; Nov. 7, 1964; Dec. 7, 1964; Jan. 27, 1965.) *NYT*, Feb. 14, 1965. *PG*, p. 255.

LAST-DITCH EFFORT TO POSTPONE EVICTION: L & T #4845, Queens Civil Court (Special Term, Part I), 1964: Jan. 29, 1965 affidavit by Malcolm X. Little; Jan. 29, 1965 affidavit by Oliver Sutton; Feb. 9, 1965 letter from Percy Sutton to Judge Wahl; Feb. 12, 1965 requisition for warrant; Feb. 15, 1965 order by Judge Wahl vacating stay of execution. *NYT*, Feb. 15, 1965.

AROUND 2:30 A.M.: Malcolm's widow told an interviewer that the fire occurred "at 2:30 in the morning." (Fletcher Knebel, "A Visit with the Widow of Malcolm X," *Look*, March 4, 1969, p. 77.) *SPKS*, p. 157. Also see *New York Herald Tribune*, Feb. 15, 1965 and *New York Daily News*, Feb. 15, 1965. The first alarm was turned in at 2:38 a.m., according to what the New York City Fire Department told me. Other sources assert that the first alarm was sounded at 2:45 or 2:46 a.m. (*FBI*, Feb. 16, 1965, p. 1; *NYT*, Feb. 15. 1965; *PG*, p. 262.)

THE SAME TIME 1929 FIRE HAD OCCURRED: Michigan State Police Report #2155 concerning Nov. 8, 1929 fire.

CAB DRIVER AND PASSENGER SPOT FLAMES AND TRY TO WARN OCCUPANTS: 1965 Fire Department report: statement of taxi driver (whom I was unable to locate). *FBI*, Feb. 16, 1965, p. 2.

354 MALCOLM WAS SMILING: Interview: Kenneth Kopp.

STILL SMILING HOURS AFTER THE FIRE: UPI photo negative #1459986. (It is unclear if the photo, which was transmitted to UPI's customers Feb. 15, 1965, was taken Feb. 14 or Feb. 15.) Original, unedited tape-recording of Stan Bernard's Feb. 18, 1965 talk show "Contact," New York City radio station WINS.

UNBURNED GASOLINE DISCOVERED IN BOTTOM OF SHATTERED BOTTLES: Interview: Thomas Barry.

THE WICK WAS NOT EVEN SCORCHED: 1965 Fire Department Report. *FBI*, Feb. 16, 1965, p. 3.

AT THE BASE OF THE DRAWN VENETIAN BLIND THAT HUNG ALL THE WAY TO THE BOTTOM OF THE WINDOW: *FBI*, Feb. 16, 1965, p. 2 and accompanying diagram.

Interview: Ralph Aiello.

CLAIMED FIREMEN RUINED SUITS DELIBERATELY: Interview: Anas Mahmoud Luqman.

355 SO FEW BOOKS: Interview: Hugo Mazzu.

HAD REMOVED BOOKS BEFORE THE FIRE: Interview: Tom Wallace.

GLASS FROM WINDOW, STORM WINDOW, AND BURNED-OUT MOLOTOV COCK-TAIL DISCOVERED OUTSIDE, NOT INSIDE, CHILDREN'S BEDROOM: 1965 Fire Department report. *FBI*, Feb. 16, 1965, p. 3 and accompanying diagram. Undated, written reply from Ralph Aiello to author's written Oct. 19, 1976 inquiry. Interview: Ralph Aiello.

SPREADING, FAN-SHAPED PATTERN THAT INDICATED THAT THE FIREBOMB HAD BEEN THROWN FROM THE HOUSE INTO THE YARD: Interview: Ralph Aiello. Diagram sent by Ralph Aiello in response to author's written Oct. 19, 1976 inquiry. The Feb. 16, 1965 *FBI* report on the fire mentions the scorched ground and fence. (See pp. 2-3.) Malcolm asserted that the burned-out firebomb had landed in the back yard because it had been thrown at a forty-five-degree angle and had glanced off the glass window instead of shattering it. (*BP*, p. 141.)

UNBROKEN, UPRIGHT, WICKLESS, GASOLINE-FILLED WHISKEY BOTTLE: Testimony of Thomas Barry [in] 1965 Fire Department report. *FBI*, Feb. 14, 1965, p. 1; Feb. 16, 1965, p. 3. *New York Daily News*, Feb. 16, 1965. *NYT*, Feb. 17, 1965. *JHC*, p. 88. Interviews: Hank Thoben, Marvis Rogoff, Thomas Barry. Also see Betty Shabazz's statement in the 1965 Fire Department report.

POLICEMEN OR FIREMEN ALLEGEDLY PLANTED THE BOTTLE: *The Realist*, Feb., 1967, p. 12. Stan Bernard's talk show "Contact," Feb. 18, 1965, supra. But detective Joe McCormack went to the fire station and asked each fireman who had been inside the house whether he had brought an unbroken bottle into it. They all replied no, says McCormack. (Interview: Joe McCormack. Also see *FBI*, Feb. 16, 1965, p. 3.)

ABSENCE OF SMUDGE BENEATH THE BOTTLE: Interviews: Hank Thoben, Marvin Rogoff.

ANOTHER UNSHATTERED, UNEXPLODED MOLOTOV COCKTAIL: Interviews: Joe McCormack, Ralph Aiello, Hank Thoben, Dennis James, Tom Wallace. See Tom Wallace's undated, written response to author's written August 26, 1976 inquiry.

AFTER PENETRATING STORM WINDOW AND DRAWN VENETIAN BLINDS?: The storm windows were closed and the venetian blinds were fully extended and drawn. (*FBI*, Feb. 16, 1965, p. 2. Statement by Betty Shabazz [in] 1965 Fire Department report. Interviews: Ralph Aiello, Richard Nielsen, Joe McCormack, Marvin Rogoff.)

WOULD NOT PERMIT POLICE TO QUESTION THE CHILDREN, WHO SEEMED UNFAZED: Interview: Ralph Aiello.

WOULD NOT LET BETTY TALK MUCH: Interview: Marvin Rogoff. At the offices of the New York City Fire Department, Betty would not answer questions until Malcolm gave the okay. (Interview: Joe McCormack.) Years later, as she described the way Malcolm had behaved during the fire, she said his conduct had "almost frightened" her. (*Look*, March 4, 1969, p. 77.)

FIRED PISTOL: Interview: Ralph Aiello.

AS HE SAID HIS FATHER HAD DONE: *MX*, p. 4.

NO ONE HEARD SHOTS: Interview: Matthew Conlan.

PISTOL MISFIRED: *FBI*, Feb. 17, 1965, p. 2. See Malcolm's statement in 1965 Fire Department report. Also see *JHC*, pp. 86-87.

356 COOL AND COLLECTED; AS SOON AS EACH QUESTION WAS ASKED: Interviews: Milton Klein, Vincent Canty. Also see *FBI*, Feb. 16, 1965, p. 4, which emphasizes the lack of emotion.

SUTTON READ NEWSPAPER: Interview: Joe McCormack.

LAUGHED WHEN ASKED WHY HIS HOME HAD BEEN SET ABLAZE: *New York Daily News*, Feb. 15, 1965. Interview: Jack Mallon. *Afro-American* (National Edition), Feb. 20, 1965.

IN RESPONSE TO THE QUESTION WHO HAD SET THE FIRE: *PG*, p. 263. *FBI*, Feb. 16, 1965, p. 4.

FINANCIALLY IN DESPERATE STRAITS: *MX*, pp. 429-430, 445-446. *PG*, p. 4 and footnote on p. 233. "Like It Is," WABC-TV, Feb. 22, 1969 (a rebroadcast). In the Dec. 4, 1964 issue of

Muhammad Speaks, Louis X said that Malcolm was "not capable of even putting his family in a home."

PUBLICITY AND SYMPATHY: *New York Post*, Feb. 16, 1965. *New York Daily News*, Feb. 16, 1965. *NYT*, Feb. 16, 1965; Feb. 17, 1965. *TKBM*, p. 229. *MX*, p. 428.

EFFORT TO DISCREDIT ELIJAH MUHAMMAD: The Feb. 19, 1965 issue of *Muhammad Speaks* declared that "the Honorable Elijah Muhammad came through the smoke and flames completely unscathed."

REVENGE: Detective Ralph Aiello came to the conclusion that the motive had been revenge. (Interview: Ralph Aiello.) And see the way Percy Sutton uses the phrase "striking back" on p. 32 of the transcript of "Like It Is," WABC-TV, Feb. 22, 1969.

"IF HE CAN'T HAVE [THE HOUSE], WE CAN'T EITHER": Warner Brothers film documentary entitled "Malcolm X."

USES "BURN" TO MEAN "PUNISH": *MX*, p. 295. (Recall Malcolm's admonition that "it is better to marry than to burn." Also see *FBI*, May 19, 1959, p. 37 and Malcolm's Dec. 13, 1950 petition to the Massachusetts Commissioner of Correction.)

VOWED THE NOI WOULD NEVER GET THE HOUSE: Interview: Matthew Conlan.

JAIL A ROAD TO MARTYRDOM AND POLITICAL LEADERSHIP: "I'll go to jail. I'll go to prison. Stick me in jail. Let me go to prison." (Excerpt from phonograph record entitled "Malcolm X Speaks to the People in Harlem" [Up Front Records; record #UPF-152].) One NOI spokesman charged that Malcolm wanted to appear the martyr. (*New York Post*, Feb. 15, 1965.)

LOOKED POLICE OFFICIAL IN THE EYE AND SAID HE OWNED A PISTOL: *JHC*, pp. 86-87. *FBI*, Feb. 17, 1965, p. 2. Malcolm also told Detective Aiello that he owned a pistol. (Interview: Ralph Aiello.)

ALSO TOLD THE FIRE MARSHALL AND THE MEDIA: Statement by Malcolm [in] 1965 Fire Department report. *NYT*, Feb. 22, 1965. Warner Brothers film documentary entitled "Malcolm X." Interview: M.S. Handler.

MICHIGAN AUTHORITIES HAD JAILED HIS FATHER ON A GUN-CARRYING CHARGE: Michigan State Police Special Report #2155 concerning Nov. 8, 1929 fire.

"HE DIDN'T CARE": Interview: Ralph Aiello.

AIELLO AND ANOTHER POLICE OFFICIAL RECOMMENDED MALCOLM'S ARREST: Interviews: Ralph Aiello, Marvin Rogoff.

OVERRULED BY SUPERIORS: Interviews: Hugh O'Donnell, Ralph Aiello, confidential source.

357 MALCOLM CHANGED THE WORD "I" TO "II": Unedited tape-recording of Feb. 14, 1965 Detroit speech. Phonograph record entitled "The Last Message" (Discus Hablands; record #LP-1300). Malcolm's slip of the tongue was edited out of the version of his remarks that appears in *SPKS*, p. 157.

"SUPPORTERS": *New York Post*, Feb. 15, 1965. Undated *New York Journal-American* article that was published after Malcolm's assassination.

"WELL AWARE": *BP*, p. 126.

"LET THE CHIPS FALL": *BP*, p. 142.

HE SAID THE PROGRAM WOULD BE ONE OF HIS LAST: *BP*, p. 149.

ACTION-PROGRAM: "We didn't want to bring up our program," Malcolm acknowledged. (*BP*, p. 133.) The "program" was not even ready February 21. (Undated transcript of grand jury testimony by Benjamin Goodman, pp. 17-18. *PG*, pp. 244, 271.)

HIGH-SOUNDING RESTATEMENT: *LYMX*, pp. 113-124.

"QUITE CERTAIN" BOMB-THROWERS KNEW WHERE EACH MEMBER OF FAMILY SLEPT: *BP*, P. 111.

HAD KNOWN "NOTHING" ABOUT EVICTION PROCEEDINGS: *BP*, p. 140. *FBI*, Feb. 16, 1965, p. 1.

MEN WHO PLACE INNOCENT CHILDREN IN THE LINE OF FIRE: *BP*, P. 131. *NYT*, May 11, 1963.

"IF ANYBODY CAN FIND WHERE I BOMBED MY HOUSE, THEY CAN PUT A RIFLE BULLET THROUGH MY HEAD": Original tape-recording of Feb. 15, 1965 speech at Audubon Ballroom. (Also see the edited version in the Warner Brothers film documentary entitled "Malcolm X." The version published in *BP*, pp. 141-142, says "I've bombed" instead of "I bombed.") Malcolm did not say, "If anybody can find that I bombed my house, . . . " He said, "If anybody can find where I bombed my house, . . . "

AUDIENCE'S ATTENTION DIVERTED: *New York Newsday*, July 23, 1989. *PG*, p. 265. Interviews: Ken Gross, Tom Wallace. Also see the part of the tape-recording of Malcolm's Feb. 15, 1965 speech where he tells a number of people in the audience, "Y'all sit down and be cool."

57. Political Martyr

358 MOVED TO TOM WALLACE'S HOME: Interviews: Tom Wallace and confidential source. *PG*, p. 264.

CASH IN SUITCASE: Interviews: Tom Wallace, Jr., confidential source.

SAID HE HAD TO TAKE MONEY TO SWITZERLAND: Interview: Tom Wallace.

HAD RECEIVED FINANCIAL HELP FROM ABROAD: Interview: James 67X.

LEAVING HIS FAMILY AT WALLACE'S: According to two members of Tom Wallace's family, the Feb. 16, 1965 *New York Daily News*, the medical examiner's report that was completed the following week, pages 264 and 267 of *PG*, and pages 429-430 of *MX*, Malcolm had already left Tom's house by Feb. 16, 1965 and had moved elsewhere, despite the contradictory, self-serving account in *JHC*, pp. 90-91 and the March 8, 1965 issue of *Newsweek*, which omits Malcolm's brief stay at Wallace's house altogether.

TO SAFEGUARD WIFE AND CHILDREN: Interviews: Oliver Sutton, Tom Wallace.

RUMORED ARGUMENT: Interview: Philbert Little.

EXPECTED TO DIE PREMATURELY: *Afro-American*, Feb. 23, 1965. *MX*, pp. 2, 138, 378, 380-381, 410. *JHC*, p. 90. *PG*, p. 246. Interviews: Malik Hakim, Milton Henry, Lawrence Henry, Billy Rowe.

"IT WILL BE ALL OVER SOON": *JHC*, p. 90.

BY FEBRUARY 26: *FDL*, p. 221. Also *NYT*, Feb. 22, 1965.

ROOT AND OTHERS SENSED: Interview: Gladys Towles Root. *PG*, pp. 220, 240, 246-247, 265. *FDL*, pp. 213-215. "Like It Is," WABC-TV, Jan. 6, 1980. Leon Ameer, who had been beaten and severely injured by NOI enforcers, also feared for his life. One day, he and Malcolm met with James Hicks in Hicks's Amsterdam News office. After Ameer left the office, Malcolm told Hicks, "If he's that frightened, you can imagine how I feel." (Interview: James Hicks.) Also see the relevant sources cited below.

PREPARING HIS FOLLOWERS FOR A RETRACTION: Minutes before he died, Malcolm told his associates he was going to announce that he had been hasty to accuse the NOI of firebombing his home. (*MX*, p. 433.) A day earlier, he had told Alex Haley, "I think I'm going to quit saying it's the Muslims." (*MX*, pp. 430-431.)

359 OTHER INDICATIONS: For example, recall Malcolm's habit of sitting in the rear of airplanes in the apparent hope of being thrown clear in the event of a crash, just as the stewardesses who had survived the crash near Paris had been thrown clear. (Interviews: James 67X, Charles 37X, confidential source.)

THE NEED TO PUT DISTANCE BETWEEN HIMSELF AND ELIJAH'S HENCHMEN: *PG*, p. 220. Interview: John Elton Bembry. *Al Gumhuriya*, Feb. 24, 1965, reprinted in March 3, 1965 airgram from American Embassy, Cairo, to U.S. Dept. of State.

BRIDLED AT SHADOWS: *PG*, p. 240,

"BANG": *PG*, p. 246. Also interview with Elizabeth Gethers, who recalls how jittery unexpected noises made Malcolm.

LOOKING BACK OVER SHOULDER: *PG*, pp. 212, 265.

NEVER SIT WITH BACK TO DOOR: *MX*, p. 129. Interview: Wilfred Little.

SECURED HOOD OF CAR: Interview: Tom Wallace, Jr.

CONFLICTING REPORTS WHETHER MALCOLM COMPLETED APPLICATION FORM: *PG*, pp. 265-266. *NYT*, Feb. 22, 1965. *New York Herald Tribune*, Feb. 19, 1965. *MX*, p. 438. Clipping of Feb. 23, 1965 newspaper article by Edward Kirkman, William Travers, & Lester Abelman. (The clipping is in Malcolm Jarvis's scrapbook of articles on Malcolm X.) But cf: *JHC*, p. 90; *New York Post Daily Magazine*, Feb. 23, 1965; undated article by Sam Crowther from the *New York Journal-American; New York Amsterdam News,* Feb. 19, 1966. Also see section 1903 (formerly section 1837) of the New York State Penal Law and sections 436-5.0 and 436-6.6 of the Administrative Code of New York City.

DISCLOSURE OF SECRET NOI-KKK CONTACTS: *New York Post,* Feb. 16, 1965. *NYT,* Feb. 16, 1965. *BP,* pp. 122-124. *FBI,* May 17, 1961, p. 19; Feb. 16, 1965, pp. 2-3; Feb. 19, 1965, pp. 1-2. FBI file on the Nation of Islam, April 14, 1961, pp. 96-97. *PG,* pp. 253, 265. Also see *Muhammad Speaks,* Sept. 11, 1964. *BP,* pp. 122-123 says that the meeting occurred in December of 1960, but the April 14, 1961 and May 17, 1961 FBI files indicate that the meeting occurred Jan. 28, 1961.

REMINISCENT OF JAMES EASON'S DISCLOSURE OF GARVEY'S CONTACTS WITH KKK: According to Jarvis, Malcolm was very well read about Marcus Garvey. (Eason's provocative disclosure is described in Theodore G. Vincent, *Black Power and the Garvey Movement,* (The Ramparts Press, 1978), pp. 190-191, 196-197.)

TOLD THE KKK OFFICIALS WHAT THEY WANTED TO HEAR: FBI file on the Nation of Islam, April 14, 1961, pp. 96-97.

COULD NOT UNDERSTAND WHY THE KKK ALLOWED KING TO LIVE: FBI file on the Nation of Islam, April 14, 1961, p. 97.

DISCLOSURE ABOUT NOI CONTACTS WITH NAZI LEADER ROCKWELL: *New York Post,* April 30, 1963, June 5, 1963. *Muhammad Speaks,* August 28, 1964. *NYT,* Feb. 16, 1965. *New York Post,* Feb. 16, 1965. *BP,* p. 124. *PG,* p. 253. FBI file on the Nation of Islam, April 24, 1962, pp. 122-125; Oct. 24, 1962, p. 132. *FBI,* Feb. 16, 1965, pp. 2-3; Feb. 19, 1965, pp. 1-2. FBI correlation file on Elijah Muhammad, April 9, 1969, p. 30. Charles E. Fager, *Selma, 1965* (Scribner's, 1974), p. 27. Compare Malcolm's 1965 disclosure, and especially *BP,* p. 124, with the way he tried, when he was in the NOI, to justify Rockwell's appearance at the NOI's 1962 convention. (Kenneth B. Clark, ed., *The Negro Protest* [Beacon Press, 1963], pp. 29-30.)

360 "MAN IS ACTUALLY THE TOOL OF HIS OWN DESTRUCTION": Undated 1949 letter to Bazely Perry.

"BECAUSE I'M ME": *PG,* p. 266. Perhaps his self-destructiveness, which Elijah Muhammad had noted in the Jan. 15, 1965 issue of *Muhammad Speaks,* stemmed from the guilt Gus Newport had sensed. (See Chapter 53.)

ACKNOWLEDGED HE SOMETIMES DELIBERATELY INVITED DEATH: *MX,* p. 138.

"A TIME FOR MARTYRS": *PG,* p. 267. *MX,* p. 429.

SAMSON, GANDHI, JESUS, SAMSON: *MX,* pp. 242, 395. Undated petition to the Massachusetts Commissioner of Correction. Undated 1949 letter from Malcolm to Bazely Perry. Page 10 of unidentified document in C. Eric Lincoln Collection, Atlanta University Library. Also see July 22, 1949 letter from Malcolm to Bazely Perry, April 18, 1977 letter from J. Prescott Adams to author, and *PG,* p. 404.

KNOWING FULL WELL I WILL BE DESTROYED: *WWG,* p. 178.

NO DESIRE TO BE MOURNED: Interview: Saladin Matthews.

CHARACTERIZED DEATH AS A REFUGE: *MX,* p. 417. He characterized suicide as an act of inspired, fleeting happiness. (Phonograph record entitled "Malcolm X Speaks to the People in Harlem," Up Front Records, record #UPF-152).

PREDESTINED; BEYOND HIS CONTROL: *PG,* p. 252. Interviews: Malcolm Jarvis, Christine Johnson, John Elton Bembry, Elizabeth Gethers, Richard Friedman, Oliver Sutton, Malik Hakim. "Everything that happens . . . is written," Malcolm said. (*MX,* p. 211. Also see p. 149.)

"THERE'S NOTHING I CAN DO": Interview: Oliver Sutton. The feeling of helplessness is often engendered by youthful conditioning. See, inter alia, Charolotte Olmsted, *Heads I Win, Tails You Lose* (Macmillan, 1962), pp. 159-165.

OMAR VAINLY TRIES OUTRUNNING DEATH: *PG,* p. 239. Interview: Percy Sutton. (Several versions of the apocryphal tale exist.)

"HE WANTED TO DIE": *PG,* p. 3. Interviews: Charles 37X, confidential source.

"IT WOULD MAKE A MARTYR OUT OF HIM": *PG,* p. 203. Malcolm said he would not direct his followers to take action against NOI members. (*BP,* p. 136.)

361 CONFIDENT DEMEANOR: Interview: Maurice Wahl.

TEARS IN HIS EYES: Interview: Charles 37X.

NOT THE ONLY TEARS; "I LOOKED AT HIS EYES. THEY SEEMED BLUE": Interview: Ella Little.

UNDISCLOSED SUM: *New York Herald Tribune*, March 1, 1966. *PG*, pp. 350-353. Philbert Little heard rumors that money had been offered. (Interview: Philbert Little.)

ASKED WHAT ROOM: *New York Daily News*, Feb. 22, 1965. *New York Journal-American*, Feb. 22, 1965. *MX*, p. 431. Also *PG*, p. 268.

TALMADGE HAYER: *PG*, pp. 312, 337-339. *FBI*, Feb. 25, 1965, p. 1; Feb. 25, 1966, pp. 2-3.

HIT SQUAD: *Newsweek*, May 7, 1979, p. 39.

FAMILIAR TO POLICE: Clipping of unidentified Feb. 23, 1965 newspaper article by Edward Kirkman, William Travers, & Lester Abelman. (The clipping is in Malcolm Jarvis's scrapbook of newspaper clippings on Malcolm X.)

SMALL ARSENAL: Ibid. *New York Herald Tribune*, Feb. 23, 1965. *Afro-American*, Feb. 23, 1965. *PG*, p. 288.

NOT AN NOI MEMBER; NEVER TOOK MONEY: *PG*, pp. 350-353.

HAYER LATER CHANGED HIS STORY: Nov. 30, 1977 affidavit by Talmadge Hayer, reproduced in Dec. 5, 1977 petition by attorney William Kunstler; Motion to Vacate Judgments, *People of the State of New York vs. Norman 3X Butler and Thomas 15X Johnson* (indictment #871/65; Supreme Court of the State of New York.) The court documents and Peter Goldman's *The Death and Life of Malcolm X* detail the many twists and turns in Hayer's testimony. See especially pp. 421-423 of the second edition of Goldman's book. Note the way Hayer talks and averts his eyes as he proclaims his newest truth. ("Malcolm X's Death: Other Voices," Tony Brown's Journal, WNET-TV, Jan. 28, 1980.) Also see "Sixty Minutes," CBS-TV, Jan. 17, 1982, where Hayer tries to justify some of his earlier misstatements.

"BIG": Peter Goldman, *The Death and Life of Malcolm X* (U. of Illinois Press, 1979), p. 415.

WENT TO AUDUBON BALLROOM: Nov. 30, 1977 affidavit by Talmadge Hayer, supra. *New York Times Magazine*, August 19, 1979, p. 30. Goldman, supra., p. 418.

"ANNUAL CLASS CLOSING": *PG*, p. 314. *Muhammad Speaks*, Feb. 5, 1965. *Muhammad Speaks* enclosed the words "annual class closing" in quotation marks. The announcement describing the event did not reappear in the newspaper's February 12 issue.

DIDN'T HOLD CLASS CLOSINGS: Interviews: James 67X, Sharon 10X, and a confidential source who had been one of "Malcolm's ministers."

KEEN INTEREST IN THE EXITS: *PG*, p. 314.

HAD PARTICIPATED IN ASSASSINATION REHEARSAL: *PG*, p. 352.

362 THE POLICE KNEW AND HAD OFFERED PROTECTION: Interviews: Joe McCormack, Walter Arm. *PG*, pp. 260-262. *MX*, p. 438. *New York Journal-American*, Feb. 22, 1965. *Afro-American*, Feb. 23, 1965. Eric Norden, "The Murder of Malcolm X," *The Realist* (Feb., 1967), pp. 14-15. George Breitman, Herman Porter, & Baxter Smith, *The Assassination of Malcolm X* (Pathfinder Press, 1976), p. 57.

THE POLICE KNEW MALCOLM WOULD LIKELY REFUSE: *New York Times Magazine*, Aug. 19, 1979, p. 30. *PG*, pp. 261, 364.

FRANK ABOUT HIS RELUCTANCE TO ACCEPT POLICE PROTECTION: New York Police Dept., Bureau of Special Services file on Malcolm X, entry dated Jan. 27, 1964.

PRIDE: Interview: Charles 37X. *New York Times Magazine*, Aug. 19, 1979.

HIS OWN MEN HAD TO URGE PROTECTION ON HIM: Interview: Clifford Hyman. Also see *JHC*, p. 91.

"I'M GOING TO BE DEAD BY TUESDAY": Malcolm repeatedly said he'd be dead by Tuesday. *PG*, p. 266.

MARKED FOR DEATH BY FEBRUARY 21: Phonograph record entitled "The Search for Black Identity: Malcolm X" (Guidance Associates of Pleasantville, N.Y.).

"NOBODY . . . BUT A MUSLIM": *MX*, p. 429.

REFUSAL TO REQUEST POLICE PROTECTION: On a Jan. 14, 1965 talk show called "Talk of Philadelphia," Bill Campbell asked Malcolm if he expected an attempt on his life. "Almost everybody you see here is a policeman, " Malcolm replied. Then he added: "I didn't, and have never asked, for any kind of police protection or escort."

REFUSAL TO ACCEPT POLICE PROTECTION: Interviews: Joe McCormack, Walter Arm, Percy Sutton, Gene Roberts. *NYT*, Feb. 22, 1965. *New York Journal-American*, Feb. 22, 1965. *Afro-American*, Feb. 23, 1965. *PG*, pp. 261-262.

"OFF THE HOOK": *PG*, p. 262.

363 QUESTIONED ABOUT LOCATION OF MALCOLM'S ROOM: *New York Daily News*, Feb. 22, 1965.

"WAKE UP, BROTHER": *MX*, p. 431. *PG*, p. 268.

"MALCOLM KNEW HE WAS GOING TO DIE": *Afro-American*, Feb. 24, 1968. Also Eric Norden, supra., p. 13.

TURNS TO BETTY; CHANGES MIND ABOUT HER ATTENDING: *MX*, pp. 429-431. *PG*, pp. 267, 268. Warner Brother film documentary entitled "Malcolm X."

LONG JOHNS AND VEST: *PG*, p. 268. The autopsy report describes Malcolm's "sweater vest." *MX*, p. 431 describes the weather.

PARKED CAR AND STOOD AT BUS STOP: *New York Herald Tribune*, Feb. 23, 1965. *PG*, pp. 268-269.

AMBUSHED IN CAR: Benjamin Brown's description of where and how he was shot appears in a clipping of an unidentified newspaper article by Alvin Davis entitled "Another Victim Talks."

SEVERAL DOZEN PEOPLE ALREADY INSIDE: *PG*, p. 269. *JHC*, pp. 92-93. *Afro-American* [Baltimore edition], Feb. 24, 1970. Also see *MX*, p. 432.

364 THOMAS 15X JOHNSON SEEN INSIDE AUDITORIUM: *New York Herald Tribune*, Jan. 22, 1966. *Afro-American* [Baltimore edition], Jan. 25, 1966. *PG*, p. 321. *The Assassination of Malcolm X*, supra., pp. 74-75, 80. Also see pp. 662-665, 799 of Vernon Temple's 1966 testimony in *The People of the State of New York vs. Norman 3X Butler and Thomas 15X Johnson* (Supreme Court of the State of New York; New York County).

JOHNSON AND BUTLER SEEN INSIDE AUDITORIUM BY BROTHER JAMIL: Interview with Brother Jamil (who doesn't want his full name disclosed).

BUTLER'S CRIMINAL RECORD: New York City police record of Norman Butler. *New York Daily News*, Feb. 27, 1965.

REPORTEDLY ADMITTED FIRING THE SHOT; RIFLE DISCOVERED IN HIS HOME: *New York Post*, Feb. 26, 1965. Years later, when Peter Goldman interviewed Johnson, the latter vehemently denied shooting Brown. At the time, Johnson was reappealing his conviction for Malcolm's assassination. He asserted that someone else had given him the rifle that had been used to shoot Brown. (Second edition, Goldman, supra., p. 420.)

JOHNSON DID NOT HIDE HIS HATRED FOR MALCOLM, WHOM HE SAID DESERVED TO DIE: Mike Wallace interviewing Thomas Johnson, "Sixty Minutes," CBS-TV, Jan. 17, 1982.

HAD REPORTEDLY BEEN SUSPENDED FOR CARRYING WEAPONS: Interviews: Brother Jamil, Philbert Little.

THE SLACK SECURITY: *PG*, pp. 269-270.

MALCOLM HAD INSTRUCTED HIS MEN NOT TO SEARCH ANYONE: Second edition, Peter Goldman, supra., pp. 252, 269, 418. *MX*, p. 432. July 21, 1978 affidavit by Benjamin Goodman, The People of the State of New York vs. Norman 3X Butler and Thomas 15X Johnson (Supreme Court of the State of New York; New York County.) *Afro-American*, Jan. 29, 1966, Feb. 24, 1970. Sara Mitchell, *Shepherd of Black Sheep* (Atlanta: Heritage Celebrations International, 1981), p. 6. *Life*, March 5, 1965, p. 28. Interviews: Robert 35X, Sharon 10X, Brother Jamil, Tom Wallace, Pat Robinson, confidential source.

STANDARD PRACTICE FOR MONTHS: Interviews: Sharon 10X, Robert 35X, Tom Wallace, Brother Jamil, Pat Robinson, confidential source.

THE REASONS THERE WAS NO SEARCHING: *PG*, p. 252. Interviews: Sharon 10X, Benjamin Goodman. Also see *MX*, p. 432; *Life*, March 5, 1965, p. 28; and *Afro-American* [Baltimore edition], Feb. 24, 1970.

SEEMED DETERMINED TO TRUST; "AMONG MY OWN KIND": Interview: Robert 35X. *MX*, p. 432. (Also see *MX*, pp. 422-423.)

"I'D RATHER DIE": Interview: Brother Jamil.

REFUSED TO AUTHORIZE HIS MEN TO CARRY GUNS: *PG*, pp. 4, 269. *NYT*, Feb. 9, 1966. *JHC*, p. 90. Interview: Robert 35X.

MIGHT PRECIPITATE UGLY INCIDENT: Sara Mitchell, supra., p. 21.

"DROPPING DIMES": Interview: Robert 35X.

365 SOME BROTHERS CONTINUED CARRYING WEAPONS: *PG*, pp. 4, 252, 269. *JHC*, pp. 89-90. Interview: Robert 35X.

THE PART OF HIM THAT LONGED TO STAY ALIVE: In addition to acquiescing to the weapons that some of his aides carried, Malcolm kept a pistol and a rifle at home. (*PG*, p. 252. *JHC*, p. 86. See photograph in *Ebony*, Sept., 1964.) According to M. S. Handler, he also kept a gun in his car.

POLICEMEN OUTSIDE; HIS OWN MEN INSIDE: *PG*, p. 261.

ALL BUT THREE WITHDRAWN: *PG*, pp. 261, 269, 365. *New York Times Magazine*, August 19, 1979, p. 30.

INEFFECTIVE DEFENSE: *PG*, pp. 4, 269-270. Interviews: Robert 35X, Tom Wallace. "I look for protection from Allah," Malcolm told one questioner. (*BP*, p. 135.)

NOI MEMBERS COULD BE ADMITTED: July 21, 1978 affidavit by Benjamin Goodman, supra. "Sixty Minutes," CBS-TV, Jan. 17, 1982. Second edition, Goldman, supra., p. 421. Interviews: Tom Wallace, Sharon 10X. Malcolm said Muhammad's followers were welcome to attend his rallies. (CBS newsfilm dated Feb. 15, 1965.)

ARRIVED AT AUDUBON: According to *MX*, p. 433 and *PG*, p. 270, Malcolm arrived at the Audubon shortly before 2:00. According to Earl Grant, Malcolm arrived soon after 2:30. (*JHC*, p. 93.)

"I FEEL THAT I SHOULD NOT BE HERE": *JHC*, p. 93. Also see *PG*, p. 4.

366 LOOKED LIKE AN OLD MAN: Sara Mitchell, supra., p. 7. *PG*, p. 270. *MX*, p. 433. *JHC*, p. 95.

DISTRAUGHT; LOSES SELF-CONTROL; FLARES AT AIDES: *PG*, pp. 270-271. *MX*, pp. 433-434. *JHC*, pp. 93-94. *Afro-American* [Baltimore edition], Feb. 24, 1970. Sara Mitchell, supra., p. 21.

CALLER'S VOICE SOUNDED LIKE WALLACE MUHAMMAD'S: Interviews: Tom Wallace, confidential source.

WALLACE MUHAMMAD CONCERNED THAT PEOPLE WOULD HOLD HIM RESPONSIBLE: *Chicago's American*, Feb. 25, 1965. Wallace, who had been urging his father to readmit him into the Nation of Islam, met with Elijah the day before Malcolm's assassination. Elijah told him he could return to the fold if he publicly repented. A few days after Malcolm was killed, Wallace did so. "I will take orders from my father," he told the press. He also expressed concern that people would think he had something to do with Malcolm's death. (*Chicago's American*, Feb. 25, 1965. *Chicago Tribune*, March 2, 1975 [four-star final edition].)

"I NEVER GOT A CHANCE TO GET A HEARING BEFORE MALCOLM X": Wallace Muhammad interview, "Like It Is," WABC-TV, Jan. 6, 1980.

"I OUGHT NOT TO GO OUT THERE": *MX*, p. 433.

"A MAN WHO WOULD GIVE HIS LIFE FOR YOU": *PG*, pp. 4, 271-273. *MX*, p. 434.

367 "I WONDER IF ANYBODY REALLY UNDERSTANDS": Sara Mitchell, supra., p. 21. *MX*, p. 434.

"OUT OF MY POCKET": *New York Journal-American*, Feb. 22, 1965. *Philadelphia Tribune*, Feb. 22, 1965. *PG*, p. 273. *FBI*, Feb. 24, 1965, p. 1. Interview: Pat Robinson. Some witnesses later testified that the statement was, "Take your hand out of my pocket!" (See *MX*, p. 434.)

THE MAN WITH THE SHOTGUN: Whether Hayer's Muslim confederates were Johnson and Butler or other Muslims is discussed at length in Part V of the second edition of Peter Goldman, supra. In an effort to overturn Johnson's and Butler's 1966 convictions, Hayer later asserted that he had had four accomplices. He did not disclose their last names. He said their first names were Lee, Ben, Willie, and "Willbour [sic] or a name like it." The latter two names were those of two of Butler's former criminal associates. (New York City Police record of Norman Butler.)

SEVEN INCHES HIGH AND SEVEN INCHES ACROSS: New York City, Office of Chief Medical Examiner, Autopsy Report dated February, 1965. Also see William Brashler, "Black on Black," *New York Magazine*, June 9, 1975, p. 56.

368 GHASTLY SMILE: "It was almost as if he was glad it was over," Pat Robinson later recalled. The ghastly death smile, which Peter Goldman notes in *PG*, p. 277, appeared in photographs in the *New York Times Magazine*, Aug. 19, 1979, p. 29; in *Newsweek*, May 7, 1979, p. 39, and in *PG*.

58. America's Lumumba

JOHN ALI; BUTLER'S ENMITY; BUTLER'S DENIAL: *FBI*, March 3, 1966, p. 2. Second edition, Peter Goldman, *The Death and Life of Malcolm X* (University of Illinois Press, 1979), pp. 314, 343-344, 432. *Chicago Tribune*, March 2, 1966. *New York Herald Tribune*, March 3, 1966. *NYT*, March 3, 1966.

ANTIPATHY: Interviews: TW and two confidential sources.

"FAT JOSEPH": *BP*, p. 137. In 1952, Malcolm said, he had rescued Joseph from "the garbage can." (Ibid., p. 111.) And on Stan Bernard's talk show "Contact," he called Joseph "the fat one." (Stan Bernard, "Contact," New York radio station WINS, Feb. 18, 1965.)

BUTLER DID NOT DENY: *PG*, pp. 341-343.

"HIT PARADE": *New York Herald Tribune*, Feb. 22, 1965.

ASSISTED BUTLER'S LAWYERS: *Afro-American* [Baltimore edition], Jan. 25, 1966. *PG*, p. 345.

INNOCENT: *New York Herald Tribune*, Feb. 23, 1965. *PG*, p. 289. See disclaimers cited in *FBI*, Feb. 26, 1965, pp. 1-2; Feb. 27, 1965, pp. 1-2.

NOT HIS FOLLOWER: *PG*, p. 289.

HAYER LATER ACKNOWLEDGED HE WAS A FOLLOWER OF ELIJAH MUHAMMAD, AND THAT THE ASSASSINATION HAD BEEN AN ACT OF REPRISAL FOR MALCOLM'S ATTEMPTS TO DISCREDIT MR. MUHAMMAD: Goldman, supra., pp. 409-410. *New York Times Magazine*, Aug. 19, 1979.

HAD TROUBLE SLEEPING: Interview: Christine Johnson.

"I HAVE PROOF. . . . DO YOU HAVE PROOF?": *Muhammad Speaks*, March 19, 1965.

"EVEN WHEN YOU ARE DEAD": Interview: Malcolm Jarvis. *Fables of Aesop* (Penguin Books, 1969), p. 47.

FORMER PROTEGE. Interview. Philbert Little.

"PREPOSTEROUS"; "AS LONG AS HE STOPPED HIS UNDULY BITTER CRITICISM"; "KILL HIM": *Muhammad Speaks*, March 5, 1965.

BELATED DEATH SENTENCE: *Muhammad Speaks*, Feb. 26, 1965.

PUBLISHED RAM'S DENIAL: *Philadelphia Daily News*, Feb. 24, 1965. *Chicago Tribune*, Feb. 24, 1965. *Muhammad Speaks*, March 5, 1965.

JAMES FARMER'S ASSERTIONS: *Chicago Tribune*, Feb. 24, 1965. *NYT*, Feb. 25, 1965. Clipping of undated *New York World-Telegram* article by Paul Meskil. *MX*, pp. 443-444. *PG*, pp. 300, 309, 372.

IN ORDER TO AVERT OPEN WARFARE: *PG*, p, 300.

"SECOND SUSPECT" Eric Norden, "The Murder of Malcolm X," *The Realist* (Feb., 1967). George Brietman, Herman Porter, and Baxter Smith, *The Assassination of Malcolm X* (Pathfinder Press, 1976), Chapter Two & pp. 88-89. (Also see the centerfold photograph of the three policemen rescuing Hayer from his pursuers.) *PG*, pp. 276 (note), 287-288, 365-366, 411. *NYT*, Feb. 22, 1965. *Afro-American*, Feb. 23, 1965.

COINTELPRO: "Supplementary Detailed Staff Reports on Intelligence Activities and the Rights of Americans," Book III of the "Church Committee" Report, pp. 3-5, 15-22. [U.S. Senate, Select Committee to Study Governmental Operations with respect to Intelligence Activities (94th Congress, 2d Session), Senate Report 94-755 (April 23, 1976).] George Breitman, Herman Porter, & Baxter Smith, supra., pp. 179-181, 183. Second edition, Peter Goldman, supra., p. 432. Compare with Oba T'Shaka's polemical, inaccurate account in *The Political Legacy of Malcolm X* (Third World Press, 1983), pp. 224-229.

LIKED AND ADMIRED: Interview: Gene Roberts.

POLICEMEN HAD TAKEN THEIR TIME: *PG*, pp. 277, 295. Sara Mitchell, *Shepherd of Black Sheep* (Atlanta: Heritage Celebrations International), p. 20.

DIFFICULTY CLOSING ELEVATOR DOOR: Sept. 13, 1982 letter from V. R. Back, M.D. to author.

PEACEFUL LOOK: Malcolm was described as "looking at peace," by an unidentified, undated newspaper article entitled "In Harlem, the Quiet Line of Mourners." See the relevant photograph in *PG*.

SEVEN SHROUDS: *New York Herald Tribune*, Feb. 28, 1965. *JHC*, p. 104.

LIFE INSURANCE: *FBI* electronic surveillance file, Feb. 23, 1965. "Like It Is," WABC-TV, Feb. 22, 1969. *Afro-American*, March 2, 1965. *NYT*, Feb. 22, 1965. *MX*, pp. 11, 445-446. Interview: Tom Wallace.

CHECKS FROM ALL OVER; "FOR MALCOLM'S BABIES": *Village Voice*, May 29, 1990, p. 45.

COMMITTEE OF CONCERNED MOTHERS: Minutes of the May 5, May 11, and May 18, 1965 meetings of the Committee of Concerned Mothers. *New York Herald Tribune*, August 8 and 9, 1965. *New York Post*, June 16, 1965. *NYT*, March 2, 1965. *Afro-American*, March 2, 1965. June 21, 1965 letter from Florynce R. Kennedy, Esq., asking officials of the disbanded Committee of Concerned Mothers to forward all records, especially bank records, to Betty Shabazz's attorney Oliver Sutton. Undated letter from President of Committee of Concerned Mothers to Ruby Dee. Draft, unmailed, handwritten June 6, 1965 letter from Committee of Concerned Mothers to Gwendolyn Mallett. Sept. 29, 1979 letter from Pat Robinson to author. Written responses by Pat Robinson to author's written Nov. 15, 1979 and Nov. 23, 1979 inquiries. Interview: Pat Robinson.

BLACK CLERGYMEN RAISE MONEY FOR MALCOLM'S DAUGHTERS: *NYT*, Feb. 25, 1965, March 2, 1965. Sept. 25, 1979 letter from Freedom National Bank of New York to author.

MEMORIAL TO MALCOLM: May 31, 1965 letter from Sylvester Leaks, Chairman, Malcolm X Memorial Committee, to the Committee of Concerned Mothers. Minutes of the May 5 and May 11, 1965 meetings of the Committee of Concerned Mothers. (Also see March 25, 1965 letter from Pat Robinson to Robert Sine. The letter describes the planned memorial service.)

BETTY SHABAZZ FLIES TO SWITZERLAND, THEN TO SAUDI ARABIA: April, 1965 postcard from Mecca to Gladys Towles Root from "Mrs. Malcolm X." (The date of the postmark is unclear; Gladys Towles Root received the postcard April 27, 1965.) *Philadelphia Inquirer Daily Magazine*, May 12, 1988. Interviews: Said Ramadan, Tom Wallace, confidential source. Written response by Tom Wallace to author's written June 3, 1976 inquiry. *New York Amsterdam News*, April 3, April 10, and May 8, 1965. Also see March 3, 1965 airgram from U.S. Embassy, Cairo, to U.S. Dept. of State. (The airgram indicates there was a rumor circulating that financial support for Malcolm's widow would be forthcoming from abroad.)

"EXCELLENT" REMEDY: *Philadelphia Inquirer Daily Magazine*, May 12, 1988. The minutes of the May 11, 1965 meeting of the Committee of Concerned Mothers indicate that Mrs. Shabazz's trip "restored her emotional balance."

MORE THAN TWO AND A QUARTER MILLION COPIES: July 25, 1978 letter from Grove Press to author. Also see *Look*, March 4, 1969, p. 76.

MOVIE RIGHTS: Estate of Malcolm X, Surrogate's Court, Queens County. File #6554-1965. (Also see *Philadelphia Inquirer*, May 30, 1972 and *MX*, p. 408.)

BLOSSOMED: *Detroit Free Press*, Feb. 15, 1969.

GOOD HUSBAND: *JHC*, pp. 132-143.

SHE BECAME A PUBLIC FIGURE: See, for instance: *Newsweek*, Nov. 3, 1969. *Chicago Daily News*, May 22, 1972. *Philadelphia Inquirer Daily Magazine*, May 12, 1988. *New York Times*, July 9, 1989, Section 2, pp. H1, H23.

"I'M NOT JUST MALCOLM'S WIDOW: *The Philadelphia Inquirer*, May 24, 1972.

SPAWNED BY UNHAPPY CHILDHOOD RELATIONSHIPS: *Philadelphia Daily News*, May 20, 1972.

IT WAS PRECISELY WHAT SHE MEANT: *The Philadelphia Inquirer*, May 24, 1972.

"CARETAKER HEAD": *New York Herald Tribune*, Feb. 26, 1965.

CHOOSE LEADERS; VETO DECISIONS: *New York Post*, Feb. 26, 1965. *Afro-American*

[Baltimore edition], Feb. 27, 1965. *MX*, p. 446. *Jet*, March 11, 1965, p. 17.

ASSUMED LEADERSHIP HERSELF; MALCOLM HAD APPOINTED HER; EVERYONE CONCURRED: *Chicago's American*, March 2, 1965; March 16, 1965. *New York Herald Tribune*, March 16, 1965. *Chicago Sun-Times*, March 16, 1965. *Afro-American*, March 16, 1965. *NYT*, March 16, 1965; May 20, 1966. *New York Amsterdam News*, March 20, 1965. Also see *New York Herald Tribune*, Feb. 1, 1967; *Chicago Sun-Times*, March 18, 1967; *NYT*, May 20, 1970; and Bobby Seale, *Seize the Time* (Random House), p. 133.

VISIBLY SHAKEN; "NO SENSE IN GETTING EMOTIONAL"; "ONCE YOU ARE DEAD, YOUR TROUBLES ARE OVER": *FBI*, Feb. 21, 1965, pp. 1-2.

CURTAIN OF SILENCE; "NOTHING WE CAN DO": *Afro-American*, Feb. 23, 1965. *NYT*, Feb. 22, 1965. *MX*, p. 439.

REPORTEDLY THE ONLY ONE WHO ATTENDED: *New York Amsterdam News*, March 13, 1965; March 27, 1965. Undated clipping from the files of *The Philadelphia Tribune*. Also see *Chicago Tribune*, Feb. 27, 1965; *New York Herald Tribune*, Feb. 27 and 28, 1965; *Chicago Daily News*, Feb. 27, 1965; and the *New York Daily News*, Feb. 28, 1965.

UNSMILING; UNUSUALLY QUIET: *Chicago Daily News*, Feb. 27, 1965.

STRANGLING AND STABBING: *New York Daily News*, Feb. 28, 1965.

"THE RECKLESSNESS OF HIS PATH NO DOUBT BROUGHT ABOUT HIS EARLY DEATH": *Chicago Daily News*, Feb. 27, 1965. Also *Chicago Tribune*, Feb. 27, 1965 and *PG*, p. 301.

HAD TRIED TO PERSUADE; "NO MAN": *NYT*, Feb. 27, 1965. *Chicago Daily News*, Feb. 27, 1965. *Jet*, March 11, 1965. *MX*, p. 450.

RELUCTANT TO TALK: Interviews: Bob High, Carlton Barnette.

THE GHOST OF MALCOLM; "IN THOSE DAYS, MALCOLM WAS SAFE"; "TRYING TO MAKE ENEMIES": *Afro-American* [Baltimore edition], March 10, 1970. *MX*, pp. 449-450.

"HE CRITICIZED . . . ": *Washington Post*, Feb. 27, 1965.

"THE MAN WHO TAUGHT HIM ALL HE KNEW": *Afro-American* [Baltimore edition], March 10, 1970.

HE TRIED TO MAKE WAR AGAINST ME: *Chicago Daily News*, Feb. 27, 1965. *PG*, p. 302. *MX*, p. 450.

PROVOKED HIS OWN DEATH: *Muhammad Speaks*, March 5, 1965. *MX*, p. 450.

"WE DIDN'T WANT TO KILL MALCOLM": *Chicago Daily News*, Feb. 27, 1965. The versions quoted in *MX*, p. 450, *PG*, p. 301, and *Jet*, March 11, 1965 are slightly different. Also see *NYT*, Feb. 27, 1965 and the *New York Post*, Feb. 28, 1965.

"CRACKPOTS": *NYT*, Feb. 27, 1965. (See incorrectly quoted version in *MX*, p. 450.)

"NO MAN WILL BE SUCCESSFUL IN OPPOSING ME": *Chicago's American*, March 1, 1965.

59. No More Fear

AFTER ABOUT ONE MINUTE: *Newsweek*, March 22, 1965, p. 19. David Garrow, *Protest at Selma* (Yale University Press, 1978), pp. 74-75. (Televised versions of the event apparently edited out the time that elapsed between Cloud's ultimatum and his order for the troopers to "advance.")

SELECTED BIBLIOGRAPHY

The following bibliography is not meant to be exhaustive; it contains only a fraction of the sources cited in the Notes. Yet I hope it will help convey my biographical approach, for it includes works that contributed to the way the narrative was fashioned. Some are books or articles about racial prejudice. Others probe the deeper-seated origins of youthful criminality and drug addiction.

Wherever bibliographical data was available for a given source, I inserted it. The absence of dates or other identifying characteristics for some of the collections listed below is due to the failure of the issuing agency to supply such information. (The dates of individual documents within those collections are cited in the Notes.)

Abernathy, Ralph. *And the Walls Came Tumbling Down*. Harper Perennial paperback, 1990.

Allport, Gordon. *The Nature of Prejudice*. Addison-Wesley, 1954.

Angelou, Maya. *All God's Children Need Traveling Shoes*. Random House, 1986.

A Tribute to Malcolm. Film produced by the National Educational TV and Radio Center.

Atyeo, Don and Felix Dennis. *The Holy Warrior: Muhammad Ali*. Simon and Schuster, 1975.

Baasit, Muhammad Abdul. "The Malcolm X They Didn't Know." *Showcase* (Vol. 17, No. 1), ca. 1978.

Baldwin, Lewis V. "Malcolm X and Martin Luther King, Jr.: What They Thought About Each Other." *Islamic Studies* (Winter 1986), pp. 395-416.

Baldwin, Lewis V. "A Reassessment of the Relationship between Malcolm X and Martin Luther King." *The Western Journal of Black Studies* (Vol. 13, No. 2), 1989.

Ballots or Bullets. First Amendment Records. Distributed by Jamie/Guyden Distributing Corp. Phonograph record #100.

Baptism certificate for Louisa Little. St. Andrew's Parish, Grenada. Jan.

10, 1894.

Barnette, Aubrey. "The Black Muslims Are a Fraud." *Saturday Evening Post*, Feb. 27, 1965, pp. 23-29.

Benson, Thomas W. "Rhetoric and Autobiography: The Case of Malcolm X." *Quarterly Journal of Speech* (Vol. 60, No. 1), 1974, pp. 1-13.

Bergler, Edmund. *The Psychology of Gambling*. International Universities Press, 1970.

Bontemps, Arna, and Conroy, Jack. *Anyplace But Here*. Hill and Wang, 1966.

Booker, Simeon. *Black Man's America*. Prentice Hall, 1964.

Boulware, Marcus H. "Minister Malcolm, Orator Profundo." *Negro History Bulletin* (Vol. 30), Nov. 1967, pp. 12-14.

Bovell, Gilbert Balfour. "Psychological Considerations of Color Conflicts Among Negroes." *Psychoanalytic Review* (Vol. 30), 1943, pp. 447-459.

Bowlby, John. *Forty-Four Juvenile Thieves: Their Characters and Home Life*. London: Bailliere, Tindall, and Cox, 1946.

Branch, Taylor. *Parting the Waters: America in the King Years, 1954-63*. Simon and Schuster, 1988.

Brashler, William. "Black on Black: The Deadly Struggle for Power." *New York Magazine*. June 9, 1975, pp. 44-57.

Breitman, George (editor). *By Any Means Necessary*. Pathfinder Press, 1970.

Breitman, George (editor). *Malcolm X Speaks*. Grove Press, 1965.

Breitman, George. *Malcolm X: The Man and His Ideas*. Merit Publishers, 1969.

Breitman, George and Porter, Herman. *The Assassination*. Merit Publishers, 1969.

Breitman, George. *The Last Year of Malcolm X*. Schocken Books, 1968.

Breitman, George, Herman Porter, and Baxter Smith. *The Assassination of Malcolm X*. Pathfinder Press, 1976.

Broderick, Francis L. and August Meier. *Negro Protest Thought in the Twentieth Century*. The Bobbs-Merrill Co., 1965.

Brody, Eugene B. "Color and Identity Conflict in Young Boys: Observations of Negro Mothers and Sons in Urban Baltimore." *Psychiatry* (Vol. 26), 1963, pp. 188-201.

Brookline, Massachusetts Police Department. Police record of Malcolm Little.

Brother Malcolm. Pamphlet published May 1965 by the Malcolm X Memorial Committee.

Burns, W. Haywood. *Voices of Negro Protest*. Oxford University Press, 1963.

By Any Means Necessary. Douglas Communications Corp. Phonograph record #Z 30743.

Capeci, Dominic, Jr. *The Harlem Riot of 1943.* Temple University Press, 1977.

CBS News Film Library. Newsfilm on Malcolm X.

Central Intelligence Agency documents on Malcolm X.

Chicago's American.

Chicago Defender.

Chicago Sun-Times.

Chicago Tribune.

City of Detroit. Recorder's Court. Warrant #A-39931 and related court papers. March 14, 1945, et seq.

City of New York. Office of Chief Medical Examiner. Report of autopsy on Malcolm X performed February 21, 1965. (Case #1686.)

Clark, Kenneth Bancroft. *Prejudice and Your Child.* Beacon Press, 1955.

Clark, Kenneth Bancroft. *The Negro Protest.* Beacon Press, 1963.

Clarke, John Henrik (editor). *Malcolm X: The Man and His Times.* Collier Books, 1969.

Cleage, Albert and Breitman, George. *Myths About Malcolm X.* Pathfinder Press, 1971.

Commonwealth of Pennsylvania. Allegheny County. Coroner's Jury Verdict concerning the August 19, 1929 death of Oscar Little. August 29, 1929.

Cone, James H. *Martin & Malcolm & America.* Orbis Books, 1991.

"Contact," by talk show host Stan Bernard. New York City radio station WINS. Feb. 18, 1985. (Important parts of this recording were deleted from the transcript of Malcolm's remarks that was later published in *Malcolm X Speaks.*)

Cook County (Illinois) Circuit Court, Probate Division. Probate file #75-P-4128, entitled "Estate of Elijah Muhammad."

Corsino, Louis. "Malcolm X and the Black Muslim Movement." *The Psychohistory Review* (Vol. 10, Nos. 3-4), 1982, pp. 165-184.

County of Los Angeles. Coroner's Inquest for Ronald Townsend Stokes. May 14, 1962.

Criminal proceedings against Ella Little. The relevant court documents, which span the years 1930-1973, are housed in the archives of the Roxbury Municipal Court, the Boston Municipal Court, and the Suffolk County Superior Court.

Darling, Birt. *City in the Forest.* Stratford House, 1950.

Detroit Police Department. Police record of Malcolm Little.

District Court of East Norfolk County (Massachusetts). Complaint

#31293 filed against Malcolm Little by Stephen J. Slack. Jan. 10, 1946.

Drake, St. Clair, and Horace R. Cayton. *Black Metropolis*. Harcourt Brace, 1945.

Draper, Theodore. *The Rediscovery of Black Nationalism*. Viking Press paperback, 1970.

Epps, Archie (editor). *The Speeches of Malcolm X at Harvard*. William Morrow, 1968.

Essien-Udom, E. U. *Black Nationalism*. University of Chicago Press, 1962.

Estate of Earl Little. Ingham County Probate file #A-8783 (1931).

Fager, Charles. *Selma, 1965: The Town Where the South Was Changed*. Scribners, 1974.

Federal Bureau of Investigation files on Elijah Muhammad.

Federal Bureau of Investigation files on Malcolm X. (See the introduction to the Notes.)

Federal Bureau of Investigation files on The Nation of Islam.

Fenichel, Otto. "The Counter-Phobic Attitude," *International Journal of Psychoanalysis* (Vol. 20), 1939, pp. 263-274.

Flick, Hank and Larry Powell. "Animal Imagery in the Rhetoric of Malcolm X," *Journal of Black Studies* (Vol. 18, No. 4), 1988, pp. 435-451.

Erich Fromm. *Escape from Freedom*. Holt, Rinehart, and Winston, 1941.

Galamison, Milton. Unpublished manuscript about the campaign to integrate New York City's schools.

Galdston, Iago. "The Gambler and His Love." In *Gambling*, edited by Robert D. Herman. Harper and Row, 1967.

Gambino, Ferruccio. "Malcolm X, Laborer: From the Wilderness of the American Empire to Cultural Self-Determination." In *Studies on Malcolm X* (No. 1), date unclear. Published by Malcolm X Work Group.

Gardner, George E. "The Primary and Secondary Gains in Stealing." *The Nervous Child* (Vol. 6), 1947, pp. 436-446.

Garrow, David J. *Bearing the Cross: Martin Luther King, Jr., and the Southern Christian Leadership Conference*. William Morrow, 1986.

Garrow, David J. *Protest at Selma: Martin Luther King, Jr., and the Voting Rights Act of 1965*. Yale University Press, 1978.

Georgia, State of. Taylor County Superior Court records concerning the larceny conviction of Earl Little and Wright Little. Minute Book J, 1915, p. 198.

Glanville, Brian. "Malcolm X." *New Statesman*, June 12, 1964, pp. 901-902.

Goldman, Peter. *The Death and Life of Malcolm X*. Harper & Row, 1973. Also second edition, University of Illinois Press, 1979.

Goodman, Benjamin (editor). *The End of White World Supremacy*. Merlin House, 1971.

Grier, William H. and Price M. Cobbs. *Black Rage*. Bantam Books, 1968.

Gurr, Ted Robert. *Why Men Rebel*. Princeton University Press, 1970.

Gustin, John C. "Psychology of the Actor." *Psychoanalysis* (Vol. 4), 1955-1956, pp. 29-36.

Halleck, Seymour. *Psychiatry and the Dilemmas of Crime*. Harper and Row, with Hoeber Medical Books, 1967.

Hapgood, David. *The Purge that Failed: Tammany vs. Powell*. McGraw Hill, 1959.

Haynes, Gideon. *Pictures from Prison Life: An Historical Sketch of the Massachusetts State Prison*. Second edition; Lee and Shepard, 1871.

H. D. Christman, Co. Employment record of Earl Little.

Heinz, G. and H. Donnay. *Lumumba: The Last Fifty Days*. Translated by Jane Clark Seitz; Grove Press, 1969.

Hernton, Calvin. "The Negro Male." *The Black Male in America*, edited by Doris Y. Wilkinson and Ronald C. Taylor. Nelson-Hall, 1977.

Hernton, Calvin. *White Papers for White Americans*. Doubleday, 1966.

Hickey, Neil and Ed Edwin. *Adam Clayton Powell and the Politics of Race*. Fleet Publication Corp., 1965.

Hoffer, Eric. *The True Believer*. Harper and Row, 1951.

Howard, Jan. "The Provocation of Violence: A Civil Rights Tactic?" *Dissent*, January-February, 1966, pp. 94-99.

Hubbard, Howard, "Five Long Hot Summers and How They Grew," *The Public Interest*, Summer, 1968 (No. 12), pp. 3-24.

Ingham County (Michigan) Coroner. Coroner's report on the Sept. 28, 1931 death of Earl Little.

Ingham County Circuit Court. *Capital View Land Company and James W. Nicoll v. Earl Little, Louise Little, and Cora I Way*. Docket #14215 (1929).

Ingham County Circuit Court. *In the Matter of the Petition of Oramel B. Fuller, Auditor General of the State of Michigan, for the Sale of Certain Lands Delinquent for Taxes*. Docket #14569 (1930).

Ingham County Probate file #4053 (1939). The file contains the documents relating to the court's decision to send Malcolm to the county juvenile home.

Ingham County Probate file #B-4398 (1938-1939). The file contains the documents relating to the court's decision to commit Louise Little to Kalamazoo State Hospital.

Ingham County Probate file #B-4556 (1939). The file contains the documents relating to the appointment of a guardian for Louise Little's children.

Isaacs, Susan. "Rebellious Children." *Mother and Child* (Vol. 5, 1934), pp. 83-85.

Jamal, Hakim A. *From the Dead Level: Malcolm X and Me.* Warner paperback, 1973. Also the original unedited manuscript.

Jarvis, Malcolm. *Myself and I.* Carleton Press, 1979.

Johnson, James Weldon. *Black Manhattan.* Knopf, 1930.

Kampel, Stuart. "Menace or Messiah?" *Memories*, Feb./Mar., 1989, pp. 85-88.

Kanza, Thomas. *The Rise and Fall of Patrice Lumumba: Conflict in the Congo.* Schenkman and G. K. Hall, 1979.

Kardiner, Abram and Lionel Ovesey. *The Mark of Oppression.* World Publishing Co., 1962.

Katz, L. N., et al. "Psychosomatic Aspects of Cardiac Arrythmias," *Annals of Internal Medicine* (Vol. 27), 1947, pp. 261-274.

Keniston, Kenneth. *Young Radicals.* Harcourt, Brace, and World, 1968.

Kly, Y. N. (editor and compiler). *The Black Book: The True Political Philosophy of Malcolm X.* Clarity Press, 1986.

Knebel, Fletcher. "A Visit with the Widow of Malcolm X." *Look*, March 4, 1969, pp. 74-80.

Kulsky, J. K., P. E. Hartmann, and D. H. Gutteridge. "Composition of Breast Fluid of a Man with Galactorrhea and Hyperprolactinaemia." *The Journal of Clinical Endocrinology and Metabolism* (Vol. 52, No. 3), March 1981, pp. 581-582.

Lansing, Michigan Public Schools. Transcript of scholarship record of Malcolm Little. October 31, 1939.

Lansing State Journal

Lee, Spike. *School Daze.*

Lemberg Center for the Study of Violence. Undated, tape recorded speech by Malcolm X.

Lesch, Michael, et al. "Paroxysmal Ventricular Tachycardia in the Absence of Organic Heart Disease." *Annals of Internal Medicine* (Vol. 66), 1967, pp. 950-960.

Letters from Louise Little and Edgerton Langdon to Gertrude Langdon and Joseph Orgias, 1918-1929.

Letters from Malcolm X to Bazely Perry, 1949.

Letters from Malcolm X to Gloria Strother, 1950.

Lewis, Anthony and The New York Times. *Portrait of a Decade: The Second American Revolution.* Random House, 1964.

Lewis, Claude. *Adam Clayton Powell.* Gold Medal Books, 1963.

Lewis, David. *King: A Biography.* Praeger, 1970.

"Like It Is," WABC-TV, Feb. 22, 1969.

"Like It Is," WABC-TV, Jan. 6, 1980.

Lindner, Robert. "Raise Your Child to Be a Rebel." *McCall's* (Vol. 83),

Feb. 1956, pp. 31 ff.

Lincoln, C. Eric. *The Black Muslims in America*. Beacon Press paperback, 1961.

Lomax, Louis E. *The Negro Revolt*. Harper and Row, 1962.

Lomax, Louis E. *To Kill a Black Man*. Holloway House, 1968.

Lomax, Louis E. *When the Word Is Given*. . . . Signet Books, New American Library, 1963.

"Malcolm and Elijah." WNET-TV, New York City. Feb. 21, 1982.

Malcolm X. Address at Audubon Ballroom. Feb. 15, 1965. Tape recording.

Malcolm X. Address at Howard University. Oct., 1961. Mimeographed.

Malcolm X. Address at London School of Economics. Feb., 1965. Tape-recording.

Malcolm X. Collection of tape-recorded speeches housed in the Schomburg Center for Research in Black Culture, New York City.

Malcolm X. Collection of tape-recorded speeches owned by Milton Henry.

Malcolm X. Film documentary produced by Warner Brothers.

"Malcolm X: A Candid Conversation with the Militant Major-Domo of the Black Muslims." *Playboy*, May, 1963, pp. 53 ff.

"Malcolm X: A Retrospective." WBAI-FM, New York City. March 30, 1965.

Malcolm X: A Tribute. Steppingstones, Winter, 1983.

Malcolm X on Afro-American History. Pathfinder Press, 1970.

Malcolm X Speaks. Film distributed by Grove Press.

Malcolm X Speaking. Phonograph record produced by Ethnic Records. Record #1265.

Malcolm X Speaks to the People in Harlem. Up Front Records. Record #UPF-152.

Malcolm X: Struggle for Freedom. Film distributed by Grove Press.

Malcolm X Talks to Young People. Douglas International Recording Corp. Phonograph record #SD795.

"Malcolm X, The Black Vigilante." Portion of transcript of television show taped in Toronto, Jan. 19, 1965. In Pierre Berton, *Voices from the Sixties*. Doubleday, 1967.

"Malcolm X's Death: Other Voices." WNET-TV, New York City. Jan. 28, 1980.

Massachusetts Department of Correction. Prison record of Malcolm Little, #22843.

Medical Superintendent, Kalamazoo State Hospital, to Charlestown State Prison, May 6, 1946.

Menninger, Karl A. *Man Against Himself.* Harcourt, Brace, and World paperback, 1938.

Menninger, Karl A. and William C. Menninger. "Psychoanalytic Observations in Cardiac Disorders." *American Heart Journal.* (Vol. 11), 1936, pp. 10-21.

Michigan Department of Health. Certificate of death for Earl Little. Date of death: Sept. 28, 1931. Date certificate registered: Sept. 30, 1931.

Michigan State Police. Special Report #2155 concerning the November 8, 1929 Lansing fire.

Michigan State Police. Report by Trooper Baril about complaint #4578, concerning Earl Little's Sept. 28, 1931 death.

Middlesex County (Massachusetts) Superior Court, Criminal Dockets #31752-31756 (1946). (Court proceedings against Malcolm and his burglary associates.)

Militant Labor Forum. Collection of tape-recorded speeches by Malcolm X.

Miller, Jill Barbara Menes. "Children's Reactions to the Death of a Parent: A Review of the Psychoanalytic Literature." *Journal of the American Psychoanalytic Association* (Vol. 19), 1971, pp. 697-719.

Miller, Ross. "Autobiography as Fact and Fiction: Franklin, Adams, Malcolm X." *Centennial Review* (Vol. 16, No. 3), 1972, pp. 221-232.

Mitchell, Sara. *Shepherd of Black Sheep.* Second edition; Heritage Celebrations, International, 1981.

Montreal Superior Court. Prothonotary's Office. Marriage certificate for Early Little and Louisa Norton. May 10, 1919.

Movietone News Film Library. Newsfilm on Malcolm X.

Muhammad, Elijah. *Message to the Blackman in America.* Muhammad Mosque of Islam No. 2, 1965.

Muhammad, Wallace Deen. *As the Light Shineth from the East.* WDM Publishing Co., 1980.

Muhammad Speaks (The Newspaper of the Nation of Islam.)

Myers, Henry J. and Leon Yochelson. "Color Denial in the Negro." *Psychiatry* (Vol. 11), 1948, pp. 39-46.

Nadle, Marlene. "Malcolm X: The Complexity of a Man in the Jungle." *Village Voice,* Feb. 25, 1965.

New York Amsterdam News.

New York City Fire Department. Records of the February 14, 1965 fire that severely damaged Malcolm's home.

New York City Police Department. Bureau of Special Services ("BOSS") files on Malcolm X.

New York Herald Tribune.

New York Times.

Norden, Eric. "The Murder of Malcolm X." *The Realist*, Feb., 1967.

Norfolk County (Massachusetts) Superior Court. Criminal dockets #21550-21553 (1946). (Court proceedings against Malcolm and his burglary associates.)

Oates, Stephen B. *Let the Trumpet Sound: The Life of Martin Luther King, Jr.* Harper and Row, 1982.

Ohmann, Carol. "The Autobiography of Malcolm X: A Revolutionary Use of the Franklin Tradition." *American Quarterly* (Vol. 22, No.2, Part 1), 1970, pp. 131-149.

Osofsky, Gilbert. *Harlem: The Making of a Ghetto.* Harper and Row, 1966.

Ostow, Mortimer and Ben-Ami Scharfstein. *The Need to Believe.* International Universities Press, 1954.

Peeks, Edward. *The Long Struggle for Black Power.* Scribner's, 1971.

Perl, Arnold. "Malcolm X," a 1970 filmscript.

Perry, Bruce. "Escape from Freedom Criminal Style: The Hidden Advantages of Being in Jail." *The Journal of Psychiatry and Law*, Summer, 1984, pp. 215-230.

Perry, Bruce. "Neither White Nor Black." *Ethnic Groups* (Vol. 6, No. 4), 1985, pp. 293-304.

Perry, Bruce (editor). *Malcolm X: The Last Speeches.* Pathfinder Press, 1989.

Petitions from Malcolm X to various prison officials, 1946-1952.

Plank, Emma N. "Memories of Childhood in Autobiographies." *The Psychoanalytic Study of the Child* (Vol. 8), 1953, pp. 381-393.

Powell, Adam Clayton, Jr. *Adam by Adam: The Autobiography of Adam Clayton Powell, Jr.* Dial Press, 1971.

Prospects for Freedom in 1965. Tape-recording. Jan. 7, 1965.

Queens County Surrogate's Court. *Estate of Malcolm X.* File #6554/1965.

Queens County Civil Court. *Muhammad's Temple of Islam, Inc. v. Malcolm X. Little.* Landlord and Tenant Index #4845/1964.

Reddick, Lawrence Dunbar. *Crusader Without Violence.* Harper and Row, 1959.

Reik, Theodore. *Masochism in Modern Man.* Farrar, Straus, & Co., 1941.

Robinson, Cedric J. "Malcolm Little as a Charismatic Leader." Paper presented at the 66th annual meeting of the American Political Science Association, Sept., 1970.

Rohn, Reuben D. "Galactorrhea in the Adolescent." *Journal of Adolescent Health Care* (Vol. 5, No. 1), Jan., 1984.

Salzman, Leon. "The Psychology of Religious and Ideological Conversion." *Psychiatry* (Vol. 16), 1953, pp. 177-187.

Selective Service System records on Malcolm Little, #20-219-25-1377.

Shabazz, Betty. "The Legacy of My Husband, Malcolm X." *Ebony*, June, 1969, pp. 172-182.

Shapiro, Fred C. and James W. Sullivan. *Race Riots: New York, 1964.* (Crowell, 1964.)

Sherman Grinberg Film Library. Newsfilm on Malcolm X.

"Sixty Minutes." CBS-TV. Jan. 17, 1982.

Socarides, Charles W. *Homosexuality.* J. Aronson, Inc., 1978.

Spencer, Cora. "A Psychological Evaluation of the Political Perspectives of Malcolm X." Unpublished paper. Jan., 1970.

Sperling, Otto E. "Exaggeration as a Defense." *Psychoanalytic Quarterly* (Vol. 32), 1963, pp. 533-548.

Sperling, Samuel J. "On the Psychodynamics of Teasing." *Journal of the American Psychoanalytic Association* (Vol. 1), 1953, pp. 458-483.

Stein, Judith. *The World of Marcus Garvey.* Louisiana State University Press, 1986.

Stein, Martin H. "Premonition as a Defense." *The Psychoanalytic Quarterly* (Vol. 22), 1953, pp. 69-74.

Stern, Karl. *The Flight from Woman.* The Noonday Press, 1965.

Stringfellow, William. *My People Is The Enemy.* Holt, Rinehart, and Winston, 1964.

Sullivan, George. *The Cassius Clay Story.* Fleet Publications, 1964.

Supreme Court of the State of New York. *Johnson Hinton v. The City of New York, Ralph Plaissance, and Michael Dolan.* Index #5742/1958.

Supreme Court of the State of New York. *The People of the State of New York v. Thomas Hagan, Norman Butler, and Thomas Johnson.* Indictment #871/1965 (New York County.)

Superior Court for the State of California. County of Los Angeles. Evelyn Williams, et al v. Elijah Muhammad. Docket #D652475, 1964.

Szasz, Thomas. "The Role of the Counterphobic Mechanism in Addiction." *Journal of the American Psychoanalytic Association* (Vol. 6), 1958, pp. 309-325.

"Talk of Philadelphia," WCAU talk show, Philadelphia, April 10, 1964.

"Talk of Philadelphia," WCAU talk show, Philadelphia, Jan. 14, 1965.

Terry Gross interviews Alex Haley, "Fresh Air," WHYY-FM, March 15, 1985.

The Autobiography of Malcolm X. Grove Press paperback, 1965. The autobiography, which was published after Malcolm's death, was written by Alex Haley.

"The Crisis of Racism." New York radio station WBAI. May 1, 1962.

"The Hate that Hate Produced," Mike Wallace Show, televised in New York City July 9-13, 1959.

The Last Message. Phonograph record of Feb. 14, 1965 Detroit speech. Discus Hablands record #LP 1300.

The Wisdom of Malcolm X. Mo' Soul Records. Record #MS-8001.

T'Shaka, Oba. *The Political Legacy of Malcolm X.* Third World Press, 1983.

Two Speeches by Malcolm X. Merit Publishers, 1969.

U.S. Parole Commission. Documents relating to the parole of Elijah Muhammad, alias Gulam Bogans, prisoner # 10039-MM.

U.S. Secret Service documents regarding Malcolm X.

U.S. Senate. 94th Congress, Second Session. Senate Report #94-755 (popularly known as the Church Committee Report): Final Report of the Select Committe to Study Governmental Operations with Respect to Intelligence Activities. *Intelligence Activities and the Rights of Americans*, Books II and III.

U.S. State Department documents regarding Malcolm X.

Vincent, Theodore G. *Black Power and the Garvey Movement.* The Ramparts Press, 1975.

Vincent, Ted. "The Garveyite Parents of Malcolm X." *The Black Scholar* (Vol. 20, No. 2), March/April, 1989, pp. 10-13.

Washington Daily News.

Washington Post.

Weatherby, W. J. *James Baldwin: Artist on Fire.* Donald J. Fine, 1989.

Weiss, Samuel. "The Ordeal of Malcolm X." *South Atlantic Quarterly* (Vol. 76, No. 4), 1977, pp. 53-63.

"Who Killed Malcolm X?" Channel 13-TV, Dallas, Texas. Feb. 22, 1972.

Wolfenstein, E. Victor. *Personality and Politics.* Dickenson Publishing Co., 1969.

Wolfenstein, E. Victor. *The Revolutionary Personality.* Princeton University Press, 1967.

Wolfenstein, E. Victor. *The Victims of Democracy.* University of California Press, 1981.

Yarrow, Leon J. "Separation from Parents in Early Childhood." In *Review of Child Development Research*, edited by Martin L. Hoffman and Louis W. Hoffman. Russell Sage Foundation, 1964.

Zulliger, Hans. "Unconscious Motives for Theft." *Journal of Delinquency* (Vol. 1), 1951, pp. 198-204.

LIST OF PEOPLE INTERVIEWED

I am indebted to the people who agreed to be interviewed for this book. The majority of them were interviewed more than once. Some were reinterviewed dozens of times, usually by telephone, sometimes in person. The follow-up interviews were often more informative than the initial ones. Though most of the latter interviews were conducted during the 1970's, a few occurred as recently as 1990.

I carefully scrutinized each interviewee's testimony. One criterion I used to assess it was whether it was supported or contravened by other evidence. I also probed each interviewee's motives. I interviewed people again and again to ensure that what they told me one time was consistent with what they told me the next.

I would like to thank the interviewees, most of whom are listed below. The names of those with whom I spoke only by phone, and not in person, are followed by an asterisk. Many of them have changed their names since Malcolm knew them, either because they have married or because they have adopted Muslim names. For the most part, the names I have used are those that Malcolm himself used. Thus, Abdullah Abdur-Razzaq is James 67X. Khalil Islam is Thomas Johnson. Mrs. Phyllis Gilbert is Phyllis Davis. To underscore the relevant family ties, Ella Collins is Ella Little and Mary Riley is Mary Little.

Esther Abrams, friend.

J. Prescott Adams, who gave Malcolm bible lessons in Norfolk Prison.*

Tony (Godfrey) Agrieste, parole officer.*

Ralph Aiello, detective, New York City Police Department.

Farrow Allen, one of Malcolm's physicians.*

Mary Allen, neighbor.

Stanley Allen, teen-age friend.*

Maynard Allyn, social worker.

Tom Amiss, playmate.

Walter Arm, Deputy Commissioner, New York City Police Department.*

Ernestine Artz, social worker.*

Issam Azzam, Azzam Pasha's youngest son.

Don Bachman, who witnessed Malcolm's behavior at a number of Mason Jr. High School dances.*

Maury Baldwin, classmate.

Anne Lee Bannister, friend.

Howard Bannister, friend.

Laurence J. Baril, the Michigan State Police trooper who may have been the last person to talk to Earl Little.*

Aubrey Barnette, fellow Muslim.

Carlton Barnette, friend.*

Thomas Barry, Captain, New York City Fire Department.

Lionel Beane, friend.

Bob Bebee, friend.

Ray Bebee, younger brother of Bob Bebee.

John Elton Bembry, the well-read prison intellectual who encouraged Malcolm to educate himself.

Coleman Bender, Malcolm's debate coach at Norfolk Prison.*

Helen Bentley, classmate.*

Donald Bergus, Counsellor for Political Affairs, U.S. Embassy, Cairo, 1964.*

Mary Bibbs, former sister-in-law.*

Robert Block, Boston Municipal Court worker.

Jimmy Booker, journalist.*

Nada Bowen, a warm, compassionate elementary school teacher. (Had more of Malcolm's teachers been like Nada Bowen, the story of his youth might have been quite different.)

John Brassil, Superintendent, Charles Street Jail.*

John Breathour, friend and classmate.

Mamie Breedlove, friend.*

George Breitman, socialist author.

William Brennan, traffic court judge.*

Hugh Bronson, Lincoln Community Center playground supervisor.*

Richard Brown, schoolmate.*

Clement Brunelli, Norfolk Prison house officer.*

Clara Busby, prominent member of Lansing's black community.

Malcolm Byrd, intelligent, perceptive friend.

Mrs. Clyde Byrd, neighbor.*

Helen Bywater, classmate and friend.

Weldon Caldwell, teen-age friend.

Eugene Callender, minister.*

Jim Campbell, OAAU associate.

Vincent Canty, Deputy Chief Fire Marshall, New York City.

Mildred Cardwell, nurse.

James Carol, Brookline, Mass. police detective.*

Willard Chandler, fellow railroad employee.*

Herb Chapman, schoolmate.*

Albert ("Junior") Clark, friend.

Kenneth Clark, psychologist and author.

Lewis Clark, West Jr. High School science teacher.*

Evelyn Smith Clarke, Roxbury resident.*

Sam Clay, schoolmate and friend of Philbert.

Virginia Colby, classmate.*

Richard Colleton, senior corrections officer, Concord Reformatory.*

Kenneth Collins, Ella Little's third husband.

Matthew Conlan, Chief, New York City Fire Department.*

Tom Connally, Charlestown Prison guard.*

Harold Conrad, public relations director for the first Clay-Liston bout.*

George Conway, prison guard.*

Irene Cooley, classmate.

Allie Cooper, the outgoing, warm-hearted woman who mothered half of Lansing's West Side.

Arlington Cooper (Alpheus Cooper), son of Allie Cooper; friend of Malcolm and Philbert.

Robert Corbin, Hill boy.*

Nick Cordasco, Peace Corps volunteer stationed in Ethiopia in 1964.

Jim Cotton, classmate.

Alton ("Pappy") Cousins, dining car steward.

Herb Craigwell, a friend who later became a Deputy Police Commissioner in Boston.

Howard Cramer, schoolmate.

Henry Crawford, Charlestown Prison staff.*

Howard Cruse, professor and author.*

Max Cunningham, classmate.

Katherine Curtis, schoolmate.*

Malburne Curtis, teammate*

J. D. Driggers, prison guard.*

Katie Darling, classmate.

Rollin Dart, friend and classmate.

O.R. Dathorne, who publicly challenged Malcolm when he spoke at the University of Ibadan.*

Ted Davenport, friend.

James Davis, Sr., friend.*

Johnny Davis, Jr., friend.

Phyllis Davis, classmate.

Vearl Davis, schoolmate.*

William Davis, U.S.I.S. officer who was stationed in Ethiopia in 1964 when Malcolm visited Addis Ababa.

Bill Gordon Dawson, football team coach.*

Tom Decker, staff attorney, Illinois Attorney General's office.

Byron Delamarter (Arthur Delamarter's son), neighbor.

Richard Diehl, classmate.*

Charlice Doane, next-door-neighbor.

John ("Buster") Doane, next-door-neighbor.

Watoga Doane, next-door-neighbor.

Joyce Dolbee, classmate.*

William Dorsey, friend of Betty Shabazz.

Bill Downs, friend.

Bertha Dressel, social worker.*

Wilfred Duprey, dining car steward, New Haven Railroad.*

Josephine English, physician.*

Archie Epps, Harvard University.*

Chauncey Eskridge, one of Elijah Muhammad's lawyers.

Hazel Fairbotham, classmate.*

Shirley Feight, classmate.

Rodney Felton, schoolmate.*

Joe Ferstl, business associate of Elijah and Herbert Muhammad.*

Elaine Flynn, classmate.

Robert Foggie, barber.

Mo Foner, Executive Secretary & historian of Hospital Union Local #1199, New York City.*

Frank Ford, talk show host.*

Retha Fowler: friend.

Herb Fox, classmate.*

Leon Friedman, Esq., who was in the audience when Malcolm first addressed the Harvard Law School Forum.

Richard Friedman, staff attorney, Illinois Attorney General's office.

Hank Fries, schoolmate.*

Rev. Milton Galamison, who led the fight to integrate New York City's schools.

Dale Gardner, schoolmate.*

Mrs. Pearl Gardner, whose husband was a member of the Pleasant Grove School Board.

John Gavin, Charlestown prison guard who later became Massachusetts Commissioner of Correction.*

Elizabeth Gethers, political follower.*

George Gill, friend.*

Katherine Gillion, who frequently spent weekends, and sometimes entire summers, with the Doanes, who lived next door to the Littles.

Betty Girven, friend and classmate.

Peter Goldman, journalist and biographer.*

Benjamin Goodman, one of Malcolm's chief assistants.

M. Arthur Gordon, one of Malcolm Jarvis's attorneys.*

Charlie Grand, prison guard.*

Clara Gray, A relative of Earl Little's mother, whose maiden name was Ella Gray.*

Homer Gray, a relative of Earl Little's mother, Ella Gray.*

Samantha Gray, daughter of Clara.*

Fred Green, friend of Malcolm's parents.

Clifford Green, friend.

Sonny Greer, musician.*

Dick Gregory, prominent comedian and activist.

Eleanor Gretton, classmate.*

Chester Grill, Philbert's friend and neighbor.

Geraldine Grill, neighbor and classmate.

Ken Gross, *New York Post* reporter.*

Mrs. Lloyd Hackenberg, who helped take care of Louise Little while she was at Kalamazoo State Hospital.

Malik Hakim, fellow Muslim.

Alex Haley, who wrote Malcolm's autobiography.

Edna Mae Hamlin, classmate.

Heywood Hampton, prison-mate.

M.S. Handler, journalist.

Muhammad Haqqui, Egyptian Embassy, Washington, D.C.*

James Harmon, schoolmate.*

Jewel Harris, a friend of the Littles.

Allen Hart, classmate.*

Lemuel Hassan, NOI minister.

Halen Hazel, classmate.*

Ethel Helmeker, teacher.

Milton Henry, one of the organizers of the short-lived Freedom Now Party.

Rev. Lawrence Henry.

James Hicks, *New York Amsterdam News.*

Olive Hicks, Malcolm's kintergarden teacher.

Robert Higdon, classmate.

Bob High, friend.

Raymond Hightower, friend and fellow Muslim

Erwin Frederick Hoffman, physician.*

Zelma Holman, friend.*

Hugh ("Chico") Holmes, friend.*

Vera Hoover, schoolmate.*

Violet Houze, one of Ella Little's assault and battery victims.

George Howard, West Jr. High School gym teacher.*

Hayward Howard, friend.

Mrs. Celia Howard, friend of the Littles; mother of Hayward Howard.

Virginia Hunter, classmate.

Barbara Hyde, classmate.

Clifford Hyman, fellow Muslim.

Harold Hyman, fellow Muslim.

Heshaam Jaaber, sunni Muslim and friend.

Edward Jacko, attorney.

Louis Jackson, Mozelle Jackson's son.

Mozelle Jackson, cousin.

Oceola Jackson, friend.

Phil Jackson, friend.

Cecille Jacobson, perceptive Pleasant Grove teacher.*

Hakim Jamal, friend and author.*

Dennis James, fireman, New York City.

Brother Jamil, fellow Muslim.

Malcolm Jarvis, teen-age friend; prison-mate; fellow Muslim.

Richard Jenkins, a friend of the Littles.

Luther Jermany, friend.

Christine Johnson, Muslim teacher and friend.

Frank Johnson, Ella Little's second husband.*

John H. Johnson, nephew of Daisy Mason, Earl Little's first wife.

Roy Johnson, one of Malcolm's barbers.

Godfrey Joiner, prison-mate.

Art Jones, friend of the family; son of Earl Little's friend Chester Jones.

Betty Jones, friend of the family; daughter of Chester Jones.

Johnny Jones, friend.*

Loren Keeney, schoolmate.*

Charles Keil, a Yale undergraduate who used to rap with Malcolm at Temple Seven's restaurant and tease him about his adherence to Elijah Muhammad's teachings.*

Betty Kennedy, classmate and friend.

Alladin Kharufa, ex-director, New York City office, Islamic World League.*

Toni Ardelle Killings, political follower and co-worker.

Arden Kimmel, schoolmate.*

Kenneth Kimmel, schoolmate.

Maxine Kitchen, classmate.

Milton Kline, Supervising Fire Marshall, New York City.

Fletcher Knebel, journalist.*

Kenneth Kopp, New York City fireman.

Irv Kupcinet, journalist and talk show host.

George Landon, employer.*

Ruth Lane, Hill girl.*

Ilene Lassen, classmate.*

Lucille Lathrop, who cooked and assisted Lois Swerlein at the Ingham County juvenile home.

Harold Lavis, who avoided an icy "bottom" because of Malcolm's timely intervention.*

Jill Layton, classmate.*

Joseph LeBlanc, guard at Charlestown State Prison.*

Robert Edmund Lee, Acting Assistant Secretary of State for Congressional Relations, 1964.*

Louis Lee, schoolmate.*

Geraldine Lerg, West Junior High School teacher.*

Louis Lerner, business associate of Elijah and Herbert Muhammad.*

Dick Letts, an older West Side boy whom Malcolm had difficulty competing with.

Stan Levandowski, son of Walter Levandowski, the local grocer.*

Walter Levandowski, Senior, owner of the neighborhood grocery store.*

Reggie LeVong, who worked for radio station WWRL, which specialized in programs for New York City's African-American population.

Earl Levy, dentist at Charlestown State Prison.*

Al Lewis, prison-mate.

Claude Lewis, journalist.*

Alicia Lewkowicz, the "little blonde co-ed" described on page 286 of Malcolm's autobiography.*

C. Eric Lincoln, author of The Black Muslims in America.

Margaret Lisco, friend of Malcolm's parents.*

Clara Little, cousin.

Ella Little, Malcolm's oldest half-sister. Ella was the eldest daughter of Earl Little and his first wife, Daisy Mason.

J.C. Little, cousin.

John Little, cousin.

Louise Little (real name Louisa), Malcolm's mother.

Mary Little, Ella's younger sister.

Philbert Little, older brother.

Reginald Little, the oldest of Malcolm's younger brothers.

Robert Little, Malcolm's youngest brother.

Rose Little, aunt. (Rose was Oscar Little's wife.)

Wilfred Little, Malcolm's eldest brother.

Yvonne Little, Malcolm's younger sister.

Margaret Long, schoolmate.*

Anas Mahmoud Luqman, sunni Muslim.

Dick Lyon, classmate.*

Chuck Lyons, son of Harold and Ivy Lyons.

Marie Lyons, daughter of Harold & Ivy Lyons.

Norman Lyons, son of Harold and Ivy Lyons.

Robert Lyons, son of Harold & Ivy Lyons.

Willie MacDonald, cousin of Blanche Mitchell.

George Magraw, who taught school at Charlestown Prison.*

Enos Major, Sr., neighbor.

Jack Mallon, journalist.*

Vivian Mann, Hill girl.*

Katherine Marling, social worker.

Saladin (Milton) Matthews, fellow Muslim.

Hugo Mazzu, New York City fireman.*

Martha McAdoo, Hill girl.*

Ed McClellan, Sergeant, Chicago Police.

Joe McCormack, New York City police detective.*

Sarah Taylor McDaniel, teacher.

David McElroy, co-producer of the WBKB-TV talk show "Off the Cuff."*

Cecelia McGee, friend.*

Cyril McGuire, son of Bea McGuire, who was appointed Malcolm's legal guardian after his mother was institutionalized.

Johnny McIlvaine, professional gambler.

Walter H. McLaughlin, attorney.*

Ken Mead, in charge of Lansing School District records.

Anthony Paul Meleski, Head Corrections Social Worker, Norfolk Prison.

Pearl Merchant, Jr., friend.

Kendal Merlau, classmate.*

Louis Michaux, bookstore owner and prominent activist.

Harvey ("Junior") Miller, classmate.

Mrs. Richard Mills, Mason teacher.*

Ethel Minor, who eventually left the NOI and came to work for Malcolm.

Mildred Mitchell, Philbert's first wife.*

Leon Moffett, friend of Malcolm and Reginald.

Robert B. Moore, officer at Charlestown State Prison who later became warden of Walpole State Prison.*

Marjorie Morrow, friend.

Akbar Muhammad, Elijah Muhammad's youngest son.*

Lucille Muhammad, fellow Muslim.

Tom Mulchern, prison guard, Charlestown State Prison.*

Don Myers, Charlestown State Prison social worker.*

Daniel Nagle, attorney for one of the litigants in EOEM.*

Geraldine Nelson, to whom Malcolm was apparently attracted.

Austin Norman, Hill boy.*

Laurence Neblett, friend.

Gus Newport, activist.*

James Nicholson, crime reporter.

Richard Nielsen, New York City fireman.

Hugh O'Donnell, detective, New York City police.*

Don Oesterle, classmate.

Adeline Oleson, classmate.*

Sy Oliver, musician.*

Mildred O'Neill, who worked in the Philadelphia office of the *Afro-American.*

Constance Orgias, Aunt Gertie's daughter and Louise Little's cousin.

Daphne Orgias, Louise Little's niece.

Malcolm Orgias, Aunt Gertie's son. (Louise, who was his cousin, apparently named Malcolm after him.)

Olive Orgias, Aunt Gertie's daughter and Louise Little's cousin.

Phyllis Ostrom, classmate.

June Palmer, friend.*

Ken Palmer, friend and classmate.

Emerson Parker, classmate.

Merle Parker, Ingham County Probate Court worker.*

Paul Parker, waiter at the Braddock Bar, a well known Harlem nightspot that Malcolm frequented before he was imprisoned.*

Bazely Perry, friend and correspondent.*

Helen Pfiester, classmate.*

Philip Picard, officer at Norfolk Prison.*

Al Pierce, friend.

Reva Pierce, classmate.*

Mrs. O. F. Poindexter, Ingham County Welfare Dept. supervisor.*

Bobby Pointer, Jack Pointer's cousin.*

"Jack" Pointer, Michigan friend who accompanied Malcolm on a number of hustling expeditions.

Lawrence Pointer, Jack Pointer's cousin.*

Ted Poston, journalist.*

Adam Clayton Powell, III.*

George W. Power, one of Malcolm's house officers at Norfolk Prison Colony.*

Wahneta Preuss, social worker.*

Lloyd Price, schoolmate.*

Charles Pritchett, prison-mate.

Said Ramadan, Geneva Office, Islamic World League.*

Katie Randall, schoolmate.*

S. DeWitt Rathbun, Esq., a Lansing attorney who assisted Malcolm's mother after her husband died.

Marvin Ray, friend.*

Jim Reed, intelligent, understanding friend.

Pearl Reist, neighbor.

Harold Relyea, classmate.*

Ray Riddle, friend of Malcolm's father.

Viva Riker, teacher.*

Howard Riley, a Georgian friend of Earl Little's family.*

Lawson Riley, friend.

Arthur Roach, officer at Concord Reformatory.

Gene Roberts, undercover BOSS operative, New York Police Intelligence.

Herb Roberts, an older West Side boy with whom Malcolm tried to compete.

Pete Robertson, owner of Creole Pete's speakeasy.

Pat Robinson, activist and leading member of The Committee of Concerned Mothers.

Marvin Rogoff, detective, New York City Police.

Olive Roosenraad, the teacher who became the principal after Arthur Delamarter left Pleasant Grove Elementary School.

Gladys Towles Root, attorney.

Ed ("Big Boy") Roper, who lived with the Gohannas. Most people called him Dave Roper.

George Ross, an elderly gentleman who knew Malcolm's father.*

Norman Ross, co-producer of WBKB-TV talk show "Off the Cuff."*

Billy Rowe, journalist.*

Joe Rull, prison guard.*

Madeline Rusch, classmate.*

Morris Sayburn, court stenographer at Malcolm's 1964 eviction trial.*

Charles Scafati, guard at Charlestown State Prison.*

Colleen Schaft, classmate.*

John Scott, Peace Corps volunteer who served in Ethiopia in 1964, when Malcolm visited Addis Ababa.*

Phyllis Ashby Scott, family friend.

Clarence Seaton, an elder of the church Louise Little began attending after her husband's death.

Arlene Seaton, sister of Jean Seaton; daughter of Clarence Seaton.*

Bethel Seaton, daughter of Clarence Seaton.

Emily Seaton, niece of Clarence Seaton.*

Jean Seaton, the daughter of Clarence Seaton that Malcolm appeared to like so much.

Chuck Seeley, member of Mason school band.*

Attallah Shabazz, Malcolm's eldest daughter.*

Vivian Shaffer, classmate.

Osman Sharrieff, a Muslim who opposed Elijah Muhammad's efforts to inherit the leadership of Wallace D. Fard's movement.*

Margaret Shreve: classmate and friend.

Forrest Dwain Shultis, friend and classmate.

Gwynneth Shultis, who lived, for a while, at the Ingham County Juvenile Home.

Carl ("Sonny") Simmon, brother of Tom and Marion.*

Tom Simmon, schoolmate.

Marion Simmon, sister of Tom Simmon and classmate of Malcolm's.

Mary Simpson, friend.*

Stephen Slack, police detective.

Audrey Slagh, friend and classmate.

Bernard Snow, classmate.*

Glenn Snyder, classmate.*

Wesley South, talk show host.*

Bessie Springer, friend of the Littles.

Betty Stohrer, daughter of Anna Stohrer.

Anna Stohrer, friend and neighbor of Louise Little.

William Stohrer, son of Anna Stohrer.

Joe Stokes, Hill boy.*

Chuck Stone, Administrative Assistant to Congressman Adam Clayton Powell.*

Gloria Strother, the first woman Malcolm seriously considered marrying.

Oliver Sutton, attorney.

Percy Sutton, attorney and prominent political figure.*

Elsie Taylor, classmate.*

Lorraine Tellier, classmate.*

Joyce Tellier, schoolmate.*

John K. Terry, friend.*

Agnes Thiel, neighbor and Betty Jean Thiel's mother.

Betty Jean Thiel, neighbor and friend.

John Thimas, fellow Muslim.

Hank Thoben, New York City fireman.

Jay V. Thomas, fellow Muslim.*

Albert Thompson, Assistant Deputy Warden, Charlestown State Prison. (As assistant deputy, Mr. Thompson was in charge of prisoner discipline.)*

Dolphin Thompson, who did public relations work for Malcolm and the Nation of Islam.*

Daryl Thurston, schoolmate.

Dick Turbin, a boy whom Malcolm respected.

Ralph Taylor, friend and schoolmate.

Viola Thacker, friend of Gloria Strother.*

Martha Thayer, social worker.*

Ruby Thomas, schoolmate.*

C. P. ("Paddy") Thorne, friend.

Mildred Thurston, classmate.

Mary Tripp, classmate.*

Leona Turner, family doctor.

Hope Underwood, classmate.*

Junius Thomas Vaughan, fellow railroad employee.*

Harold Vaughan, friend.

Jean Wade, friend and neighbor.*

Hon. Maurice Wahl, the judge at Malcolm's 1964 eviction trial.

Clifford Walcott, principal, Mason Jr. High School.

Eulalia Walker, another daughter of Herb Walker.

Betty Walker, daughter of Herb Walker, who sheltered the Littles after the 1929 fire.

Jesse Walker, journalist.*

Mrs. Van D. Walker. Mrs. Walker and her husband were friends of Malcolm's parents.

Frank Walker, son of Herb Walker; brother of Betty and Eulalia Walker.*

Barbara Wallace, schoolmate.*

Gail Wallace, daughter of Tom Wallace; friend of Attallah Shabazz.

Mike Wallace, television producer.*

Thomas V. Wallace, schoolmate.*

Tom Wallace, Jr., son of Tom Wallace.*

Tom Wallace, who followed Malcolm out of the NOI and sheltered his family after the 1965 fire.

Beatrice Walline, classmate.*

Frances Walter, classmate.

Tom Washington, a resident of Lansing who was convinced that Earl Little was a businessman.*

J. J. Webster, friend.*

Hamburg E. D. Wells, who attended school with Louise Little in Grenada.

George ("Porky") White, friend.

Nettie Whitney, Ores Whitney's mother.*

Pauline Whitney, Ores Whitney's sister.*

Doris Wiegman, classmate.*

Charles W. Wiley, journalist.*

Charles Willhauck, guard at Charlestown State Prison.*

Margaret Williams, a childhood friend of Louise Little.

Alvin ("Shorty") Williams, classmate.*

Cornelia Williams, daughter of Delia Williams, who owned the rooming house where Malcolm lived in Flint, Mich.*

Delia Williams, who owned the rooming house where Malcolm lived in Flint, Mich.*

Evelyn Williams, fellow Muslim and friend.

J. D. Wilson, dentist who took care of Earl Little's teeth.*

Gertrude Wilson, newspaperwoman whose real name was Justine Smodbeck.

Clara Windsor, Pleasant Grove teacher.*

Ernie Wolf, neighbor who tried to help the Littles during the 1929 fire.

Mrs. Samuel Woolcock, neighbor.*

Bob Worthy, neighbor and schoolmate. Son of Mr. & Mrs. Marvon Worthy.

Mr. & Mrs. Marvon Worthy, neighbors.

Sharon 10X, a dedicated young Muslim.

Robert 35X, fellow Muslim.

Charles 37X, a loyal aide who later changed his name to Charles Kenyatta.

James 67X, one of Malcolm's chief aides.

Ulysses X, one of "Malcolm's ministers."

Dorothy Young, friend of Malcolm's sister Hilda. Dorothy became "Heather's" guardian and married Ella's third ex-husband Ken Collins.

AUTHOR'S ACKNOWLEDGEMENTS

I am deeply indebted, not only to the people I interviewed, but also to the hundreds of people who assisted me in the preparation of this book, which was partly inspired by the work of Cora Spencer, one of the finest students I have ever had. Leon Friedman and Richard Dannay furnished the requisite legal advice. David Garrow, Shelby Steele, Robert Coles, Stanley Crouch, Lewis Baldwin, Charles Trout, and David Bradley encouraged me when my spirits sagged. Similar encouragement came from Jonathan Galassi, Hillel Black, Ken Stuart, Gerard Van der Leun, Paul Aaron, William Goodman, Grant Ujifusa, Steve Wasserman, William Zinsser, M. B. Schnapper, Laura Brown, Arno Karlen, Barbara Karlen, Bill Whitaker, Seymour Kurtz, and the late Shirley Fisher. Frances Walter, Robert Higdon, Catherine Darling, and Helen and Clara Bywater furnished photographs of Malcolm that had been taken when he was young. The reference librarians who helped me included Adrian Love, Holly Lukas, Pam Gawronski, Maret Cheek, Charles Lockwood, Tim Wyatt, Bernard Pasqualini, Joan Bernstein, Joe Holub, David Azilena, and most of the members of the staff of the reference department of the University of Pennsylvania's Van Pelt Library. Editorial advice was provided by Susan Meigs, Herbert Lust, and Jon Weinstein, as well as Gil Gilmore, Karen Lawrence, Terry Supple, and others. First-rate typing was provided by Diane Weinstock and the book was typeset by Jeffra Ruesink. Elias Sanders and Bill Barnes were equally helpful.

Scores of people went out of their way to help me obtain important information. Among them were John H. Sengstacke, Peter Goldman, Ed Reardon, Commissioner John J. Fitzpatrick and his secretary Millie, Arthur Isberg, Esq., Nancy White, Esq., Vicki Palmer, Jerome Honore, Roger Street, Doug Ruby, Jim Gorzenski, Tom Winick, Tom Huff, Lilian Evans, Betty Alexander, Paul Akst, Jesse Walker, John Dolan, Judge

James Benton Parsons, Tom Gormely, Judge Thomas L. Brown, Judge Donald Owens, Judge Earl Broady, Florieut Johnson, Jeanie Leyden, Helen Service, Commander Fred Audner, Dallas Piper, Oscar Handlin, Roger Allen, John Day, Robert Kraft, Thomas Moshang, Morton Halperin, Philbert Little, Malcolm Jarvis, Carol Ross, Muriel Kaplan, Barbara Williams, Harriette Dorson, Ed Harvey, Estelle Redd, J. G. Robins, Ray Mowman, Gloria Thorne, Bazely Perry, Edward Ziegele, Patricia Rick, Ken Mead, Samuel Beetly, Captain Glenn Dafoe, Lieutenant Teddy, John McCarthy, Sharon Brown, Michael J. Codd, Pam Delaney, I. Carl Candoli, William Webb, Merlin Duncan, David G. Moore, Jack Conroy, James G. Bellows, Barbara Boucher, C. E. Mervine, Jr., Michael T. Hooper, Edmund R. Dewing, Carl Carter, Myron Bresnik, Henry Shultz, Doris Dynamite, S. N. Phelps, Harold Goldberg, John Gavin, Baron H. Martin, Donald Romine, James Callanan, Linda Wilson Fujimoto, Davis Meltzer, Robert E. Colville, Liz Koonter, Captain Clarence Wheeler, Derold Husby, Dan Mulqueen, George W. Owens, Arnold Perl, Rosemary Carroll, Wayne Moss, Allen Alpert, Marjorie Krome, William Bacherman, Ruth Bowen, Doris Hartman, Ruth Dressel, Verna Sheffield, Minnie Dahlgren, Roy Oberg, Fred Covert, Walter and Margaret Maag, Ruth Schilperoot, Mrs. Elmer Metz, F. Roy Phillips, Doris Wheeler, Stephen Van Note, Donald Guy, Eva Smith, Jim Bury, Louie Ruggles, John Briggs, Lee Alexander, Clarence Schier, John Petrie, Ralph Houston, Mildred Anderson, Agnes Huxtable, Rev. Thomas Toy, Donald Thurston, Roy Nelson, Dick Vincent, Diane Geis, Dennis Bolen, Hyman Pleasure, Harry Conrad, Lila Nitschke, Sam McGuire, James Newby, Beverly Chalker, C. T. Stoner, Dale Gorsline, Howard White, Shirley Grinnell, Madeline Hewell, Laurence Carrow, Howard McCowan, Howard Oesterle, Mrs. Richard Mills, Myrlan Grimes, Matthew Kane, Daniel Worthing, John Stickevers and Dr. and Mrs. John B. Kantner. I regret any inadvertent omissions that I may have made from the foregoing list.

The support and guidance I received from J. Edward Taylor, Shirley Rashkis, and the late Leon J. Saul was indispensable, as was the support of my parents and the following members of my family: Ben Perry, Anne Sutland, Arlene Leventhal, Phil Gilbert, Howard Dukes, Richard Dukes, and Robert Dukes. My brother David and sister-in-law Sherryl read part of the manuscript and provided a word processor. And my wife supplied the companionship and encouragement that made the discouraging junctures easier to bear.

INDEX

PHOTOGRAPHIC ACKNOWLEDGEMENTS

The publisher gratefully acknowledges the following sources for permission to reprint the photographs in this book. Photos in the text are designated here according to the page number upon which they appear:

Cover: photo by Laurance Henry by permission of the Laurance Henry Collection at the Schomburg Center for Research in Black Culture; The New York Public Library; Astor, Lenox and Tilden Foundations.

Page ii: by permission of the Schomburg Center for Research in Black Culture; The New York Public Library; Astor, Lenox and Tilden Foundations.

Page viii: by permission of the Schomburg Center for Research in Black Culture; The New York Public Library; Astor, Lenox and Tilden Foundations.

Page 136: by permission of the Schomburg Center for Research in Black Culture; The New York Public Library; Astor, Lenox and Tilden Foundations.

Page 200: both photos are by permission of UPI/Bettmann Newsphotos.

Page 368: by permission of UPI/Bettmann Newsphotos.

Page 544: photo by Laurance Henry by permission of the Laurance Henry Collection at the Schomburg Center for Research in Black Culture; The New York Public Library; Astor, Lenox and Tilden Foundations.

Photographic insert following page 304: all photographs on the fifth through eighth pages are by permission of UPI/Bettmann Newsphotos.